FOURTH EDITION

Designing Effective Mathematics Instruction

A Direct Instruction Approach

MARCY STEIN
University of Washington, Tacoma

DIANE KINDER
University of Washington, Tacoma

JERRY SILBERT
University of Oregon

DOUGLAS W. CARNINE
University of Oregon

Upper Saddle River, New Jersey
Columbus, Ohio

Library of Congress Cataloging in Publication Data

Designing effective mathematics instruction : a direct instruction approach.—
4th ed. / Marcy Stein . . . [et al.].
    p. cm.
  Rev. ed. of: Designing effective mathematics instruction / Marcy Stein,
Jerry Silbert, Douglas Carnine. 3rd ed. c1997.
  Includes bibliographical references and index.
  ISBN 0-13-119244-2
  1. Mathematics—Study and teaching (Elementary) I. Stein, Marcy.
II. Stein, Marcy. Designing effective mathematics instruction.
  QA135.6.D48 2006
  372.7'2—dc22

                     2005016531

Vice President and Executive Publisher: Jeffery W. Johnston
Senior Acquisitions Editor: Allyson P. Sharp
Editorial Assistant: Kathleen S. Burk
Senior Production Editor: Linda Hillis Bayma
Production Coordination: Mike Remillard, Pine Tree Composition
Design Coordinator: Diane C. Lorenzo
Cover Designer: Ali Mohrman
Production Manager: Laura Messerly
Director of Marketing: Ann Castel Davis
Marketing Manager: Autumn Purdy
Marketing Coordinator: Brian Mounts

This book was set in Garamond by Pine Tree Composition. It was printed and bound by
Edwards Brothers Malloy. The cover was printed by Edwards Brothers Malloy.

Pearson Education Ltd.
Pearson Education Singapore Pte. Ltd.
Pearson Education Canada, Ltd.
Pearson Education—Japan

Pearson Education Australia Pty. Limited
Pearson Education North Asia Ltd.
Pearson Educación de Mexico, S.A. de C.V.
Pearson Education Malaysia Pte. Ltd.

16
ISBN: 0-13-119244-2

To Wes Becker, a leader in showing how science can serve education.

Preface

Mathematics instruction is becoming increasingly holistic in nature, stressing the application of mathematics in a variety of contexts. Although current approaches to mathematics instruction have reasonable goals, often the methods for achieving those goals are lacking. The need for improvement in mathematics instruction has been well documented by national, even international, evaluations. Moreover, research also has suggested that many teachers are not prepared to meet the needs of a diverse student population. In our interactions with teachers, they were particularly vocal about the lack of specific guidance in how to support students who have difficulty learning mathematics. This text explains the inadequacies of some instructional programs and provides teachers with the information needed to modify the programs.

Although we believe the procedures suggested in this book to be effective, we do not claim they are panaceas. Implementing our suggestions requires hard work on the teacher's part. It is our hope that the systematic procedures and teaching strategies recommended here will stimulate the development of even better techniques.

FEATURES OF THIS BOOK

Designing Effective Mathematics Instruction: A Direct Instruction Approach includes these features:

- A description of essential skills and procedures for teaching these skills
- Procedures for evaluating, selecting, and modifying mathematics programs to meet the needs of all students

- Techniques for effectively presenting lessons, including techniques for pacing tasks, motivating students, and diagnosing and correcting errors
- Suggestions for classroom organization that maximize the amount of time students spend engaged in math instruction
- A *Topics of Interest* table (printed on the inside front cover) that summarizes how the book might be used by primary, intermediate, and remedial teachers

STRUCTURE OF THIS BOOK

The book is organized into two parts: Part I, "Perspective," and Part II, "Skills and Concepts." Chapter 1 in the "Perspective" section discusses the philosophy and techniques of direct instruction. Chapter 2 presents a framework for evaluating commercially developed mathematics programs. This framework is based on principles of instructional design derived from a direct instruction approach. Chapter 3 provides a brief review of relevant research on effective mathematics instruction.

The "Skills and Concepts" chapters in Part II are the heart of the book. Each chapter covers a specific skill area: counting skills, symbol identification and place value, basic facts, addition, subtraction, multiplication, division, problem solving, fractions, decimals, percent, telling time, money, measurement, study skills, geometry, pre-algebra. These chapters include suggestions for introducing each skill or concept, procedures for teaching specific strategies, and analyses of the major problem types within each skill area.

Each chapter also contains an Instructional Sequence and Assessment Chart. The sequence is designed to minimize student failure and to provide the practice and review necessary for student mastery. The assessment items can serve as a diagnostic test and as the basis for constructing short-term goals for Individualized Education Programs (IEPs).

Also included in some skills and concepts chapters are descriptions of the ways in which various skills are presented in commercial programs and discussions of how and why these procedures must often be modified in order to meet the needs of diverse students.

REVISIONS IN THE FOURTH EDITION

In this edition we have added a chapter (Chapter 2) on evaluating and modifying commercially developed mathematics instructional materials. This chapter will assist teachers in evaluating their current mathematics textbooks as well as curriculum adoption committees at the individual school or district level that are involved in selecting a mathematics program.

Chapter 3, devoted to relevant mathematics research, has been updated and includes a brief history of mathematics instruction, a report of current mathematics performance of U.S. students, followed by a discussion of existing reviews of research in mathematics instruction and research on critical elements important to the design of effective mathematics instruction. In addition, readers are encouraged to read the article in Appendix A that includes an overview and summary of the research of published direct instruction mathematics programs. Appendix B addresses questions that are frequently asked about the implementation of direct instruction.

Since the publication of the third edition, there has been increased public interest in the preparation of students for higher order mathematics. In response to this interest, we have added a chapter on pre-algebra skills. Other less extensive revisions were made throughout the book that incorporate feedback from various instructors and students.

Finally, a comprehensive Instructor's Manual that includes answers to the application items is available online at **www.prenhall.com.** The password-protected materials are available in the Resources for the Instructor module under the book's description.

ACKNOWLEDGMENTS

Foremost among the many people to whom we are grateful are the direct instruction teachers who prove that math failure is not inevitable. We also are grateful to Zig Engelmann, whose melding of logical analysis and empiricism has resulted in the development of numerous highly effective mathematics programs. Many of the procedures described in this book were derived from *DISTAR Arithmetic, Corrective Mathematics, Core Concepts in Mathematics,* and *Connecting Math Concepts* authored by Engelmann and his colleagues. Special thanks go to Bernadette Kelly, Don Crawford, and Paul Hill, whose suggestions and ideas contributed greatly to this edition. Additional ideas have been contributed by our colleagues and students, including Randy Williams, Kathy Jungjohann, Linda Carnine, Linda Olen, and Frank Falco. We also appreciate the extraordinary efforts of Sara Contreras. We are particularly indebted to our reviewers, Ann L. Lee, Bloomsburg University; Carol Moore, Troy State University; Kay Reinke, Oklahoma State; Dorothy Spethmann, Dakota State University; and John Woodward, University of Puget Sound, who provided us with invaluable feedback and suggestions.

Discover the Merrill Education Resources for Special Education Website

Technology is a constantly growing and changing aspect of our field that is creating a need for new content and resources. To address this emerging need, Merrill Education has developed an online learning environment for students, teachers, and professors alike to complement our products—the *Merrill Education Resources for Special Education* Website. This content-rich website provides additional resources specific to this book's topic and will help you—professors, classroom teachers, and students—augment your teaching, learning, and professional development.

Our goal is to build on and enhance what our products already offer. For this reason, the content for our user-friendly website is organized by topic and provides teachers, professors, and students with a variety of meaningful resources all in one location. With this website, we bring together the best of what Merrill has to offer: text resources, video clips, web links, tutorials, and a wide variety of information on topics of interest to general and special educators alike. Rich content, applications, and competencies further enhance the learning process.

The *Merrill Education Resources for Special Education* Website includes:

RESOURCES FOR THE PROFESSOR—

- The **Syllabus Manager**™, an online syllabus creation and management tool, enables instructors to create and revise their syllabus with an easy, step-by-step process. Students can access your syllabus and any changes you make during the course of your class from any computer with Internet access. To access this tailored syllabus, students will just need the URL of the website and the password assigned to the syllabus. By clicking on the date, the student can see a list of activities, assignments, and readings due for that particular class.
- In addition to the **Syllabus Manager**™ and its benefits listed above, professors also have access to all of the wonderful resources that students have access to on the site.

RESOURCES FOR THE STUDENT—

- Video clips specific to each topic, with questions to help you evaluate the content and make crucial theory-to-practice connections.
- Thought-provoking critical analysis questions that students can answer and turn in for evaluation or that can serve as basis for class discussions and lectures.
- Access to a wide variety of resources related to classroom strategies and methods, including lesson planning and classroom management.
- Information on all the most current relevant topics related to special and general education, including CEC and Praxis standards, IEPs, portfolios, and professional development.
- Extensive web resources and overviews on each topic addressed on the website.
- A message board with discussion starters where students can respond to class discussion topics, post questions and responses, or ask questions about assignments.
- A search feature to help access specific information quickly.

To take advantage of these and other resources, please visit the *Merrill Education Resources for Special Education* Website at

http://www.prenhall.com/stein

Educator Learning Center: An Invaluable Online Resource

Merrill Education and the Association for Supervision and Curriculum Development (ASCD) invite you to take advantage of a new online resource, one that provides access to the top research and proven strategies associated with ASCD and Merrill—the Educator Learning Center. At **www.educatorlearningcenter.com,** you will find resources that will enhance your students' understanding of course topics and of current educational issues, in addition to being invaluable for further research.

HOW THE EDUCATOR LEARNING CENTER WILL HELP YOUR STUDENTS BECOME BETTER TEACHERS

With the combined resources of Merrill Education and ASCD, you and your students will find a wealth of tools and materials to better prepare them for the classroom.

Research

- More than 600 articles from the ASCD journal *Educational Leadership* discuss everyday issues faced by practicing teachers.
- A direct link on the site to Research Navigator™ gives students access to many of the leading education journals, as well as extensive content detailing the research process.
- Excerpts from Merrill Education texts give your students insights on important topics of instructional methods, diverse populations, assessment, classroom management, technology, and refining classroom practice.

Classroom Practice

- Hundreds of lesson plans and teaching strategies are categorized by content area and age range.
- Case studies and classroom video footage provide virtual field experience for student reflection.
- Computer simulations and other electronic tools keep your students abreast of today's classrooms and current technologies.

LOOK INTO THE VALUE OF EDUCATOR LEARNING CENTER YOURSELF

A four-month subscription to Educator Learning Center is $25 but is **FREE** when packaged with any Merrill Education text. In order for your students to have access to this site, you must use this special value-pack ISBN number **WHEN** placing your textbook order with the bookstore: 0-13-218878-3. Your students will then receive a copy of the text packaged with a free ASCD pincode. To preview the value of this website to you and your students, please go to **www.educatorlearningcenter.com** and click on "Demo."

Brief Contents

Contents

Note: Every effort has been made to provide accurate and current Internet information in this book. However, the Internet and information posted on it are constantly changing, and it is inevitable that some of the Internet addresses listed in this textbook will change.

Formats for Teaching Major Skills

Perspective

CHAPTER 1

Direct Instruction

Many mathematics texts discuss the philosophy and theory of mathematics instruction. Most methods texts provide activities and games involving mathematics. Few, however, deal extensively with the instructional specifics. *Designing Effective Mathematics Instruction: A Direct Instruction Approach* focuses on what teachers can do to maximize the likelihood that students will learn. The learning theory underlying this book is elaborated in detail elsewhere (Engelmann & Carnine, 1991) and cannot be adequately summarized here. Direct instruction provides a comprehensive set of prescriptions for organizing instruction so that students acquire, retain, and generalize new learning in as humane, efficient, and effective a manner as possible.

The need for effective instruction is growing rapidly. While many variables influence students' acquisition of mathematics, these variables are certainly central: (a) instructional design, (b) instructional delivery, and (c) classroom organization and management. These three variables are *all* essential ingredients of a successful mathematics program. A well-designed program and a good teacher do not produce significant gains if the classroom is poorly managed. Similarly, a well-designed program and a well-managed classroom do not lead to success if the teacher is not skilled. Finally, adequate organization and a skilled teacher do not adequately serve students if the materials are poorly designed. A discussion of these three critical variables follows.

INSTRUCTIONAL DESIGN

To effectively teach mathematics, teachers must construct the kinds of lessons and develop the specific teaching procedures that best meet the needs of their students. Throughout the chapters in this text, five basic instructional design components are emphasized to assist teachers in designing mathematics instruction or in evaluating and modifying the commercial programs that have been adopted for use in their school or district:

1. Sequence of skills and concepts
2. Explicit instructional strategies
3. Preskills
4. Example selection
5. Practice and review

Before designing instruction or modifying it, teachers must clearly identify the objectives they want to teach. Most commercial programs specify student objectives for each instructional unit; also, many districts have developed curriculum frameworks that specify grade-level objectives that align with the curriculum they have adopted. Regardless of how the objectives are initially identified, the objectives must be written so that teachers can determine when the objectives have been met. That is, the objectives should be stated as specific, observable behaviors and include, if possible, both accuracy and rate criteria. For example, a clear first-grade objective for single-digit addition is, "Given 25 single-digit addition problems, students will correctly solve at least 22 in one minute with no more than one error." Poorly stated objectives contain vague descriptions of student behavior that are difficult to measure, such as, "Students will *understand the concept of addition.*"

Teachers can use the Instructional Sequence and Assessment Charts found at the beginning of most chapters in this book as a guide to selecting important grade-level objectives. These charts offer a sequence of instruction based on the difficulty level of the given problem types. Teachers can use the charts to help prioritize objectives, deciding which problem types to teach, which to delete, and which to add to the unit. Teachers of students who perform poorly initially should focus their instruction on higher priority skills. Higher priority skills are those skills that are used more frequently or are prerequisites for more advanced skills.

Once the teacher has determined the problem types students should be able to work when they have completed the unit, the teacher must decide on appropriate levels of mastery. Both accuracy and fluency must be considered when specifying levels of mastery. Unfortunately, there is little research available to guide decisions about determining accuracy and fluency criteria. Generally, teachers should provide supervised practice until students reach an 85% to 90% accuracy level for worksheet assignments containing a review of previously introduced types of problems. A fluency criterion usually depends on the relative complexity of the problem type. Most educators agree that students who work problems with relative fluency are more likely to retain strategies over a longer period of time. More detail about fluency criteria can be found in the section "Progress Monitoring" later in this chapter.

Sequence of Skills and Concepts

The order in which information and skills are introduced affects the difficulty students have in learning them. Sequencing involves determining the optimum order for introducing new information and strategies. Following are three general guidelines for sequencing the introduction of new skills:

1. Preskills of a strategy are taught before the strategy.
2. Easy skills are taught before more difficult ones.
3. Strategies and information that are likely to be confused are not introduced consecutively.

Generally, the more steps in a strategy and the greater the similarity of the new strategy to previously taught strategies, the more likely some students will find it difficult to master. For example, in column subtraction, problems that require renaming (borrowing) are more difficult than problems that do not require renaming. However, not all problems that require renaming are of equal difficulty. A problem such as 3,002 − 89 is significantly more difficult than a problem such as 364 − 128, largely due to the presence of zeroes.

One of the preskills for renaming with zeroes in problems like the one above is hundreds-minus-one problems (e.g., 300 − 1 = 299). That preskill should be taught prior to introducing problems such as 3002 − 89, which requires renaming 300 tens to 299 tens. This example of identifying and teaching the appropriate preskills illustrates the first sequencing guideline.

$$3002$$
$$-\ 89$$

Since problems with zeroes can be confusing to many students, subtraction with renaming should be introduced first with problems without zeroes, such as 4362 − 67. The instruction of easier skills before more difficult ones is the essence of the second sequencing guideline.

The third sequencing guideline is to separate the introduction of information and/or strategies that are likely to be confused. The more similar two tasks are, the more likely students are to confuse them. For example, students are likely to confuse the numerals 6 and 9. Thus, 6 and 9 should not be introduced consecutively. Likewise, the skip-counting series for 6s and 4s are quite similar in that they both contain 12, 24, and 36 (6, **12**, 18, **24**, 30, **36** and 4, 8, **12**, 16, 20, **24**, 28, 32, **36**). Introducing these series consecutively is likely to cause confusion for some students.

Teachers can use these sequencing guidelines in analyzing commercial programs. When teachers find instructional sequences that may cause confusion, they can modify the programs by providing additional instruction or changing the sequence of introduction for various skills.

Explicit Instructional Strategies

Research suggests that teaching students explicit instructional strategies increases their performance in mathematics. Explicit strategies are described as clear, accurate, and unambiguous instruction. (See Chapter 3 for this research.) In addition to being explicit, well-designed instructional strategies must be generalizable. That is, well-designed instructional strategies apply to a range of different problem types. For example, many programs teach strategies for identifying proper fractions using a single unit like a cookie divided into thirds or fourths. When students encounter improper fractions (e.g., 5/4), the strategies they were taught using a single unit don't work. Students cannot show 5/4 if given only a single unit (e.g., one cookie). A well-designed strategy for teaching students fraction concepts is one that applies to both proper *and* improper fractions. (See Chapter 12 for examples of well-designed fraction strategies.)

Some commercially developed mathematics programs suggest that students generate a number of alternative problem-solving strategies for the same skill. Rather than developing a conceptual foundation that highlights mathematical relationships, the introduction of alternative problem-solving strategies often confuses instructionally naive students. Teachers need to select the most generalizable, useful, explicit strategies to teach their students—strategies that draw attention to the relationships among the mathematical skills and concepts being taught.

Preskills

As mentioned previously, instruction should be sequenced so that the component skills of a strategy are taught *before* the strategy itself is introduced. The component skills, therefore, can be called preskills. For example, in order to solve a percent problem (e.g., What is 23% of 67?), the student must be able to (a) convert percent to a decimal (23% = .23); (b) work multiplication problems with multi-digit factors (.23 × 67); and (c) place the decimal point correctly in the product (15.41).

$$
\begin{array}{r}
67 \\
\times\ .23 \\
\hline
201 \\
134 \\
\hline
15.41
\end{array}
$$

It is possible that the necessary preskills for strategies presented in a specific unit were taught in previous levels. However, to ensure that the students have mastered the preskills before introducing a new instructional strategy, teachers should test students on those preskills. Each chapter in this text identifies critical preskills for the strategies presented so that teachers can design tests to determine whether the preskills have been mastered or must be taught.

Example Selection

Selecting examples means constructing or choosing appropriate problems to be used during teaching demonstrations and student practice. Several guidelines for example selection assist teachers in systematically designing their instruction so that students experience success. The first example-selection guideline is simply to include only problems that students can solve by using a strategy that has been explicitly taught. For example, if students have been taught a renaming strategy for solving subtraction problems without zeroes, but have not yet been taught to solve with zeroes, the teacher should not give them a problem such as 3004 − 87. As mentioned previously, teaching students to rename in problems containing zeroes requires additional instruction in specific preskills. If students have not yet learned the preskill of hundreds minus one (e.g., 300 − 1 = 299) including examples with zeroes would cause many students to fail.

The second guideline is to include not only examples of the currently introduced type (introductory examples) but also examples of previously introduced problem types that are similar (discrimination examples). The purpose of including previously introduced problem types is to provide students with practice in determining *when* to use the new strategy and when to use previously taught strategies. For example, after students learn how to regroup from ones to tens in column addition, the examples they practice should include both problems that require regrouping and problems that do not. Working a set of discrimination problems encourages students to examine the problems more carefully to determine *when* to apply the regrouping strategy instead of merely engaging in the rote behavior of just "putting one on top of the tens column." The importance of including discrimination examples cannot be overemphasized. Unless previously taught problem types are included, students will likely forget or misapply earlier taught strategies.

Many commercial programs do not include sufficient numbers of examples in their initial teaching presentations to enable students to develop mastery. Also, the programs rarely provide an adequate number of discrimination problems. Teachers, therefore, must be prepared to construct worksheets or other practice activities to supplement the practice provided by the program.

The second reason for including various problem types in practice activities is to provide the review necessary for students to maintain mastery of the previously taught skills. Without systematic review, students, particularly those with low performance, may forget and/or confuse earlier taught strategies. A discussion of example-selection guidelines is provided for each topic in the book.

Practice and Review

A critical instructional goal of direct instruction is to teach skills or concepts in a manner that facilitates retention over time. Providing sufficient practice for initial mastery and adequate review for retention is an essential aspect of instructional design. Research suggests a strong relationship between student achievement and sufficient practice and review. Two guidelines can help teachers provide adequate practice and review. First, teachers must provide massed practice on an individual skill until mastery is reached. Mastery is attained when the student can work problems accurately and fluently. Following this guideline requires that teachers monitor their students carefully and frequently to determine if and when mastery has been achieved. If students have not mastered a skill in the time originally allotted, teachers must provide additional practice opportunities.

Second, teachers must provide systematic review of previously introduced skills. Once students have reached a specified level of mastery on a given skill, the teacher can gradually decrease the amount of practice on that skill. However, practice should never entirely disappear. The skill should be reviewed systematically over time to ensure retention. In some cases, the review of previously introduced skills requires deliberate planning, since many commercial programs do not provide an opportunity for that review. In other cases, built-in review is naturally provided because the skill serves as a component skill for a more advanced problem type. For example, as subtraction problems with renaming are mastered, those problems are integrated into problem-solving activities. Practice in the higher level skill of problem-solving provides review on the previously introduced skill of subtraction with renaming. Many Web sites are now available to help teachers construct additional practice worksheets focused on specific skills.

INSTRUCTIONAL DELIVERY

Once teachers have designed their mathematics instruction using the five components discussed above, they need to integrate instructional delivery components into their teaching plans. While the instructional design components focus on *what to teach,* instructional delivery components address *how best to teach:* They address issues of program implementation. Included in this section on instructional delivery are

1. Initial assessment and progress monitoring
2. Presentation techniques
3. Error-correction procedures
4. Diagnosis and remediation

Initial Assessment and Progress Monitoring

In order for teachers to deliver mathematics instruction in the most efficient manner to all of their students, they must design and implement an assessment system for determining how students are currently performing and must monitor student progress once instruction has begun. Progress monitoring serves two major functions. First, through monitoring student progress, teachers can determine to what extent students have mastered the material. Second, progress monitoring helps teachers make instructional decisions regarding how quickly to advance through the instructional program.

INITIAL ASSESSMENT. Before teaching a specific unit, the teacher must construct and administer a pretest to determine what skills need to be taught. Pretesting prevents the teacher from overlooking a preskill that needs to be taught prior to the introduction of an important skill or concept. Pretesting also prevents teachers from spending instructional time on skills students have already mastered. The pretest can be used as an informal posttest, as well, to measure skill acquisition after the unit has been completed. The pretest for a specific unit should include the following:

1. Problem types in that skill area that were taught in earlier grades
2. Preskills required to solve the new problem types taught in the unit
3. Examples of the new problem types presented in the unit

Problem types taught in earlier grades are included so that the teacher can identify any deficits that should be remedied before new strategies are introduced. Generally, these items should be selected from the two previous grades. The preskills and problem types from the current unit are included so that the teacher can determine where instruction should begin—that is, whether preskills must be taught and/or what problem types require teacher-directed instruction.

Two or three problems of each problem type should be assessed. The Instructional Sequence and Assessment Charts in Chapters 4 through 20 provide a bank of pretest items to draw from. These charts include a sequential list of problem types by estimated grade level with several illustrative problems listed for each type. A fifth-grade teacher about to introduce a unit on multiplication, for example, can construct a pretest that includes all the multiplication problem types listed on the Instructional Sequence and Assessment Chart from grades three through five. Since these charts do not include every problem type students will encounter, teachers need to add any problem types that are not on the charts but are included in the unit.

A form that can be used to record student performance on pretests appears in Figure 1.1. Students' names are listed in the first column. Across the top of the form are spaces to indicate the specific problem types. Student performance on both the pretest and the posttest is recorded in the "Pre" and "Post" columns: a+ indicates the student got all the problems of a particular type correct, and a− indicates the student missed one or more problems of that type.

After pretesting the students, the teacher must decide where to begin instruction. As a general guideline, instruction should begin with the problem type failed by more than one-fourth of the students in the group. Starting at this point ensures that the teacher is presenting material that is new to a significant proportion of the students in the group. However, teachers must be extremely cautious in following this procedure. Teachers are responsible for teaching *all* students. Therefore, teachers need to allocate time to work individually with the students who missed earlier problem types until those students have caught up with the rest of the group.

PROGRESS MONITORING. A major goal of progress monitoring is to determine whether students have mastered the material presented through teacher-directed activities. Therefore, the problems selected to monitor student progress should be similar, but not identical, to those used during instruction.

A second goal of progress monitoring is to determine whether students are progressing at an optimal rate. One research-based approach to monitoring student progress that assists teachers in determining an optimal rate is called curriculum-based measurement (CBM). (See Chapter 3 for a discussion of research on CBM.)

CBM offers an alternative both to informal observations, which tend to lack consistency, and to achievement tests, which are administered too infrequently to help teachers make instructional decisions. According to Shinn (1998), CBM has two distinctive features that separate it from other curriculum-based assessments. First, the recommended procedures are as reliable and valid as most standardized achievement tests; second, the procedures are designed to be administered frequently enough to provide teachers with ongoing performance data.

The development of CBM procedures generally involves a four-step process (Fuchs, Fuchs, Hamlett, & Stecker, 1990):

1. Identifying a long-range goal; for example, given a set of computational problems representing a fifth-grade math curriculum, the student will work a specified number of problems and write a specified number of symbols correctly in two minutes;
2. Creating a pool of test items from the local curriculum;
3. Frequently measuring student performance;
4. Evaluating the results and making instructional changes as necessary.

(For more detailed information on CBM, see the relevant resources in Appendix B.)

One of the strongest advantages of using CBM is that by monitoring progress frequently, teachers can identify and remedy problems by making instructional changes before students fall too far behind their peers. Likewise, teachers can use CBM data to accelerate instruction.

Presentation Techniques

A major aspect of direct instruction involves attention to a group of presentation techniques. How skillfully a teacher presents instruction significantly affects both the student's rate of learning and the student's self-concept. The relationship between success and self-concept, a primary tenet in the direct-instruction approach to teaching, was articulated by Engelmann in 1969:

> The sphere of self-confidence that can be programmed in the classroom has to do with the child's ability to stick to his guns, to have confidence in what he has learned, and to approach school tasks with the understanding that he is smart and will succeed. For a child to maintain such an impression of himself, he must receive demonstrations that these descriptions of himself are valid. If he finds himself failing in school, displeasing the teacher, feeling unsure about what he has

FIGURE 1.1 Pretest Record Form

Unit _____

Pretest Date _____

Posttest Date _____

Student Names	Problem Type																				
	Pre	Post	Pre	Post	Pre	Post	Pre	Post	Pre	Post	Pre	Post	Pre	Post	Pre	Post	Pre	Post	Pre	Post

learned, he must reevaluate himself and perhaps conclude that he is not a complete success. (p. 68)

In general, mathematics instruction in the early grades relies more on teacher-directed instructional activities. Therefore, teachers in grades K–2 must be proficient in the variety of presentation techniques designed to maintain student participation in oral question-answer exchanges. It is during these exchanges that teachers carefully monitor the performance of their students. Although well-designed mathematics instruction requires teacher-directed presentations at all levels, intermediate-grade students will be asked to work more independently or in groups. For students at those levels, teachers must be skilled in orchestrating cooperative activities and managing students who are working independently.

The presentation techniques addressed here are those skills needed for effective teacher-directed group instruction. One means of determining whether teacher-directed instruction is effective is by examining the extent to which the teachers maintain student attention during the lesson. The more attentive students are during instruction, the higher the probability that the teaching demonstration will be successful. Attention is maintained by structuring tasks to keep students actively involved.

Several factors contribute to a successful teacher-directed lesson. For example, the length of a teacher's explanation or demonstration affects the likelihood that students will be attentive. Teachers should make explanations brief and concise. The more time the teacher spends talking, the fewer opportunities exist for student involvement. Teachers working with primary-grade and lower performing intermediate-grade students should structure their presentations so that students are required to answer frequent questions.

Since teachers cannot call on every individual student, unison responses should be incorporated into the teacher-directed lessons. Unison responses help ensure that *all* of the students in the classroom actively participate in the lesson. Two very specific presentation skills are necessary for teachers who incorporate unison responses into their instruction: appropriate use of signals and pacing.

SIGNALS. A signal is a cue given by the teacher that tells students when to respond in unison. The effective use of signals allows participation by all students, not just the highest performing students who, if allowed, tend to dominate the activity.

To signal a unison response, the teacher (a) gives directions, (b) provides a thinking pause, and (c) cues the response. When giving directions, the teacher tells the students the type of response they are to make and asks the question. For example, if presenting an addition fact task, the teacher might say, "Listen. Get ready to tell me the answer to this problem: 4 + 6."

After the directions comes the thinking pause. The duration of the thinking pause is determined by the length of time the lowest performing student needs to figure out the answer. (If one student takes significantly longer to answer than the other students in the group, the teacher should consider providing extra individual practice for that student.) For easier questions (simple tasks involving review of previously taught skills), the thinking pause may be just a split second, while for more complex questions, the thinking pause may last 5 to 10 seconds. Carefully controlling the duration of the thinking pause is a very important factor in maintaining student attention.

The final step in the signaling procedure is the actual cue to respond. A cue or signal to respond may be a clap, finger snap, hand drop, touch on the board, or any similar type of action. This procedure can be modified for use with most tasks. On tasks calling for a long thinking pause, the teacher would say, "Get ready" an instant before signaling. The purpose of the get-ready prompt is to let the students know when to expect the cue to respond. Since the length of thinking pauses varies with the difficulty of the question, students do not know when to respond following a pause. Therefore, in order to elicit a group response in which each student has an equal opportunity to respond, the cue "Get ready" is given. This cue is particularly useful for teacher-directed worksheet tasks, since students are looking at their worksheets and cannot see a hand signal from the teacher.

The essential feature of a good signal is its clarity. The signal must be given so that students know exactly when they are expected to respond. If a signal is not clear, students cannot respond in unison. The teacher can use the student responses to evaluate the clarity of her signals. A repeated failure to respond together usually indicates that the signals are unclear or that the teacher has not provided adequate thinking time.

Giving individual turns (i.e., called individual tests) is an essential part of any instructional activity in which students are asked to respond in unison. With unison responses, a teacher can never be absolutely certain whether each student has produced a correct response independent from the responses of nearby students. Giving individual turns helps teachers verify that all students are participating appropriately in the activity.

The teacher should give individual tests only after all the students in the group appear to be answering correctly during unison practice. Calling on a student who has not had enough practice to master the task may needlessly embarrass the student in front of his peers. Since individual tests are time consuming, they should not be given to every student after every task. As a general rule, turns should be given to all lower performing students each time a new or difficult task is presented. Higher performing students, on the other hand, can be tested less often.

PACING. Anyone who has observed young children watching TV shows or playing video games can attest to the role that pacing plays in maintaining attention. Teachers should be familiar enough with their material to present it in a lively, animated manner and without hesitation. Teachers who are well practiced with their instructional materials not only can teach at a more lively pace, but also can focus their attention more fully on the student performance.

Error-Correction Procedures

The first step in correcting errors made by students during group instruction is to determine the cause of the error. Teachers must decide if the error resulted from inattentiveness or from a lack of knowledge.

Teachers can judge whether a student error was caused by inattentiveness by checking where the student was looking or what the student was doing when the question was asked. Teachers must be careful in responding to errors that appear to be caused by inattentiveness. Teachers do not want to inadvertently give students their attention for being off task.

Most error corrections follow a three-step procedure of *model, test,* and *delayed test.* If an error occurs when the teacher is presenting a strategy, the teacher should model the correct response or ask leading questions from the strategy so that students can generate the correct response. Next, the teacher tests the students by presenting the same task again, this time providing no assistance. The teacher then returns to the beginning of the original task and presents the entire task again, the delayed test. The function of a delayed test is to check whether the

student remembers the correct responses when starting from the beginning of the task.

Teachers should also correct students who respond late or don't respond at all during tasks requiring unison responding. For these errors, teachers should inform the students that because not all students responded (or because some students failed to respond on signal), they have to repeat the task. Teachers should not direct any attention to the students who made the errors but should praise students who performed well and attended to the task.

Specific recommendations are outlined in each chapter for corrections of errors students are likely to make for a given topic. Specific teacher wording is often provided along with additional recommendations for how to ensure that the corrections were effective.

Diagnosis and Remediation

Diagnosis is determining the cause of a pattern of errors; remediation is the process of reteaching the skill. Diagnosis and remediation, as used in this text, are not the same as a simple error correction. An error correction *immediately* follows the mistake a student makes during teacher-directed instruction. An error correction requires minimal diagnosis, since the teacher knows exactly what question the student missed.

A diagnosis, on the other hand, consists primarily of an analysis of the errors students make on independent work. The first decision to make in diagnosing errors is determining whether they are "can't-do" or "won't-do" problems. Won't-do problems occur when students have the necessary skills but are careless, do not complete their work, or are inattentive. A diagnosis of won't-do errors requires a remediation that focuses on increasing student motivation. A diagnosis of can't-do problems requires a remediation that focuses on the student's confusion or skill deficit.

The teacher diagnoses can't-do errors by examining the missed problems on worksheets and/or by interviewing the students about how they worked the problems they missed. The following basic steps apply to diagnosing and remedying errors on most types of problem:

1. Analyze worksheet errors and hypothesize what the cause of the errors might be.
2. Interview the student to determine the cause of the errors if it is not obvious.
3. Provide reteaching through board and/or worksheet presentations.

4. Test the student on a set of problems similar to the ones on which the original errors were made.

An error can be one of three basic types: a fact error, a component-skill error, or a strategy error. Basic facts are the addition and multiplication facts formed by adding or multiplying any two single-digit numbers and their subtraction and division corollaries. Students often miss problems solely because they don't know their basic math facts.

Component skills are previously taught skills that are integrated as steps in a lengthier problem-solving strategy. Below is an example of a fraction problem a student missed due to a component-skill error:

$$\frac{3}{4} + \frac{2}{5} =$$

$$incorrect: \frac{3}{20} + \frac{2}{20} = \frac{5}{20} \qquad correct: \frac{15}{20} + \frac{8}{20} = \frac{23}{20}$$

Note that in the incorrectly solved problem, the student knew to convert both fractions to a common denominator but did not know the component skill of rewriting a fraction as an equivalent fraction. To remedy this component-skill error, the teacher presents instruction only on the component skill of rewriting fractions. Once the student masters the component skill, the teacher gives students problems to solve that are similar to the one originally missed.

A strategy error occurs when the student demonstrates that he does not know the sequence of steps required to solve the particular problem type. In the following example, the student subtracts the denominator from the numerator when instructed to convert an improper fraction to a mixed number, illustrating that the student does not have a strategy for reducing improper fractions. To remedy this problem, the teacher must teach the entire strategy of rewriting fractions to the student.

$$\frac{13}{6} = 7 \qquad\qquad \frac{15}{2} = 13$$

The diagnosis and remediation procedures recommended here are designed to increase instructional efficiency by helping teachers determine exactly how much additional teaching is necessary to bring students to mastery. If a teacher determines that student errors are due to deficient math fact knowledge, it is unnecessary to reteach lengthy problem-solving strategies. Similarly, if an error pattern reflected in a student's independent work is due to a problem with a single component skill, then only that skill, not the entire instructional strategy, must be retaught. These diagnosis and remediation procedures can save teachers valuable instructional time by focusing on only those skills that require remediation.

CLASSROOM ORGANIZATION AND MANAGEMENT

The final component of direct instruction involves organizing instruction in the classroom and throughout the school to ensure effective use of resources, particularly the use of time. Clearly, many books have been written addressing only issues of classroom organization and management that contain important recommendations for effective teaching. For the purposes of this text, however, this section discusses only the critical elements of daily mathematics lessons.

Elements of Daily Math Lessons

A daily mathematics lesson should include three parts: teacher-directed instruction, student independent work, and a teacher workcheck.

TEACHER-DIRECTED INSTRUCTION. The amount of time allocated in most classrooms for teacher-directed instruction in mathematics is generally no less than 30 minutes and as much as 90 minutes. The evidence from the teacher effectiveness literature suggests that the more time students are successfully engaged in math instruction, the more they learn. (See Chapter 3 for a discussion of this research.) Therefore, teachers must carefully manage and utilize the instructional time allocated in their daily schedules.

As mentioned previously, well-designed and well-delivered teacher-directed instruction is characterized by high rates of student–teacher interaction in a quickly paced instructional lesson. The lesson typically consists of the introduction of new skills and concepts and remediation of previously taught skills.

Introduction of New Skills. The teacher introduces new skills to students typically by demonstrating the conceptual basis for the skill, modeling how to apply the skill, then leading students through several examples, gradually fading assistance until the students can perform independently.

In direct instruction, general teaching procedures are translated into teaching formats or scripts that specify teacher wording, examples, and often error-correction procedures. Formats are designed so that teacher explanations are clear and unambiguous and so teachers do not have to worry if the explanation they use one day is consistent with the explanations they've given previously.

The teaching formats reflect a carefully designed instructional sequence, beginning with a teacher demonstration of the strategy and followed by teacher-guided worksheet practice, worksheet practice with less teacher direction, supervised worksheet practice, and, finally, independent work.

Chapters 4 through 20 contain teaching formats that address the major topics in most elementary and some middle school classrooms. Most of the formats in each chapter reflect the instructional sequence mentioned above and include four parts: a structured board presentation, a structured worksheet presentation, a less structured worksheet presentation, and supervised practice. During daily teacher-directed instructional time, teachers present structured board presentations, structured worksheet presentations, and less structured worksheet presentations. Supervised practice is usually done during independent work time.

Remediation of Previously Taught Skills. During the lesson, the teacher should remedy any of the previously taught skills or problem types with which several students demonstrate difficulty. If only one or two students experience difficulty, the teacher should work with these students individually, independent of group instructional time. Remediation exercises should be based on student performance on independent worksheets.

INDEPENDENT WORK. Independent work refers to the exercises that students complete without assistance from the teacher at a designated time other than the teacher-directed instructional time. Exer-

cises for independent work can include those found in workbooks or textbooks, problems written on the board, or cooperative activities designed for groups. Independent work should include massed practice on the most recently introduced problem types as well as practice and review of earlier introduced problem types. Teachers who use a direct instruction approach never assign independent work that the students haven't first demonstrated they can complete successfully during supervised practice.

WORKCHECK. A workcheck is an activity specifically designed to correct the errors students make during independent work time. Students' independent work should be checked daily in order to provide useful feedback to both students and teachers. The sooner a student's weakness or deficit can be identified, the easier it is to remedy. At the same time, the longer a student practices completing a problem the wrong way, the more difficult it is to correct.

Teachers of younger students will find it most efficient to check all student papers themselves prior to the workcheck and to have students correct errors only during the allocated time. Teachers of older students can conduct a group workcheck in which the teacher reads the answers and the students mark their own papers and then correct their errors. The workcheck affords teachers the opportunity to correct errors and to carefully examine independent work to determine skills that might require additional remediation during teacher-directed instructional time.

In Chapter 2, the instructional design features discussed in this chapter shape a framework for evaluating published mathematics programs. The framework also includes evaluation of teaching procedures and assessment. Suggestions for large-scale evaluations, such as district curriculum adoptions, are provided.

Mathematics Curriculum Evaluation Framework

ABSTRACT

In this paper, we present a framework for evaluating commercially developed mathematics programs. This framework is based on principles of instructional design derived from a Direct Instruction approach to education. Given the role that instructional programs play in the classroom, especially for teachers who have not been well prepared to teach mathematics, the quality of commercially developed mathematics programs needs to be closely scrutinized. The Mathematics Curriculum Evaluation Framework outlined here is designed to help teachers evaluate mathematics programs to select new programs or modify the mathematics programs available to them. While this framework is not exhaustive, it will give teachers a focus for their curriculum evaluation efforts and will also help teachers identify areas in mathematics programs that can be easily modified. Finally, this framework can serve as the first stage in the development of a reliable and valid curriculum evaluation instrument for determining the quality of commercially developed mathematics programs.

According to the 2003 National Assessment of Educational Progress (NAEP), only 32% of fourth-grade students and 29% of eighth-grade students scored at the proficient level in mathematics (National Center for Educational Statistics, 2003). According to the National Assessment Governing Board, students reaching *proficiency* have demonstrated competency over challenging mathematics content including mathematics knowledge, application to real-world situations, and analytical skills. Similarly, Schmidt, Houang, and Cogan (2002) reported that by the end of high school, students from the United States performed near the bottom of the international distribution in the Third International Mathematics and Science Study (TIMSS), the most extensive comparative study of math and science achievement and curriculum to date. Furthermore, research suggests that many students who are learning disabled lag behind their typically achieving peers in the area of mathematics (Carnine, Jones, & Dixon, 1994). These reports of poor student performance in both general and special education have compelled educators to examine the mathematics instruction in this country more closely.

The National Council of Teachers of Mathematics (NCTM), in an attempt to ensure the highest quality mathematics instruction for all students, outlined several principles of effective mathematics instruction. These broad principles address several important areas including curriculum and teaching (NCTM, 2000). For example, the NCTM principles highlight the need for well designed curricula as well as the need for quality teacher preparation that provides teachers with core mathematics knowledge. Ma

From the *Journal of Direct Instruction*, Vol. 4, No. 1, pp. 41–52. Copyright 2004 by the Association of Direct Instruction. Reprinted with permission.

(1999), in an extensive study of Chinese and American teachers' knowledge of mathematics, confirmed that the knowledge of most American elementary mathematics teachers was not nearly as robust as that of Chinese educators she interviewed. Schmidt et al. (2002), in their analysis of the TIMSS data, also addressed issues of curriculum and teaching. They stated, "American students and teachers are greatly disadvantaged by our country's lack of a common coherent curriculum and the text, materials, and training that match it" (p. 10).

Historically, few experimental studies have investigated specific instructional methods *or* curricular components in the area of mathematics (Gersten, 2002). An exception to this dearth of research on mathematics methods and materials comes from Direct Instruction. As reported by Adams and Engelmann (1996) and Przychodzin, Marchand-Martella, Martella, and Azim (2004), using a Direct Instruction approach to teach mathematics results in increased achievement when compared to other instructional approaches.

One of the ways in which Direct Instruction differs from most educational approaches is in the application of precise principles of instructional design to curriculum development (Carnine, 1997; Dixon, 1994; Engelmann & Carnine, 1991; Harniss, Stein, & Carnine, 2002). These design principles have been applied to a wide range of curricular areas including reading, writing, spelling, and critical thinking. The purpose of this paper is to present a framework for evaluating mathematics programs based on these principles. Educators involved in adopting a mathematics program can use this framework to assist them in selecting well designed commercially developed materials. In addition, educators can use this framework for evaluating and modifying their current mathematics programs to better meet the instructional needs of their students.

THE CURRICULUM ADOPTION PROCESS

The process of curriculum adoption is critical to the selection of high quality instructional materials. Therefore, educators should not only employ a systematic framework for evaluating those materials but should also conduct the adoption process in an equally systematic manner. Stein, Stuen, Carnine, and Long (2001) described some of the critical features of a systematic adoption process for the selection of reading programs. Not surprisingly, these features should also be present when selecting

mathematics programs. Although a thorough discussion of the adoption process is beyond the scope of this article, we have highlighted the features from Stein et al. that we believe are essential to conducting an effective curriculum adoption in the area of mathematics. These features include: time allocation, committee responsibilities, and the screening process.

Time Allocation

A major consideration in the adoption of curriculum materials is allocating sufficient time for the screening and evaluation of those materials. Many curriculum adoption committees work only after school for brief periods of time. However, meaningful and thorough examination of instructional materials requires large blocks of uninterrupted time. Therefore, committee members must be given adequate release time to review the materials and discuss their findings with their colleagues. Stein et al. (2001) offer an example of a timeline for curriculum adoption that allocates approximately 15 release days for teachers on the adoption committee. During those days teachers review research, generate screening and evaluation criteria, screen all submitted programs, thoroughly evaluate three to four of those programs, deliberate, and then select a program.

Committee Responsibilities

Commonly, teachers in schools or districts are given the opportunity to vote on the selection of a mathematics program from a short list generated by an adoption committee. Given that the adoption committee members are given adequate time to evaluate the mathematics programs thoroughly, the final selection of an instructional program should rest with the adoption committee. To feel comfortable with a committee decision, however, most teachers need to be kept informed at all stages of the adoption process. Therefore, adoption committee members must communicate regularly and effectively with the groups they represent.

Members of mathematics curriculum adoption committees are often selected based on seniority and knowledge of mathematics. However, additional selection factors also should be considered when forming adoption committees. Committees should include individuals representing a range of grade levels, those representing both special and general education students, and those with excellent communication skills.

Screening Process

To expedite the task of evaluating instructional programs, we recommend that the adoption committee first screen all the programs submitted for consideration. Given that evaluating programs thoroughly requires a substantial time commitment, screening is recommended to reduce the number of programs that the committee must eventually evaluate.

The first step in the screening process is to determine the criteria that will be used. Table 2.1 illustrates an example of criteria that we believe will facilitate the screening process. The criteria include questions that address three important areas: (a) General Instructional Approach, (b) Evidence of Effectiveness, and (c) Critical Content. The questions under General Instructional Approach direct evaluators to ascertain the program's theoretical approach—that is, whether the program represents an explicit or direct approach, a constructivist approach, or another approach to the teaching of mathematics. The questions under Evidence of Effectiveness direct evaluators to determine if the program has been systematically evaluated in controlled research studies that are subsequently published in the research literature. In addition to published research, evidence of whether the program has been field-tested is considered in this section as well.

The questions under Critical Content can be used to compare how different programs teach important skills or concepts. We recommend that for screening purposes, evaluators compare two skills from each program in two grade levels (e.g., one primary grade, one intermediate grade). By comparing how programs teach these two skills, evaluators can get a sense of the overall program design. The questions in this section were selected for screening purposes from a more comprehensive set of evaluation questions that appear in the Mathematics Evaluation Framework outlined later in this article.

MATHEMATICS CURRICULUM EVALUATION FRAMEWORK

On the following pages we describe a curriculum evaluation framework for examining commercially developed mathematics programs. We have developed a form that may assist teachers in using the framework to evaluate materials (see Table 2.2). The framework contains four sections: *General Program Design, Instructional Strategy Design, Teaching Procedures,* and *Assessment.* This form has three columns: Evaluation Criteria, Comments, and Examples. The Examples column is included to provide specific references to examples (i.e., page numbers from the program) that illustrate and support the evaluator's comments. These examples are necessary to engage in an objective discussion about program quality with other committee members.

I. GENERAL PROGRAM DESIGN

The purpose of the General Program Design criteria is to provide evaluators with an overview of the program's goals/objectives and degree of program coherence. The questions in this section address design features relevant to all levels in a given program. To answer these questions, we recommend that evaluators examine the scope and sequence of each level as well as examine sample lessons in a primary and intermediate level. Program coherence in this framework refers to the

---

Table 2.1 Mathematics Curriculum Evaluation Framework: Screening Criteria

A. General Instructional Approach

1. Does the program contain explicit instruction (i.e., steps in the strategies are clearly identified for both teachers and students)?

OR

2. Does the program represent a constructivist approach (i.e., student discovery and exploration is emphasized)?

B. Evidence of Effectiveness

1. Is there published evidence of the effectiveness of the program?
2. Is there evidence that the program has been field tested with large groups of students?

C. Critical Content

1. Are the steps in the selected strategies explicitly identified in the program?
2. Does the instruction follow a logical sequence?
3. Are there sufficient practice opportunities for mastery distributed across the grade level?

Table 2.2   Mathematics Curriculum Evaluation Framework

| Evaluator(s) _____ | | Grade Level _____ |
| Program/Publisher/Year _____ | | Date _____ |

Evaluation Criteria	Comments	Examples
I. General Program Design		
A. Program Goals/Objectives		
1. Are the "big ideas" in the program obvious?		
2. Are objectives stated as observable behaviors?		
B. Program Coherence		
1. Does the program use a strand or spiral design?		
2. Is there a balance between computation instruction and problem-solving instruction?		
II. Instructional Strategy Design		
A. Strategy		
1. Are the steps in the strategy **explicitly** identified in the program?		
2. Is the strategy of intermediate **generalizability**— not too narrow or too broad?		
B. Sequence and Integration		
1. Are the necessary **component skills** (preskills) taught prior to introducing the strategy?		
2. Does the program **strategically integrate** the new strategy with previously introduced strategies and related skills?		
C. Examples		
1. Is there a sufficient number of **practice examples** for initial mastery?		
2. Are there opportunities for **discrimination practice**?		
3. Does the program provide opportunities for **cumulative review** of previously introduced skills?		
III. Teaching Procedures		
A. Scaffolded Instruction		
1. Is teacher modeling specified?		
2. Is teacher assistance gradually faded?		
3. Does the program recommend specific correction procedures?		
IV. Assessment		
A. Assessment and Instruction Link		
1. Does the program contain placement tests?		
2. Do the program assessments contain recommendations for acceleration and remediation?		
3. Are the program assessments carefully aligned with instruction?		

extent to which the content of the program is integrated within and across grade levels and to the balance and integration of computation and problem solving.

A. Program Goals/Objectives

1) *Are the "big ideas" in the program obvious?* According to principles of Direct Instruction, well designed mathematics programs are organized around major principles (i.e., big ideas or goals) that are applicable in many situations and contexts (e.g., place value, equivalence, number sense). Although all programs will contain instruction on big ideas, evaluators should determine the extent to which the big ideas are well articulated and obvious by looking at the program's scope and sequence. A significant amount of instructional time should be devoted to these concepts, and evaluators should be able to determine the extent to which the concepts appear in many related contexts.

2) *Are objectives stated as observable behaviors?* The objectives in a program help teachers determine exactly what students should be able to do as a result of the instruction provided. Not only should objectives be aligned with the instruction but they should also be aligned with the program assessment procedures. The objectives should contain a statement of a measurable behavior. Many programs contain objectives that describe teacher behavior and not student behavior. For example, we found objectives similar to this one in several mathematics programs: "Review telling time." Note that the objective identifies what the teacher does but not what the students do. Alternatively this time telling objective is stated as a measurable behavior: "Students will express time as minutes after the hour." Teachers would have little difficulty assessing whether students met this objective.

B. Program Coherence

1) *Does the program use a strand or spiral design?* As Snider (2004) notes, programs using a strand design teach fewer topics over a long period of time with the goal of student mastery. Programs using a spiral design, in contrast, present a large number of topics for a short period of time with relatively little depth or integration with the goal of exposure. Evaluators can use the scope and sequence of individual grade levels and the overviews of the programs provided by the publishers to ascertain the overall approach

to the design of the content. For more detailed information on strand versus spiral design, see Snider, this issue.

2) *Is there a balance between computation instruction and problem-solving instruction?* Wu (1999) was among the first to identify the false dichotomy between computation and problem solving. He wrote that a common mathematics misconception held by many educators and the general public is, "...that the demand for precision and fluency in the execution of basic skills in school mathematics runs counter to the acquisition of conceptual understanding" (p. 14). Wu articulated concern over the practice of increasing instruction in abstract conceptual understanding while decreasing (or even eliminating) instruction in basic skills. As a mathematician, he fully realizes that understanding mathematics at the deepest level requires instruction that addresses both computation and problem solving and that the two processes are not mutually exclusive. Therefore, we recommend that evaluators carefully examine the scope and sequence of each program to determine the extent to which it provides an instructional balance between computation and problem solving.

II. INSTRUCTIONAL STRATEGY DESIGN

The criteria for Instructional Strategy Design were developed to help evaluators determine how critical content is taught in each of the programs. We recommend that grade-level committees select three to four different skills or concepts for each grade level, preferably ones that have been identified as big ideas, and use the criteria specified in Table 2.2 to examine how systematically those skills or concepts are taught.

To best evaluate the instructional strategies, we recommend that evaluators conduct a skill trace for each of the core skills or concepts they choose to evaluate. A skill trace involves locating every instance where the target strategy appears in the program. The skill trace helps evaluators isolate the instructional strategy to best evaluate its explicitness and generalizability. The skill trace also allows evaluators to determine whether component skills are identified and taught prior to the introduction of the strategy. Finally, a skill trace will also provide evidence of the degree to which the strategies are integrated with each other.

A. Strategy

1) *Are the steps in the strategy **explicitly** identified in the program?* To determine the explicitness of a strategy, evaluators should examine where in the program the strategy is first introduced and determine whether the program clearly articulates the steps that students are to follow in using the strategy to solve a problem (either a computation problem or word problem). The following is an example of a strategy for solving word problems that would *not* be considered explicit: "1. Decide what to do. 2. Do it. 3. Does my answer make sense?" (The University of Chicago School Mathematics Project, 1995, p. 44). Although the steps in the strategy are clearly articulated, the above strategy is not considered to be explicit because the cognitive processes required by students to solve the problem are not overtly taught.

In contrast, an explicit direct instruction strategy for solving classification word problems is outlined in Figure 2.1 (Stein, Silbert, & Carnine, 1997). Before students are introduced to this strategy, they are taught several component skills including the language skill of identifying class names for groups of objects (e.g., saws, hammers, and screwdrivers are all tools) and how to use a fact number family strategy to solve addition and subtraction facts (e.g., 2, 4, 6 comprise a fact family used to generate 2 + 4 = 6, 4 + 2 = 6, 6 − 2 = 4, 6 − 4 = 2). Also, prior to being introduced to this strategy, students would be familiar with the graphic conventions of big and little boxes. Figure 2.1 provides an example of an explicit strategy for teaching students how to solve a complex type of word problem.

2) *Is the strategy of intermediate **generalizability**—not too narrow or too broad?* A well designed strategy results in the greatest number of students correctly solving the greatest number of problems. The strategy should reliably lead to the solution of the problem for all students. The steps in the general word problem strategy mentioned above ("Decide what to do. Do it. Does my answer make sense?") are so broad that only students who already know how to solve the problem will correctly answer the question.

Similarly, teachers do not want to spend valuable instructional time teaching a narrow strategy that it is of limited use. Teaching students a shortcut for finding 1/3 of 9 by teaching them to divide 9 by 3 only works when the fraction in the problem has a 1 in the numerator. Low performing students are likely to overgeneralize this strategy when asked to find 2/3 of 9 and answer incorrectly.

We feel strongly that the quality of the instructional strategies included in mathematics programs should be a defining component in the evaluation of these programs. A practical approach to the evaluation of the strategies is for evaluators to assume the characteristics of naïve learners. Evaluators should pretend that they do not already know how to solve the problem and follow the steps in the strategy as specified in the teacher's manual. By doing this,

---

Figure 2.1

Solving classification word problems.

There are 8 children. Three are boys. How many are girls?

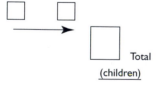

(children)

1. Read the problem. The problem talks about children, boys, and girls. Which is the big class?
2. If children is the big class then children is the total number. Write children on the line under the total box.
3. Does the problem tell how many children? So the total number is given. What is the total number? Write 8 in the box for Total number.
4. Now we write the values for boys and girls. In the boxes over the arrow. How many boys? Write 3 in the first box. We don't know how many girls so we don't write anything in the other box.
5. Is the total number given? So what do you have to do to work the problem? I start with 8 children and subtract 3 boys to find out how many girls. Write the equation and figure out the answer.
6. If there are 8 children and 3 are boys, how many are girls?

evaluators can determine whether the steps in the strategy are explicit and useful.

B. Sequence and Integration

1) *Are the necessary* **component skills** *(preskills) taught prior to introducing the strategy?* Often mathematics programs introduce the component skills and the new strategy simultaneously. For example, a program will introduce estimation at the same time that it introduces long division, a skill requiring the use of estimation. Most students need time to master the component skills prior to being introduced to a strategy that requires the application of that component skill. Students should have mastered estimation prior to the introduction of long division.

2) *Does the program* **strategically integrate** *the new strategy with previously introduced strategies and related skills?* Although we acknowledge the advantages of introducing new strategies in isolation, we also understand that students must learn the relationship among strategies to understand mathematics concepts fully. Therefore, one of the features of a well designed program is the strategic integration of mathematics strategies throughout the program. One way to determine the integration is to examine the skill trace for evidence that the newly taught strategy has been integrated with related previously taught strategies. Ideally, this integration would occur at the end of the instructional sequence after students have demonstrated mastery of the strategy in isolation. For example, well designed programs carefully integrate long division into word problems after students have demonstrated mastery on solving long division problems in isolation.

C. Examples

1) *Is there a sufficient number of* **practice examples** *for initial mastery?* Technically, this question can only be answered using information about student performance (i.e., Did students master this skill with the number of practice examples available?). Therefore, evaluators should compare programs with respect to the number of examples provided and err in selecting programs with *more* rather than *fewer* examples. Reducing the number of practice examples presented is far easier than creating additional examples for students who need more practice.

2) *Does the program contain opportunities for* **discrimination practice?** Discrimination practice refers to including a set of practice examples that requires students to determine when to apply a strat-

egy and when not to. For example, after presenting subtraction with regrouping, the program should give students the opportunity to practice regrouping using a set of examples in which some problems require regrouping and some do not. Without that practice, some students will try to apply the regrouping strategy to any multi-digit subtraction problem they encounter.

3) *Does the program provide opportunities for* **cumulative review?** Cumulative review refers to the notion that all strategies taught should be systematically reviewed throughout the grade level. Cumulative review is related to the notion of strategic integration in that the review of newly introduced strategies should be integrated and reviewed with previously introduced strategies. Well designed programs alert both the teacher and the students to the fact that this review is cumulative and that it requires careful attention to *when* as well as *how* a strategy should be applied.

III. TEACHING PROCEDURES

The Teaching Procedures criteria focus on how well the program supports the teacher by providing specific teacher instructions. Traditionally, mathematics programs suggest teachers demonstrate a strategy with a couple of problems, then direct teachers to have students complete a number of problems independently (Harniss, Carnine, Silbert, & Dixon, 2002). In contrast, one of the most critical teaching procedures derived from Direct Instruction design principles is the use of scaffolded instruction. Scaffolded instruction begins with the teacher modeling a strategy followed by *gradually* fading support until students can implement the strategy independently. We recommend that evaluators look for evidence that the program assists teachers in using scaffolded instruction. Another critical teaching procedure is the use of correction procedures during instruction. Without adequate provisions for correcting student errors, teachers will have difficulty helping students achieve mastery. The questions in this section also can be answered by examining the skill trace for any given instructional strategy.

A. Scaffolded Instruction

1) *Is teacher modeling specified?* Evaluators should examine the initial instruction provided for the target skill or concept to determine whether the program includes procedures that clearly require the

teacher to model the steps in the instructional strategy. It should be noted that some programs may suggest teacher modeling but may not explicitly provide the steps for the strategy in the teacher's manual, making modeling more difficult for teachers.

2) *Is teacher assistance gradually faded?* Scaffolded instruction provides temporary support to students as they begin to apply their new strategies. Scaffolding may take several forms. Programs might provide a series of questions for the teacher to use in guiding students through the steps necessary to complete problems. As students become more proficient, the teacher asks fewer guiding questions as students complete problems. Alternately, the program may supply graphic support for students in applying their new strategy. For example, a graphic organizer may prompt students to find the common denominators prior to adding or subtracting fractions. Scaffolded instruction provides teachers with the support necessary to ensure that students solve mathematics problems with fewer errors as they become more independent.

3) *Does the program recommend specific correction procedures?* Although modeling and carefully scaffolded instruction reduce the number of errors students make, the program should provide procedures for teachers to correct any errors that students might make. The correction procedure may suggest that teachers return to using the support provided in earlier instruction such as guiding questions or graphics. Other correction procedures may involve simply modeling the correct answer and repeating the question. The most important consideration is that the program specifies correction procedures.

IV. ASSESSMENT

Finally, the assessment criteria address the quality of the placement and evaluation procedures recommended in the programs with respect to the link between assessment and instruction. Evaluators examine the teacher's manuals as well as any supplementary assessment materials to answer the questions in this section. We suggest that evaluators first determine whether programs contain a placement test with alternative placement options so that students can be placed at appropriate levels of the program. Next, evaluators should determine if recommendations for acceleration and remediation are provided based on the program assessment results. Finally, evaluators establish the extent to which program assessments are aligned with instruction. This

alignment is necessary for teachers to make informed instructional decisions regarding student progress and mastery of the content.

A. Assessment and Instruction Link

1) *Does the program contain placement tests?* Program placement tests provide important information regarding the appropriateness of the program placement for individual students. The placement tests should provide teachers with information to determine if the students have the background knowledge and skills required for entrance into a given level of the program. Additionally, the tests could provide multiple entry points for students who have already mastered some of the program content.

2) *Do the program assessments contain recommendations for acceleration and remediation?* Related to issues of assessment/instruction alignment is the question of whether the program provides specific recommendations for acceleration or remediation based on student performance. Ideally, the program assessments would help teachers identify those students who need more or less assistance in mastering the content so that instruction could be differentiated appropriately.

3) *Are the program assessments carefully aligned with instruction?* Since the purpose of the in-program assessments is to help teachers make more informed instructional decisions, the assessments must be aligned with program content. The assessment items should test both newly taught skills and concepts as well as previously introduced content.

CONCLUSION

Teachers of elementary mathematics need well designed programs to teach their students more effectively. The Mathematics Curriculum Evaluation Framework outlined in this paper is designed to help teachers screen mathematics instructional programs and evaluate the extent to which the programs incorporate instructional design features that appear to be related to student achievement. While little research on these features in isolation is available, research on commercially developed Direct Instruction mathematics programs suggests that these features contribute to increased mathematics achievement.

Clearly, systematic research is necessary to develop reliable and valid criteria and objective procedures for the analysis of commercially developed mathematics programs. Currently, there are no reli-

able and valid evaluation instruments for analyzing these programs. The Mathematics Curriculum Evaluation Framework presented here outlines criteria that may be included in such an instrument. Educators interested in pursuing the development of these instruments will need to validate those criteria, develop objective evaluation procedures, and determine reliability. Moreover, educators will need to design the evaluation process with practitioners in mind. That is, evaluation instruments will need to be easy to use and provide information that is useful to the consumer. Until a reliable and valid curriculum evaluation instrument is designed, we suggest that using this framework will result in a much more thorough examination of the quality of a commercially developed mathematics program.

REFERENCES

Adams, G., & Engelmann, S. (1996). *Research on Direct Instruction: 25 years beyond DISTAR*. Seattle, WA: Educational Achievement Systems.

Carnine, D. (1997). Instructional design in mathematics for students with learning disabilities. *Journal of Learning Disabilities, 30,* 130–141.

Carnine, D., Jones, E. D., & Dixon, R. (1994). Mathematics: Educational tools for diverse learners. *School Psychology Review, 23,* 406–427.

Dixon, B. (1994). Research based guidelines for selecting mathematics curriculum. *Effective School Practices, 13*(2), 47–61.

Engelmann, S., & Carnine, D. (1991). *Theory of instruction: Principles and applications.* Eugene, OR: ADI Press.

Gersten, R. (2002). *Mathematics education and achievement.* Retrieved August 6, 2002, from http://www.ed.gov/offices/OESE/esea/research/gersten/html.

Harniss, M. K., Carnine, D. W., Silbert, J., & Dixon, R. C. (2002). Effective strategies for teaching mathematics. In E. J. Kame'enui, D. W. Carnine, R. C. Dixon, D. C. Simmons, & M. C. Coyne, *Effective teaching strategies that accommodate diverse learners.* (2nd ed., pp. 121–148). Columbus, OH: Merrill/Prentice Hall.

Harniss, M. K., Stein, M., & Carnine, D. (2002). Promoting mathematics achievement. In M. R. Shinn, G. Stoner, & H. M. Walker (Eds.), *Intervention for academic and behavior problems II: Preventive and remedial approaches* (pp. 571–587). Bethesda, MD: National Association of School Psychologists.

Ma, L. (1999). *Knowing and teaching elementary mathematics.* Mahwah, NJ: Lawrence Erlbaum Associates.

National Center for Educational Statistics. (2003). *The nation's report card:* Retrieved December 1, 2003, from http://nces.ed.gov/nationsreportcard/mathematics/

National Council of Teachers of Mathematics. (2000). *Principles and standards for school mathematics: An overview of principles and standards.* Retrieved December 1, 2003, from http:// standards.nctm.org

Przychodzin, A. M., Marchand-Martella, N. E., Martella, R. C., & Azim, D. (2004). Direct Instruction mathematics programs: An overview and research summary. *Journal of Direct Instruction, 4,* 53–84.

Schmidt, W., Houang, R., & Cogan, L. (2002). A coherent curriculum: The case of mathematics. *American Educator, 26*(2), 10–26.

Snider, V. E. (2004). A comparison of spiral versus strand curriculum. *Journal of Direct Instruction, 4,* 29–39.

Stein, M., Silbert, J., & Carnine, D. (1997). *Designing effective mathematics instruction: A Direct Instruction approach* (3rd ed.). Columbus, OH: Merrill/Prentice Hall.

Stein, M. L., Stuen, C., Carnine, D., & Long, R. M. (2001). Textbook evaluation and adoption practices. *Reading and Writing Quarterly, 17*(1), 5–23.

University of Chicago School Mathematics Project. (1995). *Third grade everyday mathematics: Teacher's manual and lesson guide.* Evanston, IL: Everyday Learning Corporation.

Wu, H. (1999). Basic skills versus conceptual understanding. *American Educator, 23*(3), 14–19, 50–52.

CHAPTER 3

Handwritten notes:
Constructivist vs. explicit
- Piaget/Vygotsky
- Student-centered
- discovery-oriented (inquiry)
- research oriented
- direct instructional approach

Research Relevant to Mathematics Instruction

This chapter addresses the broad topic of mathematics research by organizing information relevant to mathematics instruction into four major sections—history of mathematics instruction—issues and conflicts, current mathematics performance of students in the United States, general reviews of research in mathematics instruction, and research on critical instructional elements important to the design of effective mathematics instruction.

HISTORY OF MATHEMATICS INSTRUCTION: ISSUES AND CONFLICTS

The Math Wars

In his recently published chapter in *Mathematical Cognition,* Klein (2003) provides a brief history of K–12 mathematics education in the 20th century. The chapter chronicles some of the political struggles and resulting policy changes throughout the century and offers a context for understanding the "math wars" of the 1990s. In his discussion, Klein characterizes the math wars as a conflict between content and pedagogy. He explains that although what to teach and how best to teach shouldn't necessarily be in conflict, depending on a teacher's priority (i.e., content or pedagogy), one or the other may well be affected. For example, if a student-centered, discovery-oriented pedagogical approach to mathematics instruction takes priority over the selection of content, then students are limited to the

content that they discover or "construct" during their explorations. Likewise, Klein points out, if a predetermined amount of content has been established, the pedagogical approach to teaching content must be the most efficient and therefore may preclude other approaches to teaching.

To understand the longstanding conflicts in mathematics instruction, teachers and administrators must be able not only to discriminate content from pedagogy, but also to discriminate among different pedagogical approaches. Currently, the two major approaches to mathematics instruction are most frequently characterized as constructivist and explicit. Constructivist approaches, derived from the work of Jean Piaget and Lev Vygotsky, appear to be consistent with student-centered, discovery-oriented approaches. Explicit teaching approaches are embodied in direct instruction and derived from the research literature on teacher effectiveness.

Klein identifies two major reports on K–12 education published in the 1980s that represent the viewpoints of those who eventually would serve as the opposing factions in the math wars: "An Agenda for Action" (National Council of Teachers of Mathematics, 1980) and "A Nation at Risk" (National Commission of Excellence in Education, 1983).

"An Agenda for Action" called for a new direction in mathematics instruction that foreshadowed the 1989 Curriculum and Evaluation Standards published by the National Council of Teachers of Mathematics (NCTM). The Agenda recommended a strong emphasis on problem solving, suggesting that be-

implication for Mathematics instructor? (SPED)?

cause of increased technology (i.e., calculators and computers), students no longer needed to master basic skills prior to learning more challenging problem-solving strategies. The Agenda also recommended more collaborative work, the use of manipulatives, and alternative means of assessing student performance. "A Nation at Risk" documented the failure of education reform efforts in the 1960s and 1970s to address the discrepancy between the math and science achievement of U.S. students and those in other developed nations. The report highlighted the increased need for remedial mathematics at the college level, a shortage of qualified mathematics teachers, and lack of rigor in textbooks. Both reports are credited for motivating the development of the 1989 curriculum, pedagogy, and assessment standards in mathematics developed by the NCTM.

NCTM Standards

Much public debate was generated among mathematicians, math educators, and parents regarding the validity and usefulness of the 1989 Standards. (See Klein, 2003, for a more thorough discussion of the math wars.) In response to this academic and very public debate on the 1989 Standards, NCTM released an updated document called Principles and Standards for School Mathematics (PSSM) (NCTM, 2000). For this revision, NCTM sought input from many respected mathematics organizations (e.g., the American Mathematical Society) not consulted during the development of the previous version. As a result, PSSM includes more emphasis on computational fluency and slightly more attention to arithmetic algorithms. Despite the changes in the document, however, the mathematicians and educational researchers expressed significant concerns about the relative value of the changes and the lack of research validation for the recommendations (Hofmeister, 2004).

CURRENT MATHEMATICS PERFORMANCE OF STUDENTS IN THE UNITED STATES

Unfortunately, both international and national studies of student performance indicate that American students are not achieving in mathematics at a deep level of understanding. The Third International Mathematics and Science Study (TIMSS) is one of the most extensive cross-national comparative studies of student achievement in math and science, with the participation at some level of 42 countries

(Schmidt, Houang, & Cogan, 2002). Results of this international comparison found that although U.S. fourth-grade students ranked high, by eighth grade U.S. students were below average, and by twelfth grade U.S. students scored near the bottom of the list. No other country's scores revealed as sharp a decline in math achievement (Loveless & Diperna, 2000).

The Programme for International Student Achievement (PISA) is another cross-national study of reading, mathematics, and science literacy of 15-year-olds in 32 industrialized countries. Results from PISA were similar to those from TIMSS in that the U.S. students scored below the international average (Organization for Economic Co-Operation and Development, 2004).

National tests confirm the decline of student performance in the upper grades. The National Assessment of Educational Progress (NAEP), called the "Nation's Report Card," has been assessing the performance of fourth-, eighth-, and twelfth-grade students in several subject areas since the 1970s. Recent reports (National Center for Educational Statistics, 2000, 2003) show that, in general, mathematics scores have increased slowly and steadily over the last 30 years. However, the data do indicate that although fourth-grade students have made the greatest improvement over the years, students in twelfth grade have made no significant gains since 1990 (National Center for Educational Statistics, 2003).

GENERAL REVIEWS OF RESEARCH IN MATHEMATICS INSTRUCTION

In an era of increased accountability, where a well-educated populace implies greater participation in the global economy, the need for research-validated, "effective" instructional practices seems even greater. A call for additional research on the "...nature, development, and assessment of mathematical proficiency" was one of five major recommendations articulated by the National Research Council in its report of the current state of school mathematics (National Research Council, 2001, p. 14). Many (e.g., Baker, Gersten, & Lee, 2002; Gersten et al., under review) feel that the only way that the math wars will be resolved is with a strong focus on "what works." Basic research on cognition and learning in mathematics, translating that research into viable instructional practices, and assessing the outcomes of those practices on student performance form the foundation of educational reform that advances knowledge. Toward that end, the remaining sections in this chapter highlight a number of research reviews, syntheses, and meta-analyses in the area of mathematics instruction that should help guide teachers in designing, evaluating, and modifying mathematics instruction. The reviews of research address the following topics: teacher effectiveness, Direct Instruction, students at risk for academic failure, and students with learning disabilities.

Teacher Effectiveness Research

"Teacher effectiveness research" includes a number of studies that investigated the relationship between teacher behavior and student outcomes using classroom observations and student achievement on standardized tests. In a review of this largely correlational research, Rosenshine (1983) concluded that highly interactive, briskly paced, clearly presented instruction is related to high rates of student success. In his review, he called this type of instruction "direct instruction."

Good and Grouws (1979) conducted one of the earliest experimental teacher effectiveness studies in the area of mathematics instruction. In this study, called the Missouri Mathematics Effectiveness Project, the researchers compared the achievement of students in control classrooms in which teachers used their traditional instructional procedures to the achievement of students in classes of teachers who were given extensive professional development in the implementation of five key instructional features: daily review, lesson development, seatwork, homework assignment, and special review. (See Good, Grouws, & Ebmeier, 1983 for more details on this approach to teaching mathematics.)

The study is important for several reasons. First, the researchers demonstrated that extensive, focused professional development could have an impact on the performance of students who are at risk for academic failure. Second, the researchers highlighted specific instructional features that are likely to contribute to the improvement of mathematics performance. Third, and perhaps most enlightening, the researchers found that the initial lesson development (design of instructional strategies) proved to be the most difficult aspect of the intervention for most teachers to grasp. While this finding is not surprising, it highlights the need for commercially developed programs to provide sound instructional strategies for teachers to implement.

Research on Direct Instruction

While the term *direct instruction* was used by Rosenshine to characterize effective teaching, the Direct Instruction (DI) model described in this section and on which this book is based is a comprehensive instructional model originally developed for one of the largest educational studies sponsored by the U.S. Department of Education: Project Follow Through. A defining feature of Direct Instruction (as opposed to direct instruction) is the use of carefully designed curriculum based on a theory of instruction developed by Engelmann and Carnine (1991).

Project Follow Through, an extension of Head Start, was designed to compare different educational approaches for teaching low-income students in kindergarten through third grade. Nine different educational approaches were implemented in 170 communities ranging from inner-city to rural settings, serving nearly 100,000 children (Adams & Engelmann, 1996; Watkins, 1997; Watkins & Slocum, 2004). In addition to Direct Instruction, other Follow Through models included an approach based on applied behavior analysis, one based on open education that emphasized student-directed learning, and a cognitively oriented curriculum based on Piagetian theory. Importantly, each Follow Through intervention site was matched with a comparable non-Follow Through comparison group from the same community. Three types of standardized tests were given to all students; these measures included basic skills tests, tests of cognitive abilities, and self-concept measures.

Abt Associates was contracted by the Department of Education to conduct an independent evaluation of Follow Through. The results showed that the Direct Instruction approach was the only model in which Follow Through students consistently outperformed their comparison groups on all measures (Stebbins, St. Pierre, Proper, Anderson, & Cerva, 1977). With respect to mathematics achievement specifically, results revealed that students who received 3 to 4 years of Direct Instruction scored significantly higher than their non-Follow Through comparison groups and those students in other Follow Through intervention models. More importantly, the data indicate that the performance of students receiving Direct Instruction math was commensurate with their middle-class peers.

Results from a follow-up study of fifth- and sixth-grade students who received Direct Instruction in the primary grades but not in the intermediate grades indicated consistent positive findings in the areas of mathematics problem solving, weaker but significant effects in mathematics concepts, but no effects in computation (Becker & Gersten, 1982). These findings suggest that the students who received Direct Instruction maintained the skills that were most generalizable, such as problem solving. When students were taught later computation skills (i.e., multiplication and division) using more traditional methods, they apparently did less well on measures of computation.

Subsequent research provides additional support for using a Direct Instruction approach to teaching mathematics. Adams and Engelmann (1996) analyzed 34 intervention studies involving Direct Instruction programs compared to other treatments. Thirty-two of the 34 studies they reviewed resulted in positive scores. In their analysis of the studies that addressed math, they found an effect size of 1.11 in favor of Direct Instruction math programs, which is substantial and considered rare in educational research.

Much of the research on Direct Instruction mathematics involves the use of commercially published Direct Instruction curricular materials. An overview of these programs and a synthesis of research studies investigating their effectiveness are presented in Appendix A.

Research on Students Who Are at Risk for Academic Failure

Recently, Baker, Gersten, and Lee (2002) conducted a meta-analysis of the effects of mathematics interventions developed to improve the achievement of students who are at risk for academic failure. They identified and synthesized 15 high-quality research studies published from 1971 to 1999. Their results suggest that four types of interventions lead to significant improvement in at-risk students' mathematical performance. The first involves providing teachers and students with progress-monitoring data. Results from the analysis showed that when teachers received data about their students' performance on a regular basis using curriculum-based measurement (CBM) procedures, student performance improved; even greater improvements were achieved when teachers also received computer-generated teaching recommendations to accompany the CBM data.

The second successful intervention identified in the research review is peer tutoring. Baker and colleagues found that peer tutoring had moderate effects on students' computation performance and smaller effects on overall mathematics performance. The third intervention is providing feedback to parents. Although the positive effects of this intervention were small, Baker and colleagues point out that the intervention is relatively easy to implement and requires little extra effort for teachers. Finally, the meta-analysis showed moderately strong effects for the use of explicit, teacher-led instruction in instructional studies that addressed both problem solving and computation.

Research on Students with Learning Disabilities

Gersten and colleagues (under review) used meta-analytic techniques to analyze the experimental and quasi-experimental research on mathematics instructional approaches designed to improve the performance of students with learning disabilities. After an exhaustive search, the researchers located only 26 studies that met the criteria established for inclusion in this analysis. The studies fell into three categories: curricula and broad instructional approaches, progress monitoring, and peer tutoring. In the area of curricula and broad instructional approaches, Gersten and colleagues found small but instructionally significant effects for the use of diagrams and visual scaffolding and for highly explicit instruction, including self-verbalization. They also reviewed curricular approaches that were found to be effective in a single study, but a discussion of these studies is beyond the scope of this review.

Additional findings from this meta-analysis are similar to the findings from the previously mentioned meta-analysis of studies with students at risk for academic failure (Baker et al., 2002). Both analyses suggest that progress monitoring and tutoring are effective. Gersten and his colleagues reported that the mathematics performance of students with learning disabilities improved when their teachers used progress-monitoring data regardless of whether instructional recommendations accompanied the data. Also, the students with learning disabilities improved regardless of whether special education teachers or general education teachers were using the data. They also reported positive effects for tutoring. The tutoring interventions included studies with both peer and cross-age tutors and studies in which tutors provided both minor support and more systematic assistance. Overall, tutoring interventions led to significantly better student performance for students with learning disabilities.

RESEARCH ON CRITICAL INSTRUCTIONAL ELEMENTS

In an extensive interview study comparing Chinese and American teachers' knowledge of mathematics, Ma (1999) found the American teachers lacked a "profound understanding of the fundamentals of mathematics." She reported that U.S. teachers displayed procedural knowledge with some algorithmic competence, while Chinese teachers more often displayed algorithmic competence with conceptual understanding. When asked to what they attribute their knowledge of mathematics, Chinese teachers mentioned their own elementary education, their teacher preparation, and their work as math specialists. Based on the analysis of her interviews with teachers, Ma recommends refocusing U.S. teacher preparation, encouraging more "on-the-job" study of mathematics, and providing teachers with well-constructed textbooks. The recommendation to use well-constructed textbooks is the topic of the next section on research findings as well as the major focus of the remaining chapters in this textbook.

As part of the TIMSS, researchers examined the content of the mathematics curriculum in 37 countries. For many countries, the curriculum examined was represented by their national curriculum. For other countries, including the United States, both state and district standards and textbooks were examined. This analysis found that the U.S. math curricula were unfocused, repetitive, undemanding, and incoherent. Further, they were described as "a mile wide, an inch deep" (p. 3). The researchers hypothesize that the poor performance of U.S. students can be attributed to the lack of a common, coherent curriculum.

The analysis of mathematics curricula and textbooks provided by the TIMSS evaluation together with evidence that U.S. teachers lack critical mathematics knowledge have enormous implications for classroom teachers committed to the education of their most difficult-to-teach students. The remainder of this section on research provides some insight regarding the instructional design elements that appear critical to the development of mathematics instruction that will meet the needs of all teachers and students. These elements include explicit strategy instruction, prior knowledge, sequencing, examples, practice and review, and progress monitoring. These elements also, not incidentally, are the elements around which the instruction in this text has been developed.

Explicitness

Explicit approaches are described as clear, accurate, and unambiguous instruction often including teacher modeling and, in some cases, verbal descriptions. The two recent meta-analyses discussed in the previous section (Baker et al., 2002; Gersten et al., under review) found moderate to strong effects for the use of explicit instruction with students at risk for academic failure and for students with learning disabilities.

A number of studies focused on individual topics in mathematics also provide support for the use of explicit strategies in mathematics. Carnine and Stein (1981) found that explicitly teaching a counting strategy to learn basic math facts resulted in greater accuracy and better retention. Later, Darch, Carnine, and Gersten (1989) investigated the effects of a highly explicit, step-by-step method for teaching story problems. This explicit instruction was contrasted with traditional problem-solving instruction commonly found in basal mathematics texts at that time. In this study, even though the students receiving traditional teaching received more instructional time, the students taught using the explicit approach outperformed them. Cardelle-Elawar (1992, 1995) also explored the effects of explicit instruction in problem solving. Teachers extensively modeled an instructional strategy and then carefully monitored students as they worked individually. This explicit instructional approach was found to have a significant, positive effect on student performance.

Moore and Carnine (1989) assessed students' understanding and accuracy in solving elementary problems with decimals and proportions after the students received explicit instruction in discriminating relevant and irrelevant information in word problems. This instruction resulted in significant, positive effects for the experimental group. Woodward, Baxter, and Robinson (1999) compared the effects of explicit instruction based on the principles of direct instruction to instruction in *Everyday Mathematics*. *Everyday Mathematics* encourages students to develop or construct their own models or strategies for solving problems. Both the explicit instruction group and the *Everyday Mathematics* group studied computation with decimals. The results showed that the at-risk students in the explicit instruction group significantly outperformed the students instructed with *Everyday Mathematics*.

In summarizing the research on explicit strategy instruction in their review of effective mathematics instruction, Dixon, Carnine, Lee, Wallin, and Chard

(1998) concluded that there is strong support for explicit instruction. However, they pointed out that one study (Christensen & Cooper, 1991) found fact practice along with fluency building was more effective than explicit strategy instruction alone. Dixon and colleagues suggested that increased practice and fluency building combined with a research-based explicit strategy should be investigated.

Prior Knowledge

Prior or background knowledge is the related knowledge required in order to understand a new skill or concept (Kame'enui, Carnine, & Dixon, 2002). A firm understanding of necessary prerequisite skills (prior knowledge) is fundamental not only to understanding the new content, but also to understanding the relationship and connection between concepts (Bransford, Sherwood, Hasselbring, Kinzer, & Williams, 1990). In his early work, Carnine (1980) established the importance of prior knowledge in learning multiplication. Jackson and Phillips (1983) found that preskill instruction in vocabulary significantly improved the achievement of seventh-grade students in solving ratio and proportion problems. Barron, Bransford, Kulewicz, and Hasselbring (1989) identified basic mathematics facts as essential prior knowledge for even simple word problems. Darch and colleagues (1989) found that identifying and preteaching skills that represent prerequisite knowledge for problem solving was critical to improving student performance.

Sequencing

The order in which skills are introduced appears to have an impact on student performance. Van Patten, Chao, and Reigeluth (1986) identified two levels of sequencing: macro and micro strategies for sequencing. Macro-sequencing involves the order in which concepts and skills are introduced. However, macro-sequencing first involves identification and prioritization of instructional content. Micro-sequencing strategies refer to the order of examples, practice, and definitions associated with a given concept or skill. In a 1990 study, Kelly, Gersten, and Carnine compared the effects of two approaches to macro-sequencing of concepts and operations involving fractions. The intervention group received content in which concepts and operations were sequenced carefully, confusing concepts and terms were separated, but opportunities were provided for selecting and using the appropriate skill in mixed problem sets. The other group received traditional instruction with a new concept introduced each day and no opportunity for mixed practice. The group that received the carefully sequenced instruction outperformed the other group on posttests. Analyses of the data suggested that specific features of the instructional design, like sequence of concepts, might have accounted for the difference in outcomes.

A small number of mathematics studies have examined the issue of micro-sequencing. Petty and Jansson (1987) found that when teaching the concept of parallelograms, the order of examples had an effect on student achievement. Students who were taught with examples carefully sequenced to show the range covered by the concept and examples to show minimal differences outperformed students receiving traditionally sequenced instruction. Brown (1970) had similar results using a logical sequence to teach problem solving to high school trigonometry students.

Examples

Leinhardt, Zaslavsky, and Stein (1990) stated, "The selection of examples is the art of teaching mathematics" (p. 25). The importance of example selection is supported by both the mathematics research and the instructional design research. Instructional design theorists Markle and Tiemann (1970) proposed that four different learning outcomes are predictable from the relationships among examples: accurate generalizations, undergeneralizations, overgeneralizations, and misconceptions.

Trafton (1984) also identified several problems related to example selection. Trafton pointed out that students commonly have difficulty subtracting when there are zeroes in the subtrahend and have problems with division problems when they have zeroes in the quotient. These difficulties might occur because the selection of examples used for instruction did not include adequate examples with zeroes.

Van Patten and colleagues (1986), based on their review of the research literature, suggested the following sequencing principles.

1. Match examples and nonexamples in a way that highlights the critical attributes of the generalization being taught. For example, during initial instruction in identifying fractions, juxtapose proper and improper fractions in practice exercise.

2. Make successive examples divergent (either by varying noncritical attributes across examples or critical attributes between examples and nonexamples).

For example, in teaching regrouping in addition, provide practice in discriminating problems that require regrouping from those that do not.

3. Present examples to show the range of generalization, moving from easier to more difficult examples. For example, in teaching long division, introduce division without zeroes first, followed by instruction in division with zeroes.

Practice and Review

Research in the area of practice and review includes topics relevant to both the design of mathematics instruction (e.g., rate of introduction and curricular organization) and specific instructional procedures (e.g., scaffolding). The following sections present research in each of those areas.

RATE OF INTRODUCTION. Porter (1989) makes a strong case for the need to carefully plan the rate at which mathematical concepts are introduced. In his examination of mathematics curricula, he found that approximately 70% of the topics covered within a school year are given less than 30 minutes of instructional time each across the entire school year. Only 10 to 20 topics received as much as two hours of instructional time. Porter referred to this situation as teaching for exposure. In the TIMSS analysis of mathematics curricula, Schmidt and colleagues (2002) arrived at similar conclusions: they found that no math textbooks in the world cover as many topics as U.S. math books do.

CURRICULAR ORGANIZATION. Schmidt and colleagues (2002) also point out that the content in U.S. textbooks tends to be repetitive; topics are introduced early and repeated year after year with little added depth. Snider (2004) refers to this as spiral design. Spiral design rarely gives students who have not mastered the concepts adequate instruction or practice to be successful. Snider suggests an alternative curricular organization called strand design. In contrast to a spiral design, instruction organized around a strand design focuses on a small number of topics taught for a relatively long period of time. Strand design is the organizational feature of all Direct Instruction commercial programs. Porter; Schmidt and colleagues; and Snider all conclude that teaching less content more thoroughly will promote a deeper understanding of mathematics concepts.

SCAFFOLDING. Scaffolding is the process of fading instructional support as students become more independent. Scaffolding can consist of teacher prompts,

structured worksheets, diagrams or other visual supports, as well as the type of peer support common in cooperative learning and peer tutoring.

Paine, Carnine, White, and Walters (1982) conducted two related studies on the effects of fading instructional support during instruction of arithmetic problem-solving skills. One study evaluated the effects of gradually building student independence by moving from instruction in which every step was prompted to instruction with few key prompts. In the second study, the effects of more rapid fading were investigated. In both cases, the groups who received the scaffolding outperformed the control groups who received demonstration and practice but no assistance phase. Higher performing students benefited more from the rapid-fading schedule than did lower performing students. Since the time of the Paine and colleagues study, different forms of scaffolding have been implemented as an effective teaching component in other studies with similar results (Woodward, Carnine, & Gersten, 1988; Kame'enui, Carnine, Darch, & Stein, 1986; Kelly, Carnine, Gersten, & Grossen, 1986).

Gersten and colleagues (under review) found evidence that use of diagrams, graphic organizers, or other types of visual scaffolding was effective for students with learning disabilities. Walker and Poteet (1989/90) and Baker (1992) in separate studies both taught students to create diagrams for math word problems. In these studies, the diagramming groups outperformed students who were taught without this type of support.

More recently, Jitendra, Griffin, McGoey, and Gardill (1998) investigated the effects of what has been termed a "schema-based" problem-solving strategy. In this study, students were taught to categorize word problems, create a diagram that represented that problem type, and solve the problem. The assistance provided by these student-created diagrams appears to account for the higher success of students who used the strategy compared to those who received more traditional instruction. Although the studies discussed above in which support was provided via diagrams resulted in relatively small positive effects, they suggest promising practice (Gersten et al., under review).

Scaffolding also can be delivered through peer-assisted instructional interventions. A substantial number of studies have investigated the effects of peer support in the forms of cooperative learning or peer tutoring (Baker et al., 2002; Dixon et al., 1998; Gersten et al., under review). Dixon and colleagues identified a number of studies (e.g., Johnson, Skon, & Johnson, 1980; Nichols, 1996; O'Melia & Rosenberg, 1994; Rzoska & Ward, 1991; Slavin & Karweit, 1984; Slavin, Madden, & Leavey, 1984) using cooperative learning in mathematics. One study (O'Melia & Rosenberg, 1994) showed no advantage for the approach. In this study, students were assigned to do homework in cooperative groups. All of the other studies Dixon and colleagues (1998) reviewed found positive effects for cooperative learning; but in these studies cooperative work was done in conjunction with teacher-directed instruction.

Peer tutoring also has been shown to be successful in a number of studies (Baker et al., 2002; Dixon et al., 1998; Gersten et al., under review). Fuchs, Fuchs, Phillips, Hamlett, & Kaarns (1995) and Fuchs and colleagues (1997) investigated a tutoring intervention in which students worked in pairs, usually in a reciprocal relationship, alternating between the role of tutor and tutee. In these studies, students were carefully trained in the tutoring procedures with specific methods to help struggling tutees. In their 1997 study, tutors gave feedback on each step of the problem-solving strategy that they were taught. Results from both studies supported using peer tutoring interventions to scaffold learning.

Fantuzzo and colleagues (Fantuzzo, Davis, & Ginsburg, 1995), used peer tutoring only for mathematics computation, not for problem solving. Heller and Fantuzzo (1993) used peer tutoring for varied computation problems with low-income fourth and fifth graders also demonstrating a strong effect on student achievement.

Progress Monitoring

Recent reviews of research provide strong support for the use of progress monitoring to improve student performance (Baker et al., 2002; Gersten et al., under review). Fuchs and colleagues conducted a number of studies investigating the use of CBM in mathematics (e.g., Fuchs, Fuchs, Hamlett, Phillips, & Gentz, 1994; Fuchs et al., 1997). CBM is a group of simple, short, fluency measures that monitor student performance in math over time (Shinn & Bamonto, 1998). Fuchs and colleagues (1994) compared two approaches to CBM feedback. One group of teachers and students were provided with individual graphs illustrating students' performance on weekly tests plus computer-generated instructional recommendations. The other group of teachers used their own methods to monitor student progress. Both methods had positive effects on student achievement; however, student achievement was higher when teachers received the instructional suggestions in addition to test results.

CONCLUSIONS

In summary, although research in the area of mathematics instruction is limited, a number of outcomes have been reported consistently across studies conducted during the last 30 years. The Direct Instruction research, teacher effectiveness studies, and recent literature reviews on effective math instructional practices consistently support approaches to instruction that includes the use of explicit rather than discovery-oriented strategies, careful sequencing of instruction, identification and instruction of prior knowledge, logical selection of examples, adequate practice and review, and systematic monitoring of student performance.

It is hoped that the research briefly summarized here and elsewhere will inform instructional practice. Ideally, publishers of commercial programs will attend to research findings such as these as they develop new developmental and remedial programs. Teachers, administrators, and curriculum specialists also must use research findings as they select instructional materials for use in their classrooms. The curriculum evaluation framework described in the previous chapter is based on much of the research reported in this chapter and can be used to assist educators in the curriculum adoption process. As teachers evaluate their own instructional materials, they may find the need to supplement and modify those materials. In Part II, "Skills and Concepts," teachers will find specific recommendations based on the research literature that will help them in their task of modifying published materials and designing and implementing effective mathematics instruction for all learners.

PART TWO

Skills and Concepts

CHAPTER 4

Counting

TERMS AND CONCEPTS

set A collection of concrete or abstract elements.

cardinal number The number that identifies the number of elements or members of a set.

numeral The symbol representing a cardinal number.

rote counting Identifying number names in sequence.

rational counting Identifying the cardinal number of a set, i.e., object counting; sometimes called one-to-one correspondence.

ordinal numbers Numbers associated with position, e.g., first, second, third.

manipulatives Concrete objects often used to facilitate instruction of mathematics concepts.

skip counting Identifying every nth number in the counting series; e.g., in skip counting by twos, students say every second number: 2, 4, 6, 8.... for eights, every eighth number: 8, 16, 24....

SKILL HIERARCHY

Counting skills are not only important in and of themselves, but they are also important prerequisite skills for many problem-solving strategies. The Instructional Sequence and Assessment Chart outlines a recommended instructional sequence for the major counting skills: rote counting, rational counting, counting from a number, skip counting, and ordinal counting. Note that counting instruction forms a major component of first-grade instruction and should be continued in second and third grades.

Rote counting is identifying number names in sequence (e.g., 1, 2, 3, 4, 5, 6). During first grade, students are taught to count to 99; in second grade, through 999; in third grade, into the thousands.

Rational counting is coordinating counting with the touching of objects to determine the quantity of a particular set. Rote counting is a prerequisite skill for rational counting. Students should be able to say numbers in sequence before they are expected to coordinate saying numbers while touching objects. We recommend that students be able to rote count to 10 before rational counting is introduced. Initial rational counting exercises involve counting a group of objects. Later exercises involve counting two groups of objects, a prerequisite skill for early addition.

Counting from a number is also a prerequisite skill for addition. In counting-from-a-number tasks, students begin with a number other than 1; for example, they begin with 6 and then count 7, 8, 9. In early addition problems such as 6 + 3, students would be taught to say 6, extending the pronunciation for a few seconds, and then count markers for the second addend: *sssiiixxx,* 7, 8, 9.

Instructional Sequence and Assessment Chart

Grade Level	Problem Type	Performance Indicator
K–1	Counting by ones from 1 through 20	Verbal test: teacher asks students to count to 20.
K–1	Counting a group of lines	Teacher writes four lines, asks how many lines. Repeat with seven lines, five lines.
K–1	Counting two groups of lines	Teacher writes | | | | | | | | | and asks how many lines all together?
K–1	Counting from a number other than 1	Verbal test: teacher asks students to begin counting at 6, at 11, at 8.
K–1	Counting by ones from 1 through 30	Verbal test: teacher asks students to count to 30.
K–1	Ordinal counting first through tenth	Verbal test: teacher draws 10 lines on board, asks students to touch third line and seventh line.
K–1	Skip counting by tens 10 to 100	Verbal test: teacher asks students to count by 10 to 100.
K–1	Counting backward from 10 to zero	Verbal test: teacher asks students to count backward from 10 to zero.
K–1	Counting by ones from 1 through 100	Write the number that comes next:* 26, _____, _____, 29, _____ 46, _____, _____, 49, _____
K–1	Skip counting by 2, 5, 100	Fill in the missing numerals:* 2, 4, 6, _____, _____, _____, _____ 5, 10, 15, _____, _____, _____, _____ 100, 200, 300 ____, ____, ____, ____, ____, ____, ____, ____
2a	Counting by ones 100 to 999	Write the numeral that comes next:* 349 _____ 299 _____ 599 _____ 699 _____ 499 _____ 704 _____ 889 _____ 509 _____
2b	Skip counting	Fill in the missing numerals:* 9, 18, 27 ____, ____, ____, ____, ____, ____, ____, ____ 4, 8, 12 ____, ____, ____, ____, ____, ____, ____, ____ 3, 6, 9 ____, ____, ____, ____, ____, ____, ____, ____ 8, 16, 24 ____, ____, ____, ____, ____, ____, ____, ____ 7, 14, 21 ____, ____, ____, ____, ____, ____, ____, ____ 6, 12, 18 ____, ____, ____, ____, ____, ____, ____, ____
3	Counting by ones 1,000 to 9,999	Write the numeral that comes next:* 3,101 _____ 2,529 _____ 5,499 _____ 7,308 _____ 3,999 _____ 7,999 _____
4	Counting by ones 10,000 to 999,999	Write the numeral that comes next (similar to above):*

*If a student fails a written test, the teacher should check student performance with a verbal test.

Skip counting is counting in which the students say multiples of a base number; for example, when counting by fives, students say 5, 10, 15, 20, 25, 30. We recommend that skip counting by tens be taught early to facilitate teaching rote counting to higher numbers. From skip counting, students learn that 40 follows 30; therefore, they more easily learn to say 40 after 39. Similarly, they learn to say 50 after 49, 60 after 59.

Skip counting by tens is taught after students can rote count to 30. Skip counting by twos and fives is taught later in first grade. Other skip-counting series are taught in second and third grades. Learning the skip-counting series in early grades also facilitates solving basic multiplication problems. For example, 2×3 is skip counting by twos three times and yields 6 (see Chapter 9, "Multiplication").

Ordinal counting (counting associated with position) is introduced when the students have mastered rational counting. Ordinal counting is taught because of the common use of ordinal numbers. Teachers often use ordinal numbers in directions— for example, "Touch the third problem."

INTRODUCING THE CONCEPT

The teaching procedures for the major counting skills appear in this section. The skills are listed in their relative order of introduction. Rote counting by ones to 30 is discussed first. Rational counting is discussed next. Rational counting would be introduced when students can rote count to about 10. Thereafter, daily lessons would include both rote and rational counting exercises. After students learn to count one group of objects, they count two groups of objects and determine the total quantity. Next, procedures for teaching students to count from different numbers, to ordinal count, to rote count between 30 and 100, to rote count between 100 and 999, and to skip count are discussed.

Initial instruction for rational counting is most efficient with pictorial representations of objects. Teachers can better monitor student performance during group instruction if the students are touching and counting pictures. As soon as students are proficient in counting pictures of objects, they can apply their skills to different types of manipulatives. Many low-performing students learn to count manipulatives more easily by first receiving instruction on counting pictorial representations of objects.

Rote Counting by Ones to 30

On the first day of instruction, the teacher tests the students to determine how high they can rote count without error. The teacher tests the students individually simply by asking them to count as high as they can. The teacher records the highest number each student counts. The performance of the group determines which new numbers are introduced. The teacher notes the lowest number correctly counted to by any members of the group and adds the next two or three numbers in the counting sequence. If a student counts to 11 on the pretest, the new part would be 11, 12, 13 (the last number said correctly on the pretest, 11, and the next two numbers, 12 and 13). The teacher should test students at the beginning of each lesson to determine whether new numbers can be introduced. If the students count correctly, the teacher introduces several new numbers. If the students make errors, the teacher repeats the format with the previously introduced numbers.

The format for introducing new numbers in the counting sequence appears in Format 4.1. The teacher first tests students on previously introduced numbers (1–10). Next, the teacher models counting from 1 to 13, then models just the new part, 11, 12, 13 (see step 2 in Format 4.1). In step 3, the teacher leads the students in saying the new part. When introducing new numbers, during both the model and lead (steps 2 and 3), the teacher should emphasize the new numbers by saying them in a loud voice so that students are always hearing a correct answer. When the students appear able to say the new part by themselves, the teacher tests (step 4), then has them say the entire counting series from 1 through the new part (step 5). The students should repeat the counting sequence until they say it correctly several times in a row. Providing sufficient practice for students to count correctly several times is important to facilitate retention. Teachers should not forget to have individual students count by themselves. Finally, teachers should give a delayed test to ensure that students have mastered the sequence. Summary Box 4.1 outlines the critical steps in the teaching format.

The teacher often must provide practice for students in counting at a lively pace. To do this, she uses a model-lead-test presentation, first modeling how fast she wants the students to count. Counting at a lively pace helps keep students attentive and facilitates learning the number sequence. Initially, the teacher should establish a counting speed that is approximately one number per second. In future

---

Summary Box 4.1
Rote Counting: Introducing New Numbers into a Counting Sequence

1. Teacher tests students on the previously introduced counting sequence.

2. Teacher models counting sequence, emphasizing new part.

3. Teacher models and tests students on the new part of the sequence until students can say the new part correctly three times in a row.

4. Teacher tells students the number they will be ending with.

5. Teacher tests students from the *beginning* of the sequence through the new part.

6. Teacher practices new counting sequence frequently throughout the day.

---

lessons, as the students become more proficient, the rate should be increased to two numbers each second and a half.

Counting at a lively pace is difficult for lower performers and requires lots of practice. Some students may need 15 to 20 trials before they can say a new part of the counting sequence correctly. If teachers provide adequate repetition during the first weeks of instruction, they will find that they save time in later weeks. When students can count familiar numbers at a lively pace, the teacher introduces new numbers in the counting sequence.

When presenting a counting task, the teacher must be quite careful not to give the students inappropriate cues. For example, some teachers have a tendency to count quietly when students are supposed to be counting alone (steps 4 and 5). Sometimes teachers just move their lips. This movement cues the students on the next number and precludes the students from initiating their own responses. If teachers find a number of students who have no trouble counting in groups but cannot perform the task on an individual test, the teacher might be providing extra help during group instruction.

Teachers also must be careful to correct all student errors. If students fail to stop at the appropriate number, the teacher models the correct response, emphasizing the last number in the counting sequence. "I am going to count and end with 6—**end with 6:** 1, 2, 3, 4, 5, **6**. I counted and *ended with 6.*" If students leave out a number (counting 1, 2, 3, 4, 6), they should be stopped immediately, and the teacher should model the "hard part" by saying four numbers, beginning two numbers before the missed number (3, 4, 5, 6). Next, the teacher leads the students on the hard part, tests them on the hard part, then has them begin counting again from 1.

The teacher should be quite careful when making this correction. If a counting error is corrected inappropriately, students may become quite confused. The mistake teachers should avoid is saying the skipped number after the student has made the error. For example, the student says, "1, 2, 3, 4, 6," and the teacher says, "5." What the student hears is "1, 2, 3, 4, 6, 5." The teacher can avoid this mistake by saying "stop" when a student makes an error and then modeling the entire hard part. The teacher should repeat a rote counting exercise until students can respond correctly to the complete series three times in a row. Sometimes students make errors several times before responding correctly. If the teacher does not provide sufficient practice, students are less likely to remember the correct sequence the next day.

Mastering rote counting requires even more practice for lower performing students. One way to prevent students from becoming frustrated while practicing counting is to spend only 2 to 3 minutes on rote counting tasks at any one time, but to present counting tasks several times during a lesson. This distributed practice is better than spending 10 to 15 minutes on counting all at once, because when a counting task is too grueling, students will stop trying and just respond randomly until the task is over. Also, counting practice should not be restricted to the instructional time allotted for arithmetic. The teacher can have students practice counting when they are lining up for recess, just before they go to lunch, during opening exercises in the morning, or during the last 5 minutes of class. These extra few minutes of practice during the day will be reflected through increased retention of newly taught numbers. Finally, the teacher should treat counting as a fun exercise. One way this can be done is to incorporate gamelike activities into counting exercises. For example, having students count one time with their hands on their knees, the next time with hands on their heads, and so on.

Rational Counting: One Group

Rational counting is the one-to-one correspondence of touching objects and counting. As mentioned previously, we recommend that teachers initially use pictures to teach rational counting skills for reasons of efficiency. The preskill for rational counting is rote counting. The initial exercises in rational counting can begin when the students can rote count to 10. Initially, rational counting involves coordination of touching pictures of objects and/or lines while saying a number in the counting sequence.

The format (Format 4.2) has two parts. In Part A, the teacher touches lines as the students count and then asks what number they ended with. The teacher must use very clear signals when touching the lines. In Part B, the students count illustrations of objects on their worksheets. The objects in the illustrations in Part B should be placed about a half inch from each other so that the students won't become confused about which object they are touching. Note that the students are to begin the task by *pointing at,* not touching, the first object. The teacher signals by saying "Get ready," and then clapping. If the students are already touching the first object, they might touch the second object when they hear the clap. The teacher claps at about 1- to 1½ -second intervals. The teacher should not go too fast, as this might result in coordination errors. The cadence should be kept very predictable so that students do not make unnecessary errors.

Monitoring student performance is particularly critical in this format. Since coordinating touching and counting is the key behavior, listening to the students count is not sufficient. When the skill is first taught, the teacher must repeat the task until he has watched each student touch some objects as the student counts. Monitoring at the very start of the task is also important. If students do not begin at the first picture, they will make mistakes. Note that during step 1 of Part B, the teacher demonstrates that counting can be done from left to right or right to left. However, to facilitate monitoring, the students should always count from left to right.

Students may make coordination or rote counting errors. If a student makes a coordination error—that is, says the number before touching the picture of an object—the teacher tells the student to count *only* when the student touches an object. The teacher then repeats the task, saying, "Go back to the first object and point to it." The teacher checks to make sure students are pointing, and then repeats the task. As with all corrections in early counting instruction, after an error is made, a student should repeat the task until she performs it correctly several times in a row. If a student has a lot of difficulty coordinating counting and pointing, the teacher can slow the cadence to a clap each 2 seconds and prompt the student by taking the student's hand, counting with her, and moving the student's index finger from object to object. The teacher might need to repeat this procedure at least three times before testing the student by having her touch and count the objects without assistance.

If students make many rote counting errors (e.g., counting 1, 2, 3, 5, 6), the teacher should delay rational counting and provide extra practice on rote counting. Exercises in counting objects on worksheets should be done daily for several weeks. After students can quickly and accurately count lines and pictures of objects, they should be given manipulatives to count. Initially, the objects can be arranged in a row, which makes counting manipulatives easier. Counting objects in rows is like counting pictures in rows. After students can count objects in rows, objects should be placed randomly. The teacher models, leads, and tests counting random objects, if necessary.

Rational Counting: Two Groups

Counting two groups of lines is introduced when students are able to count a single group of six to eight lines. The format for counting two groups of lines teaches students the function of the word *all* and prepares them for addition. When students first add, they count two groups of lines—*all* of the lines. The format for counting two groups appears in Format 4.3. In Part A, the teacher draws two groups of lines on the board and has the students count and tell how many lines in the first group, in the second group, and finally in both groups. Part B is a worksheet exercise in which the students count two groups of objects on their worksheets.

The error students are likely to make in Part A occurs when they are asked to count all of the lines. After counting the lines in the first group, a student is likely to say "one" for the first line in the second group instead of continuing to count. To correct, the teacher models and tests students on that step, and then repeats from step 2. For example, if in counting the lines in this diagram | | | | | |, the student counts 1, 2, 3, 4, 1, 2 the teacher models counting, saying "When we count *all* of the lines, we keep on counting. My turn: 1, 2, 3, 4, **5,** 6." The teacher then tests the students on counting all of the lines and then repeats the steps that are linked. Students count the lines in the first group, then the lines in the second group, and finally count *all* the lines, providing a delayed test for the original task on which the error occurred.

Manipulative Extensions

Once students are proficient at counting groups of picture objects, many practice opportunities can be provided for counting manipulatives and classroom objects. Students can count the windows in the room, the students at each table, the pencils in a box, as the teacher points or touches. Paired practice can be provided wherein one student drops an object or counter into a container while another counts. Roles are reversed as the other student removes objects one at a time while the first student counts. Students can count, rearrange, and recount the same group of objects, or practice counting objects not arranged in rows.

Once students are proficient at counting two groups of picture objects, different colored manipulatives can be combined by pairs of students, or teachers can pose questions that prepare students for later problem-solving applications. For example, the teacher arranges a group of three girls and a group of five boys at the front of the class. "How many girls in this group?" "How many boys in this group?" "Now let's count *all* the children." "How many children in all?" And so forth.

Counting from Different Numbers

Counting from numbers other than 1 saves time when teaching rote counting to higher numbers. For example, in teaching students to count 38, 39, 40, the teacher would model and test from 36 (36, 37, 38, 39, 40) rather than model and test counting from 1. If students can start at numbers other than 1, teachers can focus on the relevant parts of number sequences. A second reason for teaching counting beginning at a number other than 1 is that this counting skill is a component skill of the early addition strategy. Students solve a problem such as $4 + 3 = \Box$ by saying 4 for the first group and then counting each line in the second group: 5, 6, 7.

Format 4.4 shows how to teach students to count beginning at a number other than 1. This format is introduced when students can rote count to about 15. The format contains two parts. The first part

teaches students the meaning of the term *get it going*. (When the teacher says "Get it going," the students say the designated number verbally, holding the number as long as the teacher signals, e.g., 4 is said *ffoouurr*.) The signal used is quite different from signals used in other rote counting tasks. To prompt the students to say the number for a longer time, the teacher signals by moving her hand from side to side. The students are to begin saying the number as the teacher begins the signal (moving her finger) and to stop saying the number when the teacher stops the signal (dropping her hand). The purpose of the get-it-going signal is to better enable the students to respond in unison.

The teacher should present a set of at least three examples each time Part B is presented. Initially, the examples should all be less than 10. The exercise is repeated until students respond correctly to the entire set, which increases the likelihood that they can generalize the skill to other numbers. Responding correctly to the entire set implies that if a mistake is made on one example, the teacher repeats all of the examples until the students can respond to them consecutively with no errors. Students will need several repetitions before they master the entire set. However, if a high criterion is maintained initially, the amount of practice needed to master subsequent sets will be reduced.

Sometimes students make the error of starting over at 1—for example, "ffoouurr, 1, 2, 3, 4." The teacher corrects by modeling and then leading the students several times with an emphasis on the first counted number. However, if the students continue to make errors, the teacher can introduce a procedure in which she counts quickly from 1 to the get-it-going number and then signals for the students to respond on the next number. For example, the teacher would say, "I'll start counting and when I signal, you count with me: 1, 2, 3 (signal), ffoouurr, **5,** 6, 7, 8, 9." The teacher responds with students several times, then tests. After the students begin responding correctly to several consecutive examples, they no longer need the prompt of beginning the sequence at 1.

Ordinal Counting

Ordinal counting involves saying the number associated with relative position, such as first, second, third, fourth, fifth, sixth. Ordinal counting is introduced only when students can rote count to 15 and can tell the cardinal number for a group. A model-lead-test procedure is used to introduce ordinal counting. Teachers might introduce ordinal counting by having children participate in a race, after which the teacher discusses the positions of the runners: "Who came in first? Who came in second?" The teacher then models and tests ordinal counting sequences.

Counting by Ones from 30 to 100

The procedure for counting by ones from 30 to 100 should demonstrate the relationship between each tens grouping; that is, each decade has a sequence in which the numerals 0, 1, 2, 3, 4, 5, 6, 7, 8, 9 appear in the ones column: 4**0**, 4**1**, 4**2**, 4**3**, 4**4**, 4**5**, 4**6**, 4**7**, 4**8**, 4**9**. Two preskills related to counting higher numbers are rote counting beginning at a number other than 1 (e.g., starting at 5 and counting 6, 7, 8) and skip counting by tens (10, 20, 30, 40, 50, 60, 70, 80, 90, 100), which is discussed later in the chapter.

The format for counting numbers from 30 to 100 is similar to Format 4.1 for introducing new numbers in the early counting sequence, with these modifications. First, the new part begins at a tens number ending in 7 and continues through the next tens number ending in 2 (e.g., 27, 28, 29, 30, 31, 32, or 47, 48, 49, 50, 51, 52). Starting at a higher number (e.g., 8 or 9), gives students too little time to prepare for transition to the next decade. Starting at the beginning of the decade (e.g., 21, 22) makes the task too time consuming. Second, instead of testing the students on counting from 1, the teacher has them count from a number approximately 10 to 20 numbers lower than the new part.

The first exercises should teach students to count from the thirties to the forties. Counting from the forties to the fifties, and higher should be introduced several days later or whenever students master the lower numbers. After students practice counting through a new decade for 2 days, the examples are modified daily to promote generalizability. For example, students might count from 27 to 42 one day, from 25 to 47 the next, and from 27 to 49 the next.

Counting Backward

Once students can count to 50, counting backward can be introduced. Counting backward is an important preskill for some beginning subtraction strategies. Students initially learn to count backward from 5, then the starting number may be gradually in-

creased to 20. A beginning exercise might have the teacher write a number line from 0 to 5:

The teacher models, leads, and tests on counting backward while touching the numbers on the number line. Numbers may then be erased one at a time, each time the students count backward from 5. Ideally, the teacher provides delayed tests throughout the day. If students perform the sequence correctly the next day with no visual prompt, two or three more numbers may be added to the count backward sequence.

Counting Between 100 and 999

Students are usually taught to count from 100 through 999 during second grade. First, students are taught to count by hundreds from 100 to 1,000. The hundreds skip-counting series is usually quite easy for students to learn, requiring only a few days of practice. Once students can count by ones through 99 and by hundreds from 100 to 1,000, the teacher can introduce counting by ones in the hundreds numbers. A three-stage procedure is used. In the first stage, the teacher has students count a single decade within a single hundred (e.g., 350–359). The teacher uses a model-lead-test procedure on four to five sets of examples each day. Examples similar to the following are presented daily until students demonstrate mastery:

350, 351, 352, 353, 354, 355, 356, 357, 358, 359
720, 721, 722, 723, 724, 725, 726, 727, 728, 729
440, 441, 442, 443, 444, 445, 446, 447, 448, 449
860, 861, 862, 863, 864, 865, 866, 867, 868, 869

The objective of the second stage is making the transition from one decade to the next (e.g., 325–335). An example set should include several series extending from a number with 5 in the ones column to the next number in the counting sequence that has 5 in the ones column. Examples similar to those below are presented daily until students demonstrate mastery. Lower performing students may require 2 to 3 weeks of practice.

325, 326, 327, 328, 329, 330, 331, 332, 333, 334, 335
785, 786, 787, 788, 789, 790, 791, 792, 793, 794, 795
435, 436, 437, 438, 439, 440, 441, 442, 443, 444, 445
115, 116, 117, 118, 119, 120, 121, 122, 123, 124, 125

The third stage focuses on the transition from a hundreds series to the next hundreds series (e.g., 495–505). The example set should include several series extending from a hundreds number ending with 95 to the next number in the counting series that has a 5 in the ones column. A daily lesson might include these examples:

495, 496, 497, 498, 499, 500, 501, 502, 503, 504, 505
295, 296, 297, 298, 299, 300, 301, 302, 303, 304, 305
795, 796, 797, 798, 799, 800, 801, 802, 803, 804, 805
595, 596, 597, 598, 599, 600, 601, 602, 603, 604, 605

Review can be provided through written worksheets in which the teacher writes a number on a worksheet with 10 spaces across from it. The students are to fill in the next 10 numbers. For written exercises, teachers should be careful to use number sequences that involve only those numbers students can write accurately from dictation.

Skip Counting

Skip counting refers to counting each number of a specified multiple. When a student skip counts by fives, the student says, "5, 10, 15, 20, 25, 30, 35, 40, 45, 50." When skip counting by eights, the student says, "8, 16, 24, 32, 40, 48, 56, 64, 72, 80." Throughout this book, we refer to a skip-counting sequence as a *count-by series*. Knowledge of the count-by series for multiples of 2, 3, 4, 5, 6, 7, 8, 9, and 10 is an important component skill for the memorization of basic multiplication and division facts. Students should learn to count 10 numbers for each series (except fives): 2 to 20, 3 to 30, 4 to 40, 6 to 60, and so on. Students should learn to count by fives to 60, since telling time requires this skill. Teachers also may want to teach counting by twenty-fives to 100 as a prerequisite to counting money.

The first count-by series to be introduced should be the tens, since knowledge of this series is a component skill for rote counting to 100. Counting by tens is introduced when students can rote count by ones to about 30, usually several months into first grade. The next count-by series, the twos, might not be introduced until several weeks later. Thereafter, a new series may be introduced when students can say each of the previously introduced series accurately and fluently. Students are fluent on a specific series when they can say the series within approximately 8 seconds.

We suggest teaching the count-by series cumulatively in the following sequence: 10, 2, 5, 9, 4, 25, 3, 8, 7, 6. This order is designed to initially separate those count-by series that contain many of the same numbers. For example, several numbers in the fours series also appear in the eights series: 4, **8**, 12, **16**, 20, **24**. Therefore, the introductions of the fours and eights series are separated by two other dissimilar series.

Separating similar series helps prevent errors in which students switch series. Switching series, a common count-by error, involves counting by one number and then switching to another series after saying a number common to both series. For example, students may begin counting by fours and switch to eights when they come to 16, 24, or 32 (e.g., 4, 8, 12, 16, 24, 32, 40). The chances of making that error are reduced when the two series are not introduced consecutively. Therefore, the recommended sequence for teaching count-by series can make learning them easier.

The count-by format includes two parts (see Format 4.5). Part A demonstrates to students that they end up with the same number whether they count by ones or count by another number. Also, the demonstration is intended to show that counting by a number other than 1 can save time. Part A would be presented just for the first lessons in which count-by twos and fives are taught. Part B is designed to teach students to memorize the various count-by series. Part B of the count-by format also includes a review of previously introduced count-by series. Two or three previously taught series should be reviewed daily.

The teacher uses a model-lead-test procedure, saying the numbers of the new series alone, saying the numbers of the new series with the students, and finally having the students say the numbers themselves. Teachers working with more naive students would introduce just the first three numbers of a series, while teachers working with more sophisticated students might introduce five or six numbers. For example, the first day the count-by nines series is presented to a group of lower performing students, the teacher would introduce just the first three numbers of the series: 9, 18, 27. On the other hand, a teacher working with higher performing students might present several additional numbers: 9, 18, 27, 36, 45, 54. Teachers working with average students might introduce a whole series in several days, while teachers working with lower performing students may expect the students to require about two weeks to master a series.

On the second day of instruction on a series, the teacher tests the students on the part of the series taught during the previous lesson. If the students make an error, the teacher repeats the model-lead-

---

Summary Box 4.2
Skip Counting: Introducing a New Count-by Series

1. Teacher writes part of the new count-by series on the board and models saying the series. (The teacher determines how much of the series to introduce at once, based on previous performance of the students.)

2. Teacher leads the students in reading the new series from the board.

3. Teacher gradually erases numbers in the series as students practice saying the series.

4. Teacher tests students on saying the series from memory.

5. Teacher alternates practice with previously introduced series and the new series.

---

test procedure from steps 2 and 3 of Part B. If the students know the part of the series previously taught or require just a couple of practice trials to say the previously taught part correctly, the teacher introduces the next several numbers of the count-by series. The new part includes the last two familiar numbers and the next two or three numbers in the series. For example, if students have been previously taught the nines series to 36: (9, 18, 27, 36), the new part would include 27 and 36, the last two numbers from the previously taught part, plus the next two numbers in the series, 45 and 54. The teacher uses a model-lead-test procedure, first on 27 to 54 and then on the series from the beginning.

As with any rote counting task, adequate repetition must be provided for student mastery. A teacher may have to lead lower performing students five to ten times through a series until they can say it fluently without errors. When leading students, the teacher should initially use a loud voice, particularly when saying difficult parts of a counting sequence. The purpose of using a loud voice is to ensure that all students are hearing the correct response and to prevent them from cueing on students who may be responding incorrectly. A brisk rhythm should be established by the teacher's tapping his foot or clapping his hands to make mastering the series easier. The numbers in a series should be said at a rate slightly faster than a number a second, saying, for example, 9, 18, 27...90 in about 8 seconds.

Corrections for skip-counting errors follow the model-lead-test correction procedure. When the teacher hears an error, he stops all the students, models the hard part (the two numbers just before the missed number and the one number following the missed number), leads the students on the hard part several times, tests the students on the hard part, and then has them say the entire series from the beginning. For example, if students count "8, 16, 24, 32, 40, 48, 54," the teacher stops them as soon as he

---

APPLICATION ITEMS: COUNTING

1. A student counts "5, 6, 7, 9." Immediately after the student says "9," the teacher says "8" to correct her. What is the problem with this correction? What *should* the teacher say and do? Give specific teacher wording.

2. In counting from 1 to 10, a student makes an error at 8. The teacher models and tests the student on the hard part. The student responds correctly. Is this correction sufficient? Explain.

3. Two days ago, the teacher introduced rote counting to 16. At the beginning of today's lesson, the teacher tests the students and they can all count to 16. What should the teacher do for the rote counting exercise today? What if the students had not been able to count to 16?

4. The teacher tells the students to count to 45. A child counts correctly until 39 and then says 50. What should the teacher say to correct the mistake?

5. When counting this group of lines, | | | | |, a student ends up with 8. What are two possible causes of the error? How would the correction procedures differ?

hears 54 instead of 56. Next, he models, leads, and tests on the hard part: 40, 48, **56**, 64. After students perform acceptably on the test of the hard part, the teacher has the students begin counting with 8.

A new series is introduced only when students know all of the previously introduced series. Teacers should expect students to make frequent errors when a series similar to one previously taught is presented.

When the sixes series is presented, the teacher may find that students make errors on the fours series. Both series include 24. A student might count 4, 8, 12, 16, 20, 24, 30, 36, 42, switching from the fours to the sixes series at 24. With adequate practice, this confusion can be eliminated. Practice on previously taught series can also be provided through peer tutoring or other partner practice activities.

FORMAT 4.1 Introducing New Numbers

TEACHER	STUDENTS
1. You are going to count and end up with 10. What number will you end up with? Start at 1, get ready, count.	10 1, 2, 3, 4, 5, 6, 7, 8, 9, 10
2. I'm going to count and end up with 13. What am I going to end up with? Yes, 13. Listen: 1, 2, 3, 4, 5, 6, 7, 8, 9, 10, **11, 12, 13**. *(Quickly count to 10 and then emphasize 11, 12, 13.)* Listen to the new part: *11, 12, 13.*	13
3. When I drop my hand, say the new part with me. *(Extend pronunciation of 10.) Teeenn (drop hand and respond with students), 11, 12, 13.* Again. *Teeenn (drop hand),* 11, 12, 13. *(Repeat until students respond correctly several times in a row.)*	11, 12, 13 11, 12, 13
4. Say the new part all by yourselves: *teeenn.*	11, 12, 13
5. Now you're going to count and end up with 13. What number will you end up with? Starting at 1, get ready, count. *(Call on individuals.)*	13 1, 2, 3, 4, 5, 6, 7, 8, 9, 10, 11, 12, 13

FORMAT 4.2 Rational Counting

TEACHER	STUDENTS
PART A: STRUCTURED BOARD PRESENTATION	
1. *(Draw four lines on the board.)* My turn. Every time I touch a line, I count. Watch. *(Touch lines at 1-second intervals.)* 1, 2, 3, 4. What number did I end with? *(Repeat step 1 with seven lines.)*	4
2. *(Draw six lines on the board.)* Every time I touch a line, you count. *(Point to left of line.)* Get ready. *(Touch lines from left to right at 1-second intervals as students count.)* *(If students count before you touch a line, tell them,* watch my finger. Count *only* when I touch a line.)*	1, 2, 3, 4, 5, 6
3. What number did we end with?	6
4. So, how many lines are there?	6
5. *(Repeat steps 2–4 with three lines, then seven lines. Give individual turns to several students.)*	

TEACHER   **STUDENTS**

PART B: STRUCTURED WORKSHEET PRESENTATION

Sample worksheet items:

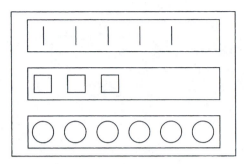

1. *(Hold up a worksheet, and point to a group of objects.)* We're going
   to count all the objects. Watch me count. *(Touch the objects from left
   to right and count.)* 1, 2, 3, 4, 5. Watch me count again. *(Touch objects
   from right to left and count.)* 1, 2, 3, 4, 5.

2. Everyone, hold your finger over the first picture. *(Check to see that all
   students are pointing to but not touching the appropriate picture.)* Each
   time I clap, you touch an object and say the number. Get ready. *(Clap   1, 2, 3, 4, 5
   one time per second. Count with students while monitoring their
   touching.)*

3. All by yourselves, you're going to count the pictures. Hold your finger   1, 2, 3, 4, 5
   over the first picture. *(Check.)* Get ready. *(Clap one time per second.)*
   How many lines are there?   5

4. *(Repeat steps 2 and 3 with other examples. Give individual turns to
   several students.)*

FORMAT 4.3 Counting Two Groups of Lines

TEACHER   **STUDENTS**

PART A: STRUCTURED BOARD PRESENTATION

1. *(Write the following lines on the board.)* | | | | | | | | |
   Here are two groups of lines. *(Touch the first group.)* Here is the **first**
   group. *(Touch the second group.)* Here is the second group.

2. Let's count the lines in the **first** group. *(Touch as students count.)*   1, 2, 3, 4, 5
   How many in the **first** group?   5

3. Let's count the lines in the **second** group. *(Touch as students count.)* 1, 2, 3
   How many in the **second** group?   3

4. Now let's count all the lines. You count the lines in the **first** group, and   1, 2, 3, 4, 5, 6, 7, 8
   then you keep on going and count the lines in the **second** group.
   (Touch as students count.)

5. How many lines in all?   8

6. *(Repeat steps 1–5 with | | | | | then | | | | | | |.)*

(continued on next page)

FORMAT 4.3   (continued)

TEACHER	STUDENTS

PART B: STRUCTURED WORKSHEET PRESENTATION

a. ||| |||| b. ▢▢▢▢ ▢▢

c.   ⁀⁀⁀ ⁀⁀⁀⁀   d. ◯◯◯◯ ◯◯◯

1. Touch a. *(Check.)*

2. Touch the first group of lines. I'll clap. You count the objects in the first group. Put your finger over the first line. *(Pause and check.)* Get ready. *(Clap at 1-second intervals.)* How many in the first group?   **3**

3. *(Repeat step 2 with the second group.)*

4. Now you're going to count all the lines. Start counting with the first group. Put your finger over the first line. *(Pause and check.)* Get ready. *(Clap at 1-second intervals.)*   **1, 2, 3, 4, 5, 6, 7**

5. How many in all?
   (Call on individual students.)   **7**

6. *(Repeat steps 1–5 with b, c, and d.)*

FORMAT 4.4   Counting from Numbers Other Than 1

TEACHER	STUDENTS

PART A: PRESKILL—GET-IT-GOING SIGNAL

1. Get it going means to say a number for as long as I move my finger.

2. *(Hold up hand.)* My turn. I'm going to get 4 going. *(Move hand in circular motion, saying ffoouurr with extended pronunciation. After several seconds, drop hand and stop saying 4.)*

3. *(Repeat step 2 with the numbers 6 and 9.)*

4. Let's do it together. We have 4. How many do we have?   **4**
   Get it going: *ffoouurr.*   *ffoouurr*
   (Repeat step 4 with the numbers 8 and 2.)

5. You have five. How many do you have?   **5**
   Get it going.   *ffiivve*
   (Repeat step 5 with the numbers 7 and 3.)

PART B: ORAL PRESENTATION

1. We're going to get it going and count. My turn. We have four. Get it going. *(Signal by moving hand in circular motion. After 2 seconds, drop hand.)* Ffoouurr, 5, 6, 7, 8, stop. *(Count at a rate of about two numbers a second.)*

2. Get it going and count with me. You have 4. How many do you have?   **4**
   Get it going. *(Begin signal.)* Foouuurr.   *ffoouurr*
   (After about 2 seconds drop hand.) 5, 6, 7, 8.   *5, 6, 7, 8*

TEACHER	STUDENTS

3. All by yourselves. You have 4. Get it going. *(Begin signal; after 2 seconds, drop hand. Say "stop" after children say 8.)* — ffoouurr, 5, 6, 7, 8

4. *(Repeat steps 1–3 with the number 7 and then 3. Give individuals turns with 7, 4, or 3.)*

FORMAT 4.5   Count-By

TEACHER	STUDENTS

PART A: INTRODUCING THE COUNT-BY

1. *(Draw lines in groups of two on the board.)* || || || || ||
   Let's find out how many lines we have. I'll touch and you count. — 1, 2, 3, 4, 5, 6, 7, 8, 9, 10
   How many lines are there? *(Write 10 next to the last group.)* — 10
   Now I'll show you a fast way to count those lines. *(Circle each group of two lines with your finger. For each group, ask, "How many lines in this group?"* — 2
   After asking about all five groups, ask, "How many lines are in each group?")
   When we count groups of 2, we count lines the fast way.

2. Let's figure out the numbers we say when we count by 2. Count the lines in the first group. *(Point to each line as students count.)* — 1, 2
   Yes, there are two lines, so I write 2 above the first group. *(Write 2 above the first group.)*
   Count the lines in the first and second groups. — 1, 2, 3, 4
   You counted four lines so far, so I'll write 4 above the second group. *(Write it.)*
   (Continue to have the students count each successive group from the beginning, writing the appropriate numeral above each group, such as the following:
   2   4   6   8   10
   || || || || ||
   When the students have finished, the lines should look like the above example.)

3. Now you know what numbers to say when you count by 2. Let's count the lines again, but this time we'll count by 2. *(Point to each numeral as students count.)* — 2, 4, 6, 8, 10

4. How many did you end up with when you counted by 2? — 10
   (Point to the 10 written next to the last group.) How many did you end up with when you counted the regular way? — 10
   See, the fast way really does work.

PART B: STRUCTURED BOARD PRESENTATION

1. *(Write the following numbers on the board.)* 6, 12, 18, 24, 30
   Today we are going to learn to count by 6.

2. I will say the numbers in the series: 6, 12, 18, 24, 30.

3. Say the sixes with me as I touch each number. Get ready. *(Signal)* 6, 12, 18, 24, 30. — 6, 12, 18, 24, 30

4. Say the series by yourselves. Get ready. *(Signal.)* — 6, 12, 18, 24, 30
   (Give individual turns to several students.)

(continued on next page)

FORMAT 4.5   (continued)

TEACHER	STUDENTS
5. (*Erase one of the numbers in the series.*) Say the sixes again, including the missing number. (*Repeat step 5, erasing another number each time, until students can say the series without help.*)	6, 12, 18, 24, 30
6. (*Alternate previously learned count-by series with practice on new series.*)	

CHAPTER 5

Symbol Identification and Place Value

TERMS AND CONCEPTS

number   The number that identifies the quantity of elements or members of a set; a cardinal number.

numeral   A symbol used to represent a number.

place value   The system by which the value of a digit is determined by the position it occupies relative to the decimal point.

expanded notation   A numeral written as a sum in which each digit's value is expressed as an addend; e.g., in 342, the digits 3, 4, and 2 are written as the addends 300 + 40 + 2.

column alignment   Writing numerals one above the other so that the ones, tens, and hundreds positions are in columns: 32 + 426 is written

$$
\begin{array}{r}
32 \\
+\ 426 \\
\hline
\end{array}
$$

SKILL HIERARCHY

Symbol identification and place value may be divided into three major areas: (a) reading and writing numerals, (b) column alignment, and (c) expanded notation. The skill hierarchy shows the relationship of specific skills within these areas. Not that numeral identification (reading and writing the numerals 0 through 10) and the concept of numeral/object correspondence form the foundation of the skill hierarchy. Numeral/object correspondence requires students to write the numeral that corresponds to the number

of objects in a group: or, con-versely, draw a group of lines to show the number represented by a numeral:

Place value concepts are introduced through the remaining instructional activities: reading and writing ten's, hundreds, thousands, and millions numbers; expanded notation; and column alignment. In reading multi-digit numbers, students translate each digit into a value according to its position and then identify the entire numeral. For example, in reading 58, students must note that the 5 represents five tens and that five tens is read as "fifty." Eight ones is read as "eight." The students then put the parts together and identify 58 as "fifty-eight." Writing numerals requires the reverse—breaking a number into parts rather than putting parts together. When students are told to write 58, they break the number into parts: 50 and 8. Fifty is represented by a 5 in the tens column, so students write that part. Eight is represented by an 8 in the ones column, so students write that part. In summary, to read numerals, students determine the value of each part and then put the values together. To write numerals, students break the number into parts and write the digit representing the value of each part.

The introduction of column alignment and expanded notation parallels that of reading and writing numbers. For example, when teachers see that students can read and write hundreds numbers, they

Instructional Sequence and Assessment Chart

Grade Level	Problem Type	Performance Indicator
K-1	Reading numerals zero through 10	Read these numerals: 4 2 6 1 7 3 0 8 5 9 10
K-1	Writing numerals zero through 10	Write these numerals: 4 2 6 1 7 3 0 8 5 9 10
K-1	Writing members of set (lines) to represent a numeral	4 6
K-1	Writing a numeral to represent members of a set	||| |||||||
1a	Reading teen numbers	Read these numerals: 15 11 13 12 17 19 14 16 18
1b	Writing teen numbers	Write these numerals: 15 11 13 12 17 19 14 16 18
1c	Reading numbers from 20 to 99	Read these numerals: 64 81 44 29
1d	Writing numbers from 20 to 99	Write these numerals: 47 98 72 31
1e	Column alignment Rewriting horizontal addition and subtraction problems	$85 + 3 = $ _____ $4 + 25 = $ _____ $37 - 2 = $ _____
1f	Expanded notation	$63 = $ _____ $+$ _____ $92 = $ _____ $+$ _____
2a	Reading and writing numbers between 100 and 999 except those with a zero in the tens column	Read: 320 417 521 Write seven hundred fifteen _____ Write four hundred thirty-six _____ Write three hundred fifty _____
2b	Reading and writing numbers between 100 and 999 with zero in tens column	Read: 502 708 303 Write four hundred eight _____ Write seven hundred two _____ Write three hundred three _____
2c	Rewriting horizontal equations; one number is a hundreds number	$305 + 8 + 42 = $ _____ $428 - 21 = $ _____ $31 + 142 + 8 = $ _____
2d	Expanded notation with hundreds numbers	$382 = $ _____ $+$ _____ $+$ _____ $417 = $ _____ $+$ _____ $+$ _____ $215 = $ _____ $+$ _____ $+$ _____

Grade Level	Problem Type	Performance Indicator
3a	Reading and writing thousands numbers between 1,000 and 9,999 with no zeroes in hundreds or tens column	Read: 3,248 7,151 1,318 Write five thousand three hundred fourteen _____ Write two thousand six hundred forty-three _____ Write one thousand one hundred forty-one _____
3b	Reading and writing thousands numbers between 1,000 and 9,999 with a zero in the hundreds column	Read: 7,025 8,014 2,092 Write five thousand seventy-two _____ Write one thousand forty _____ Write six thousand eighty-eight _____
3c	Reading and writing thousands numbers between 1,000 and 9,999 with zeroes in the hundreds and/or tens columns	Read: 7,025 2,002 1,409 Write six thousand eight _____ Write nine thousand four _____ Write five thousand two _____
3d	Column alignment: Rewriting horizontal problems	35 + 1,083 + 245 = _____ 4,035 − 23 = _____ 8 + 2,835 = _____

4a	Reading and writing all thousands numbers between 10,000 and 999,999	Read: 300,000
		        90,230
		        150,200
		
		Write two hundred thousand _____
		Write ninety thousand four hundred _____
		Write one hundred thousand two hundred _____

4b	Reading and writing numbers between 1 million and 9 million	Read: 6,030,000
		        5,002,100
		        1,340,000
		Write seven million _____
		Write three million, eighty thousand _____
		Write eight million, six hundred thousand _____

5	Reading and writing numbers between 10 million and 999 million	Read: 27,400,000
		        302,250,000
		        900,300,000
		Write ten million _____
		Write forty million two hundred thousand _____

introduce column alignment problems with hundreds numbers:

$$342 + 8 \text{ is rewritten as } \begin{array}{r} 342 \\ + 8 \\ \hline \end{array}$$

and then expanded notation problems with hundreds numbers:

$$342 = 300 + 40 + 2$$

The Instructional Sequence and Assessment Chart lists specific skills, indicating their relative order of introduction. Note that many of the tasks in kindergarten and first grade require teachers to test students individually. In later grades, only tasks requiring students to read numerals need be tested individually.

INTRODUCING THE CONCEPT

This section deals with skills normally taught during kindergarten and early first grade. These skills are prerequisites for the equality-based strategies that provide a conceptual understanding of addition and subtraction. The skills, listed in the order they are discussed in this section, are as follows:

1. Numeral identification (zero through 10)
2. Numeral writing (zero through 10)
3. Symbol identification and writing (+, −, ☐, =)
4. Equation reading and writing
5. Numeration tasks

Numeral Identification

Numeral identification tasks begin when students can rote count to 8. Introducing numeral identification is delayed until after students can rote count to 8 in order to avoid confusion between counting and numeral identification. Students who enter school knowing how to count can begin learning to identify numerals immediately.

The sequence in which numerals are introduced is important. A basic guideline in sequencing the introduction of numerals is to separate similar-looking and similar-sounding numerals. Students are likely to confuse 6 and 9 because they look so much alike; likewise, students may have difficulty discriminating 4 and 5 because they sound alike, both beginning with the same sound. Therefore, a good sequence of introduction would separate both pairs of numerals by several lessons. One possible sequence for introducing numerals 0 to 10 is 4, 2, 6, 1, 7, 3, 0, 8, 5, 9, 10. Note the separation of 6 and 9; 1, 0, and 10; and 4 and 5. This sequence is included as an example and is certainly not the only sequence that will minimize student errors.

A second sequencing guideline is to introduce new numerals cumulatively. A new numeral is not presented until students have demonstrated mastery of the previously introduced symbols. Teachers working with students who enter school with little or no previous knowledge of numerals can generally introduce new symbols at a rate of one new symbol each three to five lessons.

The format (see Format 5.1) for introducing new numerals to students consists of a model in which the teacher points to the numeral and tells the students the name of the numeral; a test in which the teacher asks the students to identify the new numeral; and discrimination practice in which the teacher asks students to identify the new numeral and previously introduced numerals.

In this format, the teacher first writes a set of numerals on the board. Each of the previously introduced numerals is written once. The new numeral is written several times to ensure that the student attends to the *appearance* of the numeral rather than its position on the board. The most important part of the introduction is the discrimination practice in steps 2 and 3 of the format. Note that the presentation of the numeral follows an alternating pattern: new numeral, one previously introduced numeral, new numeral, two previously introduced numerals, new numeral, three previously introduced numerals, and so on. The time the student has to remember the new numeral is gradually increased by adding more familiar numerals. This pattern is designed to help students better remember a new or difficult numeral. Individual turns are given after the teacher presents the discrimination practice. If, when giving an individual turn, a student misidentifies or does not respond, the teacher identifies the numeral and uses the alternating pattern, focusing on that numeral and previously identified numerals.

A clear point-and-touch signal is essential for clear presentation of this format. The features of a good point-and-touch signal are illustrated in Figure 5.1. When signaling, the teacher points under the numeral (not touching the board), making sure that no student's vision is blocked by any part of the teacher's hand or body. After pointing under the numeral for 1 to 2 seconds, the teacher signals by moving her finger away from the board and then back toward it, touching under the numeral. The out-and-in motion is done crisply with the **finger** moving away from the board (about 6 inches) and then immediately back to the board. When the finger touches below the numeral, the students are to respond. The out-and-in motion should be done the same way every time it is used. Any hesitation or inconsistency makes unison responding difficult be-

FIGURE 5.1   Point, Out, In, and Touch Signal

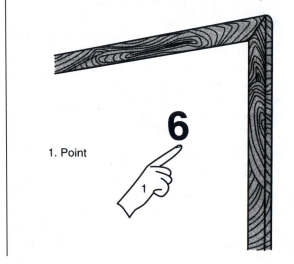

1. Point

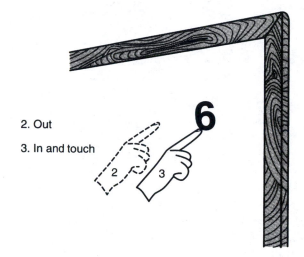

2. Out

3. In and touch

cause the students cannot tell when they are supposed to respond.

Pacing is extremely important for an effective presentation. As a general rule, the teacher should point to a numeral for a second or two, then signal. After the students respond, the teacher should confirm the response ("Yes, this is a 6") or correct the error ("This is a **6**. What numeral?"). Then, the teacher immediately points to the next number in the task, pauses a second or two, then signals. When pointing to numerals that have been newly introduced or that have caused students difficulty in the past, the teacher might initially pause 3 to 4 seconds before signaling. The primary goal of good pacing is to give students sufficient practice, with feedback, in a short amount of time.

As with rote counting, the numeral identification tasks are more efficiently taught if presented for 3 to 5 minutes at several different times during the lesson rather than in one long session. Numeral identification can also be practiced at various times of the day. Many teachers make cardboard numerals and put them on a bulletin board or wall in the room. The teachers then ask the students to identify the symbols during early morning exercises, before going to recess or lunch, or at other opportune times. The practice provided by these brief tasks, interspersed throughout the day, can make a great difference in how quickly low-performing students learn to identify symbols.

Numeral Writing

Numeral writing is an important skill in itself and also reinforces numeral identification. As a general rule, a new numeral can be introduced into numeral writing exercises several lessons after it first appears in a numeral identification format. As noted in symbol identification, symbols are introduced cumulatively. Instructionally naive students will be ready to practice writing a new numeral every three to five lessons. There are three basic stages in teaching students to write single-digit numerals:

1. Tracing numerals written on worksheets
2. Copying numerals
3. Writing numerals from dictation

For worksheet tracing exercises, we recommend that dots and dashes be used to prompt the students in writing the numerals.

During the first several lessons, the teacher leads the students through tracing, monitoring them quite carefully and, if necessary, moving the students' hands to help them make the lines. The students say the name of the numeral each time they write it. When the students are able to trace a numeral without assistance, the teacher introduces copying. In initial copying exercises, dashed lines and dots appear for the first numeral but only dots for the remaining numerals.

When students can do this exercise, a more sophisticated copying exercise is introduced in which no dots or dashed lines are used as prompts. The students should practice writing each numeral at least 10 to 20 times each day for the first week the symbol is introduced. The number of repetitions can be gradually reduced as student performance improves.

The third and final stage of numeral writing includes numeral dictation exercises in which the teacher says a number, and the students write the numeral. Some students find dictation exercises quite difficult in that they have to remember not only what a numeral looks like but also how to write it. The prerequisites for introducing a numeral in dictation exercises are being able to identify and copy the numeral.

In a numeral dictation exercise, the teacher follows the same alternating pattern used in numeral identification tasks. For example, if students have learned to write 4, 2, 6, 1 and are being introduced to 7 in a dictation exercise, the sequence of examples presented by the teacher might be 7, 4, 7, 6, 1, 7, 4, 2, 6, 7. The worksheet on which the students are to write the numerals should have blank spaces or boxes large enough to write each symbol.

Monitoring and pacing are both important teacher presentation behaviors for numeral dictation. The teacher should check the responses of all low-performing students after each numeral is written. The responses of higher performing students can be checked after every second or third numeral. As soon as the last student has finished writing a symbol, if no mistakes were made, the teacher should dictate the next numeral. Too much time between tasks can result in off-task behavior.

The correction procedure for errors involves a model-test-alternating test procedure. The teacher shows the students how to write the numeral, has the students copy it, and then alternates between having students write the missed numeral and other numerals.

Teachers must be careful in setting reasonable criteria for neatness. Students with little prior writing experience may require many months of practice before they consistently write numerals neatly. The teacher should gradually increase criteria for legibility and neatness. In initial exercises, writing a reasonable facsimile of a numeral is the critical student behavior. If a student writes a number backward, the teacher may respond by acknowledging that the correct numeral was written but correct the positioning: "Good. That is a 4, but here's how to write it." Note that the correction is made in a positive manner.

Symbol Identification and Writing

The symbols for plus, minus, equal sign, and empty box are taught with the same procedures as for numerals. An empty box can be introduced as "how many," which facilitates reading equations; for example, 6 + 5 = ☐ is read: "Six plus five equals how many?"

Introduction of the various symbols should be interspersed throughout the lessons in which numerals are introduced. The first symbol would be introduced after several numerals; subsequent symbols would be introduced after two to three additional numerals had been introduced.

Equation Reading and Writing

Equation reading is a prerequisite skill for problem solving and learning math facts. Students must be able to read an equation fluently if they are to be able to derive the answer and see its relationship to other equations.

Children may have difficulty reading a problem such as 6 − 3 = ☐, even though they can identify each symbol in isolation. When they read a problem, they must connect the numerals and symbols together, which requires some practice.

Equation reading is introduced when the students know enough numerals and symbols for the teacher to create equations. Students should be able to identify the numerals almost instantaneously prior to equation reading. If students have not received adequate practice to quickly identify numerals when they appear in isolation, they will have much difficulty reading equations. Because the procedure for teaching the reading of equations is quite straightforward, a format is not included. Following the model-lead-test procedure, the teacher writes several equations on the board:

$$4 + 3 = \square \qquad 7 - 3 = \square$$

The teacher models reading the first equation at a rate of about a numeral or symbol each second. (Reading at a faster rate should be avoided initially, since it may encourage guessing.) The teacher then responds with the students as they read the statement. Lower performing students may need 10 or more trials. When the students can read the statement by themselves, the teacher tests the group and then individuals. The same model-lead-test procedure is used with each statement.

Equation reading is practiced daily for several weeks. It can be discontinued when addition is introduced, since the addition formats begin with the students reading an equation. The rate at which students read statements should be increased gradually.

Equation writing requires students to write equations dictated by the teacher; for example, "Listen: Four plus three equals how many? Say that … Write it." Equation writing is introduced when the students can read equations with relative ease and are somewhat fluent in writing numerals and symbols, writing most numerals within 2 to 3 seconds after the teacher says the numeral in a dictation exercise.

The format for equation writing (see Format 5.2) involves the teacher dictating a statement, the students repeating the statement at a normal rate, then repeating the statement at a slow rate (a word each 2 to 3 seconds), and finally writing the statement. The purpose of having students say the statement slowly is to help students remember the latter part of the statement as they are writing the earlier part.

A common error is writing a numeral or symbol out of order. As soon as the teacher notices an error in a written equation, she points to each symbol while saying the correct statement. For example, if a student writes 6 + □ = 2 for 6 + 2 = □, the teacher says, "6" and points to 6; says "plus" and points to +; says "2" and points to the box that the student has written. The teacher immediately says, "This is not 2; let's try the problem again." The teacher has the student cross out or erase the problem, then repeats the equation, has the student say the equation, and then has the student write the equation.

Numeration Tasks: Numeral/Object Correspondence

There are two types of numeration tasks. For the first, the student identifies a symbol and then writes the appropriate number of lines; for example, the student identifies the numeral 2 and then draws two lines under the 2. For the second, the student counts the number of lines or other objects and writes the numeral that represents the number; for the task below, the student writes a 2 in the box.

Both tasks are component skills for the equality-based strategies students are taught to solve addition and subtraction; therefore, they should be taught relatively early in the instructional sequence, after students have learned to identify and write about five numerals and can count objects in a group. Both numeration skills can be introduced within a short period of time, since they are usually easy for students to learn. As soon as the students learn to identify a new numeral, teachers should incorporate it into numeration tasks.

IDENTIFYING A SYMBOL, THEN DRAWING LINES. Prior to introducing tasks in which the students draw lines to correspond to a numeral, the teacher may need to provide practice for lower performing students in simply drawing lines. The teacher gives students a piece of paper with a series of dots about 1/4 inch apart and 1/2 inch above a horizontal line. The teacher then models how to draw lines. This initial exercise is followed by an exercise in which students write a line each time the teacher claps (at a rate of about a clap each 2 seconds).

Students may write crooked lines or crowd them together—for instance, \/\\/\. Either error may cause overlapping or crossed lines. The teacher should carefully monitor and correct by modeling and then, if necessary, guiding the student's pencil as the student makes the lines. When students can draw lines as the teacher claps, the teacher introduces an exercise in which the students also count as they draw lines. When the students can count and draw lines as the teacher claps, exercises with numerals can be introduced.

Format 5.3 includes the format for teaching students to draw lines for numerals. In the format, students first identify a numeral, state that the numeral tells them to draw a certain number of lines, and then draw the lines. Since most students readily learn this skill, presentations in two to four lessons are often sufficient before including this problem type on independent worksheets. Note that a how-many box is included in the teacher presentation because it is easy to learn and because students must know that not every symbol tells them to draw lines.

If students make errors on independent worksheet items, the teacher should test to determine the cause of the error. Did the student identify the numeral correctly? If not, the misidentification caused the error. If the student identified the numeral correctly, the error resulted from a line drawing error, which is corrected by reviewing Format 5.3.

COUNTING OBJECTS, THEN WRITING A NUMERAL. Writing a numeral to represent a set of objects is important in itself and is also an integral part of the strategy to teach a conceptual base for addition and subtraction. After students draw a set of lines for one side of an equation, they must write the numeral for that set. For example,

$$4 + 2 = \Box$$
$$||||\ \ ||$$

Students count six lines and write a 6 in the box. The format for writing a numeral for a set of objects (see Format 5.4) begins with an explanation of the function of the lines under a box: "The lines under a box tell what numeral goes in the box." The students are then told to count the lines under the box and write the numeral for the number they end with. If students have mastered the necessary preskills of rational counting and numeral writing, they will have little difficulty. After presentations in two or three lessons, items of this kind can be included on worksheets as independent activities.

The two mistakes students might make on this task are miscounting the lines and writing the wrong numeral. Often it is not clear by looking at a worksheet how a student derived an answer. In such a situation, the teacher should ask the student to work several items in front of him, counting aloud so that the cause of the error can be identified and an appropriate correction provided. If the student cannot correctly count lines in several problems, the teacher should provide practice on line counting (see Chapter 4). If a student writes the wrong numeral, the teacher needs to provide practice in numeral identification and numeral dictation.

Mistakes involving mechanics such as writing a numeral backward are not critical. If the teacher can identify the numeral the student has written, the answer is acceptable, and the student should be praised. After praising the student, however, the teacher should point out that the numeral is written backward. Some students need months of practice writing numerals before they consistently write them in the correct form. The teacher should *not* put undue pressure on students who write numerals backward.

Manipulative Extensions

Once students are proficient with drawing lines for a symbol and writing a numeral for a group of objects, the tasks may be extended to equivalent tasks involving manipulatives. For example, rather than drawing lines for a symbol, students may be provided with counters or other objects. They place the appropriate number of objects in a space below or next to each numeral. Students can work in pairs and check one another's work by reading each numeral and counting the corresponding objects.

A large display can also be provided at a workstation with numerals and an empty box below each numeral. A variety of objects are made available with the display (e.g., 10 each of pencils, identical plastic toys, blocks, shapes, etc.). Students can create sets of objects for each numeral, placing the correct number of similar objects in each box. Other students can then check the sets and create different sets for each numeral.

PLACE VALUE SKILLS

Three skills related to place value are discussed in this section: (a) reading and writing numerals, (b) column alignment, and (c) expanded notation. Teaching procedures are discussed for reading and writing each type of number: teens, tens, hundreds, thousands, and millions. The procedures are quite similar for the different number quantities. In reading numbers, the students identify the number in each column (e.g., two tens and four ones), their value (e.g., two tens equal 20), and combine the values to read the entire number (e.g., 20 + 4 = 24). In writing numbers, students first expand the numbers into their component parts (e.g., 24 = two tens and four ones) and then write each component.

Variations in the teaching procedures are called for with teen numbers and numbers with zero. With teen numbers, students say the ones number first (e.g., 16 is read "sixteen," not "teensix") but write the tens number first (e.g., in writing 16, students write the 1, then the 6). Numbers with zeroes are difficult because students must omit the zeroes when reading (e.g., 306 is read "three hundred six," not "three hundred zero six") but include them when writing, even though the students don't hear them. Instructions in reading and writing should be carefully coordinated. Students should be introduced to numeral identification first and then to numeral writing for that numeral type.

Reading and Writing Teen Numbers

READING TEEN NUMBERS. Reading teen numbers is introduced when the students can read all numerals between zero and 10. Regular teens are introduced before irregular teens. The numbers 14, 16, 17, 18, and 19 are regular teens. The irregular teens are 11, 12, 13, and 15. For example, 14 is pronounced **four**teen, but 12 is not pronounced **two**teen and 15 is not pronounced **five**teen.

The format for teaching students to read teen numbers appears in Format 5.5. The format has three parts. In part A, a structured board exercise, the teacher makes a chart on the board, with spaces for the tens and ones columns. The teacher tells the students that they read one 10 as "teen" and models reading teen numerals. Then the students read them. On the first day of instruction, examples are limited to regular teen numbers: 14, 16, 17, 18, and 19. The next day, one irregular teen is introduced. A new irregular teen is introduced each day unless students have difficulty with previously introduced teens. When a new irregular teen is introduced, the teacher alternates between the new number and previously introduced numbers (e.g., 13, 14, 13, 16, 18, 13, 17, 14, 19, 13).

Part B is a less structured exercise in which the students read teen numbers with no prompting. Part B is presented daily for several weeks. Part C is a worksheet exercise designed to reinforce the place value concept. In Part C, the students are shown pictures of counters and instructed to circle the appropriate numeral. After the writing of teen numbers has been introduced, students can write the appropriate numeral rather than circle it.

WRITING TEEN NUMBERS. Writing teen numbers is introduced when students can read teen numbers accurately and with a moderate degree of fluency. As in the procedure for reading teen numbers, regular teen numbers (14, 16, 17, 18, and 19) are introduced first, then irregular teen numbers (11, 12, 13, and 15). Irregular teens can be introduced about two days after regular teens. If students have no or little difficulty, a new irregular teen can be taught each day.

Format 5.6 includes the format for teaching students to write teen numbers. Part A contains a model-test procedure for teaching students to tell the component parts of a teen number: 14 = a 1 for the teen (10) and a 4. Part B is a structured board presentation. The teacher refers to the chart on the board and writes the digits in the appropriate columns. Part C is a structured worksheet exercise in which the teacher prompts the students as they write numerals. Part D is an independent dictation exercise in which the teacher says teen numbers and the students write them. If students are able to decode (read words) adequately, the dictation exercise can be replaced with a written worksheet in which students write the numerals indicated by written words.

Practice in writing teen numbers is continued daily for several weeks to facilitate the development of fluency. The place value chart is included in writing exercises only for the first several weeks and then dropped.

Manipulative Extension

The worksheet exercise in Figure 5.2 contains pictures of a group of 10 objects and several single objects. The students are to fill in numerals in the tens

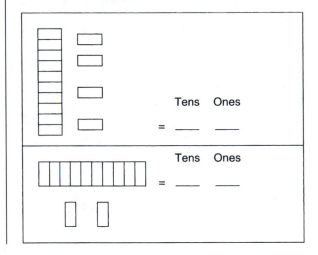

FIGURE 5.2   Teen Numbers Worksheet Activity

and ones columns. This exercise, which reinforces the place value concept, can be introduced after students become proficient in writing dictated numerals.

Additional worksheets to reinforce place value may include pictures of groups of common objects, such as a bundle of pencils, or a box of 10 crayons, and single objects. Finally, students can be presented with groups of manipulative objects—for instance, a bundle of ten toothpicks with six single toothpicks, a bouquet of ten silk flowers and individual flowers—or, if students know the value of dimes and pennies, a dime and nine pennies. Students write the teen numeral for each example.

Reading and Writing Numerals 20–99

READING NUMBERS 20–99. The reading of numbers from 20 through 99 is introduced when students can read teen numbers accurately and with modest fluency (i.e., reading a group of five teen numbers within 8 seconds). Students should also be able to count by ones and skip count by tens to 100 (10, 20, 30, 40, 50, 60, 70, 80, 90, 100). The format for teaching students to read numerals between 20 and 99 appears in Format 5.7.

Parts A and B utilize piles of 10 blocks to reinforce the place value concept for tens numbers. In Part A, the teacher draws several sets of 10 blocks. The teacher then has the students count by tens to figure out the total number of blocks, and verifies the tens place value (e.g., five tens equal 50).

In Part B, the teacher uses a model-test procedure to facilitate memorization of the various place value facts for tens numbers. Some students can be expected to have difficulty with translating two tens, three tens, and five tens, since the names for these numbers are irregular. While four tens equal forty, and eight tens equal eighty, two tens do not equal "twoty." Likewise, three tens do not equal "threety" and five tens do not equal "fivety."

Part C and Part D actually involve reading numbers in the place value chart. In Part C, the teacher instructs students to start reading in the tens column. He asks what numeral is in the tens column and what number that group of tens equals. Finally, the teacher asks for the sum of that number and the number in the ones column (30 + 5 = 35).

In Part D, students read numerals with no prompting from the teacher. If students have a lot of difficulty with Part D, it implies that they have transitioned too quickly from Part C to Part D. Return to the structured board presentation with several examples. When students appear very confident, proceed to the less structured format in Part D. (Note that for the last five lessons in which Part D is used, the place value chart should not be included.) About a fourth of the examples in Part D should be teen numbers.

In Part E, the student is to select the numeral that represents a group of blocks. The worksheet shows diagrams with sets of 10 and individual blocks. The students determine the total by first counting the piles of 10. Then they figure out what number the groups of 10 equal (three tens equal 30). Finally, they count the single blocks, starting with the tens number they ended with (e.g., 31, 32, 33, 34), which assumes the preskill of counting from different numbers.

WRITING NUMERALS 20–99. Writing numerals for 20 through 99 is introduced after students can read these numerals. The format for teaching students to write these numerals appears in Format 5.8. Parts A and B are preskills. Part A teaches the student to say the composite parts of the number (e.g., 97 is 90 and 7). Part B teaches the students to tell how many tens in a tens number (e.g., 50 is five tens). Part C introduces writing numbers from 20 through 99. The teacher says a number and has the students say its component parts. The teacher then asks how many 10s in the tens number and writes the tens digit. The teacher then asks, for example, "84 equals 80 and what else?" After the student says "4," the teacher writes the 4 in the ones column. Part D has the same steps as Part C, except the students write the numerals. Part E is a dictation exercise. The teacher dictates numbers, and the students write the appropriate numerals. About a third of the examples in this part should be teen numbers. As with reading

numerals, if students make frequent mistakes with the less structured exercise, they have moved too quickly from the prompted to the unprompted task. Return to the structured worksheet presentation (Part D). When students respond confidently to several consecutive examples, return to the dictation exercise in Part E.

Teachers working with remedial students can expect these students to have particular reversal problems with numbers ending in 1. For example, students may write 31 as 13, 71 as 17, or 21 as 12. To remedy these reversal problems, the teacher presents Parts B, C, and D of the writing teens format (Format 5.6) for one or two lessons concurrently with the writing tens numbers format (Format 5.8), excluding all tens numbers ending with 1 (e.g., 21, 31, 41, 51). The purpose of excluding the tens numbers ending in 1 is to ensure students' mastery of easier numbers before introducing numbers students typically reverse. After the student writes teen and tens numbers without assistance for several days, the teacher begins working directly on the reversal problem. She presents Part C of the writing teens format (Format 5.6) with minimally different examples, focusing on the discrimination between tens and teen numbers like 13 and 31, 17 and 71. Part C may have to be reviewed daily for several weeks for students who are confused. Note that minimally different pairs are used only for remedial students, not for younger students learning the skill for the first time.

Reading and Writing Numbers 100–999

READING HUNDREDS NUMBERS. The reading of hundreds numbers is usually taught during second grade. Students should be able to read and write numerals for numbers below 100 prior to the introduction of numbers from 100 to 999. The teaching procedure is very similar to that used for teaching students to read tens numbers. The format for reading hundreds appears in Format 5.9. In Part A, the teacher introduces the hundreds column, explaining that numerals in that column tell how many hundreds. The teacher then leads students in reading numerals. He points to the digit farthest to the left, asks what column it is in, and then asks what number the digit represents: "What column does this number start in?... How many hundreds do we have?... What do five hundreds equal?" The teacher then does the same for each remaining digit in the numeral. "How many tens do we have?... What do four tens equal?... How many ones do we have?... What do eight ones equal?" A slight modification of the basic procedure is used for numbers with a 1 in the tens column. This modification appears at the end of Part A. In Part B, the students read the numbers without teacher prompting.

Daily exercises in reading numbers are continued for several weeks. Thereafter, practice in reading numbers should be incorporated into computation strategies in which the first step always involves reading the problem. Practice can also be provided through worksheet exercises like that in Figure 5.3, where students read numerical words and then circle the correct numeral. Obviously, such written exercises are appropriate only for students who can decode the words.

The sequence in which hundreds numbers are introduced is important. Hundreds numbers that do not include a zero in the tens column should be introduced first. Numbers with a zero in the tens column are difficult because the student says nothing for the zero. This more difficult type would be introduced in Part A about a week after the easier numbers. A slight modification in the format is required: In step 3 of Part A, the teacher would say, "We have zero tens, so we don't say anything when I point to the numeral zero." In step 5, the students should not say anything when the teacher points to the zero. For example, for 608, students say "600" when the teacher points to 6, remain quiet when the teacher points to 0, and then say "8" when the teacher points to 8.

When presenting exercises to teach students to read hundreds numbers with a zero in the tens column, the teacher would include several sets of examples like these: 38, 308, 380; 42, 420, 402; 703, 730, 73. Note that each set contains three minimally different numbers: a tens number and two hundreds numbers. The hundreds numbers include the same numerals that appear in the tens number, plus a zero. In one of the hundreds numbers, the zero appears in the tens column, and in the other hundreds number, the zero appears in the ones column.

WRITING HUNDREDS NUMBERS. Students usually have more difficulty learning to write hundreds numbers than to read them. The sequence in which hundreds numbers are introduced in writing tasks is the same as for reading. We recommend that hundreds numbers be introduced in two stages. During the first stage, hundreds numbers with a zero in the tens column should be excluded; 248 would be acceptable, but 208 wouldn't. Two hundred eight is troublesome because no tens number is heard. During the second stage, numbers with a zero in either the tens or the ones column may be used.

Format 5.10 includes the format for teaching students to write the first type of hundreds numbers (those without a zero in the tens column). In Part A, the teacher presents a verbal exercise in which she has the students tell the component parts of a hundreds number (e.g., 382 = 300 + 80 + 2). Note the wording in steps 3 and 4 of Part A: The teacher asks the students if they heard a tens number and a ones number. This wording is intended to prepare students for numbers in which there is a zero in either the tens or the ones column.

In Part B, the teacher guides the students in writing numerals for numbers through 999. For example, in guiding the students through writing 486, the teacher asks students to say the first part of the number (400) and points out that since it's a hundreds number, they start writing the numeral in the hundreds column. The teacher asks how many hundreds and has the students write the numeral (4) in the hundreds column. The teacher then asks what column comes next (tens). This question is designed to remind students that they must always write a numeral in the tens column. The teacher has the students say the tens number (80), asks how many tens in that number (8), and has the students write that numeral (8) in the tens column. The ones column is completed next. The students write 6 in that column.

Part C is a supervised practice exercise in which numbers are written as words and students must write the numerals. Teachers working with students unable to decode well would read the words to the students. Daily practice would be continued for several weeks. A place value chart would be incorporated into exercises for the first several weeks and then dropped.

Note that several tens numbers are included in Part C to reinforce the concept of proper column alignment. The first digit in a tens number is written in the tens column, while the first digit in a hundreds number is written in the hundreds column.

Numbers with a zero in the tens column are introduced in writing exercises after students can accurately write three-digit numerals without a zero in

FIGURE 5.3 Worksheet Exercise for Reading Hundreds Numbers

Circle the correct numeral:			
three hundred sixty-two	320	362	360
four hundred eighty-six	48	468	486
two hundred seventy-one	217	270	271
nine hundred thirty-two	732	932	923

the tens column. For numbers with a zero in the tens or ones column, step 3 in Part B of Format 5.10 must be modified. For example, after the students indicate that they do not hear a tens number, the teacher asks, "So what do we write in the tens column?" "Zero." "Write a zero in the tens column." The teacher then proceeds to step 4.

Examples would be the same as for exercises focusing on reading numbers with a zero in the tens column; minimally different sets such as 902, 92, 920; 48, 480, 408; and 702, 72, 720 should be used. Note that for the tens numbers, once students identify the tens column as the column they start writing in (step 1), they can simply write the number.

Reading and Writing Numbers 1,000–999,999

READING THOUSANDS NUMBERS. Thousands numbers are usually introduced during third grade. The format for introducing students to thousands numbers is fairly simple (see Format 5.11). Students are taught that the numeral in front of the comma tells how many thousands. They read that number, say "thousand" for the comma, and then read the rest of the number. In reading 3,286, they say "3," then "thousand" for the comma, and finally "286."

Students should read 8 to 10 numbers in the format. The sequence in which thousands numbers are introduced should be carefully controlled. We recommend that thousands numbers be introduced in this sequence:

1. Numbers between 1,000 and 9,999 without zeroes in the tens or hundreds column
2. Numbers between 1,000 and 9,999 that have zero in the tens and/or hundreds column
3. Numbers between 10,000 and 99,999
4. Numbers between 100,000 and 999,999

We recommend not including numbers with zeroes in the tens or hundreds column initially, since students may mistakenly develop the misrule that thousands have something to do with the number of zeroes in a numeral rather than the number of places. When numbers with zeroes are introduced, the teacher should pay careful attention to example selection. A fourth of the numbers should have a zero in the hundreds and a zero in the tens column, a fourth should have a zero in just the hundreds column, another fourth should have a zero in just the tens column, and a final fourth should have no zeroes at all. A sample set might include 2,000, 2,058, 2,508, 2,815; 7,002, 7,020, 7,200, 7,248; and 9,040, 9,400, 9,004, 9,246.

During fourth grade, students should be introduced to thousands numbers between 1,000 and 9,999 that do not have a comma. Some reference materials that students encounter will have thousands numbers written without a comma. In presenting thousands numbers without a comma, the teacher tells the students that when a number has four digits, it is a thousands number and then presents a list that includes a mix of thousands and hundreds numbers.

WRITING THOUSANDS NUMBERS. Writing thousands is taught in four stages, just as reading thousands is. During the first stage, all numbers have a digit other than zero in the hundreds column and tens column. In the second stage, numbers with a zero in the hundreds column and/or the tens column are introduced. (The example in Format 5.12 is from the second stage, numerals with a zero.) Numbers with a zero in the hundreds column are difficult because students may omit the zero. Students will often write the number four thousand-eighty-five as 4,85, leaving out the zero in the hundreds column. Often students simply write the numbers they hear: four thousand, eighty, and five. The teaching procedure for writing numbers must be designed to reinforce the place value concept that digits must be written in the thousands, hundreds, tens, and ones columns. Writing numbers with a zero in the hundreds or tens column might be introduced about a week after the easier number types are taught. Just as with reading thousands numbers, sets of minimally different examples should be presented in numeral writing exercises: 4,028, 4,208, 4,218, 4,280; 6,200, 6,002, 6,020, 6,224; 5,090, 5,900, 5,009, 5,994.

Note that Format 5.12, writing thousand numbers, is very similar to the one for writing hundred numbers (Format 5.10). Before students write a number, the teacher tells them to make a long line for the thousands and shorter lines for the hundreds, tens, and ones numbers. The teacher then has the students tell how many thousands and instructs them to write the appropriate numeral. The students then write a comma for the word *thousand*. Note that the comma should be started on the line with a slightly curved downward-pointing line. Many students will write the comma in the middle of the line so that it looks like the numeral 1. The teacher should watch for this error and immediately correct mistakes by modeling where to write the comma. After the comma is written, the teacher repeats the number, asking the students if they hear a hundreds number. If the answer is no, the student writes a zero. The same procedure is used with the tens and ones column. In Part B, the students write numbers without assistance.

Practice in writing thousands numbers should be continued daily for several weeks. Practice can be provided through worksheet exercises similar to those in Figure 5.3 for reading hundreds. Students read number words, then write the appropriate numerals.

Reading and Writing Millions

The millions numbers are usually taught during late fourth grade and fifth grade. Reading millions can be taught using a procedure similar to that used for reading thousands. The teacher instructs students to identify millions by examining the number of commas in the number. Students are taught that when two commas appear, the numbers in front of the first comma signify millions, while the numbers in front of the second comma signify thousands. The teacher initially prompts students by having them say the number a part at a time. See Summary Box 5.1.

Example selection for reading millions numbers should include a mix of millions numbers and thousands numbers so that the students receive practice in discriminating what to do when there are two commas instead one comma.

Writing millions numbers is taught by using a blank line for each figure in the number and placing the two commas correctly for students:

_____, _____ _____ _____, _____ _____ _____.

The teacher leads the students through writing the numerals, using basically the same steps as in the format for writing thousands numbers (see Format 5.12): "Listen. 5 million, 203 thousand, 450. How many million?... Write 5 in the millions column ... 5 million, 203 thousand. How many thousands?... Write 203 in the spaces before the thousands

comma ... Listen. 5 million, 203 thousand, 450. Write the rest of the number."

Numbers with zeroes in either the hundred-thousands, the ten-thousands, or the thousands columns, such as 3,064,800, 2,005,000, or 8,000,124, are especially difficult for students to write. These numbers are introduced in writing exercises only after the students can write easier numbers. Again, as with thousands numbers, minimally different sets should be used (e.g., 6,024,000, 6,204,000, 6,024, 6,240,000, 6,240). The sets should include a mix of millions and thousands numbers. A great deal of practice reading and writing millions numbers is necessary before students develop mastery. This practice should be provided through oral and worksheet exercises over a period of several months.

Column Alignment

Column alignment involves writing a series of numerals so that the appropriate digits are vertically aligned. Column alignment is an important skill because it is a prerequisite for advanced computation and story problems in which the numbers to be computed do not appear in a column in the story: For example, "Fred has 4,037 marbles. He gives 382 marbles to his younger brother. How many does he have left?" Column alignment exercises also test students' understanding of place value. For example, students who try to solve the problem about Fred's marbles by writing

$$\begin{array}{r} 4,037 \\ -\ 362 \\ \hline \end{array}$$

not only will arrive at the wrong answer but also have not mastered important place value skills.

Column alignment problems usually involve numerals with different numbers of digits written as row problems. The complexity of these column alignment problems increases as the number of

---

Summary Box 5.1
Symbol Identification: Reading Millions

1. Teacher asks students to identify how many commas are in the number.

2. Teacher asks what the number in front of the first comma tells about and has students identify that number.

3. Teacher asks what the numbers in front of the second comma tell about and has students identify that number.

4. Teacher asks students to identify the entire number.

digits increases. At first, problems should involve adding tens numbers and ones numbers (32 + 5 + 14); later, hundreds, tens, and ones (142 + 8 + 34); then thousands, hundreds, tens, and ones (3,042 + 6 + 134 + 28).

The strategy we recommend involves rearranging the order of the numbers: The number with the most digits is written first, and the other numbers are written under that number. The purpose of writing the largest numeral first is to establish the columns. The teaching procedure involves a simple model-test procedure in a structured worksheet format (see Format 5.13). The teacher tells the rule about the numeral with the most digits being written first and then guides the students in determining in which column to begin writing the other numerals. The structured worksheet exercise is presented for several lessons. Thereafter, practice on about five problems daily should be given on independent worksheets for several weeks.

Expanded Notation

Expanded notation involves rewriting a number as an addition problem composed of the numerals that each digit represents. For example, the number 3,428 is rewritten as 3,000 + 400 + 20 + 8, or vertically as:

$$
\begin{array}{r}
3,000 \\
400 \\
20 \\
+ \quad 8 \\
\hline
\end{array}
$$

The sequence in which expanded notation problems are introduced parallels the order in which students are taught to read and write numerals: teens, 20–99, 100–999, 1,000–9,999, and so on.

The teaching procedure for the verbal component of expanded notation is included in the previously discussed numeral writing formats; for example, "Do you hear a tens number in 382?... What tens number?" (see Format 5.10). With this background, students should have relatively little trouble saying a number as an addition problem (354 = 300 + 50 + 4), which is the focus of the structured board presentation (see Format 5.14). On the structured worksheet, students say numbers as addition problems and then write the problems. Since a less structured format is unnecessary, supervised practice can follow the structured worksheet.

APPLICATION ITEMS: SYMBOLS AND PLACE VALUE

1. The teacher is presenting a task on which the numerals 4, 2, and 5 appear. When the teacher points to 4 and asks, "What number?" a student says, "5." What is the correction procedure?

2. A child writes a 7 in an empty box over a group of five lines. Tell two possible causes of this error. How could you determine the exact cause? Describe a remedy.

3. During a test of writing numbers, a student writes a 2 as a 5. What should the teacher do?

4. Below is a worksheet item done independently by a child. The item required the student to write the appropriate number of lines to represent a numeral. Note the errors made by the student and describe the probable cause. Describe a remedy.

5. When in Format 5.7, Part C, in which the students are being taught to read tens numbers, a student identifies 71 as 17. What does the teacher say in making the correction?

6. Two teachers are introducing the reading of hundreds numbers. Below are the examples each included in the lesson. Which set is more appropriate? Tell why.

   Teacher A: 306, 285, 532, 683, 504
   Teacher B: 724, 836, 564, 832, 138

7. During the supervised practice for writing hundreds numbers, students make frequent errors (e.g., some students write 38 for three hundred eight). How should the teacher respond to these errors?

8. The numerals below are representative of various types. Tell the type each numeral illustrates. List the order in which the types would be introduced.

    836; 13; 18; 305; 64; 5,024; 5,321

9. Construct a set of six to eight examples to be used in presenting the specified parts of the following formats.

    a. Format for reading hundreds numbers: the less structured board presentation used when teaching hundreds numbers with a zero in the tens column.
    b. Format for reading thousands numbers: the less structured board presentation used when teaching thousands numbers with zeroes in the hundreds and/or the tens column.

FORMAT 5.1   Introducing New Numerals

Note: This format is used with each new symbol. In this example, we assume that the numerals 1, 4, 6, and 2 have been introduced and that the numeral 7 is being introduced.

TEACHER	STUDENTS
1. *(Write the following numbers on the board.)*	

    7 2
 4 6 7
    7 1

TEACHER	STUDENTS
(Model and test. Point to 7.) This is a seven. What is this? *(Touch 7.)*	7
2. *(Discrimination practice.)* When I touch it, tell me what it is.	
3. *(Point to 2, pause a second.)* What numeral? *(Touch 2.)* *(Repeat step 3 with these numerals: 7, 1, 6, 1, 7, 2, 1, 6, 7, etc.)*	2
4. *(Individual turns: Ask individual students to identify several numerals.)*	

FORMAT 5.2   Equation Writing

TEACHER	STUDENTS
1. *(Give students paper and pencil.)*	
2. You are going to write a problem. First you'll say it. Listen: Six plus two equals how many? Listen again. Six plus two equals how many? Say that. *To correct: Respond with students until they can say the statement at the normal rate of speech.*	Six plus two equals how many?
3. Now we'll say it the slow way. Every time I clap, we'll say a part of the statement. *(Respond with the students.)* Get ready. (Clap) six *(Pause 2 seconds; clap.)* plus *(Pause 2 seconds; clap.)* two *(Pause 2 seconds; clap.)* equals *(Pause 2 seconds; clap.)* how many?	six plus two equals how many?

(continued on next page)

FORMAT 5.2   (continued)

TEACHER	STUDENTS
Repeat step 3 until students appear able to respond on their own.)	
4. Now I'll clap and you say the statement by yourselves. *(Pause.)* Get ready. *(Clap at 2-second intervals.)*	Six plus two equals how many?
5. Now write the problem.	Students write 6 + 2 = ☐
6. *(Repeat steps 1–5 with three more equations, e.g., 8 − 3 = ☐; 4 + 5 = ☐; 7 − 2 = ☐).*	

FORMAT 5.3   **Identifying a Symbol and Then Drawing Lines: Structured Worksheet**

4	6	☐	2

TEACHER	STUDENTS
1. Everybody touch the first numeral on your worksheet. *(Hold up worksheet and point to 4.)* What is it?	4
A 4 tells you to make four lines. What does a 4 tell you to do?	Make 4 lines.
Each time I clap, draw a line and count. *(Signal by clapping once each 2 seconds.)*	Students draw lines and count. 1,2,3,4
How many did you end up with?	4
Yes, 4	
2. Touch the next symbol. What is it?	6
A 6 tells you to make six lines. What does a 6 tell you to do?	Make 6 lines.
Each time I clap, draw a line and count. *(Signal by clapping once each two seconds.)*	Students draw lines and count.
How many did you end up with?	6
Yes, 6	
3. Touch the next symbol. What is it?	Box
Does a box tell you to draw lines? No. A box does not tell you to draw lines.	
Does a box tell you to draw lines?	No
So are you going to draw lines?	No
4. Touch the next symbol. What is it?	2
What does 2 tell you to do?	Make two lines.
Do it.	Students draw two lines.
Get ready to count the lines. Get ready. *(Signal by clapping once each 2 seconds.)*	1, 2
How many did you end up with?	2
(On subsequent days, once students appear confident, use step 4 wording for each new example.)	

FORMAT 5.4   **Writing a Numeral for a Set of Objects: Structured Worksheet**

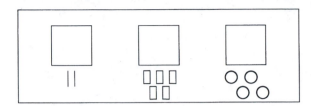

TEACHER	STUDENTS
1. Everybody, here's a rule: The objects under a box tell what numeral goes in the box. Get ready to count the objects under this box. *(Point to the first problem on the worksheet and pause while the students point to the first line.)* Count as I clap. Get ready. *(Clap each second.)*	1, 2
How many objects are under this box?	2
So what numeral are you going to write in the box?	2
Write that numeral.	
2. *(Repeat step 1 for additional examples.)*	

FORMAT 5.5   **Reading Teen Numbers**

TEACHER   **STUDENTS**

PART A: STRUCTURED BOARD PRESENTATION

1. *(Write the following chart on the board.)*

tens	ones
1	4
1	6
1	7
1	8
1	9

2. *(Point to the tens column.)* This is the tens column. *(Point to the ones column.)* This is the ones column.

3. These numerals all start with one ten. For one ten, we say *teen.* Listen to me read the numerals. *(Point to 14)* 14. *(Point to 16)* 16. *(Point to 17)* 17. *(Point to 18)* 18. *(Point to 19)* 19.

4. Your turn to read these numerals. *(Point to numerals in random order as students read.)*

5. *(Give individual turns to several students to read two numerals.)*

PART B: LESS STRUCTURED BOARD PRESENTATION

1. *(Write 14 on the board. Point to 14.)* What number?   14

2. *(Repeat step 1 with 19, 17, 18, 16.)*

(continued on next page)

FORMAT 5.5   (continued)

TEACHER	STUDENTS

PART C: PLACE VALUE WORKSHEET

1. *(Give students worksheets with problems such as these.)*

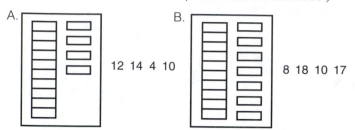

2. Look at picture A. The big pile has 10 blocks in it. The small pile has 4 blocks in it. I'll count: 10 *(pause)*, 11, 12, 13, 14. How many blocks?

        14

3. There are 14 blocks. Put a circle around the numeral 14.

4. Look at picture B. The big pile has 10 blocks in it. Start with 10 and count. Get ready.

        10, 11, 12, 13, 14, 15, 16, 17

5. How many blocks are there?

        17

6. Circle the numeral 17.

    (Repeat steps 4–6 with other examples.)

FORMAT 5.6   Writing Teen Numbers

TEACHER	STUDENTS

PART A: COMPONENTS OF TEEN NUMBERS

1. You're going to write teen numerals. Remember, the ending "teen" tells you the numeral has one ten. Listen: 16. Write a 1 for the teen and then a 6. Listen: 19. What do I write for 19? Listen: 14. What do I write for 14?

    I write a 1 for the teen and a 9.
    I write a 1 for the teen and a 4.

2. Your turn. 14. What do you write?

    A 1 for the teen and a 4.

3. *(Repeat step 2 with 16, 19, 17, 18.)*

4. *(Give individual turns to several students on step 2 or 3.)*

PART B: STRUCTURED BOARD PRESENTATION

1. *(Write the following chart on the board.)*

tens	ones

2. *(Point to the tens column.)* This is the tens column. This is where we write a 1 for teen, for one ten.

TEACHER	**STUDENTS**

3. What do you write for 14?
   (Write 1 in tens column, 4 in ones column.)   A 1 for the teen and a 4.

4. *(Repeat step 3 with 17, 19, 16, 18.)*

5. *(Call on students.)* Read each numeral. *(Point as students read.)*

PART C: STRUCTURED WORKSHEET—DICTATION

1. *(Give students a worksheet similar to the one below.)*

            tens | ones

   a. _____|_____

   b. _____|_____

   c. _____|_____

   d. _____|_____

2. Touch the space for problem a. You're going to write 14.
   What number?   14

3. What do you write for 14?   A 1 for the teen and a 4.

4. Write 14. Read the number you just wrote.   (Students write 14) 14

5. *(Repeat steps 1–4 for 16, 19, 14, 17, 18.)*

PART D: LESS STRUCTURED WORKSHEET—DICTATION

1. *(Give students worksheet with place value chart.)* You're
   going to write 14 on the first line. What are you going to write?   14
   Write 14.

2. *(Repeat step 1 with 16, 18, 19, 17.)*

FORMAT 5.7   Reading Numbers 20–99

TEACHER	**STUDENTS**

PART A: INTRODUCING TENS PLACE VALUE FACTS (PRESKILL)

1. *(Show students a diagram like the following.)*

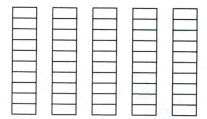

2. Each pile has 10 blocks. How many blocks in each pile?   10

3. Count by 10 each time I touch a pile. *(Touch piles.)*   10, 20, 30, 40, 50

4. How many blocks in all?   50
   Right, five tens equal 50.
   (Repeat steps 3 and 4 with two tens and four tens.)

(continued on next page)

FORMAT 5.7 (continued)

TEACHER	STUDENTS

PART B: PRACTICING TENS FACTS (PRESKILL)

1. *(Erase board. Model.)* Let's practice what groups of 10 equal. Listen. Three tens equal 30. What do three tens equal? *(Repeat with two tens and five tens.)* — 30

2. *(Test.)* What do two tens equal? — 20
   (Repeat with five tens, three tens, six tens, eight tens, and four tens until students can respond correctly to all examples.)

3. *(Present individual turns on step 2.)*

PART C: STRUCTURED BOARD PRESENTATION

1. (Write the following chart on the board.)

tens	ones
4	6

2. *(Point to tens column.)* What column? — tens column
   (Point to ones column.) What column? — ones column

3. How many tens? — 4
   What do four tens equal? — 40

4. How many ones? — 6
   What is 40 and 6? — 46
   So what does the whole numeral say? — 46
   (Repeat steps 1–4 with 52, 38, 93, 81.)

PART D: LESS STRUCTURED BOARD PRESENTATION

1. *(Write the following chart on the board.)*

tens	ones
7	2

   What does this whole numeral say? — 72
   (Pause 2–3 seconds, then signal.)

2. *(Repeat step 1 with 95, 20, 16, 31, 47, 50, 12.)*

3. *(Give individual turns to several students.)*

PART E: LESS STRUCTURED WORKSHEET

43   30   40   34

1. *(Hold up student worksheet.)* Let's find out how many blocks are in this picture. How many piles of tens are there? — 3

2. What do three tens equal? — 30

TEACHER	**STUDENTS**
3. But we're not done. *(Point to four remaining blocks.)* We have to count these blocks. *(Point to tens group.)* We have 30 blocks here. Start counting at 30 then touch these blocks as we count. *(Count 30, 31, 32, 33, 34.)*	30, 31, 32, 33, 34
4. How many blocks in the picture?	34
Put a circle around the numeral 34.	

FORMAT 5.8   Writing Numbers 20–99

TEACHER	**STUDENTS**
PART A: EXPANDED NOTATION PRESKILL	
1. Say this number: 84	84
2. Eighty-four equals 80 and 4. What does 84 equal?	80 and 4
What's the first part of 84?	80
3. Eighty-four equals 80 and what else?	4
4. *(Repeat steps 1–3 with 72, 95, 88, 43.)*	
PART B: TENS NUMBERS PLACE VALUE FACTS (PRESKILL)	
1. Twenty has two tens. How many tens in 20?	2
2. *(Repeat step 1 with 60 and 30.)*	
3. How many tens in 40?	4
4. *(Repeat step 3 with 80, 30, 60, 20, 50.)*	
5. *(Give individual turns to several students.)*	
PART C: STRUCTURED BOARD PRESENTATION	
1. *(Write the following chart on the board.)*	

tens	ones

2. I want to write some big numbers. When we write big numbers, we write the tens first. Then we write the ones.	
What do we write first?	the tens
What do we write next?	the ones
3. Listen: 84. What is the first part of 84?	80
4. How many tens in 80?	8
So I write 8 in the tens column. *(Write 8 in the tens column.)* Eighty equals eight tens.	
5. Listen: Eighty-four equals 80 and what else?	4
So I write 4 in the ones column. *(Write 4 in the ones column.)*	
6. What number did I just write?	84
7. How many tens in 84?	8
How many ones in 84?	4
8. *(Repeat steps 3–6 with several examples.)*	

(continued on next page)

FORMAT 5.8   (continued)

TEACHER	STUDENTS

PART D: STRUCTURED WORKSHEET PRESENTATION

1. *(Give students the following worksheet.)*

	tens	ones
a.		
b.		
c.		
d.		
e.		
f.		

2. Touch a. Next to a you are going to write 79.
   What are you going to write?   79

3. What is the first part of 79?   70
   How many tens in 70?   7
   Write 7 in the tens column.

4. Seventy-nine equals 70 and what else?   9
   Write 9 in the ones column.

5. What number did you write?   79

6. How many tens in 79?   7

7. How many ones in 79?   9

8. *(Repeat steps 1–6 with several examples.)*

PART E: LESS STRUCTURED WORKSHEET—DICTATION

1. (Give students worksheets labeled like the example below.)

   a. _____
   b. _____
   c. _____
   d. _____
   e. _____
   f. _____

2. You're going to write a numeral on each line.

3. Touch line a.

4. You're going to write 49. What are you going to write?   49

5. Write 49.   Students write 49.

6. *(Repeat steps 2–4 with 73, 20, 99, 14, 51, 42, 61, 17.)*

FORMAT 5.9   Reading Numbers 100–999

TEACHER	STUDENTS

PART A: STRUCTURED BOARD PRESENTATION

1. *(Write the following chart on the board.)*

hundreds	tens	ones
5	4	8

(Point to appropriate column as you say the following.)
This is the hundreds column.
This is the tens column.
This is the ones column.
Tell me the names of the columns.
(Point to the columns, starting with hundreds; repeat until students are firm.)   hundreds, tens, ones.

2. The first thing we do when we read a number is identify the column the number starts in. *(Point to 5 in 548.)*
   What column does this number start in?   hundreds
   How many hundreds do we have?   5
   What do five hundreds equal?   500

3. *(Point to 4.)* What column is this?   tens
   How many tens do we have?   4
   What do four tens equal?   40

4. *(Point to 8.)* What column is this?   ones
   How many ones do we have?   8
   What do we say?   8

5. Let's read the whole number. When I touch a numeral, you tell me what it says.
   (Point to 5, pause a second, touch 5.)   500
   (Point to 4, pause a second, touch 4.)   40
   (Point to 8, pause a second, touch 8.)   8

6. Say the whole number.   548

7. *(Repeat steps 2–6 with 697, 351, 874, 932, all written in place value charts.)*
   Note: When presenting examples with a 1 in the tens column, present the following steps instead of steps 3, 4, and 5 in the format. The following example shows how to teach the number 514.

8. What column is this?   tens
   How many tens do we have?   1

9. How many ones do we have?   4
   We have one 10 and four ones, so what do we say?   14

10. Let's read the whole number. *(Point to 5.)* What do we say for this?   500
    (Point to 14.) What do we say for these?   14

PART B: LESS STRUCTURED BOARD PRESENTATION

1. *(Write the following chart on the board.)*

hundreds	tens	ones
4	4	6

(continued on next page)

FORMAT 5.9 (continued)

TEACHER	STUDENTS

2. Now we are going to read the numbers without saying the parts first.
   This time when I point, you are going to tell me the whole number.
   (Point to 446 and then pause 2–3 seconds.)

3. *(Repeat step 1 with 249, 713, 321, 81, 720, 740.)*

4. *(Give individual turns to several students.)*

FORMAT 5.10 Writing Hundreds Numbers

TEACHER	STUDENTS

Part A: Expanded Notation

1. Count by hundreds to 900. Get ready, count.

   Now count by tens to 90. Get ready, count.

   Students: 100, 200, 300, 400, 500, 600, 700, 800, 900
   10, 20, 30, 40, 50, 60, 70, 80, 90

2. Listen to this number: 362. Do you hear hundreds in 362?
   What hundreds number?

   Students: yes
   300

3. Listen again: 362. Do you hear a tens number in 362?
   What tens number?

   Students: yes
   60

4. Listen again: 362. Do you hear a ones number in 362?
   What ones number?

   Students: yes
   2

5. 362 = 300 + 60 + 2. Say it with me.
   Say it yourselves.

   Students: 362 = 300 + 60 + 2
   362 = 300 + 60 + 2

6. *(Repeat steps 2–5 with 428, 624, and 139.)*

7. *(Give individual turns on steps 2–5 to several students.)*

Part B: Structured Worksheet Presentation—Dictation

1. *(Give students a worksheet in which columns and spaces are written as illustrated.)*

hundreds	tens	ones
a.		
b.		
c.		
d.		
e.		

   You are going to write hundreds numbers. Touch the hundreds column. Touch the tens column. Touch the ones column. *(Monitor responses.)*

2. What's the first part of 648?
   So what column do you start writing in?
   How many hundreds in 600?
   Write 6 in the hundreds column.

   Students: 600
   hundreds
   6

3. What column comes next?
   Do you hear a tens number in 648?

   Students: tens
   yes

TEACHER	STUDENTS

What tens number?
Write 4 in the tens column.

4

4. What column comes next?
Do you hear a ones number in 648?
What ones number?
Write 8 in the ones column.

ones
yes
8

5. We finished. How many hundreds in 648?
How many tens in 648?
How many ones in 648?
Read the number you wrote.

6
4
8
648

6. *(Repeat steps 2–5 with 326, 463, 825, 253, 866.)*

PART C: SUPERVISED PRACTICE

1. *(Give students a worksheet like the one below.)*
Write these numerals on the sample worksheet:

	hundreds	tens	ones
a. two hundred sixty-one	a.		
b. four hundred eighteen	b.		
c. eight	c.		
d. nine hundred sixty-two	d.		
e. forty-eight	e.		
f. four hundred eighty	f.		
g. twelve	g.		
h. nine hundred seven	h.		
i. forty-one	i.		
j. three hundred ninety-seven	j.		

2. The instructions tell you to write the numerals.

3. Item a. Read the words.   Two hundred sixty-one.

4. Write the numeral.

5. *(Repeat steps 2 and 3 with the remaining examples.)*

FORMAT 5.11   Reading Thousands Numbers

TEACHER	STUDENTS

PART A: STRUCTURED BOARD PRESENTATION

1. When a big number has one comma, the comma tells
about thousands. Here's the rule: The number in front
of the comma tells how many thousands. What does
the number in front of the comma tell?
(Write 6,781 on the board.)

how many thousands

2. What number comes in front of the comma?
So what is the first part of the number?

6
6 thousand

3. *(Point to 781.)* Get ready to read the rest of the number.

781

(continued on next page)

FORMAT 5.11 (continued)

TEACHER	STUDENTS
4. Now you are going to read the whole number. *(Point to 6, then comma, then 781.)*	6,781
5. *(Repeat steps 2–4 with these numbers: 2,145; 3,150; 5,820; 6,423.)*	
6. *(Give individual turns to several students.)*	

PART B: LESS STRUCTURED BOARD PRESENTATION

1. *(Write 3,820 on the board.)* Get ready to read this number. *(Pause several seconds.)* *To correct: Repeat steps 2–4 from Part A.*	3,820
2. *(Repeat step 1 with 9,270; 3,174; 3,271; 9,563; 4,812.)*	
3. *(Give individual turns to several students.)*	

FORMAT 5.12 Writing Thousands Numbers

TEACHER	STUDENTS

PART A: STRUCTURED WORKSHEET

1. (Write the following on the board.)

   _____ _____ _____ _____

   The big line is for thousands. The other lines are for the hundreds, tens, and ones. Write lines for the thousands, hundreds, tens, and ones on your paper.

2. Listen to this number: 8,024. How many thousands? Write 8 on the thousands line. And what do you write after the thousands number? Write a comma.	8 Students write 8. a comma Students write a comma.
3. Listen again: 8,024. You already wrote 8 thousand. What do you have left?	24
4. Are there any hundreds in 24? So write zero in the hundreds column.	no Students write zero.
5. Are there any tens in 24? What do you write in the tens column? Write it.	yes 2 Students write 2.
6. Are there any ones in 24? What do you write in the ones column? Write it.	yes 4 Students write 4.
7. *(Repeat steps 1–6 with 8,204; 8,042; and 8,240; then with 6,008; 6,806; 6,800; 6,080.)*	

PART B: SUPERVISED PRACTICE—DICTATION

1. Now you are going to write some numerals without help.

2. Make a long line for thousands and shorter lines for hundreds, tens, and ones.

TEACHER	STUDENTS
3. Listen to this number: 9,028. What number? Write 9,028. *(Monitor responses.)*	9,028
4. *(Repeat step 3 with these numbers: 9,208; 9,218; and 9,280; then 8,004; 8,400; 8,420; and 8,040.)*	

FORMAT 5.13 **Teaching Column Alignment: Structured Worksheet**

TEACHER	STUDENTS
1. *(Give students the following worksheet.)*	

    a. 42 + 361 + 9

$$\begin{array}{r} 361 \\ 42 \\ +\ 9 \\ \hline \end{array}$$

    b. 7 + 604 + 32

TEACHER	STUDENTS
Touch problem a. I'll read it. 42 + 361 + 9. Problem a has been rewritten in a column. Touch the column problem. The largest number is on top. That's 361. The 4 in 42 is in the tens column. The smallest number is on the bottom. Touch 9. It's in the ones column.	
2. Touch problem b. Read the problem.	Students touch 7 + 604 + 32. 7 plus 604 plus 32
3. We're going to write the numerals in a column so we can add them. We write the largest number first. What's the largest number? Write it and then cross out 604 in the row problem.	 604 Students write 604.
4. Now get ready to write 32 under 604. What column does 32 start in? Write 32 and cross it out in the row problem.	 tens Students write 604. 32

5. Now get ready to write 7. What column will you start writing in?
Write 7 and cross it out in the row problem.
	ones
	
	 604
	  32
	   7

6. Have you crossed out all the numerals in the row problem? What kind of problem is this? Write in the sign. You're done writing the problem. Now work it.	yes addition 604 32 + 7
7. *(Repeat steps 2–6 with four more problems.)*	

FORMAT 5.14 Expanded Notation

TEACHER	STUDENTS
PART A: STRUCTURED BOARD PRESENTATION	
1. Listen to this number: 624. Say the number.	624
2. Now listen to me say 624 as an addition problem: 600 + 20 + 4	
3. Your turn. Say 624 as an addition problem.	600 + 20 + 4
4. *(Repeat step 3 with 55, 406, 317, 29, 871, 314.)*	
PART B: STRUCTURED WORKSHEET	
1. Listen. Say 472 as an addition problem. I'll write 472 as an addition problem. *(Write on the board 400 + 70 + 2.)*	400 + 70 + 2
2. Listen. Say 528 as an addition problem. Write 528 as an addition problem.	500 + 20 + 8 Students write problem.
3. *(Repeat step 2 with 94, 427, 35, 53, 704, 266.)*	
PART C: SUPERVISED PRACTICE	
1. *(Give the students worksheets with problems like the following.)*	

    a. 624 = _____ + _____ + _____

    b. 386 = _____ + _____ + _____

CHAPTER 6

Basic Facts

There are 390 basic arithmetic facts: 100 addition, 100 subtraction, 100 multiplication, and 90 division. Basic addition facts include all possible combinations in which each of the addends is a whole number under 10. Basic subtraction facts include all possible combinations in which the subtrahend and the difference (a and b in $c - a = b$) are one-digit numbers. Tables 6.1 and 6.2 include all the basic addition and subtraction facts.

Basic multiplication facts include all possible combinations in which each of the factors is a single-digit number (i.e., in $a \times b = c$, a and b are single digits). Basic division facts include all possible combinations in which the divisor and quotient are single-digit numbers (e.g., in $c \div a = b$, a and b are single-digit numbers and a does not equal 0). Table 6.3 includes all basic multiplication and division facts.

TEACHING PROCEDURES

Ashlock (1971) outlines three different types of instructional activities designed to teach basic facts: activities for understanding, activities for relating, and activities for mastery. The activities for understanding involve concrete demonstrations of the

Table 6.1   Basic Addition Facts

					Addends					
Addends	0	1	2	3	4	5	⑥	7	8	9
0+	0	1	2	3	4	5	6	7	8	9
1+	1	2	3	4	5	6	7	8	9	10
2+	2	3	4	5	6	7	8	9	10	11
3+	3	4	5	6	7	8	9	10	11	12
4+	4	5	6	7	8	9	10	11	12	13
5+	5	6	7	8	9	10	11	12	13	14
6+	6	7	8	9	10	11	12	13	14	15
⑦+	7	8	9	10	11	12	⑬	14	15	16
8+	8	9	10	11	12	13	14	15	16	17
9+	9	10	11	12	13	14	15	16	17	18

Note: Problems are formed by an addend from the column on the left, an addend from the row on top, and their intersection; e.g., the numerals for 7 + 6 = 13 are circled.

Table 6.2   Basic Subtraction Facts

Minuends	Subtrahends									
	0	1	2	3	4	5	6	⑦	8	9
1−	1	0								
2−	2	1	0							
3−	3	2	1	0						
4−	4	3	2	1	0					
5−	5	4	3	2	1	0				
6−	6	5	4	3	2	1	0			
7−	7	6	5	4	3	2	1	0		
8−	8	7	6	5	4	3	2	1	0	
9−	9	8	7	6	5	4	3	2	1	0
10−		9	8	7	6	5	4	3	2	1
11−			9	8	7	6	5	4	3	2
12−				9	8	7	6	5	4	3
⑬−					9	8	7	⑥	5	4
14−						9	8	7	6	5
15−							9	8	7	6
16−								9	8	7
17−									9	8
18−										9

Note: Problems are formed by a minuend from the column on the left, followed by a subtrahend from the top row, and finally, the difference, which is the intersection; e.g., the numerals for 13 − 7 = 6 are circled.

operations, similar to those we have included in chapters 7 through 10.

Relating activities are exercises designed to teach the relationships among various facts. The primary way of teaching these relationships is through the introduction of fact families. Fact families can be constructed as a series, such as the plus ones (3 + 1, 4 + 1, 5 + 1, etc.), the plus fours (5 + 4, 6 + 4, 7 + 4, etc.), the plus doubles (2 + 2, 3 + 3, 4 + 4, etc.), and as sets of three related numbers that generate four facts. Following are examples of fact families constructed from three related numbers:

Addition and subtraction
3, 5, 8

3 + 5 = 8
5 + 3 = 8
8 − 3 = 5
8 − 5 = 3

Table 6.3   Basic Multiplication/Division Facts

÷/×	0	1	2	3	4	5	6	⑦	8	9
0	0	0	0	0	0	0	0	0	0	0
1	0	1	2	3	4	5	6	7	8	9
2	0	2	4	6	8	10	12	14	16	18
3	0	3	6	9	12	15	18	21	24	27
4	0	4	8	12	16	20	24	28	32	36
5	0	5	10	15	20	25	30	35	40	45
⑥	0	6	12	18	24	30	36	㊷	48	54
7	0	7	14	21	28	35	42	49	56	63
8	0	8	16	24	32	40	48	56	64	72
9	0	9	18	27	36	45	54	63	72	81

Note: Problems are formed by a number from the column on the left, a number from the top row, and their intersection; e.g., the row and column for the numerals 6 and 7 intersect at 42; these circled numbers form 6 × 7 = 42 and 42 ÷ 6 = 7.

Multiplication and division
3, 5, 15

$$3 \times 5 = 15$$
$$5 \times 3 = 15$$
$$3\overline{)15} = 5$$
$$5\overline{)15} = 3$$

Note how the commutative relationship between each pair of addition facts (3 + 5 = 8, so 5 + 3 = 8) and multiplication facts (3 × 5 = 15, so 5 × 3 = 15) greatly reduces the memorization load for students. Instead of memorizing each fact individually (5 + 3 *and* 3 + 5), students can be taught that if they know one fact, they also know the reverse. Instructional procedures based on the commutative principle are discussed later.

Our recommendations for grouping facts into sets of fact families appear in Figures 6.2 through 6.5. These sets form the basis for presenting facts. The relationship formats listed in these figures are discussed after the next section.

Mastery activities are designed to facilitate fact memorization. The activities we have identified for building mastery require a sequence for introducing facts, coordination of relationship activities with memorization activities, intensive and systematic review, specific performance criteria that define when new facts can be introduced, record-keeping procedures that allow the teacher to monitor each student's mastery of facts, and motivation procedures.

RELATIONSHIP ACTIVITIES

Since the understanding activities Ashlock recommends are presented in the chapters for each respective operation, this chapter focuses only on the relationship and mastery activities. The teaching procedures for the relationship activities include (a) exercises with number families based on a series (e.g., 3 × 1, 3 × 2, 3 × 3) and (b) exercises demonstrating inverse relationships between addition and subtraction and between multiplication and division (e.g., 4 + 2 = 6, 2 + 4 = 6, 6 − 4 = 2, 6 − 2 = 4). While the teaching procedures include strategies similar to those in the other chapters, the intent of the strategies in this chapter is different. Although the relationship strategies can be used to solve problems, their purpose is to show the relationship among number families so that fact memorization is easier. It appears that memorization of *related* bits of information, as represented by number families, is easier than memorization of random bits of infor-

mation. Following a discussion of the teaching procedures for relationship activities, mastery activities are discussed.

Preskill

Prior to introducing basic addition facts, teachers should teach students a strategy to figure out plus-one facts. (Students who know 30 or more facts do not need to receive instruction on this preskill.) Prior to instruction in facts, students most likely have been using picture representations or concrete objects to solve simple equations. The format for plus-one facts (see Format 6.1) not only teaches plus-one facts but also begins teaching students that numbers are related in systematic ways. Plus-one facts, which should be introduced in first grade, are taught through the application of this rule: When you plus one, you say the next number. From the rule, students learn that the first addend is systematically related to the sum:

$$6 + 1 = 7 \qquad 9 + 1 = 10$$

To prepare students for the plus-one rule, the term *next number* is taught in Part A of the format. At first, the teacher counts several numbers, holding the last number for several seconds (e.g., "3, 4, 5, sssiiixxx"). The students say the next number, 7. After presenting several examples in which the teacher says a series of numbers and asks students the next number (step 2), the teacher presents examples in which she says just a single number, not a series of numbers (step 3), and the students say the next number. A common error made by students is that they continue counting rather than stopping at the next number. The teacher should stop students immediately if they say more than the next number, model saying just the next number, then repeat the same example before presenting additional examples.

Part B should not be introduced until students have mastered the next number skill taught in Part A. In Part B, the teacher presents the plus-one rule, models several examples, and then tests. As a prompt, the teacher emphasizes the first addend, stretching it out for several seconds, and de-emphasizes the words *plus one* (e.g., in *sssiiixxx* plus one, the *plus one* is said quietly so that students can make the six–seven counting association).

In Part C, the teacher presents the plus-one facts without any prompting. The teacher should initially pause for 2 to 3 seconds before signaling for a response so that the students have time to figure out the answer. After several days of practice, the teacher can decrease the pause to a second. The teacher continues to provide practice on plus-one facts until students can respond instantly to any plus-one problem.

Series Saying

Series saying, one of the major relationship activities, involves teaching the students to say a consecutively ordered set of fact statements. Series saying prompts students to notice the counting relationship among facts, as indicated by the circled numerals in the following series:

$$\begin{array}{c} 6 + 2 = 8 \\ 7 + 2 = 9 \\ 8 + 2 = 10 \end{array}$$

Series saying may be incorporated into instruction for any of the four types of basic facts: addition, subtraction, multiplication, and division. Format 6.2 includes a series-saying format. Although the format illustrates an addition series, the same format can be used to present other types of series.

There are four parts to the series-saying format. In Part A, students read the consecutively ordered statements. In Part B, the teacher erases the answers and the students read the statements. In Part C, the teacher erases everything and requires the students to say the series from memory. Part D is a drill on randomly presented facts. The teacher writes the fact questions on the board without the answers. The facts are written in random order (e.g., 7 + 2, 5 + 2, 8 + 2, 6 + 2). The teacher points to each fact, pauses, and then signals the students to respond. He repeats the facts until the students can respond after a 1-second pause. The facts are written in random order so the students will not memorize the order of the answers.

Teaching students to read statements (Part A) in a rapid, crisp fashion is critical for instructionally naive students because they often read statements slowly or inaccurately. If students cannot *read* the series of statements in a crisp, rapid fashion, they will have a great deal of difficulty saying the series from memory and remembering facts during the random drill (Part D). The teacher must provide adequate practice to enable the students to say the series of statements at a fast rate.

The teacher should set a pace for saying the statements so that each statement in the series is said in approximately 2 to 3 seconds (2 seconds for older students, 3 seconds for younger students). There should also be a slight pause, about 1 second, between each statement. The pacing of the task is illustrated in Figure 6.1. The top row indicates seconds elapsed. Across the bottom row are the statements the teacher would say. The same pace should be continued in Parts B and C.

The correction for slow pacing is to keep leading (responding with the students) at a brisk pace and gradually fade the lead so that the students are saying the statements independently. The teacher must be quite careful to provide the adequate repetition in an enjoyable manner. Teachers working with lower performing students may find that several days of practice on Parts A and B are needed before continuing on to Parts C and D. Teachers working with higher performing students may be able to present all parts in a day or two.

The first day that Part D is presented, only the first three facts in the series should be presented. A new fact can be included in Part D each of the next two days.

Three-Number Fact Families

The other major format designed to demonstrate the relationships among facts is taught through the introduction of three-number fact families. These are sets of three numbers from which students can be taught to generate four statements, either addition and subtraction or multiplication and division. For example, given the numbers 3, 4, and 7, students are taught to construct the addition statements 3 + 4 = 7 and 4 + 3 = 7. Later, students learn to construct the subtraction statements based on the same three numbers: 7 − 4 = 3, 7 − 3 = 4.

There are two formats for teaching number families. The first teaches students to use the commutative properties of addition (if $a + b = c$, then $b + a = c$) and multiplication (if $a \times b = c$, then $b \times a = c$). The second teaches students to generate subtraction statements from addition statements and division

FIGURE 6.1 Pacing of Series Saying

Seconds	1	2	3	4	5	6	7	8	9	10	11
Statements	6 + 2 = 8			pause	7 + 2 = 9			pause	8 + 2 = 10		

statements from multiplication statements. The commutative property is extremely important in that it greatly reduces the number of facts students need to memorize. For every fact that students learn, they can derive the answer to the inverse fact quickly and easily by using the commutative property. For example, if students have memorized that 5 + 3 = 8, they also know the answer to 3 + 5. Note that the term *commutative property* is not explicitly taught; only the function of the property is taught.

The first format, which consists of three parts, appears in Format 6.3. Although the example shown illustrates the commutative property with addition, the same format can be used to teach the commutative property of multiplication. In Part A, students are taught how to construct a pair of addition statements from a set of three numbers. For example, given 2, 5, and 7, the students construct 2 + 5 = 7 and 5 + 2 = 7. One member of each pair has been previously presented in a series-saying format. The second member of each pair is the reverse fact. For example, if students have been taught the plus-two facts (e.g., 5 + 2, 6 + 2, etc.), the new facts would be the two-plus facts (2 + 5, 2 + 6, etc.). In Part B, the students are orally tested on the new "reversed" facts. Part C is a worksheet exercise in which the students are given a diagram like this:

$$\Box \quad \boxed{2} \atop \boxed{5}$$

$$\underline{} + \underline{} = \underline{}$$
$$\underline{} + \underline{} = \underline{}$$

They are asked to fill in the sum (called the "big number") and generate two addition statements.

The second format for teaching three-number families demonstrates how facts can be related across operations (see Format 6.4). It is used to generate subtraction facts from addition facts and division facts from multiplication facts. The teacher demonstrates how to generate the subtraction or division statements. For example, after constructing 3 + 4 = 7 and 4 + 3 = 7, students are taught to generate the subtraction statements of 7 − 4 = 3 and 7 − 3 = 4.

The format for subtraction and division facts includes two parts. Although examples in Figure 6.4 illustrate subtraction, the same format can be used to introduce division facts. In Part A, the teacher demonstrates how three related numbers such as 3, 5, and 8 can generate two subtraction statements. The teacher first has the students add the two

smaller numbers (3 and 5), then points out that two subtraction statements can be made. The teacher introduces the rule that *when you subtract, you always start with the big number,* which helps avoid errors like 3 − 8 = 5. Part B is a worksheet exercise in which the students construct four statements, two addition and two subtraction, from three numbers.

Sequence for Introducing Facts

Basic facts should be introduced in a carefully planned sequence. New sets of facts should be introduced systematically to avoid potential confusion and to facilitate learning. Figures 6.2, 6.3, 6.4, and 6.5 suggest orders for introducing addition, subtraction, multiplication, and division facts. Each figure lists about 25 sets of facts, each set comprised of three or four facts. The sets are lettered in their order of presentation: The facts in Set A would be introduced first, followed by the facts in sets B, C, D, and so on. Across from each set of facts is the relationship format recommended for introducing the facts. For example, in Figure 6.3 for subtraction facts, the teacher presents the Set G facts (6 − 3, 8 − 4, 10 − 5, 12 − 6) using the three-numbers subtraction format. For the 6 − 3 fact, the teacher writes

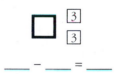

in Part A. The teacher writes blanks for only one statement because only one subtraction statement, 6 − 3, can be generated from the numbers 6, 3, and 3. The teacher presents Part A with all four sets of numbers and then presents Part B with the four sets of numbers. While the teacher is introducing the new set of facts, memorization worksheet exercises on the previous sets continue. Each relationship exercise, as illustrated with Set G for subtraction, is presented for several days before the facts are introduced into mastery exercises.

In constructing these sequences, three guidelines were followed: (a) easier facts were introduced first, (b) related facts were introduced together, and (c) the reverse of specific series of facts was taught relatively soon after the initial series was presented. These sequences illustrate just one possible order for introducing facts and are not intended to represent the only or best sequence for teaching facts.

In developmental math programs, addition facts are introduced first, followed by subtraction,

FIGURE 6.2   Sequence of Addition Facts

Plus-one format is Format 6.1.
Series-saying format is Format 6.2.
Three-number format is Format 6.3.

Sets of New Facts	Relationship Formats
A. 2 + 1, 3 + 1, 4 + 1, 5 + 1	Plus-one, series saying
B. 6 + 1, 7 + 1, 8 + 1, 9 + 1	Plus-one, series saying
C. 2 + 2, 3 + 2, 4 + 2, 5 + 2	Series saying
D. 6 + 2, 7 + 2, 8 + 2, 9 + 2	Series saying
E. 3 + 3, 4 + 4, 5 + 5, 6 + 6	Series saying
F. 2 + 3, 3 + 3, 4 + 3, 5 + 3	Series saying
G. 6 + 3, 7 + 3, 8 + 3, 9 + 3	Series saying
H. 1 + 2, 1 + 3, 1 + 4, 1 + 5	Three numbers—addition (1, 2, 3) (1, 3, 4) (1, 4, 5) (1, 5, 6)
I. 1 + 6, 1 + 7, 1 + 8, 1 + 9	Three numbers—addition (1, 6, 7) (1, 7, 8) (1, 8, 9) (1, 9, 10)
J. 2 + 4, 2 + 5, 2 + 6	Three numbers—addition (2, 3, 5) (2, 4, 6) (2, 5, 7) (2, 6, 8)
K. 2 + 7, 2 + 8, 2 + 9	Three numbers—addition (2, 7, 9) (2, 8, 10) (2, 9, 11)
L. 3 + 4, 3 + 5, 3 + 6	Three numbers—addition (3, 4, 7) (3, 5, 8) (3, 6, 9)
M. 3 + 7, 3 + 8, 3 + 9	Three numbers—addition (3, 7, 10) (3, 8, 11) (3, 9, 12)
N. 7 + 7, 8 + 8, 9 + 9, 10 + 10	Series saying
O. 1 + 0, 2 + 0, 3 + 0...9 + 0	Series saying
P. 0 + 1, 0 + 2, 0 + 3...0 + 9	Three numbers—addition (1, 0, 1) (2, 0, 2)
Q. 5 + 4, 6 + 4, 7 + 4	Series saying
R. 7 + 6, 8 + 6, 9 + 6	Series saying
S. 4 + 5, 4 + 6, 4 + 7	Three numbers—addition (4, 5, 9) (4, 6, 10) (4, 7, 11)
T. 6 + 7, 6 + 8, 6 + 9	Three numbers—addition (6, 7, 13) (6, 8, 14) (6, 9, 15)
U. 7 + 4, 8 + 4, 9 + 4	Series saying
V. 7 + 7, 8 + 7, 9 + 7	Series saying
W. 9 + 8, 8 + 9, 4 + 8	Three numbers—addition (8, 9, 17) (8, 4, 12)
X. 6 + 5, 7 + 5, 8 + 5, 9 + 5	Series saying
Y. 7 + 8, 7 + 9, 4 + 9	Three numbers—addition (7, 8, 15) (7, 9, 16) (9, 4, 13)
Z. 5 + 6, 5 + 7, 5 + 8, 5 + 9	Three numbers—addition (5, 6, 11) (5, 7, 12) (5, 8, 13) (5, 9, 14)

FIGURE 6.3   Sequence of Subtraction Facts

Series-saying format is Format 6.2.
Three-number format is Format 6.3.

Sets of New Facts	Relationship Format
A. 3 – 1, 4 – 1, 5 – 1, 6 – 1	Series saying
B. 7 – 1, 8 – 1, 9 – 1, 10 – 1	Series saying
C. 4 – 2, 5 – 2, 6 – 2, 7 – 2	Series saying
D. 8 – 2, 9 – 2, 10 – 2, 11 – 2	Series saying
E. 1 – 0, 2 – 0, 3 – 0, 4 – 0, 5 – 0, 6 – 0, 7 – 0, 8 – 0, 9 – 0	Three numbers—subtraction (1, 0, 1) (2, 0, 2) (3, 0, 3) (4, 0, 4) ...
F. 1 – 1, 2 – 2, 3 – 3, 4 – 4, 5 – 5, 6 – 6, 7 – 7, 8 – 8, 9 – 9	Three numbers—subtraction (1, 1, 0) (2, 2, 0) (3, 3, 0) (4, 4, 0) ...
G. 6 – 3, 8 – 4, 10 – 5, 12 – 6	Three numbers—subtraction (6, 3, 3) (8, 4, 4) (10, 5, 5) (12, 6, 6)
H. 5 – 3, 6 – 3, 7 – 3, 8 – 3	Series saying
I. 9 – 3, 10 – 3, 11 – 3, 12 – 3	Series saying
J. 3 – 2, 4 – 3, 5 – 4, 6 – 5	Three numbers—subtraction (3, 2, 1,) (4, 3, 1) (5, 4, 1) (6, 5, 1)
K. 7 – 6, 8 – 7, 9 – 8, 10 – 9	Three numbers—subtraction (7, 6, 1) (8, 7, 1) (9, 8, 1) (10, 9, 1)
L. 5 – 3, 6 – 4, 7 – 5	Three numbers—subtraction (5, 3, 2) (6, 4, 2) (7, 5, 2)
M. 8 – 6, 9 – 7, 10 – 8, 11 – 9	Three numbers—subtraction (8, 6, 2) (9, 7, 2) (10, 8, 2) (11, 9, 2)
N. 6 – 3, 7 – 4, 8 – 5, 9 – 6	Three numbers—subtraction (6, 3, 3) (7, 4, 3) (8, 5, 3) (9, 6, 3)
O. 10 – 7, 11 – 8, 12 – 9	Three numbers—subtraction (10, 7, 3) (11, 8, 3) (12, 9, 3)
P. 14 – 7, 16 – 8, 18 – 9	Three numbers—subtraction (14, 7, 7) (16, 8, 8) (18, 9, 9)
Q. 8 – 4, 9 – 4, 10 – 4, 11 – 4	Series saying
R. 12 – 6, 13 – 6, 14 – 6, 15 – 6	Series saying
S. 9 – 5, 10 – 6, 11 – 7	Three numbers—subtraction (9, 5, 4) (10, 6, 4) (11, 7, 4)
T. 13 – 7, 14 – 8, 15 – 9	Three numbers—subtraction (13, 7, 6) (14, 8, 6) (15, 9, 6)
U. 10 – 4, 11 – 4, 12 – 4, 13 – 4	Series saying
V. 14 – 7, 15 – 7, 16 – 7	Series saying
W. 17 – 8, 17 – 9, 12 – 8	Three numbers—subtraction (17, 9, 8) (12, 8, 4)
X. 11 – 5, 12 – 5, 13 – 5, 14 – 5	Series saying
Y. 15 – 8, 16 – 9, 13 – 9	Three numbers—subtraction (15, 8, 7) (16, 9, 7) (13, 9, 4)
Z. 11 2 6, 12 2 7, 13 2 8, 14 2 9	Three numbers—subtraction (11, 6, 5) (12, 7, 5) (13, 8, 5) (14, 9, 5)

FIGURE 6.4   Sequence of Multiplication Facts

Series-saying format is Format 6.2.
Three-number format is Format 6.3.

Sets of New Facts	**Relationship Format**
A. Any problem with a one	Series saying
B. $5 \times 2, 5 \times 3, 5 \times 4, 5 \times 5$	Series saying
C. $2 \times 2, 3 \times 2, 4 \times 2, 5 \times 2$	Series saying
D. $2 \times 5, 3 \times 5, 4 \times 5, 5 \times 5$	Three numbers—multiplication
E. $2 \times 2, 2 \times 3, 2 \times 4, 2 \times 5$	Three numbers—multiplication
F. Any problem with a zero	Series saying
G. $5 \times 6, 5 \times 7, 5 \times 8, 5 \times 9$	Series saying
H. $2 \times 6, 2 \times 7, 2 \times 8, 2 \times 9$	Series saying
I. $6 \times 5, 7 \times 5, 8 \times 5, 9 \times 5$	Three numbers—multiplication
J. $6 \times 2, 7 \times 2, 8 \times 2, 9 \times 2$	Three numbers—multiplication
K. $2 \times 0, 3 \times 0, 4 \times 0, 5 \times 0$	Series saying
L. $0 \times 6, 0 \times 7, 0 \times 8, 0 \times 9$	Three numbers—multiplication
M. $9 \times 2, 9 \times 3, 9 \times 4, 9 \times 5$	Series saying
N. $4 \times 2, 4 \times 3, 4 \times 4, 4 \times 5$	Series saying
O. $2 \times 9, 3 \times 9, 4 \times 9, 5 \times 9$	Three numbers—multiplication
P. $2 \times 4, 3 \times 4, 4 \times 4, 5 \times 4$	Three numbers—multiplication
Q. $9 \times 6, 9 \times 7, 9 \times 8, 9 \times 9$	Series saying
R. $4 \times 6, 4 \times 7, 4 \times 8, 4 \times 9$	Series saying
S. $6 \times 9, 7 \times 9, 8 \times 9, 9 \times 9$	Three numbers—multiplication
T. $6 \times 4, 7 \times 4, 8 \times 4, 9 \times 4$	Three numbers—multiplication
U. $3 \times 6, 3 \times 7, 3 \times 8, 3 \times 9$	Series saying
V. $6 \times 6, 6 \times 7, 6 \times 8, 6 \times 9$	Series saying
W. $6 \times 3, 7 \times 3, 8 \times 3, 9 \times 3$	Three numbers—multiplication
X. $7 \times 6, 8 \times 6, 9 \times 6$	Three numbers—multiplication
Y. $7 \times 7, 8 \times 7, 9 \times 7$	Series saying
Z. $7 \times 8, 8 \times 8, 9 \times 8$	Three numbers—multiplication

FIGURE 6.5   Sequence of Division Facts

Three-number format is Format 6.3.

Sets of New Facts	**Relationship Format**
A. Any number divided by one	Three numbers—division (8, 1, 8) (4, 1, 4) (7, 1, 7)
B. Any number divided by itself	Three numbers—division (3, 1, 3) (9, 1, 9) (8, 1, 8) (2, 1, 2)
C. $10 \div 5, 15 \div 5, 20 \div 5, 25 \div 5$	Three numbers—division (2, 5, 10) (3, 5, 15) (4, 5, 20) (5, 5, 25)
D. $4 \div 2, 6 \div 2, 8 \div 2, 10 \div 2$	Three numbers—division
E. $10 \div 2, 15 \div 3, 20 \div 4, 25 \div 5$	Three numbers—division
F. Zero divided by any number	
G. $4 \div 2, 6 \div 3, 8 \div 4, 10 \div 5$	Three numbers—division
H. $30 \div 5, 35 \div 5, 40 \div 5, 45 \div 5$	Three numbers—division
I. $12 \div 2, 14 \div 2, 16 \div 2, 18 \div 2$	Three numbers—division
J. $30 \div 6, 35 \div 7, 40 \div 8, 45 \div 9$	Three numbers—division
K. $12 \div 6, 14 \div 7, 16 \div 8, 18 \div 9$	Three numbers—division
L. $18 \div 9, 27 \div 9, 36 \div 9, 45 \div 9$	Three numbers—division
M. $8 \div 4, 12 \div 4, 16 \div 4, 20 \div 4$	Three numbers—division
N. $18 \div 2, 27 \div 3, 36 \div 4, 45 \div 5$	Three numbers—division
O. $8 \div 2, 12 \div 3, 16 \div 4, 20 \div 5$	Three numbers—division
P. $54 \div 9, 63 \div 9, 72 \div 9, 81 \div 9$	Three numbers—division
Q. $24 \div 4, 28 \div 4, 32 \div 4, 36 \div 4$	Three numbers—division
R. $54 \div 6, 63 \div 7, 72 \div 8, 81 \div 9$	Three numbers—division
S. $24 \div 6, 28 \div 7, 32 \div 8, 36 \div 9$	Three numbers—division
T. $18 \div 3, 21 \div 3, 24 \div 3, 27 \div 3$	Three numbers—division
U. $36 \div 6, 42 \div 6, 48 \div 6, 54 \div 6$	Three numbers—division
V. $18 \div 6, 21 \div 7, 24 \div 8, 27 \div 9$	Three numbers—division
W. $42 \div 7, 48 \div 8, 54 \div 9$	Three numbers—division
X. $49 \div 7, 56 \div 7, 63 \div 7$	Three numbers—division
Y. $56 \div 8, 64 \div 8, 72 \div 8$	Three numbers—division

multiplication, and division facts. The question of exactly when to introduce subtraction, multiplication, and division facts is a difficult one. More specifically, it is difficult to say whether students should master all of one type of fact before the next type is introduced or whether different facts should be introduced concurrently, using the three-number relationship that extends across operations. For example, should subtraction facts be introduced while students are still learning addition facts (and, if so, when?), or should subtraction facts be introduced only after students have mastered all addition facts? A similar question can be raised about multiplication and division facts.

Unfortunately, little experimental research has been done to answer the questions about when to introduce the various fact strands. In our observations of lower performing students, we have found that students have more difficulty when a set of addition facts and the inverse subtraction facts are introduced concurrently. Consequently, we recommend introducing related subtraction or division facts for a particular set a month or more after the original addition or multiplication set has been introduced. More specifically, teachers might begin introducing subtraction facts when the students have learned about half of their addition facts. The teacher then alternates between introducing sets of addition and subtraction. Following this recommendation, teachers first introduce addition sets A through M, then introduce subtraction set A. Thereafter, the teacher alternates between addition and subtraction fact sets. Addition set N is followed by subtraction set B, which is followed by addition set O, then subtraction set C, and so on.

The question of when to introduce multiplication facts is important. Many students will not have mastered all basic addition and subtraction facts at the time a program calls for the introduction of multiplication. We recommend that the teaching of multiplication facts begins no later than third grade, even though addition and subtraction facts have not been completely mastered. Knowledge of basic multiplication facts is a critical prerequisite for more advanced operations and thus should be mastered no later than fourth grade. Teachers might devote extra time to basic facts for students who have not mastered the basic addition and subtraction facts by third grade. Two practice sessions might be conducted daily, one focusing on addition and subtraction facts and one focusing on multiplication and, later, division facts.

We recommend that multiplication and division facts be presented to intermediate grade remedial students before addition and subtraction. The reason for this recommendation is that these students are likely to have some type of finger strategy that allows them to compute addition and subtraction facts correctly. (More advice on the use of fingers appears at the end of the chapter.) On the other hand, these students are likely to have no viable strategy for figuring out multiplication and division facts. Teaching multiplication and division facts first allows the teacher to present a wider range of operations during the school year. After multiplication and division facts are mastered, the teacher can go back and work on addition and subtraction facts.

COORDINATING MASTERY AND RELATIONSHIP ACTIVITIES

As a general rule, new sets of facts should be presented in relationship exercises before appearing in mastery exercises. The teacher introduces a set of facts through a relationship exercise and then provides practice to develop mastery on that set of facts. Figures 6.2 through 6.5 suggest the relationship format to present before introducing each new set of facts. The specific format to present is listed across from each respective set of facts. Remember, the relationship format is presented for several days *before* facts from that set are included in memorization exercises.

Exercises for Memorizing

Practice to aid memorization of basic facts can be provided in a number of ways: paired drill in which students practice with each other, teacher drill in which the teacher presents facts to a group, worksheet exercises, flash card exercises in which students are given a specific set of facts to study independently, and fact games. Memorization exercises should be cumulative. That is, newly introduced facts receive intensive practice, while previously introduced facts receive less intensive, but still systematically planned, practice.

Setting Up a Program to Promote Mastery

A program to facilitate basic fact memorization should have the following components:

1. a specific performance criterion for introducing new facts
2. intensive practice on newly introduced facts
3. systematic practice on previously introduced facts

4. adequate allotted time
5. a record-keeping system
6. a motivation system

PERFORMANCE CRITERION. We consider mastery of a basic fact as the ability of students to respond immediately to the fact question. For example, after the teacher asks students the answer to 8 + 7, the students immediately answer 15. Students should practice a new set of facts until they can answer each member of the new set and members of previously introduced sets immediately.

An acceptable criterion of performance for an oral exercise, assuming students say an entire statement, would be a rate of one fact each 2 seconds. The criterion for written exercises depends on the students' motor coordination. That is, rate criteria for written work should be based on the speed with which students can write numerals. Obviously, a student who writes numerals slowly will not be able to complete a worksheet as quickly as a student whose motor skills are more developed and is able to write numbers more quickly. Our basic recommendation is that the criterion be set at a rate that is about two-thirds of the rate at which the student can write digits. A student's writing ability can be easily determined by giving a 1-minute timed test. The student is instructed to write the numbers 1 through 9 as many times as he can. It is appropriate to provide several practice trials before the timing. The student's writing rate is determined by counting the number of digits written during this 1-minute period. By multiplying that number by 2/3, the teacher can estimate how many digits a student should be able to write as answers during a 1-minute fact timing. For example, a student who writes 60 digits in 1 minute should write 40 digits in 1 minute in a fact timing (60 × 2/3 = 40).

INTENSIVE PRACTICE AND SYSTEMATIC REVIEW. In addition to providing intensive practice on new facts, the teacher must provide practice on previously taught facts. Unless earlier introduced facts are systematically reviewed, students are likely to forget them. We recommend that daily practice of new facts be followed immediately by review of previously introduced facts. (See sections on materials later in this chapter.)

ADEQUATE ALLOTTED TIME. The amount of time allocated to fact practice must be sufficient. We recommend that teachers allocate 10 to 15 minutes per day for basic fact–learning activities. This time allotment is much more than what is provided in most classroom schedules. Teachers should keep in mind that work on basic math facts is time well spent. Children who know facts will be able to compute efficiently and are more likely to encounter success in later problem-solving activities.

RECORD-KEEPING SYSTEM. A record-keeping system is needed to monitor student progress so that the teacher knows when a student needs additional encouragement and when a student is ready to progress to the next set of facts. This system should involve a minimum of paperwork so that little time is taken from actual fact practice.

MOTIVATION. A motivational system should be integrated within the record-keeping procedure. The motivation system must be carefully designed so that students see a clear relationship between working hard and receiving recognition for their work.

Manageability is an important aspect of any instructional program and is especially important in a fact program. Procedures must be simple. Materials must be easy to prepare, pass out, collect, and score. Teachers cannot follow procedures that consume inordinate amounts of time.

TWO FACT MASTERY PROGRAMS

Two examples of fact mastery programs are presented in this section. The first program is designed for teachers working with homogeneous groups of students who are all functioning near the same instructional level. The second program is designed for teachers working with heterogeneous groups, groups composed of students functioning at different levels, or for one-to-one tutoring in which an adult or a peer tutors a student.

Homogeneous Group Program

The homogeneous group system is designed for teachers working with a group of students functioning at approximately the same level. The basic system consists of teacher-directed instruction, with students completing daily exercises on a fact worksheet. In these exercises, the teacher first presents a drill in which the students orally practice newly introduced facts. The oral drill is followed by a written exercise on which the students are timed.

MATERIALS. The system requires specially prepared sequences of worksheets for each type of fact: addition, subtraction, division, and multiplication. A worksheet is prepared for each set listed in figures 6.2 through 6.5. Each worksheet is divided into two parts. The top half of the worksheets should provide practice on new facts, including fact from the currently introduced set and from the two preceding sets. More specifically, each fact from the new set should appear four times. Each fact from the set introduced just earlier should appear three times, and each fact from the set that preceded that one should appear twice. If this pattern were applied to sets, each containing four facts, the top part of the worksheet would have 36 facts: 16 new facts (4 × 4), 12 facts from the previously learned set (4 × 3), and 8 facts from the set before that (4 × 2).

The bottom half of the worksheet should include 30 problems. Each fact from the currently introduced set should appear twice. The remaining facts are taken from previously introduced sets. All previously introduced facts appear just one time. *Note:* At the beginning of a fact program, students will not know many facts; thus, facts from previous sets may appear several times on the bottom half of the worksheet. Only when 30 facts have been introduced can each fact appear just once. On the other hand, after more than 30 facts have been introduced, review should be planned so that each fact appears at least once every second or third worksheet.

Figure 6.6 is a sample worksheet for introducing facts according to the guidelines for worksheet construction. The new set consists of 5 + 6, 5 + 7, 5 + 8, and 5 + 9. Each of these facts appears four times in the top half. The previously introduced set includes 7 + 8, 7 + 9, and 4 + 9, each presented three times. Finally, the next earlier introduced set includes 6 + 5, 7 + 5, 8 + 5, and 9 + 5, each presented twice. The top half of the worksheet has 33 facts. The bottom half of the worksheet includes the four facts from the new set, each written twice, along with previously introduced facts, each appearing just once.

PRETESTING. Before beginning instruction, teachers should determine which type of fact to start with (addition, subtraction, multiplication, division) and where students should be placed in that fact program.

Groups with students who know few facts start at Set A. Students who know more facts begin at later points. To determine the set at which students might begin, the teacher administers a written pretest that includes the 100 basic facts with the easier facts listed at the top. The teacher allows students 2 minutes to work as many problems as they can. A teacher with 10 or more students in a group must compromise when selecting a starting point. As a general rule, we recommend a point slightly lower than the average starting point for the students in the group.

GROUP ORAL PRACTICE. The teacher begins the lesson with a group drill in which the students orally practice the facts on the top half of the worksheet. The students say each problem in unison as the teacher signals. The teacher begins the lesson by instructing students on the procedure: "When I signal, you'll read the first problem and say the answer. Then you'll touch the next problem and figure out the answer. When I signal again, you'll read that problem and say the answer."

FIGURE 6.6 Sample Worksheet

5 +6	8 +5	5 +8	6 +5	7 +9	5 +7	4 +9	5 +6	7 +8	5 +9	7 +9
5 +8	7 +5	5 +7	7 +8	5 +6	5 +8	4 +9	5 +9	4 +9	7 +9	5 +7
8 +5	5 +6	5 +9	6 +5	5 +7	7 +5	5 +8	9 +5	7 +8	5 +9	9 +5

5 +8	6 +4	7 +5	4 +7	5 +6	9 +8	7 +9	5 +9	4 +8	5 +7
8 +9	7 +8	8 +5	5 +6	8 +7	9 +5	7 +7	5 +8	8 +4	4 +9
9 +7	6 +7	5 +9	7 +4	6 +9	4 +6	5 +7	9 +4	6 +5	6 +8

The teacher then instructs the students to touch the first problem. After allowing 2 or 3 seconds for students to figure out the answer, the teacher says, "Get ready," and signals by clapping her hands. After the students respond, the teacher instructs them to touch the next problem, pauses to let them figure out the answer, then says, "Get ready," and signals. The teacher should keep her talk to a minimum. "Next problem" (pause). "Get ready" (signal). "Next problem" (pause). "Get ready" (signal).

The teacher repeats this signaling procedure with each fact across the first line of the worksheet and repeats the line until students are able to answer each fact correctly with no more than a 2-second thinking pause. This may take several repetitions of the entire line. The same procedure is repeated with each subsequent line on the top half of the worksheet.

TIMED TEST. The timed test is done on the bottom half of the worksheet. The teacher sets a specified time. A minute and 15 seconds is a realistic goal for intermediate-grade students. The teacher allows the students a minute or two to study the bottom half of the worksheet, then tells them to get ready for the test. The teacher tells the students how much time they have and to start. At the end of the specified time, the teacher says, "Stop," has the students trade papers, and reads the answers. Students are to mark all mistakes, write the total number correct at the top of the page, and then return the worksheet to its owner.

MASTERY CRITERIA. After the lesson, the teacher inspects the students' papers and records the number of facts each student answered correctly on the written timed drill. In the next lesson, the teacher either repeats the same worksheet or presents the worksheet for the next set of facts. The teacher presents the next worksheet if three-quarters or more of the students answered 28 of the 30 facts correctly. The teacher repeats the same worksheet if less than three-quarters of the students answered 28 facts correctly. Keep in mind that students generally need anywhere from 3 days to 2 weeks to master a set. During this time, the teacher should keep presenting the relationship exercises for the new fact set and encourage the students.

SUMMARY. The advantage of this system is that it allows the teacher to coordinate the presentation of relationship activities and memorization exercises. Also, the system makes monitoring the performance of the students relatively easy. The disadvantage of this group system is that it does not allow individual students to progress at optimal rates. However, if only one or two students are performing at a much lower rate than other students in the group, the teacher could provide extra practice for those students.

Heterogeneous Group Program

The heterogeneous group program is designed for teachers working with a group of students who demonstrate significant differences in their knowledge of facts. This system also can be adapted for use in tutoring programs (peer tutoring, cross-age tutoring, or tutoring by adult volunteers).

MATERIALS. Before the school year begins, teachers should make booklets for each type of fact—addition, subtraction, division, and multiplication—consisting of the worksheets for each fact set. The same worksheets used in the homogeneous system is used in the heterogeneous system. Two types of booklets should be prepared, one with answers and one without (i.e., the test booklet). The answer book can be used in subsequent years, while the test booklets must be replaced annually.

PRETESTING. Students may start with different types of facts (addition, subtraction, multiplication, division) and at various sets within a type of fact. Pretesting to determine a starting set can be done in a group setting or individually. In a group setting, the teacher administers a written pretest that includes the 100 basic facts with the easier facts listed at the top.

As mentioned previously, the teacher allows students 2 minutes to work as many problems as they can. Students who answer 30 or more facts in two minutes might start at set G. Students who answer 45 or more might start at set M. Students who answer 60 or more might start at set R. Students who answer 85 or more facts in the 2-minute pretest probably do not need to be placed in a program for that type of fact.

Individual testing allows for a more accurate starting point for most students. To test individuals, the teacher uses the sequences in Figures 6.2 through 6.5. The teacher begins by testing the facts in set A, then set B, and so on, until reaching a set in which the student makes two or more errors. (Any fact problem that a student cannot answer within several seconds should be counted as wrong.) This set should be the student's starting point.

DAILY ROUTINE. In this program, students work in pairs. As a general rule, teachers should pair students who are working near the same level. Each student has one booklet with answers and one booklet without answers. The student with the answer sheet acts as a tutor, while the other student acts as the pupil.

The teacher has each student practice the top half of the worksheet twice. Each practice session is timed. The teacher says, "Get ready, go," and starts a stopwatch; the student practices by saying complete statements (e.g., 4 + 2 = 6) rather than just answers. Saying the entire fact statement makes it easier for the tutor to follow along. If the student makes an error, the tutor corrects by saying the correct statement and having the student repeat the statement. The teacher allows students a minute and a half when practicing the top part and a minute when practicing the bottom part. After the allotted time, the teacher has the second student begin practicing. This procedure is repeated twice for the facts on the top half and twice for the facts on the bottom half of the worksheet.

After allowing each student to practice the top and bottom sections of their individual fact sheets twice, the teacher tells the students to get ready for a test. Students work in their individual test booklets. The teacher stops students at the end of a minute. The students are to stop answering immediately. The students trade test booklets and answer booklets to correct each other's work. They count the number of facts answered correctly and record that number across from the letter for the respective set of facts on the student's record form (see Figure 6.7 and the discussion under "Student Record Form").

The next day, the same procedure is followed. However, if a student answered all but two of the facts correctly on the previous day's testing, the student moves on to the next worksheet in the sequence. The teacher begins the lesson by having students inspect their record forms to determine the series they are to practice.

FIGURE 6.7 Student Record Form

page	TRY 1	TRY 2	TRY 3	TRY 4	TRY 5	TRY 6	TRY 7	
Z								Z
Y								Y
X								X
W								W
V								V
U								U
T								T
S								S
R								R
Q								Q
P								P
O								O
N								N
M								M
L								L
K								K
J								J
I								I
H								H
G								G
F								F
E								E
D								D
C								C
B								B
A								A

Cooperative student behavior is essential to make this system work. The teacher should provide strong positive consequences for cooperative behavior among students. Rules for the activity might include (a) talking softly, (b) following teacher instructions, and (c) honestly recording performance. Students may be tempted to record inaccurate scores on the test. To guard against cheating, the teacher must monitor student performance carefully during practice. If a student performs quite poorly during practice, yet turns in an excellent testing record, testing may be inaccurate. These students should be tested by the teacher to ensure accuracy of the recorded performance.

STUDENT RECORD FORM. A record form that can be used during this exercise appears in Figure 6.7. In the first column, the worksheet letters are listed. Across from each letter are seven columns used to record the number of facts answered correctly on a test. The first day the student does a particular worksheet, the number of facts answered correctly is written in the first column across from that worksheet letter. The second day, the number is written in the second column across from the worksheet letter, and so on. On the right side of the chart is a progress rocket. Each time the student meets the criterion for a worksheet (28–30 correct problems), the student shades in the space for that worksheet on the rocket. On the next lesson, the student works on the next worksheet in the sequence.

MODIFICATIONS. The heterogeneous group program requires extensive preparation by the teacher at the beginning of the school year, because several booklets of worksheets must be made. Also, instruction is necessary to teach students the procedure. The advantage of this system, though, is that once worksheets are prepared and students know what to do, the system provides the individualization needed to allow each student to progress at her optimal rate.

This system also is easily adapted for use in tutoring programs. Whether same-age students work together in pairs (peer tutoring), older students work with younger students (cross-age tutoring), or adults work with individual students (volunteer or parent tutoring), the same materials and basic procedures can be used. That is, students practice orally with feedback from their tutors, then take a timed test and record their performance.

If students require additional practice for mastery, the teacher or tutor can make flash cards for particularly difficult facts and use the flash cards prior to the oral worksheet practice. The flash cards can be sent home for additional practice (see next section,

"Parental Involvement") or turned into a game that might be played at recess. Flash cards also are an excellent way to provide cumulative review. Tutors might begin each session with a flash card review of the 15 previously introduced facts before introducing a new set.

Motivation is an important factor in all fact mastery programs. If students practice at home or at other times during the school day, their learning rate will likely increase. Teachers can encourage students to study by establishing incentive programs based on their performance. The incentives need not be material rewards, but might include time earned on a computer, extra minutes at recess, or other activities that are highly desirable.

Parental Involvement

Parents who would like to help their children at home are often not sure what to do, how to do it, or whether they will interfere with what the teacher is doing at school. Math fact practice is a good way to involve parents. Teachers should try to secure a commitment from parents to work with their children on facts at home for about 10 minutes, three or four days a week. This practice is easily coordinated with classroom activities. If possible, parents should be invited to a training session during which the teacher explains the fact system she is using and reviews suggestions for working with children at home.

The teacher should prepare a tutoring guide for the parents, specifying exactly how to implement a home practice program. During the training session, the teacher would demonstrate recommended procedures and talk about motivation. Teachers must encourage parents to interact with their children in positive ways so that home practice becomes an opportunity for students to experience success. A communication system should be set up to inform parents about which facts they should include in the exercises. A weekly letter including the facts to work on might be sent home along with progress reports.

Additional Practice Activities

Supplemental exercises should be available for practicing facts throughout the school day. One exercise that is motivating for most students is the math fact race. The teacher puts a scorecard on the board with one row for teacher points and one for student points:

☺ T	
☺ S	

The teacher then presents a fact or shows a flash card, pauses a second or two, and calls out a student's name. The teacher then hesitates a second more and says the answer. If the student responds correctly before the teacher says the answer, the students get the point. Note that pausing before calling on a student (but after stating the fact) increases the probability that all students will attend to the question.

The race game can also be modified so that one group of students competes with another group. The teacher divides the class in half, placing an equal number of higher and lower performers in each group. The teacher conducts the game by saying a fact, pausing a second or two, and then calling on a student. The student earns a point for her team if she responds correctly.

Note that the games should be played in a way to avoid embarrassing low-performing students. Rules encouraging appropriate behavior should be discussed before playing the game and enforced during the game. Rules such as "No arguing" or "No complaining" are helpful in playing the game.

During free times, students can play board games in which the students pick a card from a deck of fact flash cards. If they say the fact correctly, they get to hit the spinner and move their marker on the board the number of spaces indicated by the spinner.

REMEDIAL STUDENTS

Many remedial students rely on their fingers to figure out facts. Teachers should not initially discourage students from using their fingers, since memorizing basic facts may require months and months of practice. Teachers may tell students that eventually they will not have to use their fingers to figure out facts, but for the time being, using fingers is fine, except during fact memorization exercises. Teachers can expect some students to be inaccurate even when using their fingers. These students may be divided into two groups: those who have an effective finger strategy to figure out facts but are careless, and those students who do not have any effective finger strategy.

The errors made by a student indicate whether or not he has an effective finger strategy. Students whose answers are correct about 80 to 90% of the time, and when wrong are usually just one number off (e.g., 15 − 9 = 5, 8 + 6 = 15, 9 + 7 = 15), probably have an effective strategy but are careless in applying it, counting too quickly or not coordinating counting and moving their fingers. The remediation procedure for these students is simply to provide

daily exercises in conjunction with a strong incentive program. Students should be given worksheets containing 30 to 50 basic addition and subtraction facts. The incentives should be contingent on the number of problems worked correctly. Daily exercises are continued until students perform with over 95% accuracy consistently for about a week.

Students who miss more than 20% of basic facts and/or make what seem to be random errors, having answers several numbers away from the correct answer (e.g., 15 − 8 = 4, 8 + 6 = 19, 9 − 3 = 8), are likely not to have an effective strategy to figure out facts. The teacher should watch these students as they work problems in order to determine the students' specific deficits. The teacher would then provide remediation or, if the students are quite confused, teach them an alternative strategy. Below are finger strategies, one for addition and two for subtraction, that can be taught to students who by third grade have not developed an effective strategy for figuring out addition or subtraction facts.

For addition, the strategy involves the following:

1. Noting which of the addends is smaller and putting up that number of fingers (e.g., in 8 + 5 the student puts up five fingers, in 3 + 6 the student puts up three fingers).
2. Counting from the other addend, saying one number for each finger (e.g., in 8 + 3, student puts up three fingers and counts "*eeighht*, 9, 10, 11").

The teacher demonstrates the strategy with several problems, then provides guided practice by asking, "Which number is smaller? . . . Hold up your fingers . . . Count and figure the answer." Daily supervised practice is provided until the student performs at a 95% accuracy level for about 2 weeks on a group of about 30 to 40 random addition facts.

The strategy for subtraction facts is not introduced until students are proficient in figuring out addition facts. One of two possible finger strategies might be taught for figuring out basic subtraction facts: a counting-backward strategy or an algebra-based counting-forward strategy.

In the counting-backward strategy, the student puts up the number of fingers representing the number being subtracted. For example, in 12 − 7, the student puts up seven fingers, says the larger number, then counts backward for each raised finger ("*tweellve*, 11, 10, 9, 8, 7, 6, 5"). Note that the student does not count a raised finger when saying the larger number.

In the algebra counting strategy, the student counts from the smaller number to the larger number (e.g., to work $11 - 6$, the student counts from 6 to 11, putting up a finger each time she counts).

If the student does not have too much difficulty with counting backward, we recommend that the counting-backward strategy be taught, since the steps are basically the same as the addition strategy except for the direction students count. Another advantage of the backward strategy is that students are less likely to become confused when renaming is introduced. Regardless of which strategy is taught, the teacher should provide daily practice on a group of 30 to 40 random subtraction facts.

COMMERCIAL PROGRAMS

Basic Facts

INSTRUCTIONAL STRATEGIES. In most programs, addition and subtraction facts are taught by emphasizing fact families. In several programs, alternative strategies that organize facts differently also are taught. This emphasis on teaching related facts is supported by current research on basic fact acquisition.

One caution about initial teaching procedures for addition and subtraction facts, however, involves the use of pictures. While pictures aid students in using a counting strategy to solve computation problems, pictures are a deterrent to memorization; if pictures are available, some students invariably resort to counting the pictures instead of trying to remember the answer. For example, in one program, a third of the exercises given to students for basic facts practice contain illustrations. For those problems, students need only count the pictures and write the answer rather than recall the answers from memory. The amount of actual fact practice provided is thereby reduced. Teachers need to remember that if the objective of an exercise is to promote acquisi-

tion of facts, then no pictures or other prompts should be available to students during the activity.

PRACTICE AND REVIEW. The most important aspect of any fact program is the provision of adequate practice to develop mastery. A critical part of adequate practice is the cumulative review of previously introduced facts mixed with the presentation of new facts. This type of practice and review is not present in most basal programs. For example, in the third-grade level of one program, all basic addition facts are introduced in only three lessons (six student practice pages). Those same facts (sums to 18) are not reviewed until six lessons later, when the relationship between addition and subtraction is taught. The program does not provide another opportunity for students to practice addition facts in that level.

Practice provided for learning basic multiplication facts is often less than adequate as well. Basal programs typically teach basic multiplication facts within a single unit. Multiplication facts are introduced most often in sets of common factors, such as, 3×0, 3×1, 3×2, 3×3, and so on (see Figure 6.8). Note that all of the three facts are introduced at once.

One type of fact practice noticeably absent from the programs we examined was fluency practice (i.e., timed fact drills). Whereas programs traditionally address issues of accuracy (number right, number wrong), they have not included exercises whereby students must meet a specified rate criterion as well. For students to be able to recall facts quickly in more complex computation problems, research tells us the students must know their math facts at an acceptable level of "automaticity." Therefore, teachers using these programs must be prepared to supplement by providing more practice and establishing rate criteria that students must achieve.

APPLICATION ITEMS: FACTS

1. Your principal asks you to describe the procedure you are using to facilitate learning basic facts. Assume that you are using the heterogeneous fact program system in your text. Write a description of the system.

2. The parents of the children in your class want to know why you spend so much time on memorization activities. What would your reply be?

3. Assume you are constructing worksheets for subtraction facts. More specifically, you are now preparing a worksheet for set U. (a) List the facts that would appear on the upper half of the worksheet. Next to each fact, write how often it would appear on the top half. (b) Describe the guidelines you would use in preparing the bottom half of the student worksheet.

4. You are presenting the relationship format to prepare students for the facts in set M of the multiplication sequence. Write what you do.

5. You are going to train a volunteer to work with a new student who is not fluent with multiplication facts. Write out directions for a volunteer who will work with this student.

6. Assume the students have learned the basic multiplication facts in sets A through M in the fact sequence of this text. Which computation problems would be appropriate to assign to students, and which would not be appropriate?

34	82	34
×5	×6	×9
65	87	48
×7	×8	×2

FORMAT 6.1   Plus-One Facts

TEACHER	STUDENTS
PART A: NEXT NUMBER	

1. When I put my hand down, you say the next number.

2. *(Hold up hand.)* 1, 2, 3, 4, *ffiivve*
   (drop hand).   6

   To correct: My turn: 1, 2, 3, 4, *ffiivve*
   (drop hand), 6.

   New problem. Tell me the next number: 3, 4, 5, 6, *ssevvenn*
   (Drop hand. Repeat step 2 with 3, 4, 5 and 7, 8, 9.)   8

3. When I put my hand down, you say the next number.
   Sssiiixxx (drop hand).   7

   To correct: My turn: *sssiiixxx (drop hand),* 7.

4. *(Repeat step 3 with 8, 4, 9, 2, 5. Give individual turns to several students.)*

PART B: PLUS-ONE RULE WITH STRETCH PROMPT

1. Everyone listen to the rule. When you plus one, you say the next number. My turn: *ffoouurr* + 1 = 5. *Eeighht* + 1 = 9.

2. Get ready to tell me the answers to some plus-one problems. Remember to say the next number: 5 + 1, *ffiivve* + 1 = *(signal).*   6

   Yes, 5 + 1 = 6.

   To correct: Listen: 5. What number comes next? So 5 + 1 = 6.

3. Listen: 3 + 1. *Thrreee* + 1 = ? *(Signal.)*   4
   Yes, 3 + 1 = 4.

   (Present step 3 with examples like the following until students answer all plus-one problems in a row correctly: 9 + 1, 7 + 1, 2 + 1, 8 + 1, 4 + 1.)

TEACHER	**STUDENTS**

PART C: PLUS ONE RULE WITHOUT PROMPT

1. Remember, when you plus one, you say the next number.

2. 8 + 1 = (pause, then signal). Say the whole statement.

	9
	8 + 1 = 9

3. *(Repeat step 2 with the following examples: 4 + 1, 7 + 1, 5 + 1, 9 + 1.)*

FORMAT 6.2   **Series Saying**

TEACHER	**STUDENTS**

PART A: READING STATEMENTS

1. *(Write the following problems on the board.)*

   5 + 2 = 7
   6 + 2 = 8
   7 + 2 = 9
   8 + 2 = 10

Everybody, I'll touch them. You read. Get ready. *(Point to numerals and symbols in each statement. Repeat step 1 until students can read statements at a rate of a statement each 3 seconds.)*	5 + 2 = 7 6 + 2 = 8 7 + 2 = 9 8 + 2 = 10

PART B: READING STATEMENTS WITH ANSWERS ERASED

1. Now I'm going to erase the answers. *(Erase answers.)* Now read the statement and tell me the answer.	5 + 2 = 7 6 + 2 = 8
To correct: Respond with students until they appear able to respond without assistance.	7 + 2 = 9 8 + 2 = 10

PART C: SAYING STATEMENTS

1. Now I'll make it even harder and erase everything. *(Erase everything.)* Get ready to say the statements starting with 5 + 2. *(Either clap or snap fingers to set pace for students to respond.)*	5 + 2 = 7 6 + 2 = 8 7 + 2 = 9 8 + 2 = 10

2. *(Repeat Part C until all students respond correctly and then present individual turns.)*

PART D: RANDOM FACT DRILL

1. *(Write facts in random order on board.)*

7	5	6	8
+2	+2	+2	+2

   When I signal, say the whole statement with the answer.

2. *(Point to left of 7 + 2, pause 2 seconds, then touch board.)*   7 + 2 = 9

3. *(Repeat step 2 with remaining facts.)*

4. *(Repeat steps 2 and 3 with only a 1-second pause.)*

5. *(Repeat step 4 until students can respond to all facts with the 1-second pause.)*

FORMAT 6.3   Three-Number Fact Families: Addition and Multiplication Facts

TEACHER	STUDENTS

PART A: STRUCTURED BOARD PRESENTATION

1. *(Write the following boxes and numbers on the board.)*

☐ 8
2

_____ + _____ = _____
_____ + _____ = _____

I want to make addition statements using the numbers 8 and 2. What is the big number that goes with 8 and 2? *(Pause.)*

I'll write the big number in the big box. *(Write 10 in the big box.)* What is 8 + 2?
(Write 8 + 2 = 10.)

                10

                10

2. We can make another addition statement. If 8 + 2 = 10, then 2 + 8 = 10. *(Write 2 + 8 = 10.)* Say the statement that begins with 8. Say the statement that begins with 2.

        8 + 2 = 10
        2 + 8 = 10

3. *(Erase statements.)* Let's say both statements we can make with the numbers 8, 2, and 10. Say the statement that begins with 8. Say the statement that begins with 2.

        8 + 2 = 10
        2 + 8 = 10

4. *(Write the following boxes and numbers on the board.)*

☐ 5
2

What's the big number that goes with 5 and 2?

To correct: What does 5 + 2 equal?

Say an addition statement using those numbers. Start with 5. *(Pause.)*

Say the other addition statement that starts with 2. *(Pause.)*

(Repeat step 4 with 6 and 2; 9 and 2.)

        7

        5 + 2 = 7

        2 + 5 = 7

PART B: DISCRIMINATION PRACTICE

1. Now let's see if you can tell me the answers to some problems. What is 2 + 6? *(Pause.)*

(Repeat step 1 with 2 + 8, 2 + 5, 2 + 7. Repeat Part B until students can respond to any fact with only a 1-second pause.)

        8

PART C: SUPERVISED WORKSHEET

☐ 2 / 7	☐ 6 / 8	☐ 2 / 5	☐ 8 / 2
__ + __ = __	__ + __ = __	__ + __ = __	__ + __ = __
__ + __ = __	__ + __ = __	__ + __ = __	__ + __ = __

TEACHER	STUDENTS

1. Fill in the big number and write the two addition
   statements that can be made from those numbers.

FORMAT 6.4   Three-Number Fact Family: Subtraction and Division Facts

TEACHER	STUDENTS

PART A: STRUCTURED BOARD PRESENTATION

1. *(Write the following lines and symbols on the board.)*

☐   ☐   ☐

___ – ___ = ___   ___ – ___ = ___   ___ – ___ = ___

___ – ___ = ___   ___ – ___ = ___   ___ – ___ = ___

   What big number goes with 5 and 3? *(Pause.)*   8

   To correct: 5 + 3 = what number?

   (Write 8 in box.)

2. We can use the numbers 5, 3, and 8 to figure out
   subtraction statements. When you subtract, you always
   start with the big number. What is the big number?   8
   I'll write 8 at the start of these subtraction problems.

3. Listen: 8 – 3. What will I end up with? Say   5
   the first statement. *(Write 8 – 3 = 5.)*   8 – 3 = 5
   8 – 5.
   What will I end up with?   3
   Say the second statement. *(Write 8 – 5 = 3.)*   8 – 5 = 3

4. Say both subtraction statements.   8 – 5 = 3
                                             8 – 3 = 5

   (Repeat steps 1–4 with 3 and 4; 6 and 3.)

PART B: STRUCTURED WORKSHEET

1. *(Give students worksheets with problems similar to these.)*

a. ☐7 ☐3 ☐4	b. ☐8 ☐5 ☐3	c. ☐9 ☐3 ☐6
__ + __ = __	__ + __ = __	__ + __ = __
__ + __ = __	__ + __ = __	__ + __ = __
__ – __ = __	__ – __ = __	__ – __ = __
__ – __ = __	__ – __ = __	__ – __ = __

(continued on next page)

FORMAT 6.4   (continued)

TEACHER	STUDENTS
Touch box a. You have to use the three numbers to make up statements. First, say the addition statements.	
2. Say an addition statement that starts with 3. (Pause.) Say the other addition statement. Write the addition statements.	3 + 4 = 7 4 + 3 = 7 Students write addition statements.
3. Now we'll write the subtraction statements. Which number will go first in both subtraction statements? Say the subtraction fact that begins 7 − 3 Say the subtraction fact that begins 7 − 4. Write the subtraction statements.	7 7 − 3 = 4 7 − 4 = 3 Students write subtraction statements.
(Repeat steps 1–3 with remaining examples.)	

CHAPTER 7

Addition

TERMS AND CONCEPTS

addition   Addition is (a) the process of combining smaller sets to form a larger set and then determining the total number of the larger set, or (b) the union of two disjoint sets. Disjoint sets have no members in common.

addend   The numbers of the smaller sets in an addition statement (e.g., in 4 + 3 = 7, the addends are 4 and 3).

missing addend   A problem type in which students solve for an addend (e.g., 6 + ☐ = 9).

sum   The number of the new set formed by combining the smaller sets (e.g., in 4 + 3 = 7, the sum is 7).

Commutative Law of Addition   The sum is the same, regardless of the order in which the numbers are added (e.g., 4 + 3 = 7 and 3 + 4 = 7).

Associative Law of Addition   Any method of grouping may be used to obtain the sum of several addends:

$$(1 + 2) + 3 = 6 \text{ or } 1 + (2 + 3) = 6$$

Identity Element for Addition   When any whole number and zero are added, the result is the whole number.

renaming   Converting a sum of 10 or more to the number of tens groups and the number of ones; e.g., 17 is renamed as 10 and 7. In 19 + 28, the sum in the ones column (17) is renamed as 10 and 7 so that the 10 can be written in the tens

column. This process had previously been called carrying. When used in addition, renaming is quite similar to expanded notation. In subtraction, a tens number is usually renamed as one 10 and the number of remaining tens; e.g., 70 is renamed 10 and 60. In a problem such as 74 − 16, the 70 is renamed so that a 10 and the 4 can be combined, allowing a student to subtract a 6 from 14. Six tens remain in the tens column.

regrouping   The same process as renaming, except it is carried out with objects or counters rather than numerals; just as 8 + 4 can be renamed 10 + 2, so ||||||||||||| can be regrouped as ||||||||| ||

SKILL HIERARCHY

Our discussion of addition is divided into two parts. The first part discusses strategies designed to establish a conceptual understanding of the process of addition. These strategies, usually taught with concrete objects or representations, are usually introduced in kindergarten or first grade. The second part addresses teaching students to work problems that require them to rely on mental computation rather than on representations of concrete objects. The second stage begins during the latter part of first grade and continues into the intermediate grades. For purposes of remediation, teachers

Instructional Sequence and Assessment Chart

Grade Level	Problem Type	Performance Indicator		
1a	Begin fact memorization	See Chapter 6		
1b	Adding a two-digit and a one- or two-digit number; no renaming	35 +21	64 +23	35 + 2
2a	Adding three single-digit numbers	1 3 +2	4 4 +3	1 3 +5
2b	Adding two three-digit numbers; no renaming	325 +132	463 +124	386 +100
2c	Adding a three-digit and a one- or two-digit number; no renaming	326 + 21	423 + 5	570 + 21
2d	Adding one-, two-, and three-digit numbers; no renaming	4 21 + 2	14 71 + 10	21 14 + 33
2e	Adding two two-digit numbers; renaming from ones to tens	37 +46	48 +14	57 +27
2f	Adding a three-digit and a one-, two-, or three-digit number; renaming from ones to tens	247 +315	258 + 13	276 + 8
3a	Complex facts; adding a single-digit number to a teen number—sum below 20	Test students individually; teacher asks: 13 + 3 = 14 + 4 = 12 + 2 =		
3b	Adding two two- or three-digit numbers; renaming from tens to hundreds	374 +261	83 +43	187 + 81
3c	Adding two three-digit numbers; renaming from ones to tens and tens to hundreds	376 +185	248 +164	437 +275
3d	Adding three two-digit numbers; renaming—ones column totals less than 20	98 14 +12	39 16 +23	74 24 +12
3e	Adding three or four numbers; renaming from ones to tens and from tens to hundreds—sums of columns below 20	385 6 24 +120	157 23 245 + 3	8 156 280 + 42
4a	Complex facts; adding a single number to a teen number—sum 20 or over	Test students individually; teacher asks: 16 + 6 = 18 + 8 = 17 + 6 =		
4b	Adding three two-digit numbers—ones column totals 20 or more	28 17 +28	29 16 +35	38 18 +15
4c	Adding three, four, or five multi-digit numbers; renaming in all or some columns totaling 20 or more	892 1486 38 286 + 35	8 4086 85 193 + 242	3856 2488 1932 +1583

should not revert to the conceptual introduction but should consider teaching basic facts and the operations specified in the Instructional Sequence and Assessment Chart.

During the beginning stage, students are taught to solve simple addition problems with concrete or semiconcrete objects representing each addend. For example, when solving the problem 4 + 2, the students are taught to draw four lines under the numeral 4 and two lines under the numeral 2. The students then figure the sum by counting all of the lines. Note that counting, numeral, and equality preskills must be mastered in order to work these problems. Missing addend problems in which an addend must be computed (e.g., 4 + ☐ = 7) are also presented during this stage. An understanding of equality is also essential to solving missing addend problems.

In the second stage, when multi-digit numbers are added, students work problems without making concrete representations for each addend. A new preskill necessary for solving column addition problems is knowledge of basic addition facts. (The 100 possible combinations of single-digit addends are referred to as basic addition facts.) The ability to accurately and quickly respond to a fact problem is a component skill of all multi-digit problems. Too little attention is usually given to the process by which students learn to memorize basic addition facts. In order to aid the teacher in teaching this critical preskill, we have devoted an entire chapter to the process of teaching addition, subtraction, multiplication, and division facts (see Chapter 6).

The first type of column problem introduced involves adding multi-digit numbers in which the sum in each column is less than 10; thus, renaming is not required (36 + 13). The next major type of problem involves adding two or more multi-digit numbers in which the sum of one or more columns is greater than 10 and requires renaming (36 + 15). The initial problem in this group involves adding two double-digit numerals such as 45 + 37. Problems with hundreds and thousands numbers are introduced after students have been taught to read and write those numerals.

The third major type of problem involves addition of three or more multi-digit numbers. The difficulty of these problems increases as the sum of each column becomes greater. For example, adding 23 + 14 + 32 is not difficult, since a sum never reaches 10. On the other hand, in a problem such as 39 + 16 + 27, the sum for the first two numbers is more than 10 (9 + 6 = 15). The student must not only rename but also be able to figure out facts in which a single-

digit number is added to a two-digit number. The sum of the first two digits in the ones column, 9 and 6, is 15. The students must then add 7 to 15 to figure the sum of the ones column. We refer to problems in which a student must mentally add a single-digit number to a two-digit number as *complex addition facts*. A great deal of practice is necessary for students to master complex addition facts.

The Instructional Sequence and Assessment Chart includes our recommended instruction and assessment sequence.

INTRODUCING THE CONCEPT

The major objective of beginning addition instruction is to develop a conceptual understanding of addition as a union of disjoint sets. Most educators agree that, at this stage, demonstrations should involve concrete objects. Math educators recommend a variety of methods for introducing addition. Using the term *sets* and giving demonstrations of joining two sets are suggested in some commercial programs:

Demonstrations through number lines also are suggested:

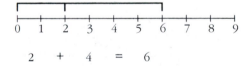

The direct instruction strategies recommended in this text use lines as semiconcrete objects to represent the members of sets. While nothing is wrong with using concrete manipulatives, having students draw lines has several advantages. Drawing lines graphically demonstrates equality (the same number of lines are on both sides of the equal sign); teachers can more readily monitor student performance with groups of students; and the lines provide a written record of student performance, which makes diagnosis of skill deficits easier.

A unique feature of the direct instruction strategies for introducing the addition process is the integration of the equality principle into the strategy. It is important that initial strategies demonstrate the application of the equality principle, since a grasp of equality is necessary for success in more complicated exercises, e.g., $7 + n = 12$.

Equality can be taught by presenting a functional definition and a series of positive and negative examples. The definition is functional in that it describes a condition that must be met for the equality principle to apply. *We must end with the same number on this side and the other side of the equal sign.* Format 7.1 includes a format for introducing equality. This format should be presented during the beginning stage before addition is introduced. The format includes three parts. In Part A, the teacher introduces the equal sign and equality rule. In Part B, the teacher demonstrates instances when the equality rule applies and does not apply. Diagrams like the one below in which lines are written inside two adjoining circles are written on the board.

The teacher leads the students in determining whether or not an equal sign would be drawn between the circles. Part C is a less structured worksheet exercise similar to Part B. Note that in parts B and C, students are asked to say the rule. Saying the rule may be quite difficult for lower performing students. To ease this difficulty, the teacher might first model, lead, and test, saying just the first half of the rule: *We must end with the same number.* Lower performers may need five to ten corrected repetitions. After several days, the teacher provides practice in saying the last half of the rule and then the entire rule.

Making lines for each addend and then counting the lines is called *addition the slow way.* Students draw the appropriate number of lines under each numeral:

$$4 + 2 = \square$$
$$\text{IIII} \quad \text{II}$$

Students count the lines, then draw the same number of lines on the other side of the equal sign and write the answer in the box:

$$4 + 2 = \boxed{6}$$
$$\text{IIII} \quad \text{II} \quad \text{IIIIII}$$

By counting the lines one by one and drawing the same number on the other side, the concept of equality is reinforced. Note that in this strategy, *plus* is used as a verb; students are taught "The plus sign

says to count all the lines." Later the term *addition* is introduced.

Problems with missing addends are introduced after students demonstrate mastery of beginning addition exercises. In solving problems with missing addends:

$$4 + \square = 7$$
$$\text{IIII} \qquad \text{IIIIIII}$$

The teacher points out that the sides are not equal. The students must add lines to make the sides equal and then write the numeral representing the number of lines added.

After the students can solve addition and missing addend problems, using a line-drawing strategy, a new strategy, called *addition the fast way*, is introduced. In addition the fast way, students make lines only under the numeral that is added, count the lines, beginning with the first numeral (*ffoouurr*, 5, 6), and then write the answer in the box. Addition the fast way represents a transition from the semi-concrete stage in which objects are drawn to represent each member of the set to the stage in which no concrete representations are used. A similar fast-way strategy can be taught for missing addend problems.

Addition the Slow Way

Addition the slow way is an important strategy, since it is the first problem-solving strategy taught. The following preskills are those that students should have mastered before addition the slow way is introduced:

1. identifying and writing the numerals 0–10 and the symbols +, −, =, and $\square$
2. equality rule
3. reading an equation
4. drawing the appropriate number of lines to represent a numeral
5. counting the lines in two groups
6. writing the numeral that represents a set of objects

The format for teaching students to work addition problems the slow way appears in Format 7.2. In Part A, the teacher works the problem on the board. The teacher draws circles around the sides of the equal sign: to emphasize the concept of *side*. The steps in the strategy are summarized in the Summary Box 7.1.

Summary Box 7.1
Beginning Addition Strategy

1. Students read equation: 5 + 2 = how many?

2. Students recite equality rule: "You must end up with the same number on this side AND the other side."

3. Students draw lines under the first addend, then under the second addend.

4. Students count all lines on that side of the equal sign.

5. Students apply the equality rule and makes lines under the box on the other side of the equal sign.

6. Students write a numeral to represent the number of lines.

When presenting Part A, the teacher should repeat a problem until students can correctly respond to all of the questions. If a student hesitates or responds incorrectly, the teacher should repeat the question, model the correct answer, then repeat the question again, and ask the students to respond. Following the correction, all the steps from the beginning are repeated one more time. This last presentation demonstrates how all the steps fit together.

Part B is a structured worksheet exercise, and Part C is a less structured worksheet exercise. Example selection for all worksheet exercises should include only numerals that students can identify and write. Sums should not exceed 10. On the worksheets, spaces should be left under numerals for students to draw lines. Once they develop 80 to 90% accuracy in working the problems, students no longer need supervised practice. Eight to 10 problems should appear daily on student worksheets for several more weeks. Note that on worksheets, spaces are drawn below each numeral to prompt drawing the lines.

Missing Addend Strategy

The strategy discussed in this section teaches students to find the missing addend in a problem such as 5 + ☐ = 8. The strategy is based on the equality rule *(You must end with the same number on both sides of the equal)*. Students are presented this form of problem to enhance their understanding of the equality principle and to demonstrate that the equality principle may be used to solve a variety of problem types.

To solve this simple form of missing addend problems, the students first find the side of the equal sign that tells how many they end with. The teacher then points out that the sides are not equal

until the students end with the same number on both sides. The teacher directs the students to draw lines on the side with the box so that the sides will be equal and to fill in the missing numeral.

Format 7.3 includes the format for presenting the missing addend strategy. Part A teaches students the component skill of determining the side to start working on. The exercise points out that since a box doesn't tell how many lines to draw, it can't be the side to start on. Parts B and C are structured board and worksheet exercises, respectively. Note that in step 5 of Part B and step 7 of Part C, the teacher reminds the students that the lines under a box tell what numeral goes in the box. This prompt prevents errors like 5 + 7 = 7 in which students write how many lines are on the whole side in the box.

Part D is a less structured worksheet exercise that includes an equal mixture of missing addend and regular addition problems. In Part D, the teacher leads the students through steps designed to teach the students when to apply the missing addend strategy. The teacher then instructs the students to make both sides equal and finally to fill in the missing numeral. Lower performing students may need a great deal of practice on this part and on the supervised practice part before they can discriminate when and how to apply the regular addition and missing addend strategies. Examples should be limited to problems in which the sum is 10 or less. This limitation is suggested to prevent the tasks from becoming too cumbersome.

When the missing addend is zero, as in 8 + ☐ = 8, the teacher can use this wording to replace steps 6, 7, and 8 in Part C:

6. This is a special kind of problem. The sides are already equal. Eight on both sides. So you shouldn't make any more lines. You plus zero lines. Write a zero in the box.

7. Eight plus how many equals 8?
8. Say the whole statement.

Teachers should present two similar problems on the last day that Part C is presented, for example, 8 + ☐ = 8 and 2 + ☐ = 2. Teachers should continue to present problems in which the missing addend is zero in Part D.

Addition the Fast Way

Addition the fast way (see Format 7.4) is taught as a transitional step between the strategy in which students draw lines for each member of the sets represented by each addend and later exercises in which students memorize addition facts. When time for math instruction is limited, teachers can skip addition the fast way and move directly into fact teaching (see Chapter 6). The addition the fast way strategy differs from addition the slow way in that the student draws lines only to represent the addend following the plus:

$$7 + 4 = \square$$
$$||||$$

When solving the problem, the student starts counting at the number represented by the numeral in the first addend position and then counts the lines (e.g., in the problem above, students count "*ssevvenn*, 8, 9, 10, 11"). Then the student writes the numeral representing the sum in the box on the other side of the equal sign. The student does not draw lines under the box. The only new preskill for this strategy is rote counting beginning at a number other than 1.

Addition the fast way is introduced when students are able to work a mixture of addition and missing addend problems with 80 to 90% accuracy. Teachers can expect some students to have difficulty coordinating counting from a number other than 1 and touching lines. For students who consistently have difficulty with this step, the teacher should present an exercise focusing solely on this component skill. The teacher might write a series of problems in which the lines are drawn:

5 + 3	7 + 2
3 + 4	9 + 5

The teacher models and tests counting until the students can do four problems in a row correctly.

For example, for 5 + 3, the teacher says, "*Ffiivve*," then touches each line and counts "6, 7, 8." The teacher then tests by presenting another example, 7 + 2, touching 7 and saying, "Get it going," to indicate that students begin with 7 and then count each line.

Example selection criteria for addition the fast way problems are somewhat different from those for addition the slow way. Larger numerals can be written in the first addend position, since the student no longer has to draw lines to represent that amount. The second addend, however, should remain a smaller number (e.g., 1–8). Teachers must design the problems so that the sum is represented by a numeral the students have been taught to write.

After students work addition problems the fast way accurately, subtraction instruction can begin (see Chapter 8). After students work addition problems fluently, memorization of addition facts should begin (see Chapter 6).

Diagnosis and Remediation

This section presents basic procedures for diagnosing and remedying errors in beginning addition. The teacher first decides whether the problem is one of can't-do or won't-do. In this section, we consider only the can't-do problems. The basic steps below apply to diagnosing and remedying errors on any type of problem.

1. The teacher analyzes worksheet errors and hypothesizes about the cause of each error.
2. The teacher interviews the student to determine the cause of the error if it is not obvious.
3. The teacher provides reteaching through board and/or worksheet presentations.
4. The teacher tests the student on a set of problems similar to the ones on which the original errors were made.

Once students begin working problems independently using a specific strategy, the errors they make on their worksheets fall into two main categories (fact errors are not possible at this stage because facts are not used, nor have they been taught):

1. Component-skill errors, indicating a deficit on one or more of the component skills that make up the strategy.
2. Strategy errors, indicating problems with the application of the strategy (strategy errors often are the result of a student's forgetting certain steps in a procedure).

Our discussion of diagnosis and remediation of each problem-solving strategy addresses both types of errors. The similarities in the suggested remediation for each type of error should be noted.

COMPONENT-SKILL ERRORS. Component-skill errors may be made on symbol identification and writing, counting and/or drawing lines, and application of the equality rule. When errors are due to component-skill deficits, error patterns are more readily apparent. Therefore, a teacher often can determine the cause of these errors by carefully analyzing worksheets. For example, on an addition the fast way worksheet, a student made the following errors:

a. (6 + 2) = 7

b. (2 + 3) = 4

c. (7 + 4) = 10

By analyzing the errors made by the student, the teacher can determine whether the student had trouble coordinating counting from a number or incorrectly said the number representing the first group while touching the first line in the second group. For example, in problem a above, the student may have touched the first line under 2 while saying *sss-iiixxx,* and then would have said 7 when touching the second line.

To remedy a component skill error, the teacher presents practice exercises on the component skill in isolation for several lessons before returning to the more advanced problems. For example, to remedy the errors made by the student above, the teacher would present an exercise on coordinating counting and touching lines. The teacher would focus on that one skill until the student reached a criterion of about 90% correct responses on the examples. Then the teacher would give the student addition problems to work independently.

Another possible component error involves symbol identification. If a student missed a problem because of numeral misidentification (e.g., identifying 6 as 9), the teacher would focus on the numeral 6 in numeral identification exercises for several lessons. During this time, the student would not be asked to solve problems including the numeral 6.

STRATEGY ERRORS. A strategy error indicates a fundamental lack of understanding of how to sequence the steps in the problem-solving strategy. A strategy error would occur when, after drawing lines under each numeral, the student writes the next number in the counting sequence (10) in the box instead of the total number of lines counted (9). This behavior clearly indicates that the student is not employing the strategy.

$$3 + 6 = 10$$
||| ||||||

To remedy a strategy error, the teacher reintroduces the format to the student, beginning with the structured board presentation, then progresses to the structured and less structured worksheet presentations. A common strategy error students make when solving problems with missing addends involves adding the addend and the sum: 6 + 15 = 9. Such errors indicate students are not applying the equality principle. For these types of errors, the teacher begins with the structured board presentation, Part B of Format 7.3, then progress to Parts C and D.

DIRECT INSTRUCTION PROCEDURES FOR MULTI-DIGIT ADDITION PROBLEMS

Column addition problems may be divided into three groups. Simplest are those that do not require renaming:

$$\begin{array}{r} 24 \\ +15 \\ \hline \end{array}$$

Next are problems with two multi-digit addends, where renaming is necessary:

$$\begin{array}{r} 424 \\ + 317 \\ \hline \end{array}$$

Most difficult are problems with more than two multi-digit addends with renaming:

$$\begin{array}{r} 671 \\ 424 \\ +317 \\ \hline \end{array}$$

Students work column addition problems by using their knowledge of facts. Therefore, problems should be constructed from facts the students have been taught.

Problems Not Requiring Renaming

Column addition problems without renaming are usually introduced in first grade after students have learned to read and write numerals through 99 and are able to figure out mentally about 25 basic addition facts. Remember that basic addition facts include all possible pairings in which the addends are single-digit numbers. Students need many months of practice before they have memorized all basic facts. However, the introduction of multi-digit addition problems need not be delayed until students have memorized all basic addition facts. Initial examples, however, should be designed to include the easier addition facts. Exercises to help memorize basic addition facts are discussed in detail in Chapter 6.

The procedure for teaching students to work these problems is relatively simple. The teacher has the students read the problem, then points out the place value columns, telling students to first add the ones and then add the tens. Teaching students to always begin working in the ones column helps prevent errors on more difficult renaming problems. Although students can compute the correct answer if they begin in the tens column on problems that don't require renaming, they will eventually have difficulty when they start working problems that do require renaming. Therefore, students should be taught to always begin solving the problem in the ones column.

$$
\begin{array}{ccccccc}
24 & & 24 & \text{BUT} & 24 & & 24 \\
+12 & \text{then} & 12 & \text{NOT} & +17 & \text{then} & +17 \\
\hline
6 & & 36 & & 3 & & 311 \\
\end{array}
$$

After learning where to solve the problem, students add the ones and then the tens, writing the sum for each column. The teacher asks about the number of tens rather than the quantity represented by the tens number; that is, for

$$
\begin{array}{r}
34 \\
+21 \\
\hline
\end{array}
$$

the students indicate they are adding 3 tens and 2 tens, not 30 and 20, to remind students they are working in the tens columns. We do not include a format in the book for this problem type, because the teaching procedure is quite simple: A teacher first uses a structured board presentation, then structured and less structured worksheet exercises. The transition from structured board to independent worksheet can be made in about four lessons.

Problems Requiring Renaming

Problems requiring renaming are usually introduced during second grade. Preskills include working addition problems without renaming, reading and writing numerals, figuring out basic addition facts, and expanded notation with teen and tens numbers.

PRESKILL. A unique preskill for renaming involves adding three single-digit numbers. For example, when adding tens in

$$
\begin{array}{r}
1 \\
37 \\
+29 \\
\hline
6 \\
\end{array}
$$

the student must add 1 + 3 to get the sum of 4, then add the sum to 2. Adding three numbers is significantly more difficult for low performers than adding two numbers. When adding three numbers, the student must add the first two numbers, remember the answer, and then add the third number to that sum.

Adding three single-digit numbers should be taught several weeks prior to the introduction of renaming problems. The format for teaching students a strategy to solve these problems appears in Format 7.5. The format contains only three parts: a structured board presentation, a structured worksheet presentation. Since relatively few steps are involved, a less-structured worksheet format is not needed.

The most common error made on this format occurs in step 6 of Part A and step 4 of Part B when students are asked to identify the next two numbers to be added. Students often respond with the second and third numbers instead of the sum of the first two numbers and the third number. For example, in the following problem

$$
\begin{array}{r}
2 \\
3 \\
+4 \\
\hline
\end{array}
$$

the students answer 3 + 4 rather than 5 + 4. In Part A, the teacher tries to prompt the correct response by referring to that question as the "hard part." If students do make the error, the teacher must model and test the answer and then repeat the entire problem from the beginning. ("Now we're adding 5 + 4. What are we adding now? What is 5 + 4?... Let's do the whole problem again from the beginning.")

There are two example selection guidelines for this format. In about half of the examples, the top numeral should be 1, since in most renaming, a 1 is carried to the tens column. Initially, the sum of the three single digits should be 10 or less so that students will be able to concentrate on adding the three numbers rather than figuring out more difficult basic facts.

INTRODUCING THE PROBLEMS. The first type of renaming problem should involve adding a two-digit numeral to another one- or two-digit numeral. Renaming is explained to students by pointing out that a tens number may not appear in the ones column and therefore must be carried to the tens column. For example, leading the students through the problem

$$\begin{array}{r} 37 \\ +25 \\ \hline \end{array}$$

the teacher asks the students what 7 + 5 equals. After the students say 12, the teacher says, "We have a problem. Twelve equals 1 ten and 2 ones. We can't have a ten in the ones column. So, we put the 1 ten at the top of the tens column (teacher writes 1 over 3) and the 2 ones below the line" (teacher writes 2 under 5). Format 7.6 can be used for introducing renaming.

While Part A focuses student attention on the fact that they cannot have a ten in the ones column, Part B sets up the chain of steps the students will follow when working problems on their own. The vocabulary used in this format was selected to foster the students' understanding of the operation. For example, under step 6 in Part A, it is important to remind the students that they are adding tens ("How many tens do we end up with?") so that they remember the values of the numbers and do not just think of the numbers as individual numerals. Note that in Part B, step 3, the teacher prompts the students less on determining what 13 equals. Instead of just telling the students that 13 = 10 + 3, the teacher encourages the students to figure out the answer by themselves.

A common error made on renaming problems involves carrying the wrong number. For example, in working the problem 37 + 27, the student carries the 4 and writes 1 under the ones column. If the students write the numerals in the wrong places, the teacher should not merely model where to write the numbers but should ask students the critical questions (Part B, step 3) so that they can see why the numerals need to be in the appropriate places. After the students correctly answer the questions, the teacher can demonstrate how to put a ten on top of the tens column.

If a student hesitates in answering on a particular step, the teacher should say the answer, repeat the question, and have the student respond again. After using this correction procedure, the teacher should then present the entire problem to give students the opportunity to successfully work through all of the steps in the strategy.

As students learn to read and write larger numbers, renaming problems with these numbers are introduced. First, problems in which students carry a hundred to the hundreds column are introduced. The format for presenting problems in which the students must rename a sum from the tens column would be very similar to the format for renaming a sum from the ones column (Format 7.6). For example, the students are working this problem:

$$\begin{array}{r} 283 \\ +185 \\ \hline \end{array}$$

After asking the students what 8 tens + 8 tens equal, the teacher would say, "We have a problem. Sixteen tens equal 1 hundred plus 6 tens. We can't have a hundred in the tens column, so we put it at the top of the hundreds column (teacher writes 1 over the 2) and put the 6 tens here" (teacher writes 6 under answer line in tens column).

Problems in which students rename twice, from the ones column and then from the tens column, are introduced next. These problems and future problem types will require just a 2 to 3 day pattern of introduction, since once students understand the process of renaming, they usually have little difficulty generalizing. Lower performing students, however, may need more supervised practice with worksheets containing a variety of problem types.

When introducing the strategy using the structured board and worksheet parts of a format, the teacher should use only examples of the type being introduced. When presenting the less structured and supervised parts of the format, the teacher should give the students a cumulative review worksheet. Worksheets are designed to provide cumulative review so that previously taught types of problems receive systematic practice. One-third to one-half of the problems on the worksheet should be of the most recently introduced type. The others should be addition problems of previously introduced types and subtraction problems. The problems should be written in random order. Several examples of the new problem type can appear at the beginning of the worksheet. Otherwise, no more than two or three problems of the same type should appear consecutively.

Cumulative review is especially important when introducing renaming. A student has not mastered renaming until he can discriminate when renaming is appropriate. Addition problems that do not require renaming must be included so that students do not

FIGURE 7.1   Sample Worksheet for Adding with Renaming

356	486	395	495	386
+277	+281	−243	+235	−241
489	37	523	924	924
+232	+28	+206	−201	+31
372	938	356	284	565
+472	−214	+217	+382	+265
87	87	299	468	98
+47	−47	+91	−354	+97

get into the habit of always putting a 1 at the top of the tens column. Likewise, subtraction problems must be included so that the students receive continued practice discriminating addition from subtraction.

An example of a worksheet for a lesson that takes place several days after introducing double renaming (e.g., from ones to tens and from tens to hundreds) appears in Figure 7.1. Note that over one-third of the problems contain double renaming. Of the other addition problems, several involve just renaming from the tens to the hundreds columns, and several involve no renaming at all. About one-third of the problems are subtraction problems.

Three or More Addends

The last major problem type includes those problems with three or more multi-digit addends. Some of these problems are particularly difficult because the student is required to mentally add a number represented by a single-digit numeral to a number represented by a two-digit numeral. For example, note the problems below:

$$\begin{array}{c} 36 \\ 16 \\ +24 \end{array} \Big] 12 + 4 \qquad \begin{array}{c} 47 \\ 24 \\ +13 \end{array} \Big] 11 + 3$$

$$\begin{array}{c} 5839 \\ 2467 \end{array} \Big] 16 + 9$$

$$\begin{array}{c} 3589 \\ +2849 \end{array} \Big] 25 + 9$$

In each problem, the sum of the first two addends in the ones column is a teen number (12, 11, and 16). The next step in each problem involves adding a single-digit number to a teen number (e.g., 12 + 4, 11 + 3, 16 + 9). As mentioned earlier, we call facts in which a single-digit number is added to a two-digit number *complex addition facts*. Learning complex addition facts is a critical preskill that takes many months of practice to master. Teachers should begin practice exercises on this preskill after students know about 50 basic addition facts. Students progressing at an average rate in a developmental program would be introduced to these problems sometime in early- to mid-second grade.

The first type of complex fact introduced is that in which a single-digit number is added to a teen number, and the total does not exceed 19 (e.g., 14 + 3, 15 + 2, 15 + 3, 15 + 4). Format 7.7 shows how to present this skill. The students learn to transform a complex fact into two simple facts; for example, students transform 16 + 3 into 10 + 6 + 3, add 6 + 3, then add 10 + 9. Note that daily practice on this skill should continue for about 30 days to develop fluency.

After students can solve this first type of complex addition fact mentally, they can begin column addi-

---

Summary Box 7.2
Addition with Renaming

1. Students read the problem.

2. Students begin adding in the ones column.

3. If the sum of the ones column is 10 or more, students determine they must rename.

4. Students use expanded notation to determine the number of tens and ones in the sum of the ones column.

5. Students rename by putting the tens in the tens column and the ones under the line in the ones column.

6. Students add the first 2 tens in the tens column, then add the next ten to that sum.

7. Students write the sum of tens under the line in the tens column.

tion problems involving three or more numbers that require renaming. These problems can be introduced with a relatively simple format. The teacher has the students add all the numbers in the ones column. After the sum of the ones column is computed, the students carry the 10 and write the remaining ones under the line. A similar procedure is followed with the tens, hundreds, and thousands columns. Note that examples should be carefully selected so that students do not encounter complex addition facts that have not been previously taught.

The second type of complex addition fact includes facts in which a single-digit number is added to a teen number and the sum totals 20 or more (e.g., $16 + 6 = 22$, $18 + 7 = 25$, $14 + 7 = 21$, $15 + 8 = 23$). This type of fact is introduced in late third or early fourth grade. There are 44 more difficult complex addition facts (see Table 7.1), which can be introduced in sets of two or three facts.

Format 7.8 shows how to teach this more difficult type of complex addition fact. Students transform a fact with a sum over 20 in the following way: $17 + 9$ becomes $10 + 7 + 9$, and then students add $7 + 9$. Then they add the sum of 16 to 10. In Part A, students learn to add the 10 to teens numbers (e.g., $14 + 10$, $18 + 10$). This skill is used in Part B (e.g., the last step in adding $19 + 3$ is adding 10 and 12; the last step for $13 + 8$ is adding 10 and 11). Part C provides supervised practice on the new complex facts and those introduced in the previous set.

Part D, an independent worksheet, should include a variety of problems, including problems that yield a sum of 20 or more and some that yield sums less than 20. This mix is needed to prevent students from possibly overgeneralizing and always adding 10 to a complex addition fact (e.g., $14 + 4 = 28$). Worksheet exercises to develop fluency in this skill are similar to those discussed in Chapter 6. A set of two or three complex facts are introduced each several days. The new facts appear several times on the independent worksheet along with previously introduced facts. Problems should be written horizontally. Instructions on the worksheet should tell students to work the problems mentally. The number of practice problems should increase as more complex facts are introduced.

SELF-CHECKING. After students become proficient in working renaming problems with three addends, they should be taught to check their answers. A checking procedure for addition is adding from the bottom digit in each column, assuming the students start with the top digit in each column when they originally work the problem. The teacher introduces checking on a worksheet exercise. Students complete the first problem, and the teacher says, "Here's how to check your work to make sure you have the right answer. Start with the bottom number and add up the column. What are the first two numbers?... What's the answer?... What's the answer for the next two numbers?... Is that what you wrote in the answer for ones and at the top of the tens column?... Let's start from the bottom again ... What are the first two numbers you add in the tens column?... What's the answer for the next two numbers?... Is that what you wrote for the answer?"

Determining whether students check their work is difficult because checking doesn't require any additional writing. An exercise to encourage checking involves giving students already worked problems, about half of which have incorrect answers, and instructing students to check the answers and correct mistakes.

Diagnosis and Remediation

As mentioned previously, once it is determined that the errors on student worksheets are not caused by a lack of motivation, the teacher must identify specific skill deficits and provide remediation accordingly.

Table 7.1 Complex Addition Facts

	Sums of 20 or more				*Sums less than 20*							
1.	11 + 9				11 + 1	11 + 2	11 + 3	11 + 4	11 + 5	11 + 6	11 + 7	11 + 8
2.	12 + 8	12 + 9				12 + 1	12 + 2	12 + 3	12 + 4	12 + 5	12 + 6	12 + 7
3.	13 + 7	13 + 8	13 + 9				13 + 1	13 + 2	13 + 3	13 + 4	13 + 5	13 + 6
4.	14 + 6	14 + 7	14 + 8	14 + 9				14 + 1	14 + 2	14 + 3	14 + 4	14 + 5
5.	15 + 5	15 + 6	15 + 7	15 + 8	15 + 9				15 + 1	15 + 2	15 + 3	15 + 4
6.	16 + 4	16 + 5	16 + 6	16 + 7	16 + 8	16 + 9				16 + 1	16 + 2	16 + 3
7.	17 + 3	17 + 4	17 + 5	17 + 6	17 + 7	17 + 8	17 + 9				17 + 1	17 + 2
8.	18 + 2	18 + 3	18 + 4	18 + 5	18 + 6	18 + 7	18 + 8	18 + 9				18 + 1
9.	19 + 1	19 + 2	19 + 3	19 + 4	19 + 5	19 + 6	19 + 7	19 + 8	19 + 9			

Students make three major types of errors: facts, component, and strategy. In the area of addition, the most common errors involve facts, the component skills of renaming (either carrying the wrong number or failure to carry), and inattention to the sign in the problem.

FACT ERRORS. Fact errors cause most column addition errors. Such errors are sometimes easy to identify, as in the problems below:

a.
$$\begin{array}{r} {}^{11} \\ 357 \\ +\ 248 \\ \hline 606 \end{array}$$

b.
$$\begin{array}{r} {}^{1} \\ 228 \\ +\ 744 \\ \hline 971 \end{array}$$

c.
$$\begin{array}{r} {}^{1} \\ 648 \\ +\ 281 \\ \hline 919 \end{array}$$

Note that in each example, the student missed the problem because of a fact error (e.g., in problem a, the student wrote 16 for 7 + 8). In some cases, however, teachers cannot easily determine if a fact error caused the incorrect answer. For example, in the following problems, the errors could have been caused by failing to add the carried number or by a fact deficit. In problem d, the student might have incorrectly added 1 + 5 + 4 in the tens column or simply failed to add the carried ten.

d.
$$\begin{array}{r} {}^{1} \\ 357 \\ +\ 248 \\ \hline 595 \end{array}$$

e.
$$\begin{array}{r} {}^{1} \\ 228 \\ +\ 743 \\ \hline 961 \end{array}$$

In order to determine the specific cause of the errors, the teacher should look for error patterns. For example, the teacher should check the problems with errors to see if the same facts were consistently missed. Also, the teacher should utilize the information she has about the student's performance on recent fact worksheets. To confirm the diagnosis, the teacher should observe the student reworking some of the missed problems.

The remediation procedure depends on the nature of the fact errors. If a student consistently misses the same facts, the teacher merely provides extra practice on those facts. On the other hand, some students are erratic in their performance, answering a fact correctly one time and missing it the next. For such students, the teacher should increase the incentives for accurate work.

A final note on facts concerns teachers who work with older remedial students who rely on their fingers to figure out basic facts. Unfortunately, since lower grade classrooms often do not provide adequate practice on fact mastery, many students may be using their fingers to figure out basic facts.

Teachers should be careful not to forbid the students to use their fingers if that is their only strategy for deriving an answer. Rather, the teacher should ensure that students are using a finger strategy that is relatively efficient and that students use the strategy accurately. Mistakes in finger operations may occur because a student makes errors in counting or does not coordinate putting up his fingers and counting (i.e., the student does not put up a finger for each number counted).

If the cause of the fact errors is determined to be an inappropriate finger strategy, the teacher should devote several minutes each day to reviewing that strategy. Keep in mind that correcting a finger strategy deficit is done only with students who have not mastered their basic facts and have no other strategy to use. In addition to correcting the finger strategy, teachers should spend more instructional time reviewing the exercises recommended in Chapter 6 to facilitate basic fact mastery. The ultimate goal of fact remediation is to teach students to master their facts and to stop relying on finger counting altogether.

COMPONENT-SKILL ERRORS. The first component-skill deficit involves renaming. Note the errors in the problems below:

$$\begin{array}{r} {}^{6} \\ 48 \\ +28 \\ \hline 121 \end{array}$$

$$\begin{array}{r} {}^{5} \\ 39 \\ 27 \\ +19 \\ \hline 112 \end{array}$$

The student carried the ones instead of the tens. Errors in which students carry the wrong number are quite serious because they indicate a fundamental misunderstanding of basic place value concepts. A possible remediation exercise for the component skill involves a set of problems containing boxes in which the sum of the ones column and the carried number are to be recorded. For each problem, the teacher tells the student the sum of the numbers in the ones column, then asks how many tens and ones make up that sum. The student answers, then fills in the numbers. The remediation set should contain approximately 10 examples that look similar to the following.

$$\begin{array}{cccc} \square & \square & \square & \square \\ 68 & 45 & 24 & 86 \\ +19 & +29 & +18 & +27 \\ \square & \square & \square & \square \end{array}$$

The first three to four examples in the remediation set should be problems in which renaming is required. However, the examples in the remediation set should also contain some discrimination examples in which renaming is not required so that students do not get into the habit of always writing a 1 above the tens column. If students demonstrate place value deficits during the remediation, the teacher may need to reteach expanded notation. After students can do four to six modified problems in a row filling in the correct numbers, the teacher leads the students through a set of four to six addition problems using Part C of Format 7.6, then has them do four to six problems with no teacher direction. This remediation procedure is repeated until students' performance on renaming problems is 90% or better.

A component-skill deficit similar to renaming the wrong number involves not renaming the ten at all. Problems in which student fails to rename the ten look like the following:

$$\begin{array}{r} 48 \\ +36 \\ \hline 74 \end{array} \qquad \begin{array}{r} 32 \\ +19 \\ \hline 41 \end{array}$$

Since the student wrote the ones number in the appropriate place, it is likely that the student just forgot to carry the ten to the tens column. The remediation procedure for this error pattern is the same as for the previously discussed error in which the student carried the ones instead of the tens. Again, remember it is necessary to individually test students to determine if the error resulted from a renaming error or from a fact error.

Failure to attend to the sign is a common cause of errors in column addition problems. This deficit is characterized by worksheet errors in which the wrong operation is performed:

$$\begin{array}{r} 342 \\ +131 \\ \hline 211 \end{array} \qquad \begin{array}{r} 304 \\ -201 \\ \hline 505 \end{array}$$

If such errors occur on more than 10% of the problems, students should be given a special worksheet with an equal mix of addition and subtraction problems in random order:

$$\begin{array}{r} 37 \\ -15 \end{array} \quad \begin{array}{r} 28 \\ +13 \end{array} \quad \begin{array}{r} 47 \\ +24 \end{array} \quad \begin{array}{r} 38 \\ -16 \end{array} \quad \begin{array}{r} 47 \\ +25 \end{array} \quad \begin{array}{r} 86 \\ -23 \end{array} \quad \begin{array}{r} 48 \\ +20 \end{array}$$

The teacher presents the less structured worksheet exercises, instructing students to circle and say the sign before working each problem.

STRATEGY ERRORS Strategy errors are caused by incorrectly carrying out several steps in the strategy. An example of one type of strategy error appears below:

$$\begin{array}{r} 35 \\ +27 \\ \hline 512 \end{array} \qquad \begin{array}{r} 68 \\ +18 \\ \hline 716 \end{array}$$

This is quite a serious error, indicating the student does not understand the concept of renaming. The remediation procedure for all strategy deficits involves reteaching the format for that particular type of problem. The teacher presents several problems using a structured board presentation, then leads the students through several worksheet problems using the structured, then less structured, parts of the format.

A summary of the deficits common to column addition and the diagnosis and remediation procedures appropriate for each appear in Figure 7.2. Unless otherwise noted, after each remediation procedure, the teacher needs to give students worksheets similar to the ones on which the original errors were made in order to test whether the remediation was effective.

COMMERCIAL PROGRAMS

Addition: Regrouping

INSTRUCTIONAL STRATEGIES In most programs, students are taught a strategy for regrouping in addition by using bundles of sticks or other manipulatives. The steps in the strategy (with minor variations) in four basals we reviewed are

Step 1 Add the ones.
Step 2 "Trade" if equal to 10 or more.
Step 3 Add the tens.

The strategies for addition with regrouping appear to be straightforward. Our analysis reveals, however, that the programs may not sufficiently address necessary prerequisite skills or provide enough systematic guided practice to ensure student success.

PREREQUISITE SKILLS. Basals often attempt to teach the prerequisite place value skills by having students trace numbers already placed in the proper columns. Then students are expected to progress from tracing numbers to independently solving problems. The problem with tracing should be obvious. If the numbers are placed for the students, students do not have to think about where to place them. As a result, some students will have difficulty on similar problems when the prompts are removed.

To remedy this potential problem, include intermediate steps in the strategy that require students to identify where they are going to write their answers

FIGURE 7.2   Diagnosis and Remediation of Addition Errors

Sample Patterns		Diagnosis	Remediation Procedures	Remediation Examples
Fact Errors				
a. 46 +17 64	263 +174 447	Basic fact errors. Student doesn't know the fact 6 + 7.	Emphasize 6 + 7 in fact memorization exercises. See Chapter 6.	
Component-Skill Errors				
b. 3 46 +17 81	2 53 +29 91	Renaming errors. Student carries the ones to the tens column, writes the tens in the ones column.	Steps from structured worksheet exercise that focus on renaming. (Format 7.6, Part B, steps 1–3)	10 problems in this form: ☐ ☐ 69 46 +36 +29 ☐ ☐
c. 46 +17 53	25 +17 32	Renaming errors. Student forgets to carry.	Same as above.	Same as above.
d. 49 +17 32	253 −174 427	Sign discrimination error. Student substracts instead of adding, vice versa.	Less structured worksheet exercise. Have students circle the sign before working each problem. (Format 7.6, Part C, steps 1, 4)	Mix of addition and subtraction problems.
Strategy Errors				
e. 46 +17 513	253 +174 3127	Student does not carry; writes the entire number in the sum.	Test and/or teach appropriate preskills. Preset format beginning with structured board exercise. (Format 7.6, Part A)	

before they write them. Then teachers can correct any errors that occur and prevent error patterns from forming.

Another major problem results from the lack of coordination between basic fact teaching and the facts students encounter in regrouping problems.

Students often do not receive adequate practice to memorize basic facts before they encounter these facts in workbook exercises. Thus, students often use their fingers to figure out the facts, which can slow down or interfere with learning the computation process.

APPLICATION ITEMS: ADDITION

1. Describe the problem type that each example below represents. List the problems in the order they are introduced. Write the grade level when each type is typically introduced.

   a. 462
       +371

   b. 35
       16
       +24

   c. 46
       87
       +19

   d. 84
       +13

   e. 348
       +135

   f. 368
       +259

2. Below is an excerpt from the independent worksheet to be given to students who have just demonstrated accuracy in solving problem type 2e from instructional sequence and assessment chart, adding two two-digit numbers, renaming from ones to tens columns. The teacher has made some errors in constructing the worksheet.

   a. Indicate the inappropriate examples.

   b. Identify any omitted problem types that should be included on the worksheet.

Worksheet

a. 462	b. 75	c. 141	d. 38	e. 582
+183	+16	+324	+26	+ 15

f. 1	g. 46	h. 617	i. 58
3	+15	+124	+ 25
+6			

3. At the beginning of the unit, the teacher tested Leslie. Her performance on the performance indicators for problem types 2e–3c appear below.

Specify the problem type with which instruction should begin for Leslie. Explain your answer.

2e.
$$
\begin{array}{r} {}^1\,37 \\ +\,46 \\ \hline 83 \end{array}
\quad
\begin{array}{r} {}^1\,48 \\ +\,14 \\ \hline 61 \end{array}
\quad
\begin{array}{r} {}^1\,57 \\ +\,27 \\ \hline 84 \end{array}
$$

2f.
$$
\begin{array}{r} {}^1\,247 \\ +315 \\ \hline 562 \end{array}
\quad
\begin{array}{r} {}^1\,258 \\ +\,13 \\ \hline 272 \end{array}
\quad
\begin{array}{r} {}^1\,276 \\ +\,8 \\ \hline 284 \end{array}
$$

3a. 13 + 3 = *16*
    14 + 4 = *18*
    12 + 2 = *14*

3b.
$$
\begin{array}{r} 374 \\ +261 \\ \hline 535 \end{array}
\quad
\begin{array}{r} 248 \\ +364 \\ \hline 511 \end{array}
\quad
\begin{array}{r} 437 \\ +285 \\ \hline 652 \end{array}
$$

3c.
$$
\begin{array}{r} {}^1\,276 \\ +185 \\ \hline 461 \end{array}
\quad
\begin{array}{r} {}^1\,248 \\ +365 \\ \hline 512 \end{array}
\quad
\begin{array}{r} {}^1\,437 \\ +285 \\ \hline 622 \end{array}
$$

4. Below are 11 problems that appeared on the worksheets to be done independently by the students in Mrs. Ash's math group. Next to each student's name are the problems missed by the student. For each student, specify the probable cause or causes of the student's errors.

Describe the remediation procedure. Be specific. For each remediation, indicate the format and the part of that format you would begin remediation with. If no format appears in the book for that problem type, indicate the page in the text that discusses that problem type.

37	364	57	36	48	72	58	57	48	34	514
+26	+212	−23	+22	+28	+26	−32	+34	−24	+26	+ 23

Errors: Bill
$$
\begin{array}{r} {}^3\,37 \\ +26 \\ \hline 91 \end{array}
\quad
\begin{array}{r} {}^6\,48 \\ +28 \\ \hline 121 \end{array}
$$
Ann
$$
\begin{array}{r} 37 \\ +26 \\ \hline 513 \end{array}
\quad
\begin{array}{r} 48 \\ +28 \\ \hline 616 \end{array}
\quad
\begin{array}{r} 34 \\ +26 \\ \hline 510 \end{array}
$$
Julie
$$
\begin{array}{r} 37 \\ +26 \\ \hline 11 \end{array}
\quad
\begin{array}{r} {}^1\,48 \\ -24 \\ \hline 72 \end{array}
$$

5. The following is an excerpt from Format 7.3 for solving missing addends. Student responses are included. Specify teacher wording for the correction required.

Missing Addend Format

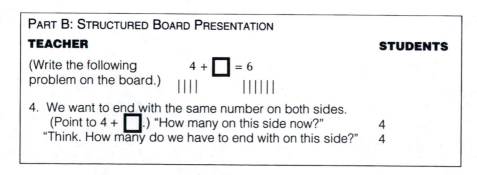

6. Specify a diagnosis and remediation for each of the students listed below.

   a. For each student, describe the probable cause or mistaken strategy responsible for the errors.

   b. For each remediation, indicate the format and the part of that format you would begin remediation with. If no format appears in the book for that problem type, indicate the page in the text that discusses that problem type.

Student A

3 + [7] = 7   5 + [8] = 8
||||| ||||

4 + [9] = 9   2 + [6] = 6
|||||| ||||

Student B

6 + 3 = [8]   7 + 2 = [8]
||| ||

2 + 4 = [5]   3 + 5 = [7]
|||| |||||

7. Write the wording the teacher uses in the structured worksheet part in presenting the following problem:

   162
   +283

8. Below are worksheets made by three teachers for the less structured part of the format for teaching students to work problems with renaming from the ones to tens columns. Two teachers constructed unacceptable lists. Identify these teachers and tell why each is unacceptable. For the unacceptable lists, specify what could be done to make the list acceptable.

   a. 37   37   237   481   374   48   786
       +25   −25   + 86   +110   −213   +24   +346

   b. 48   78   37   58   73   57
       +26   +25   + 8   +24   +28   +18

   c. 47   47   385   68   28   74   92   75   342
       +25   −25   +214   +48   +36   +23   −31   +38   + 26

FORMAT 7.1   Equality Introduction

TEACHER   **STUDENTS**

PART A: STRUCTURED BOARD PRESENTATION

1. *(Write the following problem on the board.)*

   (Point to equal sign.) This is an equal sign. What is this?   Equal

2. Here's a rule: We must end with the same number on this side *(point to left side of equal)* and the other side of the equal sign.

3. *(Point to left side.)* Let's see if we end with the same number on this side and on the other side.

4. *(Point to left side.)* Count the lines on this side as I touch them. *(Point to each line as students count.)*   1, 2, 3, 4, 5

5. How many did we end with on this side?   5

6. So we must end with 5 on the other side. *(Point to right side.)*

7. Let's count the lines. *(Point as students count.)*   1, 2, 3, 4, 5

TEACHER

Did we end with 5?
So the sides are equal. We ended with the same number on this side and the other side.

PART B: LESS STRUCTURED BOARD PRESENTATION

1. *(Write the following problem on the board.)*

Listen to the equal rule: We must end with the same number on this side and the other side of the equal sign. Say the equal rule. *(Repeat rule with students until they can say it without assistance.)*

2. Let's see if the sides are equal.

3. *(Point to left side.)* How many do we end with on this side? *(Pause, signal.)*

4. *(Point to right side.)* How many do we end with on this side? *(Pause, signal.)*

5. Do we end with the same number on this side? *(Point to right side.)* And the other side? *(Point to left side.)*

6. Are the sides equal?

7. The sides are not equal, so I don't write an equal sign.

(Repeat 1–7 with several examples, half equal and half unequal. Give individual turns to several students.)

PART C: LESS STRUCTURED WORKSHEET

1. *(Give students worksheet with these problems.)*

Touch problem a.

2. Say the equal rule.

3. Count and see if the sides are equal. *(Pause.)* Are the sides equal?

   To correct: (Point to left side). Count these lines. Tell me how many you end with. *(Point to right side.)* Count these lines. Tell me how many you end with. Did you end with the same number on this side and the other side?

4. Do you write in an equal?

5. *(If answer to 3 is yes)* Write the equal.
   (Repeat steps 1–5 with remaining problems.)

STUDENTS

Yes

4

2

No

No

We must end with the same number on this side and the other side of the equal sign.

No

No

No

FORMAT 7.2 **Teaching Addition the Slow Way**

TEACHER	**STUDENTS**

PART A: STRUCTURED BOARD PRESENTATION

1. *(Write the following problem on the board.)*

   5 + 3 = ☐
   ___ ___ ___

   Read the problem.
   (Point to the equal sign.) What is this?

| | 5 + 3 = how many? |
| | Equal |

2. Listen to the equal rule: We must end with the same number on this side *(circle 5 + 3)* and the other side *(circle box)* of the equal sign.

3. *(Point to 5.)* How many in the first group?
   I'll draw five lines under the 5. Count as I draw the lines.
   (Draw five lines.)

| | 5 |
| | 1, 2, 3, 4, 5 |

4. *(Point to + 3.)* This says "plus three." Plus tells us to draw more lines, so I draw three more lines under the 3. Count as I draw the lines. *(Draw three lines.)*

| | 1, 2, 3 |

5. We've drawn all the lines on this side. Let's count and see what we end with. Count as I touch the lines. *(Touch lines.)*
   What number did we end with?
   We must end with the same number on this side and the other side of the equal sign.

| | 1, 2, 3, 4, 5, 6, 7, 8 |
| | 8 |

6. *(Point to 5 + 3.)* We must end with 8 on this side. So what number must we end with on the other side?
   I'll draw the lines. You count and tell me when to stop.
   (Draw lines under box.)

| | 8 |
| | 1, 2, 3, 4, 5, 6, 7, 8, stop |

   5 + 3 = ☐
   ‖‖ ‖ ‖‖‖‖

   To correct: If children don't say stop after 8, keep drawing lines, then say, We made a mistake. You have to tell me to stop.
   (Repeat from step 5.)

7. The lines under a box tell what numeral goes in the box.
   How many lines are under the box?
   So what number goes in the box?
   (Write 8 in the box.) What does 5 + 3 equal?

	8
	8
	8

8. Say the whole statement.

| | 5 + 3 = 8 |

9. *(Repeat steps 1–8 until students can answer with no errors. Repeat steps 1–9 with several problems.)*

PART B: STRUCTURED WORKSHEET PRESENTATION

   (Here is a sample worksheet item.)

   a. 5 + 3 = ☐
   ___ ___ ___

1. Touch problem a.

2. Read the problem as I clap. Get ready. *(Clap at 1-second intervals.)* 5 + 3 = how many?

TEACHER	STUDENTS
3. How many in the first group? Make the lines.	5 Students draw five lines.
4. The next part of the problem says plus 3. What do you do when you plus 3?	Make three more lines.
5. Make the lines under the 3.	Students draw three lines.
6. Let's count all the lines on that side. Put your finger over the first line. *(Check.)* Touch and count the lines as I clap. *(Clap one clap per second.)*	1, 2, 3, 4, 5, 6, 7, 8
7. How many lines did we end with?	8
8. So how many must we end with on the other side of the equal?	8
9. Make the lines and write the numeral.	
10. What does 5 + 3 equal?	8
11. Say the statement. *(Repeat steps 1–11 with remaining problems.)*	5 + 3 = 8

PART C: LESS STRUCTURED WORKSHEET

1. *(Give students worksheets with problems.)* Touch problem a. 6 + 3 = ☐	
2. Read the problem.	6 + 3 = how many?
3. First you make six lines, then you plus. How do you plus 3?	Make three more lines.
4. Make the sides equal and fill in the missing numeral. *(Check.)*	
5. What does 6 + 3 equal?	9
6. Say the statement. *(Repeat steps 1–5 with remaining problems.)*	6 + 3 = 9

FORMAT 7.3 **Solving Missing Addends**

TEACHER	STUDENTS

PART A: PRESKILL—SIDE TO START ON

1. *(Write the following problems on the board.)*

    4 + ☐ = 6
    1 + ☐ = 3
    3 + 2 = ☐
    8 + ☐ = 9
    5 + 3 = ☐

    Listen: I'm going to tell you something about the side you start with. You start with the side that tells how many lines to draw. Listen again: You start with the side that tells how many lines to draw.

2. My turn. *(Point to 4 + ☐ in the first problem.)* Can I start on this side? No. How do I know? Because the box does not tell me how many lines to draw. *(Point to 6.)* Can I start on this side? Yes. How do you know? Because a 6 tells how many lines to draw.

(continued on next page)

FORMAT 7.3   (continued)

TEACHER	STUDENTS
3. Now it is your turn. *(Point to 4 +* ☐ *in the first problem.)* Can I start on this side? How do you know?	No Because a box does not tell how many lines to draw.
4. *(Point to 6.)* Can I start on this side? *(Repeat steps 1–4 with remaining problems.)*	Yes

PART B: STRUCTURED BOARD PRESENTATION

1. *(Write the following problem on the board.)*
 	
  4 + ☐ = 6
 	
  _____ _____ _____
Read this problem.
	4 + how many = 6

2. This is a new kind of problem. It doesn't tell us how many to plus. We have to figure out how many to plus. What must we figure out?	How many to plus
3. We use the equal rule to help us. The equal rule says we must end with the same number on this side *(point to 4 +* ☐*)* and the other side *(point to 6)* of the equal sign. First we figure the side we start counting on. *(Point to 4 +* ☐*.)* Do I start counting on this side? Why not? *(Point to 6.)* Do I start counting on this side? The 6 tells me to make six lines. *(Draw six lines under the 6.)*	No The box does not tell how many lines to make. Yes Yes
4. We want to end with the same number on both sides. *(Point to 4 +* ☐*.)* How many on this side now? I'll draw four lines. *(Draw four lines under 4.)* Think. How many do we need to end with on this side? *To correct:* We want to end with the same number we end with on the other side. What number do we end with on the other side? We have 4. We want to end with 6. Count as I make the lines. Tell me when to stop. *(Point to 4.)* How many in this group? Get it going. *(Draw lines under box as students count.)* *To correct:* If students do not say stop after saying 6, tell them, We ended with 6 on the other side. We must end with 6 on this side. *Then repeat from step 4.*	4 6 4 ffoouurr, 5, 6, stop
5. What number did we end with? We made the sides equal. Are we going to write 6 in the box? *To correct:* If children say yes, We must count the lines under the box to see what number goes in the box. The number of lines under the box tells us what numeral to write in the box. What numeral? *(Write 2 in box.)*	6 No 2
6. 4 + how many = 6? Say the whole statement. *(Repeat steps 1–6 with remaining problems.)*	4 + 2 = 6

TEACHER	STUDENTS

PART C: STRUCTURED WORKSHEET PRESENTATION

(Below is a sample worksheet item.)

   5 + ☐ = 8

   ____ ____ ____

1. Touch problem a. Read the problem.	5 + how many = 8
2. Touch the side you start counting on.	Students touch side with 8.
3. Make the lines under the 8.	Students make eight lines.
4. Touch the side that says "5 + how many."	Students touch that side.
5. How many do we have on that side now? Make five lines under the 5.	5 Students make five lines.
6. Think: How many do we have to end with on that side? *To correct:* We want to make the sides equal. We ended with 8 on the other side, so we must end with 8 on this side.	8
7. Touch the 5. You have five lines so far. Make more lines under the box so that we end with 8 on that side. How many did you end with on that side? Are you going to write 8 in the box? No, the lines under the box tell us what numeral to write in the box.	Students draw more lines. 8 No
8. Count the lines you made under the box and write the numeral. 5 + how many = 8? Say the whole statement.	Students write 3. 5 + 3 = 8

PART D: LESS STRUCTURED WORKSHEET

1. *(Give students a worksheet with an equal mix of addition and missing addend problems.)* a. 5 + 3 = ☐ d. 3 + 4 = ☐ b. 4 + ☐ = 6 e. 6 + ☐ = 7 c. 3 + ☐ = 8 f. 5 + 3 = ☐ Touch problem a. Read the problem.	5 + 3 = how many?
2. Touch the side you start counting on.	
3. Make the lines on that side and get ready to tell me how many you end with. *(Pause.)* What do you want to end with?	8
4. Touch the other side. *(Pause.)* What do you want to end with?	8
5. Make lines to make the sides equal.	Students make lines.
6. Count the lines under the empty box and write the numeral.	Students write 8 in the box.

FORMAT 7.4   Teaching Addition the Fast Way

TEACHER	STUDENTS

PART A: STRUCTURED BOARD PRESENTATION

1. *(Write the following problem on the board.)*
   5 + 3 = ☐
 	
   ____
 	
   I'll touch and you read.
	5 + 3 equals how many?

(continued on next page)

FORMAT 7.4 (continued)

TEACHER	STUDENTS
2. We're going to work this problem a fast way. We draw lines under the number after the plus. *(Point to + 3.)*	
What does this say?	Plus three
So how many lines are we going to draw?	3
I'll make the lines. *(Draw 3 lines under the 3.)*	
3. Watch me count the fast way. *(Touch 5 and then each line.)* Ffiivve, 6, 7, 8. Now it's your turn to count the fast way. How many are in the first group? Get it going … count. *(Touch 5 for 2 seconds and then touch each line.)*	ffiivve, 6, 7, 8
4. How many did we end with on this side? So how many must we end with on the other side?	8
I'll write an 8 in the box. *(Write 8 in the box.)*	8
5. Read the whole statement. *(Repeat steps 1–5 with 7 + 4, 9 + 5.)*	5 + 3 = 8

PART B: STRUCTURED WORKSHEET

1. *(Write the following problem on the board.)*

$$4 + 2 = \square$$

(Point to 4 + 2 = $\square$.) Touch this problem on your worksheet. *(Pause.)* Read the problem out loud. Get ready. *(Clap for each symbol.)*	4 + 2 = how many?
2. Let's work this problem the fast way. Touch the numeral after the plus. *(Pause.)*	
How many lines are you going to plus?	2
Make the lines under the 2. *(Check.)*	
3. Touch the 4 and get ready to count the fast way. Four. Get it going. *(Clap as students touch and count.)* Count.	Ffoouurr, 5, 6
To correct: (Teacher models.) My turn … *(If necessary, moves student's finger as he counts.)*	
4. How many did you end with on the side you started with?	6
How many must you end with on the side with the box?	6
Yes, 6 equals 6. What numeral will you write in the box?	6
Do it.	
5. Read the whole statement.	4 + 2 = 6

PART C: LESS STRUCTURED WORKSHEET

1. *(Read problem and determine side.)* Everybody, read the first problem on your worksheet. Get ready. *(Clap for each symbol.)*	4 + 3 equals how many?
2. *(Work problem.)* Now you're ready to plus lines and count the fast way. What are you going to do?	Plus the lines and count the fast way.
Do it. *(Check students as they work.)*	
3. Read the whole statement.	4 + 3 = 7

FORMAT 7.5   Adding Three Single-Digit Numbers

TEACHER	STUDENTS

PART A: STRUCTURED BOARD PRESENTATION

1. (Write the following problems on the board.)

$$\begin{array}{ccc} 1 & 1 & 3 \\ 3 & 2 & 1 \\ +2 & +4 & +6 \end{array}$$

You're going to learn how to work a special kind of problem today. Read this problem. $1 + 3 + 2$

2. Watch me work it. First I add 1 + 3. What do I add first? $1 + 3$
What is 1 + 3? (Pause.)   4

3. 1 + 3 = 4. Now I add 4 + 2. What do I add next? $4 + 2$
What is 4 + 2? (Pause.)   6

4. So I write the 6 below the equal.

5. Let's see if you remember. What are the first numbers I add? $1 + 3$

6. What is 1 + 3? (Pause.)   4
Here's the hard part. What are the next numbers I add? $4 + 2$

   To correct: (If student says 3 + 2, repeat steps 2–6.) What is
   4 + 2? (Pause. Write 6.)   6

7. Read the problem now. $1 + 3 + 2 = 6$

   (Repeat with two more examples. Give individual turns
   to several students.)

PART B: STRUCTURED WORKSHEET PRESENTATION

   (Students have worksheets with 10 problems of the type below.)

$$\begin{array}{ccc} 2 & 1 & 5 \\ 4 & 4 & 2 \\ +3 & +3 & +2 \end{array}$$

1. Touch the first problem. Read it. $2 + 4 + 3$

2. Touch the first numbers you add. (Monitor responses.) What
   are they? $2 + 4$

3. What is 2 + 4? (Pause.)   6

4. Now tell me the next numbers you add.(Pause.) $6 + 3$
   Yes, 6 + 3.

5. What is 6 + 3? (Pause, signal.)   9
   Write 9 below the line.

6. Read the problem now. $2 + 4 + 3 = 9$
   (Repeat Part B with two more examples.)

FORMAT 7.6 Adding Two Numerals with Renaming

TEACHER	**STUDENTS**

PART A: STRUCTURED BOARD PRESENTATION

(Write the following problems on the board.)

```
 36     48     26
+27    +26    +16
```

1. Read this problem as I point.	36 + 27 = how many?
2. What column do we start working in?	The ones column
3. What are the first two numbers we're going to add?	6 + 7
To correct: Point to 6 and 7. Repeat step 3.	
4. What is 6 + 7?	13
5. We have a problem. Thirteen equals 1 ten and 3 ones. We can't have a 10 in the ones column, so we put the 1 ten at the top of the tens column. Where do we put the 10? *(Write 1 over 3.)* We write three ones under the ones column. Where do we put the three ones? *(Write 3 under 7.)*	On top of the tens column Under the ones column
6. What are the first two numbers to add in the tens column? What does 1 + 3 equal? *(Pause.)* Now what two numbers will we add? What is 4 + 2? How many tens do we end up with? We end up with 6 tens, so I'll write 6 under the tens column. *(Write 6 in the tens column.)*	1 + 3 4 4 + 2 6 6 tens
7. We are finished. *(Point to 63.)* What does 36 + 27 equal? Read the problem and say the answer. *(Repeat steps 1–5 with remaining problems.)*	63 36 + 27 = 63

PART B: STRUCTURED WORKSHEET PRESENTATION

(Students have worksheets with the following problems.)

```
 45     57     36     47
+38    +37    +16    +26
```

1. Touch the first problem on your worksheet. Read the problem.	45 + 38 = how many?
2. What column do you start working? What are the first two numbers you're going to add? What is 5 + 8? *(Pause.)*	The ones 5 + 8 13
3. There's a problem. What does 13 equal? Can we have a ten in the ones column? So where do you put the ten? Write a 1 on top of the tens column. *(Monitor student responses.)* How many ones are left? Write them under the ones column. *(Check.)*	1 ten and 3 ones No On top of the tens column 13 equals 1 ten and 3 ones 3
4. Look at the tens column. What are the first two numbers to add in the tens column? What is 1 + 4? *(Pause.)* Now what numbers will you add? What is 5 + 3?	1 + 4 5 5 + 3 8

TEACHER	STUDENTS
How many tens do you end up with?	8 tens
Write the tens under the tens column. *(Monitor student responses.)*	
5. You're finished. What does 45 + 38 equal?	83
Read the problem and say the answer.	45 + 38 = 83
(Repeat steps 1–5 with remaining examples.)	

PART C: LESS STRUCTURED WORKSHEET

(Give students a worksheet containing some problems that involve renaming and some that do not.)

47	53	42	78
+25	+24	−31	+18
78	56	75	26
+21	+36	−23	+43

TEACHER	STUDENTS
1. Everyone, read problem one on your worksheet.	47 + 25
What type of problem is this, addition or subtraction?	Addition
2. What are the first two numbers you add?	7 + 5
What is 7 + 5? *(Pause.)*	12
3. Do you have to move a ten over to the tens column?	Yes
4. Now work the problem on your own. *(Pause.)*	
5. What does 47 + 25 equal?	72
(Repeat steps 1–5 with remaining problems.)	

FORMAT 7.7   Complex Addition Facts with a Total Less than 20

TEACHER	STUDENTS
PART A: STRUCTURED PRESENTATION	
1. I want to add 15 + 3 in my head.	
2. Fifteen equals 10 + 5, so when we add 15 + 3, we add 10 and *(pause)* 5 + 3. When we add 15 + 3, we add 10 and what numbers?	5 + 3
3. What is 5 + 3? *(Pause.)*	8
What is 10 + 8?	18
So what is 15 + 3?	18
4. Say the whole statement.	15 + 3 = 18
(Repeat steps 1–4 with 14 + 2, 11 + 4, 14 + 3, 15 + 3, 12 + 2. Give individual turns on steps 1–3.)	
PART B: LESS STRUCTURED PRESENTATION	
1. Listen: 14 + 3. What does 14 equal?	10 + 4
2. So when we add 14 + 3, we add 10 plus what numbers?	4 + 3
3. What is 4 + 3? *(Pause.)*	7
4. Say the whole statement.	14 + 3 = 17
5. What is 14 + 3?	17

(continued on next page)

FORMAT 7.7 (continued)

TEACHER	STUDENTS
(Repeat with 14 + 5, 12 + 3, 16 + 3, 13 + 4, 15 + 3. Give individual turns to several students.)	

PART C: SUPERVISED PRACTICE

1. What does 11 + 4 equal? *(Pause.)*	15
To correct: *(Use step 1 from Part B.)* Say the whole statement. *(Repeat step with 17 + 2, 14 + 5, 12 + 6, 16 + 3, 11 + 6, 13 + 5. Give individual turns to several students.)*	11 + 4 = 15

FORMAT 7.8   Complex Addition Facts with a Total More Than 20

TEACHER	STUDENTS
PART A: PRESKILL—PLUS-10 FACTS	
1. 14 + 10 is 24. What is 14 + 10? Say the statement. *(Repeat with 17 + 10, 12 + 10.)*	24 14 + 10 = 24
2. What is 13 + 10?	23
To correct: *(Tell answer. Repeat question.)* Say the statement. *(Repeat step 2 with 10 + 10, 18 + 10, 11 + 10, 13 + 10, 15 + 10. Repeat the question until all are consecutively answered correctly.)*	13 + 10 = 23
3. *(Give individual turns to several students.)*	
PART B: STRUCTURED BOARD PRESENTATION	
1. When we add 15 + 7, we add 10 and what numbers?	5 + 7
2. What is 5 + 7? *(Pause.)* What is 12 + 10? So what is 15 + 7? Say the whole statement. *(Repeat steps 1 and 2 with 17 + 7, 16 + 5.)*	12 22 22 15 + 7 = 22
PART C: SUPERVISED PRACTICE	
1. What does 15 + 7 equal? *(Pause.)*	22
To correct: When we add 15 and 7, we add 10 and what? What is 5 + 7? What is 10 + 12? So what is 15 + 7?	
2. *(Repeat step 1 with 17 + 7, 16 + 5, 18 + 8, 15 + 5, 17 + 8.)*	
PART D: INDEPENDENT WORKSHEET	

(Give students worksheets with a mix of complex facts that total 20 or more and complex facts that total less than 20.) Work these problems in your head. Write the answers.

CHAPTER 8

Subtraction

TERMS AND CONCEPTS

subtraction   The removal of a subset from a set. Subtraction is the inverse of addition.

subtrahend   Quantity to be taken away.

minuend   Original quantity from which an amount is subtracted.

difference   The quantity remaining after the subtrahend is taken away from the minuend.

renaming   Rewriting a numeral as a greater unit and a lesser unit; e.g., in 75 − 19, 75 is renamed as 60 + 15.

borrowing   A term formerly used to describe subtraction with regrouping or renaming.

regrouping   Rearranging a quantity of *objects* (not numerals) as a greater and lesser unit; for example, |||||||||||||||||||||||| can be regrouped as ||||||| |||||||||||||||||.

SKILL HIERARCHY

Subtraction instruction, like addition instruction, may be divided into two stages (see the Instructional Sequence and Assessment Chart). During the first stage, introducing the concept, the teacher presents strategies for solving simple subtraction problems with a single-digit minuend, such as 9 − 6 = ; the strategy at this stage involves semiconcrete objects that represent each member in the subtraction problem. The counting, numeral, and equality preskills on the subtraction skill hierarchy are the same as for addition. After subtraction has been taught, problems with a missing subtrahend can be presented. In these problems, all numerals should be below 10 to simplify computation (e.g., 7 − ☐ = 3 and 5 − ☐ = 3). Again, the strategy involves using semiconcrete objects to represent the numerals in a problem. Note that for the purposes of remediation, when working with older students, teachers should not revert to the conceptual introduction but should teach basic facts and the multi-digit operations specified in the Instructional Sequence and Assessment Chart.

In the second stage, multi-digit operations, which usually begins late in first grade, students compute basic facts mentally (without semiconcrete prompts). Basic subtraction facts are the 100 possible combinations in which a one-digit subtrahend is subtracted from a one- or two-digit minuend and the difference is a one-digit number. Procedures for teaching students to answer and eventually memorize basic subtraction facts are discussed in Chapter 6.

Three basic types of column subtraction problems are included in the multi-digit operations stage. The easiest is the problem in which the subtrahend is smaller than the minuend in each column; renaming is not required:

$$
\begin{array}{r}
49 \\
-24 \\
\hline
\end{array}
$$

Instructional Sequence and Assessment Chart

Grade Level	Problem Type	Performance Indicator			
1a	Conceptual introduction				
1b	Subtracting a one- or two-digit number from a two-digit number; no renaming	57 −20	45 −3	28 −4	
2a	Subtracting a one- or two-digit number from a two-digit number; renaming required	54 −18	46 −9	70 −38	
2b	Subtracting a one-, two-, or three-digit number from a three-digit number; renaming tens to ones	382 −37	393 −174	242 −6	
3a	Subtracting a two- or three-digit number from a three-digit number; renaming from hundreds to ten	423 −171	418 −83		
3b	Subtracting a two- or three-digit number from a three-digit number; renaming from tens to ones and hundreds to tens	352 −187	724 −578	534 −87	
3c	Tens minus 1 facts	70 − 1 = ☐ 40 − 1 = ☐ 80 − 1 = ☐			
3d	Subtracting a two- or three-digit number from a three-digit number, zero in tens column; renaming from tens to ones and hundreds to tens	503 −87	504 −21	700 −86	905 −164
3e	Subtracting a three- or four-digit number from a four-digit number; renaming from thousands to hundreds	4689 −1832	5284 −4631	3481 −1681	
3f	Subtracting a one-, two-, three-, or four-digit number from a four-digit number; renaming required in several columns	5342 −68	6143 −217	5231 −1658	
4a	Subtracting a two-, three-, or four-digit number from a four-digit number; a zero in either the tens or hundreds column	4023 −184	5304 −1211	5304 −418	
4b	Hundreds minus 1 facts	700 − 1 = ☐ 400 − 1 = ☐ 800 − 1 = ☐			
4c	Subtracting a one-, two-, three-, or four-digit number from a four-digit number; a zero in the tens and hundreds column	4000 −1357	2001 −1453	8000 −4264	
4d	Same as 4c, except 1,000 as top number	1000 −283	1000 −82	1000 −80	
4e	Same as 4c, except 1,100 as top number	1100 −241	1100 −532	1100 −830	
4f	Subtracting involving five- and six-digit numbers; renaming	342,523 −18,534	480,235 −1,827	38,402 −15,381	

Grade Level	Problem Type	Performance Indicator		
5a	Thousands minus 1 facts	$5000 - 1 = \square$		
		$3000 - 1 = \square$		
		$1000 - 1 = \square$		
5b	Subtracting from a number with four zeroes	$\begin{array}{r}80000\\-826\end{array}$	$\begin{array}{r}50000\\-8260\end{array}$	$\begin{array}{r}10000\\-284\end{array}$

In the second type of problem, one or more columns have a subtrahend which is larger than the minuend:

$$\begin{array}{r}374\\-28\end{array} \qquad \begin{array}{r}5437\\-2859\end{array}$$

Such problems require renaming, or *borrowing:*

$$\begin{array}{r}34\\-15\end{array} \quad \text{becomes} \quad \begin{array}{r}{}^{2}\!\!\!\not3{}^{1}\!4\\-15\end{array}$$

Students need not have memorized all basic subtraction facts before problems with renaming are introduced. They should, however, know enough facts to allow teachers to include a variety of renaming problems.

The third type includes more complex column subtraction problems that require renaming. Included are problems with zeroes in the minuend:

$$\begin{array}{r}306\\-216\end{array} \quad \text{becomes} \quad \begin{array}{r}{}^{2}\!\!\not3{}^{9}\!\!\not0{}^{1}\!6\\-219\end{array}$$

$$\text{and} \quad \begin{array}{r}4000\\-258\end{array} \quad \text{becomes} \quad \begin{array}{r}{}^{3}\!\!\not4{}^{9}\!\!\not0{}^{9}\!\!\not0{}^{1}\!0\\-258\end{array}$$

and problems with renaming in consecutive columns:

$$\begin{array}{r}421\\-247\end{array} \quad \text{or} \quad \begin{array}{r}6342\\-4971\end{array}$$

A more complete listing of problem types and a suggested sequence of introduction appears in the Instructional Sequence and Assessment Chart.

INTRODUCING THE CONCEPT

Subtraction is usually introduced in first grade through demonstrations with semiconcrete objects. A number of alternative demonstrations are sug-

gested in elementary mathematics textbooks. Among these are diagrams using pictures of objects; for example, $5 - 3$ is represented as

Another approach is the use of number lines; for example, $8 - 3$ is represented as

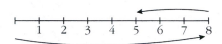

This text recommends a strategy that uses lines as semiconcrete objects. The strategy teaches minusing as crossing out; for example, $7 - 4$ is represented as

We recommend delaying the introduction of subtraction until students have demonstrated mastery of the regular addition strategy. However, subtraction may be introduced prior to or after addition problems with missing addends.

Beginning Subtraction Strategy

In the crossing-out strategy recommended here, the student first draws the number of lines for the minuend, then subtracts by crossing out the number of lines indicated by the subtrahend:

$$6 - 4 = \blacksquare$$

Next, the student counts the remaining lines and draws an equal number of lines on the other side of the equal:

$$6 - 4 = \blacksquare$$

Finally, the student writes the numeral representing that set of lines:

$$6 - 4 = \boxed{2}$$
$$|\,|\,|\!\!\!/\!\!\!/\!\!\!/\!\!\!/\qquad|\,|$$

Format 8.1 shows the format for introducing subtraction. Note that *minus* is used as a verb: "How many lines are you going to minus?" Since students have already learned to identify the minus sign, they learn that the minus sign tells them to cross out lines. Later, the term *subtraction* is introduced, and students learn that a minus tells them to subtract.

In parts A and B of the format, the teacher presents structured board and worksheet exercises focusing solely on the preskill task of crossing out lines and counting the remaining lines. Since line drawing is a fine motor skill, many students in beginning arithmetic instruction may require extensive practice before they become proficient in crossing out the appropriate number of lines. Part C is a structured worksheet exercise in which the teacher leads students as they work entire problems, drawing lines for the first group, crossing out lines for the amount to be "minused," counting how many lines they end with, and then applying the equality rule. The minuend in subtraction problems should be 10 or less so that drawing lines does not become too cumbersome. Part D, the less structured worksheet exercise, is the critical part of the format. The worksheet includes a mix of addition and subtraction problems. Instructionally naive students often have difficulty discriminating which of the two similar problem-solving strategies to use. The format must provide a

great deal of systematic practice in helping students make this discrimination. The less structured and supervised practice worksheets should also contain an equal mix of addition and subtraction problems. Supervised practice is continued until students can work problems with 80 to 90% accuracy.

Missing Subtrahend Problems

Missing subtrahend problems (e.g., $7 - \square = 3$, $8 - \square = 1$) can be introduced when the students can do a worksheet including a mix of addition, regular subtraction, and addition problems with missing addends with 80 to 90% accuracy. Since the strategy for working this type of problem is relatively difficult to teach (students must circle some lines and cross out the remaining lines), we recommend not presenting the strategy during the beginning stage unless specified by the school district's curriculum guidelines. The missing addend problems provide an ample demonstration of the equality principle.

The strategy for missing subtrahend problems includes the steps shown in Summary Box 8.1.

A specific format is not included for missing subtrahend problems, since many programs do not teach the skill. The format is similar to that for the missing addend operation. The teacher has the students (a) draw lines under the numeral, (b) circle the number of lines representing the difference, (c) cross out the remaining lines, and (d) count crossed-out lines and write the appropriate numeral in the empty box.

The teacher introduces the entire strategy in structured board and worksheet exercises, stressing the equality principle. Finally, the teacher presents a

---

Summary Box 8.1
Subtraction: Missing Subtrahend Strategy

1. Students read problem.

2. Students draw lines under minuend.

3. Students determine the number they must end with on both sides.

4. Students circle three of the seven lines, since they must end with three to make sides equal.

5. Students cross out uncircled lines.

6. Students count crossed-out lines and write numeral in the box.

Seven minus how many equals three?

$$7 - \boxed{} = 3$$
$$|\,|\,|\,|\,|\,|\,|$$

$$7 - \boxed{} = 3$$
$$\textcircled{|\,|\,|}\,|\,|\,|\,|$$

$$7 - \boxed{} = 3$$
$$\textcircled{|\,|\,|}\,/\!\!\!/\!\!\!/\!\!\!/$$

$$7 - \boxed{4} = 3$$
$$\textcircled{|\,|\,|}\,/\!\!\!/\!\!\!/\!\!\!/$$

less structured worksheet exercise that includes a mix of subtraction, missing subtrahend, addition, and missing addend problems.

Diagnosis and Remediation

Diagnosis and remediation procedures for beginning subtraction problems are very similar to those discussed for beginning addition problems. The basic steps below apply to diagnosing and remedying errors:

1. The teacher analyzes worksheet errors and hypothesizes the cause of the errors.
2. The teacher interviews the student to determine the cause of the errors if the cause is not obvious.
3. The teacher provides reteaching through board and/or worksheet presentations.
4. The teacher tests the student on a set of problems similar to the ones on which the original errors were made.

Once students begin working problems independently on their worksheets, their errors usually fall into two main categories:

1. Component-skill errors that indicate a deficit on one or more of the component skills that make up the strategy.
2. Strategy errors in which steps are omitted, applied in the wrong order, or replaced by incorrect steps. Strategy errors are remedied by reintroducing the structured board or worksheet format. Until the remedy is complete, problems of that type should not appear on the independent worksheets.

COMPONENT-SKILL ERRORS. Component-skill errors are often difficult to diagnose. Note that in this problem, the student's error may have resulted from misidentifying 3 as 4 or simply not crossing out the correct number of lines: 9 − 3 = ⑤

The teacher can determine the specific cause of errors by looking for patterns. If a student works all of the problems correctly except those that include the numeral 3, the cause of errors would be the misidentification of the numeral 3. In addition to looking for patterns, the teacher can observe students working problems, asking the students to read each problem and describe what they are doing as they work it.

Once the teacher determines the specific component-skill deficit, he works on that specific skill for

several lessons. If the skill is one that would cause students to miss many problems (e.g., a skill such as crossing out lines), the teacher would not present any subtraction problems until the students can perform the component skill independently. If the component skill is one which causes students to miss just some problems (e.g., numeral misidentification), the teacher excludes subtraction problems with that feature from independent worksheet assignments until the students demonstrate mastery of that component skill.

A common component-skill error, which occurs soon after subtraction appears on worksheets, is confusing signs and adding rather than subtracting. Teachers can expect most students to make this error occasionally. However, a remediation procedure is necessary when the error occurs frequently (in more than 10% of problems). The remediation procedure involves reintroducing the less structured worksheet format that provides guided practice on discriminating addition and subtraction problems.

Fact Memorization

Students need an understanding of the subtraction operation, which the crossing-out strategy provides. However, students also must learn to memorize the subtraction facts to reduce difficulties in learning multi-digit operations. Fact memorization instruction should begin as soon as students reach the 80 to 90% accuracy criterion during supervised practice.

MULTI-DIGIT SUBTRACTION PROBLEMS

This section deals with subtraction problems with multi-digit numbers. A critical component skill of multi-digit problems is renaming (borrowing). Two basic renaming strategies are suggested in mathematics texts. The first, the additive balancing or equal addends method, involves adding a tens unit to both the subtrahend and the minuend. In solving a problem with two digit numbers, the tens unit is added to the ones column of the top numeral, while the tens unit is added to the tens column of the bottom numeral:

$$\begin{array}{r} 73 \\ -48 \\ \hline 25 \end{array} \quad \text{becomes} \quad \begin{array}{r} {}^{1}73 \\ -5\llap{/}48 \\ \hline 25 \end{array}$$

This involves application of the compensation principle for subtraction: *The difference between two numbers is unaltered by the addition of the same amount to both terms.* In turn, the compensation principle includes the equality principle. Since few students know the compensation principle, and many don't know the equality principle, the equal addends strategy tends not to be understood by most students.

The second method, sometimes called the decomposition or borrowing method, involves renaming the minuend so that a unit from a higher order column is written in a lower order column:

$$
73 \quad \text{becomes} \quad \overset{6}{\cancel{7}}\overset{1}{3}
$$

$$
\begin{array}{r} 73 \\ -48 \\ \hline 25 \end{array} \qquad \begin{array}{r} \overset{6}{\cancel{7}}\overset{1}{3} \\ -48 \\ \hline 25 \end{array}
$$

Note that the minuend 73 has been rewritten as 60 and 13.

Teaching Procedure

The direct instruction procedures are based on the renaming (borrowing) method, since this method is used by most teachers in North America. The procedures emphasize knowing when to rename and the mechanics of renaming. The conceptual understanding of renaming is also emphasized, but in separate exercises from those for teaching the mechanics of working problems. This separation is done to simplify the formats for teaching the mechanics.

Three main groups of problems are discussed in this chapter: (a) problems that do not require renaming, (b) problems that require renaming and in which the student may "borrow" from the next column, and (c) problems requiring renaming in two consecutive columns, including problems with a zero in the column that must be renamed.

Column Subtraction—No Renaming

Since column subtraction problems that do not require renaming are taught in basically the same way as addition problems that do not require renaming, we have not included a format. Also, as was the case for addition, we recommend not introducing column problems until students have memorized approximately 12 facts. In working subtraction problems, students subtract in the ones column and then in the tens column. Also, as in addition, students read the number of tens in the tens column rather than the quantity represented by the numerals: They

would say, "Three tens minus two tens," rather than "30 minus 20."

Subtraction with Renaming

Simple renaming problems include types 2a, 2b, 3a, and 3b from the Instructional Sequence and Assessment Chart. Problem type 2a is the first subtraction problem type that involves renaming. It is usually introduced during mid-second grade. The three preskills for solving this problem type are (a) the place-value-related skills inherent in reading and writing numerals over 10, (b) knowledge of at least six facts that can be used for borrowing (i.e., facts in which the first number is ten or more), and (c) a conceptual understanding of renaming. Format 8.2 includes a process to teach the concept of regrouping (with objects), which builds the foundation for renaming (with numerals).

Format 8.2 presents a diagram showing several packages, each of which contains 10 objects and several single objects. The teacher tells a story that involves giving away some of those objects: "A boy has 34 nails. He wants to give 8 nails to his sister." The teacher points out that to give 8 nails to his sister, the boy will have to open a package of 10. The teacher erases one pack of 10 nails and draws 10 single nails. The teacher then erases 8 nails and counts the remaining packages and single nails. This format, with similar examples, is presented for several days prior to introducing the renaming format.

The procedures for introducing the computation for renaming appears in Format 8.3, which contains five parts. In Part A, students discriminate when renaming is necessary. This discrimination is critical in preventing mistakes in which students subtract the smaller from the larger number regardless of which number is on top (e.g., in $74 - 38$, students take 4 from 8). The teacher presents this rule: *When we take away more than we start with, we must rename.* This rule is not intended to be absolutely mathematically correct but serves as a functional rule to teach the concept. After presenting this rule, the teacher leads students in applying the rule. The teacher points to the top number in the ones column and asks the students how many they are starting with, then points to the numeral below it and asks whether they must rename if they take away that number. Example selection is critical in this format. The teacher must include an unpredictable mix of problems, some requiring renaming and some not.

Part A should be presented for several lessons. The teacher should then test each student individually on a set of about seven problems, asking of each, "Do we have to rename in this problem?" Student performance determines what the teacher does next. If students miss no more than one of the seven problems, the teacher can present Part B, in which the strategy for working problems is presented. If students miss more than one question, Part A is presented for several more lessons.

Part B introduces the renaming component skill. The teacher explains to the students that they rename by borrowing a ten and putting it with the ones number. In 75 − 38, they borrow a ten from the seven tens and put it with the five ones. After modeling several problems, the teacher tests students, making sure they can follow the steps for renaming.

Parts C and D are structured board and worksheet exercises in which the entire strategy is presented. Part E is a less structured worksheet exercise that includes an equal mix of problems that do and do not require renaming. Supervised practice exercises should be included in lessons until students can perform with 80 to 90% accuracy. After several days of supervised practice with only subtraction problems, the teacher should include some addition problems for discrimination practice.

Problems requiring renaming become more difficult as the number of digits in the minuend and subtrahend increase. The structured format for presenting each new problem type is quite similar to the structured format just discussed. For example, when problems involving renaming hundreds are introduced, the teacher would first ask the students to identify what they are starting with and taking away in the tens column and then ask if it is necessary to rename to work the problem. The teacher then leads students through solving the problem. In multidigit problems that require renaming in several columns, the teacher leads the students through working each column, always asking, "What does the column tell us to do?... Must we rename?"

The examples for the less structured, supervised practice, and independent worksheets should include a mix of the currently introduced and previously introduced problem types. When the first problems requiring borrowing from tens are introduced, about three quarters of the problems should involve subtraction and one quarter, addition. Of the subtraction problems, only about half should require renaming. When problems involving borrowing from the hundreds are introduced, half of the subtraction problems should require borrowing from the hundreds; a quarter, from the tens; and a quarter should not require borrowing.

Some addition problems should also be included. Figure 8.1 is an example of a worksheet that could be presented after problems requiring borrowing

FIGURE 8.1   Sample Worksheet with Renaming Problems

a. 392	b. 346	c. 423	d. 728	e. 547
− 81	−118	−180	+324	− 83

f. 547	g. 285	h. 248	i. 347	j. 236
+38	−84	−58	−109	−46

from the hundreds are taught. Note the mixture of problem types: c, e, h, and j require borrowing from hundreds; b and i, from tens; a and g do not require renaming; and d and f are addition.

SELF-CHECKING. After students become proficient in working renaming problems, they should be taught to check their answers. A checking procedure for subtraction is adding the subtrahend and the difference. The teacher introduces checking on a worksheet exercise. After the students complete the first problem, the teacher says,

> Here's how to check your answer to a subtraction problem. Add the bottom two numbers. What's the answer?... Is that the same as the top number in the problem? So your answer is correct.

To demonstrate why the checking procedure works, teachers should use simple problems like 12 − 8 = 4. The teacher uses the same questions: "Add the bottom two numbers ... What's the answer?... Is that the same as the top number? ..." With familiar facts, students more readily see that the procedure "makes sense." The same type of exercise suggested for encouraging students to use the addition self-check can be used to encourage students to check their subtraction work. Teachers give students a worksheet with some problems worked correctly and some incorrectly. Students are asked to find the problems worked incorrectly by using the self-check strategy.

Complex Renaming Problems

This group includes problems in which several consecutive columns must be renamed. First we discuss problems that do not include zeroes in the minuend. Working such problems does not involve new skills, just applying the renaming skill in consecutive columns. Errors often occur because students become confused over the crossed-out digits. When the problem 327 − 149 is worked, the number in the tens column is 11, neither digit of which comes from the original problem:

$$
\begin{array}{r}
\overset{2}{}\overset{1}{}\overset{1}{} \\
\cancel{3}\cancel{2}7 \\
-149 \\
\hline
178
\end{array}
$$

An important aspect of the teaching procedure is closely monitoring students as they write on their worksheets. Students who are not careful will make errors because of extensive crossing out and rewriting. Therefore, teachers should stress precisely where numerals are to be written.

Students encounter more difficulty with problems that require renaming zero. Types 3d, 4a, 4c, 4d, 4e, and 5b from the Instructional Sequence and Assessment Chart are examples of problems in which a number with a zero is renamed. The basic strategy students are taught is to rename several digits at once. For example, in the problem

$$
\begin{array}{r}
304 \\
-87 \\
\hline
\end{array}
$$

students treat the 3 hundreds as 30 tens. When they do this (borrow 1 ten from the 30 tens), the 30 is crossed out and replaced with 29:

$$
\begin{array}{r}
\overset{2\ 9}{}\overset{1}{} \\
3\cancel{0}4 \\
-87 \\
\hline
\end{array}
$$

Students would follow a similar procedure when working problems containing zeroes in both the tens and hundreds columns:

$$
\begin{array}{r}
3\cancel{0}\cancel{0}2 \\
-89 \\
\hline
\end{array}
$$

The students would treat the 3000 as 300 tens, crossing out the 300, writing 299 in its place, and putting a 10 in the ones column. This procedure was suggested by Cacha (1975) as a means of simplifying renaming that involved zeroes.

A preskill for solving problem types that involve renaming numbers with zeroes is learning the tens-numbers-minus-one facts, such as $60 - 1$, $90 - 1$, $40 - 1$. These facts are presented about a week prior to introducing problems such as

$$
\begin{array}{r}
407 \\
-129 \\
\hline
\end{array}
$$

The format for teaching tens-numbers-minus-one facts consists of two steps. First, the teacher says a tens number (a two-digit number ending in zero) and asks the students to indicate what number precedes it. "What number comes before 80?" Second, the teacher introduces the rule that when you minus 1, you say the number that comes just before. Then the teacher has the students apply the rule to a series of examples. The entire procedure appears in Format 8.4.

Once students have mastered the tens-minus-one preskill, they can be presented with the format for renaming numbers with a zero, which appears in Format 8.5. The format has three parts. Part A includes a board demonstration by the teacher of how to work the problem. Part B includes steps in which the teacher guides students through solving problems on their worksheets. Part C is a less structured worksheet guide. During the structured board and worksheet exercises, each problem should require renaming. In Part C, the less structured worksheet exercise, students are presented with a mix of problems—half require renaming and half do not. For example, a typical worksheet might look like Figure 8.2. In about half of the problems, the numbers in the ones column require borrowing; in the other half of the problems, borrowing in the ones column is not required. The mix is very important to prevent students from developing the misrule of always borrowing when they see a zero in the tens column. The importance of mixing problems on the less structured, supervised practice, and independent worksheets cannot be overemphasized. If the examples used are not carefully designed to provide discrimination practice, the students might develop a serious misrule of always crossing out the hundreds number and zero, as in the problem below:

$$
\begin{array}{r@{\qquad}r}
\overset{2\ 9}{} & \overset{3\ 9}{} \\
3\cancel{0}2 & 4\cancel{0}2 \\
-41 & -52 \\
\hline
251 & 340
\end{array}
$$

Problem types become more complex as the number of digits increases, particularly the number of zeroes involved in renaming. In problem type 4c of the Instructional Sequence and Assessment Chart, numbers with two zeroes are renamed, as in

FIGURE 8.2 Worksheet Problems for Renaming with Zeroes

1. 402 – 69	2. 503 –161	3. 305 – 65	4. 302 – 86	5. 504 –128
6. 703 – 42	7. 500 – 36	8. 300 – 40	9. 700 – 4	10. 206 – 36
11. 508 – 32	12. 500 – 26	13. 300 – 20	14. 501 – 61	15. 302 – 48

3004
−86

The preskill for this type of problem is hundreds-minus-one facts (e.g., 800 − 1, 300 − 1). The teaching procedure for hundreds-minus-one facts is basically the same as for tens-minus-one facts. The teacher presents the structured board and worksheet formats using basically the same wording as in Format 8.5. The only difference is that the teacher points out that in a problem such as

3004
−128

students borrow from 300 tens. "What are you going to borrow one ten from? What is 300 minus 1 ?... So cross out 300 and write 299." Again, the less structured worksheet exercise is the critical part of the format. The worksheet should include a mix of problems like that in Figure 8.3.

In some problems, students must rename in the ones column. In some problems, students rename in the tens column. In still others, students must rename in the hundreds column. Teachers can expect students to need a great deal of supervised practice on this before they reach an acceptable accuracy criterion.

Two additional problem types that may cause students difficulty require borrowing from the numbers 10, 100, 1000, or 1100 (problem types 4d and 4e). Problems in which the student must borrow from 10, 100, or 1000 may cause difficulty because the students do not replace each digit with another digit, as in

7991
8004

Instead, they only replace two of the three digits, as in

99
100

991   7991
1004   with   8004

FIGURE 8.3   Sample Worksheet: Renaming with Two or More Zeroes

a. 3004	b. 3004	c. 3001	d. 7005	e. 7005
− 289	− 302	−1394	−2101	−2104

f. 7005	g. 6000	h. 6000	i. 4000
−1149	− 80	− 8	− 50

Without instruction, students may write the nines in the wrong columns:

99
1000
−193
9807

The teaching procedure for these problems need not be elaborate. The teacher merely models working several problems and then supervises students as they work the problems.

Diagnosis and Remediation

FACT ERRORS. Basic fact errors usually are obvious. For example, in problems a and b below, the student has made obvious errors involving the facts 13 − 6 and 12 − 8 respectively.

a.   31
     435
     −162
     283

b.   41
     528
     −186
     352

The remediation procedure for fact errors depends on their frequency. An occasional error is addressed by stressing the missed fact in practice exercises. A pattern in which students make several errors on different facts requires a more complete remediation procedure. The teacher determines the strategy used by the students to derive the basic facts. This can be done by observing students as they work problems. Teachers may find some students relying on their fingers. The remediation procedure for such students is discussed in Chapter 6. Other students may not rely on using their fingers but, nonetheless, may be inaccurate, answering a basic fact correctly in one problem but incorrectly in the next problem. The remediation procedure for such students involves first working on developing accuracy in computing basic facts. The emphasis on facts should result in improved performance on column subtraction problems. If, however, the student continues making random fact errors in column subtraction problems, the teacher may tentatively consider the problem to be one of motivation and consider implementing strategies to increase student motivation.

STRATEGY ERRORS. Errors caused by failure to rename are illustrated below. In problem a, the error is in the ones column. In problem b, the error is in the hundreds column.

```
a.   342        b.   2584
    −128            −1827
    ‾‾‾‾            ‾‾‾‾‾
    226             1361
```

Again, the frequency of the error must be considered before remediation is planned. An occasional error, occurring no more than in 1 out of 10 problems, needs no extensive remediation. The teacher merely has students rework the problem. More frequent errors of this type require more in-depth remediation, beginning with Part A of Format 8.3. Part A focuses on when renaming is required. The teacher writes several problems similar to the ones missed by the student. The teacher points to each column in a problem, asking if renaming is required to work that column. This exercise is continued until students can respond correctly to four or five problems consecutively. Next the teacher leads the students through a structured worksheet exercise with several problems (Part D in Format 8.3), then through less structured worksheet problems (Part E). Finally, the teacher has students work a group of problems as she closely monitors. This set of problems should include a mix of problem types so that the teacher can be sure students are discriminating when renaming is required. The exercise is continued daily until students perform accurately on independent assignments for several days in a row.

COMPONENT-SKILL ERRORS. These errors in the mechanics of borrowing are illustrated below:

```
        1              6 1            20 1
a.     35      b.      5̶4̶     c.     3̶0̶2
      −16            −28            −54
      ‾‾‾            ‾‾‾            ‾‾‾
       29             46              8
```

In problem a, the student forgot to subtract a 10 from the three 10 after borrowing. This error is not uncommon when borrowing is first introduced. For remediation, students are given practice rewriting two-digit numerals. Teachers might use the following wording:

> You're going to practice renaming. Touch the first numeral (check). What do you do first to rename this number? Do it. Write a 1 to show one ten. Remember to cross out and write a new tens number.

The error in problem b indicates the student is adding rather than subtracting the 10 when renaming. The remediation procedure begins with the teacher drawing attention to the fact that when you borrow a 10, you must *take away* a 10. The teacher then follows the same procedure as described for problem a.

The error in problem c indicates that the student either is having difficulty with tens-numbers-minus-one facts or is confused regarding the strategy to use. The teacher should watch the student work several problems. If the problem relates to tens-minus-one facts, the teacher reteaches tens-minus-one facts (e.g., 60 − 1, 30 − 1, 80 − 1, etc.) from Format 8.4. When students demonstrate mastery of tens-minus-one facts, they are presented with the less structured part of the format for that type of problem. If the error reflects a strategy error, the teacher repeats the entire format.

A special group of problems that may cause students difficulty are problems with a zero in the ones column of the minuend or subtrahend:

```
    70          74
   −34         −30
```

Students often become confused working problems with zero, answering 70 − 34 as 44 or 74 − 30 as 40. If teachers note errors with this problem type, a special exercise comprised of problems like the ones below should be given. Teachers would first review minus-zero facts, pointing out that when you minus zero, you end with the same number you start with, then lead students through working the problems. The exercise is continued until students can work the problems with 90% accuracy for several days in a row.

```
    60        64        40        43
   −34       −30       −20       −20

    40        78        70
   −23       −30       −38
```

A summary of the diagnosis and remediation procedures for subtraction appears in Figure 8.4.

COMMERCIAL PROGRAMS

Subtraction: Renaming

INSTRUCTIONAL STRATEGIES. As in addition with renaming, most basal programs advocate the use of manipulatives when introducing renaming in subtraction. Interestingly, many programs we examined also include picture representations of the manipulatives on the introductory pages (e.g., pictures of sticks). However, little direction is given to the students on how to work the problems without the manipulatives.

PREREQUISITE SKILLS. Most programs identify key prerequisite skills and preteach these skills before the instructional strategy is introduced. However,

FIGURE 8.4   Diagnosis and Remediation of Subtraction Errors

Sample Patterns		Sample Diagnosis	Remediation Procedures	Remediation Examples
a. $\overset{\scriptstyle 3\,1}{\cancel{4}37}$ $\underline{-180}$ 247	63 $\underline{-28}$ 34	Fact error: 13 – 8	Emphasis on 13 – 8 in fact drill.	
b. $\overset{\scriptstyle 1}{34}$ $\underline{-18}$ 26	$\overset{\scriptstyle 1}{352}$ $\underline{-\;71}$ 381	Component skill: Student did not rename column borrowed from.	You're going to practice rewriting. Touch the first numeral (check). What do you do first to rewrite this number? . . . Do it. Write a 1 to show one ten. Remember to cross out and write a new number for the first digit.	For examples, present a worksheet with these numerals: a. 27 b. 38 c. 71 d. 42
c. 34 $\underline{-18}$ 24	72 $\underline{-36}$ 44	Strategy: Renaming not done.	Present renaming format starting with Part A, in Format 8.3.	Examples specified for Format 8.3.
d. $\overset{\scriptstyle 29\,1}{\cancel{3}\cancel{0}4}$ $\underline{-\;21}$ 2713	$\overset{\scriptstyle 5\,1}{\cancel{6}4}$ $\underline{-24}$ 310	Strategy: Renaming was done unnecessarily.	Same as c	Same as c
e. $\overset{\scriptstyle 7\,1}{\cancel{6}3}$ $\underline{-48}$ 35	$\overset{\scriptstyle 3\,1}{\cancel{6}1}$ $\underline{-\;2}$ 39	Fact error: Minus 1.	a. Present minus-1 facts b. Present less-structured worksheet for the particular problem type.	Mix: some problems require renaming, and some do not. Renaming problems sample all types introduced to date.
f. 35 $\underline{-14}$ 49		Component skill: Sign discrimination; student added instead of subtracting.	a. Present less-structured part of Format 8.3 Have student circle sign, then work the problem.	Equal mix of addition and subtraction.
g. $\overset{\scriptstyle 21\,1\downarrow}{\cancel{3}04}$ $\underline{-\;26}$ 288		Component skill: Problems with zero in tens column; inappropriate renaming.	a. Present tens-minus-1 preskill (if necessary). b. Present the format for renaming numbers with zeroes (Format 8.5)	6–8 problems Examples specified for Format 8.5
h. $\overset{\scriptstyle 29\,1}{\cancel{3}\cancel{0}2}$ $\underline{-\;41}$ 2511	$\overset{\scriptstyle 39\,1}{\cancel{4}\cancel{0}2}$ $\underline{-\;52}$ 3410	Strategy: Renaming unnecessarily.	Format 8.5, Part C	Example specified for Format 8.5

often the prerequisites are introduced with only a few examples the same day or a day before the strategy instruction. Teachers should allow time for students to master the prerequisites prior to introducing the strategy. Also, they should determine whether *all* necessary prerequisites have been addressed. (See chapter 7 for a thorough discussion of the preskills to teach before introducing a renaming strategy.)

PRACTICE AND REVIEW. Some programs provide sufficient initial practice on two-digit subtraction problems with renaming. While this is an adequate amount of practice initially, little further review of subtraction typically occurs until the next level of the series. This lack of review can be attributed to the spiral curriculum design employed by the majority of math programs. To maintain student success over time, adequate review on a continual basis must be provided.

Application Items: Subtraction

1. Below are Mary's and Alex's performances on a set of performance indicators. Specify the problem type with which instruction should begin for each student.

Mary

3a.
$$\begin{array}{r} \overset{3}{4}23 \\ -171 \\ \hline 252 \end{array} \quad \begin{array}{r} \overset{3}{4}18 \\ -83 \\ \hline 335 \end{array} \quad \begin{array}{r} \overset{1}{2}\cancel{2}8 \\ -137 \\ \hline 91 \end{array}$$

3b.
$$\begin{array}{r} \overset{4}{3}\overset{1}{5}2 \\ -187 \\ \hline 245 \end{array} \quad \begin{array}{r} \overset{1}{7}\overset{1}{2}4 \\ -578 \\ \hline 266 \end{array} \quad \begin{array}{r} \overset{2}{5}\overset{1}{3}4 \\ -87 \\ \hline 567 \end{array}$$

3c. 70 − 1 = **69**
    40 − 1 = **39**
    80 − 1 = **79**

3d.
$$\begin{array}{r} \overset{4}{5}03 \\ -87 \\ \hline 486 \end{array} \quad \begin{array}{r} \overset{4}{5}\overset{1}{0}4 \\ -26 \\ \hline 428 \end{array} \quad \begin{array}{r} 700 \\ -86 \\ \hline 786 \end{array}$$

3e.
$$\begin{array}{r} 4689 \\ -1832 \\ \hline 3257 \end{array} \quad \begin{array}{r} \overset{4}{5}\overset{1}{2}84 \\ -4631 \\ \hline 653 \end{array} \quad \begin{array}{r} 3481 \\ -1681 \\ \hline 2201 \end{array}$$

Alex

3a.
$$\begin{array}{r} \overset{3}{4}\overset{1}{2}3 \\ -171 \\ \hline 252 \end{array} \quad \begin{array}{r} \overset{3}{4}\overset{1}{1}8 \\ -83 \\ \hline 335 \end{array} \quad \begin{array}{r} \overset{1}{2}28 \\ -137 \\ \hline 91 \end{array}$$

3b.
$$\begin{array}{r} \overset{4}{3}\overset{1}{5}2 \\ -187 \\ \hline 245 \end{array} \quad \begin{array}{r} \overset{1}{7}\overset{1}{2}4 \\ -578 \\ \hline 266 \end{array} \quad \begin{array}{r} \overset{2}{5}\overset{1}{3}4 \\ -87 \\ \hline 567 \end{array}$$

3c. 70 − 1 = **69**
    40 − 1 = **39**
    80 − 1 = **79**

3d.
$$\begin{array}{r} \overset{49}{5}\overset{1}{0}3 \\ -87 \\ \hline 415 \end{array} \quad \begin{array}{r} \overset{49}{5}\cancel{0}4 \\ -26 \\ \hline 478 \end{array} \quad \begin{array}{r} \overset{69}{7}\cancel{0}0 \\ -86 \\ \hline 614 \end{array}$$

3e.
$$\begin{array}{r} \overset{1}{4}689 \\ -1832 \\ \hline 3857 \end{array} \quad \begin{array}{r} 5284 \\ -4631 \\ \hline 1453 \end{array} \quad \begin{array}{r} 3481 \\ -1681 \\ \hline 2200 \end{array}$$

2. Below is an excerpt of the independent worksheet to be given to students who have just demonstrated accuracy in solving problem type 3a. The teacher made some errors in constructing the worksheet.

   a. Indicate the inappropriate examples and specify the problem type.
   b. Identify any omitted problem types that should be included on the worksheet.

   a. $\begin{array}{r} 524 \\ -186 \end{array}$ b. $\begin{array}{r} 504 \\ -328 \end{array}$ c. $\begin{array}{r} 324 \\ -192 \end{array}$ d. $\begin{array}{r} 533 \\ -261 \end{array}$

   e. $\begin{array}{r} 824 \\ -161 \end{array}$ f. $\begin{array}{r} 602 \\ -159 \end{array}$ g. $\begin{array}{r} 523 \\ -186 \end{array}$ h. $\begin{array}{r} 65 \\ -32 \end{array}$

3. Describe the problem type that each example below represents. List the problems in the order they are introduced. Write the grade level when each problem type is typically introduced.

   $\begin{array}{r} 63 \\ -18 \end{array}$ $\begin{array}{r} 353 \\ -182 \end{array}$ $\begin{array}{r} 48 \\ -23 \end{array}$ $\begin{array}{r} 523 \\ -486 \end{array}$ $\begin{array}{r} 346 \\ -128 \end{array}$ $\begin{array}{r} 503 \\ -87 \end{array}$

4. Below are 12 problems which appeared on the worksheet to be done independently by the students in Mr. Dean's math group. Next to each student's name are the problems missed by the student.

For each student:

   a. Specify the probable cause or causes of the student's error.

   b. Describe the remediation procedure. Be specific (i.e., name format part).

4023	4702	8346	342	7304	430
−1857	−2563	−1895	−185	−1286	−82

2036	3248	3852	402	3826	8306
−518	−1026	−1624	−81	−63	−1243

James

$$\begin{array}{r} \overset{39}{4\cancel{0}2} \\ -81 \\ \hline 311 \end{array} \qquad \begin{array}{r} \overset{29}{\cancel{8306}} \\ -1243 \\ \hline 7053 \end{array}$$

Debbie

$$\begin{array}{r} \overset{391}{4\cancel{02}3} \\ -1857 \\ \hline 2165 \end{array} \qquad \begin{array}{r} \overset{69}{47\cancel{0}2} \\ -2563 \\ \hline 1138 \end{array}$$

Dylan

$$\begin{array}{r} \overset{79}{47\cancel{0}2} \\ -2563 \\ \hline 2239 \end{array}$$

Jack

$$\begin{array}{r} 342 \\ +185 \\ \hline 157 \end{array} \qquad \begin{array}{r} 3852 \\ +1624 \\ \hline 228 \end{array}$$

5. Specify the wording the teacher would use in the structured worksheet presentation for the problem.

$$\begin{array}{r} 314 \\ -182 \\ \hline \end{array}$$

6. In presenting Format 8.3, Part A, a board format for introducing renaming problems, the teacher asks for this problem, "Must we rename?" The student says "No." Specify the wording the teacher uses in making the correction.

$$\begin{array}{r} 57 \\ -28 \\ \hline \end{array}$$

7. Below are partial worksheets made by several teachers for the less structured part of the format for teaching students to work problems that require borrowing from the hundreds column. Two teachers constructed unacceptable lists. Identify these teachers and tell why each list is unacceptable. For each unacceptable list, specify what could be done to make the list acceptable.

a.	342	623	483	362	534	235	427	329	427
	−181	−182	−193	−181	−184	+132	−193	−152	−121

b.	383	432	342	282	346	425	524	473	392
	−195	−150	−186	−195	−138	+132	−187	−197	−161

c.	428	328	526	48	362	364	325	436	329
	−368	−209	−385	−29	−182	−148	+132	−214	+142

FORMAT 8.1   Subtraction with Lines

TEACHER	STUDENTS

PART A: STRUCTURED BOARD PRESENTATION—PRESKILL OF MINUSING LINES

1. *(Write the following problem and lines on the board.)*

   6 – 2
   | | | | | |

Everyone, read this problem.	6 – 2
This is a minus problem. What kind of problem is this?	A minus problem

2. *(Point to minus 2.)* What does this say? | Minus 2
   Minus 2 tells us to cross out two lines. |

What does minus 2 tell us to do? Watch me cross out two lines. *(Draw two minuses through two lines and count each time.)* Minus 1, Minus 2.	Cross out two lines.

3. Let's see how many lines we have left. I'll touch and you count. | 1, 2, 3, 4

   How many did we end up with? | 4
   (Repeat steps 1–3 with 7 – 4, 5 – 3.)

PART B: STRUCTURED WORKSHEET—PRESKILL OF MINUSING LINES
   (Students have worksheets with four to six problems like the one below.)

   6 – 2
   | | | | | |

   (Note that the lines under the first numeral in each problem are already drawn.)

1. Touch problem a on your worksheet. *(Check.)* Read the problem.	6 – 2
What kind of problem is this?	A minus problem
2. Touch the first group. How many lines are in the first group?	6
How many lines are you going to minus?	2
Minus the lines. *(Check that students minus two lines.)*	
To correct: When you minus 2, you cross out two lines.	
3. Now count and see how many lines you have left. *(Pause.)*	
How many did you end with?	4

   (Repeat steps 1–3 with remaining examples.)

PART C: STRUCTURED WORKSHEET—ENTIRE STRATEGY

   5 – 3 = ☐

1. Touch this problem on your worksheet. *(Point to first problem.)* Read the problem.	5 – 3 = how many?
2. What kind of problem is this?	A minus problem
Touch the first group. How many lines are you going to draw? Draw five lines under the 5.	5
3. How many lines are you going to minus?	3
Minus the lines. *(Monitor worksheet responses.)*	
4. Now count and see how many lines you end with. *(Pause.)* How many?	2

TEACHER	STUDENTS

5. So how many must you end with on the other side of the equal?

   Draw two lines and write the numeral in the box.

   2

6. Now read the whole statement.

   5 − 3 = how many?

   Say the statement again.

   5 − 3 = 2

   2

   5 − 3 = 2

(Repeat steps 1–5 with remaining examples.)

PART D: LESS STRUCTURED WORKSHEET

1. *(Give the students a worksheet with an equal mix of addition and subtraction problems.)*

   a. 4 + 3 = ☐   f. 7 − 0 = ☐
   b. 8 − 2 = ☐   g. 8 − 2 = ☐
   c. 7 − 5 = ☐   h. 2 + 4 = ☐
   d. 5 − 4 = ☐   i. 5 + 3 = ☐
   e. 7 + 0 = ☐

   This worksheet is tricky. In some problems you plus, and in some problems you minus. When you plus, you make more lines. What do you do when you plus?

   When you minus, you cross out lines. What do you do when you minus?

   Make more lines.

   Cross out lines.

2. Touch problem a. Read it.
   Is that a plus or minus problem?
   What do you do when you plus?

   4 + 3 = how many?
   Plus problem
   Make more lines.

3. Make the lines under the first group. Then plus/minus.

4. Now make the sides equal and fill in the empty box.

   (Repeat steps 2–4 with the remaining problems.)

FORMAT 8.2 Teaching Regrouping

TEACHER	STUDENTS

1. *(Draw the following boxes on the board.)*

   A boy has nails. He has three packages with 10 nails in each package and 4 nails not in a package. Let's figure out how many nails he has in all. *(Point as you count.)* 10, 20, 30, 31, 32, 33, 34.

2. The boy wants to give 8 nails to his sister. We have a problem. He can't give 8 nails to his sister the way the nails are now. He has 4 nails and packages of 10 nails. He has to regroup the nails. When we regroup, we put a group of 10 with the 4 nails. What do we do when we regroup in this problem?

   Put a group of 10 with 4.

3. We open a pack of 10 nails *(erase a group of 10 nails)* and put the 10 nails over here.
   (Draw the following on the board.)

(continued on next page)

FORMAT 8.2 (continued)

TEACHER	STUDENTS

```
            | | | | |    |
            | | | | |    |
  [10]  [10]             |
                         |
```

4. We still have 34 nails. They're just in different groups. We
   have two groups of 10 and a group of 14.
   Now let's give 8 away. *(Erase 8.)* Let's see how many we
   have left. *(Point to 6)* How many here?   6
   And 2 tens equal how many?   20

   What is 20 and 6? Right, 26. The boy starts with 34. He   26
   gives away 8 and ends with 26.

5. *(Present one or two more problems.)*

FORMAT 8.3 Subtraction with Renaming

TEACHER	STUDENTS

PART A: WHEN TO RENAME

1. *(Write the following problem on the board.)*

   ```
     75
   −49
   ```

   Here's a rule about renaming with subtraction problems:
   When we take away more than we start with, we must
   rename. My turn. When must we rename? When we take
   away more than we start with. Your turn. When do we rename?   When we take away
                                                                    more than we start with.

   (Repeat statement with students until they can say it by themselves.)

2. *(Point to the 5.)* What number are we starting with in the
   ones column?   5

   We're starting with 5 and taking away 9. Must we rename?
   (Pause and signal.)   Yes

   Right, we have to rename because we're taking away more
   than we start with; 9 is more than 5.

3. *(Write the following problem on the board.)*

   ```
     75
   −43
   ```

   What number are we starting with in the ones column?   5
   What are we taking away?   3
   Must we rename if we take away 3? *(Pause, signal.)*   No
   We don't rename. We're not taking away more than we start with.

4. *(Write the next problem on the board.)*

   ```
     38
   −27
   ```

TEACHER	**STUDENTS**
What are we starting out with now in the ones column?	8
What are we taking away?	7
Must we rename? *(Pause, signal.)*	No
Why?	We're not taking away more than we start with.

5. *(Repeat step 4 with these problems.)*

$$\begin{array}{r} 38 \\ -29 \end{array} \qquad \begin{array}{r} 42 \\ -37 \end{array} \qquad \begin{array}{r} 42 \\ -30 \end{array} \qquad \begin{array}{r} 42 \\ -33 \end{array}$$

(Give individual turns to several children.)

PART B: STEPS IN RENAMING

1. *(Write these problems on the board.)*

$$\begin{array}{r} 53 \\ -26 \end{array} \qquad \begin{array}{r} 75 \\ -28 \end{array} \qquad \begin{array}{r} 92 \\ -15 \end{array}$$

(Point to first problem.) Read this problem.	53 − 26
The ones column tells us to start with 3 and take away 6. What does the ones column tell us to do?	Start with 3 and take away 6.
Do we have to rename? *(Pause, signal.)* Right. We start with 3 and take away more than 3.	Yes

2. Here's how we rename: First we borrow a ten from the 5 tens. What do we do first? | Borrow a ten from the 5 tens.

Next we put that ten with the 3 ones. What do we do next?	Put that ten with the 3 ones.

(Repeat steps 1 and 2 with the second and third problems.)

3. Let's go back to the first problem. Read it.	53 − 26
What does the ones column tell us to do?	Start with 3 and take away 6.
Do we rename?	Yes
4. Tell me how we rename. What do we do first?	Borrow a ten from the 5 tens.
What do we do next?	Put that ten with the 3 ones.

(Repeat steps 3 and 4 with the remaining problems.)

PART C: STRUCTURED BOARD PRESENTATION

1. *(Write this problem on the board.)*

$$\begin{array}{r} 53 \\ -26 \end{array}$$

Read the problem.	53 − 26
What does the ones column tell us to do?	Start with 3 and take away 6.
Do we rename? *(Pause, signal.)*	Yes

To correct: What are we starting with in the ones column? Are we taking away more than 3? So, do we rename?

(continued on next page)

FORMAT 8.3 (continued)

TEACHER	STUDENTS
2. What do we do first to rename?	Borrow a ten from the 5 tens.
(Point to 5.) If we borrow 1 ten from the 5 tens, how many tens will be left?	4 tens
So I cross out the 5 and write 4 to show that 4 tens are left. *(Cross out 5 and write 4.)*	
3. We borrowed a ten. What do we do next?	Put the ten with the 3 ones.
Right, put the ten with the 3 ones. *(Write 1 in front of 3.)*	
Now we have 13 in the ones column.	
Figure out what 13 − 6 is. *(Pause.)* What's 13 − 6? *(Pause, signal.)*	7
We write 7 in the ones column. *(Write 7 under the line.)*	
4. The tens column says 4 tens minus 2 tens.	
How many is 4 tens minus 2 tens? *(Pause, signal.)*	2 tens
We write 2 in the tens column. *(Write 2 under the line.)*	
5. What is 53 take away 26?	27
(Repeat steps 1–5 with remaining problems.)	

PART D: STRUCTURED WORKSHEET

TEACHER	STUDENTS
1. *(Give students worksheets with these problems.)*	

$$\begin{array}{ccc} 92 & 86 & 64 \\ -35 & -17 & -49 \end{array}$$

TEACHER	STUDENTS
Read the first problem on your worksheet.	92 − 35
2. What does the ones column tell you to do?	Start with 2 and take away 5.
Do you rename? *(Pause, signal.)*	Yes
3. What do you do first to rename?	Borrow a ten from the 9 tens.
If you borrow a ten from the 9 tens, how many will be left?	8
So cross out the 9 and write 8 above it. *(Check papers.)*	*(Students cross out the 9 and write 8.)*
4. What do you do now?	Put the ten with the 2 ones.
Do that. Put the ten with the 2 ones. *(Check papers.)* How many do you have in the ones column?	12
5. What is 12 − 5? *(Pause, signal.)*	7
Write 7 under the line in the ones column.	
6. Look at the tens column. What does the tens column tell us to do?	Start with 8 and take away 3.
What is 8 tens minus 3 tens?	5 tens
Write 5 under the line in the tens column.	
7. How many is 92 take away 35?	57
(Repeat steps 1–7 with remaining problems.)	

TEACHER	STUDENTS

PART E: LESS STRUCTURED WORKSHEET

1. *(Give students a worksheet with a mixture of subtraction problems that do and do not require renaming.)*

a. 84   b. 95   c. 46   d. 56   e. 78
   −23   −38   −8   −32   −38

f. 42   g. 34   h. 58
   −26   −26   −52

   Touch problem a.

2. Read the problem.

3. Look at the ones column and get ready to tell me if you need to rename. *(Pause.)* Must you rename?   No

   (If the answer is yes, present step 4. If the answer is no, go to step 5.)

4. Where do you get the ten from?

   How many tens will you have left?

5. Work the problem.

   (Repeat steps 1–5 with remaining problems.)

FORMAT 8.4   Preskill: Tens Numbers Minus One

TEACHER	STUDENTS

1. I'll say numbers, and you say the number that comes just before. Listen: 60. What comes just before? *(Pause 2 seconds. Signal.)*   59

   To correct: *(Tell answer, then repeat the problem.)*

2. *(Repeat step 1 with 30, 80, 40, 70.)*

3. Listen: When you minus one, you say the number that comes just before. I'll say a problem, and you tell me the answer. Listen: 60 − 1 is ... *(Pause, signal.)*   59

   To correct: *(Ask)* What number comes just before 60?

   (Repeat step 3 with 30 2 1, 80 2 1, 40 2 1, 70 2 1.)

FORMAT 8.5   Renaming Numbers with Zeroes

TEACHER	STUDENTS

PART A: STRUCTURED BOARD PRESENTATION

1. *(Write this problem on the board.)*

    304
   −186

   Read the problem.   304 − 186

(continued on next page)

FORMAT 8.5 (continued)

TEACHER	STUDENTS
2. What do we do in the ones column?	Start with 4 and take away 6.
Do we have to rename? *(Pause, signal.)*	Yes
3. We have a problem. We can't borrow from zero tens, so we have to borrow from the 30 tens. We're going to borrow 1 ten from 30 tens. *(Circle 30 with finger.)*	
What are we going to borrow one ten from?	30 tens
What is 30 tens minus 1 ten?	29 tens
So I cross out 30 and write 29 above it.	
4. Now I'll put the 1 ten with the 4 ones. What is 1 ten and 4 ones?	14
What is 14 − 6? *(Pause, signal.)*	8
So I write 8 in the ones column.	
5. Now look at the tens column. How many tens are we starting with now?	9
What is 9 − 8?	1
So I write 1 under the tens column.	
6. How many hundreds are we starting with now?	2
What is 2 − 1?	1
So I write 1 in the hundreds column.	
7. What is the answer to this problem?	118
(Repeat steps 1–7 with these examples: 504 − 327, 602 − 148.)	

PART B: STRUCTURED WORKSHEET

$$\begin{array}{r} 406 \\ -287 \end{array} \qquad \begin{array}{r} 905 \\ -626 \end{array} \qquad \begin{array}{r} 403 \\ -248 \end{array}$$

TEACHER	STUDENTS
1. Touch the first problem. Read it.	406 − 287
2. What does the ones column tell us to do?	Start with 6 and take away 7.
Do you have to rename? *(Pause.)*	Yes
3. Can you borrow 1 ten from zero tens?	No
Where are you going to get the 1 ten?	From 40 tens
What is 40 tens minus 1 ten?	39 tens
Cross out the 40 and write 39 above it. *(Monitor responses.)* Now put the 1 ten with the 6 ones. *(Monitor responses.)*	
4. Now work the problem in the ones column.	
What is 1 ten and 6 ones?	16
What is 16 − 7?	9
5. How many tens are you starting with now?	9
What is 9 − 8?	1
Write it.	
(Monitor responses.)	
6. How many hundreds are you starting with now?	3
What is 3 − 2?	1

TEACHER	**STUDENTS**
Read the whole problem and say the answer.	406 − 287 = 119
(Repeat steps 1–6 with remaining examples.)	

PART C: LESS STRUCTURED WORKSHEET

a. 804   b.   905   c. 609
   −619   −164   −426

d. 605   e.   302   f. 508
   −197   −42   −349

1. Touch problem a.

2. Read the problem.   804 − 619

3. Look at the ones column and get ready to tell me if you
   need to rename. *(Pause.)* Do you need to rename?   Yes

   Where do you get the ten from?   From 80 tens

4. Work the problem.

   (Repeat steps 1–4 with remaining problems.)

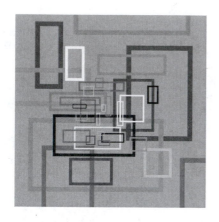

CHAPTER 9

Multiplication

TERMS AND CONCEPTS

multiplication   The process of combining a specific number of sets, each including an equal number of elements, into a single larger set.

multiplicand   The number of units in each equal set.

multiplier   The number of sets in the multiplication process.

factors   The multiplicand and the multiplier in a multiplication problem.

product   The answer in a multiplication problem. The number designating elements in the combined set of a multiplication problem; i.e., the sum of all the equal sets.

Commutative Property   The commutative property for multiplication states that changing the order of two numbers in a multiplication equation does not change the answer. If a and b are whole numbers, then $a \times b = b \times a$; e.g., $3 \times 4 = 4 \times 3$. The commutative property is very helpful in teaching multiplication facts. Once students learn that $3 \times 4 = 12$, they do not need to learn $4 \times 3 = 12$ as a new fact; rather, they can relate 4×3 to the known fact (3×4) and learn the new fact more quickly.

Associative Property   The associative property for multiplication states that if a, b, and c are whole numbers, then $(a \times b) \times c = a \times (b \times c)$; e.g., $(3 \times 2) \times 4 = 3 \times (2 \times 4)$.

Identity Element   The identity element for multiplication is 1. Any number times 1 equals that number; e.g., $4 \times 1 = 4$, $6 \times 1 = 6$. (The identity element for addition is zero: $4 + 0 = 4$, $6 + 0 = 6$. However, in multiplication, a factor of zero results in a product of zero: $4 \times 0 = 0$, $6 \times 0 = 0$.)

The identity element for multiplication is often applied in operations with fractional numbers. For example, before students add ¼ and ½, they must change ½ to an equivalent fraction by multiplying by a fraction equal to 1: $½ \times 2/2 = 2/4$. Students substitute 2/4 for ½ and complete the equation. Students must realize that multiplying by 2/2 is acceptable only because the fraction equals the identity element for multiplication, which means the value of ½ has not been changed.

Distributive Property   The distributive property of multiplication over addition says that if a, b, and c are whole numbers, then

$$a \times (b + c) = (a \times b) + (a \times c)$$

This property is essential to understanding multiplication of multi-digit numbers such as 4×27. Expanded notation allows 27 to be rewritten as $20 + 7$. The problem 4×27 then becomes $4 \times (20 + 7)$, which equals $(4 \times 20) + (4 \times 7)$. It is also important for later work with fractions, equations, and algebra.

SKILL HIERARCHY

Our discussion of multiplication is divided into two stages. The first stage involves presenting strategies designed to establish a conceptual understanding of the process of multiplication. These strategies are usually taught to students in second grade. The second stage deals with teaching students to work multi-digit problems in which students rely on mental computation rather than on representations of concrete objects. This stage typically begins during third grade and continues into the upper grades.

During the beginning stage, a procedure for solving simple multiplication problems with concrete or semiconcrete objects to represent the members in each group is presented. For example, when determining the total in an array such as the one below, students are shown that they can count by 3, four times, and end with 12. When solving the problem 3×4, the students are taught to hold up four fingers for the second factor and then skip count by threes for each of the four extended fingers: 3, 6, 9, 12. (The teaching procedures for skip counting are discussed in Chapter 4.) Students should have mastered at least three skip-counting series before multiplication is introduced.

```
O  O  O  O
O  O  O  O
O  O  O  O
```

Missing-factor problems, in which one factor and the product are given and a missing factor must be computed (e.g., $4 \times \square = 12$), are also presented during this stage. In the missing-factor strategy, students do not know the number of fingers to extend, since the second factor is represented by a box or unknown. For these problems, students hold up a fist and extend a finger every time they skip count, stopping at the product. In $3 \times \square = 15$, students extend a fist, count 3 (extending one finger), count 6 (extending a second finger), count 9 (extending a third finger), count 12 (extending a fourth finger), and count 15 (extending a fifth finger). They do not count beyond 15 because they must end with 15 on both sides of the equal sign. Since they extended five fingers, the unknown factor is 5: $3 \times \boxed{5} = 15$. The teacher then summarizes by asking how many threes are in 15. Teachers working with intermediate-grade remedial students who have some knowledge of multiplication might consider beginning instruction immediately with basic fact exercises and not presenting finger strategies. Teaching finger strategies for multiplication to older remedial students could result in an overreliance on using fingers rather than memorizing facts.

In the second stage, when multi-digit numbers are multiplied, students work problems without holding up fingers for the second factor and without using skip counting. Since students do not skip count, a new preskill is implied: knowledge of basic multiplication facts. The 100 possible combinations of single-digit factors are referred to as basic multiplication facts. Exercises to facilitate memorization of basic facts can begin a month or so after students have learned to use the count-by strategy to work multiplication problems. (See Chapter 6 for a discussion of teaching basic facts.) Besides basic multiplication facts, renaming and advanced addition facts (adding a single digit to a multi-digit addend) are also preskills. Knowledge of advanced facts such as $72 + 4$ is required in many problems with multi-digit factors. For example, in working 95×8, students first multiply 5×8 and then must add the 4 from the 40 to 72, the product of 9×8:

$$
\begin{array}{r}
4 \\
95 \\
\times\ 8 \\
\hline
760
\end{array}
$$

The need for teaching advanced facts can be avoided by presenting a low-stress multiplication algorithm. In the low-stress multiplication algorithm, students write out the complete answer every time they multiply. This strategy requires no carrying:

$$
\begin{array}{r}
32 \\
\times 24 \\
\hline
8 \\
120 \\
40 \\
600 \\
\hline
768
\end{array}
$$

Then they add the products, a process that seldom involves advanced facts. The major disadvantage of the low-stress algorithm, which is discussed at the end of this chapter, is its limited acceptance in U.S. schools.

Another preskill for multi-digit operations is expanded notation. When students multiply 34×7, they should understand that they are multiplying 4×7 and 30×7, which assumes the expanded notation skill of translating 34 into 30 and 4 (see Figure 9.1).

There are two basic types of multi-digit problems. The first type involves a single-digit factor and a multi-digit factor. This type includes problems that do not require renaming and problems that do require renaming. In the easier group, the first product is less than 10, and renaming is not required; for example,

Instructional Sequence and Assessment Chart

Grade Level	Problem Type	Performance Indicator		
1a	Count by tens to 100 Count by twos to 20 Count by fives to 60			
2a	Count by nines to 90			
2b	One digit times one digit	$2 \times 7 =$ $9 \times 3 =$ $5 \times 6 =$		
2c	Missing factor multiplication; both factors are one-digit numbers	$2 \times \square = 8$ $5 \times \square = 10$ $9 \times \square = 36$		
2d	Count by fours to 40 Count by twenty-fives to 100 Count by sevens to 70 Count by threes to 30			
3a	Count by eights to 80 Count by sixes to 60			
3b	One-digit factor times two-digit factor; no carrying	$\begin{array}{r} 43 \\ \times 2 \\ \hline \end{array}$	$\begin{array}{r} 31 \\ \times 5 \\ \hline \end{array}$	$\begin{array}{r} 32 \\ \times 4 \\ \hline \end{array}$
3c	One-digit factor times two-digit factor; carrying	$\begin{array}{r} 35 \\ \times 5 \\ \hline \end{array}$	$\begin{array}{r} 43 \\ \times 9 \\ \hline \end{array}$	$\begin{array}{r} 17 \\ \times 2 \\ \hline \end{array}$
3d	One-digit factor times two- or three-digit factor; problem written horizontally	$5 \times 35 =$ $9 \times 34 =$ $7 \times 56 =$		
4a	One-digit factor times three-digit factor	$\begin{array}{r} 758 \\ \times 2 \\ \hline \end{array}$	$\begin{array}{r} 364 \\ \times 5 \\ \hline \end{array}$	$\begin{array}{r} 534 \\ \times 9 \\ \hline \end{array}$
4b	One-digit factor times three-digit factor; zero in tens column	$\begin{array}{r} 405 \\ \times 3 \\ \hline \end{array}$	$\begin{array}{r} 302 \\ \times 5 \\ \hline \end{array}$	$\begin{array}{r} 105 \\ \times 9 \\ \hline \end{array}$
4c	One-digit factor times three-digit factor; horizontal alignment	$352 \times 9 =$ $7 \times 342 =$ $235 \times 5 =$		
4d	Two-digit factor times two-digit factor	$\begin{array}{r} 37 \\ \times 25 \\ \hline \end{array}$	$\begin{array}{r} 26 \\ \times 52 \\ \hline \end{array}$	$\begin{array}{r} 34 \\ \times 25 \\ \hline \end{array}$
4e	Two-digit factor times three-digit factor	$\begin{array}{r} 324 \\ \times 29 \\ \hline \end{array}$	$\begin{array}{r} 343 \\ \times 95 \\ \hline \end{array}$	$\begin{array}{r} 423 \\ \times 29 \\ \hline \end{array}$
5a	Three-digit factor times three-digit factor	$\begin{array}{r} 284 \\ \times 346 \\ \hline \end{array}$	$\begin{array}{r} 242 \\ \times 195 \\ \hline \end{array}$	$\begin{array}{r} 624 \\ \times 283 \\ \hline \end{array}$
5b	Three-digit factor times three-digit factor; zero in tens column of multiplier	$\begin{array}{r} 382 \\ \times 506 \\ \hline \end{array}$	$\begin{array}{r} 320 \\ \times 402 \\ \hline \end{array}$	$\begin{array}{r} 523 \\ \times 703 \\ \hline \end{array}$

FIGURE 9.1   Using Expanded Notation to Explain Multi-digit Multiplication

$$\begin{array}{ccccc} 27 & & 20 & & 7 \\ \underline{\times 4} & = & \underline{\times 4} & + & \underline{\times 4} & = 108 \\ & & 80 & & 28 \end{array}$$

20 × 4   +   7 × 4

80   +   28   = 108

32 × 3 does not require renaming in the first product (2 × 3 = 6). Problems in the harder group, such as 32 × 7, require renaming; in 2 × 7 = 14, the 10 from 14 is carried. The second major type of problem involves multiplying two multi-digit numbers (e.g., 32 × 13, 189 × 43, 342 × 179). A more detailed specification of the various multiplication problem types appears in the Instructional Sequence and Assessment Chart.

INTRODUCING THE CONCEPT

The meaning of multiplication can be conveyed in various ways. Underhill (1981) lists five: sets, arrays, linear models, cross products, and addition. Jerman and Beardslee (1978) suggest that the most common ways of introducing the concept are equivalent sets and cross products. Multiplication as cross products is illustrated for 2 × 3 in Figure 9.2. Note that the

display symbolized by 2 × 3 contains six pairs of objects as the product and the display symbolized by 3 × 5 contains 15 pairs of objects as the product. The product, formed by all possible pairings of two sets, is also called the Cartesian product. Multiplication as equivalent sets is illustrated for 2 × 3 as

BEGINNING MULTIPLICATION

Single-Digit Multiplication

Multiplication with single-digit factors can be introduced when students have mastered three count-by series (e.g., twos, fives, nines) and can read and write all numerals between 1 and 99. Single-digit

FIGURE 9.2   Multiplication as Cross Products

for 2 x 3 as

$$\begin{array}{c|ccc} & & 3 & \\ & a & b & c \\ \hline 2 \quad \bullet & \bullet a & \bullet b & \bullet c \\ \triangle & \triangle a & \triangle b & \triangle c \end{array}$$

and for 3 x 5 as

$$\begin{array}{c|ccccc} & & & 5 & & \\ & a & b & c & d & e \\ \hline 3 \quad \square & \square a & \square b & \square c & \square d & \square e \\ \circ & \circ a & \circ b & \circ c & \circ d & \circ e \\ \triangle & \triangle a & \triangle b & \triangle c & \triangle d & \triangle e \end{array}$$

multiplication is typically introduced in mid-second grade. The format for teaching it is divided into five parts (see Format 9.1). Since an equivalent-sets representation is easier for students to understand than a Cartesian product, we introduce the multiplication concept in Part A with illustrations of equivalent sets. The students are shown a group of equivalent sets and told they can figure the total a "fast way" when each set has the same number. After verifying that each set has the same number, the teacher demonstrates how to write the problem as a multiplication problem. Next, the teacher demonstrates how to use skip counting to determine the total. In the final step of Part A, students count the members of the sets one at a time to verify that the answer derived through multiplication is correct. Part A should be included only the first two or three days the format is presented.

In Part B, students learn to translate a multiplication statement into terms that indicate how the problem is to be solved. For example, in initial problems, the multiplication sign (×) is read as "count by." Students are taught to read the multiplication statement 5 × 2 = as "count by 5, two times." By reading the statement this way, students know exactly what to do to derive an answer. "Count by 5, two times" tells them to extend two fingers for the number of times they skip count and then to skip count by fives. After several weeks, students learn to read problems in the conventional manner (e.g., 4 × 3, is read as "4 times 3").

When reading multiplication problems in Part B, students begin with the multiplication sign, saying "count by" and then the first number; 5 × 3 is read "count by 5, three times." Since translating multiplication problems differs from reading addition or subtraction problems, in which students read in a strict left to right order, multiplication problems require a slightly different signal. The teacher should point under both the numeral and the times sign when having students translate problems. For some students, the teacher may even need to point under the sign first, then point to the first number to emphasize that the multiplication sign is read before the numeral.

In Part C, the teacher guides students in solving several multiplication examples in a structured board presentation. First, students read and translate a problem. They hold up the appropriate number of fingers, and the teacher models skip counting while touching each extended finger. Next, the students skip count each time they touch an extended finger. Finally, the students work three new problems without any teacher modeling.

Part D is the structured worksheet presentation. The teacher has the students extend the appropriate number of fingers, identify the skip-counting number, and then work the problem. Part E is the less structured worksheet part of the format. Students work a set of problems on their own with the teacher carefully monitoring their performance. After students demonstrate accuracy during group instruction, they are given 5 to 10 problems daily in independent worksheet exercises.

When having the students count and touch their fingers in step 2, Part C, the teacher must be sure that students coordinate saying the numbers with touching their extended fingers. Low-performing students may say the first number in the skip-counting series before touching the first extended finger; in 2 × 5, for example, students may say 2, and then when they touch their finger, count 4, continuing to count 6, 8, 10, 12. The correction for this error is to model, then lead by actually guiding the student's hand to coordinate touching and counting, and then test by watching while the student touches and counts alone. The teacher should then present a series of examples for the students to practice only the touching and counting and not the entire sequence of steps in Part C. Instead of presenting all of the steps, the teacher tells the student the problem and how many fingers to hold up and then has the student touch and count. For example, the teacher would present a series of examples using this wording: "You're going to count by 5, three times. Hold up three fingers. Good. Now count by 5. Remember to touch each finger as you count by 5." With this correction, the teacher is providing intensive practice on an important component skill prior to reintroducing the strategy.

There are two example-selection guidelines for this format. First, example selection should be coordinated with count-by instruction. The first digit in the multiplication problem should be taken from a skip-counting series the students have previously mastered. For example, a problem such as 6 × 7 would not be included until students have mastered counting by sixes. As a general rule, problems with a specific number as the first digit should be included in multiplication tasks after students have reviewed that count-by series for about 2 weeks. Second, there should be a mix of problems. As a general rule, no more than two or three problems in a row should have the same numeral as the multiplicand or multiplier. Following is an example of an acceptable set of examples:

5 × 2	2 × 2
2 × 4	5 × 4
9 × 3	9 × 1
9 × 5	5 × 3

The mix of problems helps to ensure that students develop the habit of carefully attending to both factors.

Missing-Factor Multiplication

Missing-factor multiplication, or algebra multiplication, is not only a useful skill in its own right, but also a critical preskill for the simple division strategies, which are discussed in the next chapter. In order to solve a missing-factor multiplication problem, students must determine the number of times they count by a certain number. For example, in the problem $5 \times \square = 15$, students figure out how many times they have to count by 5 to get to 15. Students extend a finger every time they skip count; they extend one finger when they say 5, a second when they say 10, and a third when they say 15. The three extended fingers represent the answer.

Missing-factor multiplication problems can be introduced after students have demonstrated mastery in solving regular multiplication problems. A time frame of at least 3 to 4 weeks between the introduction of regular multiplication and problems with missing factors is recommended to enable students to develop this mastery.

The format appears in Format 9.2. In Part A, students learn to translate the problem type; $5 \times \square = 20$ is translated as "Count by 5 how many times to end with 20?" Next, the strategy is modeled. The teacher holds up a closed fist to indicate that the number of times to count is unknown and then extends a finger every time she skip counts. Then the teacher tests the students by guiding them through several examples. In Part B, the structured worksheet, students apply the strategy as the teacher guides them to hold up a fist, to identify the skip-counting number and the product, and to extend a finger each time they count. Part C is the less structured worksheet in which students are taught to discriminate between regular problems and algebra problems (e.g., $2 \times 8 = \square$, $2 \times \square = 8$).

Example-selection guidelines are basically the same as for regular multiplication. The first factor in the problem should represent a count-by series the students have mastered. Different numbers should appear as the first factor. Independent practice worksheets should include an equal mix of regular multiplication and multiplication problems with missing factors.

Diagnosis and Remediation

Four errors—two component-skill and two strategy—account for the majority of errors in beginning multiplication. The first type of error results from skip counting incorrectly. Students may either forget a number or switch from one series to another while counting. Although this count-by component-skill error is usually obvious on worksheets, it can only be diagnosed accurately by asking students to work problems aloud. A worksheet illustrating this count-by component skill error appears below:

$$5 \times 4 = 20 \qquad 9 \times 3 = 27$$
$$10 \times 3 = 30 \qquad 10 \times 6 = 60$$
$$2 \times 7 = 14 \qquad 9 \times 5 = 47$$
$$9 \times 6 = 50 \qquad 5 \times 2 = 10$$

Note that of the eight problems on the worksheet, only two were missed. Both these missed problems had 9 as one factor and a number of 5 or more as the other factor. The errors indicate that the student may have had difficulty remembering the higher numbers in the count-by-9 series. To remedy the count-by skill deficit, the teacher provides practice on counting by nines for several lessons. The student shouldn't be required to solve any multiplication problems involving counting by nines until he has demonstrated that he can accurately count by nines.

The second error pattern is one in which answers are consistently off by one count-by number. For example, in regular multiplication problems, a student might answer a set of problems like this: $9 \times 6 = 63$, $7 \times 6 = 49$, $5 \times 6 = 35$. Quite often the cause of this error is that the student says the number for the first group and then begins counting as opposed to touching and counting simultaneously. For example, a student working 4×3 may say the number 4 before touching his fingers and then say 8, 12, and 16 as he touches the three raised fingers.

To remedy this type of error, the teacher presents Part C, the structured board part of the multiplication format, correcting by modeling and leading. The exercise is continued until the students can respond correctly to four consecutive problems. Several days of practice on this exercise should be provided before students are given problems to work independently again.

The third type of error occurs when students confuse the multiplication and addition operations. The remediation procedure involves presenting the less structured format for regular multiplication, which includes a mix of multiplication and addition problems. For remediation purposes, the teacher could instruct students to circle the sign in the problems before working them.

The fourth type of error common to single-digit multiplication occurs when students confuse regular and missing-factor multiplication, writing $5 \times \boxed{50} = 10$

or $2 \times \boxed{8} = 4$. The remediation procedure involves reviewing the less structured part of the missing-factor multiplication format, which contains a mixture of regular and algebra multiplication problems. The teacher should present the less structured worksheet with about 10 problems, observing and correcting errors. This remediation is continued daily until students correctly answer 9 of 10 problems without teacher assistance for several days in a row. The diagnosis and remediation information is summarized in Figure 9.3.

MULTI-DIGIT MULTIPLICATION

There are two algorithms presented in most commercial programs to solve problems with a multi-digit factor. One algorithm is commonly called the long-form or low-stress algorithm. The other algorithm is called the short form. Both forms are illustrated in Figure 9.4.

Both algorithms are based on the distributive property of multiplication, which states that the product of a multiplier and a multiplicand will be the same as the sum of a series of products from multiplying individual number pairs. For example, $3 \times 24 = (3 \times 20) + (3 \times 4)$.

The advantages of the long-form algorithm are that it does not alternate between multiplication and addition and seldom requires renaming. Moreover, it clearly shows the distributive property of multiplica-

tion. Its disadvantage, however, is that in problems involving multi-digit factors, many numerals must be written as partial products:

$$
\begin{array}{r}
245 \\
\times 37 \\
\hline
35 \\
280 \\
1400 \\
150 \\
1200 \\
6000 \\
\hline
9065
\end{array}
$$

The advantage of the short-form algorithm lies in its relative efficiency in solving problems with multi-digit factors and its widespread usage. Its disadvantage lies with the difficulty a student may have in understanding the process when he alternates between addition and multiplication and with the inclusion of complex addition facts.

In this section, we discuss in detail the procedures for teaching the short-form algorithm, primarily because it is the one used in most classrooms. The section on the short-form algorithm is divided into two parts. The first addresses problems in which one of the factors is a single-digit number and the other factor a multi-digit number. The second part deals with problems in which each factor is a multi-digit number.

FIGURE 9.3 Diagnosis and Remediation of Single-Digit Multiplication Errors

Error Patterns	Diagnosis	Remediation Procedures	Remediation Examples
a. $9 \times 6 = 51$ $8 \times 4 = 32$ $6 \times 5 = 30$ $9 \times 3 = 26$	Component skill: Student doesn't know count-by-nines series.	Part B—Count-by Preskill Format 4.5.	Practice on counting by nines.
b. $9 \times 6 = 63$ $8 \times 4 = 40$ $6 \times 5 = 36$	Component skill: Student not coordinating touching and counting.	Part C—Format 9.1 for single-digit multiplication.	Regular multiplication problems.
c. $9 \times 6 = 15$ $8 + 4 = 12$ $6 \times 5 = 11$	Strategy: Student is confusing addition with multiplication; not attending to the sign in the problems.	Less structured worksheet of regular multiplication format, Format 9.1. Instructions to circle the sign before working the problem.	Mix of addition and multiplication problems.
d. $2 \times \boxed{16} = 8$ $6 \times 5 = \boxed{30}$ $9 \times 6 = \boxed{54}$ $4 \times \boxed{32} = 8$	Strategy: Student is confusing regular multiplication and missing factor multiplication.	Less structured worksheet of format for problems with missing factors, Format 9.2.	Mix of regular multiplication problems and problems with missing factor.

FIGURE 9.4   Two Algorithms for Multi-digit Multiplication

Long Form	Short Form
232	*21*
× 7	232
14	× 7
210	*1624*
1400	
1624	

Single-Digit Factor and Multi-digit Factor

Multiplication problems in which a single-digit factor and multi-digit factor are multiplied usually are introduced during mid-third grade. This group of problems includes problems 3b through 4c on the Instructional Sequence and Assessment Chart.

PRESKILLS. Three preskills necessary to work these problems are (a) multiplication facts, (b) place value skills, including expanded notation and placing a comma in the proper position when writing an answer in the thousands, and (c) complex addition facts in which a single-digit number is added to a two-digit number.

Basic multiplication facts include all of the possible combinations of single-digit factors. Memorizing basic facts is a very demanding and lengthy process. It is not realistic to imagine that most students will have memorized all basic multiplication facts by mid-third grade. Therefore, initially, problems should be limited so that they include only basic facts the teacher is sure students have memorized. As students learn more basic facts, these should be integrated into multiplication problems.

When introducing multiplication facts to students, teachers may find multiplication maps useful (see Table 9.1). Each map is designed to facilitate learning multiplication facts for a particular series. Students who can visualize the maps in their minds initially learn and remember facts more easily.

Each map has a unique pattern. For nines, the second digit decreases by 1, while the first digit increases by 1. For fives, the last digit of the numbers in the first column is 5; the last digit of the numbers in the second column is zero. For fours, the second digits repeat after 20 (4, 8, 2, 6, 0). The pattern for threes shows that all values below the top row have a second digit one less than the digit above it. For sevens, the second digit of each number is one more than the digit above it. It is helpful to let students discover the patterns after introducing a particular map. If *they* find it, they will remember it longer.

Teachers need to provide lots of practice with the number map in addition to practicing the count-bys orally. Practice activities may require students to write in missing digits, write missing numbers, or complete blank maps.

The place value skill of expanded notation is needed if the student is to understand the renaming procedure in the short-form algorithm. Procedures for teaching place value concepts appear in Chapter 5.

The second place value skill, placing a comma, seems trivial but needs to be taught. After completing problems with larger numbers, students are expected to place a comma in the answer. The procedure is simple. The teacher presents the following rule: The comma is written between the hundreds and the thousands. Then the teacher models and tests application of the rule. The teacher writes a series of three-, four-, and five-digit numbers on the board, then demonstrates how to find where to place the comma. Starting at the ones column, the teacher points to each numeral, saying "ones, tens, hundreds, thousands," and then places the comma between the hundreds and the thousands columns. After modeling several examples, the teacher tests the students.

Complex addition facts involve adding a single-digit number to a two-digit number mentally (e.g., 35 + 7, 27 + 3, 42 + 5). Complex addition facts were discussed earlier in the addition chapter as a preskill for adding a series of multi-digit numbers. This type of addition fact is found in the short-form multiplication algorithm, when the student adds the carried units to the product of a column. For example, in the problem 35 × 9, the student first multiplies 9 × 5 and gets 45. A 4 is carried to the tens column and a 5 written under the ones column:

$$\begin{array}{r} 4 \\ 35 \\ \times 9 \\ \hline 5 \end{array}$$

The student then multiplies 9 × 3 for a product of 27. Next, the student must mentally add the advanced addition fact, 4 + 27:

$$\begin{array}{r} 4 \\ 35 \\ \times 9 \\ \hline 315 \end{array}$$

There are easier and more difficult types of complex addition facts. In the easier type, the sum has the same number of tens as the original two-digit

Table 9.1   Multiplication Maps for 9s, 5s, 3s, 7s, and 4s

9	9	9	9	9
18		__8	1__	
27	27	__7	2__	
36		__6	3__	
45	45	__5	4__	
54		__4	5__	
63	63	__3	6__	
72		__2	7__	
81	81	__1	8__	
90		__0	9__	90

5	10	5		__1__
15	20	15		1__ 2__
25	30	25		2__ 3__
35	40	35		3__ 4__
45	50	45		4__ 5__

5	__0	5	
__5	__0		
__5	__0		30
__5	__0		
__5	__0	45	

3	6	9
12	15	18
21	24	27
30		

__	__	__
1__	1__	1__
2__	2__	2__
3__		

3	6	9
__2	__5	__8
__1	__4	__7
__0		

3		
	24	

7	14	21
28	35	42
49	56	63
70		

__	__	__
2__	3__	4__
4__	5__	6__
7__		

7	14	21
__8	__5	__2
__9	__6	__3
__0		

7		
	56	

4	8	12	16	20
24	28	32	36	40

__	__	1__	1__	2__
2__	2__	3__	3__	4__

4	8	__2	__6	__0
__4	__8	__2	__6	__0

addend: 64 + 3 = 67, 43 + 5 = 48, 75 + 4 = 79. In the more difficult type, the sum has a tens number one higher than the original two-digit addend: 36 + 7 = 43, 58 + 8 = 66, 48 + 4 = 52, 49 + 9 = 58.

Instruction on complex addition facts begins in early second grade. First, students are taught to add a single-digit number to a teen number: 14 + 3, 16 + 2, then 17 + 6, 15 + 8, and so on. After several months of practice with teen numbers, students are introduced to advanced facts with tens numbers, first with easier facts (e.g., 24 + 3, 36 + 2), then with more difficult facts (e.g., 49 + 6, 45 + 8). Practice is continued for many months to develop fluency. Procedures for teaching both the easier and more diffi-cult types of complex addition facts appear in Chapter 7.

STRATEGY. Column multiplication is introduced with simple problems involving no renaming. The product of the numbers in the ones column should be less than 10:

$$\begin{array}{cccc} 34 & 43 & 31 & 32 \\ \times 2 & \times 2 & \times 5 & \times 4 \end{array}$$

When presenting this type of problem, the teacher points out that the student first multiplies the ones and then the tens. A format is not included, since it would be quite similar to the one that involves renaming (see Format 9.3).

Problems with carrying are introduced several days after noncarrying problems have been presented. In Part A of the format (Format 9.3), the structured board presentation, the students break the problem into two parts. The two parts for 5×47 are 5×7 and 5×4 tens. After multiplying in the ones column, the teacher models how to carry, multiply the second part of the problem, add the carried number, and write the answer. Parts B and C provide structured and less structured worksheet practice.

Note in the format the balance between explaining to students the rationale for the procedure and providing clear guidance in the mechanics of working the problem. Also note the use of a place value grid. The purpose of the grid is to initially prompt the students to place numerals from the product in the proper column. Proper placement of numerals in the product, though not a critical component of these problem types, is critical in problems with two multi-digit factors. The place value grid would appear on students' worksheets for about a week and then be dropped. The day the grid is dropped, the teacher leads the students through several problems, pointing out the need to write numerals in the proper position. The teacher also examines students' worksheets carefully for column alignment errors.

Multi-digit problems written horizontally are introduced after students can correctly work vertically aligned problems. The teacher presents a strategy in which the students rewrite the problem vertically, writing the one-digit factor under the multi-digit factor. In later grades, the teacher presents a strategy in which students multiply horizontally, writing the product and carrying:

$$\overset{12}{5 \times 324} = 1620$$

This strategy is taught prior to introducing fraction multiplication and division problems with multi-digit divisors, both of which involve horizontal multiplication:

$$\frac{5}{4} \times 324 \qquad 324\overline{)1620}^{5}$$

Problems with a one-digit factor and a three-digit factor (e.g., 243×5 and 342×9) are introduced in late third grade. The format for presenting problems of this type is essentially the same as the format for introducing problems with a two-digit factor. The same basic explanation for carrying from the ones to the tens column is used in presenting carrying from the tens to the hundreds column. In 543×5, students multiply the 4 tens and add the carried ten. Then the teacher explains that they can't have 21 tens in the tens column, so they write a 2 over the hundreds column to show 20 tens and 1 ten is written under the tens column. Note that, at this point, the teacher need not require the students to say that 20 tens equal 200 but simply to write the 2 in the hundreds column.

A special problem type includes a zero in the tens column of the three-digit factor (e.g., 403×5 and 306×2). Students may have trouble adding the carried ten to zero. This type of problem is introduced a week after problems with three-digit factors are introduced. Several problems of this subgroup should be presented daily for about 2 weeks. The first several days, the teacher models a few problems, then closely supervises students as they work the problems.

EXAMPLE SELECTION. Two rules govern example selection. First, the basic facts included in problems should be those that the student has already mastered. Second, less structured, supervised practice, and independent worksheets should include a mixture of problems. About half the worksheet should contain problems of the most currently introduced type while the other half should contain previously introduced multiplication problems. About 10% of the worksheet should contain addition problems to keep students in the habit of examining the sign in a problem carefully before working it.

SELF-CHECKING. In mid-fourth grade, or whenever students become proficient in multiplying by a one-digit factor and dividing by a one-digit divisor, students should be taught to check their answers. A checking procedure for multiplication is to divide the answer by the one-digit factor. If the quotient equals the other factor, the answer is correct. The teacher introduces checking on a worksheet exercise. After her students complete the first multiplication problem (e.g., 7×35), the teacher says, "Here's how to check your work to make sure you have the right answer. We multiplied by 7, so we divide 7 into the answer. If you end with 35, your answer is correct. What's the answer to the multiplication problem? Divide 7 into 245.... Write the problem and work it.... Is the answer the same as the top number in the multiplication problem?.... So the answer for the multiplication problem must be correct."

Determining whether students check their work in multiplication is easier than in addition because checking requires writing a division problem. An exercise to encourage checking is to give students already worked problems, half of which have incorrect answers. The teacher instructs the students to check the answers and find the mistakes.

Two Multi-digit Factors

Problems with two multi-digit factors are usually introduced during mid-fourth grade and include four problem types (types 4d, 4e, 5a, and 5b from the Instructional Sequence and Assessment Chart). The simplest problems involve two two-digit factors. Next in difficulty are problems with a two-digit factor and a three-digit factor. This type is introduced during late fourth grade. The last type, which is presented during fifth grade, includes two three-digit factors.

The preskills for introducing problems with two multi-digit factors include the preskills for problems with a one-digit and multi-digit factor (i.e., basic multiplication facts, place value skills, complex addition facts) and a new preskill, column addition with renaming, which is required when the student must add the partial products.

Format 9.4 shows how to present problem type 4d in which both factors are two-digit numbers. We recommend using a place value grid the first several weeks this problem type appears. Examples of problems worked in a grid appear in Figure 9.5. The grids should already be predrawn on students' worksheets. Although drawing the grids provides extra work for the teacher, it saves instructional time that would be used to teach students how to draw them properly. The important part of the task for the student is filling in the numbers in the appropriate columns.

In Part A, the teacher simply presents the numbers in the order in which they are multiplied. For example, in the problem

$$
\begin{array}{r}
52 \\
\times\,37
\end{array}
$$

"We multiply 7×2, then 7×5, then 3×2, then 3×5." This part focuses simply on mechanics. Part B is a structured board presentation in which the teacher models the steps in solving a problem. Note in steps 3 and 5 that the teacher summarizes what has been done to that point: "First we multiplied 52×7, now we'll multiply 52 by 3 tens." Step 3 also points out that when multiplying by the tens number, a zero must first be placed in the ones column. This step is critical.

$$
\begin{array}{r}
52 \\
\times\,37 \\
\hline
175 \\
\hline
0
\end{array}
$$

Part C is a structured worksheet presentation. Step 4 of Part C, during which the teacher leads students in multiplying by the tens number, is the step in which students are most likely to have difficulty. Note the wording is very specific regarding where numerals are placed. Part D is a less structured worksheet presentation. It includes problems with a two-digit factor and problems with a one-digit factor as the bottom factor, as well as some addition problems with a one-digit addend.

Diagnosis and Remediation

The specific cause of errors is sometimes obvious, as in problem a below, and sometimes not obvious, as in problem b. In problem a, we can readily assume the student made a fact error, multiplying 7×6 and writing 58.

$$
\begin{array}{ccccc}
\text{a.} & \begin{array}{r} 5 \\ 36 \\ \times\,7 \\ \hline 268 \end{array} & & \text{b.} & \begin{array}{r} 4 \\ 36 \\ \times\,7 \\ \hline 242 \end{array}
\end{array}
$$

In problem b, we cannot be sure of the error. The student may have multiplied wrong or added wrong. If the cause of the error is not clear, the teacher should have the student rework the problem in front of her so that she can ascertain the specific cause.

FACT ERRORS. The remediation procedure for basic fact errors depends on the number of fact errors made by the student. If a student makes a few fact errors, the teacher simply records the facts the student missed and incorporates them into practice exercises for the next several lessons. If a student makes fact errors on more than 10% of the prob-

FIGURE 9.5 Using a Place Value Grid in Multi-digit Multiplication

$$
\begin{array}{r}
3\,|4\,|2 \\
\times\quad 2\,|5 \\
\hline
1\,|7\,|1\,|0 \\
+\ 6\,|8\,|4\,|0 \\
\hline
8\,|5\,|5\,|0
\end{array}
\qquad
\begin{array}{r}
4\,|6 \\
\times\quad 2\,|6 \\
\hline
2\,|7\,|6 \\
+\ 9\,|2\,|0 \\
\hline
1\,|1\,|9\,|6
\end{array}
$$

lems, the teacher should test the student individually to determine what action to take. The teacher tests the student verbally on the facts missed (e.g., What is 8×7? 9×4? 8×6?). If the student responds correctly to the missed facts, the teacher should tentatively consider the cause of errors to be the student's hurrying through the problems and not exercising enough care. The remediation procedure would involve increasing motivation to perform accurately. If the student's performance indicates she does not know many basic facts, the teacher should devote more time to basic facts and, if possible, limit problems to include only basic facts the student knows or give students alternative strategies for figuring out facts (e.g., a fact table).

COMPONENT-SKILL ERRORS. Many of the component-skill errors in column multiplication have to do with addition. Renaming errors may involve either (a) carrying the wrong number or carrying a number to the wrong column:

```
    2              1
   58            312
  × 9           ×  7
  ───           ────
  477           2274
```

or (b) forgetting to add the carried number:

```
    7              1
   58             82
  ×9             ×7
  ───            ───
  452            564
```

If students make frequent errors (more than 10%) in which they carry the ones number to the tens column, the error might be caused by the students not understanding the place value concept. The teacher would test the students on the tasks in the writing tens number format (see Format 5.8) and, if necessary, teach these place value skills in the context of writing numbers. When the students consistently respond correctly to place value tasks, such as how many tens in 57, the teacher would present the multiplication format, beginning with the structured worksheet exercise.

If students miss many problems because they fail to add the carried number, the teacher would present the structured worksheet part of the format again and then progress to the less structured worksheet exercise, emphasizing the need to carry the added tens.

Addition mistakes account for a sizable proportion of student errors. Below are several examples of addition errors:

```
a.    5         b.    3
     88              34
    × 7             × 9
    ───             ───
    626             296

c.    5
     28
    × 7
    ───
    186
```

Although, as mentioned earlier, we cannot be absolutely sure that the students' errors resulted from addition mistakes, the probability is high that they did. For example, in problem a, the student added 5 to 56 and ended incorrectly with a sum of 62. If students make frequent addition errors, the teacher places extra emphasis on teaching complex addition facts, that is, facts in which the first addend is a two-digit number and the second addend a one-digit number. Teachers working with older students who have little knowledge of basic addition facts should permit students to use their fingers in computing complex addition facts; however, they should insist on accuracy. Practice should be provided on worksheets that include just complex addition facts. Worksheets of this type would be provided daily until students perform at 95% accuracy for several days.

Students often have difficulty with problems that have a zero in the tens column:

```
   306
  × 7
  ────
```

Students may multiply the carried number:

```
   24
   306
  ×  7
  ─────
  2382
```

or treat the zero as if it were a 1:

```
   14
   306
  ×  7
  ─────
  2212
```

The remediation procedure for errors of this type begins with testing and, if necessary, teaching times-zero facts: "When you multiply by zero, you end up with zero. What is 5×0? 8×0? 3×0?" The teacher then gives students a worksheet containing 10 to 20 problems. Half of the problems should contain a zero in the tens column, a fourth should include a 1 in the tens column, and another fourth should have another numeral in the tens column. The teacher leads the students through several problems using a structured worksheet presentation, then presents a less structured worksheet exercise with several examples, and finally has the students work the problems without assistance.

Errors unique to problems with two multi-digit factors include not writing a zero in the ones column when multiplying by tens:

$$\begin{array}{r} 46 \\ \times\ 24 \\ \hline 184 \\ 92 \\ \hline \end{array}$$

and inappropriately recording the partial products so that numbers are added in the wrong columns:

$$\begin{array}{r} 425 \\ \times\ \ 37 \\ \hline 2975 \\ 12750 \\ \hline 42455 \end{array}$$

Both errors can be identified by closely examining worksheet errors.

To remedy the first error, caused by forgetting the zero, the teacher leads students through about three multiplication problems using Part D of Format 9.4, the less structured worksheet of the format for a two-digit factor times a two-digit factor. In Part D, the teacher prompts students to write a zero when multiplying by tens but does not guide them on every step. The students complete the rest of the worksheet independently. The worksheet should contain four or five multi-digit problems with a one-digit factor mixed and about 10 to 15 multiplication problems with two-digit factors. Using some problems with single-digit factors provides better practice than having students work only problems that require inserting a zero. Students must remember and apply the rule about zeroes correctly rather than write a zero by every problem. The practice exercise is done daily until students respond correctly to 9 of 10 multiplication problems for several consecutive lessons.

To remedy errors caused by students' inadvertently writing numbers in the wrong columns, the teacher should point out the errors to the students and remind them to carefully align the columns. Often, just providing feedback on why the students missed the problems is enough to encourage students to be more careful. However, if students continue to make column alignment errors, the teacher should reintroduce the use of the place value grid. The teacher should lead students through working the first couple of problems using Part C in Format 9.4, the structured worksheet, and have the students complete the remaining problems independently.

The teacher should probably continue having students use the grid for several days, then have students work problems without the grid.

Students may also answer problems incorrectly because of an error in adding the partial products. In problem a below, the student failed to carry. In problem b, the student made a basic fact error:

$$\begin{array}{cc} a. & b. \\ \begin{array}{r} 688 \\ \times\ \ 94 \\ \hline 2752 \\ 61920 \\ \hline 63672 \end{array} & \begin{array}{r} 688 \\ \times\ \ 94 \\ \hline 2752 \\ 61920 \\ \hline 64572 \end{array} \end{array}$$

Carrying errors often result from sloppiness. Teachers should insist that students write neatly. The remediation for carrying errors might involve giving the students a worksheet with about 10 problems. In each problem, the multiplication should be done already. The students' tasks is to add the partial products. After the students can perform accurately on this worksheet, the teacher supervises students as they work entire problems on their own.

STRATEGY ERRORS. Strategy errors indicate that the student simply has not learned the steps in the algorithm. Below are examples of student performance that indicate a strategy deficit:

$$\begin{array}{cc} \begin{array}{r} 428 \\ \times\ \ \ 3 \\ \hline 12624 \end{array} & \begin{array}{r} 32 \\ \times\ \ 57 \\ \hline 160224 \end{array} \end{array}$$

The remediation for such errors involves presenting the entire format for the particular problem type, beginning with the structured board presentation. The diagnosis and remediation information is summarized in Figure 9.6.

COMMERCIAL PROGRAMS

Multiplication: Multiplying by Two or More Digits

INSTRUCTIONAL STRATEGIES. Often, when teaching multi-digit multiplication, examples are given with arrows to display the order in which digits are to be multiplied. However, the actual strategy is not clearly defined in the teacher directions, and often the teacher is told to simply work through repeated examples to model the strategy.

Some basals use various multiplication algorithms to teach multiplication "shortcuts." Because the teacher directions often are vague, it is easy to see why the authors warn teachers that most students will have difficulty at first with this type of multiplication algorithm.

Practice and Review

Many commercial programs do not include a sufficient number of examples in their initial presentations to enable students to develop mastery of complex multiplication. Also, they often fail to provide an adequate variety of problem types to allow students to practice when to apply various steps in the strategies.

FIGURE 9.6 Diagnosis and Remediation of Multi-digit Multiplication Errors

Error Patterns	Diagnosis	Remediation Procedures
Two-Digit Factor × One-Digit Factor		
a. $\begin{array}{r} 34 \\ 156 \\ \times\ 7 \\ \hline 1090 \end{array}$	Fact error: Student makes an error in problems containing the factor 6 × 7.	Drill on fact 6 × 7.
b. $\begin{array}{r} 8 \\ 46 \\ \times\ 3 \\ \hline 201 \end{array}$ $\begin{array}{r} 32 \\ 156 \\ \times\ 7 \\ \hline 1074 \end{array}$	Component skill: Student carries the ones and writes the tens in the ones column.	Present place value exercise for writing tens numbers (Format 5.8). Then begin with structured worksheet exercise for multiplication (Format 9.3).
c. $\begin{array}{r} 46 \\ \times\ 3 \\ \hline 128 \end{array}$ $\begin{array}{r} 156 \\ \times\ 7 \\ \hline 752 \end{array}$	Component skill: Student does not carry the tens.	Begin with structured worksheet exercise (Format 9.3).
d. $\begin{array}{r} 1 \\ 46 \\ \times\ 3 \\ \hline 148 \end{array}$ $\begin{array}{r} 34 \\ 156 \\ \times\ 7 \\ \hline 982 \end{array}$	Component skill: Student does not add the carried number correctly.	Teach complex addition facts. Present worksheets containing complex addition facts.
Problems Containing Zero		
a. $\begin{array}{r} 1 \\ 406 \\ \times\ 3 \\ \hline 1238 \end{array}$ $\begin{array}{r} 24 \\ 106 \\ \times\ 7 \\ \hline 982 \end{array}$	Component skill: Student multiplies the carried number.	Test and teach times-zero facts. Begin with structured worksheet exercise (Format 9.3).
b. $\begin{array}{r} 1 \\ 406 \\ \times\ 3 \\ \hline 1248 \end{array}$ $\begin{array}{r} 4 \\ 106 \\ \times\ 7 \\ \hline 712 \end{array}$	Fact error: Student multiplies the zero as if it were a 1.	Test and teach times-zero facts.
c. $\begin{array}{r} 406 \\ \times\ 3 \\ \hline 1208 \end{array}$ $\begin{array}{r} 106 \\ \times\ 7 \\ \hline 702 \end{array}$	Component skill: Student does not carry tens.	Modify Format 9.3 to include single-digit times three-digit factor with zero in the tens column.
Two-Digit Factor x Two-Digit Factor		
a. $\begin{array}{r} 1 \\ 46 \\ \times 23 \\ \hline 138 \\ 92\ \\ \hline 230 \end{array}$ $\begin{array}{r} 4 \\ 56 \\ \times 17 \\ \hline 392 \\ 56\ \\ \hline 448 \end{array}$	Component skill: Student does not write zero in ones column when multiplying by tens.	Begin with less structured exercise (Format 9.4). Include mix of problems with two-digit factor and one-digit factor on bottom of problem.
b. $\begin{array}{r} 1 \\ 46 \\ \times 23 \\ \hline 138 \\ 920 \\ \hline 9338 \end{array}$ $\begin{array}{r} 4 \\ 56 \\ \times 17 \\ \hline 392 \\ 560 \\ \hline 5992 \end{array}$	Component skill: Addition error; student doesn't align numbers in columns appropriately.	Make worksheets including place value grid. Begin with structured exercise (Format 9.4).
c. $\begin{array}{r} 96 \\ \times 78 \\ \hline 768 \\ 6720 \\ \hline 6488 \end{array}$	Component skill: Addition error; student doesn't carry when adding partial products.	Give worksheet focusing on adding partial products, then supervised practice on multiplication problems.

APPLICATION ITEMS: MULTIPLICATION

1. Describe the problem type each example below represents. List the problems in the order they are introduced. Write the grade level when each type is typically introduced.

   a. 758
      × 2

   b. 9 × 4 = ☐

   c. 3 × 26

   d. 34
      × 2

   e. 37
      × 2

   f. 258
      × 37

   g. 37
      × 24

   h. 5 × ☐ = 20

2. At the beginning of a unit, the teacher tested Jack. His performance on the performance indicators for problem types 3b–4b appears below. Specify the problem type with which instruction should begin. Explain your answer.

   Jack

   3b. 43   31   32
       × 2   × 5   × 4
       ———   ———   ———
       86   155   128

   3c.   ¹   ²
         35   43   17
         × 5   × 9   × 2
         ———   ———   ———
         165   377   34

   3d. 5 × 35 = *175*
       9 × 34 = *296*
       7 × 56 = *392*

   4a. 758   364   534
       × 2   × 5   × 9
       ————   ————   ————
       1516   1820   4806

   4b. 403   302   105
       × 5   × 5   × 9
       ————   ————   ————
       2105   1600   1305

3. Below are 10 problems that appeared on the worksheet to be done independently by the students in Mrs. Ash's math group. Next to each student's name are the problems missed by the student. For each student, specify the probable cause or causes of the student's error. Describe the remediation procedure.

   24   342   61   23   203   60   21   28   432   48
   × 37   × 7   × 84   × 53   × 5   × 9   × 43   × 73   × 6   × 37

   Jill

   203
   × 5
   ————
   1105

   Alice

   48   28
   × 37   × 73
   ————   ————
   338   84
   1440   1980
   ————   ————
   1778   2064

   Sam

   203   60
   × 5   × 9
   ————   ———
   1065   549

   Jean

   24
   × 37
   ————
   168
   72
   ————
   240

   Sarah

   23   28
   × 53   × 75
   ————   ————
   69   140
   1150   1960
   ————   ————
   1119   2000

4. A student makes the following errors on the less structured worksheet presentation:

   ⁷
   43
   × 9
   ———
   2

   Assume this type of error occurs frequently. What would the teacher do?

5. Write the wording the teacher would use in the structured worksheet part of a format in presenting the following problem:

   304
   × 7

6. A student's worksheet assignment contains the following worked problems:

$$3 \times \boxed{27} = 9 \qquad\qquad 2 \times \boxed{12} = 6$$

What error is the student making? Describe the remediation procedure.

FORMAT 9.1   Single-Digit Multiplication

TEACHER	STUDENTS

PART A: PICTORIAL DEMONSTRATION

1. *(Write the following boxes on the board.)*

We're going to learn a fast way to work problems that talk about the same number time and time again. *(Point to each column and ask)* How many in this group?   5

Are we talking about the same number time and time again?   Yes

2. When we talk about the same number time and time again, we make a times problem. What number are we talking about time and time again?   5

So we write 5. *(Write 5.)*

How many fives do we have?   3

To correct: Count the groups of five. (Point to each group as students count.)

So I write times 3. *(Write × 3.)*

3. The problem says what? 5×3

We figure out 5×3 a fast way. We count by fives three times: *(Point to each group of 5 as you count.)* 5, 10, 15. There are 15 in all.

4. Let's count by ones and make sure 15 is right. *(Point to each member as students count.)* Are there 15?   Yes

So we can count the fast way when we talk about the same number time and time again. *(Repeat steps 1–4 with the following boxes.)*

PART B: ANALYZING PROBLEMS

1. *(Write these partial problems on the board.)*
   5 ×
   10 ×
   2 ×
   9 ×

(continued on next page)

FORMAT 9.1   (continued)

TEACHER	STUDENTS

Reading Partial Problems

1. *(Point to ×.)* This sign tells you to count by. What does it tell you to do?

   Count by

2. *(Point to 5 ×.)* So this tells you to count by 5. What does this tell you to do?

   Count by 5.

3. *(Point to 10 ×.)* What does this tell you to do?

   Count by 10.

4. *(Point to 2 ×.)* What does this tell you to do?

   Count by 2.

5. *(Point to 9 ×.)* What does this tell you to do?

   Count by 9.

   (Repeat step 5 with all examples.)

Reading Entire Problems

6. *(Point to 5 ×.)* What does this tell you to do?

   Count by 5.

   (Write 3 after 5 ×: 5 × 3.) Now this problem tells you to count by 5, three times. What does this problem tell you to do? *(Pause, signal.)*

   Count by 5, three times.

7. *(Point to 10 ×.)* What does this problem tell you to do?

   Count by 10.

   (Write 4 after 10.) What does this problem tell you to do now? *(Pause, signal.)*

   Count by 10, four times.

8. *(Point to 2 ×.)* What does this problem tell you to do?

   Count by 2.

   (Write 5 after 2 ×.) What does this problem tell you to do now? *(Pause, signal.)*

   Count by 2, five times.

9. *(Point to 9 ×.)* What does this problem tell you to do?

   Count by 9.

   (Write 4 after 9 ×: 9 × 4.) What does the problem tell you to do now?

   Count by 9, four times.

10. Let's start over. *(Point to 5 × 3.)* What does this problem tell you to do?

    Count by 5, three times.

    (Repeat step 10 with each problem. Give individual turns to several students.)

PART C: STRUCTURED BOARD PRESENTATION

1. *(Write this problem on the board.)*

   $2 \times 5 = \square$

   What does this problem tell us to do? *(Point to problem as students read.)*

   Count by 2, five times.

   How many times are we going to count?

   5

   So I'll put up five fingers. Watch me count by 2, five times: *(Count and touch fingers.)* 2, 4, 6, 8, 10.

2. Now it's your turn to count by 2, five times. How many times are you going to count?

   5

   Hold up your fingers. *(Monitor students' responses.)* You're counting by 2, five times. What number are you going to count by?

   2

   Touch a finger every time you count. Counting by 2. Get ready, count. *(Clap at intervals of 2 seconds.)*

   Students touch an extended finger every time they count: 2, 4, 6, 8, 10.

   What number did you end with?

   10

   So I'll write a 10 in the box. *(Write 10.)*

TEACHER	**STUDENTS**
3. *(Write the problem below on the board.)*	
$2 \times 3 = \square$	
What does this problem tell us to do? *(Pause, signal.)*	Count by 2, three times.
How many times are you going to count?	3
Hold up your fingers. *(Monitor students' responses.)* What number are you going to count by?	2
Get ready to count. *(Clap at intervals of 2 seconds.)*	Students touch an extended finger every time they count: 2, 4, 6.
How many did you end with?	6
So I'll write 6 in the box. *(Write 6.)* When we count by 2, three times what do we end with?	6
4. *(Repeat step 3 with $5 \times 4 = \square$, $10 \times 3 = \square$, $2 \times 4 = \square$, $9 \times 3 = \square$.)*	
(Give individual turns to several students.)	

PART D: STRUCTURED WORKSHEET

    a. $5 \times 3 = \square$
    b. $10 \times 4 = \square$
    c. $2 \times 6 = \square$

1. Touch problem a. What does the problem tell you to do?	Count by 5, three times.
How many times are you going to count?	3
Hold up your fingers. *(Monitor responses.)*	Students hold up three fingers.
What number are you counting by?	5
2. Get ready. Count. *(Clap at intervals of 1 second.)*	Students count 5, 10, 15, touching each extended finger.
When you count by 5, three times what do you end with?	15
Write 15 in the box.	
(Repeat steps 1 and 2 with remaining problems.)	

PART E: LESS STRUCTURED WORKSHEET

(Students have worksheets with variety of multiplication and addition problems.)

    a. $5 \times 4 = \square$
    b. $5 + 4 = \square$
    c. $10 \times 3 = \square$
    d. $10 \times 5 = \square$
    e. $10 + 5 = \square$

1. Touch problem a. Put your finger under the sign. What does the problem tell you to do, plus or count by?	Count by
Say the problem.	Count by 5, four times.
Work it and write how many you end with in the box.	
(Repeat step 1 with remaining problems.)	

FORMAT 9.2 **Missing-Factor Multiplication**

TEACHER	**STUDENTS**

PART A: STRUCTURED BOARD PRESENTATION

1. *(Write the problem below on the board.)*
   $5 \times \square = 20$

Model and Test Translation

Here's a new kind of problem. Here's what it tells us to do. *(Point to each symbol as you read.)* Count by 5 how many times to end with 20?

2. *(Point to $\square$.)* Does this problem tell how many times we count by 5?

   Right, we have to figure out how many times we count by 5.

   No

3. Your turn to read the problem. I'll touch and you read. *(Touch ×, then 5, $\square$ =, and 20. Repeat step 3 until students respond acceptably.)*

   Count by 5 how many times to end with 20?

Model Strategy

4. Let's work this problem. What are we going to count by?

   5

   Do we know how many times we count?

   No

   I hold up a fist to show that I don't know how many times to count. How many are we going to end with?

   20

5. My turn. I'm going to count by 5 and end with 20

   (Begin with a closed fist, then hold up a finger each time you count): 5, 10, 15, 20.) I put up a finger each time I counted. Here's how many times I counted. How many?

   4

   So how many fives in 20?

   4

   I write a 4 in the space. *(Write 4 in box.)*

Test Strategy

6. Now it's your turn. (Erase 4 in the space.) Say what the problem tells us to do. *(Point to $5 \times \square = 20$.)*

   Count by 5 how many times to end with 20?

   You have to figure out how many times we count. What do you have to figure out?

   How many times we count.

   What are you counting by?

   5

   Do you know how many times to count?

   No

   So hold up a fist. What number are you going to end with?

   20

7. Each time I clap, you count and put up a finger. *(Students are to hold up a finger each time you clap. Clap at 2-second intervals.)*

   Students count 5, 10, 15, 20, putting up a finger each time they count.

TEACHER	**STUDENTS**

Now count your fingers and see how many times you counted. *(Pause.)* How many fives in 20? — 4

Yes, so what do we write in the space?

Right. *(Write 4.)* — 4

(Repeat steps 5 and 6 with $2 \times \square = 14$, $10 \times \square = 30$, $9 \times \square = 36$, $2 \times \square = 6$.)

PART B: STRUCTURED WORKSHEET

    a. $5 \times \square = 20$
    b. $2 \times \square = 10$
    c. $10 \times \square = 40$
    d. $9 \times \square = 18$
    e. $5 \times \square = 30$

1. Touch problem a. What does the problem tell you to do? — Count by 5 how many times to end with 20?

2. What do you have to figure out? — How many times we count.

Put up your fist. What are you counting by? — 5

What are you going to end with? — 20

3. Count and put up a finger each time you count. Get ready. Count. *(Clap at 2-second intervals.)* — *(Students count 5, 10, 15, 20, putting up a finger each time they count.)*

How many times did you count? — 4

Write 4 in the box.

(Repeat steps 1–3 with remaining problems.)

PART C: LESS STRUCTURED WORKSHEET

(Students have worksheets with an equal mix of regular and missing factor problems.)

    a. $5 \times \square = 10$
    b. $9 \times 3 = \square$
    c. $2 \times \square = 8$
    d. $2 \times 6 = \square$

1. Touch problem a.

2. What does the problem tell you to do? — Count by 5 how many times to end with 10?

3. What are you counting by? — 5

4. Does the problem tell you how many times to count? — No

5. Show me what you hold up. — Students hold up fist.

6. Work the problem and write the answer in the box.

(Repeat steps 1–6 with remaining problems.)

FORMAT 9.3   **One-Digit Factor Times Two-Digit Factor—Renaming**

TEACHER	**STUDENTS**

PART A: STRUCTURED BOARD PRESENTATION

1. *(Write the problem below on the board.)*

$$\begin{array}{r} 4\;7 \\ \times5 \\ \hline \end{array}$$

2. Read the problem.   5 × 47

3. First we multiply 5 × 7.

4. What do we do first?   Multiply 5 × 7

   Next we multiply 5 × 4 tens.

4. What do we do next?   Multiply 5 × 4 tens.

   (Repeat steps 1–4 until students respond acceptably.)

5. What is 5 × 7?   35

   We can't write 35 in the ones column. We must carry the tens.
   How many tens are in 35?   3
   I put 3 above the tens column and put a plus sign in front
   of it to remind us to plus those tens.

$$\begin{array}{r} {}^{+3} \\ 4\;7 \\ \times5 \\ \hline 5 \end{array}$$

6. Thirty-five has 3 tens and how many ones?   5

   I write the 5 under the ones column. Now we multiply 5 × 4 tens.
   How many tens is 5 × 4 tens? *(Pause, signal.)*   20

7. Now we add the 3 tens we carried. What is 20 + 3?
   (Pause, signal.)   23

   Yes, 23 tens. I write 2 hundreds and 3 tens in the answer.

$$\begin{array}{r} {}^{+3} \\ 4\;7 \\ \times5 \\ \hline 2\;3\;5 \end{array}$$

8. What does 5 × 47 equal?   235

   (Repeat steps 1–8 with the problems below.)

36	42	34
×2	×9	×5

PART B: STRUCTURED WORKSHEET

   (Students have worksheet with these problems.)

a.	2 5	b.	1 4	c.	4 8	d.	7 6	e.	3 7
	× 9		× 7		× 2		× 5		× 2

1. Read problem a.   9 × 25

   What numbers do we multiply first?   9 × 5

   What is 9 × 5? *(Pause, signal.)*   45

TEACHER	STUDENTS
How many tens in 45?	4
Write plus 4 over the tens column. How many ones in 45?	5
Write the 5 under the ones column.	
2. What numbers do we times next?	9×2
What is 9×2? *(Pause, signal.)*	18
What do we do now?	Add 4.
What is $18 + 4$? *(Pause, signal.)*	22
Write 22 next to the 5 under the line. What is 9×25?	225
Read the whole problem.	$9 \times 25 = 225$
(Repeat steps 1 and 2 with remaining examples.)	

PART C: LESS STRUCTURED WORKSHEET PRESENTATION

(Students have worksheets with these problems.)

a. 35	b. 79	c. 35
$\times 5$	$\times 2$	$+ 5$
d. 64	e. 83	f. 83
$\times 9$	$\times 5$	$+ 5$

TEACHER	STUDENTS
1. Read problem a.	5×35
What type of problem is this?	Times
(If the problem is addition, tell students to work the problem.)	
What will you do first?	Multiply 5×5.
What is 5×5? *(Pause, signal.)*	25
Carry the tens in 25 and write the ones.	
2. What numbers do we times next?	5×3
Then what do we do?	Add the 2.
Work the rest of the problem. *(Pause.)*	
3. What is 5×35?	175
(Repeat steps 1–3 with remaining problems.)	

FORMAT 9.4   Two-Digit Factor Times Two-Digit Factor

TEACHER	STUDENTS

PART A: ORDER OF MULTIPLYING

1. *(Write these problems on the board.)*

$$\begin{array}{r} 58 \\ \times\,43 \\ \hline \end{array}$$

$$\begin{array}{r} 27 \\ \times\,95 \\ \hline \end{array}$$

$$\begin{array}{r} 42 \\ \times\,57 \\ \hline \end{array}$$

(continued on next page)

FORMAT 9.4 (continued)

TEACHER	STUDENTS

(Point to 58 × 43.) Read the problem.

43 × 58

Here's how we work multiplication problems with two numbers on the bottom. First, we multiply all the numbers on the top by this number. *(Point to 3.)* Then we multiply all the numbers on the top by this number. *(Point to 4.)*

2. My turn. *(Point to numbers as you say them.)* First we multiply 3 × 8, then 3 × 5, then 4 × 8, then 4 × 5.

3. *(Point to 3.)* What numbers do we multiply first?

3 × 8

   (Point to 3.) What numbers do we multiply next?

3 × 5

   (Point to 4.) What numbers do we multiply next?

4 × 8

   (Point to 4.) What numbers do we multiply next?

4 × 5

   (Repeat steps 2 and 3 with remaining problems. Give individual turns.)

PART B: STRUCTURED BOARD PRESENTATION

1. *(Point to the problem below.)*

```
  |5|8|
×|4|3|
```

   Read the problem.

43 × 58

2. What numbers do we multiply first?

3 × 8

   What is 3 × 8? *(Pause, signal.)*

24

   (Point above tens column.) What number do I write here?

2

   (Point under ones column.) What number do I put here?

4

   What numbers do we multiply next?

3 × 5

   What is 3 × 5? *(Pause, signal.)*

15

   What else do we do?

Add 2

   What is 15 + 2?

17

   There are no more numbers on top to multiply, so I write the 17 under the line next to the 4.

3. We multiplied 3 × 58. What is 3 × 58?

174

   I cross out the 2 we carried and the 3 to show we're finished with those numbers.

```
  |2|  |
  |5|8|
×|4|3|
 |1|7|4|
```

Now we multiply 4 tens × 58. Tens numbers have a zero, so we put a zero in the ones column to show we're multiplying tens. How do we show we're multiplying by tens?

Put a zero in the ones column.

(Write 0 under 4.)

Now we multiply 4 × 8, then 4 × 5. What is 4 × 8? *(Pause, signal.)*

32

(Point above tens column.) What number do I write here?

3

TEACHER	**STUDENTS**

(Point next to zero.) What number do I write here?   2

(Write numbers.)

```
    3
    2
   |5|8|
  ×|4|8|
  |1|7|4|
|2|3|2|0|
```

4. Now what number do we multiply? 4×5

    What is 4×5? *(Pause, signal.)*   20

    What do we do now?   Add 3

    What is 20 + 3? *(Pause, signal.)*   23

    Where do I write the 23?   Next to the 2

5. First we multiplied 3×58 and ended with 174. Then we multiplied 40×58 and ended with 2320. Now let's add those numbers and figure out what 43×58 equals. What is 4 + 0?   4

    What is 7 + 2?   9

    What is 1 + 3?   4

    What is nothing and 2?   2

6. We're finished adding. I'll put in the comma. Where does it go?   Between the 2 and 4

    What does 43×58 equal?   2,494

    (Repeat steps 1–6 with remaining problems on board.)

Part C: Structured Worksheet

(Students have worksheets with problems such as these.)

```
a. | |2|8|     b. | |6|4|     c. | |8|7|
   |×|3|6|        |×|2|8|        |×|4|5|
   | | | |        | | | |        | | | |
```

1. Touch problem a on your worksheet. Read the problem. 36×28

    What numbers are you going to multiply first? 6×8

    What is 6×8 *(Pause, signal.)*   48

    Write it; don't forget to carry the tens. *(Monitor responses.)*

2. What do you multiply next? 6×2

    What is 6×2? *(Pause, signal.)*   12

    What do you do now?   Add 4

    What is 12 + 4? *(Pause, signal.)*   16

    Write 16 next to the 8. *(Monitor responses.)*

3. Are you done multiplying by 6?   Yes

    Cross out the 6 to show you're finished, and cross out the carried number. *(Monitor responses.)*

4. We multiplied 6×28. Now we multiply 30×28. What do you write to show that you are multiplying by tens?   Write a zero.

    Write it. *(Monitor responses.)* What numbers do you multiply now? 3×8

    What is 3×8? *(Pause, signal.)*   24

    Write the 4 next to the zero. Write the 2 over the 2. *(Monitor responses.)*

(continued on next page)

FORMAT 9.4 (continued)

TEACHER	STUDENTS
5. Now what are you going to multiply?	3 × 2
What is 3 × 2? *(Pause, signal.)*	6
What do you do now?	Add 2.
What is 6 + 2? *(Pause, signal.)*	8
Write it. *(Monitor responses.)*	
6. We multiplied 6 × 28 and 30 × 28. Add the sums to see what 36 × 28 equals, then put in the comma. *(Pause.)* What is 36 × 28?	1008
(Repeat with several examples.)	

PART D: LESS STRUCTURED PRACTICE

1. *(Give students worksheets with a mix of multiplication problems with two-digit and one-digit factors and some addition problems.)*

   Touch problem _____. Read the problem. What kind of problem is this?

2. What numbers do you multiply first?

   What numbers do you multiply next?

   What numbers do you multiply next?

   What numbers do you multiply next?

3. What are you going to do just before you start to multiply by 5 tens?

   Right, don't forget to write the zero. Work the problem.

CHAPTER 10

Division

TERMS AND CONCEPTS

Division   The inverse of multiplication. When a student divides, she is finding a missing factor; $16 \div 8$ can be expressed as $8 \times \square = 16$.

Measurement Division   Performed when a set of elements is to be separated into equivalent subsets. The answer is the number of subsets; e.g., John has six hats and separates them into groups of two hats. How many groups will he have?

Partitive Division   Performed when a set of elements is to be separated into a given number of subsets. The answer is the size of each subset; e.g., John has six hats and separates them into three groups. How many hats will be in each group?

Dividend   The number being divided. It corresponds to the product in a multiplication problem:

$$6 \text{ in } 2\overline{)6}$$

Divisor   The factor that is given in a division problem. It is written in front of the division sign:

$$2 \text{ in } 2\overline{)6}$$

Quotient   The factor solved for in a division problem. It is written above the division sign:

$$3 \text{ in } 2\overline{)6}$$

Commutativity   The commutative property does not hold:

$$a \div b \neq b \div a$$
$$6 \div 2 \neq 2 \div 6$$
$$3 \neq \frac{1}{3}$$

Associativity   The associative property does not hold:

$$(a \div b) \div c \neq a \div (b \div c)$$
$$(8 \div 4) \div 2 \neq 8 \div (4 \div 2)$$
$$2 \div 2 \neq 8 \div 2$$
$$1 \neq 4$$

Distributivity   The distributive property over addition and subtraction holds:

$$(a + b) \div c = (a \div c) + (b \div c)$$
$$(8 + 4) \div 2 = (8 \div 2) + (4 \div 2)$$
$$12 \div 2 = 4 + 2$$
$$6 = 6$$

The distributive property is used extensively in the division algorithm:

$$4\overline{)48} = 4\overline{)40} + 4\overline{)8}$$

$$
\begin{array}{c}
1 \\
4\overline{)48}
\end{array}
=
\begin{array}{c}
10 \\
4\overline{)40}
\end{array}
+ 4\overline{)8}
$$

$$
\begin{array}{c}
 \\
\underline{4} \\
8
\end{array}
\qquad
\begin{array}{c}
 \\
\underline{40} \\

\end{array}
$$

$$
\begin{array}{c}
12 \\
4\overline{)48}
\end{array}
=
\begin{array}{c}
10 \\
4\overline{)40}
\end{array}
+
\begin{array}{c}
2 \\
4\overline{)8}
\end{array}
= 12
$$

$$
\begin{array}{c}
\underline{4} \\
8 \\
-\underline{8}
\end{array}
\qquad
\begin{array}{c}
\underline{40} \\

\end{array}
\qquad
\begin{array}{c}
\underline{8} \\

\end{array}
$$

Note: The distributive property does not hold when the division operation precedes addition:

$$c \div (a + b) \neq c \div a + c \div b$$
$$8 \div (4 + 2) \neq 8 \div 4 + 8 \div 2$$
$$\frac{8}{6} \neq 2 + 4$$

SKILL HIERARCHY

As with all major operations, division is introduced in two stages: the conceptual stage and the multi-digit operation stage. During the conceptual stage, exercises providing concrete demonstrations of the division concept are presented. With concrete objects or pictures, the teacher illustrates how groups of objects can be divided into equal-sized small groups, first illustrating problems that have no remainder and later, problems that have a remainder.

During the operation stage, students are taught algorithms to solve division problems that have multi-digit quotients. A significant period of time is needed between the introduction of the conceptual stage and presentation of division algorithms. During that time, the teacher should present exercises to facilitate memorization of basic division facts. Once students know their division facts, division problems with one-digit divisors (and multi-digit quotients) can

---

Instructional Sequence and Assessment Chart

Grade Level	Problem Type	Performance Indicator
3a	One-digit divisor and one-digit quotient; no remainder.	$3\overline{)15}$ $2\overline{)12}$ $5\overline{)20}$
3b	One-digit divisor and quotient with remainder.	$5\overline{)38}$ R $2\overline{)9}$ R $5\overline{)22}$ R
3c	Division equation with ÷ sign; no remainder; single-digit divisor and quotient.	$8 \div 2 = \square$ $20 \div 5 = \square$ $36 \div 9 = \square$
4a	One-digit divisor; two- or three-digit dividend; two-digit quotient; no remainder.	$5\overline{)85}$ $2\overline{)172}$ $2\overline{)54}$
4b	One-digit divisor; two- or three-digit dividend; two-digit quotient; remainder.	$5\overline{)87}$ $2\overline{)173}$ $2\overline{)55}$
4c	One-digit divisor; two- or three-digit dividend; quotient has two digits, one of which is zero; remainder	$5\overline{)53}$ $9\overline{)274}$ $9\overline{)360}$
4d	One-digit divisor; two- or three-digit dividend; two-digit quotient; express remainder as fraction.	Write the remainders as fractions. $5\overline{)127}$ $2\overline{)91}$ $9\overline{)364}$
4e	One-digit divisor; three- or four-digit dividend; three-digit quotient.	$5\overline{)635}$ $2\overline{)1343}$ $2\overline{)738}$
4f	Same as 4e; zero in quotient.	$5\overline{)2042}$ $2\overline{)1214}$ $5\overline{)520}$
4g	Four-digit quotient; one-digit divisor, four- or five-digit dividend.	$5\overline{)8753}$ $2\overline{)11325}$ $9\overline{)36286}$
4h	Rounding to the nearest 10.	76 rounds off to _____ tens 405 rounds off to _____ tens 297 rounds off to _____ tens
4i	Two-digit divisor; one- or two-digit quotient; all estimation yields correct quotient.	$23\overline{)94}$ $56\overline{)857}$ $47\overline{)1325}$
4j	Same as above except estimation procedures yield quotient which is too large or small.	$24\overline{)82}$ $67\overline{)273}$ $35\overline{)714}$

be introduced. Division problems with two-digit divisors are substantially more difficult and therefore are introduced later. A list of the specific problem types and when they are normally introduced appears in the Instructional Sequence and Assessment Chart.

INTRODUCING THE CONCEPT

There are at least four basic ways to provide concrete demonstrations of division:

1. *Removing equivalent disjoint subsets:* A picture of 6 fish is shown. The teacher says, "Let's put these fish in little bowls. We'll put 2 in each bowl. Let's see how many bowls we'll need. We put 2 in the first bowl. That leaves 4, then we put 2 in the second bowl. Then we put 2 in the third bowl. We need three bowls if we put 2 fish in each bowl."

2. *Arrays:* A group of objects aligned in equal piles is an array:

The teacher says, "Let's see how many sets of 6 there are in 30." The teacher counts each set of 6 as he circles them and then summarizes, "There are 5 sets of 6 in thirty."

3. *Linear models:* A linear model is usually characterized by use of a number line: In multiplication, students start at zero and jump to the right; e.g., 3×4 may be demonstrated as making 3 jumps of 4. Division problems are illustrated by saying, "If we start at 12, how many jumps of 4 do we make to get back to zero?"

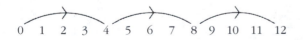

4. *Repeated subtraction:* This way of introducing division is similar to the removal of equivalent disjoint subsets. The teacher says, "We want to find out how many groups of 4 are in 12. Here's one way to find out. We keep subtracting fours until we run out. We subtract 4 from 12. That equals 8. Then we subtract 4 from 8. That equals 4, and 4 from 4 equals

zero." The teacher then has students count the number of times they subtracted to derive the answer.

Direct instruction procedures introduce the division concept through disjoint sets. Removing equivalent disjoint sets was selected because it can easily illustrate the relationship between multiplication and division as well as the concept of remainder. Initial direct instruction exercises teach students to remove equivalent sets by circling groups of lines.

Students must have mastered two preskills prior to the introduction of division. The first preskill is knowledge of basic multiplication facts. Students need not have memorized all multiplication facts before division is introduced, but they should at least have memorized multiplication facts with 2 and 5 as factors. A second preskill is column subtraction with renaming, which often is required when students subtract to find a remainder.

Division is usually presented during mid-third grade. Exercises to teach division facts are introduced about a week or two after the concept of division is introduced. Teachers present facts in related series (e.g., the facts with 5 as a divisor). Ample practice to enable students to develop fluency with a set of facts must be provided before a new set is introduced. Cumulative review of all previously introduced facts must also be provided. Practice exercises to teach basic division facts usually are provided daily for many months.

The concept of remainder is introduced after students have learned about 20 division facts. More specifically, we recommend that students know the division facts with divisors of 2 and 5 before the remainder concept is introduced. Similar to the introduction of division without remainders, the first exercises in which students are introduced to remainders require the students to circle groups of lines. After several days, exercises to teach students to compute quotients mentally in problems with remainders are presented. Practice on division facts with remainders continues for several months.

Problems Without Remainders

The procedure for introducing division appears in Format 10.1. The format contains four parts. Part A begins with the teacher modeling and testing the translation of a division problem. For example, the problem $5\overline{)20}$ is read as "5 goes into 20 how many times?" rather than "20 divided by 5." The purpose of this translation is to draw attention to the divisor, since it specifies the size of the equivalent groups—the critical feature in using lines to solve division problems. Also, the translation facilitates the use of multiplication facts. Note that the students are taught to translate problems so that they are read as a form of missing-factor multiplication.

Part B is a structured board exercise in which the teacher demonstrates with lines the process of taking a big group and making smaller, equal-sized groups. When working the problem, the teacher points out the function of the numbers in a problem. In 5 ÷ 20, the 20 tells how many lines in all, the 5 tells how many in each group, and the 4 tells how many groups. One minor, but important, aspect of Part B deals with where the quotient is written. If the dividend is a two-digit number, the quotient is written over the last digit. For example, in the problem 5 ÷ 20, the quotient 4 is written over the zero. The purpose of having students write the quotient in the correct place is to prepare them for using the traditional algorithm to solve problems with multi-digit quotients. Improper placement of digits in the quotient leads to various types of errors:

$$
\begin{array}{r}
13 \\
5\overline{)607} \\
5 \\
\hline
17 \\
15 \\
\hline
2
\end{array}
\qquad \text{or} \qquad
\begin{array}{r}
.25 \\
5\overline{)1.26} \\
10 \\
\hline
26 \\
25 \\
\hline
\end{array}
$$

Parts C and D are structured and less structured worksheet exercises. In both exercises, students are given problems for which lines are already drawn. Note that a variety of divisors can be included in these exercises, since knowledge of facts is not required. Students just make groups the size of which are defined by the divisor. Note also that students are assigned only two or three problems a day for practice. This exercise is designed to provide a conceptual basis for understanding division. Therefore, teachers need only develop accuracy in such exercises; fluency is not as important at this point.

Division Facts

A week or so after students have been introduced to division through the line-circling exercises described in Format 10.1, exercises to facilitate mastery of basic facts can begin. Exercises that demonstrate the relationship between multiplication and division facts, such as exercises in which students must generate both multiplication and division facts from fact number families, are presented first.

$$
3 \times 4 = 12 \qquad\qquad 4 \times 3 = 12
$$

$$
\begin{array}{r}
4 \\
3\overline{)12}
\end{array}
\qquad\qquad
\begin{array}{r}
3 \\
4\overline{)12}
\end{array}
$$

After relationship exercises are presented for several days for a set of facts, those facts are incorporated into memorization exercises. We recommend that students continue saying the facts in the statement form "5 goes into 20 four times" rather than "20 divided by 5 equals 4," because the former uses the language form presented when division problems with multi-digit quotients are introduced. Procedures to teach basic facts are discussed in more depth in Chapter 6.

Problems with Remainders

The concept of remainders is an important skill in and of itself and is also a preskill for the short-form division algorithm involving multi-digit quotients. Problems with remainders can be introduced when the students have learned division facts with divisors of 2 and 5, which is usually 2 to 2 weeks after division is introduced.

Format 10.2 shows how to introduce the remainder concept. In Part A, the teacher writes a problem on the board and has the students read it. After students read the problem, the teacher draws lines. For 5 ÷ 13, the teacher draws 13 lines, then asks the students for the number in each smaller group and begins drawing circles around groups of 5 lines. After drawing two groups, the teacher points out that he cannot draw a circle around the last lines because there are not 5 lines. The teacher tells the students that only two groups of 5 can be made and that the other lines are called the remainder. The teacher then states the answer to the problem: 5 goes into 13 two times, with a remainder of 3.

In Part B and Part C, the students are given a worksheet with several division problems involving remainders. Next to each problem is a diagram illustrating the problem. For example, next to the problem

$$
5\overline{)17}
$$

17 lines would be drawn with circles around groups of 5 lines:

The diagram is drawn so that the teacher may concentrate on the mechanics of where to write the number of groups, how to figure out how many parts are used (multiply 5×3), where to write the number of parts used (under the 17), and how to compute the remainder (subtract 17 minus 15). Note that practice on this exercise is continued just for a week or two, since the exercise is designed primarily to teach a conceptual understanding.

Remainder Facts

As mentioned earlier, students should have been taught at least 20 division facts before the remainder concept is introduced. About a week after the remainder concept is introduced, exercises to teach students to mentally compute division facts that include remainders should begin with problems like those below:

$$5\overline{)27} \qquad\qquad 6\overline{)34}$$

This skill is a critical preskill for division problems with multi-digit quotients, since most of these problems involve remainders. For example, in

$$3\overline{)147}$$

students must first determine that 3 goes into 14 four times with a remainder. After multiplying 3×4, they subtract to compute the exact remainder. Format 10.3 shows how to teach students to mentally compute division facts with remainders.

Part A uses a diagram like the one below to introduce remainder facts. The teacher writes numbers in a single row, circling numbers that are all multiples of a particular divisor. In the example below, numbers with a divisor of 5 are circled.

⓪   1   2   3   4   ⑤   6   7   8
9   ⑩   11   12   13   14   ⑮   16   17
18   19   ⑳   21   22   23   24   ㉕

If the teacher is introducing the second part of a series, the teacher writes the higher numbers in the series. For example, if the second half of the 5 series is being introduced, the teacher writes in a single row:

㉕   26   27   28   29   ㉚   31   32   33
34   ㉟   36   37   38   39   ㊵   41   42
43   44   ㊺   46   47   48   49   ㊿

After writing the series on the board, the teacher points out that the circled numerals are the numbers that 5 goes into without a remainder. The teacher then models answering the question of how many times 5 goes into various numbers; for example, "5

goes into 23 four times with a remainder; 5 goes into 10 two times with no remainder; 5 goes into 9 one time with a remainder." (Note that at this point, the quantity of the remainder is not stated.) The teacher then tests the students on a set of examples.

In Part B, the teacher tests the students on various numbers, letting the students refer to the diagram. Part C is a supervised worksheet exercise designed to provide practice that facilitates fluency in determining division facts. In Part C, the students are given a set of about 30 worksheet problems. The students write the quotient, then multiply and subtract to figure out the remainder. The teacher leads the students through several problems and then has them complete the work independently.

Parts A and B need to be presented only when the first several sets of facts are introduced. Once students have learned to compute division facts mentally with twos and fives and nines, problems with other divisors can be introduced without using the diagram as a prompt.

The sequence in which new division facts with remainders are introduced parallels the sequence in which basic division facts without remainders are introduced (see Chapter 6 on basic facts for the suggested sequence for introducing division facts). About two weeks after a set of division facts with a particular divisor has been taught, division facts with remainders for the same divisors and quotients are presented. For example, after students master the division facts for fives:

$$\text{e.g., } 5\overline{)30} \qquad 5\overline{)35} \qquad 5\overline{)40} \qquad 5\overline{)45}$$

problems with the same divisor and quotient but with remainders are introduced:

$$\text{e.g., } 5\overline{)32} \qquad 5\overline{)41} \qquad 5\overline{)43}$$
$$5\overline{)48} \qquad 5\overline{)36} \qquad 5\overline{)38}$$

The daily worksheet exercise includes about 30 problems. In half of the problems, the divisor is derived from the set currently being introduced; in the other half, the divisor is a number introduced in earlier sets. Although most problems should involve remainders, about a fifth without remainders should be included to prevent students from developing the potential misrule that all problems must have remainders.

Finally, several problems in which the quotient is zero should be included:

$$5\overline{)3} \qquad\qquad 9\overline{)6} \qquad\qquad 2\overline{)1}$$

Teaching students to mentally compute the answer to such problems prepares them for long division problems in which zero is in the quotient, such as

$$\begin{array}{r} 104\ R4 \\ 5\overline{)524} \end{array}$$

Figure 10.1 is a sample worksheet exercise based on the assumption that students have previously mastered problems with divisors of 2, 5, and 9 and are being introduced to the first half of the sevens series.

Worksheet exercises like Figure 10.1 should be presented daily for several months. Students who develop fluency in computing division facts with remainders are less likely to have difficulty when more complex division problems are introduced.

Diagnosis and Remediation

Determining the cause of errors while introducing the division concept is fairly easy. The more common causes, other than not knowing basic facts, are component-skill errors:

1. writing quotients that are either too small or too large
2. subtracting incorrectly
3. confusing the placement of the quotient and remainder

FACT ERRORS. Basic fact errors are illustrated below:

$$\begin{array}{ccc}
5 & 4 & 4 \\
\text{a. } 7\overline{)33} & \text{b. } 9\overline{)42} & \text{c. } 7\overline{)32} \\
\underline{30} & \underline{38} & \underline{26}
\end{array}$$

As usual, the remediation procedure for basic fact errors depends on the number of fact errors the student makes. If a student makes just an occasional fact error, the teacher simply records the facts the student misses and incorporates those facts into practice exercises for the next several lessons. If a student makes fact errors on more than 10% of the problems, he should be tested individually to determine what action to take next. If the teacher finds that the student responds correctly on the individual test to all the missed facts, the teacher should tentatively conclude that the errors resulted from hurrying through the problems. The remediation procedure is to increase the student's motivation to perform accurately. If the student's test performance indicates he does not know many previously introduced basic facts, he should be tested on all previously taught multiplication and division facts and provided systematic, intensive instruction on those facts. Also, for several weeks, the teacher should carefully control the assignments given to the student so that only facts the student knows appear on worksheet problems.

COMPONENT-SKILL ERRORS. One component skill error involves writing a quotient that is either too large or small. Examples of this error are illustrated below. Problems a and b are examples of computing too small a quotient; problems c and d are examples of computing too large a quotient.

$$\begin{array}{cc}
4 & 4 \\
\text{a. } 5\overline{)28} & \text{b. } 7\overline{)35} \\
\underline{20} & \underline{28} \\
\\
6 & 5 \\
\text{c. } 6\overline{)32} & \text{d. } 4\overline{)19} \\
\underline{36} & \underline{20}
\end{array}$$

If either type of error occurs in more than 10% of the problems students work independently, the teacher should present an exercise that teaches students to compare the remainder and divisor to determine the accuracy of their answer.

FIGURE 10.1 Sample Worksheet Exercise

7)18	9)46	7)26	7)31	2)7	5)32	7)35	9)27
7)4	7)17	9)58	9)65	7)27	5)3	7)41	9)53
5)30	7)11	7)25	7)32	9)31	5)18	7)3	7)25
9)49	9)26	5)48	2)17	7)36	7)28	7)19	7)36

The content of the remedial exercise depends on the type of error made. If the student writes quotients that are too small:

$$5\overline{)37} \quad \begin{array}{r} 6 \\ \underline{30} \\ 7 \end{array}$$

the teacher presents an exercise like the one in Format 10.4. That format contains an exercise in which students are given a worksheet comprised of division problems with the quotients written. In half of the problems the quotient is correct, and in the other half the quotient is too small:

$$9\overline{)38} \quad \begin{array}{r} 3 \\ \underline{27} \\ 11 \end{array}$$

In Part A, the teacher tells students that they must compare the remainder and the divisor to see if they worked the problem correctly. Note that the term divisor is not used by the teacher. If students divide by 9, they are taught that the remainder must be smaller than 9; if they divide by 5, the remainder must be smaller than 5; if they divide by 3, the remainder must be smaller than 3; and so on. In Part B, the teacher leads students through determining if the quotient is correct by figuring the remainder and comparing it to the divisor. In problems in which the remainder is not smaller than the divisor, the teacher points out that another group can be made and instructs the student to cross out the answer and in its place write the next higher number. For example, in the problem

$$5\overline{)16} \quad \begin{array}{r} 2 \\ \underline{10} \\ 6 \end{array}$$

the teacher has the students cross out 2 and write 3 as the answer. The student then erases 10, multiplies 3 × 5, and subtracts 15 from 16. The teacher guides students through four problems and then has them work 8 to 10 problems on their own. The format is presented daily until students can successfully solve the problems for several consecutive days.

For errors such as

$$5\overline{)32} \quad \begin{array}{r} 7 \\ \end{array}$$

in which the answer is too large, the teacher should use the process illustrated in Format 10.5. In Part A,

the teacher guides the students through a set of problems on the board, pointing out that if they can't subtract, the answer is too big, and the number in the answer must be made smaller. In Part B, the teacher has students work a set of remediation examples in which half of the problems have a quotient that is too large and half have a quotient that is correct. As with the previous format, this remediation format should be presented for several lessons.

Column subtraction errors are easy to spot and usually result from a failure to rename. Problems a and b below illustrate subtraction errors.

a. $7\overline{)41} \begin{array}{r} 5 \\ \underline{35} \\ 14 \end{array}$ b. $9\overline{)71} \begin{array}{r} 7 \\ \underline{63} \\ 12 \end{array}$

The remediation procedure includes giving students a worksheet with about 10 problems in which borrowing is necessary. The teacher guides students through the first several problems and then has students work the remaining problems on their own. For example, in the problem

$$7\overline{)41} \quad \begin{array}{r} 5 \\ \underline{35} \end{array}$$

the teacher would have the students identify the problem in the ones column, ask if they can subtract 5 from 1, then prompt students to regroup.

The final type of error involves confusing placement of the quotient and remainder. The remediation procedure is to present Part C of Format 10.3 with several problems and then supervise the students as they work several more problems.

A summary of the diagnosis and remediation procedures for beginning division appears in Figure 10.2.

MULTI-DIGIT PROBLEMS

The second stage of instruction in division focuses on multi-digit problems, which become quite complex. Multi-digit quotients are grouped in this text according to the number of digits in the divisor. Problems with one-digit divisors are discussed first, followed by a discussion of problems with two-digit divisors.

Two algorithms are taught in most commercial programs. One is commonly called the long form; the other, the short form. The long-form and short-form division algorithms are illustrated below:

FIGURE 10.2   Diagnosis and Remediation of Beginning Division Errors

Error Patterns	Diagnosis	Remediation Procedures	Remediation Examples
Component Skill Errors			
$\frac{4}{7\overline{)35}}$ $\underline{32}$	Fact error: 35 ÷ 7	High percentage of fact errors—provide systematic fact instruction. Low percentage of fact errors—increase motivation, include missed facts in fact drills.	See Chapter 6
$\frac{3}{6\overline{)24}}$ $\underline{18}$	Component skill: Student computes a quotient that is too small.	Format 10.4, "Remediation for Division with Remainders—Quotient Too Small."	Partially worked problems, containing quotients. Half of the quotients should be too small, half of them should be accurate: $\frac{3}{9\overline{)42}}$ $\frac{6}{9\overline{)56}}$
$\frac{4}{7\overline{)26}}$ $\underline{28}$	Component skill: Student computes a quotient that is too large.	Format 10.5, "Remediation for Division with Remainders—Quotient Too Large."	Partially worked problems combining quotients—half of the quotients should be too large, half of them should be accurate.
$\frac{7}{8\overline{)62}}$ $\underline{56}$ $\overline{74}$	Component skill: Student incorrectly subtracts.	Lead student through subtraction.	Partially worked problems containing accurate quotients in which students must subtract.
$\frac{1 \ R4}{7\overline{)29}}$ $\underline{28}$ $\overline{7}$	Component skill: Student misplaces remainder and quotient.	Part C of Format 10.3.	

LONG FORM

$$
7\overline{)382} \\
\underline{350} \quad 50 \\
32 \\
\underline{28} \quad 4 \\
\overline{4} \\
\overline{54}
$$

SHORT FORM

$$
\frac{54}{7\overline{)382}} \\
\underline{35} \\
32 \\
\underline{28} \\
4
$$

The advantage of the long-form algorithm is that it presents a clear interpretation of what is involved in division. The disadvantage is that most intermediate-grade teachers expect students to use the short-form algorithm. The advantage of the short-form algorithm is the relatively easy set of preskills that must be mastered prior to introducing division problems. The disadvantage of the short-form algorithm is that students may not understand why it works.

In this section, we discuss in detail the procedures for teaching the short-form algorithm. We discuss this algorithm because it is the algorithm most programs eventually encourage students to use. Remember, as mentioned earlier, we believe that lower performing students will be more successful if just one algorithm is presented. The basic steps of the short-form algorithm are presented in Summary Box 10.1.

One-Digit Divisors

Problems with one-digit divisors and multi-digit quotients are usually introduced in late third or early fourth grade. Students should know at least 30 to 40 basic division facts and the corresponding remainder facts prior to the introduction of this type of problem.

Two factors affect the difficulty level of single-digit divisor problems: the number of digits in the quotient and the presence of a zero in the quotient. The more digits in the quotient, the more difficult a problem is. For example, the first problem below is more difficult than the second problem

---

Summary Box 10.1
Division: The Short-Form Algorithm

1. Students read the problem.

2. Students underline the part of the problem that they work first.

3. Students compute the underlined part and write the answer above the last underlined digit.

4. Students multiply, subtract, and bring down the next number.

5. Students read the "new" problem and compute a quotient.

6. Students write the answer above the digit they just brought down.

7. Students multiply and subtract to determine the remainder.

8. Students say the problem and answer.

$$5\overline{)835} \qquad 5\overline{)125}$$

because the former will have a three-digit quotient while the latter will have a two-digit quotient. Each additional numeral in the quotient requires an extra set of computations. Similarly, a problem such as the first one below is more difficult than the second

$$5\overline{)52} \qquad 5\overline{)85}$$

because in the former problem, the quotient contains a zero. Without careful instruction, students are likely to leave out the zero.

$$5\overline{)\overset{1}{52}}$$
$$\underline{5}$$

This section discusses procedures for teaching students to work all of these problem types.

PROBLEMS WITH A TWO-DIGIT QUOTIENT. Format 10.6 shows the process to use for introducing division problems with two-digit quotients. The format includes five parts. In Part A, the students are taught how to determine the part of the problem to work first. This important preskill is necessary because division problems are worked a part at a time. For example, when working the problem

$$5\overline{)375}$$

the student first works the problem

$$5\overline{)37}$$

then, after multiplying and subtracting:

$$5\overline{)\overset{7}{375}}$$
$$\underline{35}$$
$$25$$

the student divides 5 into 25. The strategy to determine which part to work first involves comparing the divisor with the first digit of the dividend. If the first digit of the dividend is at least as big as the divisor, only the first digit of the dividend is underlined. For example, in this problem, the 9 is underlined:

$$7\overline{)\underline{9}45}$$

because the part of the problem to work first is 7 goes into 9. If the first digit of the dividend is not at least as big as the divisor, students are taught to underline the first two digits of the dividend. For example, in this problem, 23 is underlined:

$$7\overline{)\underline{23}6}$$

because the part of the problem to be worked first is 7 goes into 23. Note that in presenting this important preskill, the teacher does not use the words *divisor* or *dividend,* but rather refers to "the number dividing by" and "dividing into."

Examples must be carefully selected for Part A. In half of the problems, the first digit of the dividend should be smaller than the divisor. In the other half, the first digit of the dividend should be the same or larger than the divisor. A variety of divisors can be included, since students are not actually working the problems at this point. Below is a sample set of problems appropriate to use when teaching this preskill.

a. $7\overline{)243}$ b. $5\overline{)85}$ c. $4\overline{)235}$

d. $7\overline{)461}$ e. $9\overline{)362}$ f. $8\overline{)89}$

Part B of this format is a worksheet exercise in which the students practice underlining the part of the problem they work first. The teacher guides the students through several problems, then has the students work the rest on their own. The teacher repeats this part daily until students can perform accurately without teacher assistance. Part C is a structured board exercise in which the teacher demonstrates the entire short-form algorithm.

$$7\overline{)238}$$

Parts D and E in Format 10.6 are structured and less structured worksheet exercises. Note that the teacher specifies where digits in the quotient are to be written. The first digit in the quotient is to be written over the last underlined digit:

$$\overset{3}{7\overline{)2\underline{3}8}} \qquad \overset{1}{8\overline{)8\underline{2}}}$$

Each succeeding numeral is to be written over the succeeding digit in the dividend:

$$\overset{613}{7\overline{)\underline{4}291}}$$

As mentioned earlier, placing the digits of the quotient in the proper position helps students in solving problems with zeroes in the quotient as well as with problems containing decimals.

The example-selection guidelines for all worksheet exercises remain the same as for parts A and B, except that since students work the problems, the divisors should be limited to familiar facts. Half of the problems should have two-digit dividends, and half should have three-digit dividends. All problems should have two-digit quotients. Below is a sample set of problems that might appear in an exercise. This worksheet assumes students have learned division facts with 2, 9, 5, and 7 as divisors.

a. $5\overline{)87}$ b. $9\overline{)324}$ c. $5\overline{)135}$

d. $7\overline{)86}$ e. $2\overline{)134}$ f. $7\overline{)94}$

g. $2\overline{)156}$ h. $7\overline{)79}$ i. $2\overline{)29}$

ZERO IN THE QUOTIENT. Problems with zero as the last digit of a two-digit quotient, such as

$7\overline{)143}$ $2\overline{)81}$ $5\overline{)153}$

require special attention. These problems are introduced several weeks after division problems with two-digit quotients have been presented.

The critical part of the format occurs after students subtract and bring down the last digit. For example, in

$$\overset{3}{7\overline{)214}} \\ \underline{21} \\ 4$$

the teacher asks, "7 goes into 4 how many times?" Since the answer is zero, the teacher writes a zero above the 4. The teacher may have to model the answer for the first several problems. The format is presented for several days. Thereafter, three or four problems with a quotient ending in zero should be included in daily worksheet exercises.

QUOTIENTS OF THREE OR MORE DIGITS. Problems with quotients of three or more digits are introduced only when students have mastered problems with two-digit quotients. No preskills or board exercises need be presented. The teacher merely presents the less structured part of Format 10.6 for several days, emphasizing the need to keep bringing down digits until an answer has been written above the last digit of the dividend.

Problems with a zero as one of the three digits in the quotient are introduced only after students can solve problems without zeroes in the quotient. Problems with a zero as the last digit can be introduced a week or so after problems with three-digit quotients have been introduced. These problems should cause students relatively little difficulty, since two-digit quotients with a zero would have been taught earlier. On the other hand, problems with a zero as the second digit of a three-digit quotient, such as

$$\overset{103}{5\overline{)515}} \qquad \overset{407}{2\overline{)814}}$$

will be difficult for many students. A structured worksheet exercise (Part D of Format 10.6) should be presented. After bringing down the first number, the teacher can say, "The next part says 5 goes into 1; 5 goes into 1 zero times, so I write 0 in the answer. What is zero times 5? So I write zero under the 1. Now we subtract and bring down the next number."

$$\overset{1}{5\overline{)517}} \\ 5$$

The teacher presents the structured worksheet exercise for several days with three or four problems. Next, a supervised worksheet exercise containing about 10 problems, three or four of which have zero as the middle digit, is presented. Supervised practice is continued until students develop accuracy.

Problems with quotients of four or more digits are usually presented in late fourth grade or early fifth. For students who have mastered all types of problems with three-digit quotients, these longer problems should cause little difficulty.

SELF-CHECKING. After students become proficient in working division problems with remainders, they should be taught to check their answers. A checking procedure for division is to multiply the divisor and quotient and add the remainder, if there is one. The teacher can introduce self-checking on a worksheet exercise in which the problems are already worked and about half of them have incorrect answers. The teacher instructs the students to check their answers using the self-checking strategy and to correct mistakes.

Two-Digit Divisors

Solving problems with two-digit divisors requires the integration of numerous component skills into a fairly lengthy strategy. The steps in the short-form algorithm for two-digit divisors are outlined in Summary Box 10.2.

The complexity of problems with two-digit divisors is affected mainly by whether or not the estimating, or rounding off, procedure produces a correct quotient. In some cases, the estimate may yield a quotient that is too large. For example, in the problem

$$53\overline{)203}$$

students round off 53 to 5 tens and 203 to 20 tens, and then determine how many fives in 20. The estimated quotient, 4, when multiplied by 53, equals 212, which is too large to be subtracted from 203. Since the estimate yielded too large a quotient, the actual quotient must be 3, not 4.

In contrast, other estimates may yield a quotient that is too small. For example, in the problem

$$56\overline{)284}$$

when 56 is rounded off to 6 tens and 284 is rounded off to 28 tens, the estimate is a quotient of 4. However, 56 × 4 is 224, which when subtracted from 284 leaves a difference of 60, from which another group of 56 could be made. Since the estimated quotient yields too small a quotient, the actual quotient must be one larger than 4.

Problems in which the estimated quotient is too large or too small are more difficult and should not be introduced until students can work problems in which the estimated quotients prove to be correct.

PRESKILLS. Students should have mastered all of the component skills needed to solve division problems with one-digit divisors before problems with two-digit divisors are introduced. Additional preskills are rounding off numbers to the nearest tens unit, which is discussed next, and multiplying multi-digit numbers, which was discussed in Chapter 9.

Rounding off numbers to the nearest tens unit is a critical skill for problems with two-digit divisors. The first part of the strategy teaches students to estimate how many groups the size of the divisor can be made from the dividend. For the problem

$$54\overline{)186}$$

Summary Box 10.2
Division: Short-Form Algorithm—Two-Digit Divisors

1. Student reads the problem.
2. Student underlines the part to be worked first.
3. Student writes the rounded-off problem.
4. Student computes the division problem using the estimate from the rounded-off problem.
5. Student multiplies and determines if she can subtract.
6. Student adjusts the quotient if the estimate is not correct (using the rules, if you can't subtract, make the answer smaller; if the remainder is too big, make the answer bigger).
7. Student computes the division problem and reads the problem with the answer.

the teacher asks, "How many times does 54 go into 186?" The estimate is derived by rounding off and expressing both the divisor and dividend as tens units: 54 is rounded to 5 tens and 186 is rounded to 19 tens. The students then figure out how many fives in 19.

Format 10.7 shows how to teach students to round off numbers to the nearest tens unit. In Part A, the teacher models and tests converting a tens number that ends in zero to a unit of tens: 340 equals 34 tens, 720 equals 72 tens, 40 equals 4 tens. The teacher repeats a set of six to eight examples until the students can respond correctly to all of the examples. In Part B, the teacher models and tests rounding numbers that end in any digit to the nearest tens unit. The teacher writes a numeral on the board and asks the students if the number is closer to the tens number preceding it or following it. For example, after writing 238 on the board, the teacher asks the students if 238 is closer to 230 or 240. After the students respond "240," the teacher asks, "So how many tens is 238 closest to, 23 tens or 24 tens?"

Part C is a worksheet exercise in which the student must write the tens unit closest to the number (e.g., 342 = ☐ tens). Students may require several weeks of practice to master this skill. However, division problems with two-digit divisors should not be introduced until mastery of this preskill is demonstrated.

There are several example-selection guidelines for this format: (a) half of the numbers to be transformed should have a numeral less than 5 in the ones column, while the other half should have 5 or a numeral greater than 5; (b) about two-thirds of the examples should be three-digit numbers and one-third, two-digit numbers, so that practice is provided on the two types of numbers students will have to round off; and (c) numbers that may cause particular difficulty for students should not be included in initial exercises.

Two types of numbers may cause difficulty: (a) numbers in which the last two digits are 95 or greater (e.g., 397, 295, 498), which require rounding off to the next hundreds grouping (397 rounds off to 40 tens, and 295 rounds off to 30 tens), and (b) numbers that have a zero in the tens column (e.g., 408, 207, 305). Special emphasis should be given to these two types of examples about a week after the format is initially presented.

PROBLEMS WITH CORRECT ESTIMATED QUOTIENTS. Initially, division problems with two-digit divisors should be limited to problems in which the estimated quotients prove to be correct. Also, the initial problems should involve a one-digit quotient. Problems containing a two-digit quotient can usually be introduced several days after problems with a one-digit quotient are presented.

The process for teaching correct estimated quotients with two-digit divisors appears in Format 10.8. It includes four parts. Parts A and B teach component skills unique to the short-form algorithm: horizontal multiplication and estimating a quotient by rounding off the divisor and dividend.

Part A teaches students to multiply the estimated quotient and divisor, which are written horizontally, and to place the product below the dividend. In the problem

$$57\overline{)391}$$

the estimated quotient 6 and the divisor 57 are multiplied. The student first multiplies 6×7, which is 42. The 2 is placed under the 1 in the dividend, and the 4 is carried over the 5 in the divisor:

$$\begin{array}{c} 4 \quad\; 6 \\ 57\overline{)391} \\ 2 \end{array}$$

The student then multiplies 6×5 and adds the carried 4. The total 34 is written under the 39 in the dividend:

$$\begin{array}{c} 4 \quad\; 6 \\ 57\overline{)391} \\ 342 \end{array}$$

Part B presents the rounding-off strategy to determine the estimated quotient. The teacher writes a problem on the board and next to the problem writes a box with a division sign:

$$37\overline{)1582} \qquad \boxed{\overline{)}}$$

The rounded-off problem is written in the box. The teacher has students read the problem and determine the part to work first (e.g., 37 goes into 158) and then underline those numbers in the dividend. The students then round off 37 to 4 tens and 158 to 16 tens and write the rounded-off problem in the box:

$$\boxed{4\overline{)16}}$$

After rounding off, the students figure out the answer to the rounded-off problem and write the answer above the last underlined digit in the original problem:

$$\begin{array}{cc} 4 & \\ 37\overline{)\underline{158}2} & \boxed{4\overline{)16}} \end{array}$$

Parts A and B can be introduced at the same time. Also note that both parts contain two sections.

In the first section of each part, the teacher presents several problems on the board. In the second section, the teacher leads the students through several worksheet problems and then has them work several problems on their own. Each day, the students should work more problems on their own. If the students can work at least four of the five problems correctly, they are presented the next day with Part C, in which the entire strategy is introduced. If students miss two or more problems, they continue working on parts A and/or B. Students must be able to perform the multiplication and estimation skills accurately before the entire strategy is presented.

Part C is a structured worksheet exercise in which students are guided through all the steps in the strategy. For about the first two weeks, the boxes for rounding off should be written on students' worksheets. A sample problem on a worksheet would looks like this:

The upper box is for writing the rounded-off problem for the first part of the problem; the lower box is for writing the rounded-off problem for the second part of the problem.

Two example-selection guidelines are important to this format. First and foremost, all of the problems must yield estimated quotients that are correct. Second, in half of the problems, the first two digits in the dividend must be less than the divisor:

$$37\overline{)2431} \qquad 52\overline{)4681}$$

while in the other problems, the first two digits must be greater than the divisor:

$$37\overline{)441} \qquad 52\overline{)838}$$

Several problems with a one-digit quotient should be included in supervised and independent worksheets. The mixture of problems ensures that students will use the steps of determining which part to work first.

PROBLEMS WITH INCORRECT ESTIMATED QUOTIENTS. In a minor, but still significant, proportion of problems with two-digit divisors, one or more estimated quotients will prove to be incorrect. For example, in the problem

$$39\overline{)155}$$

the estimated quotient would prove too large, since 4×39 equals 156. Problems in which the estimated

quotient is incorrect should be introduced about a week after students have developed accuracy in working problems in which the estimates are correct. The first problems presented should result in a one-digit quotient. The steps for presenting these problems appear in Format 10.9.

The format includes two parts. Part A focuses only on the component skill of determining if the estimated quotient is correct and what to do if it is not correct. Separate sequences of steps are indicated for problems in which the estimated quotient is too large and for problems in which the estimated quotient is too small. The rules in the format are designed to minimize student confusion (e.g., if you can't subtract, make the answer smaller; if the remainder is too big, make the answer bigger).

In Part A, the students are given a worksheet on which the estimated quotient is written in each problem. The worksheet includes a variety of problems. One-third of the problems have a quotient that is a multiple too large:

$$34\overline{)146}^{\,5}$$

One-third of the problems have a quotient that is a multiple too small:

$$36\overline{)193}^{\,4}$$

The final third of the problems contain the estimated quotients that are correct:

$$28\overline{)153}^{\,5}$$

Students first multiply the quotient and divisor. If the product of these two numbers is greater than the dividend, the teacher points out that the answer must be less. In the problem

$$\begin{array}{r} 5 \\ 34\overline{)146} \\ \underline{170} \end{array}$$

the teacher says, "We can't subtract. We must make the answer smaller. Cross out the 5 and write 4." In problems in which the estimated quotient is too small, the teacher has the students compare their remainder to the divisor. If the remainder is as big as or bigger than the divisor, the quotient is to be made larger. For example, in the problem

$$\begin{array}{r} 4 \\ 36\overline{)193} \\ \underline{144} \\ \underline{49} \end{array}$$

the teacher points out that another group of 36 can be made from 49, so the answer is made bigger. The 4 in the answer is erased and replaced with a 5.

A special type of problem yields an estimated quotient of 10 or above. For these problems, the teacher introduces a rule that no matter how high the answer to the rounded-off problem, the highest number used in an answer is 9. Then, even though rounding off yields 11 as an estimated quotient, the student still uses 9 as the quotient. Several problems of this type should be included in the exercises.

$$24\overline{)228} \quad as \quad 2\overline{)23}$$

Practice on problems yielding an incorrect quotient is continued daily for several weeks. During this time, problems are limited to those that have one-digit quotients. Problems with multi-digit quotients are not introduced until students are successful at working problems with single-digit quotients. The teacher should prepare worksheets containing a variety of problems. In some problems, the estimate for the first digit of the quotient should prove too large or too small, while the estimate for the second digit proves correct. For example, in the problem

$$64\overline{)1803}$$

only the estimate for the first numeral in the quotient is incorrect (3 is too large). In other problems, the estimate for the first digit of the quotient should be correct, while the estimate for the second part is incorrect. For example, in the problem

$$64\overline{)3317}$$

the estimate for 64 into 331 is correct, while the second part of the problem, 64 into 117, yields an estimated quotient that is too large. Finally, in some problems, the estimate for both numerals of the quotient should be incorrect. Figure 10.3 includes sets of problems that can be used in these exercises.

Problems in which the estimated quotient is too small are particularly difficult for students. In order to prepare students for this format, the teacher should present an exercise for several days prior to introducing Format 10.11, focusing on when a remainder is too big. In this exercise, the teacher writes about six problems with two-digit divisors on the board and models how to determine if the remainder is too big.

FIGURE 10.3 Examples of Two-Digit Divisor Problems with Single-Digit Quotients

Estimate Yields Quotient That Is Correct

$34\overline{)102}$	$82\overline{)591}$	$37\overline{)1723}$	$72\overline{)3924}$	$73\overline{)2308}$	$53\overline{)230}$	$27\overline{)94}$	$52\overline{)2731}$
$53\overline{)1752}$	$29\overline{)2150}$	$48\overline{)268}$	$51\overline{)78}$	$68\overline{)1528}$	$27\overline{)941}$	$51\overline{)2398}$	$39\overline{)94}$
$90\overline{)673}$	$80\overline{)7485}$	$19\overline{)813}$	$86\overline{)5000}$	$40\overline{)289}$	$48\overline{)269}$	$12\overline{)384}$	$41\overline{)987}$
$25\overline{)896}$	$67\overline{)242}$	$82\overline{)370}$	$89\overline{)6703}$	$58\overline{)1256}$	$16\overline{)415}$	$32\overline{)197}$	$11\overline{)48}$
$45\overline{)968}$	$93\overline{)5780}$	$42\overline{)534}$	$75\overline{)183}$	$28\overline{)154}$	$36\overline{)2000}$	$84\overline{)991}$	$60\overline{)2486}$

Estimate Yields Quotient Too Large

$73\overline{)289}$	$84\overline{)246}$	$91\overline{)632}$	$64\overline{)3321}$	$53\overline{)1524}$	$16\overline{)60}$	$23\overline{)170}$	$13\overline{)68}$
$93\overline{)2724}$	$24\overline{)900}$	$44\overline{)216}$	$72\overline{)354}$	$82\overline{)2401}$	$52\overline{)1020}$	$31\overline{)1500}$	$31\overline{)180}$
$54\overline{)102}$	$71\overline{)3520}$	$41\overline{)2450}$	$72\overline{)2815}$				

Estimate Yields Quotient Too Small

$26\overline{)185}$	$35\overline{)175}$	$38\overline{)193}$	$35\overline{)1651}$	$25\overline{)1852}$	$46\overline{)283}$	$86\overline{)260}$	$75\overline{)300}$
$37\overline{)2483}$	$47\overline{)1898}$	$57\overline{)342}$	$29\overline{)114}$	$48\overline{)3425}$	$46\overline{)1823}$	$85\overline{)6913}$	$45\overline{)238}$
$58\overline{)232}$	$36\overline{)1892}$	$16\overline{)861}$	$17\overline{)698}$				

Problems in Which Estimated Quotient Is Greater Than 9

$23\overline{)214}$	$21\overline{)200}$	$34\overline{)312}$	$73\overline{)725}$	$74\overline{)725}$	$43\overline{)412}$	$24\overline{)238}$	$14\overline{)120}$
$13\overline{)104}$	$32\overline{)304}$						

FIGURE 10.4 Diagnosis and Remediation of Multi-digit Division Errors

Error Patterns	Diagnosis	Remediation Procedures
One-Digit Divisor Problems		
a. $\begin{array}{r} 64 \\ 7\overline{)483} \\ 45 \\ \hline 33 \\ 28 \\ \hline 5 \end{array}$	Fact error: Student makes a fact error ($6 \times 7 = 45$).	Depends on frequency of fact error. High % fact errors—provide systematic fact instruction. Low % fact errors—increase motivation, include missed facts in fact drills.
b. $\begin{array}{r} 56 \\ 7\overline{)413} \\ 35 \\ \hline 43 \\ 42 \\ \hline 1 \end{array}$	Component skill: Student makes a subtraction error ($41 - 35 = 4$).	Less structured worksheet part of Format 10.7. Remind students to borrow.
c. $\begin{array}{r} 81 \\ 6\overline{)493} \\ 48 \\ \hline 13 \\ 6 \\ \hline 7 \end{array}$	Component skill: Student computes an incorrect quotient: too small.	Remediation formats (formats 10.4 and 10.5) for incorrect quotients. Problems should have divisor that was in problem missed.
d. $\begin{array}{r} 49 \\ 6\overline{)288} \\ 24 \\ \hline 48 \\ 54 \end{array}$	Component skill: Student computes an incorrect quotien: too large.	
e. $\begin{array}{r} 335 \\ 7\overline{)23458} \\ 21 \\ \hline 24 \\ 21 \\ \hline 38 \\ 35 \\ \hline 3 \end{array}$	Component skill: Student computes an incomplete quotient: does not bring down a digit.	Less structured worksheet exercise (Format 10.7).
f. $\begin{array}{r} 514 \\ 4\overline{)20568} \\ 20 \\ \hline 5 \\ 4 \\ \hline 16 \\ 16 \\ \hline 0 \end{array}$	Component skill: Student computes an incomplete quotient: does not write a quotient for the last digit.	Less structured worksheet exercise focusing on need to keep working problems until each digit after underlined part has a digit over it.
g. $\begin{array}{r} 12 \\ 7\overline{)714} \\ 7 \\ \hline 14 \\ 14 \end{array}$ $\begin{array}{r} 7 \\ 5\overline{)352} \\ 35 \\ \hline 2 \end{array}$	Component skill: Student computes an incomplete quotient in problems with zero in the quotient.	Structured worksheet focusing on problems of this type.
h. $\begin{array}{r} 4 \\ 39\overline{)155} \\ 156 \\ \hline 1 \end{array}$ $\begin{array}{r} 2 \\ 25\overline{)78} \\ 50 \\ \hline 28 \end{array}$	Component skill: Student computes quotient that is too large or too small.	Present format for problems in which estimated quotient is incorrect (Format 10.11).
i. $\begin{array}{r} 7 \\ 27\overline{)2248} \\ 189 \end{array}$	Component skill: Student computes an incomplete quotient because of misplacement of products.	Present structured worksheet exercise (Format 10.10). Focus on where to place digits when multiplying.

Diagnosis and Remediation

Division problems may be worked incorrectly for numerous reasons. Common errors made by students are summarized in the diagnosis and remediation chart in Figure 10.4. The remediation procedures usually involve presenting a structured worksheet exercise focusing on the particular component-skill error made by the students. Remember, when students miss more than 10 to 20% of the problems due to a specific type of error, a remediation procedure is needed. When examining student worksheets, the teacher not only should look for the reason students missed a problem but also should examine problems solved correctly, noting if the students rounded off correctly. Students who round off incorrectly may solve problems correctly but may do much unnecessary computing. Students who make rounding-off errors in 10 to 15% or more of the problems should receive intensive remediation in rounding off. The teacher should review the rounding-off formats for several days before reintroducing the less structured presentation.

COMMERCIAL PROGRAMS

Division: Renaming with Single- and Double-Digit Divisors

INSTRUCTIONAL STRATEGIES The initial strategy presented for division with remainders does not vary significantly in the major programs. The strategy usually includes these steps:

Step 1: Divide tens.
Step 2: Regroup.
Step 3: Divide ones.

As with strategies presented for other basic operations, the strategy appears straightforward. However, upon closer inspection, we find that critical steps in the strategy are omitted, thereby making the strategy more difficult to use, especially for low-performing students. In some programs, students are encouraged to "think through" these critical steps. Also, the use of pictures tends to direct student attention away from necessary steps in the computation process, such as how to align numbers in the problem or when and where to subtract. In fact, it is often unclear from the teacher's manual whether students are supposed to operate on the pictures or on the numerals first. Naive students require more explicit instruction on all steps of this computation process to master this skill.

The strategies for division with two-digit divisors that appear in the many basals are again quite similar. Even in initial lessons, students are assumed to have mastered sophisticated prerequisites such as determining where to begin working the problem or estimation. The strategy is outlined in four basic steps: regroup thousands, regroup hundreds, regroup tens, and regroup tens again. The process of estimating the answer is already completed for the student. Whether students can estimate on their own is a question. Also, since many errors in division are caused by writing quotients in the wrong columns, it is noteworthy that many programs do not explicitly teach students how to align columns in division.

APPLICATION ITEMS: DIVISION

1. Describe the problem type that each example below represents. List the problems in the order they are introduced. Write the grade level when each type is typically introduced.

   $5\overline{)128}$ $5\overline{)23}$ $2\overline{)136}$ $5\overline{)20}$ $5\overline{)153}$

   $27\overline{)122}$ $5\overline{)736}$ $27\overline{)136}$ $5\overline{)526}$

2. Below is an excerpt from the independent worksheet to be given to students who have just demonstrated accuracy in solving problems with a one-digit divisor and a three-digit quotient (type 4e). The teacher has made some errors in constructing the worksheet.

   a. Indicate any inappropriate examples.
   b. Identify any omitted problem types that should be included on the worksheet. (Assume that students know all basic division facts.)

   $7\overline{)932}$ $5\overline{)1432}$ $3\overline{)1214}$ $5\overline{)3752}$

   $2\overline{)714}$ $9\overline{)1436}$ $5\overline{)823}$ $6\overline{)1443}$

3. Below are eight problems that appeared on a worksheet to be done independently by the students in Ms. Adams's math group. Below each student's name are the problems missed by the student. For each student, specify the probable cause or causes of the student's errors. Describe the remediation procedure.

$6\overline{)8324}$ $4\overline{)12385}$ $7\overline{)493}$ $8\overline{)7200}$ $5\overline{)5214}$ $7\overline{)9222}$ $5\overline{)8253}$ $9\overline{)72990}$

Barbara

```
      8332R2              925
  9)72990            8)7200
     70                 70
     29                 20
     27                 16
     29                 40
     27
     20
     18
      2
```

Randy

```
      396R1             142R4
  4)12385           5)524
     12                 5
     38                 21
     36                 20
     25                 14
     24                 10
      1                  4
```

Fred

```
      131R5
  7)9222
     7
     22
     21
     12
      7
      5
```

4. Below is an error made by Charles on a worksheet assignment. Describe what the teacher says in making the correction.

```
       4R40
  36)184
     144
      40
```

5. Write the structured worksheet part of a format to present this problem:

$7\overline{)213}$

6. Specify the wording the teacher uses to correct the following errors:

a. $27\overline{)482}$ $3\overline{)48}$

b. $27\overline{)482}$ $2\overline{)4}$

7. Below is an excerpt from the independent worksheet to be given to students who have just demonstrated accuracy in solving problems with two-digit divisors and one- or two-digit quotients, in which estimating produces proper quotient. Indicate the inappropriate examples.

$23\overline{)989}$ $34\overline{)148}$ $76\overline{)793}$

$58\overline{)2938}$ $31\overline{)283}$ $49\overline{)1638}$

FORMAT 10.1   Introducing Division

TEACHER	STUDENTS

PART A: TRANSLATING DIVISION PROBLEMS

1. *(Write these problems on the board.)*

$5\overline{)15}^{\;3}$ $2\overline{)18}^{\;9}$ $6\overline{)30}^{\;5}$ $3\overline{)12}^{\;4}$

$4\overline{)20}^{\;5}$ $7\overline{)28}^{\;4}$ $3\overline{)21}^{\;7}$

This is a division problem. What kind of problem?   **A division problem**

It says *(Point to 5.)* 5 goes into *(point to 15.)* 15 *(point to 3)* three times. What does the problem say?   **5 goes into 15 three times.**
(Point to 5, then 15, then 3 as students answer. Repeat step 1 with the problems below.)

$2\overline{)18}^{\;9}$ $6\overline{)30}^{\;5}$

2. (Point to $3\overline{)12}^{\;4}$.) What does this problem say?   **3 goes into 12 four times.**
   (Point to 3, then 12, then 4 as students answer.

   Repeat step 2 with the problems below.)

   $4\overline{)20}^{\;5}$ $7\overline{)28}^{\;4}$ $3\overline{)21}^{\;7}$

   (Give individual turns to several students.)

PART B: STRUCTURED BOARD PRESENTATION

1. *(Write on board: $5\overline{)15}$.)*
   What kind of problem is this?   **A division problem**
   This problem says 5 goes into 15. What does this problem
   say? *(Point to 5, then 15.)*   **5 goes into 15.**
   We have to find out how many times 5 goes into 15. When
   we divide, we start with a big group and make equal-sized
   smaller groups. *(Write 15 lines on board.)*

   |||||||||||||||

2. This is a group of 15 lines. I want to divide this group of 15
   lines into smaller groups. Each smaller group will have 5
   lines in it. How many lines in each smaller group?   **5**

3. I'll touch the lines. You count. *(Touch five lines.)* This is a   **1, 2, 3, 4, 5**
   group of 5, so I'll put a circle around it. *(Circle five lines.)*
   (Repeat step 3 with remaining groups of five lines.)

TEACHER	STUDENTS

4. We divided 15 into groups of 5. Let's count the groups. (Touch each group.) — 1, 2, 3

5. How many times does 5 go into 15? I write the 3 above the last 3 digit in 15. (Write $5\overline{)15}$ with 3 above.) — 3

Say what the problem tells us. — 5 goes into 15 three times.

(Repeat steps 1–5 with $2\overline{)8}$.)

PART C: STRUCTURED WORKSHEET

a. $5\overline{)20}$ b. $2\overline{)8}$ c. $2\overline{)12}$
||||||||||||||||||||| |||||||| |||||||||||||

1. Touch problem a. That problem says 5 goes into 20. What does the problem say? — 5 goes into 20.

2. We have to find out how many groups of 5 we can make from 20. There are 20 lines under the problem. Make groups of 5 lines each (Check students' papers.)

3. How many groups did you make? — 4

   Write 4 above the last digit in 20. (Monitor.) — Students write 4.

4. Now the problem says 5 goes into 20 four times. What does the problem say now? — 5 goes into 20 four times.

   (Repeat steps 1–4 with remaining problems.)

PART D: LESS STRUCTURED WORKSHEET

1. Touch problem a. — Students touch $2\overline{)10}$. ||||||||||

2. What does the problem say? — 2 goes into 10.

3. How many in each group? — 2

4. Make the groups and write how many groups over the last digit in 10. — Students make circles around each two lines. Students write 5.

5. Read the problem and answer. — 2 goes into 10 five times.

FORMAT 10.2   Introducing Division with Remainders

TEACHER	STUDENTS

PART A: INTRODUCING REMAINDERS

1. (Write this problem on board.)

   $5\overline{)13}$

   (Point to $5\overline{)13}$.) What does the problem say? — 5 goes into 13.

(continued on next page)

FORMAT 10.2   (continued)

TEACHER	**STUDENTS**

2. First let's solve the problem by making lines. The problem asks how many groups of 5 in 13, so I'll draw 13 lines. *(Make 13 lines on the board.)* The problem asks how many groups of 5 in 13, so I'll put a circle around each group of 5. *(Count out each group of 5 aloud; after circling each group, say,)* Here's a group of 5. *(After counting the last 3 lines, say,)* We only have 3 left so we can't make a group of 5.

3. Now let's see how many groups of 5 there are; count the groups as I touch them. *(Touch groups as students count.)*   1, 2

4. How many groups of 5 in 13?   2

Yes, there are two groups. *(Write* $5\overline{)13}^{\,2}$ *.)*

5. Are there lines left over?   Yes
We call those lines the remainder. How many lines are left over?   3

6. We say that 5 goes into 13 two times with a remainder of 3. How many times does 5 go into 13?   Two times with a remainder of 3.

(Repeat steps 1–6 with the problems below.)
$2\overline{)9}$ $9\overline{)21}$

PART B: STRUCTURED WORKSHEET

a. $5\overline{)23}$ (|||||)   (|||||)   (|||||)   (|||||) |||

b. $2\overline{)7}$ (||)   (||)   (||) |

c. $9\overline{)25}$ (|||||||||)   (|||||||||) |||||||

d. $5\overline{)14}$ (|||||)   (|||||) ||||

1. Read problem a.   5 goes into 23.

2. The problem asks how many groups of 5 we can make from 23. Next to the problem are 23 lines. A circle has been drawn around each group of 5 lines. How many groups of 5 are there? Write 4 on the line above the 3.   4

3. We want to figure out how many lines we used up, so we multiply 4 times 5. How do we figure how many lines we used up?   Multiply 4 × 5.

4. What is 4 × 5? *(Pause, signal.)*   20

TEACHER	**STUDENTS**
5. Write 20 under the 23. We started with 23 and used up 20, so write a minus sign in front of the 20. Read the subtraction problem we just wrote. Subtract and write the remainder. What is 23 minus 20?	23 – 20 3
6. We're all finished; 5 goes into 23 four times with a remainder of 3. How many times does 5 go into 23?	Four times with a remainder of 3.

(Repeat steps 1–6 with problems b, c, and d.)

PART C: LESS STRUCTURED WORKSHEET

1. Read problem _____.	_____ goes into _____.
How many times does _____ go into _____? *(Pause, signal.)* Write _____ above the _____ in _____. How do we figure how many lines we used?	_____ times Multiply _____ × _____.
2. What is _____ times _____?	_____
3. Write _____ under the _____. Put in the minus sign.	
4. Subtract. *(Remind students to borrow when applicable.)* What is the remainder?	_____
5. How many times does _____ go into _____?	_____ times with a remainder of _____.

FORMAT 10.3   **Introducing Remainder Facts**

TEACHER	**STUDENTS**
PART A: STRUCTURED BOARD PRESENTATION	
1. *(Write these numbers on the board in a single row.)*	

⓪ 1 2 3 4 ⑤ 6 7 8 9
⑩ 11 12 13 14 ⑮ 16 17 18
19 ⑳ 21 22 23 24 ㉕

Listen: 5 goes into the circled numbers without a remainder. Say the numbers that 5 goes into without a remainder.	0, 5, 10, 15, 20, 25
2. Five goes into the other number with a remainder. *(Point to 1, 2, 3, 4.)* These are numbers 5 goes into zero times with a remainder.	
3. My turn: How many times does 5 go into 2? Five goes into 2 zero times with a remainder. How many times does 5 go into 2?	Zero times with a remainder.
How many times does 5 go into 4?	Zero times with a remainder.
	(continued on next page)

FORMAT 10.3 (continued)

TEACHER	STUDENTS

4. *(Point to 5.)* Five goes into 5 one time. *(Point to 6, 7, 8, 9.)* These are numbers 5 goes into one time with a remainder. How many times does 5 go into 8?

One time with a remainder.

How many times does 5 go into 6?

One time with a remainder.

5. *(Repeat step 4 using 5 goes into 15 and then 5 goes into 19 and 5 goes into 17.)*

6. *(Repeat step 4 using 5 goes into 20, 5 goes into 24, 5 goes into 21.)*

PART B: LESS STRUCTURED BOARD PRESENTATION

1. *(Write these numbers on the board in a single row.)*

⓪ 1 2 3 4 ⑤ 6 7 8 9
⑩ 11 12 13 14 ⑮ 16 17 18
19 ⑳ 21 22 23 24 ㉕

Say the numbers that 5 goes into without a remainder.

5, 10, 15, 20, 25

2. *(Point to 13.)* Think, 5 goes into 13 how many times? *(Pause, signal.)*

Two times with a remainder.

To correct: *(Point to 10.)* Five goes into 10 two times. *(Point to 11, 12, 13, 14.)* These are the numbers 5 goes into two times with a remainder. Five goes into 13, two times with a remainder. *(Repeat step 2.)*

3. *(Repeat step 2 with 20, 24, 0, 3, 9, 16.)*

PART C: STRUCTURED WORKSHEET

a. 5)‾2‾2‾   b. 5)‾1‾6‾   c. 5)‾1‾0‾   d. 5)‾7‾

1. Read problem _____ .

_____ goes into _____ .

2. How many times does _____ go into _____ ? *(Pause, signal.)*
To correct: *(If student says number too low:*

$$\overset{3}{5)\overline{22}}$$

say,)* We can make another group of five—5 × 4 = 20.
(If student says number too high:

$$\overset{5}{5)\overline{22}}$$

say,)* 5 × 5 = 25. That's too big.

3. Write _____ above the _____ in _____ .

Student writes quotient over last number in dividend.

What do you multiply?

_____ times _____

Multiply and subtract. *(Pause.)* What is the remainder?

TEACHER	STUDENTS
How many times does _____ go into_____?	_____ times with a remainder of _____.

(Repeat steps 1–3 with several more problems and then have students work the rest on their own.)

FORMAT 10.4   Remediation for Division with Remainders—Quotient Too Small

---

PART A: RECOGNIZING QUOTIENTS THAT ARE TOO SMALL

TEACHER   **STUDENTS**

1. *(Write this problem on the board.)*

   $5\overline{)28}$

   This problem says 5 goes into 28. We're figuring 5 into a number, so the remainder must be smaller than 5.

2. What does the problem say?   5 goes into 28.

3. So what do you know about the remainder?   It must be smaller than 5.

4. *(Repeat steps 1–3 with* $7\overline{)23}$ $2\overline{)13}$ $6\overline{)14}$ $5\overline{)27}$ $3\overline{)24}$.*)*

PART B: WRITING THE CORRECT ANSWER

a. $5\overline{)28}^{\,4}$ b. $7\overline{)31}^{\,4}$ c. $9\overline{)24}^{\,2}$

d. $9\overline{)43}^{\,3}$ e. $5\overline{)42}^{\,8}$ f. $2\overline{)13}^{\,5}$

g. $2\overline{)15}^{\,6}$ h. $5\overline{)28}^{\,5}$

1. Problem a says 5 goes into 28 four times. We figure the remainder by multiplying 5×4 and then subtracting. Do that on your paper.

2. What's the remainder?   8

3. Here's a rule: If the remainder is too big, we make the answer bigger. What do we do if the remainder is too big?   Make the answer bigger.

4. Is the remainder too big?   Yes

   So what must we do?   Make the answer bigger.

   The remainder is more than 5, so 5 can go into 28 another time. Cross out the 4 and write 5. *(Check.)* Now erase 20; multiply and subtract to figure the new remainder. What's the new remainder?   3

   (Note: If the answer to step 4 is no, tell students,) so the answer is correct. Let's go to the next problem *(see step 5).*

5. Is the remainder too big?   No

   So the answer is correct. Read the problem.   5 goes into 28 five times with a remainder of 3.

6. *(Repeat steps 1–5 with several problems, and then have students work remaining problems on their own.)*

FORMAT 10.5 **Remediation for Division with Remainders—Quotient Too Large**

TEACHER	STUDENTS

PART A: RECOGNIZING QUOTIENTS THAT ARE TOO LARGE

1. *(Write the problem below on the board.)*

$$\frac{6}{5\overline{)28}}$$
$$\underline{30}$$

What does this problem say? — 5 goes into 28 six times.

2. The problem is worked for you, but there is something wrong. Can you subtract 30 from 28? — No

3. Here's a rule: If you can't subtract, make the answer smaller. What do you do if you can't subtract? — Make the answer smaller.

4. We make the answer 1 smaller. What is 1 smaller than 6? — 5

   (Erase 6 and write 5.) What is 5 times 5? — 25

5. *(Erase 30 and write 25.)* Can you subtract 25 from 28? — Yes

   What is 28 – 25? — 3

   Read the problem. — 5 goes into 28 five times with a remainder of 3.

6. *(Repeat steps 1–5 with several examples.)*

PART B: WRITING THE CORRECT ANSWER

a. $\dfrac{6}{5\overline{)28}}$ b. $\dfrac{4}{7\overline{)31}}$ c. $\dfrac{2}{9\overline{)24}}$

d. $\dfrac{5}{9\overline{)43}}$ e. $\dfrac{8}{5\overline{)42}}$ f. $\dfrac{7}{2\overline{)13}}$

1. Look at the problems on your worksheet. Some of the answers are too big. You'll have to fix them.

2. Look at problem a. What is 6 × 5? — 30

3. Can you subtract 30 from 28? — No

   What must you do? — Make the answer 1 smaller.

   (Note: Do step 4 only if answer to step 3 is no.)

4. Cross out the 6. What do you write? — 5

   Work the problem.

   (Repeat steps 2–4 with five or six problems, and then have students complete the worksheet on their own.)

FORMAT 10.6 **Division with Two-Digit Quotients**

TEACHER	STUDENTS

PART A: DETERMINING WHERE TO BEGIN

1. When a division problem has lots of digits, we work the problem a part at a time. We always begin a problem by underlining the first part we work. Sometimes we underline just the first digit. Sometimes we underline the first two digits.

TEACHER   **STUDENTS**

2. *(Write the following problem on the board.)*

$$6\overline{)242}$$

Read the problem.   6 goes into 242.

We're dividing by 6. If the first digit in the number we're
dividing is at least as big as 6, we underline the first digit in
242. If 6 can't go into the first digit, we underline the first
two digits. Look at the number we're dividing into. The first
digit we're dividing into is 2. Is 2 at least as big as 6?   No

So we underline the first two digits. *(Underline 24.)* $6\overline{)\underline{24}2}$

The underlined problem says 6 goes into 24. What does the
underlined problem say?   6 goes into 24.

(Repeat step 2 with these problems.)

a. $5\overline{)87}$ b. $9\overline{)328}$ c. $4\overline{)38}$

d. $6\overline{)62}$ e. $3\overline{)245}$ f. $7\overline{)832}$

PART B: WORKSHEET ON DETERMINING WHERE TO BEGIN

a. $7\overline{)248}$ b. $3\overline{)527}$ c. $7\overline{)486}$ d. $5\overline{)532}$

e. $5\overline{)234}$ f. $6\overline{)184}$ g. $6\overline{)932}$

h. $4\overline{)128}$ i. $4\overline{)436}$ j. $8\overline{)264}$

1. Touch problem a. Read the problem.   7 goes into 248.

You're going to underline the part of the problem you work
first. What are you dividing by?   7

Is the first digit you're dividing into at least as big as 7?   No

So what do you underline?   24

Underline 24. Say the underlined problem.   7 goes into 24.

*(Repeat step 1 with five problems. Then have students
underline the part they work first in renaming problems.)*

PART C: STRUCTURED BOARD PRESENTATION

1. *(Write the following problem on the board.)*

$$5\overline{)213}$$

Read this problem.   5 goes into 213.

Tell me the part to underline. *(Pause. Underline 21.)* $5\overline{)\underline{21}3}$ 21

To correct: Look at the first digit. Is 2 at least as big as 5?   No

So what do you underline?   21

What does the underlined problem say?   5 goes into 21.

2. How many times does 5 go into 21? *(Pause.)*   4

3. I'll write the 4 over the last digit underlined.
   (Write the following:)

$$5\overline{)213}^{4}$$

4. Now multiply 4 × 5. What is 4 × 5? *(Pause. Write 20.)*   20
   Now I subtract 20 from 21. What is 1 – 0?   1
   (Write 1.)

(continued on next page)

FORMAT 10.6 (continued)

TEACHER	STUDENTS

5. *(Point to 3.)* What's the next digit after the underlined part? — 3

I bring it down and write it after the 1.
(Write the steps in the problem so far.)

```
     4
5)213
   20
   13
```

What number is under the line now? — 13

6. The next part of the problem says 5 goes into 13.
What does the problem say now? — 5 goes into 13.

How many times does 5 go into 13? *(Pause.)* — 2

I write the 2 above the digit I brought down.
(Write this step in the problem.)

```
    42
5)213
   20
   13
```

7. Now I multiply and subtract. What is 2 × 5? *(Pause.)* — 10
I write 10 under the 13. *(Write 10.)* What is 13 minus 10? *(Pause.)* — 3

8. The problem is finished. Every digit after the underlined part
has a digit over it. 5 goes into 213, forty-two times with a
remainder of 3. How many times does 5 go into 213? — 42 times with a remainder of 3.

(Repeat steps 1–8 with 7)94   2)135   3)65 .)

PART D: STRUCTURED WORKSHEET

1. *(Write the following problem on the board.)*

   3)137

   Touch the problem. Read the problem. — 3 goes into 137.
   What numbers do you underline? *(Pause.)* — 13

2. Underline 13. What does the underlined problem say? — 3 goes into 13

3. How many times does 3 go into 13? — 4
   Write 4 above the last digit you underlined.

4. What numbers do you multiply? — 4 × 3
   What is 4 × 3? — 12

5. Write 12 under 13, then subtract. What is 13 – 12? — 1

6. What is the next digit in the number you're dividing into? *(Pause.)* — 7

   Bring down the 7 and write it next to the 1.

```
     4
3)137
   12
   17
```

7. What number is under the line? — 17
   What does this part of the problem say? — 3 goes into 17.
   How many times does 3 go into 17? *(Pause.)* — 5

TEACHER	STUDENTS

8. Write the 5 above the digit you brought down. *(Monitor student responses.)*

9. What numbers do you multiply?   5 × 3

   What is 5 × 3?   15

   Write 15 under 17 and subtract. What is 17 – 15?   2

   Is there another number to bring down?   No

10. Every digit after the underlined part has a digit over it. So you finished the problem. What's the remainder?   2

   How many times does 3 go into 137?   45 with a remainder of 2.

   (Repeat steps 1–10 with remaining problems.)

PART E: LESS STRUCTURED WORKSHEET

1. *(Write the following problem on the board.)*

   4)‾69‾

   Touch the problem. Read the problem.   4 goes into 69.

   Underline the part you work first.   4)6̲9

   Say the underlined problem.   4 goes into 6.

   How many times does 4 go into 6?   1

2. Write the 1, multiply, subtract, and then bring down the next digit. *(Pause.)* What number is under the line now?   29

3. Say the new problem.   4 goes into 29.

   How many times does 4 go into 29?   7

   Write 7 in the answer. Then multiply and subtract. *(Pause.)* Is there another number to bring down?   No

   Is the problem finished?   Yes

4. How many times does 4 go into 69?   17 with a remainder of 1.

(Repeat steps 1–4 with remaining problems.)

FORMAT 10.7   **Rounding to Nearest Tens Unit**

TEACHER	STUDENTS

PART A: EXPRESSING NUMBERS AS TENS UNITS

1. *(Write on board: 190.)*
   What number?   190

   Another way of saying 190 is 19 tens. What's another way of saying 190?   19 tens

2. *(Repeat step 1 with 80, 230.)*

3. What's another way of saying 140?   14 tens

4. *(Repeat step 3 with 280, 30, 580, 420, 60, 500, 280, 40, 700.)*

PART B: STRUCTURED BOARD PRESENTATION

1. *(Write on board: 186.)*
   What number?   186

(continued on next page)

FORMAT 10.7 (continued)

TEACHER	STUDENTS
2. Is 186 closer to 180 or 190?	190

To correct: If we have at least 5 in the ones column, we round off to the next higher tens unit. How many ones in 186? So we round off to 190.

So is 186 closer to 18 tens or 19 tens? *(Pause.)*   19 tens

To correct: 186 is closer to 190. How many tens in 190?

3. *(Repeat step 2 with these examples.)*

142	14 tens or 15 tens?
83	8 tens or 9 tens?
47	4 tens or 5 tens?
286	28 tens or 29 tens?
432	43 tens or 44 tens?
27	2 tens or 3 tens?
529	52 tens or 53 tens?

PART C: STRUCTURED WORKSHEET

Round off these numbers to the nearest ten. Write how many tens in the rounded off number:

142 ___ tens	87 ___ tens	537 ___ tens	497 ___ tens
287 ___ tens	426 ___ tens	248 ___ tens	321 ___ tens
825 ___ tens	53 ___ tens	632 ___ tens	503 ___ tens
546 ___ tens	182 ___ tens	428 ___ tens	278 ___ tens
932 ___ tens	203 ___ tens	561 ___ tens	426 ___ tens

1. *(Call on a student to read the directions.)* Read the first number.   142

2. Think: 142 is closest to how many tens?   14 tens

To correct: Is 142 closer to 140 or 150? So, is 142 closer to 14 or 15 tens? *(Write the answer.)*

3. Write 14 in the blank. *(Repeat steps 2–3 with several more examples.)*

FORMAT 10.8 **Correct Estimated Quotients with Two-Digit Divisors**

TEACHER	STUDENTS

PART A: PRESKILL—MULTIPLYING QUOTIENT TIMES DIVISOR

I. Board Presentation

1. *(Write the following problem on the board.)*

$$54\overline{)231} \quad \text{with } 4 \text{ above}$$

This problem says 54 goes into 231 four times. What does the problem say?   54 goes into 231 four times.

2. We have to figure out the remainder. We multiply 4 × 54. What do we multiply?   4 × 54

TEACHER	**STUDENTS**

3. When I multiply 4 × 54, first I multiply 4 × 4, then I multiply
   4 × 5. What is 4 × 4?   **16**

   I write the 6 under the last underlined digit and carry the 1.

   (Write the problem below on the board.)

$$\begin{array}{r} 4 \\ 54\overline{)231} \\ \hline 6 \end{array}$$

4. Now I multiply 4 × 5 and add the 1 I carried. What is 4 × 5?   **20**
   And 1 more is?   **21**

   I write the 21 in front of the 6. *(Write this step of the
   problem on the board.)*

$$\begin{array}{r} 4 \\ 54\overline{)231} \\ 216 \end{array}$$

5. What is 4 × 54?   **216**

6. We subtract 216 from 231 to figure out the remainder.
   Can we start with 1 and subtract 6?   **No**

   We must borrow. *(Write this step:)*

$$\begin{array}{cc} 2 & 1 \\ 2 \;\; \cancel{3} & 1 \end{array}$$

   What is 11 − 6?   **5**
   What is 2 − 1?   **1**

7. 54 goes into 231 four times with a remainder of 15. Say that.   54 goes into 231 four
                                                                    times with a remainder
                                                                    of 15.

   (Repeat steps 1–7 with the problems below.)

$$\begin{array}{cc} 3 & 4 \\ 48\overline{)156} & 94\overline{)413} \end{array}$$

II. Worksheet

$$\text{a.} \quad 27\overline{)103}^{\;3} \qquad \text{b.} \quad 46\overline{)278}^{\;6} \qquad \text{c.} \quad 14\overline{)80}^{\;5}$$

1. Read problem a.   27 goes into 103 three
                                                              times.

2. You need to multiply 3 × 27. When you multiply 3 × 27,
   what do you multiply first?   **3 × 7**

3. What is 3 × 7?   **21**

   Write the 1 and carry the 2 tens.

   To correct: Write the 1 under the 3. *(Pause.)* Carry the
   2 tens above the 2 in 27.

4. Now what do you multiply?   **3 × 2**

   What is 3 × 2?   **6**

   Add the 2 you carried. What's the answer?   **8**

   Write the 8.

(continued on next page)

FORMAT 10.8 (continued)

TEACHER	STUDENTS

5. Figure out the remainder. Be careful to borrow in the tens column.

6. What is the remainder?   22
   Yes, 27 goes into 103 three times with a remainder of 22.
   Say that.

     27 goes into 103 three times with a remainder of 22.

(Repeat steps 1–6 with several problems, then have students work the rest independently.)

PART B: PRESKILL—ESTIMATING

I. Board Presentation

1. *(Write the following problem and the box on the board.)*

   $37\overline{)932}$ $\boxed{)\quad\quad}$

   What does the problem say?   37 goes into 932.

2. We have to underline the part we work first. Does 37 go into 9?   No

   Does 37 goes into 93?   Yes

   So I underline the first two digits.

3. I'll read the part we work first: 37 goes into 93. Say the part we work first.   37 goes into 93.

4. To find out how many times 37 goes into 93, we must round off. The box next to the problem is for rounding off.

5. First I round off 37; 37 is rounded off to how many tens? *(Pause and then write the four.)*   4

   $\boxed{4)\quad\quad}$

   93 is rounded off to how many tens? *(Pause and then write the 9.)*   9

   $\boxed{4)9\quad}$

   Read the rounded-off problem.   4 goes into 9.

6. Four goes into nine how many times?   2
   So in the problem we started with, I write 2 over the last underlined digit. *(Write the 2.)*

   2
   $37\overline{)932}$

   (Repeat steps 1–6 with $24\overline{)136}$ $52\overline{)386}$ $34\overline{)942}$.)

II. Worksheet

a. $79\overline{)246}$ $\boxed{)\quad\quad}$ b. $49\overline{)538}$ $\boxed{)\quad\quad}$

c. $27\overline{)943}$ $\boxed{)\quad\quad}$ d. $36\overline{)193}$ $\boxed{)\quad\quad}$

TEACHER	STUDENTS

1. What does problem a say?   79 goes into 246.

2. What digits do you underline? *(Pause.)*   246

   Underline the part you work first. Say the underlined problem.   79 goes into 246.

3. Let's write the rounded-off problem for 79 into 246 in the box.
   How many tens does 79 round off to? *(Pause.)*   8

   Write 8 in the box. How many tens does 246 round off to? *(Pause.)*   25

   Write 25 in the box. Read the rounded-off problem.   8 goes into 25.

   Eight goes into 25 how many times?   3

4. Write the answer in the problem you started with. Write it
   above the last underlined digit.

   *(Repeat steps 1–4 with three more problems, then have
   students work the next problems on their own.)*

PART C: STRUCTURED WORKSHEET

1. *(Write the sample problem on the board.)*

   38)‾1‾4‾3‾2‾

   Read the problem.   38 goes into 1432.
   Underline the part you work first.
   What did you underline?   143
   Read the underlined problem.   38 goes into 143.

2. Write the rounded-off problem in the box. How many tens
   does 38 round off to? *(Pause.)*   4

   Write 4. How many tens does 143 round off to? *(Pause.)*   14

   Write 14. Read the rounded-off problem.   4 goes into 14.

3. 4 goes into 14 how many times?   3
   Write 3 above the last digit you underlined.

4. Now we multiply 3 × 38. What is 3 × 8? *(Pause.)*   24
   Write 4 below the last underlined digit and carry the 2.
   (Pause.) Now multiply 3 × 3 and add 2. *(Pause.)*

   What's the answer? *(Pause.)*   11

   Write 11 next to the 4.

5. Now subtract 114 from 143. *(Pause.)*
   What is 143 − 114?   29

6. Let's see if there's a second part to work. Is there a digit
   after the underlined part to bring down?   Yes

   *(If the answer to step 6 is no, skip steps 7–10
   and go directly to step 11.)*

7. Bring down that digit. What number is under the line now?   292
   Say the new problem.   38 goes into 292.

(continued on next page)

FORMAT 10.8 (continued)

TEACHER	STUDENTS
8. Let's write the rounded-off problem in the second box. How many tens does 38 round off to?	4
Write 4. How many tens does 292 round off to?	29
Write 29. Read the rounded-off problem.	4 goes into 29.
9. How many times does 4 go into 29? Write 7 in the problem you started with. Write it above the 2 you brought down.	7
10. Now we multiply 7 × 38. What do we multiply? Multiply and write the answer below 292.	7 × 38
(Pause.) What is 7 × 38?	266
Subtract 292 – 266 to find the remainder. *(Pause.)* What's 292 – 266?	26
Are there any more digits to bring down?	No
11. So you're done with the problem. How many times does 38 go into 1432?	37 times with a remainder of 26.

(Repeat steps 1–11 with remaining problems.)

PART D: LESS STRUCTURED WORKSHEET

1. *(Write the sample problem on the board.)*

18)604

TEACHER	STUDENTS
Read the problem.	18 goes into 604.
Underline the part you work first. What did you underline?	60
Read the underlined problem.	18 goes into 60.
2. Write the rounded-off problem in the upper box. *(Pause.)* Say the rounded-off problem.	2 goes into 6.
3. Write the answer, then multiply. *(Pause.)* Say the subtraction problem.	60 – 54
Subtract 60 – 54. *(Pause.)* What is 60 – 54?	6
4. What do you do next? Do it.	Bring down the 4.
5. Say the new problem.	18 goes into 64.
6. Write the rounded-off problem in the second box. *(Pause.)* Say the rounded-off problem.	2 goes into 6.
7. Write the answer, then multiply and subtract. *(Pause.)* What is the remainder?	10
8. Are you finished? How many times does 18 go into 604?	33 times with a remainder of 10.

FORMAT 10.9   **Incorrect Estimated Quotients**

TEACHER	**STUDENTS**

PART A: STRUCTURED WORKSHEET

a. $37\overline{)142}$ with 4 above

b. $48\overline{)299}$ with 5 above

c. $48\overline{)299}$ with 5 above

d. $79\overline{)315}$ with 4 above

e. $46\overline{)192}$ with 3 above

f. $52\overline{)148}$ with 3 above

g. $82\overline{)318}$ with 4 above

h. $34\overline{)178}$ with 5 above

i. $26\overline{)81}$ with 2 above

1. The answers to some of these problems are wrong. To find out which ones are wrong, you figure out the remainder. If you can't subtract, you must make the answer *smaller*. If you find a remainder, but it is too big, you must make the answer *bigger*.

2. Touch problem a. What does the problem say?

   37 goes into 142 four times.

3. What are you going to multiply? Do the multiplication. Write the minus sign and stop.

   4×37.

4. Say the subtraction problem.

   $142 - 148$

5. Can you subtract 142 minus 148? We can't subtract, so we must make the answer smaller.

   No

6. So you have to cross out the 4 and write a 3 above it. Do it, then erase the 148.

7. Now multiply 3×37.

8. Read the subtraction problem now.

   $142 - 111$

9. Subtract and figure out the remainder. What is the remainder? That's all we do for now.

   31

   (Steps 4a–8a are for problems in which the estimated quotient is too small, as in the following problem.)

   $48\overline{)299}$ with 5 above

4a. Say the subtraction problem.

   $299 - 240$

   Can you subtract 240 from 299? Subtract. *(Pause.)*

   Yes

5a. What is the remainder?

   59

   Is the remainder too big?

   Yes

   To correct: What are we dividing by? Is the remainder at least as big as 48? You can make another group, so we make the answer bigger. Cross out the 5 and write 6. Erase 240.

6a. Now multiply 6×48.

7a. Read the subtraction problem now. Subtract.

   $299 - 288$

(continued on next page)

FORMAT 10.9 (continued)

TEACHER	STUDENTS
8a. What's the answer?	11
Can we make another group of 48?	No
So we're all finished.	

(*Repeat steps 1–9 or 4a–8a with three of the remaining
problems. Have students work the remaining problems on their own.*)

PART B: LESS STRUCTURED WORKSHEET

a. $42\overline{)197}$ [ ) _____]   b. $36\overline{)203}$ [ ) _____]

c. $58\overline{)232}$ [ ) _____]

1. Touch problem a. Read the problem.	42 goes into 197.
2. Underline the part you work first.	
3. Write the rounded-off problem. Say the rounded-off problem.	4 goes into 20.
4. What is the answer?	5
Multiply 5×42. (*Pause.*) Can you subtract?	No

(*Note: Present step 5 or 6.*)

5. (*If the answer to step 4 is no, say,*) So what must you do?
    Fix your answer then multiply and subtract.

6. (*If the answer to step 4 is yes, say,*) Subtract _____
    from _____. What is the remainder? Is the remainder
    too big? (*Continue if answer is yes.*) So what must we do?
    Erase _____ and write _____, then multiply
    and subtract. (*Pause.*) What is the remainder? Is that remainder
    too big? So we're finished. Say the whole answer.

(*Repeat steps 1–6 with remaining problems.*)

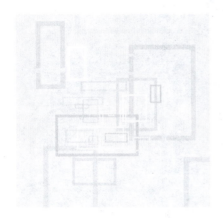

CHAPTER 11

Problem Solving

This chapter discusses procedures for teaching students to apply the four basic operations (addition, subtraction, multiplication, and division) to word problems, stories that present situations requiring a mathematical solution. Because mathematical terms and properties were introduced in the chapters for each operation, no new terms or properties are presented here. Nor does this chapter include all of the important problem-solving strategies. Procedures for teaching problem-solving strategies that include fractions, percent, decimals, time, money, and measurement are addressed in later chapters on those topics.

There are two basic kinds of math story problems: addition/subtraction and multiplication/division. Addition and subtraction word problems are introduced together to provide discrimination practice. For the same reason, multiplication and division word problems are taught together. Multiplication and division story problems are introduced as soon as students have mastered previously introduced types of story problems (i.e., problems involving addition and subtraction) and have been taught to solve multiplication and division computation problems. It is important for students to work mixed sets of word problems involving all four operations once multiplication and division problems have been introduced.

Addition and subtraction problems are usually introduced in late first grade. Analysis of addition and subtraction problems in commercial mathematics programs reveals three main problem types: tempo-

ral sequence problems, comparison problems, and classification problems. Simple versions of these three types of one-step problems are usually introduced by the end of second grade. Both initial and more sophisticated strategies for solving these problem types are introduced in this chapter.

Multiplication and division problems are usually introduced during third grade. In most initial problems, the multiplication or division operation is signaled by the presence of the word *each* or *every*. Later, the words *a* and *per* serve as signals for multiplication or division (e.g., the crew works 7 hours *a* day; there are 6 crayons *per* box). Multiplication and division problems that do not contain key words are obviously more difficult. See the Instructional Sequence and Assessment Chart for a recommended sequence of introduction.

Within the two basic groupings of story problems are problems with large numbers, multistep problems, and problems with distractors. Problems with larger numbers are usually more difficult because the computation is more difficult and the operation required is often less obvious. Multistep problems usually appear in third grade and require students to perform two or more steps, usually involving two or more different operations, to solve the problem. The simplest type of multistep problem involves adding three numbers. Multistep problems become more difficult as the number and type of computations to be performed increase. The third type of these more difficult story problems contains irrelevant quantities or information that may distract students from the

Instructional Sequence and Assessment Chart

Grade Level	Problem Type	Performance Indicator
1–2a	Addition/subtraction simple action problems with key words	Deshawn had 7 apples. He got 3 more from the store. How many apples does he have in all?
		Lisa had some apples. She bought 3 more. She ended up with 12 apples. How many apples did she start with?
2a	Addition/subtraction temporal sequence problems	Carlos had 7 apples. He gave 3 to his sister. How many does he have left?
2b	Addition/subtraction comparison problems	Bill is 7 years old. Alice is 5 years old. How much older is Bill?
		Hole A is 5 feet deep. Hole B is 7 feet deeper than Hole A. How deep is Hole B?
		Hole A is 5 feet deep. Hole B is 7 feet deep. How much deeper is Hole B?
2c	Addition/subtraction classification problems	Eight men are in the store. Three women are in the store. How many people are in the store?
		Ramona has 4 hats; 3 of the hats are blue. How many hats are not blue?
		Maria sold 5 hats in the morning. She sold 2 hats in the afternoon. How many hats did she sell?
2d	Multistep problems: add three numbers	LaToya ran 5 miles on Monday, 3 miles on Tuesday, and 4 miles on Wednesday. How many miles did he run altogether?
3a	Multiplication/division problems with the word *each* or *every*	Marcus has 4 boxes. In each box there are 6 pencils. How many pencils does Bill have?
		Tamara jogs 5 miles every day. How far will she jog in 3 days?
		There are 20 students. The teacher wants to divide them into 4 equal groups. How many students will be in each group?
3b	Multiplication/division problems with the word *per* or a phrase using *a*	The ABC Company makes pens. They put 5 pens in a box. How many pens are in 3 boxes?
		Rosa runs 2 miles per day. How many days will it take her to run 8 miles?
3c	Addition/subtraction problems with larger numbers	Travis ran 214 miles in January and 158 miles in February. How many more miles did he run in January?
		There are 153 students in the school. If there are 61 girls in the school, how many boys are there?

Grade Level	Problem Type	Performance Indicator
3d	Multiplication/division problems with larger numbers	There are 35 students in every class. There are 5 classes in the school. How many students are in the school?
		Jean worked 2 days. If she makes $16 a day, how much did she make?
		Jill has 215 pencils. She wants to make bundles with 5 pencils in each bundle. How many bundles can she make?
3e	Division problems with remainders	There are 22 students. The teacher wants to divide them into 4 equal groups. How many students will be in each group?
		A mother wants to divide a pie equally among her children. The pie has 19 pieces. There are 9 children. How many pieces should she give to each child?
3f	Addition/subtraction problems with distractors	There are 20 blue pencils, 5 red pencils, and 16 yellow pens in a bag. How many pencils are in the bag?
		Bill weighed 120 pounds. He ran 5 miles. Now he weighs 117 pounds. How much did he lose?
		Bill had 12 hats; 5 hats were old. He gave away 3 old hats. How many hats does he have left?
4a	Division and multiplication problems with larger numbers (two-digit divisor or multi-digit factors)	Sarah wants to save $385. If she puts $35 in the bank each month, how many months will it take her to save the $385?
		A factory produces 325 cars a day. How many cars will it produce in 25 days?
		A pound of apples costs 60¢. How much will 20 pounds of apples cost?
4b	Multistep problems: three numbers; the sum of two numbers is subtracted from the third number	Julie sold 12 pencils in the morning. Ann sold 15 in the afternoon. How many more must they sell before they've sold 50 altogether?
		Timmy weighed 84 pounds. He lost 4 pounds in May and 7 pounds in June. How much did he weigh at the end of June?
		Jean sold 10 pens in the morning. She began with 18. If she sells 2 more, how many will she have left?
4c	Three numbers: two quantities are multiplied; the product is added or subtracted from a third number	Tom has 3 pens in each pocket. He has 5 pockets. Ann has 16 pens. Who has more pens? How many more?

(continued)

Grade Level	Problem Type	Performance Indicator
		Ann has $7. If she works 4 hours and earns $3 each hour, how many dollars will she have at the end of the day?
4d	Three numbers: two quantities are added; the sum is divided or multiplied	There are 10 boys and 20 girls in the class. Each row can sit 5 students. How many rows will there be?
		Jill earns $2 every morning and $4 every afternoon. How much will she earn in 6 days?
5a	Four numbers: two sets of quantities are multiplied; the product of each is added	Pam ran 5 miles a day for 3 days and 6 miles a day for 2 days. How many miles did she run altogether?
		Tammy bought 3 cakes and 2 drinks. A cake cost 10¢. A drink cost 15¢. How much did Tammy spend?
5b	Five numbers: two sets of quantities are multiplied; the product of each is added; the sum is subtracted or added to a given quantity	Bill needs $30. He worked 5 hours on Monday for $2 an hour. He worked 2 hours on Tuesday for $3 an hour. How much more money does he need?
		Bill weighed 135 pounds in May. He gained 3 pounds each month for the next 2 months. Then he gained 5 pounds each month for the next 3 months. How much does he weigh now?

necessary steps to solve the problem. More information about these three problem types is presented later in the chapter.

Teachers also should be aware that story problems become more difficult as the problems include unfamiliar vocabulary and use more complex syntax. The two problems that follow illustrate the importance of vocabulary and syntax:

a. Miles wrote 6 sentences. The teacher crossed out 2 of them. How many are left?

b. When the teacher read Andrew's paper, she deleted 15 sentences and 3 commas. He had initially written 52 sentences. How many sentences did he have at the end?

Both of these word problems are temporal sequence problems—problems that state the original amount and the amount of decrease. Problem b is more difficult for several reasons. First, problem b contains more difficult vocabulary. Students may not be familiar with the words *deleted* and *initially*. If a student does not understand *deleted*, she has no basis for solving the problem. Second, the amount that

Miles began with is stated first in problem a, but in problem b the amount Andrew began with is stated *after* the amount of the decrease. When the smaller number appears first, students are more likely to add. The third difficulty is the presence of the words *deleted . . . commas,* a distractor that must be ignored. Finally, the numerals in problem b are larger, and the operation requires renaming.

Some approaches to mathematics instruction introduce problem-solving activities to students before the students have been taught efficient strategies for solving them. Commercial programs often suggest that students work word problems by using manipulatives to represent values or acting out the story. These approaches frequently confuse students because the students fail to see the relationship between their actions to solve the problem and the appropriate algorithm. Another obstacle is the amount of time required to present some of the activity-based strategies. Some of these suggested activities may not be the most efficient use of instructional time. In this chapter, we present generalizable problem-solving strategies that are useful and efficient. We endorse the use of more activity-based strategies as an introduction to the *concepts* in word problems (rather than the primary strategy for solving them) and also as opportunities for students to learn alternative strategies for confirming solutions once they have mastered the primary strategy.

ADDITION AND SUBTRACTION PROBLEMS

The procedures for teaching addition and subtraction problems are divided into two parts. The first part introduces the concept of story problems to first-grade students or remedial second-graders through the use of illustrations. The second part teaches a more sophisticated generalizable problem-solving strategy that enables students to solve temporal sequence, comparison, and classification problems. The generalizable strategy is more sophisticated because it accommodates the difficulties caused by variations in word usage. The same verb *(gave away)* appears in examples a and b below, but the usage is such that addition is called for in a and subtraction in b.

a. Nicole gave away 7 stickers. Maria gave away 3 more stickers than Nicole. How many stickers did Maria give away?

b. Nicole had 15 stickers. Then she gave away 7 stickers. How many stickers does she have now?

Introducing the Concept

In first grade, word problems can be introduced when students can work a page of simple addition and subtraction problems, using a line strategy, with 80 to 90% accuracy. It is not necessary that students know how to solve missing-addend problems or have memorized any basic facts in order to be introduced to word problems.

About three weeks prior to the introduction of word problems, the teacher should present a preskill format designed to teach students how to translate to symbols four key phrases: *get more, get rid of, end with,* and *how many.* The phrase *get more* translates to a plus sign, *get rid of* to a minus sign, *end with* to an equal sign, and *how many* to an empty box. The teacher should say each new phrase and tell students its translation. For example, the teacher might say, "Listen: When you *get more,* you write a plus sign. What do you write for *get more?*" Each second or third day, the teacher introduces a new phrase and review the phrases introduced earlier.

After the students know these four terms, the teacher presents another preskill exercise in which the teacher says a common verb and asks if the verb translates to a plus or a minus sign. Several common verbs should be presented—for example, *buys, loses, sells, eats, finds, gives away, breaks,* and *makes.* The teacher equates each verb with getting more or getting rid of before asking the students to translate the verb to a symbol. For example, the teacher asks, "When you buy something, do you get more or get rid of something? So when you buy something, do you plus or minus?"

The format for introducing word problems (see Format 11.1) is presented when the students have mastered the preskills outlined above. The format includes two parts. In Part A, a structured board presentation, the teacher begins story problem instruction by demonstrating on the chalkboard how a written or verbal story-problem can be solved with semiconcrete objects (pictures). In solving problems such as "There were six children. Two children went home. How many were left?" pictures or actions are easily used to illustrate the problem.

After demonstrating how a verbal or written word problem can be illustrated, the teacher demonstrates how a verbal or written story problem may be expressed numerically, translating it phrase by phrase into an equation.

There were six children.　　6
Two children went home.　　$6 - 2$
How many were left?　　$6 - 2 = \Box$

In Part B, the structured worksheet exercise, the teacher gives students a worksheet with a set of problems. If students can decode the words in the story, they read the problems. If the students do not have adequate decoding skills, the teacher should read the problems to them. The teacher has the students read the entire problem and then reread it phrase by phrase. After reading each phrase, students are directed to draw the appropriate picture. Then, students read the problem again, phrase by phrase, and write the appropriate symbols. After completing the equation, students are encouraged to figure out the answer by counting the pictures.

Example selection for word problems is very important. The verbs in stories should be fairly common terms such as *buy, give away, make, break, find, lose.* Also, problems should contain words that the students are able to decode, and the problems initially should be relatively short. A random mix of addition and subtraction problems should be used so that students must discriminate between the two types of problems.

For the first several weeks, the last sentence in word problems should say, "ends with how many?" These words can be literally translated to the symbols = ☐. After several weeks, final sentences such as "How many does she have now?" and "How many does she have in all?" can be presented. The teacher explains that these sentences mean the same as *ends with how many?* and thus can be translated into the symbols = ☐.

A Number-Family Problem-Solving Strategy

Most word problems cannot be translated phrase by phrase into an equation. Therefore, we recommend teaching a strategy that encourages students to integrate their knowledge of fact-number-family concepts with basic language skills involving temporal sequencing, comparison, and classification. The number-family strategy is based on the concept that three numbers can be used to form four math statements. For example, the numbers 2, 5, and 7 yield $2 + 5 = 7$, $5 + 2 = 7$, $7 - 5 = 2$, and $7 - 2 = 5$. The numbers may be represented as the following number family diagram:

$$\underrightarrow{2 \qquad 5}7$$

A standard diagram is used to represent a number family. When using the number-family strategy to solve basic facts, students are taught that the big number (total) goes at the end of the arrow. If the big number is not known, a box goes at the end of the number-family arrow. In a typical problem, two of the numbers in the family are provided. Students place these numbers where they belong in the family and then determine whether the missing number is obtained by adding or subtracting. For example, the family

$$\underrightarrow{2 \qquad 5} \; \square$$

does not give the total, and yields the problem $2 + 5 = \square$. The family does give the total, so yields the problem $7 - 2 = \square$.

$$\begin{array}{c} \square \\ \underrightarrow{2 \qquad} 7 \end{array}$$

The key to applying the number-family analysis to a range of problem types is analyzing the language in the problem to determine the name for the total. For example, in a classification problem involving boys, girls, and children, the name for the total is the superordinate class: children. If the problem gives a number for children, subtraction is implied. If the problem asks for the number of children, addition is implied. Students first *represent* the analysis of the problem in a diagram and use the diagram to determine the operation. For example, consider the following problem: There are 8 children at the party. Three are boys. How many girls are at the party? The number for children is given

$$\underrightarrow{3 \qquad \square}\; 8 \quad \overset{\text{children}}{}$$

and yields the problem $8 - 3 = \square$.

Conversely, when the number for children is not given, the analysis yields an addition problem. For example, there are 8 girls and 3 boys at the party. How many children are at the party? The number-family representation is

$$\underrightarrow{8 \qquad 3}\; \square \quad \overset{\text{children}}{}$$

and yields the problem $8 + 3 = \square$.

The number-family analysis is useful in allowing students to see the relationships between the concepts in the word problem and the values that are given. Very careful guided practice is required to teach students the language in a story problem that tells whether or not the total number is given. The analysis for each problem type is explained in detail later in this chapter.

PRESKILL FOR THE NUMBER-FAMILY STRATEGY. An essential preskill for the number-family word-problem strategy is figuring out the missing number when two of the three numbers in a fact family are given. Students are taught that if the total number is given,

$$\underrightarrow{4 \qquad \square}\; 9$$

they subtract to find the missing number:

$$9 - 4 = \square$$

On the other hand, if the total number is not given,

$$\underrightarrow{4 \qquad 9}\; \square$$

they add the two given numbers:

$$4 + 9 = \square$$

Students should be able to compute these facts mentally rather than using lines. Consequently, problems should be limited to basic facts that students already know.

This preskill, which is presented in Format 11.2, should be taught approximately 2 or 3 weeks before temporal sequence problems are first introduced, normally sometime during second grade. Note that this format is similar to those used in Chapter 6 to teach basic facts. In that chapter, the phrases *big numbers* and *small numbers* were used. Those phrases can be replaced by the phrases *total number* and *parts of the total* when preparing students to solve story problems. These phrases are substituted to prevent students from cueing on every larger number as the "big" number.

When presenting the preskill diagrams, the teacher shows an arrow with two numbers and a box. Below are examples of the diagrams. In problem a, the total number is given, while in problem b, the total number is not given. The line below the diagram is for writing the equation to find the missing number.

a. $6 \xrightarrow{\hspace{0.3cm}\square\hspace{0.3cm}} 8$ **b.** $6 \xrightarrow{\hspace{0.3cm}2\hspace{0.3cm}} \square$

Format 11.2 has four parts. Part A introduces the rule about what to do when the total number is given: *When the total number is given, we subtract.* After telling students the rule, the teacher demonstrates its application, writing on the board a diagram in which the total number is given:

$$2 \xrightarrow{\hspace{0.3cm}\square\hspace{0.3cm}} 8$$
$$8 - 2 = 6$$

The teacher points out that because the total number is given, the students must subtract to figure out the missing number ($8 - 2 = 6$). And when they subtract, they must start with the total number.

Part B introduces the rule about what to do when the total number is not given: *When the total number is not given, we add.* After telling students the rule, the teacher demonstrates its application, writing on the board a diagram in which the total number is not given:

$$3 \xrightarrow{\hspace{0.5cm}7\hspace{0.5cm}} \square$$
$$3 + 7 = 10$$

The teacher points out that because the total number is not given, the two given numbers must be added to figure out the missing number ($3 + 7 = 10$). Note that if students do not understand the terms *add* and *subtract,* the teacher can use *plus* and *minus* instead.

Part C is a structured worksheet with diagrams, half of which give the total number and half of which do not.

a. $\square \xrightarrow{\hspace{0.3cm}3\hspace{0.3cm}} 9$ **b.** $4 \xrightarrow{\hspace{0.3cm}2\hspace{0.3cm}} \square$

The student's task is to write the appropriate equation on the line under each arrow and to figure out the missing number. In problem a, the total number is given, so the student writes the subtraction problem $9 - 3$ on the line to figure out the missing number. In problem b, the total number is not given, so the student writes the addition problem $4 + 2$ on the line to derive the answer.

Part D is a less structured worksheet exercise in which the teacher asks students whether they add or subtract and then has them work the problem. In parts C and D, the problems should not be written in a predictable order. Addition and subtraction problems should appear randomly.

TEMPORAL SEQUENCE PROBLEMS. In temporal sequence problems, a person or thing starts out with a specified quantity, and then an action occurs (e.g., *finds, loses, buys, sells*) that results in the person or thing ending up with more or less. There are four basic types of temporal sequence problems (see Table 11.1). Two are types in which a verb indicates that the person ended up with more (e.g., *gets, buys, makes*). Two are types in which a verb indicates that the person ends up with less (e.g., *loses, eats, sells*).

The problems in Table 11.1 illustrate why students cannot rely solely on the verb to determine what operation is called for. Even though the presence of verbs such as *buys, gets,* and *finds* usually indicates addition, there are a significant number of problems with those verbs that require subtraction. Likewise, some story problems contain verbs that usually indicate subtraction but that are solved by adding. For example, Michael lost 17 pounds. Now he weighs 132 pounds. How much did he weigh before?

The strategy presented in the format for temporal sequence problems (Format 11.3) teaches the students to look at the overall structure of a word problem. The format utilizes the number-family

Table 11.1   Four Types of Action Problems

- Verb indicates ending up with more.
  Addition
     a. James had 12 apples. He bought 17 more apples. How many apples did he end up with?
  Subtraction
     b. James had 12 apples. He bought more apples. Now he has 17 apples. How many apples did he buy?
- Verb indicates ending up with less
  Addition
     c. James had lots of apples. He sold 17 of the apples. He ended up with 12 apples. How many apples did he start with?
  Subtraction
     d. James had 17 apples. He sold 12 apples. How many apples did he end up with?

concept. A story problem gives two quantities of the three quantities that make up a number family. If the quantity that represents the total is given in the problem, the students subtract to determine the missing quantity. If the quantity that represents the total is not given in the problem, the students add to determine the missing quantity.

Students apply a two-step strategy for solving these problems. First, they determine whether the person (or thing) in the problem *starts* or *ends* with the total. If the verb implies that the person ends with more, the person ends with the total. This is the case with the first two problems in Table 11.1: James *buys* more apples so he *ends* with the total. Students label the total accordingly:

$$\xrightarrow{\hspace{3cm}} \text{Ends}$$

Next, the students determine whether the total is given (Do we know how many James ends with?). In problem a, we do not know the total; we are asked how many James ends up with:

$$\xrightarrow{\hspace{3cm}} \overset{\text{Ends}}{\square}$$

The two numbers given are parts of the total:

$$\underset{12 \quad 17}{\xrightarrow{\hspace{3cm}}} \overset{\text{Ends}}{\square}$$

Students add to find the total. In problem b, the same label applies. Since James is *buying* apples, he *ends* with the total:

$$\xrightarrow{\hspace{3cm}} \text{Ends}$$

In problem b, however, the total *is* given. We know James ends up with 17 apples:

$$\xrightarrow{\hspace{3cm}} \overset{\text{Ends}}{17}$$

The total is given, so we must subtract to find how many he buys:

$$\underset{12}{\xrightarrow{\hspace{3cm}}} \square \overset{\text{Ends}}{17}$$

For problems c and d in Table 11.1, James *sells* apples. He ends up with fewer apples, so he *starts* with the total:

$$\xrightarrow{\hspace{3cm}} \text{Starts}$$

Next, we determine if the total is given (Do we know how many he starts with?) Problem c asks how many he starts with. The total is not given, so we add:

$$\underset{17 \quad 12}{\xrightarrow{\hspace{3cm}}} \overset{\text{Starts}}{\square}$$

For problem d, we know James starts with 17:

$$\xrightarrow{\hspace{3cm}} \overset{\text{Starts}}{17}$$

The total is given; we subtract:

$$\underset{12}{\xrightarrow{\hspace{3cm}}} \square \overset{\text{Starts}}{17}$$

Hence, all four types of temporal sequence problems are analyzed successfully with two questions: Do we start or end with the total? Is that total given? Students must be familiar with the number-family rules presented in Format 11.2 to be successful in applying this strategy to problem solving.

Format 11.3 teaches students to work temporal sequence problems. Part A is a verbal exercise to establish the relationship between various verbs (e.g., *buys*, *gives away*, *loses*) and a person starting or ending with more. Part B is a structured board exercise in which the teacher guides students through problems in two steps. First, students determine whether the person in the problem starts or ends with more (the total). Next, they figure out whether the total is given. The teacher then places the values given in the problem on the number-family arrow. After the values are in place along the arrow, students apply their knowledge of the number-family rule: *If the total, or big number, is missing, you add. If a small number is missing, you subtract.*

Part C, which is introduced when students have mastered the steps in Part B, is a structured worksheet exercise. The teacher leads students through the same two-step strategy, but the students construct the number-family diagrams that yield the correct operation. Part D is a less structured worksheet exercise in which the teacher asks the students to identify the name for the total. Students then complete the number-family diagram and figure out the answer.

Example Selection. When selecting examples for this format, the teacher constructs sets of four problems. An exercise might include two sets of four problems for a total of eight problems. Each set should contain two addition and two subtraction problems. In one addition problem, the person should start with more; in one addition problem, the person should end with more. Likewise, in one subtraction problem, the person should start with more, and in one subtraction problem, the person should end with more. The problems should be written in random order. Problems introduced initially should contain common verbs. Sentences should be relatively simple. All problems should result in equations that the students are able to work. For example, if students have not learned to regroup, subtraction problems should be limited to problems that do not require regrouping.

COMPARISON PROBLEMS. A comparison problem addresses two quantities and the difference between them. There are two basic types of comparison problems. In one type, a quantity is stated describing an attribute of one object, such as weight, length, height, or age. Also stated is the difference between that object and another object: "Brendan is 7 years old. Colleen is 3 years older." The student is asked to find the quantity of the other object: "How old is Colleen?" In the second type of problem, the quantities of two objects are stated and the student is asked to find the difference between them: "Brendan is 7 years old. Colleen is 10 years old. How much older is Colleen?" Both types of comparison problems are introduced concurrently. All comparison problems can be solved using a number family analysis. The larger of the quantities being compared represents the *total*. The smaller quantity and the difference are the *parts of the total*.

The two-step strategy for solving comparison problems is similar to that introduced for temporal

---

Summary Box 11.1
Temporal Sequence Word Problems

1. Students read the problem and determine whether the person *starts* or *ends* with more.

2. Students draw a number-family diagram and label *starts* or *ends* as the total.

3. Students fill in number-family diagram with labels and numbers that are given in the problem.

4. Students use number-family strategy to determine whether to add or subtract to find the unknown number.

Sam began with $25 in his savings account. He put another $4 into the account. How much money has he saved?

ENDS
$\longrightarrow$

25   4   ENDS
$\longrightarrow$ □

25   4   ENDS
$\longrightarrow$ 29

sequence problems. It involves (a) determining which object represents the larger quantity and (b) determining whether the larger quantity is given or not given. For example, "Andrew got 10 problems correct. Josh got 2 fewer problems correct than Andrew. How many problems did Josh get correct?" In this problem, the number of problems Josh answered correctly is fewer, so the number of problems Andrew answered correctly represents the bigger number. Because the number of problems Andrew answered correctly is given, the problem requires subtraction.

Format 11.4 shows how to present comparison problems. The format includes three parts. Part A is a preskill format designed to teach students how to determine the name for the bigger number. Note that this part assumes that students understand comparative words such as *deeper, shallower, thicker, thinner, bigger, smaller, heavier, lighter.* Students who have difficulty with Part A may not understand the meaning of the comparatives. Teachers should test students' understanding with diagrams or illustrations. For example, the teacher could present illustrations of two holes and ask, "Show me the hole that is deeper."

Another useful strategy for helping students determine which object is greater is to practice with sentences that compare two things without numerical values. For example,

a. The lake is closer than the city.
b. Brad worked longer than Ryan did.
c. The bird stored fewer nuts than the raccoon stored.

Students write partial number families for these sentences, writing the name for the larger quantity at the end of the number-family arrow. For example, in sentence a, the lake is closer than the city, so the city must be the larger value. Students would write the following number family:

$$\underset{\longrightarrow}{\overset{\text{City}}{\rule{3cm}{0pt}}}$$

After students master placing the name correctly in the number family, they can be taught to place the numbers in a comparison problem on the number-family arrow. Part B is a structured worksheet exercise with complete story problems. The teacher

leads the students in applying the two-step strategy, first writing the name for the total and then writing a box or a quantity given for the total. For the problem, "The lake is 23 miles closer than the city. The city is 59 miles away. How far away is the lake?" the students, first write *city* for the total, and then, since the quantity for city is given, write *59* under city. The students write the other quantity and a box for the small numbers on the number-family arrow.

$$\underset{\longrightarrow}{23 \quad \square \quad \overset{\text{City}}{59}}$$

Since the total is given in the number family, the number problem is written:

$$59 - 23 = \square$$

The critical step in Part B occurs when the teacher asks if the problem gives a number for the total. Students may not read the problem carefully and may give a wrong answer. For example, if a problem states that Rachel is 12 years older than Sally, who is 7 years old, the total will tell how old Rachel is. When examining the problem, the students may misread the words *Rachel is 12 years older* as *Rachel is 12 years old,* and write 12 as the total number.

If this type of error occurs frequently, the teacher should do a practice exercise that focuses only on this step. The teacher presents a series of problems verbally. For each problem, the teacher tells the students what the total number tells about and asks if the problem gives a number for the total. For example, "The total number tells how old Rachel is. Does a number in the problem tell how old Rachel is?" The teacher presents a set of six to eight problems in the exercise.

Part C is a less structured worksheet exercise in which the teacher leads students in applying the strategy.

Example Selection. Each example set should include the following types of examples to provide discrimination practice.

1. Two addition problems in which one quantity is stated. The difference indicates the other quantity is greater:

  Bill dug a hole 6 feet deep. Tim dug a hole 2 feet deeper than Bill's hole. How deep is the hole Tim dug?

Bill dug a hole 6 feet deep. Bill's hole is 2 feet shallower than the hole Tom dug. How deep is the hole Tom dug?

2. One subtraction problem in which one quantity is stated. The difference indicates the other quantity is smaller:

Bill dug a hole 6 feet deep. Jim dug a hole 2 feet shallower than Bill's hole. How deep is the hole Jim dug?

3. One subtraction problem in which both quantities are stated. Students must determine the difference.

Bill dug a hole 6 feet deep. Jim dug a hole 2 feet deep. How much deeper is Bill's hole?

Two addition problems are included in each set to provide an equal mix of addition and subtraction problems.

CLASSIFICATION PROBLEMS. Format 11.5 gives the steps for teaching students to work classification problems using the number-family strategy. Part A provides practice in the language preskill of identifying class names for groups of objects. The teacher says a superordinate class and two related subclasses and asks the students to tell which is the biggest class. This exercise assumes that students already understand classification. Teachers working with very low-performing students may find that more extensive teaching in this skill is necessary.

In Part B, a structured worksheet exercise, the teacher introduces classification story problems. Students are given a worksheet with six to eight problems. Part B begins with the teacher reviewing with students that when the total number in a number family is given, they must subtract to find the an-

swer; when the total number is not given, they must add. The teacher then states a problem and identifies the three groups mentioned in the problem: "There are eight children. Three are boys. How many are girls? This problem is about children, boys, and girls." After telling students the three groups, the teacher asks which word tells about the big class in this problem. Students are directed to write the word *children* above the total place to show the big category or class that the story problem is talking about.

Children
———→

As with the comparison and temporal sequence word problems, students next determine whether the number for the total is given. In this example, the number family is completed as follows:

                    Children
3   □   8
———————→

Students apply the number-family rule, and since a small number is missing, they subtract to find out the number of girls:

8 − 3 = 5 Answer: 5 girls

Part C is a less structured worksheet exercise. After reading a problem, the students write the name of the big class at the end of the number-family line above the place for the total. They reread the problem to figure out whether the total is given, then complete the number family with two numbers and a box. They are then ready to work the addition or subtraction to solve the problem.

Summary Box 11.2
Problem-Solving Strategy for Comparison Problems

1. Students read the problem and determine the bigger number.

2. Students fill in the number-family diagram with the label in the place for total.

3. Students complete the diagram by filling in known values.

4. Students use number-family strategy to determine whether to add or subtract.

Diane runs 3 miles each day. Mark runs 2 miles more each day. How many miles does Mark run each day?

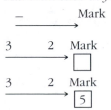

Summary Box 11.3
Classification Problem-Solving Strategy

1. Students read the problem and underline the classes.

2. Students write the biggest class in the area for total number.

3. Students write the values for the two smaller classes, if known, in the number-family diagram.

4. Students use the number-family strategy to determine whether to add or subtract.

Jose has 3 soccer balls and 4 baseballs. How many balls does Jose have?

Balls
————→

3   4   Balls
————————→

3   4   Balls
————————→ 7

Example Selection. There are several example-selection guidelines. First, there should be an equal mix of addition and subtraction problems. Second, problems should initially be written in a relatively short form with few extraneous words. Third, relatively common classes should be used. A sample set of four problems appears below:

a. There were 75 cars in all. 15 were green cars. The rest were red cars. How many red cars were there?

b. Lauren had red marbles and blue marbles. She had 23 red marbles and 16 blue marbles. How many marbles did she have in all?

c. Tom collected toy cars and airplanes. He had 43 toys in his collection. 14 were cars. How many were airplanes?

d. At Kennedy school, there are 16 girls and 15 boys in first grade. How many children are in first grade?

During the first week that classification problems are introduced, the key words in the problem can be underlined to prompt the students. For example, in problem a above, the words *cars, red,* and *green* could be underlined.

While students are learning to solve classification problems, they should continue to solve temporal sequence and comparison problems. After they have mastered classification problems, the teacher should give students worksheets that include a mix of classification, comparison, and temporal sequence problems. Worksheets should still include six to eight problems daily, with one-third representing each type of problem. When students first encounter a mix of problems, they must again receive teacher direction to be sure that they can discriminate the different kinds of problems that they should solve. Even though students have been successful at solv-

ing temporal sequence, comparison, and classification problems independently, teachers should not assume students will be equally successful when two or three types are combined on the same worksheet.

Reading Tables. An important skill related to working classification problems involves the application of classification logic to solve problems using tables. Table problems are an efficient way to present sets of data and reinforce logic skills and number facts. Students are introduced to the idea that values in rows and columns are added to obtain totals (see parts A and B in Format 11.6). To find the total for a row or column, students use a running total. In a beginning table exercise, students learn that columns run vertically and rows horizontally. After students have sufficient practice adding both columns and rows of numbers in tables, headings are presented. These headings tell about the numbers in the columns and rows. For example,

Hours Worked

	Mon.	Tues.	Weds.	Total
Josh	5	4	10	19
Jane	4	7	1	12
John	2	5	3	10
Total	11	16	14	

Students practice touching both headings and finding a particular cell. For example, students place one finger on *Tuesday* and move downwards, and another finger on *John* and move across until they meet at 5. After working with several examples, students should be ready to answer questions about a number in a particular cell, such as, How many hours did Jane work on Wednesday? Who worked the most hours on Tuesday? Who worked the most hours in all?

After students are familiar with reading tables and adding data in rows and columns, the teacher can demonstrate how to apply the number-family strategy to solving problems in tables. Students first are introduced to the concept that tables with rows and columns can work like number families. Instead of just a line for the cells, the tables in the early problems should have arrows for the rows. The arrows remind the students that each row works like a number family. The first two numbers in the row are small numbers. The total is the big number (see Part C in Format 11.6).

a.		27	52
b.	12	13	
c.	10		32
Total			

A small number is missing in row a. Students apply the number-family rule: *If the small number is missing, you subtract. If the big number is missing, you add.* Since a small number is missing in this example, students subtract to find the missing number in the row (52 − 27 = 25). In row b, a big number is missing, so students add to find the missing number in the family and write it in the table: 12 + 13 = 25.

Teachers may want to separate the introduction of the number family in rows and the number family in columns, first working only with rows, then only with columns, and finally solving for unknown cells in both. The tables below show this progression.

	15	35		10		9		35		50
20	12				22	31		10	18	
14		26		19	45					

The final step involves teaching students how to transfer the information from a word problem to a table and answer questions (see Part D in Format 11.6). Using tables to work with data that involves classification is a natural extension of what students have learned when solving addition/subtraction classification problems. The column and row headings show the names for the two subclasses (e.g., boys and girls) as well as the name for the big class (e.g., children). For example, the table might show the number of girls and boys attending soccer practice on two days, Tuesday and Thursday. The table for recording the data would look like this:

	boys	*girls*	*children*
Tuesday			
Thursday			
Total			

Part D in Format 11.6 illustrates how teachers can teach students to record information, use the number-family strategy to complete the table, and then answer questions using the information from the table. Note that teaching all parts of Format 11.6 will take a considerable amount of time. However, teaching students to use tables is an efficient and logical approach to solving several types of problems.

MULTIPLICATION AND DIVISION PROBLEMS

Multiplication and division operations are used to solve word problems that address equal-sized groups. These problems are stated in three basic forms. If a problem gives the number of groups and the number in each group, the problem is a multiplication problem; for example, "Carlos has 3 piles of toys. There are 2 toys in each pile. How many toys does Carlos have in all?" The equation representing that problem is $3 \times 2 = \square$. If the problem gives the total and asks either how many groups or how many in each group, the problem is solved with division; for example, (a) "Carlos has 6 toys. He puts 2 toys in each pile. How many piles does he end up with?" The equation is $6 \div 2 = 3$; (b) "Carlos has 6 toys. He wants to put the toys in 3 piles, with the same number of toys in each pile. How many toys will he put in each pile?" The equation is $6 \div 3 = 2$. Once the students determine that the problem is addressing equal-sized objects or groups, they will know that it is either a multiplication or a division problem. Then the students can apply the same number family strategy to determine whether the big number is given and, therefore, whether they must multiply or divide to solve the problem.

Multiplication and division problems almost always contain a word or phrase that indicates that the problem is referring to equal-sized groups. Most of the problems contain the word *each* or *every*. Other indications of equal-sized groups include the word *per* and phrases like *in a box* or *in a dozen;* for example, (a) "John walked 4 miles per day. How many miles did John walk in 3 days?" (b) "There were 3 balls in a box. There were 6 boxes. How many balls in all?"

Multiplication and division word problems should not be introduced until students have mastered addition and subtraction word problems and have a working knowledge of basic multiplication and division facts.

Word problems requiring multiplication and division may be first introduced using coins, since coins represent equal-sized groups. Later, problems that do not involve coins can be introduced using the same strategy. Initially, students do not solve the problems but learn to set up the number families correctly. If someone has 4 dimes, she has 10×4, or 40 cents. Illustrations for problems show either the number of coins for the example or the number of cents (total amount) for the example. Students complete the number family by following the convention of writing the value of each coin as the first small number of the number family. The number of coins is the second small number in the family. The total amount (cents) is the big number (see Format 11.7). For example,

$$\text{Ⓓ Ⓓ Ⓓ} \quad 10 \quad \text{Dimes}$$
$$\text{Ⓓ Ⓓ Ⓓ} \xrightarrow{} \text{cents}$$

The next step in the strategy is to introduce problems in which no coins are shown. For example,

a. You have some nickels. You have 45 cents in all. How many nickels do you have?

$$\text{Nickels}$$
$$\xrightarrow{} \text{cents}$$

To work problem a, students write the value of each nickel as the first small number and 45 as the big number for total cents, or cents in all. Since the big number is given, the answer is obtained by dividing: $45 \div 5 = 9$. There are nine nickels.

$$5 \quad \text{Nickels}$$
$$\xrightarrow{} \text{45 cents}$$

b. You have quarters. You have 5 quarters. How many cents do you have in all?

$$25 \quad 5 \text{ Quarters}$$
$$\xrightarrow{} \text{cents}$$

For problem b, the value of each quarter is written as the first small number, and 5 is written for the second small number. The number of cents is the big number in the number family and can be obtained by multiplying 25×5.

The coin strategy can be applied to a range of other types of examples. After students have mastered writing coin problems in number families, they are taught how to analyze the language in a multiplication/division problem. Each problem gives two names. As in addition/subtraction problems, the key to the number-family analysis lies in identifying the name for the big number. The name representing the larger quantity is the big number. In the coin problems, there are more cents than coins. The total number of cents gives the big number. Later, students are taught to work with equal-sized groups other than coins. For example, "Each brick weighs 3 pounds." There are more pounds than bricks, so pounds is the name for the big number. Brick is a small number. The weight of each brick is the other small number.

$$3 \qquad \text{B}$$
$$\xrightarrow{} \text{P}$$

In the beginning, students are not asked to figure out the answer to these types of problems, but rather to practice putting them in number families. After students master writing the number family, they are asked to complete problems. Students are taught that one sentence in each problem tells how to make the number family. That sentence is the one that tells about each thing.

In Part A of Format 11.8, students practice analyzing statements and determining the big number, while the teacher demonstrates how to make the number family. In Part B of Format 11.8, the students make complete number families and solve written problems in a worksheet format.

Sometimes students have difficulty determining the big number. For the sentence, "Each sack has 10 cookies," the big number is cookies and sack is a small number. But if students think about the big number as the size of things, they may reverse the components. Since sacks are generally bigger than cookies, the students may think that the number of sacks represents the big number. Teachers need to remind students that they are counting objects, not measuring size. If students have difficulty determining the name for the big number, they can be taught that the word in the problem following *each* refers to a small number. If they use the information about *each* in the sentence above, they can identify one of the objects as the big number. "Each sack has 10 cookies." The word following *each* is *sack*. Sack is the small number. The only other name in the sentence is *cookies,* so cookies must be the big number.

MULTISTEP WORD PROBLEMS

Frequently, students work temporal problems that require both addition and subtraction. These multistep problems can be solved using number families. Here is an example of such a problem:

> Shane spends $12 on stamps. Then he spends $32 on a video game. If he ends up with $6, how much did he start out with?

Because this problem contains the word *spends,* students tend to use subtraction to solve the problem regardless that there are several steps required by the problem. Using a number-family analysis guards against this kind of mistake.

An adaptation of the addition/subtraction number-family strategy can be used to solve this problem (see Format 11.9). In this adaptation, the values in the number family are labeled *in, out,* and *end up. In* stands for how much the person started with and how much more of that item came in. *In* is always the big number; *out* and *end up* are the small numbers. *Out* stands for decreases in the items. The diagram below illustrates how the problem above can be represented.

$$
\begin{array}{ccc}
\textit{End up} & \textit{Out} & \textit{In} \\
 & 12 & \\
 & \underline{32} & \\
6 & 44 & \boxed{50}
\end{array}
$$

In applying the number-family strategy, students must add both *out* numbers to find the total for *out* before adding that to the *end up* number to arrive at the *in,* or big number (the answer to the problem).

To prepare students to work multistep problems, the teacher can have students practice using the ends-in-out format with one-step subtraction and addition problems. The purpose of this practice is to teach the concepts of *in, out,* and *end up.* If a sentence tells the amount that somebody has, that is an *in* number. The sentence "Caley had $15" gives a number for *in.* If a sentence tells about a gain, it tells about a value for *in.* "McKenzie collected 34 stamps" tells the gain in stamps: 34 is the number for *in.* Values for *out* tell about losses or reductions. "Howard gave away 3 apples" tells about *out;* "1500 gallons leaked out of the tanker" tells about *out.* The value for *end up* is the amount that is left, or the difference between the amount *in* and the amount *out.* In most problems, the amount for *end up* is the amount the person has after the final loss or gain

the problem describes. Simple problems that refer to only three values permit students time to practice these conventions before proceeding to multistep problems. Following are examples of simple problems.

a. Maria starts a savings account with $567. Later, she takes some money out of her account, which leaves a balance of $329. How much money was taken out?

b. A florist starts out with no carnations. She buys 59 carnations and later sells 47 of them. How many carnations did she end up with?

c. Daniel had an empty fruit crate. He put some oranges in the crate. Then he gave away 23 of those oranges. The crate still has 19 oranges in it. How many oranges did he put in the crate?

After students have mastered these concepts, multistep problems are introduced. These problems have more than one value for *in* or more than one value for *out.* The values are shown stacked under the appropriate heading in the number family. Following is an example of a problem with values stacked under the *in* heading.

> Bill caught 12 crabs yesterday, 11 this morning, and 8 this afternoon. On his way home, he stopped at the marketplace and sold some of the crabs. He still has 15 crabs. How many did he sell at the marketplace?

$$
\begin{array}{ccc}
\textit{End up} & \textit{Out} & \textit{In} \\
 & & 12 \\
 & & 11 \\
 & & \underline{8} \\
15 & \boxed{16} & 31
\end{array}
$$

After students have mastered multistep problems with more than one value for either the *in* or *out* headings, they are introduced to problems with multiple values for both headings. For example,

> At the beginning of the work day, the elevator in the Federal Building is empty. Then 5 people get on the elevator. It stops at the fifth floor and 2 more people get on. On the next floor, 4 people get off. On the seventh floor, 7 people get on, and 8 people get off. How many people are still on the elevator?

$$
\begin{array}{ccc}
\textit{End up} & \textit{Out} & \textit{In} \\
 & 4 & 5 \\
 & \underline{8} & 2 \\
 & & \underline{7} \\
\boxed{2} & 12 & 14
\end{array}
$$

DISTRACTORS

A distractor is information given in a word problem that is not necessary to find the solution to the problem. It is called a distractor because students are accustomed to using all of the information that a problem provides, and it may distract them from the correct calculations. For example,

> Stefanie had 4 stuffed dogs, 2 stuffed rabbits, 2 stuffed pigs, and 5 stuffed cats in her collection. Four of the stuffed animals are very old. How many stuffed animals does Stefanie have in her collection?

Since the problem asks how many stuffed animals Stefanie has in her collection, the irrelevant information is about the number of old animals and must be ignored in order to solve the problem correctly.

Students are most often introduced to problems with distractors in intermediate grades. Several practice problems should be given in which students state what they have been asked to solve and cross out the information that they don't need in order to solve the problem. Problems with distractors should be distributed throughout the math curriculum and practiced frequently until students can easily discern the relevant information when solving a problem.

DIAGNOSIS AND REMEDIATION

Teachers should be monitoring student performance daily. Every effort should be made to determine the possible cause of errors in order to provide appropriate remediation. There are at least five possible causes of errors in solving story problems: (a) fact errors, (b) computation errors, (c) decoding errors, (d) vocabulary errors, and (e) translation errors.

FACT ERRORS. A fact error occurs when the student chooses the correct operation and writes the problem correctly, but fails to arrive at the correct answer. An example of a fact error follows:

> There were 9 boys and 8 girls in the class. How many students were there?

$$9 + 8 = 16$$

The equation is written using the correct numbers and the correct operation, but the student failed to add correctly. The remediation process would not require repetition of word problem strategies, but some extra practice on memorization of basic facts.

COMPUTATION ERRORS. A computation error is one that a student makes in one or more parts of computing an answer. For example, failure to rename correctly would be a computational error. Errors of this sort do not require reteaching of the word-problem strategies, but remediation in the type of computation that is giving the student difficulty.

DECODING ERRORS. Reading a word or words in a problem incorrectly is a decoding error. For example, if a student reads *broke* instead of *bought* in the following problem, he will use the wrong operation: "Taryn had 8 glasses. She bought 6. How many does she have now?" The decoding error would cause the student to subtract 6 from 8, for a solution of 2 glasses, rather than add 6 + 8. Identifying a decoding error is easily done by having the student read the problem aloud.

Teachers can help students who have difficulty decoding words in story problems by presenting difficult words in board exercises before students encounter them in word problems. Teachers of students who are unable to decode written story problems easily should not require students to read the problems, but should read the problems to the student.

VOCABULARY ERRORS. Vocabulary errors occur when students do not know the meaning of key words in the story problems. For example, in the following problem, students must know that *receives* means "to get more."

> Curt has 18 pairs of socks. He receives 4 more pairs for his birthday. How many pairs of socks does he have now?

Teachers can easily determine if the error is related to vocabulary knowledge by simply asking the student what the word *receive* means. If necessary, the meaning of crucial vocabulary words should be taught prior to teaching the word problems.

TRANSLATION ERRORS. If a student fails to translate a problem into the correct equation and uses the wrong operation, the student has made a translation error. For example,

> Andrew now has 7 video games. He started out with 2 video games that he received for his birthday. How many more video games has he gotten since then?

$$7 + 2 = 9$$

In this problem, the student added instead of subtracting. The teacher begins remediation by examining the student's work over a period of days to determine if the same type of problem is consistently missed. If a previously taught problem type is missed more than 25% of the time, the student needs remediation on this problem type. Remediation can be done through a worksheet exercise using the less structured format for that particular problem type. The worksheet should include at least 10 problems, half of which are of the difficult type, the other half a similar type involving a different operation. Students should not be allowed to work on this type of problem independently until they can perform with a 90% accuracy rate for several days in a row.

APPLICATION ITEMS: PROBLEM SOLVING

1. Tell which story problem type each of the following problems represents. Use the types described in the Instructional Sequence and Assessment Chart.

   a. Jim has 15 green apples and 17 red apples. He wants to split them equally among his four friends. How many apples should he give to each friend?
   b. Ann has been running for several months. She runs 5 miles each day. How many miles will she run in 10 days?
   c. There are 20 balls in the toy closet. Eight of the balls are baseballs. How many of the balls are not baseballs?
   d. Jill has 2 pens in each pocket. She has 8 pens. How many pockets does she have?
   e. Amy had 8 dollars. Then she earned 3 dollars. How many dollars does she have now?
   f. A girl is 15 years old. Her brother is 2 years younger. How old is her brother?

2. Story problems can be made easier or more difficult by changing one or more aspects. Name several ways in which problems can be made more difficult. For each problem in the item above, change or add to the problem to increase its level of difficulty in some way.

3. Explain the possible cause of the following errors. When there is doubt as to the cause of the error, tell how to find out the specific cause. Specify the remediation procedure called for if errors of this type occur frequently.

   a. Jill's team scored 54 points. The other team scored 19 points fewer. How many did the other team score? 36 points
   b. The ABC Company produced 1,534 pool tables last year. This year, production decreased by 112 pool tables. How many pool tables did the ABC Company produce this year? 1,646 pool tables
   c. Tim baked 6 cakes every week. He baked for 18 weeks. How many cakes did he bake? 3 cakes
   d. Tara took 20 shots in the basketball game. She made 15 shots. How many shots did she miss? 35 shots
   e. There are 10 boys and 20 girls in the class. Each row can seat 5 students. How many rows will there be? 35 rows
   f. There are 28 students. The teacher wants to divide them into 4 equal groups. How many students will be in each group? 6 students
   g. A factory produces 325 cars a day. How many cars will it produce in 25 days? 8,105 cars

4. Write a structured worksheet format using tables to guide students through solving this problem: Twenty-eight vehicles went past our house. Twelve of the vehicles were cars. How many vehicles were not cars?

5. Write a structured worksheet format to guide students through solving this problem: Ann runs 5 miles every day. So far she has run 20 miles. How many days has she run?

FORMAT 11.1 Introducing Problem-Solving Concepts

TEACHER	STUDENTS

PART A: PRESKILL: PICTURE DEMONSTRATION

Addition Problem

1. Listen: Ann has 7 apples. She gets 3 more apples. She ends with how many apples?

2. Let's draw a picture of that problem. Ann has 7 apples. *(Draw the illustration below on the board.)*

She gets 3 more apples, so I draw 3 more.
(Draw 3 more apples.)

3. Let's write the equation. Here's the first sentence again. Ann has 7 apples. How many apples does Ann have?

   7

I write 7 under the 7 apples. *(Write 7.)*

Here's the next sentence. She gets 3 more apples. How many more apples did she get?

   3

Yes, Ann gets 3 more. What do I write for gets 3 more? *(Write + 3.)*

   Plus 3

The problem says she ends up with how many apples? So I write equals and a box, like this: *(Write = ☐: 7 + 3 = ☐.)*

4. Read the equation.

   7 + 3 equals how many?

Let's count and see how many we end up with. *(Touch pictures of apples as students count.)*

   1, 2, 3, 4, 5, 6, 7, 8, 9, 10

So Ann ends with 10 apples. *(Write 10 in the box.)*

Subtraction Problem

1. Listen: Ann has 7 apples. She gives away 3 apples. She ends with how many apples?

2. Let's draw a picture of that problem. Ann has 7 apples, so I draw 7 apples. *(Draw apples.)*

She gives away 3 apples, so I'll cross out 3 apples. *(Cross out 3 apples.)*

TEACHER	STUDENTS

3. Let's write the equation. Here's the first sentence again.
   Ann has 7 apples. How many apples did Ann have?

   7

   I'll write a 7 *(Write 7.)*

   Here's the next sentence. She gives away 3 apples.
   How many apples did she give away?

   3

   What do I write for gives away 3 apples?

   Minus 3

   Yes, she gives away 3, so we write −3. *(Write − 3.)*

   The problem says she ends with how many apples?
   So I write equals and a box.

   (Write = ☐: 7 − 3 = ☐.)

4. Read the equation.

   7 − 3 equals how many?

   Let's count the apples that are left and see how many she
   ends with *(Touch the remaining apples.)*

   1, 2, 3, 4

   So, Ann ends with 4 apples. *(Write 4 in the box.)*

   *(Repeat addition or subtraction steps 1–4 with several
   more problems.)*

PART B: STRUCTURED WORKSHEET

1. *(Give students a worksheet that contains a mix of addition
   and subtraction problems and includes a box and the
   word for the unit answer, like the following.)*

   a. Jim has 6 marbles. He finds 2 more marbles. He ends
      with how many marbles?

      ☐marbles

   b. Jim has 6 marbles. He gives away 2 marbles. He ends
      with how many marbles?

      ☐marbles

   Touch problem a. Listen: Jim has 6 marbles. He finds
   2 more marbles. He ends with how many marbles?

   ◯ ◯ ◯ ◯ ◯ ◯ ◯ ◯

2. Let's draw a picture of that problem. Jim has 6 marbles.
   Draw the marbles. *(Wait while the students draw on their
   papers, then draw the marbles on the board.)*

   Students write:

   ◯ ◯ ◯ ◯ ◯ ◯   ◯◯◯◯◯◯

   He finds 2 more marbles. Draw those. *(Wait, then
   draw the marbles on the board.)*

   Students write:

   ◯◯◯◯◯◯ ◯◯   ◯ ◯ ◯ ◯ ◯ ◯ ◯ ◯

3. Let's write the equation.

   Read the first sentence again.

   Jim has 6 marbles.

   How many marbles did Jim have?

   6

(continued on next page)

FORMAT 11.1 (continued)

TEACHER	STUDENTS
Write 6 under the 6 marbles. *(Wait, then write 6 on board.)*	Student write 6.
Read the next sentence.	He finds 2 more marbles.
How many more marbles did he get?	2
Yes, Jim finds 2 more. What do you write for finds 2 more?	Plus 2
Yes, write + 2. *(Write +2 on board.)*	Students write + 2.
The problem says he ends with how many marbles? So, what do you write?	Equals box
Write equals how many. *(Write = ☐ on board: 6 + 2 = ☐.)*	Students write = ☐.
4. Read the equation.	6 + 2 equals how many?
Let's count and see how many we end with. *(Touch pictures of marbles as students count.)*	1, 2, 3, 4, 5, 6, 7, 8
Write 8 in the box after the equal sign.	Students write 8.
Now, write 8 in the answer box next to the word marbles. Jim ends with 8 marbles.	Students write 8 in box next to the word marbles.

Subtraction Problem

1. Touch the next problem. Listen: Jim has 6 marbles. He gives away 2 marbles. He ends with how many marbles?

2. Let's draw a picture of that problem. Jim has 6 marbles. Draw the marbles. *(Wait while students draw on their papers, then draw the marbles on board.)*

Students write:

○ ○ ○ ○ ○ ○   ○○○○○○

He gives away 2 marbles. Cross them out. *(Wait, then cross out two marbles.)*

Students cross out marbles:

⊘ ⊘ ○ ○ ○ ○   ⊘⊘○○○○

3. Let's write the equation. Jim has 6 marbles. How many marbles does Jim have?

Write a 6. *(Write 6 on board.)*	6
How many does he give away?	Students write 6.
What do you write for gives away 2 marbles?	2
Yes, he gives away 2, so write −2. *(Write −2 on board.)*	Minus 2
The problem says he ends with how many marbles, so what do you write?	Students write − 2.
Write it. *(Write = ☐ on board: 6 − 2 = ☐.)*	Equals box
	Students write = ☐.

4. Read the equation.

Let's count the marbles that are left and see how many he ends with. *(Touch the remaining marbles.)*	6 − 2 equals how many?
	1, 2, 3, 4
Write 4 in the box after the equal sign. *(Write 4 in the box.)*	Students write 4.
Now write 4 in the answer box next to the word *marbles*. Jim ends with 4 marbles.	Students write 4 in answer box.

(Repeat addition or subtraction steps 1–4 with several more problems.)

FORMAT 11.2   **Preskill: Fact Family—Finding the Missing Family Member**

TEACHER	STUDENTS

PART A: SUBTRACTING RULE

1. *(Write this diagram on the board.)*

$$\boxed{2} \quad \boxed{6}$$
$$\longrightarrow \boxed{8}$$

2. Three numbers go together to make a fact family. *(Point to 8.)*
   The total number is always at the end of the arrow.
   (Point to 2.) This number is part of the total.
   (Point to 6.) Here's the other part of the total.

$$\boxed{2} \quad \boxed{6}$$
$$\longrightarrow \boxed{}$$

   (Erase the 8.) Sometimes, we don't know the total and
   we have to figure it out.

$$\boxed{2} \quad \square$$
$$\longrightarrow \boxed{8}$$

   (Write the 8 back in; erase the 6.) Sometimes, we don't know
   part of the total and we have to figure it out.

3. *(Write the following diagram on the board.)*

$$\boxed{3} \quad \square$$
$$\longrightarrow \boxed{10}$$
$$\underline{}$$

Is the total number given in this problem?	Yes

   Here's the rule: When the total number is given, we subtract.
   The total number is 10. So I start with 10 and subtract 3.

(Write 10 − 3 on the bottom line.) What is 10 − 3?	7

   So, I write equals 7. *(Write = 7 on the line.)*
   Now I write 7 in the empty box. *(Write 7 in box.)*
   The numbers 3 and 7 are the parts of the total. The
   number 10 is the total number.

4. *(Write the following diagram on the board.)*

$$\square \quad \boxed{5}$$
$$\longrightarrow \boxed{12}$$
$$\underline{}$$

Is the total number given?	Yes
What do we do when the total number is given?	Subtract

(continued on next page)

FORMAT 11.2 (continued)

TEACHER	STUDENTS

Remember, when you subtract, you start with the total number. What problem do I write on the line?

$12 - 5$

(Write 12 − 5 on the line.) What is $12 - 5$?

7

(Write = 7 on the line.) What number goes in the empty box? *(Write 7 in the box.)*

7

(Repeat step 3 with these problems.)

PART B: ADDITION RULE

1. *(Write the following diagram on the board.)*

2. In this problem, the total number is not given. When the total number is not given, we add.

Is the total number given in this problem?

No

Watch. The parts are 3 and 5, so I add 3 and 5. *(Write 3 + 5 on the line.)* What is $3 + 5$?

8

So, I write equals 8. *(Write = 8 on the line.)*

Now, I write 8 in the empty box. The numbers 3 and 5 are the parts of the total. The number 8 is the total.

3. *(Write the following diagram on the board.)*

Is the total number given?

No

What do we do when the total number is not given?

Add

What problem do I write on the line? *(Write 7 + 2 on the line.)*

$7 + 2$

What is $7 + 2$? *(Write = 9 on the line.)*

9

What number goes in the empty box? *(Write 9 in the box.)*

9

(Repeat step 3 with the problems below.)

TEACHER   **STUDENTS**

PART C: STRUCTURED WORKSHEET

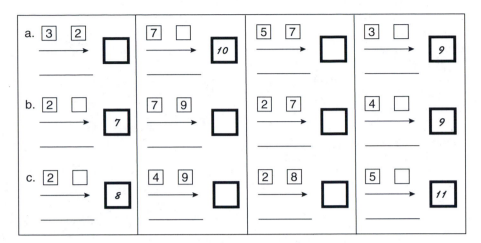

1. You must figure out the missing number in all these problems.
   It might be the total number or it might be part of the total.

   If the total number is given, what must you do?   Subtract

   If the total number is not given, what must you do?   Add

   (Repeat step 1 until students answer correctly.)

2. Touch the first problem.

   Touch the box for the total.   Students touch the box
                                                                                      after the arrow.

   Is the total given?   No

   So what must you do?   Add

   What problem do you write on the line?   3 + 2

   Write it.   Students write 3 + 2.

   What is 3 + 2?   5

   Write an equals sign and the answer.   Students write = 5

   Fill in the empty box.   Students write 5 in box.

   (Repeat step 2 with remaining problems.)

PART D: LESS STRUCTURED WORKSHEET

1. *(Give students a worksheet like that in Part C.)*

2. Touch the first problem.

3. Is the total number given or not given?

4. Do you add or subtract?

5. Write the equation on the line and write the answer.

   (Repeat steps 1–5 with all problems.)

FORMAT 11.3 Temporal Sequence Word Problems

TEACHER	**STUDENTS**

PART A: PRESKILL—DETERMINING WHETHER SUBJECT STARTS OR ENDS WITH MORE

1. We're going to figure out if a person *starts* or *ends* with more.

2. Jimmy *buys* books. Does he *start* or *end* with more?

   Jimmy *sells* books. Does he *start* or *end* with more?

   Mary *gives away* apples. Does she *start* or *end* with more?

   Mary *loses* money. Does she *start* or *end* with more?

   Mary *finds* money. Does she *start* or *end* with more?

   Sally *makes* some dolls. Does she *start* or *end* with more?

   Sally *throws away* her old shoes. Does she *start* or *end* with more?

   Mike *collects* some stamps. Does he *start* or *end* with more?

   STUDENTS:
   Ends with more.
   Starts with more.
   Starts with more.
   Starts with more.
   Ends with more.
   Ends with more.
   Starts with more.
   Ends with more.

PART B: STRUCTURED BOARDWORK

1. *(Give students a worksheet with the following problems.)*

   a. Billy buys some ties. Then he buys 8 more ties. He ends up with 23 ties. How many did he buy at first?

   b. Sandra had 8 eggs in the fridge. She ate 2 eggs for breakfast. How many eggs does she have now?

   c. Walter had some apples in a basket. After he gave away 11 apples, he had 9 apples left. How many apples did he start with?

   d. Sam began with 14 bricks on his toy truck. He put another 12 bricks on the truck. How many bricks ended up on the truck?

2. We're going to make number families for these problems. First we'll figure out if the person *starts* or *ends* with more. I'll read the first part of each problem.

3. Problem a. Billy buys some ties. Then he buys 8 more ties. Listen. Billy buys ties. So does he start or end with more?

   Yes, he ends with more, so *ends* is the name for the total.

   (Write the following diagram on the board)

   Ends
   a. ──────────→

   Ends with more.

4. Problem b. Sandra had 8 eggs in the fridge. She ate 2 eggs for breakfast. Listen. Sandra ate eggs. So does she start or end with more?

   Yes, she starts with more, so *starts* is the name for the total.

   (Write the following diagram on the board)

   Starts
   b. ──────────→

   Starts with more.

5. Problem c. Walter had some apples in a basket. After he gave away 11 apples, he had 9 apples left. Listen. Walter gave away apples. So does he start or end with more?

   He starts with more, so *starts* is the name for the total.

   (Write the following diagram on the board)

   Starts
   c. ──────────→

   Starts with more.

TEACHER **STUDENTS**

6. Problem d. Sam began with 14 bricks on his toy truck.
   He put another 12 bricks on the truck. Listen. Sam put
   more bricks on the truck. So does he start or end with more?   Ends with more.

   He ends with more, so *ends* is the name for the total.

   (Write the following diagram on the board)

             Ends
   d. —————→

7. Now let's go back and put in the numbers we know.
   Problem a. We know Billy ends with more. Let's see if
   we know how many he ends with. Billy buys some ties.
   Then he buys 8 more ties. He ends up with 23 ties.
   Do we know how many he ends with?   Yes

   How many?   23

   So I write 23 for *ends*.

   (Write 23 in the diagram.)

             Ends
   a. —————→ 23

   We don't know how many he buys at first, so I write a box.

   (Draw how-many box in the diagram.)

       ☐   Ends
   a. —————→ 23

   We know he buys 8 more.

   (Write 8 in the diagram.)

       ☐ 8 Ends
   a. —————→ 23

8. Now we have our number family. The total is given.
   Do we plus or minus?   Minus

   Say the problem we work. $23 - 8$

   When we work that problem, we figure out he
   bought 15 ties at first.

9. Problem b. We know Sandra starts with more. Let's see
   if we know how many she starts with. Sandra had 8 eggs
   in the fridge. She ate 2 eggs for breakfast. Do we know
   how many she starts with?   Yes

   How many?   8

   So write 8 for *starts*.

   (Write 8 in diagram.)

             Starts
   b. —————→ 8

   She ate 2 for breakfast, and we don't know how many
   she has now.

   (Write 2 and how-many box in diagram.)

     2   ☐ Starts
   c. —————→ 8

(continued on next page)

FORMAT 11.3   (continued)

TEACHER	STUDENTS
The total is given. Do we plus or minus?	Minus
Say the problem we'll work.	$8 - 2$
What's $8 - 2$?	6
So now she has 6 eggs left.	

10. Problem c. We figured out Walter starts with more. Let's see if we know how many he starts with. Walter had some apples in a basket. He gave away 11 apples. Do we know how many he starts with?   No

    So I'll write a box for the total.

    (Write how-many box in diagram.)

    Starts
    c. ——————→ ☐

    We know he gives away 11 and has 9 left.

    (Write 11 and 9 in diagram.)

    Starts
    c. ——11——— 9 ☐ →

11. We need to figure out the total. Do we plus or minus?   Plus

    Say the problem. $11 + 9$

    $11 + 9 = 20$, so Walter started out with 20 apples.

12. Problem d. We know Sam ends with more. Let's see if we know how many he ends with. Sam began with 14 bricks on his toy truck. He put another 12 bricks on the truck. How many bricks ended up on the truck?

    Do we know how many he ends with?   No

    So I'll write a box.

    (Write how-many box in the diagram.)

    Ends
    d. ——14——— 12 ☐ →

13. He begins with 14 and puts on another 12.

    (Write 14 and 12 in the diagram.)

    Ends
    d. ——————→ ☐

    Do we plus or minus?   Plus

    Say the problem. $14 + 12$

    When we add, we get 26.

    So 26 bricks ended up on the truck.

PART C: STRUCTURED WORKSHEET

1. *(Give students a worksheet with the following problems.)*

   a. Milly started out with $10 in her bank account. She put $8 in her account. How much money did she end up with in her account?

TEACHER   **STUDENTS**

    b. Roger dropped and broke 4 glasses. If he started
       out with 9 glasses, how many glasses does he have now?

    c. After buying some toy cars at the swap meet, Tony
       had 17 cars in his collection. Before the swap meet,
       he had 12 cars in his collection. How many cars did he buy?

    d. Joe had too many kittens. He gave away 8 kittens and
       had 3 left. How many kittens did Joe start out with?

2. You're going to make number families for these problems.
   Read problem a to yourself. Raise your hand when you
   know if Milly *starts* or *ends* with more. *(Monitor students.)*

3. Does Milly *start* or *end* with more?   Ends with more.

   Make your number-family arrow. Write *ends* over the place
   for total. *(Check.)*

   (Write the following diagram on the board.)

                    Ends
   a. ————————→

   Here's what you should have.

4. The problem asks how much she ends up with. Do we
   know how much she ends with?   No

   So what do we write for *ends*?   A box

   Write a box. Then put in the numbers the problem gives.
   (Check.)

   *(Write to show: Draw the box first, then write 10 and 8 in
   the diagram.)*

                    Ends
          10   8 ☐
   a. ————————→

   Here's the number family for problem a.

5. Read problem b to yourself. Raise your hand when you
   know if Roger *starts* or *ends* with more. *(Monitor students.)*

6. Does Roger *start* or *end* with more?   Starts with more.
   Make your number-family arrow. Write *starts* over the
   place for total. *(Check.)*

7. Read the problem again. Raise your hand when you
   know what we write for *starts*. *(Monitor students.)*

   What did you write?   9

   Yes, he starts with 9 glasses. Write 9 for the total, then
   complete the number family. *(Check.)*

8. *(Write the following diagram on the board.)*

            4   ☐   Starts
   b. ————————→ 9

   Here's the number family for problem b.

9. Read problem c to yourself. Raise your hand when
   you know if Tony *starts* or *ends* with more. *(Monitor students.)*

10. Does Tony *start* or *end* with more?   Ends with more.
    Make your number-family arrow with the word *ends*. *(Check.)*

(continued on next page)

FORMAT 11.3 (continued)

TEACHER	STUDENTS

11. Raise your hand when you know what to write for *ends*.
    (Monitor students.) What do you write?   17

    Yes, he ends with 17. Complete the number family
    with two numbers and a box. *(Check.)*

12. *(Write the following diagram on the board.)*

    c.   12   ☐   Ends
              ──────→ 17

    Here's the number family for problem c.

13. Read problem d to yourself. Raise your hand when
    you know if Joe *starts* or *ends* with more. *(Monitor students.)*

14. Does Joe start or end with more?   Starts with more.

    Raise your hand when you know what to write for *starts*.
    (Monitor students.) What do you write?   A box

    Yes, the problem asks how many kittens he starts out
    with, so you write a box.

    Complete the number family with two numbers and a box. *(Check.)*

15. *(Write the following diagram on the board.)*

    d.   8   3   Starts ☐
              ──────→

    Here's the number family for problem d.

16. Figure out the answer to each problem. Remember
    the unit names. *(Check.)*

17. Tell me the answer for each problem.
    Problem a. How much money did Milly end with?   18 dollars
    Problem b. How many glasses does Roger have now?   5 glasses
    Problem c. How many cars did Tony buy?   5 cars
    Problem d. How many kittens did Joe start out with?   11 kittens

PART D: LESS STRUCTURED WORKSHEET

1. *(Give students a worksheet with the following problems.)*

   a. Wendy found 9 shells on the beach. She already had
      15 shells in her collection. How many shells does
      she have now?

   b. Harry went on a diet and lost 25 pounds. Before his diet,
      he weighed 195 pounds. How much does he weigh now?

   c. Mike started out with lots of fish. He threw back 8 fish and
      still had 9 left. How many fish did he start with?

   d. After Emily added 12 stories to her brick tower, the tower
      is 15 stories high. How high was her tower to start with?

2. For some of these problems, the person *starts* with more.
   For some, the person *ends* with more.

3. Problem a. Read the problem. Raise your hand when you
   know if the person starts or ends with more. *(Monitor
   students.)* Which is it?   Ends with more.

TEACHER	STUDENTS

4. Make the complete number family. Remember to label the total. *(Check.)*

5. *(Write the following diagram on the board.)*

   a.
   $$\overset{\text{Ends}}{\underset{\xrightarrow{}}{\quad 9 \qquad 15 \;\; \square}}$$

   Here's what you should have.

6. Now figure out the answer. Remember the unit name. *(Check.)*

7. How many shells does Wendy have now?   24 shells

   (Repeat steps 3–7 with other items; each number family and step 7 is shown below.)

   b.
   $$\overset{\qquad\quad\; \square \;\; \text{Starts}}{\underset{\xrightarrow{} \; 195}{\; 25 \qquad\quad\;}}$$

   How much does Harry weigh now?   170 pounds

   c.
   $$\overset{\text{Starts}}{\underset{\xrightarrow{}}{\quad 8 \qquad 9 \;\; \square}}$$

   How many fish did Mike catch?   17 fish

   d.
   $$\overset{\qquad\;\; \square \;\; \text{Ends}}{\underset{\xrightarrow{} \,15}{\; 12 \qquad\quad}}$$

   How high was Emily's tower to start with?   3 stories

FORMAT 11.4   Comparison Problems

TEACHER	STUDENTS

PART A: DETERMINING THE TOTAL NUMBER—PRESKILL

1. Comparison problems tell you about two persons or things. Here are some words you'll see in comparison problems: *bigger, older, smaller, taller, wider.* If the problem tells about two people and has a word that ends in *er*, you know it's a comparison problem.

2. Let's practice figuring out which person or thing in a comparison problem tells about the big number.

3. Listen: A dog weighs 7 pounds. A cat weighs 3 pounds more than the dog. Who does that problem tell about?   A dog and a cat.

4. Listen to the problem again. *(Repeat problem.)* Who is heavier?   The cat.

5. So the big number tells how many pounds the cat weighs.

   (Repeat steps 3–5 with the problems below.)

   Jill is 10 years old. Brian is 8 years younger. Who is older?

   Hole A is 6 feet deep. Hole B is 4 feet deep. Which hole is deeper?

   Jack ran 8 miles. Ann ran 2 miles more. Who ran farther?

   Jane weighs 60 pounds. Ann is 5 pounds lighter. Who is heavier?
   A yellow pencil is 5 inches long. A blue pencil is 3 inches longer. Which pencil is longer?

(continued on next page)

FORMAT 11.4   (continued)

TEACHER	STUDENTS

PART B: STRUCTURED WORKSHEET

1. *(Give students worksheets with problems written in the form below.)*

> a. Tom's stick is 2 feet long.
>   Bill's stick is 5 feet longer.
>   How long is Bill's stick?
>
>   ——— Answer: ———
>
> b. Jack is 10 years old.
>   May is 2 years younger.
>   How old is May?
>
>   ——— Answer: ———

2. You're going to make number families for comparison problems. The name for the bigger number goes at the *end* of the arrow. The name for which number goes at the end of the arrow?   **The bigger number.**

   Yes, the bigger number tells about the total.

3. Read the problem. *(Pause.)*

4. Who does the problem tell about?   **Tom and Bill**

   Which is longer, Bill's stick or Tom's stick?   **Bill's stick**

   Write Bill on the line above the total place. *(Check.)*

5. Read the problem again. *(Pause.)*

   Does a number in the problem tell how long Bill's stick is?   **No**

   Make a box below Bill. *(Check.)*

6. The problem doesn't give a number for the total. The numbers in the problem tell about parts of the total. Write those numbers on the arrow. *(Check.)*

7. Write the problem and figure out the answer. *(Check.)*

   What's the answer?   **7 feet**

8. So Bill's stick is 7 feet long.

   Write 7 feet on the answer line.

9. Read the problem. *(Pause.)*

10. Who does the problem tell about?   **Jack and May**

11. Who is older, Jack or May?   **Jack**

    Write Jack on the line above the Total place.

12. Read the problem again. *(Pause.)*

    Does the problem tell how old Jack is?   **Yes**

    How old?   **10**

    Write 10 below Jack.

13. The problem gives a number for the total.

    Complete the number family with a number and a box. *(Check.)*

TEACHER	**STUDENTS**

14. Write the problem and figure out the answer. *(Check.)*
    What's the answer?   8

15. So May is 8 years old.

    Write 8 years on the answer line.

    *(Repeat steps 3–8 with remaining addition problems.
    Repeat steps 9–15 with remaining subtraction problems.)*

PART C: LESS STRUCTURED WORKSHEET

1. *(Give students a worksheet with a mix of addition and
   subtraction problems; for example-selection guidelines, see page.)*

    a. Martha's cat weighs 2 pounds more than Sarah's cat.
       Martha's cat weighs 12 pounds. How much does
       Sarah's cat weigh?

    b. The trip to the library is 6 miles. The trip to the zoo
       is 3 miles further than the library. How far is it to the zoo?

    c. Greg has 12 cars in his collection. Will has 15 cars
       in his collection. How many more cars does Will have
       than Greg?

    d. There are 5 fewer children in Fay's family than in
       Joe's family. There are 3 children in Fay's family. How
       many children are in Joe's family?

2. Read problem a. *(Pause.)*

3. Make a number-family arrow. Write the word that tells
   about the total above the total place. *(Check.)*

4. See if the number for the total is given in the problem.   Martha
   Then write two numbers and a box where they belong. *(Check.)*   2 _____ □ 12

5. Write a number problem and figure out the answer.
                                                                12
   Then write the whole answer. *(Check.)*   −2
                                                                10   10 pounds

6. What's the answer? *(Repeat steps 2–6 with the remaining
   problems.)*   10 pounds

FORMAT 11.5   Classification Story Problems

TEACHER	**STUDENTS**

PART A: LANGUAGE TRAINING

1. I'll say some class names. You tell me the biggest class.
   Listen: cats, animals, dogs. What is the biggest class?   Animals

   *(Repeat step 1 with hammer, saw, tool; vehicle, car, truck;
   men, women, people; girls, boys, children.)*

(continued on next page)

FORMAT 11.5 (continued)

TEACHER	**STUDENTS**

PART B: STRUCTURED WORKSHEET

1. (Give students a worksheet with 6–8 problems written like those below.)

> a. There are 8 *children;* 3 are *boys.* How many are *girls*?
>   ————
>   ————————→
>
> b. Jill has 5 *hammers* and 4 *saws.* How many *tools* does she have?
>   ————
>   ————————→

2. Let's review some rules you already know. If the total number is given, what do you do?

   Subtract

   If the total number is not given, what do you do?

   Add

3. In some problems, we don't see words like *find, lose, buy,* or *give away,* so we have to use a different way to do these problems.

4. Touch the first problem. I'll read it. There are 8 children; 3 are boys. How many are girls? The problem talks about children, boys, and girls. Which is the big class, children, boys, or girls?

   Children

   If children is the big class, then the number of children is the total number. So write *children* on the line above the total place.

5. Listen. *(Repeat the problem.)* Children is the total number. Does the problem tell how many children?

   Yes

   Make a box below children.

   So the total number is given. What is the total number?

   8

   Write 8 in the box for the total number.

   > Note: If the first answer is no, tell the students, "The total is not given, so we don't write anything in the box for the total."

6. Now we write the values for boys and girls on the arrow. How many boys?

   3

   Write 3.

   We don't know how many girls, so we write a box above the arrow.

7. Is the total number given?

   Yes

   So what do you do to work out the problem?

   Subtract

   We start with 8 children and subtract 3 boys to find out how many girls.

   Write the equation and figure out the answer.

   If there are 8 children and 3 are boys, how many are girls?

   5

   (Repeat steps 3–5 with remaining problems.)

TEACHER   **STUDENTS**

PART C: LESS STRUCTURED WORKSHEET

1. *(Give students worksheet with problems in this form.)*

> Jerry has 7 pets; 4 are *dogs*.
> How many are *cats*?
> ——————— Answer: ———————
> ————————→

2. Touch the first problem.
3. Read the problem. Then write the name for the big class above the total place.

4. Write the two numbers and box where they belong.
5. Write the equation and figure out the answer.
6. Write the whole answer on the answer line.

   (Repeat steps 1–5 with remaining problems.)

FORMAT 11.6   Using Tables to Solve Problems

TEACHER   **STUDENT**

PART A: INTRODUCING ROWS AND COLUMNS IN A TABLE

1. *(Write the table below on the board.)*

6	6	1	
2	3	2	
1	1	2	

2. This is a table problem. To work this kind of problem, you have to add the numbers in each column and the numbers in each row. Remember that columns go up and down. Rows go side to side. Point to show me which way columns go. *(Check to make sure that students go up and down.)* Point and show me which way rows go. *(Check to make sure that students point side to side. Repeat to correct.)*

3. *(Touch the first column.)* I'll read the numbers in the first column: 6, 2, 1.

4. *(Touch the second column.)* Read the numbers.   6, 3, 1

5. *(Touch the third column.)* Read the numbers.   1, 2, 2

6. *(Touch the top row.)* I'll read the numbers in the top row. 6, 6, 1.

7. *(Touch the middle row.)* Your turn. Read the numbers in the middle row.   2, 3, 2

8. *(Touch the bottom row.)* Read the numbers in the bottom row.   1, 1, 2

(continued on next page)

FORMAT 11.6 (continued)

TEACHER	STUDENTS

PART B: FINDING TOTALS IN TABLES

1. Go back to the first column. The numbers are 6, 2, 1. Here's how you work the problem. You add 6 and 2. What's the answer?   8

2. Then you add 8 and 1. What's the answer?   9

3. 9 is the *total* for the first column. *(Write 9 at the bottom of the first column.)*

4. Your turn. Add the numbers in the next column and raise your hand when you know the answer. *(Wait for students to solve the problem.)* The numbers in this column are 6, 3, and 1. What is the answer, everyone?   10

5. *(Repeat procedure with last column.)*

6. The numbers for the top row are 6, 6, and 1. What is 6 + 6?   12
   What's 12 + 1? *(Write 13 at the end of the row.)*   13

7. Your turn. Add the numbers in the middle row and raise your hand when you have the answer. *(Wait for students to solve the problem.)* The numbers in this row are 2, 3, and 2. What is the answer, everyone?   7

8. *(Repeat procedure with last row.)*

PART C: USING THE NUMBER-FAMILY STRATEGY TO SOLVE FOR MISSING DATA

1. *(Write the following table on the board.)*

a		38	45
b	15	11	
c	12		31

2. This is a table with arrows for the rows and columns. The arrows show you something interesting about the table. Each row and column works just like a number family. The first two numbers in the row are the small numbers. The total is the big number.

3. *(Touch row a.)* A number is missing in that row. Is the missing number a big number or a small number?   A small number.

   (Write the following diagram on the board.)

   $$\xrightarrow{\quad 38 \quad} 45$$

4. So do you add or subtract to find the missing number?   Subtract

5. Say the subtraction problem.   45 − 38

6. *(Touch row b. Write the diagram below on the board.)*

   $$\xrightarrow{\quad 15 \quad 11 \quad}$$

   Here is the number family for that row. Is the missing number a small number or the big number?   The big number.

7. So do you add or subtract to find the missing number?   Add

8. Say the addition problem.   15 + 11

9. *(Touch row c.)* Is the missing number a small number or the big number?   A small number.

TEACHER	STUDENTS

10. So do you add or subtract? — Subtract

11. Say the subtraction problem. — 31 − 12

12. Your turn. Write the problem and the answer for each row. Write the column problem for rows a, b, and c. *(Wait for students to finish the problems.)*

13. Everyone, read the problems and the answers. Get ready:
    row a, — 45 − 38 = 7
    row b, — 15 + 11 = 26
    row c. — 31 − 12 = 19

14. What is the missing number in row a? *(Write 7 in row a.)* — 7
    What is the missing number in row b? *(Write 26 in row b.)* — 26
    What is the missing number in row c? *(Write 19 in row c.)* — 19

15. Figure out the totals for each column. *(Wait for students to finish the column problems.)*

16. Read the totals for the columns:
    first column, — 34
    second column. — 68

PART D: USING TABLES TO SOLVE WORD PROBLEMS

1. *(Students have worksheets with several problems similar to the one below.)*
   Facts: There are 23 red cars on Al's lot and Jim's lot has 12 green cars. The total number of red and green cars on Jim's lot is 43. The total number of green cars on both lots is 30.

	Red cars	Green cars	Total for both colors
Jim's lot			
Al's lot			
Total for both lots			

Questions

    a. Are there fewer green cars or red cars on both lots?

    b. How many green and red cars are on Al's lot?

    c. There are 31 cars of some color on Jim's lot. What color?

    d. Are there more green cars on Jim's lot or Al's lot?

2. We're going to use a table to answer the questions listed above. First we need to fill in any missing information from the facts that are given. Read the first fact. — There are 23 red cars on Al's lot.

   Write the value from that fact in the correct place in the table.
   (Repeat step 1 with the remaining facts.)

3. Now you have enough information to complete the table using the number-family strategy. If one of the small numbers is missing, what do you do? — Subtract

   If one of the totals is missing, what do you do? — Add

4. Now that the table is complete, read question a and raise your hand when you know the answer. *(Call on an individual student to answer question a.)* Everyone, write the correct answer next to the question.

(continued on next page)

FORMAT 11.6 (continued)

TEACHER	STUDENTS

5. *(Repeat step 4 for each question.)*

To correct: If students make a mistake locating the correct information, have them put their fingers on the cell that has the information to answer the question. Monitor where students place their fingers to determine if they are able to read the table. If they have problems locating the correct cells, then reteach Part C of this format, adding a question about the information represented in each row and column.

FORMAT 11.7 **Introduction to Multiplication and Division Word Problems**

TEACHER	STUDENT

1. *(Write the following diagrams on the board.)*

Ⓓ Ⓓ Ⓓ ——— D
Ⓓ Ⓓ Ⓓ ———→ C

2. We are going to use a multiplication number family to find out how many cents are in this picture. Remember, in multiplication number families, if the big number is not given, you must multiply. If the big number is given, then you must divide to find the answer.

What must you do if the big number is not given?	Multiply
What must you do if the big number is given?	Divide
What coins are shown in this picture?	Dimes

3. The total number of cents is the big number. Cents is already written on the diagram.

4. How many cents is *each* dime worth? 10 cents
   So 10 is the first small number. *(Write 10.)*

   10   D
   ————————→ C

5. How many dimes are there? 6

6. So I cross out dimes and write 6. *(Cross out dimes and write 6.)*

       6
   10   D̶
   ————————→ C

7. Look at the diagram. Is the big number given? No

8. If the big number is not given, what do you need to do? Multiply.

9. What is 10 times 6? 60
   (Cross out cents and write 60.)

10. What is the total number of cents? 60 cents

11. *(Repeat steps 1–11 with similar problems using nickels, dimes, and quarters. Later prolems do not need to show pictures of coins, but can describe them as in the following problems.)*

   a. You have some nickels. You have 35 cents in all. How many nickels do you have?

   b. You have some dimes. You have 9 dimes. How many cents do you have in all?

TEACHER   **STUDENT**

    c. You have some nickels. You have 8 nickels. How many cents
       do you have in all?

    d. You have some quarters. You have 5 quarters. How many
       cents do you have in all?

    e. You have some dimes. You have 40 cents in all. How many
       dimes do you have?

FORMAT 11.8 **Setting Up Multiplication and Division Word Problems**

TEACHER   **STUDENT**

PART A: WRITING NUMBER FAMILIES—PRESKILL

1. *(Write the following problems on the board.)*

    a. Each box holds 7 cans. You have 35 cans.
       How many boxes do you have?

    b. Each room had 10 lights. There were 8 rooms.
       How many lights were there in all the rooms?

    c. Each dog had 9 bugs. There were 7 dogs.
       How many bugs were there on all the dogs?

    d. Each cat had 9 fleas. There were 36 fleas in all.
       How many cats were there?

    e. Each boy ate 2 hot dogs. There were 5 boys.
       How many hot dogs were eaten by all the boys?

2. These are word problems. To work them, you have to make
multiplication number families. One sentence in each problem t
ells how to make the family. That sentence tells about each thing.

3. Listen while I read problem a. Each box holds 7 cans. You have
35 cans. How many boxes do you have? The first sentence gives
you information for making the number family. Each box holds 7
cans. There are more cans than boxes. So cans is the big number.

4. What do we write to stand for box?   B

   (Write the following diagram on the board.)

        B
   ————————→

   What do we write to show cans?   C

   (Write the following diagram on the board.)

        B
   ————————→ C

   If can is the big number and box is a small number,
   what is the other small number?   7

   (Write the following diagram on the board.)

      7   B
   ————————→ C

5. Here is the number family. The next sentence tells you
that you have 35 cans, so we cross out C and write 35.

   (Write the following diagram on the board.)

      7   B   35
   ————————→ ~~C~~

(continued on next page)

FORMAT 11.8   (continued)

TEACHER	STUDENTS

6. Our number family shows a big number and a small number. You find the missing small number by finding out how many sevens are in 35.

7. How many boxes do you have?   5

   (Write the final diagram on the board.)

```
       5
   7   B̶      35
   ─────────→ C̶
```

8. (Repeat steps 1–5 using problems b, c, d, and e.)

PART B: STRUCTURED WORKSHEET

1. (Give students a worksheet with 6 to 8 problems similar to those below.)

   a. There are 6 chairs at each table. If there are 42 chairs, how many tables are there?

   b. Books are stacked on shelves with the same number of books on each shelf. There are 5 shelves and 40 books. How many books are on each shelf?

2. These are multiplication and division problems.

3. Read problem a to yourself. Raise your hand when you've found the sentence that tells how to make the number family. (Pause. Call on a student to read.)
   — There are 6 chairs at each table.

4. There are 6 chairs at each table. Are there more chairs or more tables?
   — Chairs

   So which name tells about the big number?
   — Chairs

5. Make the number family with two letters and a number. (Check.)
   — Students write
```
   6          T
   ─────────→ C
```

6. The problem gives a value for one of the names. Which name?
   — Chairs

7. Put that value in the number family. (Check.)
   — Students write
```
   6          T 42
   ─────────→ C
```

8. Is the big number given?
   — Yes

   So do you multiply or divide?
   — Divide

9. Work the problem and write the answer with a unit name. (Check.)

10. What's the answer?
    — 7 tables

    (Repeat steps 3–10 with other items.)

FORMAT 11.9   Introducing Multistep Word Problems

TEACHER	STUDENT

PART A: INTRODUCING ENDS–IN–OUT FORMAT

1. (Write the following problems on the board.)

   a. A wallet is empty. $432 goes into that wallet. Then some money goes out of that wallet. The wallet ends up with $85. How much went out?

TEACHER   **STUDENTS**

    b. A florist starts without any roses. She picks up 87 roses. She
       sells 54 roses. How many roses does she end up with?

    c. Chandra had an empty basket. She put some eggs in the basket.
       Then she gave away 37 of those eggs. The basket still had 14 eggs
       in it. How many eggs did Chandra put in the basket?

    End up   *Out   In*

    ——————————→

2. Listen while I read problem a. A wallet is empty. $432 goes into
   that wallet. Then some money goes out of that wallet. The wallet
   ends up with $85. How much went out?

3. In this problem, some money goes into the wallet, and some money
   goes out of the wallet. How much money does the wallet end up with? $85

   So I will write $85 under "end up" in the number family.

   (Write $85 on the board.)

   End up   *Out   In*
   $85
   ——————————→

4. Do we know how much money went out of the wallet?   No

   So we do not know the other small number.

5. Do we know how much money went into the wallet?   Yes

6. How much money went into the wallet?

   So we can write that for the big number. *(Write $432*
   under "in" on the board.) $432

   End up   *Out   In*
   $85
   ——————————→ $432

7. Now that we know two numbers for the number family,
   we can figure out the third number. What is missing,
   a big number or a small number?   A small number.

8. How do we find a missing small number?   Subtract

9. Say the subtraction problem. $432 − $85

10. *(Repeat for problems b and c.)*

PART B: STRUCTURED BOARD PRESENTATION—MULTI-STEP PROBLEMS

1. *(Write the following problems on the board.)*

   a. Josh had $17 in the bank. Later he put $12 in the bank.
      The next day he went to the bank and took out $11.50.
      How much money did Josh end up with in the bank?

   b. A water tank had some water in it. 250 gallons were
      taken from the tank. Then another 720 gallons were
      taken from the tank. The tank still had 1150 gallons
      in it. How many gallons were in the tank in the beginning?

(continued on next page)

FORMAT 11.9 (continued)

TEACHER	STUDENTS

c. A farmer had 534 bales of hay. She fed 247 bales to her cattle. She sold 85 bales to a neighbor. She threw 4 bales away because they were moldy. How many bales did she end up with?

2. Listen while I read problem a: Josh had $17 in the bank. Later he put $12 in the bank. The next day he went to the bank and took out $11.50. How much money did Josh end up with in the bank? The first part of the problem tells about the two values that went in the bank. Here is the number family:

End up   *Out   In*

———————→

3. What is the first value that went in the bank? $17

   (*Write $17 in the number family.*)

   End up   *Out   In*
                        $17
   ———————→

4. What is the second value that went in the bank? $12
   (*Write $12 on the board.*)

   End up   *Out   In*
                        $17
                        12
   ———————→

5. Do we know how much Josh took out of the bank?   Yes
   How much? $11.50

   So we write $11.50 in the number family.

   (*Write $11.50 on the board.*)

   End up   *Out*   *In*
                         $17
            $11.50   12
   ———————→

6. Now we need to add the amounts that went into
   the bank. Say the problem. $17 + $12

   What is the total? $29

   (*Write $29 on the board.*)

   End up   *Out*   *In*
                         $17
            $11.50   12
   ———————→ $29

7. Now that we have two numbers in the number family,
   we can figure out the other number. What is missing,
   a big number or a small number?   A small number.

8. How do we find a missing small number?   Subtract

9. Say the subtraction problem. $29.00 − $11.50

10. Subtract to figure out how much money Josh ended
    up with in the bank. How much? $17.50

11. (*Repeat for problems b and c.*)

CHAPTER 12

Fractions

TERMS AND CONCEPTS

Fractions   A fraction is a numeral of the form y/x where $x \neq 0$. Fractions involve division into equal-sized segments and a statement regarding the number of segments present, used, or acted upon. For example, "John ate ¼ of a pie" implies that a pie was divided into four equal parts and that John ate one of those parts.

Numerator   The top number in a fraction.

Denominator   The bottom number in a fraction.

Proper Fraction   A fraction whose numerator is less than its denominator.

Improper Fraction   A fraction whose numerator is equal to or greater than the denominator.

Mixed Number   An improper fraction expressed as a whole number and a fraction.

Greatest Common Factor   Largest factor of both the numerator and the denominator; e.g., the greatest common factor for ⅜ is 4.

Lowest Common Denominator   The least common multiple of the denominators; e.g., the lowest common denominator for ⅓ + ½ + ¼ is 12.

Rational Numbers   Rational numbers can be expressed as the quotient of two integers. (Rational numbers can be negative, −¾ or −½, as well as positive, ¾ or ½. The chapters in this text discuss only positive rational numbers.) Fractions, decimals, ratios, proportion, and percent can all be considered different forms of rational numbers. Rational numbers are usually represented in one of the following ways:

1. Portioning off units from a total number of units

$$\text{(III)} \quad \text{IIIIIII} = \frac{3}{10} = .3 = 30\%$$

2. Portioning off subsets of a group of subsets

$$\text{(III)(III)} \quad \text{(III)} = \frac{2}{3} = .67 = 66\tfrac{2}{3}\%$$

3. Dividing a whole figure into equal parts

$$\bigcirc = \frac{1}{4} = .25 = 25\%$$

4. Number line

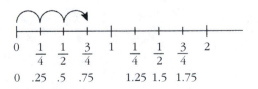

SKILL HIERARCHY

We have included a Skill Hierarchy Chart in this chapter because fractions comprise one of the most complex sets of skills covered in elementary mathe-

SKILL HIERARCHY CHART

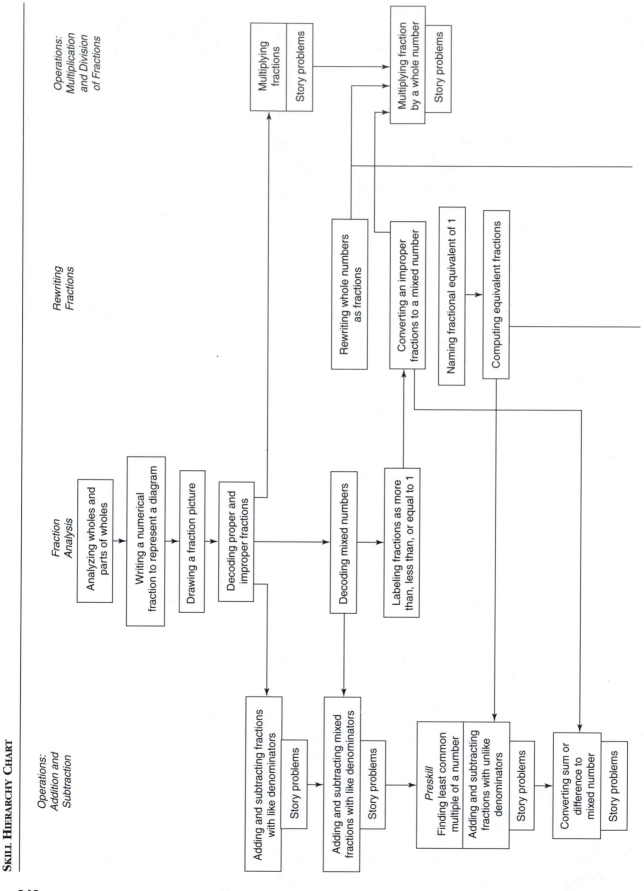

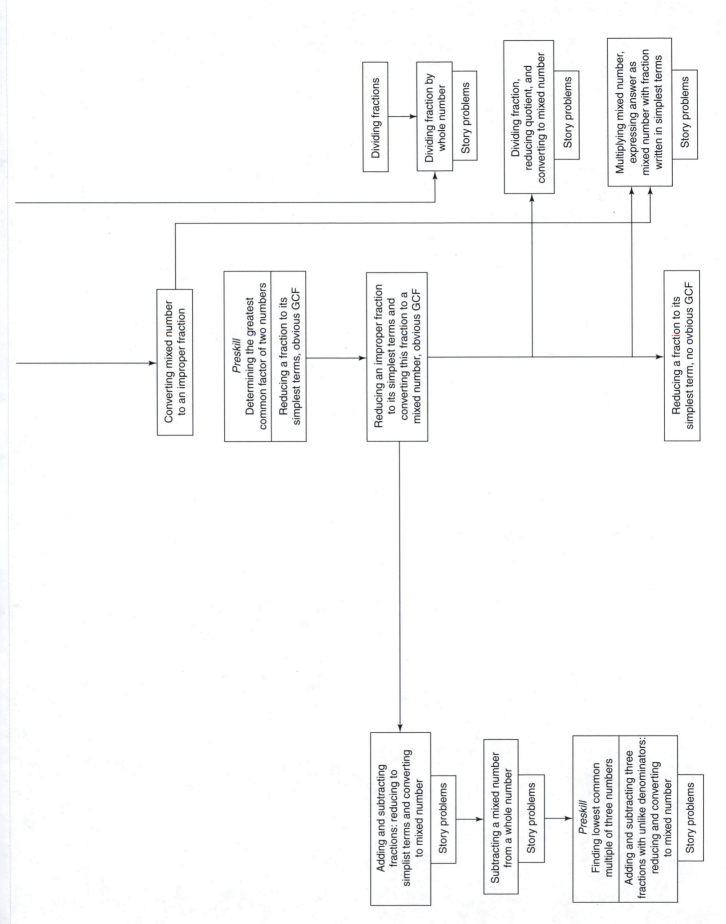

Dividing fractions

Dividing fraction by whole number

Story problems

Dividing fraction, reducing quotient, and converting to mixed number

Story problems

Multiplying mixed number, expressing answer as mixed number with fraction written in simplest terms

Story problems

Converting mixed number to an improper fraction

Preskill
Determining the greatest common factor of two numbers

Reducing a fraction to its simplest terms, obvious GCF

Reducing an improper fraction to its simplest terms and converting this fraction to a mixed number, obvious GCF

Reducing a fraction to its simplest term, no ovbious GCF

Adding and subtracting fractions: reducing to simplist terms and converting to mixed number

Story problems

Subtracting a mixed number from a whole number

Story problems

Preskill
Finding lowest common multiple of three numbers

Adding and subtracting three fractions with unlike denominators: reducing and converting to mixed number

Story problems

243

Instructional Sequence and Assessment Chart

Grade Level	*Problem Type*	*Performance Indicator*
1–2a	Identifying fractions that correspond to diagrams	a. Circle the picture that shows ¾.

b. Circle the picture that shows ¼.

c. Put X on the line below the picture that shows ⅓.

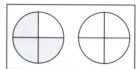

———————————   ———————————

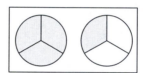

d. Put X on the line below the picture that shows ½.

———————————   ———————————   ———————————

| 1–2b | Drawing diagrams to correspond to fractions | |

$\frac{3}{4}$ =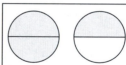

$\frac{2}{3}$ =

$\frac{3}{2}$ =

Grade Level	Problem Type	Performance Indicator
1–2c	Reading and writing fractions expressed as fractions	Write these fractions: a. two-thirds $= \dfrac{h}{h}$ b. five-halves $= \dfrac{\square}{\square}$ c. four-fifths $= \dfrac{\square}{\square}$ (Test students individually. "What does this say: $\dfrac{2}{3}, \dfrac{4}{5}, \dfrac{5}{2}$?")
2d	Determining whether a fraction is more than, equal to, or less than 1	Write *more than*, *less than*, or *equal to* in each blank. $\dfrac{4}{3}$ is _____ 1 $\dfrac{7}{7}$ is _____ 1 $\dfrac{5}{6}$ is _____ 1
2e	Adding and subtracting fractions with like denominators	$\dfrac{3}{5} - \dfrac{2}{5} = $ _____ $\dfrac{4}{7} - \dfrac{2}{7} = $ _____ $\dfrac{3}{5} + \dfrac{1}{5} = $ _____
2f	Multiplying fractions	$\dfrac{3}{5} \times \dfrac{2}{3} = $ _____ $\dfrac{2}{5} \times \dfrac{3}{5} = $ _____ $\dfrac{2}{2} \times \dfrac{3}{5} = $ _____
3a	Reading and writing mixed numbers	Write two and one-third _____ Write four and two-fifths _____ Write six and one-half _____ (Test students individually. "Read these numbers: $2\dfrac{1}{4}, 3\dfrac{2}{5}, 7\dfrac{3}{9}$.")
3b	Adding and subtracting mixed numbers: fractions with like denominators	$5\dfrac{4}{7} - \dfrac{2}{7} = $ _____ $3\dfrac{2}{5} - 1\dfrac{2}{5} = $ _____

(continued)

Instructional Sequence and Assessment Chart (continued)

Grade Level	Problem Type	Performance Indicator
3c	Story problems: adding and subtracting mixed numbers and fractions with the same denominator	Bill ran 2¾ miles on Monday and 3¼ miles on Tuesday. How many miles did he run altogether? _____ miles
		Jack had 4⅝ pounds of nails. Bill had 2⅜ pounds of nails. How much more did Jack have? _____ pounds of nails
		Bob worked 2½ hours on Monday and 3 hours on Tuesday. How many hours did he work altogether? _____ hours
4a	Rewriting fractions as mixed numbers	$\frac{12}{5} = $ _____ $\frac{8}{3} = $ _____ $\frac{21}{9} = $ _____
4b	Rewriting whole numbers as fractions	$9 = \frac{\square}{\square} \quad 6 = \frac{\square}{\square} \quad 8 = \frac{\square}{\square}$
4c	Multiplying fractions by a whole number; converting answers to whole numbers	$\frac{2}{3} \times 6 \qquad \frac{1}{3} \times 12$ $\frac{3}{5} \times 20$
4d	Multiplying fractions by whole numbers and converting answers to mixed numbers	$\frac{2}{5} \times 14 \qquad \frac{3}{7} \times 8$ $\frac{2}{9} \times 15$
4e	Story problems: multiplying fractions by whole numbers	There are 15 children in class. Two-thirds are boys. How many boys in the class?
		Jack has to study for 30 hours. He has done half of the studying. How many hours did he study?
		Ann's coach told her to run ¾ of a mile a day. How many miles will she run in 5 days?
4f	Writing a fraction as an equivalent to one whole group	$1 = \frac{\square}{4} \qquad 1 = \frac{\square}{7}$
4g	Rewriting fractions as equivalent fractions with larger denominators	$\frac{2}{5} = \frac{\square}{10}$ $\frac{3}{4} = \frac{\square}{12}$ $\frac{2}{3} = \frac{\square}{9}$

Grade Level	Problem Type	Performance Indicator
4h	Finding the lowest common multiple of two small numbers	Find the lowest common multiple of 6 and 4 _____ Find the lowest common multiple of 5 and 10 _____ Find the lowest common multiple of 5 and 2 _____
4i	Adding and subtracting fractions with unlike denominators	$\dfrac{3}{4} - \dfrac{2}{3} = \dfrac{\square}{\square}$ $\dfrac{2}{5} + \dfrac{3}{10} = \dfrac{\square}{\square}$ $\dfrac{1}{2} - \dfrac{1}{3} = \dfrac{\square}{\square}$ $\dfrac{2}{6} + \dfrac{1}{2} = \dfrac{\square}{\square}$
4j	Comparing value of fractions	Which is greater: $\dfrac{2}{3}$ or $\dfrac{4}{5}$? $\dfrac{4}{5}$ or $\dfrac{2}{3}$? $\dfrac{2}{7}$ or $\dfrac{1}{2}$?
4k	Story problems: adding and subtracting fractions with unlike denominators	Bill painted ½ of the wall. Jane painted ¼ of the wall. How much of the wall have they painted altogether? Tom ate ⅓ of the pie, and Jack ate ½ of the pie. How much of the pie did they eat?
4l	Determining all factors of a given number	Write all the numbers that are factors of 12. Write all the numbers that are factors of 8.
4m	Determining the greatest common factor	What is the greatest common factor of 8 and 12? What is the greatest common factor of 4 and 8? What is the greatest common factor of 12 and 15?
4n	Reducing a fraction to its simplest terms	Reduce these fractions to their simplest terms: $\dfrac{12}{18} = \dfrac{\square}{\square}$ $\dfrac{16}{20} = \dfrac{\square}{\square}$ $\dfrac{6}{18} = \dfrac{\square}{\square}$

(continued)

Instructional Sequence and Assessment Chart (continued)

Grade Level	Problem Type	Performance Indicator
4o	Adding fractions, reducing and converting to mixed numbers	Add these fractions; reduce the answers to simplest terms. Write answers as mixed numbers. $\frac{4}{6} + \frac{2}{5} = $ _____ $\frac{2}{4} + \frac{2}{3} = $ _____ $\frac{6}{10} + \frac{4}{5} = $ _____
4p	Converting mixed numbers to improper fractions	$2\frac{1}{4} = \frac{\square}{4}$ $3\frac{1}{2} = \frac{\square}{2}$ $1\frac{3}{5} = \frac{\square}{5}$
5a	Subtracting mixed numbers from whole numbers	$8 - 1\frac{2}{3} = $ _____ $9 - 2\frac{3}{5} = $ _____ $7 - 4\frac{1}{2} = $ _____
5b	Finding the lowest common multiple of three numbers	Find the lowest common multiple of 3, 6, and 4. Find the lowest common multiple of 2, 4, and 5. Find the lowest common multiple of 2, 5, and 10.
5c	Adding and subtracting three fractions with different denominators	Add these fractions and write the answers with fractions written in simplest terms: $\frac{3}{5} + \frac{1}{2} + \frac{3}{6} = $ _____ $\frac{2}{3} + \frac{2}{4} + \frac{1}{6} = $ _____ $\frac{3}{4} + \frac{1}{2} + \frac{2}{5} = $ _____
5d	Multiplying mixed numbers	$7\frac{3}{4} \times 3\frac{1}{2} = $ _____ $2\frac{3}{5} \times 4 = $ _____ $5 \times 2\frac{1}{2} = $ _____
5e	Dividing fractions	$\frac{3}{4} \div \frac{2}{5} = $ _____ $\frac{5}{6} \div \frac{2}{3} = $ _____ $\frac{7}{9} \div \frac{1}{3} = $ _____

Grade Level	*Problem Type*	*Performance Indicator*
5f	Dividing fractions by whole numbers	$\frac{2}{3} \div 4 =$ ______ $\frac{3}{5} \div 2 =$ ______ $\frac{2}{4} \div 7 =$ ______
5g	Dividing mixed numbers by whole numbers	$3\frac{1}{2} \div 3 =$ ______ $2\frac{1}{5} \div 2 =$ ______ $7\frac{1}{2} \div 4 =$ ______
5h	Story problems: division involving fractions	Two girls picked 5½ pounds of cherries. They want to split up the cherries equally. How much will each one get? Bill has 35 inches of ribbon. He wants to make shorter ribbons. If each ribbon is ½″ long, how many ribbons can he make?

matics. This complexity is understandable, since the entire range of operations discussed in other sections of the book is applicable to fractional numbers. Unfortunately, fractions do not represent a simple extension of familiar skills. While early instruction on whole numbers covers counting by groups of 1 or more than 1, that instruction does not help students generalize to groups of less than one. For example, in addition and subtraction of whole numbers, members of a second group relate to the members of the first group based on one-to-one correspondences. For example, in the problem 4 + 3, students increase the first set in units of 1 (5, 6, 7), producing the answer 7. To solve 4 − 3, students decrease the first set in units of 1, producing the answer 1. In multiplication and division of whole numbers, a second group is related to the first group based on a one-to-many correspondence. For example, in solving for 8 × 2, students count units of 8 for each member of the second group (8, 16), producing the answer 16. In 16 ÷ 2, students determine the answer by counting 1 for each unit of 2 in 16 (1, 2, 3, 4, 5, 6, 7, 8), producing the answer 8.

In operations containing fractions, the correspondences involve fractional numbers. For example, to solve ⅔ × 4 students count units of ⅔ for each member of the second group. While students can quickly learn to count 2, 4, 6, 8 for 2 × 4, counting ⅔, 4/3, 6/3, 8/3, for ⅔ × 4 is not easy. The problem ⅔ × ⅘ is even less comprehensible because students have no experiential basis for counting ⅘ths times. Therefore, learning fractional correspondences with both whole numbers and other fractions requires instruction in new strategies.

Another major difficulty with fractions is the incompatibility of different units. Addition and subtraction can be carried out only with equivalent units. Whole numbers represent a simple type of equivalent unit, so they can be added and subtracted in any combination. In contrast, fractional numbers do not represent one type of unit: All thirds represent equivalent units and all fourths represent equivalent units, but thirds are not the same as fourths. Consequently, thirds and fourths cannot be added or subtracted as such. Prior to adding or subtracting fractions, the fractional units must be transformed into a common unit:

$$\frac{1}{4} + \frac{2}{3} = \frac{3}{12} + \frac{8}{12} = \frac{11}{12}$$

The necessity to transform or rewrite fractional numbers is a major source of difficulty in teaching fractions. (This is one reason for the appeal of decimals; they have the uniform base of multiples of 10.)

Instruction in fractions can be organized around the three main groupings of fraction topics outlined in the Skill Hierarchy: fraction analysis, rewriting fractions, and operations (addition, subtraction, multiplication, and division of fractions).

Since application of fraction skills depends on an understanding of fractional numbers, initial instruction on the concepts and conventions characterizing fractions is critical. Therefore, early instruction must address fraction analysis skills such as constructing diagrams to represent fractions, writing the fraction represented by diagrams, decoding fractions, and determining if a fraction is proper or improper.

The second area, rewriting fractions, includes the following skills:

1. Rewriting an improper fraction as a mixed number: $\frac{13}{2} = 6\frac{1}{2}$
2. Rewriting a proper fraction using the smallest possible denominator (reducing fractions): $\frac{6}{8} = \frac{3}{4}$
3. Rewriting a fraction as an equivalent fraction: $\frac{2}{5} = \frac{4}{10}$
4. Rewriting a mixed number as an improper fraction: $2\frac{1}{2} = \frac{5}{2}$

The third area, operations, includes addition, subtraction, multiplication, and division of fractions. These operations often require several rewriting fraction skills. For example, to work the problem $\frac{3}{4} + \frac{5}{6}$, the student must rewrite $\frac{3}{4}$ and $\frac{5}{6}$ as equivalent fractions with the same denominator: $\frac{3}{4} = \frac{9}{12}$ and $\frac{5}{6} = \frac{10}{12}$. The equivalent fractions $\frac{10}{12}$ and $\frac{9}{12}$ are then added to produce a sum of $\frac{19}{12}$, which must be converted to the mixed number $1\frac{7}{12}$. When working the problem $\frac{4}{5} \times 1\frac{3}{4}$, the student must first convert the mixed number $1\frac{3}{4}$ to the improper fraction $\frac{7}{4}$. The student then multiplies $\frac{4}{5} \times \frac{7}{4}$, ending with a product of $\frac{28}{20}$, which can be converted to the mixed number $1\frac{8}{20}$. The fraction part of this mixed number can be reduced so that the final answer reads $1\frac{2}{5}$.

The Skill Hierarchy Chart illustrates the interrelationships among various fraction skills. Note on the chart the numerous fractions skills that are component skills for other skills. A sequence for teaching fractions must be arranged so that all component skills for an advanced problem type have been presented before that problem type is introduced. Note also how the focus of instruction circulates. For example, simple addition and subtraction problems involving fractions with like denominators are introduced at a relatively early stage in the sequence of instruction. Problems involving adding and subtracting fractions with unlike denominators are not introduced until significantly later in the sequence, since

several rewriting skills must be taught first. The Instructional Sequence and Assessment Chart suggests one possible order for introducing the important types of fraction-related problems. Teachers working with intermediate students will find it productive to test for and teach, when necessary, the skills appearing at the beginning of the sequence chart, since these skills lay the foundation for a conceptual understanding of fractions.

FRACTION ANALYSIS

Fraction analysis instruction usually begins in mid-second grade. The skills included in this area are listed below in their order of introduction:

1. Learning part/whole discrimination: Students learn to discriminate between whole units, the number of parts each unit is divided into, and the number of parts used.
2. Writing a numerical representation for a diagram of whole units divided into equal-sized parts, and vice versa:

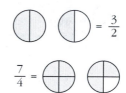

3. Reading fractions: $\frac{3}{4}$ is read as "three-fourths."
4. Determining whether a fraction equals, exceeds, or is less than one whole.
5. Reading mixed fractional numbers: $3\frac{1}{2}$ is "three and one-half."

The strategies in the fraction analysis section are designed to introduce proper and improper fractions concurrently. This feature prevents students from learning the misrule that all fractions are proper fractions. Without adequate instruction, low-performing students often learn this misrule, as evidenced by their ability to decode and draw a picture of $\frac{3}{4}$ but inability to generalize the skills to the example $\frac{4}{3}$. By introducing proper and improper fractions at the same time, teachers show students that the analysis applies to all fractions.

A second important feature of the analysis section is that students are taught initially to interpret what the denominator and numerator tell (e.g., in $\frac{3}{4}$ the 4 tells four parts in each whole unit, and 3 tells three parts are used) rather than to read the fraction in the traditional way (e.g., ¾ is read as three-fourths). The interpretive reading of fractions enables students to represent a diagram as a numerical fraction and facilitates conceptual development.

A third important feature of fraction analysis is initial limitation of fractions to figures that have been divided into parts:

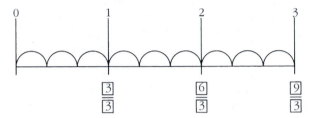

To simplify initial learning, we recommend delaying the introduction of subsets until several months after fractions are introduced.

Part–Whole Discrimination

Format 12.1 shows how to introduce fractions to students. The goal of the format is to teach basic fraction (part–whole) concepts through the use of number lines rather than separate groups. The reason for working with number lines from the onset is to ensure that students relate fractions to whole numbers. The specific objective is to teach students to discriminate between the number of parts in each whole unit and the number of whole units.

In the format, the teacher draws a number line on the board and divides each unit into an equal number of parts. The teacher tells the students that each unit is called a whole and then leads the students through determining how many parts are in each whole. Students complete the bottom number for units on the number line. They learn that the bottom number is the number of parts in each unit. (See Format 12.1.)

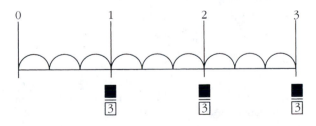

Each example set should include number lines divided into different numbers of parts, and each number line should be of a different length. For example, the first number line might end with 5, with each section divided into two parts. The next number line might end with 3, and each unit might be

divided into four parts. This format is presented for several days.

Next, the students learn to write complete fractions for whole numbers on number lines. The bottom number is the number of parts in each unit. That number is the same for all whole units on a number line. The top number is the number of parts from the beginning of the number line.

For the third step, students write three fractions for each number line, two whole-number fractions and a fraction for a shaded part. To figure out the fractions, students first count the number of parts in each unit and write the bottom number for all the fractions. They then count the units from the beginning of each number line and write the top number for the fraction at one unit, the top number at two units, and the top number for the shaded part.

After students have worked with horizontal number lines for several days, teachers can introduce number lines that are vertically oriented. The procedure is the same. The number of parts in each unit is the bottom number of each fraction. The top number is the number of parts from the beginning of the number line.

After working with number lines until students can perform flawlessly, students work with groups that are separated. Groups that are separated are figures, like circles or squares, that are divided into equal parts.

Format 12.2 includes a format for introducing groups that are separated. The goal of the format is to teach basic fraction (part–whole) concepts through the use of diagrams. The specific objectives are to teach students to discriminate between the number of parts in each whole unit and the number of whole units.

In the format, the teacher writes a row of circles on the board and divides each into an equal number of parts. The teacher tells the students that each circle is called a whole and then leads the students through determining how many parts in each whole, or unit.

Each example set should include a different number of circles (wholes). Also, the number of parts each whole is divided into should vary from set to set. For example, the first set might include three circles, each divided into two parts. The next set might include five circles, each divided into four parts; the next two circles, each divided into three parts; and so on. This format should be presented for several days.

Some students may not see the relationship between pictures of "separated" fraction groups and fractions on a number line. It is therefore very important to use the same language when teaching or correcting mistakes. Be sure to stress the word *each* if students have problems with the number-line examples. Remind them to count the parts in each unit.

Writing Numerical Fractions to Represent Diagrams

$$\oplus \oplus = \dfrac{\square}{\square}$$

Exercises in which the students write a numerical fraction to represent a diagram (e.g., ¾) are presented after the students have had ample practice, usually several days, to master the part–whole concepts presented in Format 12.2. The format for writing numerical fractions appears in Format 12.3. In Part A, the structured board presentation, students learn that the bottom number of a fraction tells how many parts in each whole, while the top number of a fraction represents how many parts are used (shaded). Parts B and C are structured and less structured worksheet exercises in which the students fill in the numerals to represent a diagram. Daily practice is provided for several weeks, followed by intermittent review.

Two guidelines are important for appropriate example selection for this skill. First, the number of parts in each whole unit, the number of whole units, and the number of parts used should vary among examples. Second, the examples should include a mixture of proper and improper fractions as well as some fractions that equal less than a whole unit:

$$\oslash = \dfrac{2}{3} \qquad \oplus = \dfrac{1}{4}$$

some examples that equal more than one unit:

$$\oslash \oslash \oslash \oslash = \dfrac{7}{2} \qquad \oplus \oplus = \dfrac{5}{4}$$

and just a few that equal one unit:

$$\oplus = \dfrac{4}{4} \qquad \oslash = \dfrac{2}{2}$$

During the first days, all examples should include circles divided into parts. After several weeks, other shapes (e.g., squares, rectangles, triangles) can be included in exercises.

Special attention should be given to examples containing a series of units that are not divided:

These diagrams need additional explanation. The teacher should point out that if a whole is not divided into parts, students should write a 1 on the bottom. The 1 tells that there is only one part in the whole unit. Examples that yield 1 as a denominator should not be introduced when fractions are initially presented, but can be introduced about a week after initial instruction. Thereafter, about 1 in every 10 diagrams should be an example with 1 as a denominator. These examples are important, since they present a conceptual basis for exercises in which students convert a whole number to a fraction (e.g., $8 = \frac{8}{1}$).

Drawing Diagrams to Represent Fractions

Prior to constructing actual diagrams, students should practice completing fractions and shading in the correct fractional parts on the number line. Monitor the work carefully. Make sure that students are relating the information shown by the number lines to the fractions.

Translating numerical fractions into diagrams is a useful exercise for reinforcing a conceptual understanding of the part–whole fraction relationship. Constructing diagrams can be introduced when students can accurately fill in the numerals to represent a diagram. For most students, this should be a week or two after fraction analysis is introduced. The procedure is relatively simple, so we haven't included a format. The teacher should begin instruction by modeling how to divide circles into equal-sized parts, stressing the need to divide the circles so that each part is the same size. Examples can be limited to fractions with 2, 3, or 4 as denominators. This allows for adequate discrimination without spending an inordinate amount of time teaching younger students to divide circles into more than four parts. After several days of practice dividing wholes into parts, the teacher presents a worksheet exercise, prompting the students as they draw diagrams. The teacher has the students say what each number tells, beginning with the bottom number. For ¾, the teacher would say, "Touch the bottom number. What does it tell you? . . . Draw four parts in each whole. . . . Touch the top number. . . . What does it tell you? . . . Shade in three parts." Figure 12.1 includes a sample worksheet. Note that each example has four circles. The purpose of keeping the number of circles constant is to prevent students from thinking that the number of whole units has something to do with the numerator and/or denominator.

Decoding Fractions

When fractions are initially introduced, students are taught to say what each numeral in the fraction tells. The fraction ¾ is read as "four parts in each whole; three parts are used up." This translation is recommended because it specifies what to do (make four parts in each whole and then shade three parts), thus facilitating conceptual understanding.

Several weeks after fractions are introduced, reading fractions in the traditional way can be taught; for example, ¾ is read as three-fourths. Format 12.4 shows how to teach students to read fractions the traditional way. The teacher writes several fractions on the board and models how to read the fractions, testing after each example. Then the teacher tests students on reading the fractions without first providing the model. The correction is a model and test. After the initial correction, the teacher uses the alternating-test pattern to provide practice on the missed example.

This decoding-fractions format should be presented daily for about 2 or 3 weeks, then once each second or third day for about 3 or 4 weeks until students can accurately read fractions. Thereafter, students receive practice in reading fractions at the same time new fraction skills are introduced. For example, in adding fractions, students receive practice decoding fractions in the step when they are asked to read the problem aloud.

Two example-selection guidelines should be followed in teaching students to decode fractions. First, the introduction of fractions with the numbers 2, 3, or 5 as denominators should be delayed several lessons, because these denominators are not pronounced by adding the suffix *ths* to the number as is the case for sixths, ninths, and fourths. When a 2 appears as the denominator, students say "halves," not "twoths"; when a 3 appears, students say "thirds," not "threeths"; when a 5 appears, students say "fifths," not "fiveths." These denominators need to be introduced one at a time, using a model-and-test procedure. Fractions with 2 as a denominator might be introduced first. When introducing 2 as a denominator, about half of the examples in the teaching set should contain 2 in the denominator, while the other half should represent a variety of previously introduced denominators:

$$\frac{1}{2} \quad \frac{1}{4} \quad \frac{3}{2} \quad \frac{3}{8} \quad \frac{5}{2} \quad \frac{5}{7} \quad \frac{1}{6} \quad \frac{4}{2}$$

When students have mastered denominators of 2, they are introduced in the same way to fractions with 5, then 3, as denominators. A second example-selection guideline addresses the numerators. In about a fourth of the examples, the number 1 should be written as the numerator. These examples are included so that the students can see the difference between how a fraction is said when the numerator is 1 and when the numerator is more than 1: one-eighth versus four-eighths.

Determining If a Fraction Is More Than, Less Than, or Equal to One

Determining whether a fraction equals, exceeds, or is less than one whole is an important skill and also serves as a prerequisite for later exercises in which students are expected to convert an improper fraction like ¹⁰⁄₄ to a mixed number: 2¾. This skill can be introduced when students can accurately decode fractions the traditional way. The teaching process appears in Format 12.5. Part A is a pictorial demonstration in which the teacher draws diagrams representing fractions of various values (more than 1, less

FIGURE 12.1 Sample Worksheet for Drawing Diagrams from Numerical Fractions

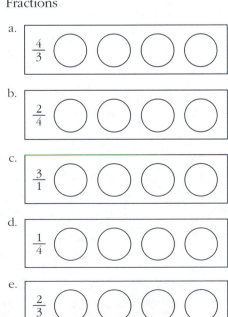

than 1, equal to 1) and asks the students if the picture shows one whole, more than one whole, or less than one whole.

In Part B, the teacher presents rules to be used in determining whether a numerical fraction equals, exceeds, or is less than one whole unit. First, students are taught the rule that when the top and bottom number of a fraction are the same, the fraction equals one whole. After this rule is presented, the teacher tests the students' application of the rule, using a series of numerical fractions, about half of which equal one whole:

$$\frac{5}{5} \quad \frac{6}{4} \quad \frac{4}{4} \quad \frac{9}{2} \quad \frac{9}{9} \quad \frac{5}{5} \quad \frac{7}{3} \quad \frac{2}{7} \quad \frac{8}{8}$$

Next, the teacher instructs students that when the top number of a fraction is greater than the bottom number, the fraction equals more than one whole; and when the top number is less than the bottom number, the fraction equals less than one whole. Finally, the students are shown fractions and asked to tell whether the fraction is equal to, more than, or less than 1. A structured worksheet exercise follows in which students must circle either *more, equal,* or *less* when given numerical fractions:

$$\frac{3}{4} \quad \text{more equal less}$$

$$\frac{8}{8} \quad \text{more equal less}$$

Note that in this format, the words *numerator* and *denominator* are not used. The purpose of excluding the terms is to avoid possible confusion for students who may be unclear about which number is the numerator and which is the denominator. Similarly, the term *improper* fraction is not included in the format. This term is best introduced in later grades.

Examples for parts B, C, and independent practice should include a variety of problems. In about a third of the examples, the numerator and denominator of the fraction should be the same:

$$\frac{4}{4} \quad \frac{8}{8} \quad \frac{3}{3}$$

In another third, the numerator should be greater than the denominator:

$$\frac{7}{5} \quad \frac{3}{2} \quad \frac{4}{2}$$

In another third, the numerator should be less than the denominator:

$$\frac{2}{3} \quad \frac{4}{7} \quad \frac{3}{4}$$

Reading and Writing Mixed Numbers

The above diagram may be expressed as the improper fraction ¾ or as the mixed fractional number 2¼. Reading and writing mixed numbers can be introduced relatively early in the fraction sequence, as soon as students can correctly determine when a fraction equals, exceeds, or is less than one whole. However, the teacher must keep in mind that exercises designed to teach students to convert mixed numbers to improper fractions and vice versa should not be introduced until much later in the fraction sequence, since these conversions require students to know basic multiplication facts. Format 12.6 is designed to teach students to read and write mixed numbers. The format begins with a pictorial demonstration exercise in which students are taught to express the diagram of an improper fraction as a mixed number by counting the number of whole units shaded and writing that number, then determining the numerator and denominator of the remaining units. Below is a sample exercise:

Part B is designed to teach students to read mixed numbers. The teacher uses a model-test procedure, having students first say the whole number, then the fraction, then the mixed number. Note that the teacher emphasizes the word *and* when reading mixed numbers. The purpose of emphasizing *and* is to prevent errors in which the student either combines the whole number and the numerator, reading 4⅔ as "forty-two thirds," or leaves out the numerator, reading 5⅓ as "five thirds."

Part C is an exercise in which students are taught to write mixed numbers. The teacher gives students lined paper and pencil and points out that when students write mixed numbers, they are to make the whole number big and the numbers in the fraction small: "The big number should be written so that it touches the top and bottom of the line. Then write the fraction line in the middle of the space." The exercise begins with the teacher dictating a mixed number and having students first say and write the whole number, then say and write the fraction part of the mixed number.

REWRITING FRACTIONS

The procedures in this section all involve the process of changing a fraction from one form to another without changing its value—that is, maintaining equivalency. Three main types of conversion skills are discussed:

1. Determining the missing number in a pair of equivalent fractions. Given a problem such as

$$\frac{3}{5} = \frac{\square}{10}$$

   the student determines the missing number. This problem type is a critical component skill for problems involving adding and subtracting fractions with unlike denominators.
2. Reducing fractions to their lowest terms. A fraction is said to be at its lowest term (or simplest form) when both the numerator and denominator have no common factor except 1:

$$\frac{20}{24} \text{ can be reduced to } \frac{5}{6}$$

3. Converting mixed numbers to improper fractions:

$$3\frac{1}{2} = \frac{7}{2}$$

   and improper fractions to mixed numbers:

$$\frac{17}{5} = 3\frac{2}{5}$$

A general preskill for all rewriting skills is knowledge of basic multiplication and division facts. To perform all three types of conversion problems, students must be able to either multiply or divide. Thus, rewriting-fraction skills usually are not introduced until early fourth grade.

The strategies presented here are designed so that students not only learn the necessary computation required to change fractions into parallel forms but also understand the underlying concepts of equivalency that govern each strategy. Without understanding equivalency, students can apply very few of the skills they learn. For example, if students do not understand that when the numerator and denominator are the same, the fraction is equal to 1, they will not understand why $\frac{3}{4}$ can be multiplied by $\frac{5}{5}$ to create the equivalent fraction $\frac{15}{20}$. Although the equivalency concept is relatively sophisticated, the language of the strategies is relatively simple because they are designed for elementary students.

Completing Equivalent Fractions

Instruction in equivalent fractions begins with problems in which the student must determine the missing numerator in an equivalent fraction:

$$\frac{3}{4} = \frac{\square}{12} \qquad \frac{1}{2} = \frac{\square}{10}$$

The basic strategy is to multiply the first fraction by a fractional equivalent to one whole. In working the first problem above, the student determines that to end up with an equivalent fraction that has 12 as a denominator, the fraction $\frac{3}{4}$ must be multiplied by $\frac{3}{3}$:

$$\frac{3}{4} \times \frac{(3)}{(3)} = \frac{9}{12}$$

Equivalency is maintained since, by definition, the identity element for multiplication is 1. When multiplying $\frac{3}{4}$ by $\frac{3}{3}$, we are multiplying $\frac{3}{4}$ by a fraction that equals 1; therefore, we are not changing the value of $\frac{3}{4}$.

PRESKILLS. Several skills should be mastered before equivalency problems are introduced: (a) knowledge of the terms *numerator* and *denominator,* (b) the ability to multiply fractions, and (c) the ability to construct a fraction that equals one whole.

The terms *numerator* and *denominator* are usually introduced in second or third grade. The teaching procedure is simple. The teacher tells students the numerator is the top number in the fraction and the denominator is the bottom number in the fraction. The teacher then provides practice by writing several fractions on the board and having students identify the numerator and denominator of each fraction. Daily practice is necessary so students won't forget or confuse the terms.

Multiplication of two fractions is also usually taught in third grade. Procedures for teaching this skill are presented later in this chapter.

Constructing fractions equal to one whole is introduced about 2 weeks prior to introducing equivalent fraction problems. Format 12.7 includes the preskill format for constructing fractions equal to 1. Part A is a board exercise in which the rule for constructing fractions equal to 1 is introduced: "When the top number is the same as the bottom number, the fraction equals 1." After introducing the rule, the teacher presents examples of its application, writing problems such as

$$1 = \frac{\square}{4}$$

in which the student must fill in the missing numerator of a fraction equal to one whole. The board exercise is followed by worksheet exercises of a similar nature.

FORMAT. The format for computing equivalent fractions is shown in Format 12.8. Part A includes a pictorial demonstration introducing the concept of equivalent fractions. The teacher first defines the term *equivalent fractions,* explaining that fractions are equal when they show that equal portions of the wholes are used. The teacher then draws two circles on clear plastic, each divided into a different number of parts, but each with equal portions shaded:

The teacher points out that these fractions are equivalent, since the same portion of each whole is shaded. The same demonstration is presented with a diagram in which nonequal proportions of the wholes are shaded:

The teacher points out that the fractions are not equivalent, since the shaded portions of the wholes do not take up the same space.

Part B introduces a very critical rule: *When you multiply by a fraction that equals 1, the answer equals the number you start with.* The teacher tells students this rule, then presents a set of problems demonstrating the rule's application. In some of the problems, the original fraction is multiplied by a fraction that equals 1, and in some, the original fraction is multiplied by a fraction not equal to 1. The students are to tell whether or not the answer will equal the original fraction.

Part C is a structured board exercise in which the teacher presents the strategy for working equivalency problems such as

$$\frac{3}{4} = \frac{\square}{20}$$

The teacher explains that the equal sign tells that the fractions are equal. The student's job is to find the missing numerator in the second fraction.

The teacher writes parentheses after the first fraction

$$\frac{3}{4}\left(\ \ \right) = \frac{\square}{20}$$

explaining that the students must multiply the first fraction by a fraction that equals 1, which will be written inside the parentheses. The parentheses indicate multiplication. The teacher demonstrates how to figure out the denominator to be written inside the parentheses by using a missing-factor multiplication strategy. In the problem above, the teacher asks, "4 times what number equals 20?"

The answer, 5, is written as the denominator inside the parentheses:

$$\frac{3}{4}\left(\frac{\ }{5}\right) = \frac{\square}{20}$$

The teacher then points out that since the fraction inside the parentheses must equal one whole, the numerator must be the same as the denominator. The missing number in the equivalent fraction can be determined by multiplying the numerator in the first fraction and the numerator in the second fraction:

$$\frac{3}{4}\left(\frac{5}{5}\right) = \frac{15}{20}$$

EXAMPLE SELECTION. There are three example-selection guidelines for this format. The denominator of the first fraction must be a number that can be multiplied by a whole number to end with the denominator of the second fraction. Therefore, problems such as

$$\frac{2}{3} = \frac{\square}{5} \qquad \frac{4}{5} = \frac{\square}{8} \qquad \frac{2}{3} = \frac{\square}{7}$$

are not appropriate to include, while problems such as

$$\frac{2}{3} = \frac{\square}{6} \qquad \frac{4}{5} = \frac{\square}{10} \qquad \frac{2}{3} = \frac{\square}{9}$$

are appropriate. Second, the numbers to appear in parentheses should vary from problem to problem. For example, in one problem, the numerator and denominator in the second fraction could be four times bigger than the original:

$$\frac{3}{5} = \frac{\square}{20}$$

in the next problem, two times bigger:

$$\frac{5}{6} = \frac{\square}{12}$$

in the next, five times bigger:

$$\frac{2}{3} = \frac{\square}{15}$$

and so on. The third guideline is that all problems should require multiplication; that is, the numbers in the fraction to be completed should be greater than the numbers in the first fraction.

Reducing Fractions

We recommend that reducing fractions be taught in two stages. During the first stage, which is presented during late fourth grade, the teacher introduces a greatest-common-factor (sometimes shortened to GCF) strategy. In this strategy, students are taught to reduce a fraction to its simplest terms by pulling out the greatest common factor of the numerator and denominator. For example, the fraction $\%_5$ is reduced by pulling out a 3, which is the greatest common factor of 9 and 15. When the factor 3 is pulled out, $\%_5$ becomes $\%$.

The greatest-common-factor strategy is a viable strategy only for problems in which it is relatively easy to find the greatest common factor (e.g., $^{18}\!/_{27}$, $^{30}\!/_{35}$, $\%_6$). Nearly all reducing problems students encounter in fourth and early fifth grades can be reduced to simplest terms using the greatest common factor strategy. During the second stage, students are taught to reduce fractions in which the greatest common factor is difficult to determine.

PRESKILLS. Teaching students to find the greatest common factor of two numbers is the critical preskill for reducing fractions. The greatest common factor of two numbers is the largest number that can be multiplied by whole numbers to end with the two target numbers. For example, the greatest common factor of 12 and 18 is 6. Six can be multiplied by whole numbers to end with 12 and 18.

The first step in teaching students to find the greatest common factor of two numbers is to teach them to determine all possible factors for a given number. For example, the numbers 1, 2, 3, 4, 6, and 12 are all factors of 12, since they can all be multiplied by another whole number to end with 12. Table 12.1 includes a list of the factors for the numbers 1 through 50. Once the students can easily determine all factors for a number, finding the greatest common factor is relatively easy.

Format 12.9 includes the format for teaching students to determine factors. In Part A, the teacher introduces the term *factor,* defining factors as any numbers that are multiplied together. In Part B, the teacher presents a strategy for figuring out all factors

Table 12.1 Factors for 1 to 50

Number Factors* (other than the number itself and 1)†	
4—2, 2	28—14, 2; 7, 4
6—3, 2	30—15, 2; 10, 3; 6, 5
8—4, 2	32—16, 2; 8, 4
9—3, 3	33—11, 3
10—5, 2	34—17, 2
12—6, 2; 3, 4	35—7, 5
14—7, 2	36—18, 2; 9, 4; 6, 6
15—5, 3	38—19, 2
16—4, 4; 8, 2	39—13, 3
18—6, 3; 9, 2	40—20, 2; 10, 4; 8, 5
20—10, 2; 5, 4	42—21, 2; 14, 3; 7, 6
21—3, 7	44—22, 2; 11, 4
22—11, 2	45—15, 3; 9, 5
24—12, 2; 8, 3; 6, 4	46—23, 2
25—5, 5	48—24, 2; 12, 4; 8, 6
26—13, 2	49—7, 7
27—9, 3	50—25, 2; 10, 5

* Factors are listed in pairs.
† Numbers not in list have only the number itself and 1 as factors.

for a target number. The teacher writes the target number on the board and beside it writes spaces for each factor. For example, if the target is 15, the teacher writes 15 on the board and puts four blanks beside it, since four numbers (1, 3, 5, 15) are factors of 15. The teacher then tells the students that they are going to find all of the numbers that are factors of 15 by asking if they can multiply a number by another number and end up with 15. The teacher always begins with the target number: "Is 15 a factor of 15?" The teacher then points out that they can find another factor by determining what number times that factor equals the target number. For example, after determining that 15 is a factor of 15, the teacher asks, "What number times 15 equals 15?" The answer, 1, is the factor of 15 that goes with 15. The teacher writes 15 in the first space and 1 in the last space.

The teacher then asks about other numbers, beginning with 10 and proceeding backward (10, 9, 8, 7, . . .): "Can we multiply 10 and end with 15? No, so 10 is not a factor of 15," and so on. The teacher instructs the students to say *stop* when she says a number that is a factor of the target number. When the students identify another factor of the target number, the teacher once again leads them in finding the other factor it goes with to produce the target number. If 15 is the target number, the students say stop after the teacher says 5. The teacher asks what number times 5 equals 15. The students answer 3. The teacher points out that 5 and 3 are both factors of 15. When target numbers over 20 are introduced, the teacher models the answer for the larger numbers. That is, the teacher tells the student any two-digit number that is a factor of the target number. For example, when introducing 28, the teacher says that 14 and 2 can be multiplied to equal 28.

Part C is a worksheet exercise. Target numbers are written on the worksheet, followed by spaces for each of the factors of that number. For the target number 7, only two spaces would be written, since 1 and 7 are the only factors for 7. For the number 12, six spaces would be written, since the numbers 12, 1, 6, 2, 4, and 3 are factors for 12. Students are to fill in the factors, beginning with the biggest factor.

The objective of this format is to develop student fluency in naming all possible factors of numbers. A systematic plan for introducing new target numbers and reviewing target numbers should be followed. One or two new target numbers can be introduced daily. (Table 12.2 contains a suggested sequence for introducing target numbers.) Part A of the format is used only with the first pair of target numbers. New numbers are introduced using the board presentation in Part B. The worksheet exercise described in Part C could be done independently after the first several lessons. A target number should appear on practice worksheet exercises daily for several weeks after it is introduced. This practice is very important to developing fluency.

Table 12.2 Sequence for Introducing Target Numbers and Their Factors

Day	Factors of These Numbers Are Introduced	Day	Factors of These Numbers Are Introduced
1	12, 7	16	27, 29
2	10, 3	17	28
3	16, 5	18	30, 31
4	8, 13	19	32, 33
5	4, 6, 9	20	34, 37
6	2, 17	21	35, 39
7	12, 19	22	36, 41
8	14, 23	23	38, 43
9	15	24	40, 47
10	18	25	42
11	20	26	44
12	21	27	45
13	22	28	46
14	24	29	48
15	25, 26	30	49
		31	50

FORMAT FOR GREATEST COMMON FACTORS. The format for teaching greatest common factors (Format 12.10) is introduced when the students are able to determine the factors of any target number below 20. The format is relatively simple. The teacher defines the phrase *greatest common factor* as the largest number that is a factor of both target numbers. The teacher then leads the students through finding the greatest common factor. First, the teacher asks students what the largest factor of the smaller target number is and if that factor is also a factor of the other target number. For example, assuming that 8 and 20 are the target numbers, the teacher asks what the largest factor of 8 is. The students reply, "8 is the largest factor of 8." The teacher then asks, "Is 8 a factor of 20?" Since the answer is no, the teacher asks the students to tell him the next largest factor of 8: "What is the next biggest factor of 8?" After the students answer 4, the teacher asks, "Is 4 a factor of 20? . . . So, 4 is the greatest common factor of 8 and 20."

After about 5 days of presenting the format, the teacher gives students worksheet exercises to work independently. The worksheet includes 8 to 12 problems daily in which students find the greatest common factor of two target numbers. A common error in independent exercises involves writing a common factor that is not the greatest common factor of the two target numbers; for example, writing 3 as the greatest common factor of 12 and 18. The correction is to point out to students that they can find a larger common factor.

Example-selection guidelines are quite important. In about half of the problems, the greatest common factor should be the smaller of the two target numbers (e.g., 6, 18; 4, 8; 2, 10; 5, 20). If examples such as these are not included, students might develop the misrule that the smaller number is never the greatest common factor. This would result in errors in which the student might identify a 4 rather than an 8 as the greatest common factor of 8 and 24. Examples should be limited to numbers for which students have been taught to find factors. Initially, both target numbers should be under 20. As students learn to determine factors for larger numbers, the larger numbers can be included. Several examples should be included in which 1 is the greatest common factor, as in 4 and 7 or 6 and 11. These prepare students for fractions that cannot be reduced (e.g., $\frac{4}{7}$, $\frac{6}{11}$).

FORMAT FOR REDUCING FRACTIONS. The format for reducing fractions (see Format 12.11) is introduced when students are able to determine the greatest common factor of any two target numbers below 20. The format includes three parts. Part A is a board exercise in which the teacher presents the strategy for reducing fractions. The teacher writes a fraction on the board with an equal sign next to it. Next to the equal sign are parentheses and a fraction bar for the reduced fraction:

$$\frac{12}{16} = (\ ) \underline{\hspace{1cm}}$$

The fraction in which the numerator and denominator are the greatest common factor of the two target numbers will be written inside the parentheses. For example, the greatest common factor of 12 and 16 is 4. Thus, the fraction in the parentheses will be $\frac{4}{4}$, which equals 1. The teacher then asks, "12 equals 4 times what number?" The answer is 3, which is the numerator of the reduced fraction. The teacher then asks, "16 equals 4 times what number?" The answer is 4, which is the denominator of the reduced fraction. Since multiplying by 1 does not change the value of the fraction, $\frac{4}{4}$ can be crossed out. Crossing out the fraction equal to 1 leaves the reduced fraction:

$$\frac{12}{16} = \left(\frac{4}{4}\right)\frac{3}{4}$$

Part B is a structured worksheet exercise in which the teacher first asks for the greatest common factor of the numerator and denominator of a fraction; in $\frac{10}{15}$ the greatest common factor is 5. The teacher then instructs the students to write the corresponding fraction equal to 1 in the parentheses. For example, the fraction written in parentheses for $\frac{10}{15}$ is $\frac{5}{5}$. The teacher then has the students determine the missing factors in the final fraction, which is the reduced fraction:

$$\frac{10}{15} = \left(\frac{5}{5}\right)\frac{2}{3}$$

There are three example-selection guidelines for exercises on reducing fractions. First, the numbers should be ones for which students have been taught to find factors. At first, both the numerator and denominator should be below 25. As students learn to find factors for larger numbers, fractions with these larger numbers can be included.

Second, a third of the fractions should have the greatest common factor as the numerator. For example, in the fractions $\frac{4}{12}$, $\frac{8}{16}$, and $\frac{5}{20}$, the numerator is the greatest common factor. Third, about a third of the fractions should already be expressed in their simplest terms (e.g., $\frac{4}{5}$, $\frac{3}{8}$, $\frac{9}{11}$). Including several fractions already expressed in their simplest terms shows the students that not all fractions can be reduced. A sample set of items appears below:

a. $\frac{12}{15}$ b. $\frac{4}{8}$ c. $\frac{5}{7}$ d. $\frac{8}{12}$ e. $\frac{3}{5}$

f. $\frac{5}{15}$ g. $\frac{4}{12}$ h. $\frac{6}{9}$ i. $\frac{9}{11}$

Items b, f, and g are fractions in which the smaller number is a factor of the larger number. Items c, e, and i are fractions that are already expressed in their simplest terms and therefore cannot be reduced any further.

REDUCING FRACTIONS WITH LARGER NUMBERS. After several weeks of practice reducing fractions using the greatest common factor, students can be introduced to the concept of pulling out successive common factors. When the greatest common factor is difficult to find, students can reduce the fraction to its simplest terms by repeatedly pulling out factors. Note the examples below:

a. $\frac{45}{75} = \left(\frac{5}{5}\right)\frac{9}{15} = \left(\frac{3}{3}\right)\frac{3}{5} = \frac{3}{5}$

b. $\frac{24}{72} = \left(\frac{2}{2}\right)\frac{12}{36} = \left(\frac{6}{6}\right)\frac{2}{6} = \left(\frac{2}{2}\right)\frac{1}{3} = \frac{1}{3}$

This strategy is useful for problems with larger numbers. The teacher guides students through sets of problems, pointing out clues students can use (e.g., if both the numerator and the denominator are even numbers, the fraction can still be reduced. If the numerator and denominator both end in either 5 or zero, the fraction can still be reduced). The teacher presents an exercise in which students check answers to determine if they're reduced to simplest terms. The teacher gives students a worksheet with problems similar to those below, some of which have not been reduced to their simplest terms. The students are asked to find those fractions that can be further reduced and to reduce those fractions.

a. $\frac{64}{72} = \left(\frac{4}{4}\right)\frac{16}{18} =$ d. $\frac{65}{85} = \left(\frac{5}{5}\right)\frac{13}{15} =$

b. $\frac{45}{75} = \left(\frac{5}{5}\right)\frac{9}{15} =$ e. $\frac{48}{64} = \left(\frac{2}{2}\right)\frac{24}{32} =$

c. $\frac{21}{30} = \left(\frac{3}{3}\right)\frac{7}{10} =$ f. $\frac{56}{84} = \left(\frac{2}{2}\right)\frac{28}{42} =$

Converting Mixed Numbers and Improper Fractions

An improper fraction, one whose numerator is greater than its denominator, is a fraction that equals more than one whole. An improper fraction may be converted to a mixed number by dividing its numerator by its denominator. For example, to convert the fraction $\frac{13}{5}$ to a mixed number, we divide 13 by 5, which equals 2 with a remainder of 3. The remainder is written as the fraction $\frac{3}{5}$; the improper fraction $\frac{13}{5}$ is converted to the mixed number $2\frac{3}{5}$.

Converting a mixed number to an improper fraction requires the reverse operation, multiplication rather than division. Students first change the whole number into a fraction by multiplying the whole number by the number of parts in each whole, indicated by the denominator:

$$\text{for } 6 = \frac{}{4}, \text{ students write } \frac{24}{4}$$

To determine the equivalent improper fraction for a mixed number, after students multiply the whole number, they add the numerator of the fraction:

$$3\frac{1}{2} = \frac{6 + 1}{2} = \frac{7}{2}$$

On the Instructional Sequence and Assessment Chart, we recommend that converting improper fractions to mixed numbers be introduced in early fourth grade. Students apply this skill when they rewrite their answers after adding or multiplying fractions. Converting a mixed number to an improper fraction should not be introduced until several months later. The time between the introduction of these two conversion skills is recommended to decrease the probability of students' confusing the two operations. Converting mixed numbers to and from improper fractions requires that students have a good understanding of the difference between a whole unit and parts of a unit. Therefore, students should have mastered all the fraction analysis skills presented earlier.

CONVERTING IMPROPER FRACTIONS TO MIXED NUMBERS. The format for converting improper fractions to mixed numbers appears in Format 12.12. Part A is a pictorial demonstration in which the teacher shows how to construct a diagram to figure out how many whole units an improper fraction equals.

Part B is a structured board presentation in which the teacher presents the strategy of dividing the numerator by the denominator. Note the special emphasis given to explaining how to write the remainder as a fraction. The teacher explains that the denominator of the fraction in the mixed number must be the same denominator as in the original fraction.

Part C is a structured worksheet exercise. The division symbol, along with boxes for the whole number and the fraction remainder, are written as prompts on the students' worksheets:

$$\frac{11}{4} = \ \overline{)\ \ \ \ \ \ \ \ \ \ \ }\begin{array}{c}\square \frac{\square}{\square}\end{array}$$

The teacher begins the exercise by instructing the students to look at the fraction and determine whether it is less than one whole, equal to one whole, or more than one whole. If the fraction is less than 1, students are instructed to leave the fraction as it is. If the fraction equals 1, they write = 1. If the fraction equals more than 1, they are instructed to divide and write the answer as a mixed number.

Part D is a less structured worksheet exercise in which students convert improper fractions to mixed numbers with minimal teacher prompting. Teachers should insist that students write the whole number part of the answer and the fraction part of the answer neatly. Teachers should watch for students writing answers in which the numerator of the fraction could easily be mistaken for a whole number:

$$\overset{3^{2}/_{5}}{5)\overline{17}}$$

Examples should be selected to provide appropriate discrimination practice. First, there should be a mixture of problems. About half of the fractions should translate to a mixed number; about a fourth should translate simply to a whole number (e.g., $\frac{9}{3}$, $\frac{16}{4}$, $\frac{10}{5}$); finally, about a fourth should be proper fractions. Including proper fractions ensures that students do not develop the misrule of inappropriately converting all fractions to mixed numbers (e.g., $\frac{3}{4} = 1\frac{1}{4}$).

After students have had several weeks of practice converting improper fractions to mixed numbers and reducing fractions to their lowest terms, they can be given exercises in which they must first convert the fractions to mixed numbers, then reduce the fractions. No special format is required for such exercises. The teacher gives students a worksheet with directions similar to these: "Change any fraction that equals one or more wholes to a mixed number. Then reduce the fractions." A set of examples would include a mix of proper and improper fractions, some of which can be reduced and some of which are written in their simplest form. A sample set might include these fractions:

$$\frac{16}{12} \quad \frac{6}{8} \quad \frac{9}{7} \quad \frac{14}{6} \quad \frac{5}{7}$$

$$\frac{8}{24} \quad \frac{20}{8} \quad \frac{9}{12} \quad \frac{24}{10}$$

Exercises of this type should be continued for several months to develop fluency.

CONVERTING MIXED NUMBERS TO IMPROPER FRACTIONS. The format for converting mixed numbers to improper fractions appears in Format 12.13. It includes three parts. Part A teaches the component skill of translating any whole number into an improper fraction by multiplying the number of whole units by the number of parts in each whole:

$$\text{In } 6 = \frac{}{4}, \text{ students multiply } 6 \times 4$$

Since this component skill is very important, both a board and a worksheet exercise are presented.

Part B, a structured board presentation, teaches the strategy to convert a mixed number into an improper fraction. First, the students determine the fraction equivalent to the whole number; then they add the fraction portion of the mixed number. For example, with 6¾, students multiply 6×4 and then add 3 to determine the answer:

$$6\frac{3}{4} = \frac{24 + 3}{4} = \frac{27}{4}$$

To ensure that students understand the purpose of the computations, the teacher might have students check several problems by drawing the diagram to illustrate the improper fraction or mixed number.

OPERATIONS—ADDING AND SUBTRACTING FRACTIONS

There are three basic problem types in addition and subtraction of fractions. The first type includes addition/subtraction problems that have like denominators:

$$\frac{3}{8} + \frac{1}{8} + \frac{2}{8} = \frac{\square}{\square} \qquad \frac{7}{9} - \frac{3}{9} = \frac{\square}{\square}$$

Problems of this type can be introduced during the primary grades, since relatively few preskills are required to work the problems. The students learn that to work such problems, they work only across the numerators; the denominator remains constant:

$$\frac{2}{5} + \frac{1}{5} = \frac{3}{5} \qquad \frac{7}{9} - \frac{3}{9} = \frac{4}{9}$$

The second type includes problems with unlike denominators. Problems in this group are limited, however, to those in which the lowest common denominator (LCD) is relatively easy to figure out. Problems of this type are usually introduced during fourth grade. The strategy for solving these problems involves first figuring out the lowest common denominator, rewriting each fraction as an equivalent fraction with that denominator, and then working the problem:

$$\frac{5}{6} \text{ becomes } \frac{5}{6}\left(\frac{2}{2}\right) = \frac{10}{12} \text{ which becomes } \frac{10}{12}$$
$$\frac{3}{4} \qquad \frac{3}{4}\left(\frac{3}{3}\right) = \frac{9}{12} \qquad \quad -\frac{9}{12}$$
$$\frac{1}{12}$$

The third type includes problems in which the lowest common denominator is difficult to determine. These problems usually have a lowest common denominator that is a relatively large number. For example, in the problem ⁷⁄₁₃ + ⁵⁄₁₈, the lowest common denominator is 234. To solve this problem, students must be taught a strategy that involves factoring. Since the discussion of the procedures to teach this strategy would take many pages, and since this type of problem is often not introduced until junior high, we have not included it.

Fractions with Like Denominators

Adding and subtracting fractions with like denominators is a relatively simple operation that can be introduced after fraction analysis skills have been taught, sometime in second or third grade. A format for teaching students to add and subtract fractions with like denominators appears in Format 12.14. Part A is a pictorial demonstration in which the teacher demonstrates adding fractions. In Part B, the teacher presents the rule that students can only add and subtract fractions in which each whole has the same number of parts.

Parts C and D are structured and less structured worksheet exercises in which the students are presented with a set of addition and subtraction problems. Half of the problems should have like denominators:

$$\frac{3}{4} - \frac{1}{4} \qquad \frac{4}{7} + \frac{2}{7}$$

and half different denominators:

$$\frac{3}{4} - \frac{1}{3} \qquad \frac{5}{7} + \frac{2}{3}$$

Students are instructed to cross out the problems with unlike denominators and work the problems with like denominators. The problems with unlike denominators are included to prevent errors caused by students' ignoring the denominators.

During the first week or two of instruction, adding and subtracting fraction problems should be written horizontally. When students can work problems written horizontally, vertically aligned problems should be introduced:

$$\frac{3}{4} \qquad \frac{4}{8} \qquad \frac{5}{7}$$
$$-\frac{1}{4} \qquad +\frac{3}{8} \qquad +\frac{2}{3}$$

The teacher introduces vertically aligned problems with a board and structured worksheet exercise. Teachers should not assume that because students can work horizontally aligned problems, they will all be able to work vertically aligned problems.

Problems with Mixed Numbers

Adding and subtracting mixed numbers in which the fractions have like denominators:

$$3\frac{2}{5} - 1\frac{1}{5}$$

can be introduced when students can read and write mixed numbers and can add and subtract fractions

with like denominators. The teaching procedure is relatively simple: The students work first the fraction part of the problem, then the whole number part of the problem. Both horizontally and vertically aligned problems should be presented.

Fractions with Unlike Denominators

Adding and subtracting fractions with unlike denominators is usually introduced during fourth grade. A strategy for solving problems with unlike denominators is outlined in Summary Box 12.1. Note the integration of several component skills.

PRESKILLS. Two preskills should be mastered before the format for adding and subtracting fractions with unlike denominators is introduced: (a) finding the least common multiple of two numbers and (b) rewriting a fraction as an equivalent fraction with a given denominator (see Format 12.8).

The least common multiple (LCM) of two numbers is the smallest number that has both numbers as factors. For example, the least common multiple of the numbers 6 and 8 is 24, since 24 is the smallest number that has both 6 and 8 as factors. Likewise, the least common multiple of 6 and 9 is 18, since 18 is the smallest number that has 6 and 9 as factors.

Format 12.15 shows how to teach students to figure out the least common multiple of two numbers. This format assumes that students are able to say the skip-counting series for twos through nines. About 2 months prior to introducing the least common multi-

---

Summary Box 12.1
Steps for Problems with Unlike Denominators

1. $\frac{3}{4} + \frac{1}{6}$

   Students read problem and say, "The problem can't be worked as it is because the denominators are not the same."

2. $\frac{3}{4} + \frac{1}{6}$

   Students determine that the least common multiple of 4 and 6 is 12. Thus 12 is the least common denominator. Both fractions must be rewritten with denominator of 12.

3. $\frac{3}{4} \left(\frac{3}{3}\right) + \frac{1}{6} \left(\frac{2}{2}\right)$

   Students determine the fraction by which each original fraction must be multiplied to equal 12.

4. $\frac{3}{4} \left(\frac{3}{3}\right) + \frac{1}{6} \left(\frac{2}{2}\right)$
   $\quad 12 \qquad\qquad 12$

   Students rewrite each fraction so that it has a denominator of 12.

5. $\frac{3}{4} \left(\frac{3}{3}\right) + \frac{1}{6} \left(\frac{2}{2}\right) = \frac{11}{12}$
   $\quad 12 \qquad\qquad 12$

   Students work the problem with equivalent fraction.

ple, the teacher should begin reviewing the skip-counting series. (See Chapter 4 for teaching skip counting.) Students who know their basic multiplication facts should have little trouble learning the series.

The strategy students are taught requires them to say the skip-counting series for each target number and to select the smallest number appearing in both series. This strategy is viable for examples in which the target numbers are small. A more sophisticated strategy must be taught to figure the least common multiple of larger numbers for which the students could not say the skip-counting series. This more sophisticated strategy, which involves factoring, is not discussed in this text.

The format includes two parts. In Part A, the teacher writes count-by series for two numbers on the board so that students can visually find the least common multiple. The teacher also introduces the term *multiple*. Part B is a worksheet presentation in which the teacher leads students in finding the least common multiple for several pairs of numbers and then monitors as students complete the worksheet on their own. Daily practice on worksheet exercises involving finding the least common multiple of two numbers is continued for several weeks.

There are two example-selection guidelines for the least-common-multiple format. First, in about half of the problems, the larger number should be a multiple of the smaller number. For the numbers 3 and 12, 12 is a multiple of 3. The least common multiple of 12 and 3 is 12. Likewise, the least common multiple of the numbers 2 and 8 is 8.

The second guideline pertains to the other half of the problems in which the larger number is not a multiple of the lower number. In these problems, both target numbers should be below 10.

FORMAT. The format for adding and subtracting fractions with unlike denominators appears in Format 12.16. The format has three parts. Part A is a structured board presentation, which begins with the teacher writing a problem on the board and asking the students if the fractions can be added (or subtracted) as they are. After the students determine the fractions cannot be added (or subtracted) because the denominators are not the same, the teacher tells the students that they can work the problem by rewriting the fractions so that both have the same denominator. The teacher then demonstrates the problem-solving strategy outlined earlier: writing the least common multiple of both denominators; multiplying each fraction by the fraction of 1, which enables it to be rewritten with the lowest common denominator; and then adding (or subtracting) the rewritten fraction.

In parts B and C, the structured and less structured worksheet exercises, the teacher leads students through working problems. Note that Format 12.16 includes problems in which both fractions are rewritten. In many problems, only one fraction will need to be rewritten (e.g., in ¾ + ⅛, only ¾ needs to be rewritten as %). When initially presenting this type of problem, the teacher has the students write the fraction 1/1 next to the fraction that does not need to be rewritten:

$$\frac{3}{4}\left(\frac{2}{2}\right) + \frac{5}{8}\left(\frac{1}{1}\right)$$
$$\phantom{\frac{3}{4}}\mathit{8}\phantom{\left(\frac{2}{2}\right) + \frac{5}{8}}\mathit{8}$$

After several weeks, the teacher can explain that if the denominator of the rewritten fraction is to be the same, nothing need be done to that fraction.

There are two example-selection guidelines. The first addresses the manner in which problems are written. During the first 2 weeks, all problems should be written horizontally. When students can work horizontal problems, they can be introduced to vertically aligned problems.

The second guideline pertains to the variety of problems. Half of the problems should have denominators in which the larger denominator is a multiple of the smaller denominator. For example, in the problem

$$\frac{3}{5} + \frac{2}{10}$$

the larger denominator, 10, is a multiple of the smaller denominator, 5. In the other half of the problems, the denominators should both be one-digit numbers:

$$\frac{3}{5} + \frac{2}{3} \qquad \frac{3}{4} + \frac{2}{5} \qquad \frac{5}{6} - \frac{1}{4}$$

Several problems involving adding and subtracting fractions with like denominators should also be included. A sample set of problems appears below. Note that problems c and f have like denominators. Problems b, e, and g have a lower denominator which is a factor of the larger denominator. In problems a, d, and h, both fractions must be rewritten.

a. $\frac{3}{4} + \frac{2}{5}$ b. $\frac{7}{9} - \frac{2}{3}$ c. $\frac{5}{6} - \frac{1}{6}$

d. $\frac{5}{6} - \frac{4}{9}$ e. $\frac{1}{5} + \frac{3}{10}$ f. $\frac{4}{9} + \frac{3}{9}$

g. $\frac{7}{10} - \frac{1}{2}$ h. $\frac{3}{4} - \frac{2}{3}$

Reducing and Rewriting Answers as Mixed Numbers

The skills of reducing fractions to their lowest common terms and converting an improper fraction to a mixed number can be integrated into problems after students have had several weeks of practice working problems with unlike denominators. Students should be given problems that require them to convert the answer to a mixed number (when necessary) and/or reduce. Teachers should lead students through determining the correct answers for several days. Daily practice with six to eight problems should continue for several weeks.

More Complex Problems with Mixed Numbers

A rather difficult problem type involving mixed numbers is illustrated below:

$$\begin{array}{r} 8 \\ -3\frac{2}{4} \\ \hline \end{array}$$

This is a subtraction problem involving renaming. The student must rewrite the 8 as 7 and $\frac{4}{4}$ to work the problem. Prior to introducing such a problem, the teacher would present an exercise like the one below in which the student must rewrite a whole number as a whole number and a fraction equivalent to 1 (e.g., $6 = 5 + \frac{4}{4}$).

$$6 = \boxed{5} + \frac{\square}{4} \qquad 9 = \boxed{8} + \frac{\square}{6}$$

$$6 = \boxed{5} + \frac{\square}{3}$$

In leading students through this preskill exercise, the teacher points out that they have to take one whole away from the original whole number and rewrite that one whole as a fraction. Once this preskill is taught, students should have little difficulty with problems that involve renaming.

Comparing Fractions

Students are often asked to compare the values of fractions. For example, which has the greater value, $\frac{1}{5}$ or $\frac{1}{3}$? Which has the lesser value, $\frac{2}{3}$ or $\frac{2}{6}$? During second and third grade, students usually are asked to compare fractions with numerators of 1 but with different denominators. The students can be prepared for early comparison questions by pictorial demonstrations illustrating that the more parts a unit is divided into, the smaller the size of each part. The rule is, *The bigger the denominator, the smaller the value of each part.* The demonstrations can then be followed by a rule-application exercise in which the teacher presents pairs of fractions and asks which fraction has a greater value.

In later grades, students are asked to compare fractions that have numerators other than 1 (e.g., $\frac{3}{4}$ and $\frac{5}{9}$). The strategy for comparing the two fractions involves rewriting fractions so that they have common denominators (e.g., $\frac{3}{4}$ would be rewritten as $\frac{27}{36}$ and $\frac{5}{9}$ as $\frac{20}{36}$).

Once fractions have been rewritten so they have common denominators, their values are readily apparent. Procedures for teaching students to rewrite fractions with common denominators are the same as those discussed in the early steps of the format to add and subtract fractions with different denominators: determining the least common multiple of the denominators and multiplying each fraction by a fraction equal to 1.

Word Problems

The basic guideline for introducing fraction word problems is that a new type of problem should be integrated into word problem exercises as soon as the students can accurately compute problems of that type. Story problems involving adding and subtracting fractions with like denominators should be introduced after students work such problems independently. Story problems with unlike denominators should be introduced only after students have mastered the strategy for adding/subtracting that type of problem. All of the various types of addition and subtraction problems described in the problem-solving chapter (Chapter 11) should be included in the exercises. Figure 12.2 is a sample of problems that could be included on a worksheet given to stu-

FIGURE 12.2 Sample Story Problem Worksheet with Mixed Numbers and Like Denominators

1. Tina ran $3\frac{2}{5}$ miles in the morning and $2\frac{1}{5}$ miles in the afternoon. How many miles did she run altogether?
2. We had $\frac{3}{4}$ of an inch of rain on Monday and $\frac{1}{4}$ of an inch of rain on Tuesday. How much more rain did we have on Monday?
3. Ricardo's cat weighed $14\frac{2}{6}$ pounds. If the cat gains $3\frac{1}{6}$ pounds how much will it weigh?
4. Joan bought $6\frac{2}{4}$ pounds of meat. After she cooked the meat, it weighed $2\frac{1}{4}$ pounds. How much less does it weigh now?

dents shortly after they learn how to add/subtract mixed numbers with fractions that have like denominators. Note the variety of story-problem types (e.g., classification, action, and comparison).

OPERATIONS—MULTIPLYING FRACTIONS

There are three types of multiplication fraction problems. The first type, which involves multiplying two proper fractions, is usually introduced in third grade:

$$\frac{3}{4} \times \frac{2}{5} \qquad \frac{4}{9} \times \frac{1}{3}$$

The second type, which also is usually introduced during third or fourth grade, involves multiplying a fraction and a whole number:

$$\frac{3}{4} \times 8$$

This type of problem is important, since it occurs often in story problems. The third type of problem, usually introduced in fifth grade, involves multiplying one or more mixed numbers:

$$5 \times 3\frac{2}{4} \qquad 4\frac{1}{2} \times 2\frac{3}{5} \qquad \frac{3}{4} \times 2\frac{1}{2}$$

Multiplying Proper Fractions

Multiplying proper fractions can be introduced several weeks after students have learned to add and subtract fractions with like denominators. The steps for multiplying fractions are presented in Format 12.17. Note that no pictorial demonstration is included, since it would be too complex. The reason

multiplying proper fractions is taught at this point is that it is a prerequisite for equivalent fraction tasks and for the second type of multiplication problem, a fraction times a whole number.

The format includes two parts. In Part A, the structured board presentation, the teacher presents the rule about multiplying fractions—"Work top times the top and bottom times the bottom"—and demonstrates how to apply the rule to several problems. Part B is a structured worksheet presentation. Note that the examples in this part include an equal mix of multiplication problems and problems that involve addition and subtraction of like denominators. This mix is essential to provide students with practice in remembering the difference between the multiplication strategy (multiply across the top and bottom) and the addition/subtraction strategy (work only across the top). Part B begins with a verbal exercise in which the teacher asks students how they work a particular type of problem (i.e., "What do you do when you multiply fractions? What do you do when you add or subtract fractions?").

Multiplying Fractions and Whole Numbers

Problems that involve multiplying a fraction and a whole number are important because they have many real-life applications. For example, consider the following problem: "A boat engine called for ⅔ quarts of oil for every gallon of gasoline. John had 9 gallons of gas. How much oil did he need?"

Multiplying fractions and whole numbers in word problems can be introduced when students have mastered multiplying proper fractions and converting an improper fraction to a mixed number. The steps in the problem-solving strategy are outlined in Summary Box 12.2.

Summary Box 12.2
Multiplying Fractions and Whole Numbers

1. Student reads the problem.
$$\frac{3}{4} \times 8$$

2. Student changes the whole number into a fraction.
$$\frac{3}{4} \times \frac{8}{1}$$

3. Student multiplies numerators and denominators.
$$\frac{3}{4} \times \frac{8}{1} = \frac{24}{4}$$

4. Student converts product into a whole number or mixed number.
$$\frac{3}{4} \times \frac{8}{1} = \frac{24}{4} = 6$$

Picture demonstrations of what takes place when multiplying a whole number by a fraction might precede the introduction of the format. In these demonstrations, the teacher explains that the bottom number tells how many groups to form and the top number tells how many groups are used. For example, for the problem ⅔ × 12, the following diagram might be drawn:

IIII   IIII   IIII

The teacher first draws 12 lines and says, "I've made three groups. Now I'm going to circle two of the groups." The teacher then circles two groups.

(IIII)   (IIII)   IIII

The teacher counts the lines within the circles: "We end up with 8. ⅔ × 12 = 8."

The format for teaching students to work such problems appears in Format 12.18. Part A introduces an essential component skill: converting a whole number to a fraction. Any whole number may be converted to a fraction by putting it over a denominator of 1. Part B is a structured board presentation. Part C is a structured worksheet presentation. Note that the worksheet is set up with a prompt for the students. After a fraction bar for the answer is a division box:

$$\frac{3}{4} \times 8 = \underline{\quad} = \overline{)\quad} = \square$$

The division box serves as a prompt for the students to divide. The box serves as a prompt to write the whole number answer. This prompt should be used the first week this problem type is presented.

Examples should be carefully controlled. Some problems should have answers that are whole numbers:

$$\frac{3}{4} \times 8 = 6$$

and some should have answers that are mixed numbers:

$$\frac{2}{3} \times 7 = 4\frac{2}{3}$$

Initially, the whole number should be a relatively small number (e.g., below 20). As students learn to multiply and divide larger numbers, the examples

should include hundreds and then thousands numbers:

$$\frac{3}{4} \times 2000$$

Multiplying Mixed Numbers

Multiplying a mixed number and a whole number is an important component skill for advanced map-reading skills. For example, if 1 inch equals 50 miles, how many miles will 3½ inches equal?

$$50 \times 3\frac{1}{2} = 175$$

Initially, we recommend a strategy in which the students convert a mixed number into an improper fraction before working the problem. See Summary Box 12.3 in which problems a and b illustrate the steps in working these problems.

Later, a more sophisticated strategy involving the distributive property may be introduced for problems in which a whole number and mixed number are multiplied. The students first multiply the whole-number factor by the whole number from the mixed-number factor, then multiply the whole-number factor by the fraction, and finally add the products. This process is shown below:

$$5 \times 3\frac{1}{2} = (5 \times 3) + \left(5 \times \frac{1}{2}\right)$$

$$= 15 + 2\frac{1}{2}$$

$$= 17\frac{1}{2}$$

OPERATION—DIVIDING FRACTIONS

Dividing fractions is usually introduced in fifth grade. Fraction division problems may be divided into three types. First are those in which a proper fraction is divided by a proper fraction:

$$\frac{2}{3} \div \frac{3}{4} \qquad \frac{4}{5} \div \frac{2}{7}$$

This type of problem, while having little practical application, is introduced first because it prepares students for the second type of problem in which a fraction is divided by a whole number:

$$\frac{3}{4} \div 2$$

Summary Box 12.3
Multiplying Mixed Numbers

Steps	*Problems*

Problems

a. $5\frac{1}{2} \times 3\frac{2}{4} =$ b. $5 \times 2\frac{3}{4} =$

1. Convert mixed number to improper fraction.

$\frac{11}{2} \times \frac{14}{4} =$ $\frac{5}{1} \times \frac{11}{4} =$

2. Multiply.

$\frac{11}{2} \times \frac{14}{4} = \frac{154}{8}$ $\frac{5}{1} \times \frac{11}{4} = \frac{55}{4}$

3. Convert answer to mixed number.

$\frac{154}{8} = 8\overline{)154}^{\;19\frac{2}{8} = 19\frac{1}{4}}$ $\frac{55}{4} = 4\overline{)55}^{\;13\frac{3}{4} = 13\frac{3}{4}}$

Problems such as the one above have everyday application. For example, John has ¾ pound of candy. He wants to split the candy up equally among his two friends. How much candy should he give to each friend?

The third type of problem involves dividing a mixed number:

$$3\frac{1}{2} \div 4 \qquad 5\frac{1}{2} \div 2\frac{1}{3}$$

The strategy taught to solve division problems involves inverting the second fraction, changing the sign to a times sign, and then multiplying (e.g., ¾ ÷ ⅔ is worked by inverting ⅔ so that the problem reads ¾ × ½ = ⅜). Because a lengthy explanation is needed for the rationale for this procedure, we recommend presenting the strategy in the elementary grades without rationale. The teacher simply presents the rules: "We cannot divide by a fraction number; we must change the problem to a multiplication problem. Here's how we do that: We invert the second fraction and change the sign." The teacher illustrates the meaning of *invert* as she demonstrates solving the problem.

Problems in which students divide by a whole number are solved by first converting the whole number to a fraction and then inverting that fraction:

$$\frac{3}{4} \div 2 = \frac{3}{4} \div \frac{2}{1} = \frac{3}{4} \times \frac{1}{2} = \frac{3}{8}$$

Problems that include a mixed number are solved by converting the mixed number to an improper fraction, inverting, and multiplying.

The relationship between fractions and multiplication/division number families is very important. Teachers should introduce the line in fractions as another way of saying "divided by." The fraction ½ can also be read "1 divided by 2." After students have practiced reading fractions in both ways, they learn that multiplication number families can be turned up on end.

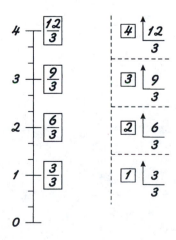

Students practice identifying the big number and the two small numbers. Later, students apply this knowledge to number lines.

Students complete the fractions for the number lines. The fraction for 1 on the number line is ⅓. The fraction for two is 6/3. Next to the numbers on the number line, students complete the number families that are turned on end. The number that goes in the box is the whole number on the number line. The numbers for the fractions are the vertically oriented numbers in the family.

This relationship is very important. It shows how multiplication/division number families imply fractions, and vice versa. The relationship between multiplication/division number families is emphasized when students learn to read fractions as division problems. Students should be presented this concept as an introduction to dividing fractions, and as early as third grade. After mastering reading fractions as division problems, students learn to write regular division problems as fractions.

Story Problems—Multiplication and Division

Multiplication and division story problems can be introduced when students can solve the respective problem types. Multiplication story problems with fractions usually involve figuring out what a fractional part of a specified group equals. Here is a typical problem:

> There are 20 children in our class; $\frac{3}{4}$ of the children are girls. How many girls are in the class?

This type of problem is introduced shortly after students can solve problems in which a fraction and a whole number are multiplied (e.g., $\frac{3}{4} \times 12$). As an intermediate step to prepare students for the story problems, the teacher can present problems like these:

$$\frac{3}{4} \text{ of } 12 = \frac{\square}{\square} = \square \qquad \frac{2}{3} \text{ of } 9 = \frac{\square}{\square} = \square$$

Students are taught that *of* in this problem can be translated to *times*. The problem $\frac{3}{4}$ of 12 would be converted to $\frac{3}{4} \times 12$ and then worked:

$$\frac{3}{4} \times \frac{12}{1} = \frac{36}{4} = 9$$

As students are able to solve operations with larger numbers, the examples in the story problems should include larger numbers. Instead of $\frac{2}{3}$ of 12, a problem might ask $\frac{2}{3}$ of 126.

The most common type of division story problem involves dividing a fraction by a whole number. Here is an example of this type of problem:

> Kate has $\frac{2}{3}$ of an apple left. She wants to share it equally with her 2 friends. How much of the apple should she give to each friend?

This type of problem can be introduced when students can work problems in which a fraction can be divided by a whole number.

DIAGNOSIS AND REMEDIATION

Students may miss fraction problems for one or a combination of the following reasons:

1. *A computational error* (e.g., dividing 18 by 3 and ending with 5, multiplying 7×8 and ending with 54). If a student misses a problem solely because of a computational error, the teacher need not spend time working on the fraction skill but should reteach the specific computational skill.
2. *A component-skill error.* The student makes an error on a previously taught fraction skill, which causes the student to miss the current type of problem. For example, when working the problem $\frac{2}{3} \times 12$, the student converts 12 to the fraction $\frac{1}{12}$ instead of $\frac{12}{1}$, writing $\frac{2}{3} \times \frac{1}{12} = \frac{2}{36}$. The remediation procedure involves reteaching the earlier taught component skill. In the example given, the teacher would first reteach the student how to convert a whole number to a fraction. When the student's performance indicates mastery of the component skill, the teacher leads the student through solving the original type of problem, using the structured worksheet part of the appropriate format.
3. *A strategy error.* A strategy error occurs when the student does not correctly chain the steps together to solve a problem. For example, when attempting to convert $\frac{12}{4}$ to a whole number, the student subtracts 4 from 12, ending with 8. The remediation procedure involves reteaching the strategy beginning with the structured board part of the format.

The following sections give examples of common errors made on the various types of fraction problems along with suggestions for remediation.

Reading and Writing Fractions and Mixed Numbers

Students should read a problem as the first step in any part of the format. If the teacher notes the student reading a fraction or mixed number incorrectly, the teacher should reintroduce the reading format, stressing the particular type of fraction missed. For example, if a student reads $5\frac{1}{3}$ as $\frac{5}{3}$, the teacher would present the formats for reading a mixed numbers.

Adding and Subtracting Fractions

When adding fractions with like denominators, students will usually make (a) strategy errors or (b) computational errors. Note the problems below:

a. $\dfrac{7}{9} - \dfrac{2}{9} = \dfrac{5}{0}$ b. $\dfrac{4}{8} + \dfrac{2}{8} = \dfrac{6}{16}$

c. $\dfrac{7}{9} - \dfrac{2}{9} = \dfrac{6}{9}$ d. $\dfrac{4}{8} + \dfrac{3}{8} = \dfrac{7}{8}$

Problems a and b illustrate strategy errors. The student does not know that the denominators are not added or subtracted. The remediation procedure involves reintroducing the format for adding and subtracting fractions, beginning with Part A. Problems c and d, on the other hand, indicate computational errors. The student knows the strategy but missed the problems because of basic fact errors. The remediation procedure depends on the number of problems missed. If a student misses less than 10% of the problems because of computational errors, the teacher merely works on the particular fact missed, writing the fact for the student and testing him periodically on it for several days. If the student misses more than 10% of the problems because of computational errors, the teacher must work on improving fact accuracy through instituting a stronger motivational system and/or providing more practice on basic facts. In neither case must the teacher reintroduce the adding and subtracting fraction format.

Problems involving adding or subtracting fractions with unlike denominators may be missed because of fact, component-skill, or strategy deficits. Note the problems in Summary Box 12.4. The cause of each error and the suggested remediation procedures are provided for many common mistakes.

COMMERCIAL PROGRAMS

Fractions: Adding and Subtracting Fractions with Unlike Denominators

INSTRUCTIONAL STRATEGIES. The main concern regarding the way fractions are taught is the lack of specificity generally found in the instruction. Structured teaching presentations become particularly important when more complex strategies are intro-

---

Summary Box 12.4
Errors in Addition with Unlike Denominators

Error Patterns	Diagnosis	Remediation Procedures
1. $\dfrac{4}{5} + \dfrac{2}{3} = \dfrac{4}{5}\left(\underset{15}{\times 3}\right) + \dfrac{2}{3}\left(\underset{15}{\times 5}\right) = \dfrac{6}{15}$	Component error: student failed to multiply numerator.	Present Format 12.16 beginning with Part A.
2. $\dfrac{4}{8} + \dfrac{2}{4} = \dfrac{4\overset{16}{\left(\times 4\right)}}{8\underset{32}{\left(\times 4\right)}} + \dfrac{2\overset{16}{\left(\times 8\right)}}{4\underset{32}{\left(\times 8\right)}} = \dfrac{32}{32}$	Component skill error: student did not find least common multiple. Note that answer is correct.	Teacher points this out but emphasizes it's important to find the least common multiple. Extra practice on finding LCM.
3. $\dfrac{4}{5} + \dfrac{2}{3} = \dfrac{6}{8}$	Strategy error: student adds denominators.	Present entire format for fractions with unlike denominators (12.16) over, beginning with Part A.
4. $\dfrac{5}{6} + \dfrac{2}{4} = \dfrac{5\overset{10}{\times 4}}{6\underset{12}{\left(\times 4\right)}} + \dfrac{2\overset{5}{\times 3}}{4\underset{12}{\left(\times 3\right)}} = \dfrac{15}{12}$	Computational errors: student multiplied 2×3 incorrectly.	Teacher works on 2×3 fact. No reteaching of fraction format necessary.

duced. However, the teacher is directed to provide minimal guidance. Typically, the teacher demonstrates one example on the board, and there is a model of one problem in the student's text. In one program, there was no demonstration for subtracting a mixed number from a whole number, yet nine problems were of this type. Considering that not only must students rename but in many problems they must also first rewrite the fractions with common denominators, it is highly likely that some students will have difficulty.

REVIEW. The second focus of concern with instruction in fractions has to do with the amount of review provided in the programs. In grades one through three, only 1 to 3 weeks are typically devoted to fraction skills. Minimal review is presented on fraction skills after the unit is presented. Because of this

minimal review, it is highly likely that many students will not retain fraction-related skills taught in these earlier grades. In intermediate grades, the critical fraction analysis skills taught in early grades are briefly reviewed prior to teaching new skills. The amount of practice provided in the programs must be significantly supplemented if the students are to develop mastery. Teachers must not go on to a new skill until students have mastered preskills. When the more complex fraction skills are introduced in the intermediate grades, the programs tend to provide enough initial practice (with all of the supplemental worksheets available). However, the practice usually is concentrated in a short amount of time with little systematic review built into the program outside of the fractions units themselves, as in the earlier grades. Low-performing students require continual review if they are to maintain acquired skills.

APPLICATION ITEMS: FRACTIONS

1. Below are various fraction-related problems. Describe the type each problem represents. List the types in their order of introduction.

    a. $\dfrac{2}{3} - \dfrac{1}{3}$

    b. Circle the picture that shows $\dfrac{2}{4}$.

    c. Read this fraction: $\dfrac{3}{5}$

    d. $\dfrac{3}{4} + \dfrac{2}{5}$

    e. $5\dfrac{4}{7} - 3\dfrac{2}{7}$

    f. $\dfrac{12}{5} = \square$

    g. $\dfrac{3}{5} = \dfrac{\square}{10}$

    h. $5\dfrac{1}{2} \times 3$

    i. $3\dfrac{4}{5} = \dfrac{\square}{5}$

2. Write a structured worksheet presentation for teaching students how to solve the following type of problem:

    Draw a picture for this fraction: $\dfrac{3}{4} = \bigcirc\bigcirc$

3. A teacher is presenting the first lesson in which she is teaching students to decode fractions in the traditional manner (e.g., ⅔ is read as two-thirds). Below are four sets of examples. Which set is appropriate? Tell why the other three sets are not appropriate.

    a. $\dfrac{2}{3}$ $\dfrac{1}{2}$ $\dfrac{4}{5}$ $\dfrac{7}{3}$ $\dfrac{1}{4}$ $\dfrac{2}{9}$ $\dfrac{3}{2}$ $\dfrac{1}{5}$

    b. $\dfrac{1}{8}$ $\dfrac{1}{4}$ $\dfrac{1}{9}$ $\dfrac{1}{6}$ $\dfrac{1}{5}$ $\dfrac{1}{7}$

    c. $\dfrac{1}{8}$ $\dfrac{3}{4}$ $\dfrac{7}{6}$ $\dfrac{1}{6}$ $\dfrac{2}{8}$ $\dfrac{9}{4}$ $\dfrac{1}{4}$

    d. $\dfrac{3}{4}$ $\dfrac{7}{9}$ $\dfrac{8}{4}$ $\dfrac{2}{9}$ $\dfrac{4}{6}$ $\dfrac{8}{6}$ $\dfrac{5}{7}$

4. A student writes the mixed number five and one-third as $\frac{5}{3}$. Specify the wording the teacher uses in making the correction.

5. Specify the wording the teacher uses in making the correction for the following error:

$$\frac{3}{4} = \frac{\boxed{3}}{8}$$

6. Cross out the examples below that would not be included in an early equivalent-fraction exercise.

   a. $\frac{2}{3} = \frac{\square}{9}$ b. $\frac{5}{7} = \frac{\square}{28}$ c. $\frac{3}{4} = \frac{\square}{6}$

   d. $\frac{4}{5} = \frac{\square}{20}$ e. $\frac{3}{5} = \frac{\square}{20}$ f. $\frac{4}{6} = \frac{\square}{10}$

7. Below are four sets of examples constructed by the teacher for an early reducing-fraction exercise. One set is appropriate. Three are not appropriate. Identify the inappropriate sets. Tell why they're inappropriate.

   a. $\dfrac{8}{12}$ $\dfrac{7}{9}$ $\dfrac{6}{18}$ $\dfrac{4}{6}$ $\dfrac{5}{20}$ $\dfrac{2}{3}$

   b. $\dfrac{8}{12}$ $\dfrac{6}{18}$ $\dfrac{4}{6}$ $\dfrac{5}{20}$ $\dfrac{3}{12}$ $\dfrac{6}{8}$

   c. $\dfrac{8}{12}$ $\dfrac{7}{9}$ $\dfrac{10}{15}$ $\dfrac{12}{20}$ $\dfrac{3}{5}$ $\dfrac{6}{8}$

   d. $\dfrac{4}{7}$ $\dfrac{5}{20}$ $\dfrac{22}{36}$ $\dfrac{8}{16}$ $\dfrac{18}{34}$ $\dfrac{5}{9}$

8. Write the structured worksheet presentation used in leading students through reducing the fraction $\frac{12}{18}$ to its lowest terms.

9. Below are sets of examples prepared by various teachers for an exercise in which students convert improper fractions to mixed numbers. Tell which sets are inappropriate.

   a. $\dfrac{9}{5}$ $\dfrac{11}{3}$ $\dfrac{9}{3}$ $\dfrac{12}{7}$ $\dfrac{14}{5}$ $\dfrac{12}{4}$

   b. $\dfrac{9}{4}$ $\dfrac{3}{7}$ $\dfrac{8}{2}$ $\dfrac{7}{5}$ $\dfrac{8}{3}$ $\dfrac{5}{9}$ $\dfrac{9}{3}$ $\dfrac{7}{3}$

   c. $\dfrac{9}{5}$ $\dfrac{3}{7}$ $\dfrac{5}{2}$ $\dfrac{4}{9}$ $\dfrac{7}{3}$ $\dfrac{9}{2}$

10. Below are sets of examples prepared by several teachers for an independent worksheet exercise focusing on adding and subtracting fractions with unlike denominators. Tell which sets are inappropriate. Explain why.

   a. $\dfrac{6}{14} - \dfrac{3}{8}$ $\dfrac{5}{8} + \dfrac{1}{5}$ $\dfrac{4}{9} - \dfrac{5}{12}$ $\dfrac{3}{8} + \dfrac{2}{8}$

   b. $\dfrac{3}{8} + \dfrac{1}{5}$ $\dfrac{5}{7} - \dfrac{1}{4}$ $\dfrac{3}{8} + \dfrac{2}{8}$ $\dfrac{3}{5} + \dfrac{2}{3}$ $\dfrac{2}{3} - \dfrac{1}{2}$ $\dfrac{4}{7} - \dfrac{2}{5}$

   c. $\dfrac{3}{4} - \dfrac{2}{3}$ $\dfrac{4}{9} - \dfrac{2}{9}$ $\dfrac{2}{9} + \dfrac{2}{3}$ $\dfrac{5}{7} - \dfrac{1}{2}$ $\dfrac{3}{8} + \dfrac{1}{4}$ $\dfrac{3}{7} + \dfrac{2}{7}$

11. Below are problems missed by students. These examples are typical of the errors made by students. Specify the diagnosis and remediation for each student.

   William

   $$\frac{7}{8} - \frac{1}{6} = \frac{6}{2}$$

Ann

$$\frac{5}{9} + \frac{2}{5} = \frac{5}{9}\left(\frac{5}{5}\right) + \frac{2}{5}\left(\frac{9}{9}\right) = \frac{5}{9}\overset{25}{\left(\frac{5}{5}\right)} + \frac{2}{5}\overset{18}{\left(\frac{9}{9}\right)} = \frac{42}{45}$$

Samuel

$$\frac{4}{5} + \frac{1}{2} = \frac{4}{5}\left(\frac{2}{2}\right) + \frac{1}{2}\left(\frac{5}{5}\right) = \frac{4}{5}\overset{8}{\left(\frac{2}{2}\right)} + \frac{1}{2}\overset{5}{\left(\frac{5}{5}\right)} = \frac{13}{10} = \frac{3}{10}$$

Jean

$$\frac{3}{5} + \frac{2}{3} = \frac{3}{5}\left(\frac{5}{3}\right) + \frac{2}{3}\left(\frac{3}{5}\right) = \frac{3}{5}\overset{15}{\left(\frac{5}{3}\right)} + \frac{2}{3}\overset{6}{\left(\frac{3}{5}\right)} = \frac{21}{15}$$

12. Write a structured worksheet exercise to lead students through solving this problem:

$$8 - 3\frac{4}{5}$$

13. Specify the diagnosis and remediation procedures for each student.

Jim

$$\frac{6}{7} \text{ of } 28 = \frac{162}{7} = 23\frac{1}{7}$$

Sarah

$$\frac{6}{7} \text{ of } 28 = \frac{6}{196} = \frac{3}{98}$$

William

$$\frac{6}{7} \text{ of } 28 = \frac{168}{7}$$

FORMAT 12.1 **Introducing Fractions**

TEACHER   **STUDENTS**

1. *(Write the following diagram on the board.)*

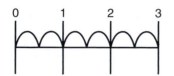

2. *(Touch the line 0.)* Pretend that I've drawn inches on the board.
   (Point to 1.) Here's 1 inch.
   (Point to 2.) Here's 2 inches.
   (Point to 3.) Here's 3 inches.

TEACHER   **STUDENTS**

3. Listen: Each inch is divided into parts. Each hump is a part.
   (Draw a line under the first inch.)

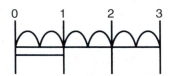

4. Look at the first inch. How many parts are in the first inch?   2
   (Signal.)
   (Underline the next inch.)

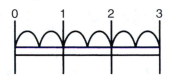

5. Look at the second inch. How many parts are in the second   2
   inch? *(Signal.)*
   (Underline the third inch.)

6. Look at the next inch. How many parts are in the next inch?   2
   (Signal.)

7. If I drew another inch, how many parts would be in that inch?   2
   (Signal.)
   To correct:

   a. *(Students do not understand the number of parts in each*
      unit. They do not write the same bottom number or the
      correct bottom number for all the fractions.)

      (First, have them show you the first unit on the number
      line.) Use your fingers. Show me where the first unit starts
      and where it stops. Now start at the beginning and count
      the parts in that unit. How many parts are in that unit? Now
      do the same thing for the next unit. Mark the beginning and
      the end of the unit. Now start at the beginning and count
      the number of parts in that unit. How many parts are in
      that unit? There were 2 parts in the first unit and 2 parts   2
      in this unit. So how many parts are in EACH unit?   2

      (Repeat the procedure until students who have problems
      are performing flawlessly. Note that some of them may
      have serious problems because they don't understand
      that the second unit starts where the first unit ends.)

   b. *(Students don't write the correct top number.)*

      (If students seem to make chronic mistakes, touch different
      places on the number line and say,) Let's say you're going
      to write a fraction right here. Figure out the top number of
      that fraction. Count from the beginning and write the number.

FORMAT 12.2 **Part–Whole Discrimination**

TEACHER	STUDENTS

1. *(Draw the following circles on the board.)*

2. *(Point to the first circle.)* This is a whole unit. What is this? — A whole unit.
   (Point to the second circle.) This is a whole unit. What is this? — A whole unit.
   How many units? — 2

3. Each whole unit has parts. The parts are all the same size.
   Let's see how many parts are in each whole unit.

4. *(Point to first unit.)* Count the parts as I touch them. Touch — 1, 2, 3
   each part in the first circle. How many parts in this whole unit? — 3

5. *(Point to the second circle.)* Now let's count the parts in this — 1, 2, 3
   whole unit. *(Touch each part as students count.)*

6. How many parts in each whole unit? — 3 parts

7. Yes, three parts in each whole unit. Say that. — 3 parts in each whole unit.

8. Now think: How many whole units? Yes, there are 2 whole units — 2
   with 3 parts in each unit. *(Repeat steps 1–7 with other examples.)*

FORMAT 12.3 **Writing Numerical Fractions**

TEACHER	STUDENTS

PART A: STRUCTURED BOARD PRESENTATION

1. *(Draw the following circles on the board.)*

2. We're going to learn to write fractions. Fractions tell us how many
   parts in each whole unit and how many parts are used.

3. The bottom number of a fraction tells how many parts in each — How many parts in each
   whole. What does the bottom number tell? *(Signal.)* whole.
   Look at this picture and think, how many parts in each whole? — 4

   To correct: Let's see how many parts are in each whole.
   (Point to first circle.) Count the parts as I touch them.
   *(Touch each part in the first circle. Repeat same procedures
   with next two circles.)* There are 4 parts in this whole and
   4 parts in this whole. There are 4 parts in each whole.

TEACHER

So what is the bottom number of the fraction?
I'll write 4 as the bottom number. That tells us 4 parts
in each whole. What does the 4 tell us?

4. The top number tells us how many parts are used.
What does the top number tell us?

We find how many parts are used by counting the
shaded parts. *(Point to each shaded part.)* Count as
I touch the parts. How many parts are shaded?

So I write 5 as the top number of the fraction. *(Write 5
on top.)* That tells us 5 parts are used. What does the 5 tell us?

5. I'll say what the fraction tells us. *(Point to 4.)* 4 parts in each
whole. *(Point to 5.)* 5 parts are used.

6. You say what the fraction tells us. *(Point to 4, Signal.
Point to 5. Signal. Repeat step 5 until students respond
without hesitation. Give individual turns to several students.)*

7. *(Repeat steps 1–4 with the problems below.)*

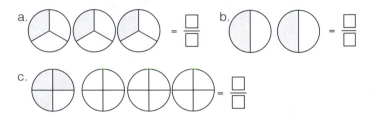

PART B: STRUCTURED WORKSHEET

1. *(Give students a worksheet with problems like those that follow.)*

a.   d.

b.   e.

c.   f.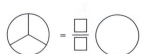

2. Touch picture a. You're going to write the fraction for
the picture.

STUDENTS

4

4 parts in each whole.

How many parts are
used.

1, 2, 3, 4, 5
5

5 parts are used.

4 parts in each whole
5 parts are used.

(continued on next page)

FORMAT 12.3 (continued)

TEACHER	STUDENTS
3. First we write how many parts in each whole.	
Where do you write the number of parts in each whole?	In the bottom box.
Look and see how many parts in each whole. *(Pause.)*	
How many parts in each whole?	3
Where do you write 3? Write the number.	In the bottom box.
4. Now we write the number of parts used. Where do you write the number of parts used?	On the top
Count the shaded parts. *(Pause.)* How many parts were used?	4
5. Touch the bottom number. *(Pause.)* What does that tell us?	3 parts in each whole
Touch the top number. What does that tell us?	4 parts are used.
(Repeat step 4 until students answer without hesitation. Give individual turns to several students on step 4. Repeat steps 1–4 with remaining diagrams.)	

PART C: LESS STRUCTURED WORKSHEET

TEACHER	STUDENTS
1. *(Give students a worksheet similar to the one in Part B.)* Touch problem a.	
2. Where do you write how many parts in each whole unit?	On the bottom
3. What do you write on the top? Write the numbers.	How many parts are used.
4. Touch the bottom number. What did you write? What does it tell us?	_____ parts in each whole.
5. Touch the top number. What did you write? What does the top number tell us?	_____ parts are used.
(Repeat steps 1–5 with remaining problems.)	

FORMAT 12.4 Reading Fractions

TEACHER	STUDENTS
1. *(Write the following fractions on the board.)*	

$$\frac{4}{9} \quad \frac{1}{9} \quad \frac{3}{4} \quad \frac{1}{4} \quad \frac{6}{7} \quad \frac{1}{7} \quad \frac{2}{4} \quad \frac{1}{4}$$

TEACHER	STUDENTS
So far we've learned what fractions tell us to do. Today we're going to learn to read fractions a new way. My turn to read this fraction. *(Point to 4.)* Four *(point to 9)* ninths.	
2. Your turn. *(Point to 4, then 9.)*	4/9
3. *(Repeat steps 1 and 2 with half the examples on the board.)*	
4. *(Repeat step 2 only with the remaining examples.)*	
To correct: Model correct answer; repeat.	

FORMAT 12.5 **Determining Whether a Fraction Equals, Exceeds, or Is Less Than One Whole**

TEACHER	**STUDENTS**
PART A: PICTORIAL DEMONSTRATIONS	

1. I'll draw a picture on the board. You tell me if we use up more than one whole, less than one whole, or just one whole. *(Draw the diagram below.)*

2. Did I shade more than one whole, less than one whole, or just one whole? *(Signal.)*

   Yes, less than one whole unit. Each circle has 4 parts, but I only shaded 3 parts.
   (Repeat step 2 with the examples below.)

	STUDENTS
	Less than one whole unit.

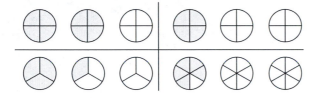

PART B: STRUCTURED BOARD PRESENTATION

1. We're going to learn some rules so we can tell if a fraction equals one whole or equals more or less than one whole without drawing a picture.

2. First rule: A fraction equals one whole when the top number and bottom number are the same. When does a fraction equal one whole?

	STUDENTS
	When the top number and bottom number are the same.

   (Write the following fraction on the board.)

   $$\frac{4}{4}$$

3. *(Point to the fraction.)* Does this fraction equal one whole?

   How do you know?

	STUDENTS
	Yes
	The top number and bottom number are the same.

   (Repeat step 3 with the problems below.)

   $$\frac{7}{4} \quad \frac{2}{3} \quad \frac{5}{5} \quad \frac{1}{4} \quad \frac{8}{8}$$

4. Listen to these new rules: If the top number is *more* than the bottom number, the fraction equals *more* than one whole. When does a fraction equal more than one whole?

	STUDENTS
	When the top number is more than the bottom number.

(continued on next page)

FORMAT 12.5 (continued)

TEACHER	**STUDENTS**
If the top number is *less* than the bottom number, the fraction equals *less* than one whole. When does a fraction equal less than one whole?	When the top number is less than the bottom number.

5. *(Write the following fraction on board.)*

$$\frac{3}{5}$$

Is the top number the same as the bottom number?	No
So does the fraction equal one whole?	No
Is the top number more or less than the bottom number?	Less
So does the fraction equal more or less than one whole? How do you know?	Less than one whole. The top number is less than the bottom number.

Yes, 5 parts in each whole and only 3 parts are used. *(Repeat step 5 with the problems below.)*

$$\frac{3}{4} \quad \frac{3}{3} \quad \frac{3}{2} \quad \frac{4}{5} \quad \frac{4}{4} \quad \frac{4}{2}$$

PART C: STRUCTURED WORKSHEET

1. *(Give students worksheets with problems like these.)*

   a. $\frac{5}{4}$ more equal less   b. $\frac{7}{7}$ more equal less   c. $\frac{3}{7}$ more equal less

2. In these problems you have to tell if a fraction is more than one whole, equals one whole, or is less than one whole.

3. Read the fraction in problem a.	$\frac{5}{4}$
4. Does the fraction equal one whole?	No
5. Is the top number more or less than the bottom number?	More
So does the fraction equal more or less than one whole?	More than one whole.
Put a circle around the word *more*.	

(Repeat steps 1–4 with remaining problems.)

FORMAT 12.6 **Reading and Writing Mixed Numbers**

TEACHER   **STUDENTS**

PART A: PICTORIAL DEMONSTRATIONS

1. *(Draw the following diagrams on the board.)*

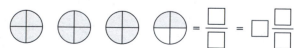

2. You're going to learn how to write the fraction in this picture a new way.

TEACHER	**STUDENTS**

3. First, let's write the fraction the old way. How many parts in each whole? *(Pause.)*

    4

   Where do I write it? Do it.

    On the bottom.

4. How many parts are used? *(Pause.)*

    14

   Where do I write it? Do it.

    On the top.

5. Now we're going to write the fraction as a mixed number. A mixed number has a whole number and a fraction. What does a mixed number have?

    A whole number and a fraction.

6. First we count the number of wholes used up. Count as I point. How many wholes are used up?

    3

   So I write 3 in the box. *(Write 3 in the box.)*

7. Now we write the fraction to tell about the whole not used up. *(Point to the last circle.)*

   What do I write as the bottom number in the fraction? *(Write 4.)*

    4

     To correct: There are 4 parts in each whole.

   What do I write as the top number in the fraction? *(Write 2.)*

    2

     To correct: There are 2 parts shaded. The fraction that tells about the whole not used up says ¾.

8. The mixed number says 3¾. What does the mixed number say?

    $3\frac{2}{3}$

   There are 3 whole units used up and ¾ of another whole unit used up.

   (Repeat steps 2–7 with these examples.)

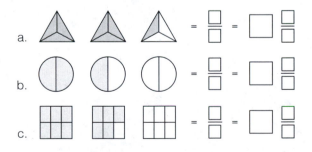

PART B: STRUCTURED BOARD PRESENTATION

1. *(Write the following on the board.)*

    $2\frac{1}{3}$

2. A mixed number is a whole number and a fraction. What is a mixed number?

    A whole number and a fraction.

(continued on next page)

FORMAT 12.6 (continued)

TEACHER	**STUDENTS**

3. *(Point to:)*

$$2\frac{1}{3}$$

What's the whole number? — 2

What's the fraction? — $\frac{1}{3}$

4. Read the mixed number. — $2\frac{1}{3}$

(Repeat steps 2 and 3 with these problems.)

$$5\frac{2}{7} \quad 7\frac{1}{2} \quad 3\frac{4}{5} \quad 6\frac{1}{2}$$

PART C: STRUCTURED WORKSHEET

(Give students lined paper.)

1. Listen: 2¾. Say that. — $2\frac{3}{4}$

   What is the whole number? — 2

   I write 2 so that it takes up the whole space:

$$\overline{\underline{2}}$$

2. Listen: 2¾. What's the fraction? — $\frac{3}{4}$

   I write the fraction line in the middle of the space next to the 2. Then I write the fraction numbers small. *(Write the number.)*

$$\overline{\underline{2\frac{3}{4}}}$$

3. What is the mixed number? — $2\frac{3}{4}$

   (Repeat steps 1–3 with the problems below.)

$$7\frac{1}{2} \quad 4\frac{2}{5}$$

4. Now it's your turn. You're going to write the mixed number

   5⅔. What mixed number are you going to write? — $5\frac{2}{3}$

5. Listen: 5⅔. What is the whole number? Write it. Make it big so that it touches both lines. *(Monitor responses.)* — 5

6. Listen: 5⅔. What is the fraction? Put the fraction line right in the middle of the space next to the 5. Then write ⅔. — $\frac{2}{3}$

   Write the numbers small.

   (Repeat step 2 with these numbers.)

$$7\frac{2}{4} \quad 9\frac{1}{3} \quad 7\frac{1}{2} \quad 5\frac{3}{8}$$

TEACHER	**STUDENTS**
7. Listen: 3⅚. Say it.	$3\dfrac{4}{6}$
Write it. *(Monitor responses. Repeat step 7 with these numbers.)*	

$$7\frac{2}{4} \quad 9\frac{1}{3} \quad 7\frac{1}{2} \quad 5\frac{3}{8}$$

***FORMAT 12.7* Constructing Fractions Equal to 1—Preskill**

TEACHER	**STUDENTS**
PART A: STRUCTURED BOARD PRESENTATION	
1. Here's a rule: When the top number is the same as the bottom, the fraction equals one whole. When does a fraction equal one whole?	When the top number is the same as the bottom number.
2. *(Write the following on the board.)*	
$\dfrac{\square}{5}$	
What number is on the bottom of this fraction?	5
What fraction with a 5 as the bottom number equals one whole?	$\dfrac{5}{5}$
To correct: A fraction equals 1 when the top number is the same as the bottom number. What's the bottom number? What must the top number be? *(Repeat step 2.)*	
Yes, 5/5 equals one whole.	
(Repeat step 2 with these problems.)	
$\dfrac{\square}{8} \quad \dfrac{\square}{3} \quad \dfrac{\square}{6} \quad \dfrac{\square}{9}$	
PART B: STRUCTURED WORKSHEET	
1. *(Give students worksheets with examples like these.)*	
a. $1 = \dfrac{\square}{4}$ b. $1 = \dfrac{\square}{7}$	
c. $1 = \dfrac{\square}{4}$ d. $1 = \dfrac{\square}{7}$	
2. When does a fraction equal one whole?	When the top number is the same as the bottom number.
3. Touch problem a. It says 1 equals how many fourths? Read the problem.	1 equals how many fourths?
4. Tell me the fraction with 4 as a denominator that equals one whole. Yes, ¼ equals one whole.	$\dfrac{4}{4}$
5. Fill in the missing number.	Students write 4 in box.
(Repeat steps 1–4 with remaining problems.)	

FORMAT 12.8 **Computing Equivalent Fractions**

TEACHER	**STUDENTS**
PART A: PICTORIAL DEMONSTRATIONS	
1. Fractions are equivalent when they show the same amounts. *(Draw these figures on clear plastic sheets. The circles should have the same radius. Use a different color for each figure.)*	
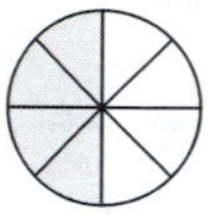 $\frac{4}{8}$ 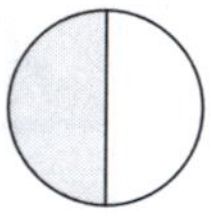 $\frac{1}{2}$	
2. This is a picture of ⁴⁄₈. *(Point to first figure.)* This is picture of ½. *(Point to second figure.)*	
3. Would a person who had ⁴⁄₈ of a pie have the same portion as a person who had ½ a pie?	Yes
To correct: (Place one figure on top of the other. Outline the shaded part.) See, the shaded portion is the same size in both pies.	
4. So are ⁴⁄₈ and ½ equivalent fractions?	Yes
5. Yes, ⁴⁄₈ and ½ both use up the same amount of a whole. *(Repeat steps 1–3 with these pairs.)*	
a. $\frac{2}{3}$  $\frac{1}{2}$ 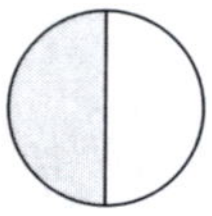 b. $\frac{2}{3}$  $\frac{4}{6}$ 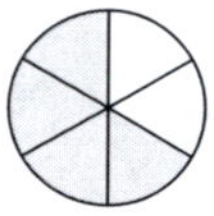 c. $\frac{3}{4}$ 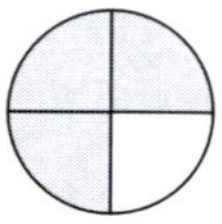 $\frac{2}{3}$ 	
PART B: MULTIPLYING OR DIVIDING BY 1	
1. When you multiply by 1, the answer equals the number you start with.	
2. *(Write the following problem on the board.)* $\frac{3}{8} \times 1$	
What number do we start with?	$\frac{3}{8}$
Will our answer equal ³⁄₈?	Yes
How do you know?	We are multiplying by 1.
(Repeat step 2 with these problems.) $\frac{1}{2} \times 1$ $\frac{1}{4} \times 5$	
3. Here's a rule about fractions: When you multiply by a fraction that equals 1, your answer equals the number you start with. Listen, again. *(Repeat rule.)*	
4. *(Write the following problem on the board.)* $\frac{4}{8} \times \frac{2}{2}$	
What fraction do we start with?	$\frac{4}{8}$
What are we multiplying ⁴⁄₈ by?	$\frac{2}{2}$

TEACHER	**STUDENTS**
5. Does $\frac{2}{2}$ equal 1?	Yes
So will our answer equal $\frac{4}{8}$?	Yes
How do you know?	We are multiplying by a fraction that equals 1.
(Repeat steps 4 and 5 with the problems below.)	

$$\frac{4}{8} \times \frac{4}{4} \qquad \frac{5}{6} \times \frac{3}{6}$$
$$\frac{5}{6} \times \frac{2}{3} \qquad \frac{3}{9} \times \frac{8}{8}$$
$$\frac{7}{2} \times \frac{9}{9} \qquad \frac{2}{4} \times \frac{4}{4}$$

PART C: STRUCTURED BOARD PROBLEMS

1. *(Write the following problem on the board.)*

$$\frac{2}{3}\left(\ \right) = \frac{\square}{12}$$

2. We don't change the value of a fraction when we multiply it by a fraction that equals 1.
3. These parentheses mean times. We're going to multiply $\frac{2}{3}$ by a fraction that equals 1. We have to figure out the fraction that equals 1.
4. We are going to end with a fraction that has the same value as $\frac{2}{3}$. *(Point to 12.)*

What's the bottom number of the fraction we end with?	12
Three times what number equals 12?	4
So we multiply by a fraction that has a denominator of 4.	

5. *(Write 4 inside parentheses.)*

$$\frac{2}{3}\left(\frac{\ }{4}\right) = \frac{\square}{12}$$

6. The fraction inside the parentheses must equal 1.

If the bottom number is 4, what must the top number be?	4
(Write a four in the numerator inside parentheses.)	

$$\frac{2}{3}\left(\frac{4}{4}\right) = \frac{\square}{12}$$

Yes, we multiply $\frac{2}{3}$ by $\frac{4}{4}$. What do we multiply $\frac{2}{3}$ by?	$\frac{4}{4}$

7. We figured out the fraction of 1 we're multiplying by. Let's multiply and figure out how many twelfths $\frac{2}{3}$ equals. 2 × 4 = how many? *(Pause.)* — 8

(Write the problem on the board.)

$$\frac{2}{3}\left(\frac{4}{4}\right) = \frac{8}{12}$$

8. We multiplied $\frac{2}{3}$ by a fraction that equals 1 and ended with $\frac{8}{12}$; $\frac{2}{3}$ has to equal $\frac{8}{12}$.

(Repeat steps 3–7 with these problems.)

$$\frac{3}{5} = \frac{\square}{10} \qquad \frac{2}{3} = \frac{\square}{15} \qquad \frac{2}{7} = \frac{\square}{21}$$

(continued on next page)

FORMAT 12.8 (continued)

TEACHER	STUDENTS
PART D: STRUCTURED WORKSHEET	
1. *(Give students a worksheet with problems similar to these.)*	
a. $\frac{3}{4}\left(-\right) = \frac{\square}{8}$ b. $\frac{5}{9}\left(-\right) = \frac{\square}{27}$ c. $\frac{1}{4}\left(-\right) = \frac{\square}{20}$	
d. $\frac{2}{5}\left(-\right) = \frac{\square}{20}$ e. $\frac{3}{5}\left(-\right) = \frac{\square}{35}$ f. $\frac{2}{3}\left(-\right) = \frac{\square}{12}$	
2. Touch problem a.	
3. It says ¾ equals how many eighths? What does the problem say?	$\frac{3}{4}$ equals how many eighths?
4. We have to multiply ¾ by a fraction that equals 1. What is the bottom number of the fraction we start with?	4
What is the bottom number of the fraction we end with?	8
Four times what number equals 8?	2
Write 2 as the bottom number in the parentheses.	
5. We're multiplying ¾ by a fraction that equals 1. What fraction with a denominator of 2 equals one whole?	$\frac{2}{2}$
Write 2 as a numerator in the parentheses.	
6. We figured out the fraction of 1. Now what do we multiply to figure out the missing numerator?	3×2
What is 3×2? *(Pause, signal.)*	
Write 6 in the box.	6
7. What fraction equals ¾?	$\frac{6}{8}$
8. How do you know that ¾ equals ⁶⁄₈?	We multiplied by a fraction that equals 1.
(Repeat steps 1–7 with remaining problems.)	
PART E: LESS STRUCTURED WORKSHEET	
1. *(Give students a worksheet with problems like the one below. Note that parentheses aren't written in.)*	
a. $\frac{5}{6} = \frac{\square}{12}$ b. $\frac{3}{4} = \frac{\square}{20}$ c. $\frac{1}{3} = \frac{\square}{12}$	
d. $\frac{1}{5} = \frac{\square}{20}$ e. $\frac{2}{5} = \frac{\square}{15}$ f. $\frac{3}{7} = \frac{\square}{14}$	
2. Touch problem a. Read the problem.	$\frac{5}{6}$ equals how many twelfths?
3. We must multiply ⅚ by a fraction that equals 1. To keep the fractions equal, put parentheses next to ⅚.	
4. Look at the numbers and get ready to tell me what we must multiply ⅚ by. *(Pause.)*	$\frac{2}{2}$
To correct: What is the bottom number of the fraction we start with? What is the bottom number of the fraction we	

TEACHER	STUDENTS

end with? Six times what number equals 12? That's the denominator. The fraction we're multiplying equals 1. What fraction goes in the parentheses?

Write ⅔ in the parentheses.

5. Multiply and write in the missing numerator.

6. What fraction does ⅚ equal?

$$\frac{10}{12}$$

(Repeat steps 1–5 with remaining problems.)

FORMAT 12.9 **Preskill: Determining Factors**

TEACHER	STUDENTS

PART A: INTRODUCING THE CONCEPT

1. *(Write the following problems on board.)*

    $5 \times 3 = 15$
    $9 \times 2 = 18$
    $7 \times 6 = 42$

Factors are numbers that are multiplied together.

2. Read the first problem. $5 \times 3 = 15$

   What numbers are being multiplied?   5 and 3

   So 5 and 3 are factors of 15. What are two factors of 15?   5 and 3

3. Look at the board and tell me two factors of 18.   9 and 2

4. Look at the board and tell me two factors of 42.   7 and 6

PART B: STRUCTURED BOARD PRESENTATION

1. *(Write 12 on board.)*

   We want to list all of the factors for 12, beginning with the smallest factor.

   Listen: A number multiplied by 1 always equals itself. So is 1 a factor of 12?   Yes

   Yes, 1 is a factor of 12. What number times 1 equals 12?   12

   12 and 1 are factors of 12; 12 is the largest factor of 12; 1 is the smallest factor of 12.

   We're going to make a list of the factors of 12.

   Let's start with 1×12.

      1×12

2. One is the smallest factor of 12.
   Let's find the next larger number we can multiply and end with 12. I'll say some numbers. You say stop when I come to a number that is a factor of 12.

   Listen, 2 *(pause).*   Stop

   To correct: (If students don't say stop at 2)

   We can multiply 2 and end with 12, so 2 is a factor of 12.

(continued on next page)

FORMAT 12.9 (continued)

TEACHER	STUDENTS

Yes, 2 is the next largest factor of 12.

2 times what number equals 12? — 6

So 6 is the other factor of 12 that goes with 2.

Let's add 2 × 6 to our list of factors of 12.

    1 × 12
    2 × 6

3. Let's find the next largest factor of 12.
I'll say some numbers. You say stop when I come
to a factor of 12. We already have 1 and 2. Listen, 3 *(pause)* — Stop

To correct: (If students don't say stop at 3)

We can multiply 3 and end with 12, so 3 is a factor of 12.

Yes, 3 is a factor of 12.

3 times what other number equals 12? — 4

So 4 is the other factor of 12 that goes with 3.

Let's add 3 × 4 to our list of factors of 12.

    1 × 12
    2 × 6
    3 × 4

4. Listen, my turn. I know there are no more factors of 12.
How do I know? Because the next number after 3 is 4,
and we already have that number. We have all the
factors of 12.

Your turn. Do we have all the factors of 12? — Yes

How do you know? — Because the next
number after 3 is 4, and
we already have that
number.

    1 × 12
    2 × 6
    3 × 4

5. When we say the factors of a number, we read the
numbers in order, and we don't have to say *times*.
My turn to say all the factors of 12 *(point to the
numbers as you say them)*.
Your turn. Say all the factors of 12. — 1, 2, 3, 4, 6, 12

6. *(Write 10 on board.)*

7. We want to list all of the factors for 10, beginning with
the smallest factor. Listen: A number multiplied by
1 always equals itself. So is 1 a factor of 10? — Yes

Yes, 1 is a factor of 10. What number times 1 equals 10? — 10

10 and 1 are factors of 10; 10 is the largest factor of 10;
1 is the smallest factor of 10.

Let's begin our list of factors of 10 with 1 × 10.

    1 × 10

8. Let's find the next largest number we can multiply and
end with 10. I'll say some numbers. You say stop when
I come to a number that is a factor of 10. 1 is the smallest
factor of 10. What number comes next? — 2

TEACHER	**STUDENTS**

Is 2 a factor of 10? · Yes

To correct: (If students say no) We can multiply 2 and
end with 10, so 2 is a factor of 10.

Yes, so 2 is the next largest factor of 10.

2 times what number equals 10?

So 5 is the other factor of 10 that goes with 2.

Let's add 2 × 5 to our list of factors of 10.

   1 × 10
   2 × 5

9. Let's find the next largest factor of 10. I'll say some numbers.
   You say stop when I come to a factor of 10. We already have
   1 and 2. Listen: 3 *(pause)*, 4 *(pause)*, 5 *(pause)* · · · · · · · · · Stop

   To correct: (If students say stop at 3, or 4), We can't
   multiply that number and end with 10.

   Yes, 5 is a factor of 10.

   Do we already have 5? · Yes

10. So, do we have all the factors of 10? · · · · · · · · · · · · · · · · Yes

   How do you know? · Because the next factor
                                                                         was 5, and we already
   1 × 10   had that number.
   2 × 5

11. When we say the factors of a number, we read the
    numbers in order, and we don't have to say times.

    Your turn. Say all the factors of 10. · · · · · · · · · · · · · · · · · 1, 2, 5, 10

    (Repeat Part B with other new examples for that day.)

PART C: STRUCTURED WORKSHEET

1. *(Give students worksheets with problems like those below
   and instructions to list all the factors for each number,
   and list the biggest factors first.)*

   a. 1 × 16

   b. 1 × 12

   c. 1 × 7

   (Touch a.) What is the smallest factor of 16? · · · · · · · · · · · · 1

   What is the other factor that goes with 1 to equal 16? · · · · · · 16

   Write 1 times 16 on the first line

      1 × 16

2. 1 is the smallest factor of 16.

   What is the next largest factor of 16? *(Pause.)* · · · · · · · · · · 2

   What is the other factor that goes with 2 to equal 16? *(Pause.)* · 8

   Write 2 × 8 below to the 16 × 1.

      1 × 16
      2 × 8

(continued on next page)

FORMAT 12.9   (continued)

TEACHER	STUDENTS
What is the next largest factor of 16? *(Pause.)*	4
What is the other factor that goes with 4 to equal 16? *(Pause.)*	4
Write 4 × 4 below 2 × 8.	
1 × 16 2 × 8 4 × 4	
3. Are there any more factors of 16? How do you know? 1 × 16 2 × 8 4 × 4	No Because the next factor was 8, we already had that number.
4. Say all the factors of 16.	1, 2, 4, 8, 16
(Repeat steps 1–4 with new target numbers. *Have students do remaining problems on their own.)*	

FORMAT 12.10   Determining the Greatest Common Factor (GCF)

TEACHER	STUDENTS
1. (Present students with a worksheet similar to the one below.)	
a. What is the greatest common factor of 12 and 16?	
b. What is the greatest common factor of 10 and 5?	
c. What is the greatest common factor of 4 and 7?	
d. What is the greatest common factor of 10 and 15?	
e. What is the greatest common factor of 18 and 9?	
f. What is the greatest common factor of 12 and 9?	
2. Find problem a on your worksheet. Read the directions.	What is the greatest common factor of 12 and 16?
Let's find the greatest common factor of 12 and 16. The greatest common factor is the largest number that is a factor of 12 and 16. What is the largest number that is a factor of 12?	12
Is 12 a factor of 16?	No
12 cannot be the greatest common factor of 12 and 16. Why?	Because 12 is not a factor of 16.
3. What is the next largest factor of 12? *(Pause.)*	6
Is 6 a factor of 16? *(Pause.)*	No
So 6 is not a factor of 12 and 16. Why?	Because 6 is not a factor of 16.
4. What is the next largest factor of 12? *(Pause.)*	4
Is 4 also a factor of 16? *(Pause.)*	Yes

TEACHER	STUDENTS
So what number is the greatest common factor of 12 and 16?	4

5. Write 4.

   (Repeat steps 1–4 with remaining examples.)

FORMAT 12.11   Reducing Fractions

TEACHER	STUDENTS

PART A: STRUCTURED BOARD PRESENTATION

1. *(Write the following problem on the board.)*

$$\frac{8}{12} = \left(\ \right)\underline{\quad}$$

2. We're going to reduce this fraction. We reduce by pulling out the greatest common factor of the numerator and denominator. How do we reduce a fraction?

   Pull out the greatest common factor of the numerator and denominator.

3. We want to reduce ⁸⁄₁₂. What is the greatest common factor of 8 and 12? *(Pause.)*

   4

   To correct: Tell correct answer. Explain why student's answer is incorrect.

4. So we pull out the fraction ¼. What fraction do we pull out of ⁸⁄₁₂?

   $\frac{4}{4}$

   (Write the new fraction on the board.)

$$\frac{8}{12} = \left(\frac{4}{4}\right)\underline{\quad}$$

5. Let's figure out the top number of the reduced fraction. *(Point to symbols as you read.)* 8 = 4 × what number? *(Pause.)*

   2

   (Write the 2.)

$$\frac{8}{12} = \left(\frac{4}{4}\right)\frac{2}{\ }$$

6. Let's figure out the bottom number of the reduced fraction. *(Point to symbols as you read.)* 12 = 4 × what number? *(Pause, signal.)* *(Write the 3.)*

   3

$$\frac{8}{12} = \left(\frac{4}{4}\right)\frac{2}{3}$$

7. The fraction in parentheses equals 1. We don't change the value of a fraction when we multiply by 1, so we can cross out ¼. *(Cross out.)* When we pull out the fraction of 1, the reduced fraction is ⅔. What is the reduced fraction?

   $\frac{2}{3}$

(continued on next page)

FORMAT 12.11 **(continued)**

TEACHER   **STUDENTS**

8. Read the statement. $\frac{8}{12} = \frac{2}{3}$

   (Repeat steps 1–7 with these problems.)

   $\frac{15}{20} = \left(\ \right)\underline{\qquad}$ $\frac{9}{36} = \left(\ \right)\underline{\qquad}$ $\frac{16}{24} = \left(\ \right)\underline{\qquad}$

PART B: STRUCTURED WORKSHEET

  1. *(Give students a worksheet with problems like those below.)*

   a. $\frac{10}{15} = \left(\ \right)$ b. $\frac{12}{16} = \left(\ \right)$

   c. $\frac{8}{24} = \left(\ \right)$

  2. We're going to reduce these fractions. How do you reduce   Pull out the greatest
     fractions?   common factor of the
                                                                     numerator and
                                                                     denominator.

  3. Touch problem a. Read the fraction. $1\frac{10}{15}$

  4. What is the greatest common factor of 10 and 15? *(Pause.)*   5

  5. So what fraction do you write in the parentheses? Write it. $\frac{5}{5}$

  6. The numbers across the top of the fraction say 10 = 5 ×
     what number? What do the numbers across the top say?   10 = 5 × what number?

  7. What do the numbers across the bottom say?   15 = 5 × what number?

  8. Fill in the numerator and denominator in the reduced
     fraction. *(Pause.)*   Students write 2 and 3

     Cross out the fraction of 1 in the parentheses.   Students cross out $\frac{5}{5}$

  9. What is the reduced fraction? $\frac{2}{3}$

 10. Read the statement. $\frac{10}{15} = \frac{2}{3}$

     (Repeat steps 1–9 with remaining problems.)

PART C: LESS STRUCTURED WORKSHEET

 1. *(Present a worksheet like the following. Note that
    parentheses are not written.)* Reduce these fractions:

    a. $\frac{15}{20}$ b. $\frac{8}{12}$ c. $\frac{6}{18}$

    d. $\frac{4}{7}$ e. $\frac{8}{16}$ f. $\frac{5}{8}$

 2. How do you reduce a fraction?   Pull out the greatest
                                                                   common factor of the
                                                                   numerator and
                                                                   denominator.

TEACHER	STUDENTS
3. Read fraction a.	$\dfrac{15}{20}$
4. Make an equal sign. Then write parentheses on the other side of the equal.	Students write $\dfrac{15}{20} = \Big(\quad\Big)$
5. What fraction are you going to write in the parentheses? *(Pause.)*	$\dfrac{5}{5}$
To correct: What is the greatest common factor of _____ and _____? *(Repeat step 4.)*	
6. Write ⅚ in the parentheses. Then figure out the reduced fraction. *(Pause.)*	
7. Cross out the fraction of 1.	
8. What is the reduced fraction?	$\dfrac{3}{4}$
To correct: Read the top numbers of the fractions. What's the answer? Read the bottom numbers of the fractions. What's the answer?	
9. Read the statement.	$\dfrac{15}{20} = \dfrac{3}{4}$

(Repeat steps 1–8 with remaining problems.)

FORMAT 12.12   Converting Improper Fractions to Mixed Numbers

TEACHER	STUDENTS
PART A: PICTORIAL DEMONSTRATION	
1. *(Draw the following diagram on the board.)* $\dfrac{13}{5}$ ◯ ◯ ◯	
2. *(Point to ¹³⁄₅.)* Read this fraction.	$\dfrac{13}{5}$
3. Does ¹³⁄₅ equal more than one whole unit?	Yes
4. Let's make a picture and see how many whole units ¹³⁄₅ makes.	
5. How many parts in each whole? *(Draw the following circles on the board.)*	5
6. How many parts do we use up? *(Shade in 13 parts.)*	13
7. Let's see how many whole units are used. *(Point to first circle.)* Is this whole unit all used up?	Yes

(continued on next page)

FORMAT 12.12 (continued)

TEACHER	STUDENTS

(Point to second circle.) Is this whole unit all used up? — Yes

(Point to third circle.) Is this whole unit all used up? — No

How many whole units are used up? — 2

Two whole units are used up. Let's look at the last unit
and count. How many parts are used up? — 3

And how many parts in each whole? — 5

So, we can say ⅗ of a unit. We have 2 whole units and
⅗ of another unit. *(Write 2⅗.)*

PART B: STRUCTURED BOARD PRESENTATION

1. We're going to learn a fast way to figure out how many
   whole units a fraction makes. We divide by the number of
   parts in each whole unit. What do we do to figure out how
   many whole units?

   — Divide by the number of parts in each whole unit.

   (Write the following on the board.)

   $$\frac{13}{5}$$

   — $\frac{13}{5}$

   Read this fraction.

   Is this fraction equal to, more than, or less than one unit?

   — More than one unit.

2. I want to figure out how many whole units this fraction
   makes. How many parts in each whole? — 5
   So I divide by 5.

   (Write the problem.)

   $$\square\frac{\square}{\square}$$
   $$5\overline{)13}$$

3. Let's divide. *(Point to box.)* How many fives in 13? — 2
   (Write 2.) We have 2 whole units. *(Point under 13.)* What
   number do I write here? — 10

   (Write −10 under 13.)

   $$\boxed{2}\frac{\square}{\square}$$
   $$5\overline{)13}$$
   $$\underline{-10}$$

4. We use up 10 parts in 2 wholes. Now let's subtract and
   see how many parts we have left. What is 13 − 10? — 3

5. Since we started with a fraction, we write the remainder
   as a fraction. Remember, there are 5 parts in each whole.
   (Point to 5 in 5)13.)

   So we write 5 on the bottom of the fraction. *(Write 5.)*
   How many parts are remaining? — 3

   So I write 3 on the top of the fraction.

TEACHER

STUDENTS

(Write the 3.)

5)13
 10
 ——
  3

6. Tell me the mixed number for the fraction ¹³⁄₅.
   Yes, 2⅗ is the same as ¹³⁄₅.

$2\frac{3}{5}$

7. (Write = 2⅗ next to ¹³⁄₅.)

   Read the statement.

$\frac{13}{5} = 2\frac{3}{5}$

   (Repeat steps 1–7 with ¹²⁄₇ and ⁹⁄₄.)

PART C: STRUCTURED WORKSHEET

1. (Give students a worksheet with problems like the following ones.)

   a. $\frac{11}{4} =$)

   b. $\frac{8}{5} =$)

   c. $\frac{7}{3} =$)

2. Touch problem a. Read the fraction.

$\frac{11}{4}$

   Is ¹¹⁄₄ less than 1, equal to 1, or more than 1?

More than 1

   So you have to change ¹¹⁄₄ to a mixed number. How many
   parts in each whole? So you divide 4 into 11.

4

3. Write the division problem.

Students write 4)11

   How many 4s in 11?

2

   We can make two whole units. Write the 2 in the big box.
   Multiply and subtract to find how many parts are left.
   How many parts are left?

3

4. Now let's figure out the fraction remainder. The bottom
   number of the fraction tells how many parts in each whole.
   How many parts in each whole?

4

   So write 4 on the bottom of the fraction.

Students write 4 in the
bottom box of the fraction.

   What do you write for the top number? Write it.

3

5. What mixed number does ¹¹⁄₄ equal?

$2\frac{3}{4}$

   Say the whole statement.

$\frac{11}{4} = 2\frac{3}{4}$

   (Repeat steps 1–4 with remaining problems.)

PART D: LESS-STRUCTURED WORKSHEET

1. (Present a worksheet like the following.)
   Rewrite the fractions that equal more than 1 as mixed numbers.

   a. $\frac{12}{5}$ b. $\frac{3}{4}$

   c. $\frac{15}{4}$ d. $\frac{5}{5}$

(continued on next page)

FORMAT 12.12   (continued)

TEACHER	STUDENTS
2. Some of these fractions equal more than one whole unit. If a fraction equals more than one whole unit, change it to a mixed number. What are you going to do if a fraction equals more than one unit?	Change it to a mixed number.
If the fraction does not equal more than one group, don't do anything.	
3. Touch problem a. Read the fraction.	$\dfrac{12}{5}$
Does the fraction equal more or less than one unit?	More than one unit.
The fraction equals more than one unit, so what must you do?	Change it to a mixed number.
What do you divide by?	5
Say the division problem.	5 goes into 12
Write the problem and work it. (Pause.)	
Remember to write the whole number as a big number and the numerator and denominator small.	
4. $\frac{12}{5}$ equals what mixed number?	$2\dfrac{5}{5}$
(Repeat steps 1–3 with remaining problems.)	

FORMAT 12.13   **Converting Mixed Numbers to Improper Fractions**

TEACHER	STUDENTS

PART A: CONVERTING WHOLE NUMBERS

Board Presentation

1. (Write the following problem on the board.)

$$6 = \dfrac{\square}{4}$$

a. This problem says 6 wholes equal how many fourths? What does the problem say?	6 wholes equal how many fourths?
b. We want to figure out how many parts are used when we have 6 wholes. How many parts in each whole?	4
c. We're talking about the same number again and again, so we multiply 6×4. What numbers do we multiply?	6×4.
d. What is 6×4? (Pause, signal; write 24 in box.)	24
e. Yes, 6 whole units equal 24 fourths. If we use 6 whole units and there are 4 parts in each unit, we use 24 parts.	

   (Repeat steps 1–4 with the problems below.)

$$5 = \dfrac{\square}{3} \qquad 2 = \dfrac{\square}{6} \qquad 4 = \dfrac{\square}{5} \qquad 6 = \dfrac{\square}{3}$$

TEACHER	**STUDENTS**

Worksheet

1. *(Give students worksheets with problems such as the ones below.)*

   a. $5 = \dfrac{\square}{3}$ b. $2 = \dfrac{\square}{4}$

   c. $7 = \dfrac{\square}{2}$ d. $5 = \dfrac{\square}{9}$

2. Touch problem a.

3. Read the problem.

5 equals how many thirds?

4. How many parts in each whole unit?
   How many whole units?

3
5

5. What do we do to figure out how many parts are used up?
   Yes, we multiply 5×3. Multiply and write your answer in the box.

Multiply

6. Five equals how many thirds?

$\dfrac{15}{3}$

   Say the whole statement.

$5 = \dfrac{15}{3}$

   (Repeat steps 1–5 with half the problems, and then tell students to do the rest by themselves.)

PART B: STRUCTURED BOARD PRESENTATION

1. *(Write the following problem on the board.)*

   $6\dfrac{1}{4} = \dfrac{}{4}$

2. This problem says $6\frac{1}{4}$ equals how many fourths?
   What does this problem say?

$6\dfrac{1}{4}$ equals how many fourths?

3. First we figure out how many fourths in 6 whole units.
   Then we add on ¼. *(Write + between 6 and ¼.)*
   What do we do first?

Figure out how many fourths in 6 whole units.

4. There are 6 wholes with 4 parts in each whole.
   What do I do to figure how many parts are used?

Multiply 6×4.

5. What is 6×4 *(Pause.)*

24

   (Write the 24.)

   $6\dfrac{1}{4} = \dfrac{24 + 1}{4}$

6. How many parts are used in the last whole?

1

7. I add one part. *(Write + 1 in the numerator.)*

   $6\dfrac{1}{4} = \dfrac{24 + 1}{4} =$

8. What is $24 + 1$?

25

   (Write the following on the board.)

   $\dfrac{25}{4}$

(continued on next page)

FORMAT 12.13 (continued)

TEACHER	STUDENTS

9. So 6¼ = ²⁵⁄₄. Say that.

$$6\frac{1}{4} = \frac{25}{4}$$

   (Repeat steps 1–8 with these fractions.)

   $3\frac{2}{5}$ $7\frac{3}{4}$ $2\frac{3}{7}$ $5\frac{1}{4}$

PART C: STRUCTURED WORKSHEET

1. (Present a worksheet like the one below.)
   Convert these mixed numbers to improper fractions.

   a. $3\frac{1}{2}$ = _____ = _____

   b. $7\frac{3}{5}$ = _____ = _____

   c. $4\frac{2}{5}$ = _____ = _____

   d. $2\frac{3}{4}$ = _____ = _____

2. Read the mixed number in problem a.

   $3\frac{1}{2}$

3. How many parts in each whole unit?

   2

   Write 2 as the denominator in the new fraction.

   Students write 2.

4. First we see how many halves in 3 whole units.
   Then we add ½. How do we figure out how many
   halves in 3 wholes? (Pause.)

   Multiply 3 × 2.

   How many halves in 3 wholes? (Pause.)

   6

   Write 6.

   Students write 6.

5. How many parts in the last whole?

   1

   Write + 1.

   Students write $\frac{6 + 1}{2}$.

6. What is ⁶⁄₂ + ½?

   $\frac{7}{2}$

   Write equals ⁷⁄₂.

   Students write $= \frac{7}{2}$.

7. What fraction does 3 ½ equal?

   $\frac{7}{2}$

   (Repeat steps 1–6 with remaining problems.)

FORMAT 12.14 **Adding and Subtracting Fractions with Like Denominators**

TEACHER	STUDENTS

PART A: PICTORIAL DEMONSTRATION

1. *(Draw the following circles and lines on the board.)*

_____ + _____ = _____

2. Let's write a problem that will tell us how many parts are used in these wholes.

3. How many parts in each whole?   4

   (Write the denominators.)

   $$\frac{\ }{4} + \frac{\ }{4} = \frac{\ }{4}$$

   We're talking about wholes with 4 parts in each whole.

4. *(Point to first circle.)* How many parts are used in this whole?   3

   (Write the following on the board.)

   $$\frac{3}{4}$$

   (Point to second circle.) How many parts are used in this whole?   2

   (Write the following on the board.)

   $$\frac{3}{4} + \frac{2}{4} =$$

5. How many parts are used altogether?   5

   (Write the following on the board.)

   $$\frac{5}{4}$$

6. What does ¾ + ¾ equal? $\frac{5}{4}$

   (Repeat steps 1–5 with the problem below.)

_____ + _____ = _____

PART B: STRUCTURED BOARD PRESENTATION

1. We can only add and subtract fractions with the same number of parts in each whole. Listen again. *(Repeat rule. Write this problem.)*

   $$\frac{3}{4} + \frac{2}{5} =$$

2. Read this problem.

3. *(Point to ¾.)* How many parts in each whole?   4

   (Point to ⅖.) How many parts in each whole?   5

(continued on next page)

FORMAT 12.14 (continued)

TEACHER	STUDENTS

4. Can we add these fractions?   No

5. Right. We can only add fractions that have the same
   bottom number.

   (Repeat steps 2–5 with the problems below.)

$$\frac{3}{5} + \frac{2}{5} \qquad \frac{5}{7} - \frac{3}{9} \qquad \frac{3}{9} + \frac{3}{5}$$

$$\frac{4}{7} + \frac{2}{7} \qquad \frac{5}{7} - \frac{5}{9} \qquad \frac{4}{9} - \frac{3}{9}$$

   (Give individual turns.)

PART C: STRUCTURED WORKSHEET

1. *(Write the following problems on the board.)*

   a. $\frac{3}{5} + \frac{1}{5} =$ _____   f. $\frac{3}{4} - \frac{1}{4} =$ _____

   b. $\frac{3}{5} + \frac{2}{7} =$ _____   g. $\frac{6}{9} - \frac{2}{8} =$ _____

   c. $\frac{4}{7} - \frac{2}{7} =$ _____   h. $\frac{6}{9} + \frac{2}{9} =$ _____

   d. $\frac{5}{9} - \frac{2}{3} =$ _____   i. $\frac{5}{7} + \frac{3}{5} =$ _____

   e. $\frac{7}{9} + \frac{1}{9} =$ _____

2. Remember, you can only add and subtract fractions that
   tell about the same number of parts in each whole.

3. Touch problem a. Read the problem. $\frac{3}{5} + \frac{1}{5}$

4. Can we add these fractions the way they are now?   Yes

   (If the answer to step 3 is no, say to students) You can't
   work the problem, so cross it out. *(If the answer to
   step 3 is yes, do steps 4–6.)*

5. We're talking about fractions with 5 parts in each whole,
   so the answer will have 5 parts in each group. Write 5
   as the bottom number in the answer.

6. Look at the top numbers. They tell the number of parts
   used. What is 3 + 1?   4

   So what do you write for the top number in the answer? Write it.   4

7. Read the whole problem. $\frac{3}{5} + \frac{1}{5} = \frac{4}{5}$

   (Repeat steps 1–6 for the remaining problems.)

PART D: LESS STRUCTURED WORKSHEET

1. *(Give students a worksheet with a mix of four addition
   and four subtraction problems. About half of the problems
   should have like denominators.)*

TEACHER   **STUDENTS**

2. Read the first problem. If you can work it, write the
   answer. If you can't work the problem, cross it out.
   (Monitor student performance.)

FORMAT 12.15   **Preskill: Finding the Least Common Multiple**

TEACHER   **STUDENTS**

PART A: STRUCTURED BOARD PRESENTATION

1. *(Write the following numbers on the board.)*

   3   6   9   12   15   18
   5   10   15   20   25

2. *(Point to 3.)* These numbers are multiples of 3. Say them.   3, 6, 9, 12, 15, 18

   (Point to 5.) These numbers are multiples of 5. Say them.   5, 10, 15, 20, 25

3. What is the smallest number that is a multiple of 3 and 5?   15

   Yes, 15 is the least common multiple of 3 and 5. *(Repeat
   steps 1 and 2 with these examples: 2 and 8, 6 and 8, 3 and 9.)*

PART B: WORKSHEET PRESENTATION

1. *(Write the number which is the least common multiple
   for each pair of numbers.)*

   a. The LCM of 6 and 9 is _____.

   b. The LCM of 8 and 6 is _____.

   c. The LCM of 5 and 2 is _____.

   d. The LCM of 5 and 4 is _____.

   e. The LCM of 6 and 12 is _____.

   f. The LCM of 4 and 3 is _____.

   g. The LCM of 6 and 2 is _____.

   h. The LCM of 4 and 12 is _____.

   i. The LCM of 5 and 3 is _____.

   j. The LCM of 3 and 9 is _____.

2. The instructions tell us to find the least common multiple of
   the numbers. LCM means least common multiple. In
   problem a you must find the least common multiple of
   6 and 9. The least common multiple is the lowest number
   that is in both count-by series.

3. Say the numbers that are multiples of 6. *(Stop students at 30.)*   6, 12, 18, 24, 30

4. Say the numbers that are multiples of 9. *(Stop students at 45.)*   9, 18, 27, 36, 45

5. What is the least common multiple of 9 and 6? *(Pause, signal.)*   18

   Write it in the space.

   *(Repeat steps 1–4 with several more problems, and then
   have students work the rest of the problems on their own.)*

FORMAT 12.16 **Adding and Subtracting Fractions
with Unlike Denominators**

TEACHER	**STUDENTS**

PART A: STRUCTURED BOARD PRESENTATION

1. *(Write the following problem on the board.)*

$$\frac{2}{3} + \frac{1}{4} = \underline{\hspace{2cm}}$$

2. Read this problem.

$$\frac{2}{3} + \frac{1}{4}$$

Can we add these fractions the way they are written?

No

3. To work this problem, we must rewrite the fractions so they both have the same denominator. First, we figure out the least common multiple of the denominators. What is the denominator of the first fraction?

3

What is the denominator of the second fraction?

4

4. What is the least common multiple of 4 and 3? *(Pause, signal.)*

12

To correct: Say the numbers that are multiples of 3. Say the numbers that are multiples of 4. What is the least common multiple?

5. We must rewrite each fraction as equivalent fractions with denominators of 12. *(Write 12 under each denominator.)*

$$\frac{2}{3} + \frac{1}{4}$$
$$\quad 12 \quad 12$$

I want to rewrite 2/3 as a fraction that has 12 as a denominator. Remember, I don't want to change the value of ⅔. What fraction do I multiply ⅔ by to end with a fraction that has a denominator of 12? *(Pause, signal.)*

$$\frac{4}{4}$$

To correct: What is the denominator of ⅔? What must I multiply 3 by to end with 12? So I must multiply ⅔ times ¼. What do I multiply ⅔ by?

(Write ¼ in parentheses.)

$$\frac{2}{3}\left(\frac{4}{4}\right) + \frac{1}{4}$$
$$\quad 12 \qquad 12$$

What is 2 × 4? *(Pause, signal.)*

8

(Write 8.) What is 3 × 4? *(Pause, signal.)*

12

(Cross out ⅔. Write the 12.)

$$\frac{2}{3}\left(\frac{\cancel{4}}{\cancel{4}}\right)^{\!8} + \frac{1}{4}$$
$$\quad 12 \qquad 12$$

We rewrote ⅔ as ⁸⁄₁₂. What did we rewrite ⅔ as?

$$\frac{8}{12}$$

TEACHER	STUDENTS

6. Now let's rewrite ¼ as a fraction that has 12 as a denominator. Remember, I don't want to change the value of ¼. What fraction must I multiply ¼ by? *(Pause, signal.)*

$\dfrac{3}{3}$

To correct: What is the denominator of ¼? What do I multiply 4 by to end with 12? So I must multiply ¼ by ⅜. What do I multiply ¼ by?

(Write ⅜.)

$$\overset{8}{\underset{12}{\frac{2}{3}}}\left(\frac{\cancel{4}}{\cancel{4}}\right) + \overset{}{\underset{12}{\frac{1}{4}}}\left(\frac{3}{3}\right)$$

What is 1 × 3?

3

(Write 3.) What is 4 × 3?

12

(Cross out ¼. Write ³⁄₁₂.)

$$\overset{8}{\underset{12}{\frac{2}{3}}}\left(\frac{\cancel{4}}{\cancel{4}}\right) + \overset{3}{\underset{12}{\frac{\cancel{1}}{\cancel{4}}}}\left(\frac{3}{3}\right)$$

We rewrote ¼ as ³⁄₁₂. What did we rewrite ¼ as?

$\dfrac{3}{12}$

7. Now the denominators are the same and we can add. The problem now says ⁸⁄₁₂ + ³⁄₁₂. What does the problem say?

$\dfrac{8}{12} + \dfrac{3}{12}$

8. What is ⁸⁄₁₂ + ³⁄₁₂?

$\dfrac{11}{12}$

(Repeat steps 1–7 with the problems below.)

$$\frac{4}{5} - \frac{7}{10} \qquad \frac{3}{6} - \frac{1}{4} \qquad \frac{1}{9} + \frac{2}{3}$$

PART B: STRUCTURED WORKSHEET

1. *(Give students worksheets with problems like the ones below.)*

   a. $\dfrac{5}{6} - \dfrac{2}{4} =$ d. $\dfrac{5}{10} - \dfrac{2}{5} =$

   b. $\dfrac{2}{9} + \dfrac{2}{3} =$ e. $\dfrac{7}{9} - \dfrac{2}{3} =$

   c. $\dfrac{2}{3} - \dfrac{3}{5} =$ f. $\dfrac{2}{5} - \dfrac{1}{3} =$

2. Read problem a.

$\dfrac{5}{6} - \dfrac{2}{4}$

   Can we work the problem the way it is?

No

   (If the answer is yes, tell the students to work the problem. If the answer is no, continue the format.)

   Why not?

The denominators aren't the same.

(continued on next page)

FORMAT 12.16 (continued)

TEACHER	STUDENTS
3. What are the denominators?	6 and 4
What is the least common multiple of 6 and 4? *(Pause, signal.)*	12
Write 12 under each fraction.	
4. The first fraction says $\frac{5}{6}$. Write parentheses next to it. What fraction do you multiply $\frac{5}{6}$ by so that you'll end with a denominator of 12? *(Pause, signal.)*	$\frac{2}{2}$
Write $\frac{2}{2}$ in the parentheses.	
To correct: The denominator is 6; 6 times what number equals 12? So we must multiply a fraction that has 2 as a denominator. We don't want to change the value of $\frac{5}{6}$, so we multiply it by $\frac{2}{2}$.	
Let's multiply $\frac{5}{6}$ by $\frac{2}{2}$ and write the new fraction. What is 5×2?	10
Write 10 over the fraction. Five-sixths equals how many twelfths?	$\frac{10}{12}$
(Cross out 5/6.)	
5. The second fraction says $\frac{2}{4}$. Write parentheses next to it. What fraction do you multiply $\frac{2}{4}$ by so that you'll end with a denominator of 12? *(Pause, signal.)*	$\frac{3}{3}$
To correct: (same as step 3).	
Multiply $\frac{2}{4}$ by $\frac{3}{3}$ and write the new fraction. *(Pause.)* Two-fourths equals how many twelfths?	$\frac{6}{12}$
(Check students' papers.) Cross out $\frac{2}{4}$.	
6. Read the problem saying the rewritten fractions.	$\frac{10}{12} - \frac{6}{12}$
Can you work the problem now?	Yes
How do you know?	The denominators are the same.
7. Work the problem and write the answer.	
8. What is the answer?	$\frac{4}{12}$

PART C: LESS STRUCTURED WORKSHEET

1. *(Give students a worksheet like that for structured worksheet exercise.)*
2. Read problem a. Can we work the problem the way it is? *(If the answer is yes, tell students to work the problem. If the answer is no, continue the format.)* Why not?
3. What is the least common multiple of the denominators? *(Pause, signal.)* Write it under the fraction.
4. What fraction will you multiply the first fraction by so that it will have a denominator of ____________? *(Pause, signal.)*
5. What fraction will you multiply the second fraction by so that it has a denominator of ____________? *(Pause, signal.)*
6. Rewrite the fractions and work the problem. *(Pause.)*
7. What is your answer?

FORMAT 12.17 Multiplying Two Proper Fractions

TEACHER	**STUDENTS**

PART A: STRUCTURED BOARD PRESENTATION

1. *(Write the following problem on the board.)*

$$\frac{3}{4} \times \frac{2}{5} =$$

2. Read this problem.

$\frac{3}{4} \times \frac{2}{3} =$ what number?

3. We work times problems with fractions by multiplying top times the top and bottom times the bottom. How do we work times problems with fractions?

Top times the top; bottom times the bottom.

4. First we multiply top times the top. What is 3 × 2? *(Pause, signal.)*

6

(Write the 6.)

$$\frac{3}{4} \times \frac{2}{5} = \frac{6}{}$$

5. Now we multiply bottom times the bottom. What is 4 × 5? *(Pause, signal.)*

20

(Write the 20.)

$$\frac{3}{4} \times \frac{2}{5} = \frac{6}{20}$$

6. What does ¾ × ⅖ equal?

$\frac{6}{20}$

(Repeat steps 1–5 with several more problems.)

PART B: STRUCTURED WORKSHEET

1. *(Give students worksheets with a mix of multiplication, addition, and subtraction problems.)*

a. $\frac{3}{4} + \frac{2}{4} = \frac{\square}{\square}$ b. $\frac{3}{2} \times \frac{4}{2} = \frac{\square}{\square}$

c. $\frac{6}{3} - \frac{1}{3} = \frac{\square}{\square}$ d. $\frac{6}{3} \times \frac{1}{3} = \frac{\square}{\square}$

2. When you times fractions, you work top times top and bottom times bottom. When you times fractions, what do you do?

Top times top and bottom times bottom.

3. But when you plus or minus fractions, you work only across the top. When you add or subtract fractions, what do you do?

Work only across the top.

4. What do you do when you add or subtract fractions?

Work across the top.

What do you do when you times fractions?
(Repeat step 3 until firm.)

Top times top and bottom times bottom.

5. Touch problem a. Read the problem.

$\frac{3}{4} + \frac{2}{4}$

What type of problem is this?

Plus

What do you do when you plus fractions?

Work across the top.

Work the problem. *(Pause.)* What's the answer?

(Repeat step 4 with remaining problems.)

FORMAT 12.18   Multiplying a Fraction and a Whole Number

TEACHER	STUDENTS

PART A: CONVERTING A WHOLE NUMBER TO A FRACTION

1. Listen to this rule: We can change a whole number into a fraction by giving it a denominator of 1. How do we change a whole number into a fraction?

   Give it a denominator of 1.

2. *(Write on board: 3.)* What number is this?

   3

   How do I change it into a fraction?

   Give it a denominator of 1.

   Watch me change 3 into a fraction.

   (Write 1 under 3.)

   $$\frac{3}{1}$$

   A 3 over 1 is the same as 3. I'll draw a picture to show you that $\frac{3}{1}$ equals 3.

   (Draw the following circles.)

   $\frac{3}{1} = \bigcirc \bigcirc \bigcirc$

   We have three wholes used up.

3. *(Write on board: 5.)* How do I change 5 into a fraction?

   Give it a denominator of 1.

   Yes, 5 over 1 equals 5 wholes. *(Write the fraction.)*

   $$\frac{5}{1}$$

   (Repeat step 3 with 2, 9, 4, 8.)

PART B: STRUCTURED BOARD

1. *(Write the following problem on the board.)*

   $$\frac{3}{4} \times 8 = \underline{\hspace{1cm}} = \overline{)\hspace{1cm}} = \square$$

2. Listen to this rule about multiplying fractions: A fraction can only be multiplied by another fraction. Listen again.

   (Repeat the rule.)

3. Read this problem. *(Point to $\frac{3}{4}$.)*

   $\frac{3}{4} \times 8$

   Is this fraction multiplied by another fraction?

   No

   So before we can work the problem we have to change 8 into a fraction. How do I change 8 into a fraction?

   Give it a denominator of 1.

   (Write the problem.)

   $$\frac{3}{4} \times \frac{8}{1} =$$

4. Now we're ready to multiply across the top and bottom. What is 3×8?

   24

   (Write 24.)

   What is 4×1?

   4

   (Write $\frac{24}{4}$.)

TEACHER	STUDENTS
5. Does ²⁴⁄₄ equal more or less than one whole?	More
How do we figure out how many whole groups ²⁴⁄₄ equals?	Divide 4 into 24.
Four goes into 24 how many times?	6
(Write 6 in box.)	
6. What does 3/4 × 8 equal?	6
(Repeat steps 2–5 with the problems below.)	

$$\frac{2}{3} \times 9 \qquad \frac{3}{5} \times 10 \qquad \frac{1}{4} \times 8$$

PART C: STRUCTURED WORKSHEET

1. *(Give students worksheets with problems similar to the following problem:)*

$$\frac{2}{3} \times 7 = \underline{\quad} = \overline{)\quad\quad} = \square$$

2. Touch problem a. Read it.	$\frac{2}{3} \times 7$ = how many?
Is ⅔ multiplied by another fraction?	No
So what do you have to do?	Change 7 into a fraction.
Do it. *(Monitor responses.)*	
3. Now multiply the fractions. *(Monitor responses.)*	
What fraction did you end up with?	$\frac{14}{3}$
4. Is ¹⁴⁄₃ more or less than one whole group?	More
How do you figure out how many whole groups?	Divide 3 into 14.
Divide—don't forget to write the remainder as a fraction.	
5. What does ⅔ × 7 equal?	$4\frac{2}{3}$

(Repeat steps 1–4 with remaining problems.)

FORMAT 12.19 **Writing Regular Division Problems from Fractions**

TEACHER   **STUDENTS**

1. *(Write the following on the board.)*

$$\frac{12}{3} \quad \overline{)\quad\quad}$$

2. I'll show you how to write fractions as regular division problems. You just read the fraction as a division problem. Then you know what to write. I will read this fraction as a division problem. Remember that we read the big number first for a division problem. This fraction can be read as 12 ÷ 3.

3. That's what I write: 12 ÷ 3. 12 is the big number and 3 is the first small number. *(Write 3 and 12.)*

$$\frac{12}{3} \quad 3\overline{)12}$$

(continued on next page)

FORMAT 12.19 (continued)

TEACHER	STUDENTS
(Write the next fraction.)	

$$\frac{40}{8}$$

4. Here's another fraction. Read it as a division problem. Get ready. *(Signal.)* — 40 ÷ 8

5. I want to write it as a regular division problem. What do I write for the big number? *(Signal.)* — 40

   What do I write for the first small number? *(Signal.)* — 8

   (Write 8 and 40.)

   $$\frac{40}{8} \qquad 8\overline{)40}$$

6. The answer to the division problem is the answer to the fraction problem. 40 ÷ 8 = what number? — 5
   (Write 5.)

   $$\frac{40}{8} \qquad 8\overline{)40}^{\,5}$$

(Continue with other fraction examples until firm.)

CHAPTER 13

Decimals

TERMS AND CONCEPTS

Decimal Fractions   Fractions with a denominator of 10 or any power of 10: ¹⁄₁₀, ¹⁄₁₀₀, ¹⁄₁₀₀₀, etc.

Decimals   Decimals are similar to fractions in that they both deal with something that has been divided into equal parts. Decimals are restricted, however, to situations with 10 parts or any power of 10 (10, 100, 1000, etc.). In a decimal, the number of equal parts is not indicated by a denominator but rather through place value. The position of a number in relation to a decimal point expresses the number of equal parts. For example, one digit after the decimal point indicates 10 equal parts; two digits after the decimal point indicate 100 equal parts. The value of the digit represents the number of parts present, used, or acted upon. For example, .5 equals ⁵⁄₁₀ and .5 represents a division into 10 equal parts with 5 parts present.

Mixed Decimal   An expression consisting of a whole number and a decimal: e.g., 3.24, 18.05.

Percent   The symbol % is read "percent." It represents the ratio of two quantities with the denominator being hundredths. The fraction ²⁄₅ may be converted to an equivalent fraction, ⁴⁰⁄₁₀₀, which in turn may be expressed as 40%. When presenting the various forms of rational numbers, teachers must consider their interrelatedness. Problem-solving strategies designed for teaching fractions should be presented in a manner that will prepare students for decimals. Likewise, the strategies presented for decimals should prepare students for percent.

The Instructional Sequence and Assessment Chart illustrates the seven main areas covered in decimal instruction:

1. Reading and writing decimals and mixed decimal numbers
2. Converting decimals to equivalent decimals
3. Adding and subtracting decimals
4. Multiplying decimals
5. Rounding off decimals
6. Dividing decimals
7. Converting values between the decimal notation system and fraction notation system

The chart also illustrates the relationship of the various skill areas to one another with respect to the sequence of their introduction. Note that analyzing fractions is a preskill for decimals. Students must understand what the numerator and denominator in a fraction represent: the denominator signifying the parts in each whole; the numerator, the parts that are used. They must also understand the concept of whole units versus parts of a whole. An understanding of fraction analysis skills is critical, since decimals are explained as an alternative representation of fractions that have 10 or a multiple of 10 (100, 1000, etc.) as a denominator.

Also, note that reading and writing decimals are component skills for all the other decimal operations. Too frequently, an insufficient amount of instructional time is allotted to teaching students to accurately read and write decimals. Without adequate practice on these basic decimal reading and writing skills, students will encounter unnecessary difficulty when more advanced decimal skills are introduced.

Instructional Sequence and Assessment Chart

Grade Level	Problem Type	Performance Indicator
4a	Reading tenths and hundredths	Circle the correct decimal: five-tenths 5 .05 .5 four-hundredths 4 .04 .4 seven-hundredths 70 .70 .07
4b	Writing tenths and hundredths	Write these fractions as decimal numbers: $\dfrac{5}{100} =$ $\dfrac{5}{10} =$ $\dfrac{19}{100} =$

4c	Reading mixed decimals: tenths and hundredths	Circle the correct mixed decimal:
		five and three-tenths
		    .53 5.03 5.3
		ten and four-hundredths
		    1.04 10.04 10.4
		eighteen and six-hundredths
		    18.6 1.86 18.06

4d	Writing mixed decimals: tenths and hundredths	Write the mixed decimal for each mixed number: $10\dfrac{14}{100}$ _____ $16\dfrac{3}{10}$ _____ $40\dfrac{18}{100}$ _____
4e	Column alignment: adding tenths, hundredths, and whole numbers	Write these problems in columns and work them: 8.23 + 12.1 + 6 = 7 + .3 + 45 = .08 + 4 + .6 =
4f	Subtracting tenths and hundredths from whole numbers	5 − 3.2 = 8 − .34 = 7 − .3 =
4g	Ordering mixed decimals	Rewrite these numbers in order, beginning with the smallest: 18.8 10.10 10.3 10.03 _____ _____ _____ _____
5a	Reading thousandths	Circle the correct decimal: five-thousands .05 .5 .005 .500 ninety-thousandths .90 .900 .090 .009

Grade Level	Problem Type	Performance Indicator
5b	Writing thousandths	Write these fractions as decimals: $\dfrac{342}{1000} =$ $\dfrac{60}{1000} =$ $\dfrac{5}{1000} =$
5c	Multiplying decimals: one-digit or two-digit factor times three-digit factor	$\begin{array}{r} 7.14 \\ \times\ .5 \\ \hline \end{array}$ $\begin{array}{r} 214 \\ \times\ .7 \\ \hline \end{array}$
5d	Multiplying decimals: zero to be placed after decimal point	$\begin{array}{r} .1 \\ \times\ .7 \\ \hline \end{array}$ $\begin{array}{r} .02 \\ \times\ .8 \\ \hline \end{array}$
5e	Rounding off decimals	Round off these numbers to the nearest whole number: 8.342 _____ 7.812 _____ Round off these numbers to the nearest tenth: 8.34 _____ 9.782 _____ Round off these numbers to the nearest hundredth: 8.346 _____ 9.782 _____
5f	Dividing: whole number divisor, no remainder	$5\overline{)32.45}$ $7\overline{)215.6}$ $2\overline{).856}$
5g	Dividing by whole number: quotient begins with zero	$9\overline{).036}$ $9\overline{).36}$ $9\overline{).0036}$
5h	Rounding off where there is a 9 or 99 after the decimal	Round off these numbers to the nearest tenth: 9.961 _____ 19.942 _____ 29.981 _____ Round off these numbers to the nearest hundredth: 14.993 _____ 14.996 _____ 29.9982 _____
5i	Dividing: whole number divisor, zeroes must be added to dividend after decimal point	Divide and write answer as mixed decimal: $2\overline{)3}$ $5\overline{)3.1}$ $4\overline{)21}$
5j	Dividing: whole number divisor, rounding off	Divide: write answer to mixed decimal; round off to the nearest hundredth: $7\overline{)3.1}$ $9\overline{)7}$ $3\overline{)2}$
5k	Converting proper fraction to decimal; no rounding off required	Rewrite these fractions as decimals: $\dfrac{2}{5} =$ $\dfrac{3}{4} =$ $\dfrac{3}{10} =$

Instructional Sequence and Assessment Chart (continued)

Grade Level	Problem Type	Performance Indicator
5l	Converting proper fraction to decimal: rounding off required	Rewrite these fractions as decimals; round off to nearest hundredth: $\frac{3}{7} =$ $\frac{4}{6} =$ $\frac{2}{9} =$
5m	Multiplying mixed decimal by 10 or 100: no zeroes added	$10 \times 34.2 =$ $100 \times 34.52 =$ $10 \times 34.52 =$
5n	Multiplying mixed decimal by 10 or 100: zeroes added	$100 \times 34.2 =$ $100 \times 3.42 =$ $100 \times 342 =$ $10 \times 342 =$
5o	Dividing: divisor is decimal, no adding zeroes in dividend necessary	$.2\overline{)23.74}$ $.2\overline{)14.26}$ $.05\overline{).345}$
5p	Same as above: adding zero in dividend required	$.5\overline{)13}$ $.50\overline{)275}$ $.02\overline{)3.1}$ $.05\overline{)2}$
5q	Converting decimal to fractions	Circle the correct answer: .75 equals $\frac{1}{4}$ $\frac{5}{7}$ $\frac{2}{3}$ $\frac{3}{4}$ .8 equals $\frac{4}{5}$ $\frac{8}{8}$ $\frac{1}{8}$ $\frac{2}{5}$ .67 equals $\frac{1}{4}$ $\frac{2}{3}$ $\frac{6}{7}$ $\frac{1}{6}$
5r	Converting mixed numbers to mixed decimals	Rewrite these mixed fractions as mixed decimals: $2\frac{3}{5} =$ $7\frac{1}{4} =$

READING AND WRITING DECIMALS AND MIXED DECIMALS

This section includes procedures for teaching students to read and write decimals and mixed decimals expressed as tenths, hundredths, and thousandths. Early direct instruction procedures for teaching students how to read and write decimals focus student attention on the number of digits after the decimal point (i.e., one digit after the decimal point indicates tenths; two digits after the decimal point indicate hundredths; three digits after the decimal point indicate thousandths).

Decimals and mixed decimals representing tenths and hundredths are usually introduced in fourth grade, while decimals and mixed decimals representing thousandths are introduced in fifth grade. The sequence for introducing these skills follows:

1. Reading decimals representing tenths or hundredths
2. Writing decimals representing tenths or hundredths
3. Reading and writing mixed decimals; decimals represent tenths or hundredths
4. Reading decimals representing thousandths
5. Writing decimals representing thousandths
6. Reading and writing mixed decimals; decimals represent thousandths

Note that students are taught to write decimal numbers immediately after they can read them.

Reading Decimals Representing Tenths and Hundredths

The format for reading decimals (Format 13.1) introduces students to decimals as an alternative system for writing fractions of tenths and hundredths. The teacher begins by writing two fractions on the board, one with 10 as a denominator and one with 100 as a denominator (e.g., $\frac{3}{10}$, $\frac{23}{100}$) and has students read the fractions. Next, the teacher explains that there is another way to express fractions that have 10 or 100 as a denominator. In this alternative method, a decimal point is used in place of the denominator. The teacher explains that if one digit is written after the decimal point, the decimal tells how many tenths; but if two digits are written after the decimal point, the decimal tells how many hundredths. (If students are unfamiliar with the term *digit*, they should be told that a digit is any written numeral from 0 to 9.)

After telling students the rule regarding the number of digits after the decimal, the teacher has the students read a list of numbers comprised of an equal mixture of tenths and hundredths decimals. Several minimally different sets (e.g., .07, .70, .7 and .4, .04, .40) are included among the examples. Included in the minimally different sets would be three decimal numbers: a decimal representing tenths (e.g., .8) and two decimals representing hundredths. In one of these hundredth decimals, a zero would precede the numeral (.08) while in the other hundredth decimal, the zero would follow the numeral (.80). The purpose of these minimally different sets is to focus student attention on the number of digits following the decimal.

The correction for errors in reading decimals is to have students identify the number of places after the decimal and then model and test identifying the decimal. For example, if a student misreads .04 as four tenths, the teacher says, "How many digits after the decimal? So what does the 4 tell about?"

A critical teacher behavior for this format is monitoring student responses. To avoid student problems in confusing whole numbers and decimal numbers, teachers should be sure that students are adding the "ths" endings to tens, hundreds, and thousands. For example, teachers should be sure .40 is pronounced as "forty hundredths," not "forty hundreds." Individual turns should be given frequently during the first several lessons. Practice on reading decimal numbers would be presented daily for 2 or 3 weeks. After the first several lessons, the teacher need not present all of the steps in Part A but would just write decimals on the board and have students read them (step 4).

Part B includes a worksheet exercise designed both to provide practice in reading decimals and to reinforce the relationship between decimal fractions and decimals. Students are given worksheets with two types of items. In the first type, a decimal number is written to the left of three fractions:

$$.8 \;=\; \frac{8}{10} \quad \frac{8}{100} \quad \frac{1}{8}$$

The students read the decimal and then circle the fraction equivalent of the decimal number. In the second type, a fraction is written, and students must find the corresponding decimal among several similar-looking decimals:

$$\frac{4}{100} \;=\; .4 \quad .40 \quad .04$$

About five of each type of item should appear daily on worksheets for several weeks.

Writing Decimals Representing Tenths and Hundredths

Writing decimals representing tenths and hundredths is introduced after students can read those decimals accurately. A format for teaching students to write these decimals appears in Format 13.2, which includes three parts. Part A is a structured board format in which the teacher demonstrates how to write a decimal fraction as a decimal. The teacher writes a fraction on the board and has the students read it. The teacher then asks how many digits there must be after the decimal point and models writing the fraction as a decimal number. Special attention must be given to fractions with a hundred as the denominator and with a numerator of less than 10 (e.g., $\frac{7}{100}$, $\frac{3}{100}$, $\frac{1}{100}$). When presenting these examples, the teacher demonstrates that in order to make two digits after the decimal, a zero must be written immediately after the decimal point. For example, in writing 7/100, the teacher would write .07.

Practice on writing decimal numbers should be provided daily for several weeks. This practice can be provided in written worksheets containing fractions with 10 or 100 as the denominator. The students would be required to write the decimal equivalents.

The example selection guideline is basically the same as that for the reading decimals format. Several minimally different sets (e.g., 3/10, 3/100, 80/100) would be included to provide students with the practice to determine when a zero is needed immediately after the decimal point. Several extra examples of hundredths fractions with a numerator below 10 also would be included to provide extra practice on this difficult type of decimal.

Reading and Writing Mixed Decimals: Tenths and Hundredths

When the students are able to read and write tenths and hundredths decimals without prompting from the teacher, mixed decimals, numbers formed by a whole number and a decimal (e.g., 9.3, 16.4, 27.02), can be introduced. Students are first taught to read mixed decimals, then to write them. The format for these skills appears in Format 13.3. In Part A, the board presentation, the teacher introduces reading mixed decimals, explaining that the numerals before the decimal point represent whole numbers, while the numerals after the decimal point tell about the decimal number. The teacher then models and tests reading several numbers, having the students say the whole number, the decimal, and then the mixed decimal. Note that in reading mixed decimals, the teacher should heavily emphasize the word *and* (e.g., 15.03 should be read "fifteen *and* three hundredths"). This voice emphasis is designed to help students discriminate between the whole number and the decimal parts of the mixed decimal in preparation for writing mixed decimals. Reading mixed decimals is practiced daily for several weeks. No prompting is recommended after the first several days.

Part B, a structured worksheet exercise, includes two types of items. In the first type, a mixed fraction is written, and the student rewrites it as a mixed decimal:

$$12 \frac{3}{100} \text{ is written as } 12.03$$

In the second type, the words representing a mixed decimal are written and the student must write the mixed decimal; for example, twenty-eight and four hundredths is written as 28.04. This type of item is appropriate, of course, only for students able to decode well.

Reading and Writing Decimals Representing Thousandths

Decimals representing thousandths are introduced after students have mastered reading and writing decimals and mixed decimals representing tenths and hundredths. Thousandths decimals are taught with the same basic formats as used for reading and writing tenth and hundredth decimals (see Formats 13.1 and 13.2) with the added explanation that if there are three digits after the decimal point, the decimal tells about thousandths.

During the first several lessons, examples should concentrate entirely on thousandth numbers. Minimally different groupings such as

.800	.080	.008
.004	.040	.400
.070	.007	.700

should be presented. In these sets, two of the three digits in each decimal are zeroes and one digit is a numeral other than zero. In each decimal, the nonzero digit is placed in another position:

.003	.030	.300

After several lessons comprised of just thousandth decimals, the teacher presents examples including tenths, hundredths, and thousandths. In these example sets, minimally different groupings should be included to focus student attention on the number of digits after the decimal point:

.4	.04	.004
.70	.070	.700

Writing decimals representing thousandths is particularly difficult because students must discriminate when to write two zeroes after the decimal point (e.g., .001, .009) from when to write one zero after the decimal point (e.g., .010, .090). Therefore, the teacher should be prepared to provide extensive practice on examples of this type.

EQUIVALENT DECIMALS

Equivalent decimals are decimals that have the same value. The mixed decimals 8.30 and 8.3 are equivalent since they both represent the same quantity. Converting a decimal, mixed decimal, or whole number to an equivalent mixed decimal is an important preskill for addition, subtraction, and division operations with decimal numbers. For example, when subtracting .39 from 5, students must convert 5 into 5.00. Students should be introduced to equivalent decimal conversions shortly after they can read and write decimals and mixed decimal numbers.

Format 13.4 shows how to teach students to convert decimals into equivalent decimals. Although the rewriting skill is simple, since the students simply add or take away zeroes, students should understand why adding or taking away zeroes is permissible. Part A illustrates the rationale behind adding zeroes by using equivalent fractions. The teacher demonstrates that changing a fraction like ³⁄₁₀ to ³⁰⁄₁₀₀ involves multiplying by a fraction equal to 1 (¹⁰⁄₁₀) and therefore does not change the value of the original fraction. Since ³⁄₁₀ = ³⁰⁄₁₀₀, then .3 = .30.

Part B is a structured board exercise demonstrating how to rewrite decimals. Part C is a worksheet exercise in which the students are given a chart containing columns for whole numbers, tenths, hundredths, and thousandths. The student's task is to write equivalent mixed decimals in other spaces across the row. For example, 9.1 is written in the tenths column. The student would add a zero, writing 9.10 in the hundredths column; and add two zeroes, writing 9.100 in the thousandths column. For whole numbers, the teacher explains that a whole number is converted into a mixed decimal by writing a decimal point after the number and writing zero(es) after the decimal point.

ADDING AND SUBTRACTING DECIMALS AND MIXED DECIMALS

Addition and subtraction problems with decimals and/or mixed decimals can be divided into two groups for instructional purposes. The first group contains those problems in which each number in the problem has the same number of decimal places; for example, in the problems below, all numbers have decimals representing hundredths:

$$
\begin{array}{r} 435.42 \\ + 17.82 \end{array}
\qquad
\begin{array}{r} 24.35 \\ - 1.48 \end{array}
$$

The second group is comprised of those problems in which the addends (in an addition problem) or the minuend and subtrahend (in a subtraction problem) have different numbers of digits after the decimal point:

$$
\begin{array}{r} 9.1 \\ - 3.87 \end{array}
\qquad
\begin{array}{r} 4 \\ + 3.64 \end{array}
\qquad
\begin{array}{r} 4.23 \\ - 3.645 \end{array}
$$

Decimals Having the Same Number of Places

Problems in which each number has the same number of digits after the decimal point can be introduced when students can read and write decimals and mixed decimals. Problems of this type are relatively easy. The only new step involves placing the decimal point in the answer. Because the teaching procedure is simple, no format has been included.

The first problems should be vertically aligned so students can be taught to bring the decimal point straight down without first having to determine if the columns are properly aligned. For these problems, the teacher just instructs students to write the decimal in the answer below the other decimal points.

Problems written horizontally (e.g., 7.24 + 19.36) can be introduced shortly after the introduction of vertically aligned problems. For horizontal problems, we recommend teaching students to rewrite the problem so that the decimal points are in a column. When horizontal problems are introduced, teachers should monitor student worksheets daily to see that students align the numbers correctly.

Decimals with Different Number of Places

Problems in which each mixed decimal has a different number of digits after the decimal point are introduced after students can rewrite decimal numbers as equivalent decimal numbers by adding zeroes after the decimal. This typically is only a week or two after the easier addition and subtraction problems are presented. The strategy for solving these more complex problems involves rewriting one or more of the mixed decimal numbers so that each mixed decimal in the problem has the same number of digits after the decimal point. Once the problem has been rewritten, students are instructed to bring the decimal point straight down, and then solve the problem. For example,

$$
\begin{array}{r} 8.1 \\ - 3.42 \end{array}
\quad \text{becomes} \quad
\begin{array}{r} 8.10 \\ - 3.42 \end{array}
$$

Horizontally written problems should be introduced once students can solve the vertical problems. The key to accurately solving horizontal problems is correctly aligning the numbers vertically. Without direct instruction, students are likely to misalign the numbers, as illustrated below:

$$3.72 + 18.4 \quad \text{becomes} \quad \begin{array}{r} 3.72 \\ + 18.4 \\ \hline \end{array}$$

The strategy for rewriting the decimal numbers so that each has the same number of digits after the decimal will prevent this alignment error from occurring. Format 13.5 shows how to present this type of problem.

Problems in which a decimal or mixed decimal is added to or subtracted from a whole number should receive special emphasis (e.g., $7 - 3.8$, $8 - .43$, $4.23 + 7 + 2.1$, $9.2 - 3$). Problems of this type are introduced several days after problems with mixed decimals expressing various decimal fractions are introduced. The teacher reminds students that a whole number is converted to a mixed decimal by placing a decimal point after it and adding zeroes. The teacher models solving several problems. About half of the problems on students' worksheets should include problems with a whole number.

ROUNDING OFF DECIMALS

Rounding off is not only a useful skill in and of itself but is also a necessary component skill for decimal division and percent. An example of rounding off in percentage problems occurs when converting ⅗ to a percent: The 3 is divided by 7, which yields a decimal:

$$7 \overline{\smash{)}3.000} \begin{array}{c} .428 \\ \end{array}$$

The decimal then is rounded off to hundredths to determine the approximate percent, 43%. Although rounding off decimals involves steps similar to those used in rounding off whole numbers, these two skills should not be introduced at the same time because of potential confusion. Rounding off whole numbers should have been presented many months before rounding off decimals is introduced.

Format 13.6 shows how to present rounding off decimal numbers to the nearest whole number, tenth, hundredth, or thousandth. The rounding-off strategy taught in this format is comprised of three steps:

1. The students determine how many digits will appear after the decimal point when the number is rounded off; for example, when rounding

off to the nearest tenth, one digit will be left after the decimal.

2. The students count that number of digits and then draw a line. If 3.4825 is to be rounded to the nearest tenth, the students place a line after the digit in the tenth place, the 4: 3.4|825. The line serves as a prompt.

3. The students look at the numeral after the line. If it is a 5 or more, they add another unit to the digit before the line. For example .54|7 rounded to the nearest hundredth is .55, since 7 appears after the line. If a number less than 5 appears after the line, no extra unit is added. For example, .54|2 is rounded to .54, since a number less than 5 follows the line.

There are three important example selection guidelines for this format:

1. Half of the decimals should require the addition of another unit; that is, the numeral after the place to be rounded off should be 5 through 9. In the other half of the decimals, the numeral after the place to be rounded off should be less than 5.

2. The numbers should have two or three places after the place to be rounded off. These extra places reinforce the concept that only the digit immediately after the line determines if another unit is added.

3. Examples should include a mix of problems that require students to round off to the nearest tenth or to the nearest hundredth. The sample worksheet in Part B of the format shows an application of these guidelines.

A particularly difficult type of rounding-off problem arises when a unit is added to a 9, because the sum is 10. For example, rounding off .498 to the nearest hundredth requires students to add a whole unit to the nine-hundredths, which changes .498 to .50. Likewise, when rounding off 39.98 to the nearest tenth, the answer is 40.0. Problems of this type should be introduced after students have mastered easier rounding-off problems. When introducing the more difficult type, the teacher should model working several problems.

Most errors in rounding off occur because students do not attend to the relevant digit. A student is likely to round off .328 to .4 if she focuses on the 8 rather than the 2. The basic correction is to emphasize the steps in the strategy by asking the student:

1. How many digits will there be after the decimal when we round off to the nearest whole (or tenth or hundredth)?

2. Where do you draw the line?
3. What number comes just after the line?
4. So do you add another whole (or tenth or hundredth)?

MULTIPLYING DECIMALS

Although the concept of multiplying decimals is difficult to illustrate, teaching students to solve a multiplication problem with decimal numbers is relatively simple. A possible demonstration to illustrate the rationale of the multiplying decimal strategy can be done with decimal fractions like these:

$$\frac{32}{100} \times \frac{4}{10}$$

The answer, $\frac{128}{1000}$, would then be written as the decimal .128. The original problem would then be written in a decimal form: .32 × .4, and the teacher would point out the three decimal places in the two fractions and make three decimal places in the answer. "The total number of decimal places in the factors is the same as the number of decimal places as the answer: .32 has two places; .4 has one place. That's three decimal places. The answer has three decimal places, too."

Format 13.7 is a strategy for multiplying decimals or mixed decimal numbers. In the board presentation, the teacher introduces the strategy for figuring out where the decimal point goes in the answer. In the worksheet presentation, the teacher gives the student a worksheet with 10 to 15 multiplication problems that have answers and leads students in determining where to place the decimal point. Note that in the problems on the worksheet, the decimal point in the factors appears in several different positions.

The less structured worksheet exercise includes a mix of multiplication and addition problems. The purpose of combining multiplication with addition is to ensure that students do not overgeneralize (to addition) the procedure of counting the places to determine where to put the decimal. A worksheet might include these examples:

9.4	9.4	3.2
× .5	+ .5	× .57
.32	40	18
+ .57	× 3	× .32
.18	31.4	3.14
+ 32	× .05	+ .05

Before the students work the problems, the teacher should remind them about placing the deci-

mal point in different types of problems. "In addition problems, bring the decimal point straight down. In multiplication problems, count the digits after the decimal points in the numbers you multiply." The teacher should then carefully monitor the students as they work the first several problems.

A potentially confusing type of multiplication problem is one in which the students must place a zero in front of the digits in the answer. For example, when multiplying .4 × .2, the student must add a zero before the 8: .4 × .2 = .08. Likewise, in .5 × .01, the student must place two zeroes after the decimal: .5 × .01 = .005. This type of problem is introduced after the easier types of problems. The teacher models solving several problems of this type, and then includes about three such problems in daily worksheet assignments.

A common error found on independent seatwork occurs when students simply forget to put the decimal point in the answer. The correction is merely to inform the students that they forgot to put in the decimal point. However, if the error occurs frequently, the teacher should prepare worksheets with about 10 to 15 problems, two-thirds of which contain decimals. In presenting the worksheet, the teacher tells students that the worksheet was designed to try to fool them, that some of the problems require decimal points in the answer and some don't. The teacher then monitors closely as students complete the worksheet so that immediate corrections can be made.

DIVIDING DECIMALS

Dividing decimal numbers is the most difficult decimal operation. Division with decimal numbers can be introduced when students can read and write decimals and perform long division. When long division with whole numbers was taught, the teacher should have stressed placing the digits in the quotient over the proper places in the dividend. For example, when working the problem 186 ÷ 2, the quotient should be written as in example a, not example b:

a. $2\overline{)186}$ with 93   b. $2\overline{)186}$ with 93

If students have not learned to write numerals in the quotient in the proper position, errors of misplacing the decimal in the quotient are likely to occur.

$2\overline{)1.86}$ with 9.3   rather than $2\overline{)1.86}$ with .93

Procedures for teaching proper placement of the digits in the quotients of long division problems are discussed in Chapter 10.

Division problems with decimals can be categorized into four types of difficulty. The first three types have whole numbers as divisors.

1. Problems in which the quotient does not have a remainder and that require no conversion of the dividend:

$$5\overline{)3.45}^{\,.69} \quad \text{or} \quad 7\overline{).21}^{\,.03}$$

2. Problems in which the dividend must be converted to an equivalent decimal so that no remainder will be present:

$$
\begin{array}{c}
5\overline{)3.7}^{\,.7} \\
\underline{3\ 5} \\
2
\end{array}
\quad \text{becomes} \quad
\begin{array}{c}
5\overline{)3.70}^{\,.74} \\
\underline{3\ 5} \\
20 \\
\underline{20}
\end{array}
$$

3. Problems with a remainder that requires rounding off:

$$
\begin{array}{c}
7\overline{)2.40\,|\,0}^{\,.34\,|\,2} = .34 \\
\underline{2\ 1} \\
30 \\
\underline{28} \\
20 \\
\underline{14} \\
6
\end{array}
$$

4. Problems in which the divisor is a decimal or mixed decimal number and must be converted to a whole number

$$.4\overline{)61.32} \quad \text{becomes} \quad .4\overline{)61.32}$$

Decimal or Mixed Decimal Divided by a Whole Number

Division problems in which the dividend is a mixed decimal or decimal number and the divisor a whole number are usually introduced in late fourth or early-to-mid-fifth grade. An elaborate format is not required to introduce the problem type in which the divisor goes into the dividend without leaving any remainder:

$$5\overline{)2.35} \qquad 7\overline{)84.7}$$

The teacher presents the rule that the decimal point must be written on the line directly above where it appears in the number being divided. For example,

when dividing 69.26 by 6, the student writes the problem:

$$6\overline{)69.26}$$

then places the decimal point on the quotient line directly above the decimal in the dividend:

$$6\overline{)69.26}^{\,.}$$

The teacher then leads students through working several sets of problems, emphasizing the need to place the digits in the quotient in their proper place.

There are two example-selection guidelines for problems without remainders. First, the decimal point should appear in different positions in various problems:

a. $5\overline{)3.725}$ b. $2\overline{)184.6}$ c. $9\overline{)1.836}$

d. $7\overline{).364}$ e. $5\overline{)23.5}$ f. $5\overline{).215}$

Second, one or two problems in which a zero must be placed immediately after the decimal point should be included. In problems d and f above, the quotients are .052 and .043. The teacher may have to provide extra prompting on these problems by explaining that a digit must be written in every place after the decimal point. Therefore, in problem d, the teacher might say, "7 doesn't go into 3, so write a zero above the 3." Daily practice would include 6 to 10 problems.

The second type of decimal division problem requires the student to eliminate a remainder by rewriting the dividend as an equivalent decimal. For example, zeroes need to be added to the dividend in each of the following problems:

a. $5\overline{)3.1} = 5\overline{)3.10}^{\,.62}$ c. $4\overline{)3} = 4\overline{)3.00}^{\,.75}$

b. $2\overline{)3.45} = 2\overline{)3.450}^{\,1.725}$ d. $5\overline{)2} = 5\overline{)2.0}^{\,.4}$

This type of problem is introduced about 2 weeks after decimal division problems without remainders.

The preskill of converting a decimal to an equivalent decimal should be taught prior to the introduction of this problem type. These problems are not very difficult and, like the previous type, do not require a lengthy format. In introducing the problems, the teacher explains that students should work them until there are no remainders. He then models working problems that require the addition of zeroes. For example, after bringing down the final digit, 9, of the dividend in this problem:

```
      5.6
  6)33.9
     30
      3 9
      3 6
        3
```

the teacher explains that he must keep dividing, since he doesn't want a remainder, "I'll add a zero after the last digit in the decimal and divide again. Remember: Adding zeroes after a decimal does not change the value of the number."

```
      5.65
  6)33.90
     30
      3 9
      3 6
        30
        30
```

Examples in these exercises should be designed so that the addition of one or two zeroes to the dividend eliminates a remainder. Several examples such as

$$4\overline{)3} \quad \text{or} \quad 5\overline{)8}$$

in which a whole number is the dividend should be included. These problems may require the teacher to remind students to write the decimal point first and then add zeroes after the whole number:

$$4\overline{)3} \quad \text{becomes} \quad 4\overline{)3.0}$$

The third type of decimal division problem requires rounding off. Students are usually instructed to work these problems to the nearest tenth, hundredth, or thousandth. Obviously, the preskill required is rounding off decimal numbers. The format for presenting this problem type appears in Format 13.8. In Part A, the teacher demonstrates how to work the problem. Students first read the directions specifying to what decimal place (tenths, hundredths, thousandths) the answer is to be rounded. The teacher asks how many digits must be written after the decimal point in the answer, then instructs students to work the problem until they have written that many digits. Students are instructed to draw a line after that last digit in the answer and divide once more so they can decide how to round off the answer. The answer is then rounded off. If the numeral after the line is 5 or greater, another unit is added; if the numeral after the line is less than 5, no additional unit is added.

Special consideration should again be given to those problems in which a whole number is divided by a larger whole number. These problems are very important, since they prepare students to compute percentages; for example, "John made 4 out of 7 basketball shots. What is his percentage for making shots?" We recommend that students round off answers in this type of problem to the nearest hundredth, since percents are based on hundredths.

Dividing by a Decimal or Mixed Decimal

The fourth type of division problem has a decimal or mixed decimal divisor. Problems of this type are relatively difficult because students must multiply the divisor and dividend by 10 or a multiple of 10 to convert the divisor into a whole number. Both the dividend and divisor must be multiplied by the same number so that the numerical value represented by the problem is not altered. For example, to work the problem 8.7 ÷ .35, students must multiply the dividend and divisor by 100, converting .35 to 35 and 8.7 to 870.

The preskill of moving the decimal to the right when multiplying by a multiple of 10 should be taught and practiced for several weeks before introducing division problems with decimal divisors. Format 13.9 teaches this preskill. Students are taught that when a decimal number is multiplied by 10, the decimal point moves one place to the right; when it is multiplied by 100, the decimal moves two places to the right; and when it is multiplied by 1000, the decimal point moves three places to the right.

Particularly difficult problems are those in which a zero must be added. For example, to multiply 8.7 × 100, the students must add a zero to the 8.7 so they can move the decimal point two places to the right: 8.7 × 100 = 870. The teacher must model several of these problems, explaining the need to add zeroes. "You have to move the decimal point two places to the right, but you've only got one decimal place to the right. Add a zero so you can move the decimal point two places."

The examples in this preskill exercise should include a mix of problem types. The decimal point should not be placed in the same position from problem to problem. In half of the problems, 10 should be a factor, and in the other half, 100 should be a factor. Several problems should require that students add zeroes to a mixed decimal (e.g., 100 × 34.2, 100 × 14.2). Also, several problems should include a whole number that must be multiplied by a multiple of 10 (e.g., 10 × 34, 25 × 100). As the decimal point is moved over, zeroes are added. For example, with 15×100, the student writes 15 and then adds two zeroes: 1500. The teacher models working several of these problems, pointing out that a whole number can be converted to a mixed decimal by adding a decimal point after the last digit in the whole number (e.g., 15 is written as 15.).

Teachers can demonstrate that moving the decimal and adding a zero when multiplying by a multiple of 10 is valid by beginning with a problem like this:

$$
\begin{array}{r}
3.4 \\
\times\ 10 \\
\hline
00 \\
340 \\
\hline
34.0
\end{array}
$$

The teacher points out that when he multiplies by 10, the answer is 34, with the decimal point moved one place to the right and a zero added. Next, the teacher writes this problem:

$$
\begin{array}{r}
3.4 \\
\times\ 100 \\
\hline
00 \\
000 \\
3400 \\
\hline
340.0
\end{array}
$$

and points out that when he multiplies by 100, the answer is 340, with the decimal point moved two places to the right.

Division problems with decimal or mixed decimal divisors are introduced when students have mastered multiplying by multiples of 10 and can work all types of problems in which the divisor is a whole number and the dividend a decimal or mixed decimal number. Format 13.10 shows how to teach students to work problems with a decimal or mixed decimal divisor.

In Part A, the teacher presents a rule, "We cannot divide by a decimal number," and demonstrates how the divisor and dividend must be revalued. Both the divisor and dividend are multiplied by whatever multiple of 10 is needed to change the divisor into a whole number. The teacher revalues the divisor first by moving the decimal point to the right. The dividend is revalued by moving the decimal point the same number of spaces to the right. Note in the format, the demonstration of how to revalue a problem is kept relatively simple to avoid confusing students with lengthy explanations.

Two example-selection guidelines are important in teaching division with decimal or mixed decimal divisor. First, the number of places in the divisor and dividend should vary from problem to problem.

For example, a worksheet might include the following problems:

a. $.5\overline{)3.75}$ b. $.05\overline{)37.5}$ c. $2.5\overline{)75}$

d. $.2\overline{)1368}$ e. $.03\overline{)24}$ f. $.5\overline{)21.85}$

Changing the type of decimal divisor forces students to attend carefully to moving the decimal. A second guideline involves including some examples in which zeroes must be added to the dividend (e.g., problems b, c, and e above). After a week or so, some problems in which a decimal or mixed decimal is divided by a whole number should be included so that students will receive adequate practice applying the strategies to the various types of problems.

If the teacher wishes to demonstrate the validity of moving the decimal point, she begins with a division problem:

$$
.5\overline{)2.4} = \frac{2.4}{.5}
$$

Let's work this division problem as a fraction. Dividing by a decimal is too hard, so I have to change .5 into a whole number. I do that by multiplying by 10. If I multiply the denominator by 10, what do I have to do to the numerator?... Right, ten-tenths equal 1, and when we multiply by 1, we don't change the value of the fraction.

The teacher writes this:

$$
\frac{2.4}{.5} \times \frac{10}{10} = \frac{24}{5}
$$

and says, "Now we can divide by a whole number." The teacher then writes this problem:

$$
5\overline{)24}
$$

CONVERTING FRACTIONS AND DECIMALS

Decimals and fractions are both numerical systems for representing part(s) of a whole. Converting a fraction to a decimal is an important skill in itself as well as a component skill of percent problems. Converting a decimal to a fraction is less important, since it has fewer practical applications.

Converting a Fraction to a Decimal

The strategy for converting a fraction to a decimal involves dividing the numerator by the denominator. For example, ⅜ is converted to a decimal by dividing 8 into 3:

$$\overset{.375}{8)\overline{3.000}}$$

The preskills for this conversion strategy, which we discussed earlier in this chapter, are (a) decimal division problems in which a whole number is divided by a larger whole number (e.g., 3 ÷ 7, 3 ÷ 5) and (b) rounding off decimals.

Because students who have mastered these preskills should have no difficulty converting a fraction to a decimal, an elaborate format is not required. The teacher merely presents the rule: *To change a fraction into a decimal, divide the numerator by the denominator.* The teacher then models application of the rule with several problems and supervises students as they complete a worksheet. Proper and improper fractions should be included in the exercise.

Initial examples of this strategy should be limited to fractions that can be divided evenly to the nearest tenth, hundredth, or thousandth:

$$\frac{4}{8} = \overset{.5}{8)\overline{4.0}} \\ \quad \underline{40}$$

Fractions that result in repeating decimals should not be introduced until several days later, since they require rounding off. When these problems are presented, instructions should specify to what place the decimal should be rounded off.

$$\frac{2}{3} \quad \overset{.6666}{3)\overline{2.0000}}$$

Mixed numbers can be converted to a mixed decimal by first converting the mixed fraction to an improper fraction:

$$3\frac{2}{5} = \frac{17}{5} = \overset{3.4}{5)\overline{17.0}}$$

$$5\frac{3}{4} = \frac{23}{4} = \overset{5.75}{4)\overline{23.00}}$$

Conversion of a mixed number is introduced about a week after the introduction of repeating decimal problems.

In a final type of problem, the denominator is a two-digit number (e.g., 6/12, 15/18). Students should be taught to first reduce the fraction to its lowest common terms before converting the fraction to a decimal:

$$\frac{6}{9} = \frac{2}{3} = \overset{.666}{3)\overline{2.000}}$$

$$\frac{15}{18} = \frac{5}{6} = \overset{.833}{6)\overline{5.000}}$$

Reducing is helpful because dividing by a one-digit divisor is easier than dividing by a two-digit divisor. If the fraction cannot be reduced, students must be able to work problems with a two-digit divisor. Daily practice including four to eight problems should be provided over a period of several weeks.

Converting a Decimal to a Fraction

Converting a decimal to a fraction can be presented when students have learned to read and write fractions and can reduce fractions to their lowest terms. The strategy for converting a decimal to a fraction involves the students' first rewriting the decimal as a decimal fraction, and then reducing this decimal fraction to its lowest terms. For example, the decimal .75 would first be converted to the fraction 75/100, which in turn would be reduced to 3/4.

Initially, students should be given a worksheet like the one below, and the teacher should lead students through completing several items.

Decimal	Decimal Fraction	Common Fraction
.8	$\frac{8}{10}$	$\frac{4}{5}$
.80		
.35		

After several lessons, the teacher could introduce a worksheet exercise like the following. The teacher guides students in converting the decimal to a decimal fraction, and then reducing this fraction to its lowest terms.

Circle the fraction that is equivalent to the decimal number.

.60	$\frac{6}{9}$	$\frac{3}{6}$	$\frac{3}{5}$	$\frac{6}{6}$
.75	$\frac{2}{3}$	$\frac{3}{4}$	$\frac{5}{7}$	$\frac{7}{5}$
.8	$\frac{8}{5}$	$\frac{1}{8}$	$\frac{4}{5}$	$\frac{3}{5}$

DIAGNOSIS AND REMEDIATION

Students may miss decimal problems for one or a combination of the following reasons:

1. *A computational error.* For example, when working the problem 9.63 ÷ 9, the student writes 1.08 as the answer. The student's only mistake was dividing 9 into 63 incorrectly.

   If a student misses a problem solely because of a computational error, the teacher need not

---

Summary Box 13.1
Diagnosis and Remediation of Decimal Errors

Error Patterns	Diagnosis	Remediation Procedures
Adding or subtracting 3.5 + 2 = **3.7** 5 − .3 = **2**	Component skill error: student doesnot convert whole number to mixed decimal.	Teach students to rewrite whole number as mixed decimal, see Format 13.4. Present structured worksheet on addition and subtraction problems, see Format 13.5.
Multiplying 3.45 × .5 **17.25**	Strategy error: placing decimal point in wrong position in answer.	Present Format 13.7. Be sure to include mix of addition and multiplication problems in less structured worksheet exercise.
Dividing $\frac{46.1}{7\overline{)32.27}}$	Component skill error: misalignment of digits in quotient	Present format for teaching long division from Chapter 10. Stress proper alignment of digits.
$\frac{.63}{.05\overline{)3.15}}$	Strategy error: failure to rewrite divisor and dividend	Present Format 13.10.
Rounding off 3.729 **3.8** 8.473 **8.4**	Strategy error	Present Format 13.6.

---

spend time working on the fraction skill but should reteach the specific computational skill.

2. *A component-skill error.* The student makes an error on a previously taught decimal skill, which causes the student to miss the current type of problem. For example, when converting ⅜ to a decimal, the student divides 3 by 7 correctly to .428, but then rounds off the answer to .42.

The remediation involves reteaching the earlier taught component skill. In the example given, the teacher would first reteach students how to round off. When the students demonstrate mastery of the component skill, the teacher would lead the students through solving the original type of problem, using the structured worksheet part of the appropriate format.

3. *A strategy error.* A strategy error occurs when the student does not correctly follow the steps to solve a problem. For example, when attempting to convert ¾ to a decimal, the student divides 4 by 3. The remediation procedure involves reteaching the strategy, beginning with the structured board part of the format.

Summary Box 13.1, which describes diagnoses and remediation procedures for common errors made on the various types of decimal problems, appears above.

APPLICATION ITEMS: DECIMALS

1. Describe the problem type that each example below represents. List the problems in the order they are introduced.

a. 14.3 + 8.5

b. 7 × 34.8

c. 9 − 3.28

d. Convert 4/7 to a decimal.

e. Convert 2/5 to a decimal.

f. Read this number 8.04.

g. $.9\overline{)28}$

h. $9\overline{)2.7}$

i. $9\overline{)2.8}$

j. Round off 3.4785 to the nearest hundredth.

2. Construct a structured board presentation to teach students to read decimals expressed as thousandths.

3. Below are the examples various teachers used in presenting reading decimals (tenths and hundredths). Tell which teacher used an appropriate set of examples. Tell why the other sets are inappropriate.

Teacher A	.04	.09	.08	.05	.01	.07
Teacher B	.7	.37	.48	.5	.28	
Teacher C	.7	.70	.07	.4	.40	.04

4. Specify the wording the teacher uses to present the following problem: $8 - .34 =$

5. Below is a set constructed by a teacher for a rounding-off exercise. It is inappropriate. Tell why.

   Round off 3.482 to the nearest tenth
   Round off 7.469 to the nearest hundredth
   Round off 4.892 to the nearest tenth
   Round off 6.942 to the nearest whole number

6. A student rounds off 3.738 to the nearest hundredth, writing 3.73. Specify the wording the teacher uses in making the correction.

7. Which problems below would not be included in the initial exercises teaching students to divide a whole number into a decimal or mixed decimal number? Tell why.

   a. $7\overline{)37.8}$ b. $4\overline{)23.5}$ c. $9\overline{)84.86}$
   d. $.7\overline{)34.3}$ e. $9\overline{)3.87}$ f. $2\overline{)1.46}$

8. Tell the probable cause of each student's error. Specify the remediation procedure for the type of error.

   Write this fraction as a decimal rounded off to the nearest hundredth: 5/7.

   Jason

   $$\frac{5}{7} = 7\overline{)5.00} = 7\overline{)5.00}^{.614} = .61$$

   Jill

   $$\frac{5}{7} = 5\overline{)7.0}^{1.4}$$

   Samuel

   $$\frac{5}{7} = 7\overline{)5.0}^{.714} = .72$$
   $$\frac{4.9}{10}$$
   $$\frac{7}{3}$$

FORMAT 13.1   Reading Decimals

TEACHER	**STUDENTS**

PART A: STRUCTURED BOARD PRESENTATION

1. *(Write the following fractions on the board.)*

   $\dfrac{3}{10}$ and $\dfrac{3}{100}$

2. Read these fractions.   3 tenths, 3 hundredths

3. We're going to learn another way to write tenths and
   hundredths. *(Write a decimal point on the board.)* This is
   a decimal point. What is this?   A decimal point

   One digit after the decimal point tells about tenths. What
   does one digit after the decimal tell about?   Tenths

   Two digits after the decimal point tell about hundredths.
   What do two digits after the decimal point tell about?   Hundredths

   Remember: If there is one digit after the decimal point, the
   number tells about tenths. If there are two digits after the
   decimal point, the number tells about hundredths.

4. *(Write .9 on board.)*
   Listen: There's one digit after the decimal point. The 9 tells
   about tenths. This says "nine-tenths."

   (Write .09 on board.) Listen: There are two digits after the
   decimal point. The 9 tells about hundredths. This says
   "nine-hundredths." Your turn.

5. *(Write .3 on the board.)*
   How many digits after the decimal point?   1

   What does the 3 tell about?   Tenths

   Say the decimal number.   3 tenths

   To correct: How many digits after the decimal point?
   There is/are _____ digit(s) after the decimal so
   the _____ tells about _____.
   The decimal says _____.

   (Repeat step 3 with .03, .30, .6, .60, .06, .58.)

6. *(Write .7 on board.)*
   Say this decimal number.

   (Repeat step 4 with .70, .07, .9, .09, .90, .05, .4, .32.)

PART B: STRUCTURED WORKSHEET

1. *(Present a worksheet like the following.)*

   a. $.4 = \dfrac{4}{100} \quad \dfrac{4}{10} \quad \dfrac{40}{1000}$ e. $.06 = \dfrac{60}{100} \quad \dfrac{6}{100} \quad \dfrac{6}{10}$

   b. $.40 = \dfrac{40}{100} \quad \dfrac{40}{10} \quad \dfrac{4}{10}$ f. $.6 = \dfrac{6}{100} \quad \dfrac{6}{1000} \quad \dfrac{6}{10}$

   c. $.04 = \dfrac{40}{100} \quad \dfrac{40}{10} \quad \dfrac{4}{100}$ g. $\dfrac{38}{100} = .3 \ .38 \ 38.$

   d. $.61 = \dfrac{61}{100} \quad \dfrac{61}{10} \quad \dfrac{61}{1000}$ h. $\dfrac{4}{100} = .40 \ .04 \ .4$

TEACHER STUDENTS

i. $\dfrac{40}{100}$ = .40 .4 .04   j. $\dfrac{8}{100}$ = .80 .08 .080

k. $\dfrac{80}{100}$ = .80 .08 .8   l. $\dfrac{7}{10}$ = .70 .07 .7

2. Read the decimal number next to a. We have to find
   the fraction that says .4.   4 tenths

3. Read the first fraction. *(Pause, signal.)*   4 hundredths

   Read the next fraction. *(Pause, signal.)*   4 tenths

   Read the next fraction. *(Pause, signal.)*   40 thousandths

4. The decimal says four-tenths. Draw a circle around the
   fraction that says four-tenths. *(Monitor student responses.)*

5. Work problems b–f on your own. Remember to circle the
   fraction that says the same thing as the decimal.

6. Read the fraction next to letter g. We have to find the
   decimal that says 38 hundredths.   38 hundredths

7. Read the first decimal.   3 tenths

   Read the next decimal.   38 hundredths

8. It says the same thing as the fraction, so draw a circle
   around it. *(Monitor student responses.)*

9. Work the rest of the problems on your own.

FORMAT 13.2 Writing Decimals

TEACHER STUDENTS

PART A: STRUCTURED BOARD PRESENTATION

1. *(Write $\dfrac{73}{100}$ on board.)*

2. Read this fraction.   73 hundredths

3. I want to write 73 hundredths as a decimal.

4. How many digits after the decimal point when a decimal
   tells about hundredths?   2

5. So I write a decimal point, then 73. What do I write after
   the decimal point to write 73 hundredths?   73

6. *(Write .73.)* Read the decimal.   73 hundredths

   (Repeat steps 1–5 with: $^7/_{10}$, $^7/_{100}$, $^{70}/_{100}$, $^4/_{100}$, $^{48}/_{100}$, $^6/_{10}$, $^6/_{100}$,
   $^6/_{10}$, $^{60}/_{100}$, $^3/_{100}$.*)*

   *(Note: When presenting fractions like $^7/_{100}$, the teacher
   says in step 4, "So I write a decimal point, then zero seven.")*

PART B: LESS STRUCTURED WORKSHEET

1. *(Write these fractions as decimals.)*

   a. $\dfrac{4}{100}$ = _____   c. $\dfrac{40}{100}$ = _____

   b. $\dfrac{4}{10}$ = _____   d. $\dfrac{7}{100}$ = _____

(continued on next page)

FORMAT 13.2   (continued)

TEACHER	STUDENTS

e. $\dfrac{7}{10}$ = _____   i. $\dfrac{9}{10}$ = _____

f. $\dfrac{70}{100}$ = _____   j. $\dfrac{92}{100}$ = _____

g. $\dfrac{32}{100}$ = _____   k. $\dfrac{9}{100}$ = _____

h. $\dfrac{28}{100}$ = _____   l. $\dfrac{5}{10}$ = _____

2. Read the directions.

Write these fractions as decimals.

3. Read the fraction next to a.

4 hundredths

4. How many digits must there be after the decimal point for hundredths?

2

5. What do you write after the decimal point to say four-hundredths?

04

6. Now write the decimal point and the numeral(s) to say seven-hundredths.

(Repeat steps 2–5 with remaining examples.)

FORMAT 13.3   **Reading and Writing Mixed Decimals**

TEACHER	STUDENTS

PART A: STRUCTURED BOARD PRESENTATION

1. *(Write a decimal point on the board.)* The numerals on this side of the decimal point *(motion to the left)* tell about whole numbers. What do the numerals on this side of the decimal point *(motion to the left)* tell about? The numerals after the decimal point *(motion to the right)* tell about the decimal number.

Whole numbers

2. *(Write 2.4 on board.)* This is a mixed decimal. It has a whole number and a decimal number. It says two and four-tenths. What is this mixed decimal?

2 and 4 tenths

What's the whole number in the mixed decimal?

2

What's the decimal?

4 tenths

Say the mixed decimal.

2 and 4 tenths

(Repeat step 2 with 9.03, 14.2, 16.23, 7.4, 9.03.)

3. *(Write 8.4 on board.)* Say the mixed decimal.

8 and 4 tenths

(Repeat step 3 with 8.04, 7.41, 19.2, 8.50, 19.02.)

PART B: STRUCTURED WORKSHEET

1. *(Write the mixed decimal.)*

   a. eight and four-tenths = _____

   b. sixteen and two-hundredths = _____

TEACHER	**STUDENTS**

    c. five and sixteen-hundredths = _____

    d. eleven and four-tenths =   _____

    e. eleven and four-hundredths = _____

    f. eleven and forty-hundredths = _____

    g. $17\frac{9}{10}$ =   _____

    h. $8\frac{45}{100}$ =   _____

    i. $16\frac{1}{100}$ =   _____

    j. $16\frac{5}{100}$ =   _____

    k. $16\frac{10}{100}$ =   _____

TEACHER	**STUDENTS**
2. Read the words in a.	8 and 4 tenths
3. What's the whole number? Write it.	8
4. What's the decimal number? Write it—don't forget the decimal point. *(Monitor responses.)*	4-tenths
5. What mixed decimal did you write?	8 and 4 tenths
(Repeat steps 1–4 with problems b–f.)	
6. Read the mixed number in problem g.	17 and 9 tenths
(Repeat steps 2–5 with remaining problems.)	

FORMAT 13.4 **Converting Decimals into Equivalent Decimals**

TEACHER	**STUDENTS**
PART A: DEMONSTRATION	
1. Listen to this rule: When we write zeroes after a decimal number, we don't change the value of the number. Say that.	When we write zeroes after a decimal number, we don't change the value of the number.
2. *(Write on board: .3)* Read this decimal.	3 tenths
I'll write a zero after the decimal. *(Add a zero: .30.)* Now read the decimal.	30 hundredths
I changed 3 tenths to 30 hundredths by adding a zero after a decimal number.	
3. I'm going to use fractions to show that 3 tenths equals 30 hundredths. *(Write on board: $\frac{3}{10}$)* Read this.	3 tenths

(continued on next page)

FORMAT 13.4 (continued)

TEACHER	STUDENTS

We start with 3 tenths and we end with 30 hundredths.

(Write on board: $\frac{30}{100}$*)*

What do I multiply 10 by to make it 100? — 10

What do I multiply 3 by to make it 30? — 10

(Write on board: $\frac{3}{10}\left(\frac{10}{10}\right) = \frac{30}{100}$*)*

I multiplied 3 tenths by 10 tenths: 10 tenths equal 1. Remember, when we multiply by 1, we don't change the value of a number. So 3 tenths equals 30 hundredths. *(Write .3 = .30.)*

4. *(Repeat steps 2 and 3, changing .5 to .500.)*

5. Here's another rule about zeroes: If we cross out zeroes at the end of a decimal number, we don't change the value of the decimal. *(Write .50.)* Read this decimal number. — 50 hundredths

   I'll cross out the zero at the end of the decimal. *(Cross out zero: .50.)* Now what does this decimal say? — 5 tenths

6. Let's use fractions to show that 50 hundredths equal 5 tenths. *(Write the problem on the board.)*

   $$\frac{50}{100} = \frac{5}{10}$$

   50 = 5 × what number? — 10

   100 = 10 × what number? — 10

   (Write the rest of the problem.)

   $$\frac{50}{100} = \frac{5}{10}\left(\frac{10}{10}\right)$$

   To make 5 tenths into 50 hundredths we multiplied it by 10 tenths. Ten-tenths equals 1. When we multiply by 1, we don't change the value of a number, so .50 = .5.

   (Repeat steps 5 and 6 with $^{300}/_{1000} = {}^{3}/_{10}.$*)*

PART B: STRUCTURED BOARD PRESENTATION

1. *(Write 8.4 on the board.)*
   Read this number. — 8 and 4 tenths

   I want to rewrite this mixed decimal so that the decimal tells about thousandths.

2. When we write a decimal that tells about thousandths, how many digits must there be after the decimal point? — 3

3. I already have one digit after the decimal point, so how many zeroes must I add? *(Write 8.400.)* — 2

4. Read the decimal number now. — 8 and 4 hundred thousandths

   Did we change the value of 8.4? — No

   No, 8.400 is the same as 8.4. When we add zeroes at the end of the decimal, we don't change its value.

   (Repeat steps 1–4 changing 5.1 to 5.10; 9.300 to 9.3, 7 to 7.00, 9 to 9.0.)

TEACHER   **STUDENTS**

PART C: LESS STRUCTURED WORKSHEET

1. *(Give students a worksheet like this one.)*

Mixed Decimals

Tenths	Hundredths	Thousandths
a. 3.7	_____	_____
b. _____	4.20	_____
c. 9.2	_____	_____
d. _____	_____	7.300
e. _____	6.20	_____

2. *(Point across row a.)* You have to fill in the missing mixed
   decimal numbers. Every mixed decimal in a row must have
   the same value. Read the number closest to a.   3 and 7 tenths

3. Touch the space in the next column. The heading says
   hundredths. We must rewrite 3.7 so that the decimal
   expresses hundredths. How many digits must be after
   the decimal point for hundredths?   2

   The mixed decimal 3.7 has one digit after the decimal.
   What must you do?   Add one zero.

   Write the mixed decimal in the hundredths column.
   What mixed number did you write in the hundredths column?   3.70

4. *(Repeat step 2 with the thousandths column.)*
   (Repeat steps 2 and 3 with remaining examples.)

   *(Note: When converting whole numbers to mixed decimals,
   the teacher explains that a decimal point is written after the
   whole number. After the decimal point, zero(es) are added:
   one zero if the decimal expresses tenths, two zeroes if it
   expresses hundredths, and three zeroes if it expresses
   thousandths.)*

FORMAT 13.5   **Addition/Subtraction of Unlike Decimals**

TEACHER   **STUDENTS**

PART A: STRUCTURED BOARD PRESENTATION

1. When we add or subtract numbers containing decimals,
   we first rewrite them so they all have the same number
   of places after the decimal point.

   (Write 13.7 − 2.14 on board.)

2. Read this problem.   13 and 7 tenths minus
                                                                   2 and 14 hundredths.

3. Which number has more places after the decimal point?   2.14

   So we have to rewrite the problem so that each number
   is talking about hundredths.

4. *(Point to 13.7.)* What can I do to 7 tenths to make it into
   a number with two places behind the decimal?   Add 0 after the 7.

(continued on next page)

FORMAT 13.5 (continued)

TEACHER	**STUDENTS**

Yes, I add a zero after the 7. *(Write 0 after 7: 13.70.)* Now
we have 70 hundredths. Read the problem now.

13.70 − 2.14

5. To work the problem, I'll write the problem in a column,
making sure the decimal points are lined up. *(Write and
solve the problem.)*

$$\begin{array}{r} 13.70 \\ -\ 2.14 \\ \hline 11.56 \end{array}$$

6. I'll write the decimal point in the answer. Remember, when
we subtract numbers with decimals, we bring the decimal
point straight down. *(Write the decimal point.)*

$$\begin{array}{r} 13.70 \\ -\ 2.14 \\ \hline 11.56 \end{array}$$

Read the answer.
(Repeat steps 1–6 with this problem: 18.9 − 3.425.)

11.56

PART B: STRUCTURED WORKSHEET

1. *(Give students a worksheet like this one.)*

a. 7.1 − 3.45	e. 19.1 − 8.34
b. 16.345 + 8.3	f. 96.4 + 86.4
c. 51.43 + 6.85	g. 4.5 + 6.35
d. 13.6 − 2.346	h. 271. − 71.42

2. Read problem a on your worksheet.

7.1 − 3.45

3. Do the numbers have the same number of places
after the decimal point?

No

4. Right. One number has tenths, and the other has hundredths.
Which number has more places after the decimal?

3.45

So which number do you have to change?

7.1

What do you do to 7.1?

Add 0 after the 1.

Add the zero. *(Monitor responses.)* Now rewrite the problem
in a column and work it. *(Pause.)* What is the answer?
(Pause, signal.)

1.65

(Repeat steps 1–3 with several more problems.)

FORMAT 13.6 **Rounding Off Decimals**

TEACHER	**STUDENTS**

PART A: STRUCTURED BOARD PRESENTATION

1. *(Write. 376 on board.)*

2. I want to round off this decimal to the nearest hundredth.
When we talk about hundredths, how many digits will
we have after the decimal?
I will count off two digits after the decimal point and then
draw a line after that digit. *(Write. 37|6.)*

2

TEACHER	STUDENTS

3. When we round off a decimal, we must look at the number that comes after the line. If the number is 5 or more, we must add another unit. What number comes after the line? **6**

So must we add another hundredth? **Yes**

If we have 37 hundredths and we add another hundredth, how many hundredths do we have? **38**

So .376 rounded to the nearest hundredth is . . . **.38**

(Write .38.)

4. *(Repeat steps 1 and 2 with the following problems.)*

   .372 rounded to the nearest tenth
   .1482 rounded to the nearest hundredth
   .382 rounded to the nearest whole
   .924 rounded to the nearest hundredth

PART B: STRUCTURED WORKSHEET

1. *(Give students a worksheet like this one.)*

   a. Round .462 to the nearest tenth   _____

   b. Round .428 to the nearest tenth   _____

   c. Round .8562 to the nearest hundredth   _____

   d. Round .8548 to the nearest hundredth   _____

   e. Round .3467 to the nearest hundredth   _____

   f. Round .3437 to the nearest hundredth   _____

   g. Round .417 to the nearest tenth   _____

   h. Round .482 to the nearest tenth   _____

   i. Round .3819 to the nearest hundredth   _____

   j. Round .3814 to the nearest hundredth   _____

2. Touch problem a. What do we round off that decimal to? **To the nearest tenth**

3. How many digits will be after the decimal point when you round off to the nearest tenth? **1**

   Count one digit after the decimal point and draw a line.

4. Let's see if you add another tenth. What number comes just after the line? **6**

   So do you add another tenth? **Yes**

   You had four tenths. If you add a tenth, how many tenths do you have? **5**

   If you round off .462 to the nearest tenth, what do you have? **5 tenths**

   Write the answer on the line. **Students write .5.**

   (Repeat steps 1–3 with remaining problems.)

PART C: LESS STRUCTURED WORKSHEET

   (Give students a worksheet like the one in Part B.)

1. Read item a.

2. Draw a line to show where you round off.

3. Round off and write your answer on the line.

4. Read your answer.

   (Repeat steps 1–4 with remaining problems.)

FORMAT 13.7 Multiplying Decimals

TEACHER   **STUDENTS**

PART A: STRUCTURED BOARD PRESENTATION

1. *(Write the following problem on the board.)*

   34.2
   × .59
   ────
   3078
   1710
   ────
   20178

2. We're multiplying mixed decimals, so we have to put a decimal point in our answer. Here's a fast way to figure out where to write the decimal point in the answer. We count the places after the decimal points in both numbers we're multiplying.

3. I'll touch the numbers after the decimal points and count them: *(touch 2)* one, *(touch 9)* two, *(touch 5)* three. How many decimal places in both numbers?   3

4. So I write the decimal point in the answer so that there are three places after it. *(Point between 7 and 8.)* One place. *(Point between 1 and 7.)* Two places. *(Point between 0 and 1.)* Three places. I put the decimal point here. *(Point between 0 and 1.)*

5. How many places after the decimal point?   3
   Read the answer.   20.178

   (Repeat steps 1–4 with the problems below.)

   34.2   34.2   351
   × 5   × .7   ×.05

PART B: STRUCTURED WORKSHEET

1. *(Give students a worksheet like the following one.)*

   a. 32.1   b. .321   c. 3.21   d. 321   e. 3.421
      × .9   × .9   × 9   × .9   × .7
      ────   ────   ────   ────   ─────
      2889   2889   2889   2889   23947

   f. 492   g. 4.92   h. .492   i. 49.2
      × .53   × .53   × 5.3   × 53
      ────   ────   ────   ────
      1476   1476   1476   1476
      24600   24600   24600   24600
      ─────   ─────   ─────   ─────
      26076   26076   26076   26076

   j. 429   k. .32   l. 3.2   m. 3.2
      × 53   × .05   × 5   × .05
      ────   ────   ───   ────
      1476   160   160   160
      24600   000   000
      ─────   ───   ───
      26076   160   160

2. These problems are worked already. All you have to do is put in the decimal points.

3. Touch problem a.

TEACHER	**STUDENTS**
4. How many places are after the decimal points in both numbers being multiplied? *(Pause, signal.)*	2
5. Where does the decimal point go in the answer?	Between the first 8 and the second 8.
6. Write it.	
7. Read the answer.	
(Repeat steps 2–6 with remaining problems.)	28.89

PART C: LESS STRUCTURED WORKSHEET

1. *(Give students a worksheet with a mix of multiplication and addition problems containing decimals and mixed decimals.)* Remember: When you multiply, you count the places after the decimal point. When you add, you bring the decimal point straight down.

2. Work problem a. *(Pause.)*

3. Where does the decimal point go?

(Repeat steps 1–3 with remaining problems.)

FORMAT 13.8   **Division with Decimals—Rounding Off**

TEACHER	**STUDENTS**
PART A: STRUCTURED BOARD PRESENTATION	
1. *(Write the following instructions on the board.)* Work the problem, and express your answer to the nearest hundredth: $7\overline{)3.24}$	
2. Read the problem.	7 goes into 3 and 24 hundredths.
The instructions tell us to work the problem to the nearest hundredth. How many digits after the decimal point when we have hundredths?	2
So we work the problem until we have two digits after the decimal point.	
(Solve the problem.)	

$$
\begin{array}{r}
.46 \\
7\overline{)3.24} \\
\underline{2\,8} \\
4\,4 \\
\underline{4\,2} \\
2
\end{array}
$$

3. We have hundredths in the answer, but we're not done because we have a remainder. We have to work the problem to thousandths and then round to hundredths. So I draw a line after the 6.

(continued on next page)

FORMAT 13.8 (continued)

TEACHER   **STUDENTS**

4. We have to divide one more time so we know how to round
   off. Here's what we do. We add a zero after the 4 in the
   number we're dividing. Remember, when you add a zero
   after the last digit in a decimal number, you don't change
   the value of the number.

   (Add a zero.)

```
     .46|
   7)3.24|0
     2 8
     ─────
     4 4
     4 2
     ─────
       2
```

   Now we can divide again. We bring down the zero. *(Write 0*   2
   next to 2.) How many sevens in 20? *(Pause, signal.)*
   (Write 14 and 2.)

```
     .46|2
   7)3.24|0
     2 8
     ─────
     44
     42
     ─────
     20
     14
     ─────
      6
```

5. Do I round off to 46 hundredths or 47 hundredths?   46 hundredths
   To correct: What number is after the rounding off line?
   That is less than 5, so we don't add another unit.

   (Repeat steps 1–4 with the problems below.)

   9)4 Round off to nearest tenth.
   7)26.3 Round off to nearest hundredth.
   3)2 Round off to nearest hundredth.

PART B: STRUCTURED WORKSHEET

1. *(Give students a worksheet like the following one.)*

   a. Work these problems and round off to the nearest hundredth.

      1. 3)7.4 =   2. 6)5 =

   b. Work these problems and round off to the nearest tenth.

      3. 4)2.31 =   4. 7)3 =

   Read the instructions for a.   Work these problems
                                                                        and round off to the
                                                                        nearest hundredth

   Read problem one.   3 into 7.4.

2. You have to round the problem to the nearest hundredth.
   How many digits will there be after the decimal point
   in your answer?   2

TEACHER	STUDENTS
Work the problem. Stop when there are two digits after the decimal point. *(Monitor students' work.)*	$$\begin{array}{r} 2.46 \\ 3\overline{)7.40} \\ \underline{6} \\ 1\,4 \\ \underline{1\,2} \\ 20 \\ \underline{18} \\ 2 \end{array}$$

3. You're not finished because you still have a remainder. Draw a line after the last digit in your answer. Now add a zero to 7.40 and divide again. *(Pause.)*

4. What numeral did you write after the line in the answer?   6

   So do you add another hundredth?   Yes

   Write your rounded-off answer. What's your answer?   2.47

PART C: LESS STRUCTURED WORKSHEET

1. *(Give students a worksheet like the one given in Part B.)*

2. Read the instructions for a.

3. Read problem one.

4. Where are you going to draw the line for rounding off:
   after the first, second, or third digit behind the decimal point?   Second digit.

5. Work the problem and write your rounded-off answer.

FORMAT 13.9   **Preskill: Multiplying Decimals by Multiples of 10**

TEACHER	STUDENTS

PART A: STRUCTURED BOARD PRESENTATION

1. Here are some rules about multiplying decimals by 10 or 100: When you multiply by 10, you move the decimal one place to the right. What do you do to the decimal point when you multiply by 10?   Move it one place to the right.

   When you multiply by 100, you move the decimal point two places to the right. What do you do with the decimal point when you multiply by 100?   Move it two places to the right.

2. *(Write on the board: 37.48 × 10)*
   Read the problem.   37.48 × 10

   We're multiplying by 10. What do you do to the decimal point when you multiply by 10?   Move it one place to the right.

3. *(Write on the board: 37.48 × 10 = 3748)*
   The decimal point was between the 7 and the 4. If I move it one place to the right, where will the decimal be?   Between the 4 and 8.

   (Write on board: 37.48 × 10 = 374.8)
   Read the answer.   374.8

   (continued on next page)

FORMAT 13.9 **(continued)**

TEACHER	**STUDENTS**

4. *(Repeat steps 2 and 3 with the problems below.)*

    37×100
    8.532×10
    7.2×100
    25×100
    2.5×10

PART B: STRUCTURED WORKSHEET

1. *(Give the students a worksheet like the following one.)*

  a. $3.74 \times 10 =$ e. $16 \times 100 =$

  b. $.894 \times 100 =$ f. $15 \times 10 =$

  c. $42.8 \times 100 =$ g. $.0382 \times 10 =$

  d. $3.517 \times 10 =$ h. $49.2 \times 100 =$

2. When you multiply by 10, what must you do?	Move the decimal one place to the right.
When you multiply by 100, what must you do?	Move the decimal two places to the right.
3. Read problem a.	3.74×10
4. You're multiplying by 10, so what must you do to the decimal point?	Move it one place to the right.
5. Where will the decimal point be in the answer?	Between the 7 and the 4.
6. Write the answer.	Students write 37.4.
7. Read your answer.	37.4

   (Repeat steps 1–6 with remaining problems.)

FORMAT 13.10 **Dividing by Decimals**

TEACHER	**STUDENTS**

PART A: STRUCTURED BOARD PRESENTATION

1. *(Write the following on the board.)*

    $.5\overline{)51.75}$

2. Here's a rule about decimal division: We don't divide by a decimal number. *(Point to .5.)* We must change the divisor to a whole number.

3. *(Point to $.5\overline{)51.75}$)* What is the divisor in this problem?	5
Can we work the problem the way it is?	No
What must we do?	Change the divisor to a whole number.

4. We make five-tenths a whole number by moving the decimal point. A number is a whole number when there are no digits after the decimal point. How many places must I

TEACHER	STUDENTS

move the decimal point over to the right to make .5 into a
whole number?

(Draw arrow: $.5.\overline{)51.75}$ *)*

I moved the decimal one place to the right. We have to
move the decimal point the same number of places in the
dividend. How many places to the right must we move the
decimal point in the dividend?

(Write on board: $.5.\overline{)51.7.5}$ *)*

Now we can work the problem. I write the decimal point
on the answer line, <u>and then</u> divide.

(Write on board: $.5.\overline{)51.7.5}$ *)*

One

One

5. I'll divide.

```
     10 3.5
 5.)51 7.5
     5
     017
      15
      25
      25
```

6. What's the answer?

(Repeat steps 1–5 with the problems below.)

103.5

$$.05\overline{)5.125} \qquad .7\overline{)28}$$
$$.0\overline{)21.9} \qquad .07\overline{)28}$$

PART B: STRUCTURED WORKSHEET

1. *(Give students a worksheet like the following one.)*

$$.05\overline{)3.25} \qquad .5\overline{)32} \qquad .04\overline{)92}$$
$$.3\overline{)9.6} \qquad .03\overline{)9.6}$$

2. Read the first problem.

.05 into 3.25

3. What is the divisor?

.05

4. Cross out the decimal point and move it to the right to
   make a whole number.

Students write
$05.\overline{)3.25}$.

5. How many places did you move the decimal point
   to the right?

   That's what you must do in the dividend. Cross out the
   decimal point and write it where it belongs. *(Monitor
   students' work.)*

2

Students write
$05.\overline{)3.25}$.

6. Now write the decimal point where it will be in the answer.

Students write
$05.\overline{)3.25}$.

7. Work the problem.

8. What's the answer?

65

(Repeat steps 1–7 with remaining problems.)

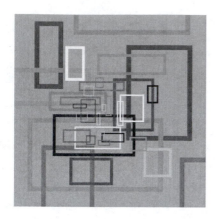

CHAPTER 14

Percent and Ratio

TERMS AND CONCEPTS

Percent   A notation for hundredths.

Percentage   The number obtained by finding the percent of another number.

Ratio   The numerical expression of the relationship between two comparable quantities. Usually the ratio is the result of dividing the first quantity by the second.

The concepts of percentage and percent are applied frequently in real-life situations.

Percentage

Prices went up 15%.

The store is having a 20% reduction sale.

The loan charges are 8%.

Percent (Ratio)

Alice made 3 of 7 shots.

Mary worked 8 of 10 problems.

Carlos saw 2 of the 3 movies.

The introduction of percentage and ratio usually follows instruction on most of the basic fraction and decimal skills discussed in the earlier chapters.

Ratio problems require students to convert a numerical relationship (ratio) between two quantities into a percent. The fraction ¾ is converted to 75%. An example of a ratio application problem is, "Ann made 3 of 7 shots. What percent of her shots did she make?"

Percentage problems require the student to figure out the quantity that represents a given percent of another quantity. For example, (a) What is 30% of 60? (b) You need to get 70% of the questions on the test correct to pass. If there are 20 problems on the test, how many must you get correct to pass?

Teachers should note that various decimal skills are preskills for percent and ratio problems. For example, to solve a percentage problem, the student must be able to multiply mixed decimals; to solve a ratio problem, the student must be able to convert a fraction to a decimal or mixed decimal and round off the decimal or mixed decimal number.

A specific sequence for introducing the major types of problems students encounter in the elementary grades appears in the Instructional Sequence and Assessment Chart. Note on the chart that we recommend introducing percentage-related skills before ratio-related skills.

PERCENTAGE PROBLEMS

Two types of percentage problems are common to elementary mathematics instruction. The easier type of problem states a percent and quantity and asks students to find the percentage:

> The teacher said that 70% was passing. There are 50 problems on the test. How many problems must I get to pass? (70% of 50 is .70 × 50 = 35)

The more difficult problem type requires the student to figure the percentage of an original quantity,

336

Instructional Sequence and Assessment Chart

Grade Level	Problem Type	Performance Indicator
5a	Converting percentages to decimal figures	Write these percents as decimals: 45% = 15% = 6% = 1% =
5b	Determining a percent of a given number	What is 8% of 20? What is 25% of 12? What is 130% of 50?
5c	Simple percentage story problems	Jane took 20 basketball shots. She made 60% of her shots. How many shots did she make? Tara scored 5% of her team's points. Her team scored 60 points. How many points did Tara score? In May a store sold 300 shirts. In June the store sold 130% of what it sold in May. How many shirts did it sell in June?
5d	Converting a decimal to a percent	.32 = % .6 = % 3.4 = %
5e	Converting a fraction to a percent: percentage comes out even	Convert these fractions to percentages: $\frac{3}{5}$ = % $\frac{7}{10}$ = % $\frac{5}{4}$ = %
5f	Converting a fraction to a percent: rounding off required	$\frac{3}{7}$ = % $\frac{4}{9}$ = % $\frac{5}{3}$ = %
5g	Simple ratio story problems: total is given	Bill took 20 basketball shots. He made 12. What is his shooting percentage? Ann has 15 friends; 9 of her friends are from Texas. What percentage of her friends are from Texas?
6a	Complex percentage problems	Jill earned $80 in May. In June she earned 30% more than she did in May. How much did Jill earn in June? Tim borrowed $200. He must pay 9% interest. How much must he pay back altogether?

Instructional Sequence and Assessment Chart (continued)

Grade Level	Problem Type	Performance Indicator
6b	Complex ratio problems; total not given	I got A's on 5 tests and B's on 4 tests. What percent of the tests did I get A's on? There are 4 boys and 6 girls. What percent of the class is boys? Bill has 5 blue pens and 15 red pens. What percent of the pens are blue?

then either add or subtract that amount from the original quantity:

Bill borrowed $80 from the bank. He must pay 8% interest on the loan. How much must he pay back to the bank? (.08 × 80 = 6.40, $80.00 + $6.40 = $86.40)

This problem type is not be introduced until students had a great deal of practice with the easier type.

Converting Percent to Decimal

Prior to introducing percentage problems, students should have mastered (a) multiplying decimal and mixed decimal numbers and (b) converting a percent figure to a decimal.

Format 14.1 introduces the percent concept and teaches students to convert a percent to a decimal. The format contains three parts. In Part A, the teacher simply presents the percent sign and teaches students to read percent numbers. In Part B, a structured board exercise, the teacher demonstrates how a percent number can be written as a decimal number by rewriting the numerals, deleting the percent sign, and placing a decimal point so that there are two decimal places. Part C is a structured worksheet exercise. Daily worksheet practice should continue for several weeks.

Example selection is quite important when teaching this format. One-third of the percent figures should be below 10%, one-third between 10 and 100%, and one-third over 100%. For example, a conversion exercise might include the following percents: 5%, 28%, 1%, 235%, 30%, 300%. Exposure to these problem types provides students with the practice needed to generalize the strategy to a wide range of examples. Percents below 10 are included to teach students that when converting a percent below 10, they must write a zero in front of the decimal number (e.g., 6% = .06, 1% = .01). Percents of 100 and above are included to show that a whole number can be produced (e.g., 354% = 3.54, 200% = 2).

Problems in which a percent that already includes a decimal, such as 87.5%, is converted to a decimal are not included initially. Problems of this type require the students to add two more decimal places (e.g., 87.5% = .875). An adaptation of Format 14.1 would be used. The teacher would explain that two more decimal places must be added.

Simple Percentage Problems

Simple percentage problems are comprised of a quantity multiplied by a given percent; students must determine the percentage (e.g., 30% × 40 = 12). This problem type can be introduced after the students can translate percent to decimals and can accurately multiply decimal numbers.

Format 14.2 shows how to teach students to solve simple percentage problems. Part A is designed to teach students rules that will help them determine if their answers to subsequent problems are correct. The students are taught that if the problem asks for 100%, then the answer is the same as the number being multiplied (e.g., 100% × 20 = 20).

Likewise, if the percent is more than 100%, the answer is more than the number being multiplied; if less than 100%, the answer is less than the number being multiplied. Students then use the rules to predict the answers to some numerical problems. Although these rules appear to be extremely simple, by examining the errors of students who have not been explicitly taught this information, it is clear that many students never figure out these relationships on their own.

Part B is a structured board presentation in which the strategy for solving percentage problems is presented: Convert the percent to a decimal, then multiply that decimal and the amount given. Students apply the rules learned in Part A to check their answers.

Part C is a structured worksheet exercise in which the students solve problems. Note that when multiplying a two-digit and a three-digit number, the student should be instructed to write the two-digit number on the bottom. For example, in solving 125% × 60, the student writes:

$$\begin{array}{r} 1.25 \\ \times\ 60 \\ \hline \end{array}$$

Examples should include sets of three problems in which the same number is multiplied. In one problem, the percent would be below 10%; in another problem, between 10 and 100%; and in another problem, more than 100%. For example, a sample set for an exercise might include these problems:

30 % × 60	25 % × 36
3 % × 60	2 % × 36
30 % × 60	125 % × 36

Including these three problem types in a set provides practice in the wide range of problems students will encounter.

Simple Percentage Story Problems

Simple percentage story problems state an amount and ask the student to determine a percentage. A distinguishing characteristic of these problems is the inclusion of the word *of.* Below are two typical simple percentage problems:

> There are 60 children in our school. 75% of the children are girls. How many girls are there in our school?

> Sarah made 60% of her shots. She took 20 shots. How many shots did she make?

Story problems of this type are introduced when students can solve problems such as 40% × 20 accurately. As preparation, teachers first give students simple equations in which the word *of* is substituted for the times sign (e.g., 75% of 48). After several lessons, the teacher introduces story problems, modeling and testing how to solve them. After solving them, the teacher repeats the problem, asking whether students multiplied by more or less than 100%, and if the answer made sense. (For example, "The problem said she got 60% of her shots in. She took 20 shots. We know the answer must be less than 20 because she made less than 100% of her shots.") A worksheet should include problems with a percent below 10, problems with a percent between 10 and 100, and problems with a percent above 100.

COMPLEX PERCENTAGE PROBLEMS

Complex percentage problems usually give the percent that an original amount has either increased (or

decreased) and asks the students to figure out the amount of the increase (or decrease) and the new total. These complex percentage problems should not be introduced until students have practiced simple percent problems for at least several weeks. This type of problem is illustrated below:

> The hat store sold 50 hats in May. In June the sales went up 20%. How many more hats did the store sell in June than in May? How many hats did the store sell in June?

The teacher models how to solve the problem: first computing the percentage increased or decreased by converting the percent to a decimal and then multiplying. This amount is then added to or subtracted from the original amount to determine the new total. For example, in the problem above, the student converts 20% to .20 and multiplies .20 × 50 to end with 10. The store sold 10 more hats in June than in May. This 10 is added to the 50 hats sold in May to determine that 60 hats were sold in June.

A special type of problem involves computing interest. (The term *interest* used here refers to simple interest. Compound interest is presented in junior or senior high.) The teacher can explain the term *interest* to students by using an explanation similar to the one below. "When you borrow money from a bank, you must pay back the bank extra money. The extra money is interest. If the bank charges 10% interest, you must pay back the money you borrowed plus 10% of the amount you borrowed."

Figure 14.1 is a sample interest exercise. Students fill in missing amounts in a table that provides practice in determining interest for various loans. More complex interest problems are introduced in later grades.

RATIO PROBLEMS

In ratio problems, students must convert a fraction to a percent figure. There are three basic types of ratio problems:

1. Numerical problems for converting a fraction to percent.

$$\frac{2}{5} = 40\ \%$$

$$\frac{5}{4} = 125\ \%$$

2. Simple ratio story problems. In these problems, the total and one partial quantity are given. The student calculates the percent.

FIGURE 14.1 Sample Interest Exercise

Amount of Loan	***Interest Rate for 1 Year***	***Amount of Interest for 1 Year***	***Amount to Be Paid Back at End of 1 Year***
a. \$500	5%	________	________
b. \$500	8%	________	________
c. \$1000	4%	________	________
d. \$1000	7%	________	________

Sarah made 10 out of 20 shots. What percent of her shots did she make?

$$\frac{10}{20} = 50\ \%$$

3. Complex story problems. In these problems, the student is required to add the amounts given prior to determining a percent.

Ann got 10 shots in and missed 10 shots. What percent of her shots did she make?

$$10 + 10 = 20 \qquad \frac{10}{20} = 50\ \%$$

Converting a Fraction to a Percent

Converting a fraction to a percent can be introduced several weeks after students have mastered simple percentage problems. Format 14.3 teaches this conversion skill. The format assumes that students have previously mastered converting fractions to decimals by dividing the numerator by the denominator, which in turn requires students to divide and round off decimal numbers.

The format includes five parts. In Part A, the teacher presents a strategy for converting decimal numbers to percent numbers: "Write a percent sign and move the decimal point two places toward the percent sign." The wording for this procedure is designed to aid students in determining the direction to move the decimal point. After presenting the rule, the teacher presents examples of its application in converting decimals to percents. Examples should include mixed decimals and decimal numbers with tenth, hundredth, and thousandth decimals.

Part B is a worksheet exercise in which students practice converting decimals to a percent. The teacher guides the students through several conversions, and then the students work the rest of the problems themselves. Several days of practice on this skill should be provided before introducing Part C. The examples selected for parts A and B should include a mix of decimals, whole numbers, and mixed decimals. Decimals expressed as tenths, hundredths, and thousandths should be included, as well as one or two whole numbers and several mixed decimals. A sample set for a worksheet exercise might include these numbers: 3.2, .475, 6, .08, .4, .37, 2, 6.1, 35, .875, and .1. When converting a tenths decimal or whole number, the teacher tells the students the number of zeroes to add:

$$.1 = .10 = .10\ \% = 10\%$$

In Part C, a structured board exercise, the teacher presents the two-step strategy for converting fractions to a percent. "First convert the fraction to a decimal, and then convert that decimal to a percent." The teacher then demonstrates its application with several fractions.

Part D is a structured worksheet exercise in which students are given a worksheet with prompts to help make the conversion. A prompted problem looks like this:

$$\frac{3}{4} = .________ = ________\%$$

Part E is a less structured worksheet exercise in which no prompts are written on the students' worksheets. There are two example-selection guidelines for parts C, D, and E:

1. Both proper and improper fractions should be included so that students can see that the strategy also applies to percents greater than 100 percent (e.g., $5/4$ = 125%, $7/5$ = 140%).

2. Problems should initially be limited to fractions that do not require rounding off to compute the percent. Problems that must be rounded off require an extra step and should not be introduced for several weeks. The fractions $3/4$, $1/2$, $7/5$, $7/10$, $6/8$ and $6/4$ are examples of fractions that do not require rounding off. The fractions $5/7$, $2/9$, $4/3$, $3/11$, and $6/5$ do require rounding off.

When problems requiring rounding off are introduced, the teacher tells the students to divide until the answer has three digits after the decimal and then instructs them to round off to the nearest hun-

Summary Box 14.1
Converting Decimals and Fractions to Percents

1. Students change a fraction to a decimal by dividing the numerator by the denominator.

$$\frac{3}{4} = \begin{array}{r} .75 \\ 4\overline{)3.00} \\ \underline{28} \\ 20 \\ \underline{20} \end{array}$$

2. Students change the decimal to a percent by writing % sign and moving the decimal two places toward the percent sign.

$$.75 = 75\%$$

dredth. For example, when converting $\frac{5}{7}$ to a percent, the student divides to hundredths, then writes a line after the 1 (the hundredths number), divides once again, and then rounds off the answer to .71:

$$\begin{array}{r|l} .71 & 4 \\ 7\overline{)5.00} & 0 \\ \underline{4\,9} & \\ 10 & \\ \underline{7} & \\ 3\,0 & \\ \underline{2\,8} & \\ 2 & \end{array}$$

For examples such as $\frac{2}{3}$ in which there is a repeating decimal, the teacher can demonstrate how to round off and express the answer as 66.7. This type of problem is potentially confusing and should not be introduced until students have mastered the rounding-off strategy.

After students have had several weeks of practice in converting fractions to decimals, the teacher can introduce the new steps of reducing the fraction before dividing, when possible. For example, $\frac{9}{12}$ can be reduced to $\frac{3}{4}$, so students would divide 3 by 4 instead of 9 by 12. Reducing fractions prior to dividing is especially helpful when dealing with two-digit denominators. If the denominator can be reduced to one digit, the division problem will be much easier.

A final consideration in teaching students to convert fractions to decimals involves providing students with adequate practice so that they can memorize the percents that more common fractions represent. The percents for these fractions should be taught: $\frac{1}{4}$, $\frac{3}{4}$, $\frac{1}{2}$, $\frac{1}{3}$, $\frac{2}{3}$, $\frac{1}{5}$, $\frac{2}{5}$, $\frac{3}{5}$, $\frac{4}{5}$ as well as $\frac{1}{10}$, $\frac{3}{10}$, $\frac{7}{10}$. Students should receive adequate practice so that they can tell the percents these fractions represent instantaneously. To facilitate this memorization, the teacher provides flash card practice or another type of memorization exercise. However, this memorization practice would not begin until after several weeks of instruction on conversions to percents.

Simple Ratio Story Problems

In simple ratio story problems, two related quantities are given, and students are asked to express the relationship between these two quantities as a percent figure. Most simple ratio problems deal with a subset of a total set. For example, shots made (subset) out of shots attempted (total set); girls (subset) out of children (total set); red apples (subset) out of apples (total set). Problems a and b are examples of this type of problem:

a. There were 20 problems on the test. Jack got 14 right. What percent of the problems did Jack get correct?

b. There are 12 children in our class; 8 are girls. What percent of our class are girls?

Simple percentage problems can be introduced when students have mastered converting fractions to a percent figure. The format for simple ratio problems contains three parts (see Format 14.4). In Part A, the board presentation, students are taught the component skill of converting the relationship expressed in the story to a fraction. The teacher presents the rule that the number that tells how many altogether is written as the denominator of the fraction; she then models and tests with several examples. For example, "Sheila took 12 shots; she made 10" translates to the fraction $\frac{10}{12}$.

Part B provides worksheet practice on converting ratio story problems to fractions. Part C is a less structured worksheet in which the teacher guides students in rewriting a fraction as a percent figure. The teacher first asks students to write the fraction indicated by the problem and then to translate that fraction to a percent.

Practice problems should include as many real-life situations pertaining to the classroom as possible (e.g., What percent of the children are girls? What percent of the days has it rained?).

Complex Ratio Story Problems

In complex ratio story problems, the students must add the two quantities to derive a sum that will be the denominator of the fraction used to compute percent. For example, a problem may state there are 4 boys and 6 girls and ask for the percent of the children that are girls. For that problem, the quantities 4 and 6 must be added to determine the denominator, since the fraction is

$$\frac{\text{girls}}{\text{boys and girls}}$$

Complex ratio story problems are not introduced until students have had several weeks of practice with simple ratio problems.

In Part A of Format 14.5, the teacher models how the total is derived for complex problems. "The problem asks what fraction of the children are girls, so the fraction will be girls over the children. How many children? So what do I write for the denominator?"

The examples used to teach complex ratio problems should include both simple and complex ratio problems, including sets of related problems such as a and b below:

a. There are 6 children in the club, and 4 are girls. What percent of the children are girls?
b. There are 4 boys and 6 girls in the club. What percent of the children in the club are girls?

Problem a is a simple ratio problem. Problem b is a complex ratio problem. Note that the total in both problems is the number of children. In problem a, the number of children is given. However, problem b does not tell the total, and the quantities 4 boys and 6 girls must be added. Presenting related simple and complex problems is necessary to provide students with practice in determining when the quantities should be added to figure the denominator of the fraction.

APPLICATION ITEMS: PERCENT AND RATIO

1. Below are errors made by students. Specify the probable cause of each error and describe a remediation procedure.

   a. What is 38% of 90?

   Jill

   ```
      90
   × .38
     720 = 3420
    2700
    3420
   ```

   Tim

   ```
   90.00
   + .38 = 90.38
   90.38
   ```

   Sarah

   ```
      90
   × .38
     720 = 9.9
     270
    9.90
   ```

   b. What is 5% of 60?

   Jack

   ```
      60
   × .5 = 30
   30.0
   ```

c. Bill took 15 shots; he made 12 of his shots. What percent of his shots did he make?

Tom

$$\frac{15}{12} = 12\overline{)15.0} = 125\%$$

$$\begin{array}{r} 1.25 \\ \hline 12\,)\,15.0 \\ 12 \\ \hline 30 \\ 24 \\ \hline 60 \end{array}$$

Zelda

$$\frac{12}{15} = 15\overline{)12.0} = 69\%$$

$$\begin{array}{r} .69 \\ \hline 15\,)\,12.0 \\ 9\,0 \\ \hline 3\,00 \\ 1\,35 \end{array}$$

Elwin

$$\frac{12}{15} = 15\overline{)12.0} = 8\%$$

$$\begin{array}{r} .8 \\ \hline 15\,)\,12.0 \\ 12.0 \end{array}$$

2. Specify the wording the teacher uses in correcting Tom's mistake.

3. Specify the wording the teacher uses in a structured worksheet presentation for converting ⅗ to a percent.

4. Below are sets of examples teachers constructed for an exercise to teach students to convert percent figures to decimals. Tell which sets are inadequate and why.

Set A:	85%	94%	30%	62%	53%	6%
Set B:	40%	5%	135%	240%	7%	82%
Set C:	130%	20%	72%	145%	80%	360%

FORMAT 14.1   Converting Percent to Decimal

TEACHER	**STUDENTS**
PART A: READING AND WRITING THE PERCENT SIGN	
1. (*Write % on board.*) This is a percent sign. What is this?	A percent sign
2. (*Write 42% on board.*) This says 42%. What does this say?	42%
3. (*Repeat step 2 with 20%.*)	
4. (*Write 30% on board.*) What does this say?	30%
(*Repeat step 4 with 8%, 142%, 96%, 300%.*)	

(continued on next page)

FORMAT 14.1 (continued)

TEACHER	STUDENTS

PART B: STRUCTURED BOARD PRESENTATION

1. Percent means hundredths. What does percent mean?

Hundredths

2. 87% means 87 hundredths. What does 87% mean?

87 hundredths

(*Repeat step 2 with 50%, 214%.*)

3. What does 30% mean?

30 hundredths

(*Repeat step 3 with 248%, 8%.*)

4. How many decimal places in a hundredths number?

Two

5. Here's rule for changing a percent number to a decimal number: Get rid of the percent sign and put in a decimal point so that there are two decimal places. How many decimal places must we have when we change a percent number to a decimal number?

Two

6. (*Write 236% on board.*) Read this.

236%

I want to change this number to a decimal. What does 236% mean?

236 hundredths

How many decimal places in a hundredths number?

Two

So I get rid of the percent sign and put in two decimal places. (*Write 2.36.*) Read this.

2 and 36 hundredths

Yes, 236% = 2.36.

7. (*Write 8% on board.*) Read this.

8%

I want to change this number to a decimal. What does 8% mean?

8 hundredths

How many decimal places in a hundredths number?

Two

So I get rid of the percent sign and put in two decimal places. (*Write .08.*) Read this

8 hundredths

Yes, 8% = .08.

(*Repeat steps 6 and 7 with 34%, 126%, 5%, 82%.*)

PART C: STRUCTURED WORKSHEET

(*Give students a worksheet with instructions and problems similar to those below.*)

1. Change these percents to decimals:

   a. 35% = _____   e. 1% = _____
   b. 200% = _____   f. 192% = _____
   c. 6% = _____   g. 374% = _____
   d. 72% = _____   h. 2% = _____

2. Read the directions.

Change these percents to decimals.

3. Read the percent number in problem a.

35%

4. What does 35% mean?

35 hundredths

5. How many decimal places in a hundredths number?

Two

6. Where will we write the decimal point?

In front of the 3

7. Write the decimal number.

Students write .35.

TEACHER	STUDENTS
8. What decimal did you write?	35 hundredths

Yes, 35% equals 35 hundredths.

(*Repeat steps 1–7 with remaining problems.*)

FORMAT 14.2 Solving Simple Percentage Problems

TEACHER	STUDENTS

PART A: MORE/LESS THAN 100%

1. (*Write 100% on board.*) I want to change 100% to a decimal, so I get rid of the percent sign and put in two decimal places.

   (*Write 1.00 on board.*) 100% equals what whole number? Yes, 100% equals one whole. So when we multiply by 100%, we don't change the value of the number we're multiplying. The answer is the same as the number we're multiplying. — 1

2. Here are some rules about other percents: If we multiply by more than 100%, our answer is bigger than the number we're multiplying. If we multiply by less than 100%, our answer is less than the number we're multiplying.

3. If you multiply by 100%, what do you know about the answer? — The answer is the same as the number we're multiplying.

4. If you multiply by less than 100%, what do you know about the answer? — The answer is less than the number we're multiplying.

   Right, when the percent is less than 100, you multiply by a number less than 1. So the answer must be less than the number we're multiplying.

5. If you multiply by more than 100%, what do you know about the answer? — The answer is more than the number we're multiplying.

   (*Repeat steps 2–5 until students respond correctly.*)

6. Here's a problem: 60% × 20. Say the problem. — 60% × 20

   What's the percent? — 60

   Is the answer more than 20, less than 20, or equal to 20? (*Pause, signal.*) — Less than 20

   To correct: Remember: If the percent is less than 100, the answer is less than the amount we're multiplying. Is the percent less than 100? So, tell me about the answer. — The answer is less than 20.

   (*Repeat step 6.*)

   How do you know? — The percent is less than 100.

(*continued on next page*)

FORMAT 14.2 (continued)

TEACHER	STUDENTS

7. (*Repeat step 6 with 140% of 20, 100% of 20, 24% of 150, 100% of 150, and 60% of 150.*)

PART B: STRUCTURED BOARD PRESENTATION

1. (*Write 75% × 20 on board.*) Read this problem.

       75% × 20

    What is the percent?

       75

    What is the amount?

       20

    Will the answer be more or less than 20?

       Less than 20

2. Here's how we find the exact answer. We change the percent to a decimal, then multiply. How do we find the exact answer?

       Change the percent to a decimal and multiply.

3. First we write 75% as a decimal; 75% equals how many hundredths?

       75

    Yes, 75% can be written as 75 hundredths. (*Write .75.*)

4. Now we multiply. (*Write the problem on the board.*)

    $$\begin{array}{r} 20 \\ \times\,.75 \\ \hline 100 \\ 1400 \\ \hline 1500 \end{array}$$

    We multiplied by a decimal number, so I must put a decimal point in the answer. Where do I put the decimal point?

       After the 5

    So what whole number do we end with?

       15

5. What is 75% × 20?

       15

    Write 75% × 20 = 15. Say the statement.

       75% × 20 = 15.

6. Let's see if that follows the rules. The amount we began with was 20. We were finding less than 100%. Our answer must be less than 20. Is 15 less than 20?

       Yes

    So our answer makes sense.

    (*Repeat steps 1–6 with these problems:* 125% × 20, 5% × 20, 120% × 65, 12% × 65, 20% × 65.)

PART C: STRUCTURED WORKSHEET

   a.   30% × 50 = ☐
   b. 130% × 50 = ☐
   c.   3% × 50 = ☐
   d. 25% × 72 = ☐

1. Read problem a.

       30% × 50 =

    What is the percent?

       30

    What is the amount?

       50

    Will the answer be more or less than 50?

       Less than 50

2. Remember, we find the exact answer by changing the percent to a decimal and then multiplying. How do we find the exact answer?

       Change the percent to a decimal and then multiply.

3. First you need to write 30% as decimal; 30% equals how many hundredths?

       30

TEACHER	**STUDENTS**
4. Write 30% as 30 hundredths.	.30
5. What do you do next?	Multiply by 50.
6. Multiply. What is 30% × 50.	15
(*Repeat steps 1–6 for problems b–d.*)	

FORMAT 14.3 **Converting Decimals and Fractions to Percents**

TEACHER	**STUDENTS**
PART A: CONVERTING DECIMALS TO PERCENT	
1. We change a decimal to a percent by adding a percent sign after the number and moving the decimal point two places toward the percent sign. Listen again.	
(*Repeat rule.*)	
(*Write. 486 on board.*)	
2. Read this decimal.	486 thousandths
I want to change this decimal to a percent number. First I write the percent sign after the number.	
(*Write. 486% on board.*)	
3. Now I move the decimal point two places, toward the percent sign. What do I do?	Move the decimal point two places toward the percent sign.
(*Erase decimal point. Move two places to right: 48.6%.*)	
4. What percent do we end with?	48.6%
(*Repeat steps 1–4 with 1.4, 2, .73, .04.*)	
PART B: CONVERTING DECIMAL TO PERCENT WORKSHEET	
1. (*Give students a worksheet with instructions and problems like the following one.*)	
Convert these decimals and mixed decimals to percents:	

a. .38 = _____ e. 3 = _____ i. 7.3 = _____
b. 4.1 = _____ f. .542 = _____ j. .485 = _____.
c. .7 = _____ g. .04 = _____ k. 8 = _____
d. .07 = _____ h. .4 = _____ l. .02 = _____

TEACHER	**STUDENTS**
2. Read the instructions.	Convert these decimals and mixed decimals to percents.
3. Where do we write the percent sign?	After the number
4. What do we do to the decimal point?	Move it two places toward the percent sign.
5. Touch a. Read the number.	.38
6. Write the digits 3 and 8 in the space next to the decimal. Write in the percent sign.	

(*continued on next page*)

FORMAT 14.3 (continued)

TEACHER	STUDENTS
7. What must you do to the decimal point?	Move it two places toward the percent sign.
Put in the decimal. What percent does 38 hundredths equal?	38%

(*Repeat steps 4–6 with several more problems; then have students work the rest on their own.*)

PART C: STRUCTURED BOARD PRESENTATION

1. (*Write ⁵⁄₄ on the board.*)

   I want to write this fraction as a percent. Here's how we change a fraction to a percent. First we change the fraction to a decimal and then change that decimal to a percent. Listen again. (*Repeat procedure.*) Read this fraction. — Five-fourths

2. I want to change this fraction to a percent. First I change the fraction to a decimal. What do I do first? How do I change ⁵⁄₄ to a decimal? — Change the fraction to a decimal. Divide 4 into 5.

   I'll work the problem. I divide until there is no remainder. (*Solve the problem.*)

$$\frac{5}{4} = 4\overline{)5.00} = 1.25$$

$$
\begin{array}{r}
1.25 \\
4\overline{)5.00} \\
\underline{4} \\
1\,00 \\
\underline{80} \\
20
\end{array}
$$

   What mixed decimal does ⁵⁄₄ equal? — 1 and 25 hundredths

3. First I changed the fraction to a decimal. Now I change the decimal to a percent. What do I do next? — Change the decimal to a percent.

   I write the percent sign and move the decimal two places toward the percent sign. (*Write 125% on board*)

   How many percent does ⁵⁄₄ equal? — 125 percent

   (*Repeat steps 1–3 with ⅗, ½, and ⅞.*)

PART D: STRUCTURED WORKSHEET

1. (*Give students a worksheet with instructions and problems like the following.*)

   Change these fractions to percents:

   a. $\dfrac{3}{4} = \overline{)}$ =. _____ = _____%

   b. $\dfrac{2}{5} = \overline{)}$ =. _____ = _____%

   c. $\dfrac{8}{4} = \overline{)}$ =. _____ = _____%

2. In these problems, you must figure out the percent a fraction equals. First you change the fraction to a decimal. What do you do first? — Change the fraction to a decimal.

TEACHER	**STUDENTS**
How do you change ¾ to a decimal?	Divide 4 into 3.
Divide 4 into 3. Don't forget to put the decimal point in the answer. (*Pause.*) What decimal does ¾ equal?	75 hundredths
Write 75 hundredths in the space next to the division problem. Now you change the decimal to a percent.	
3. What do you do?	Change the decimal to a percent.
Do it and write your answer in the last space. (*Pause.*)	
4. What percent does ¾ equal?	75%
(*Repeat steps 1–3 with remaining problems.*)	

PART E: LESS STRUCTURED WORKSHEET

1. (*Give students a worksheet with instructions and problems like the following one.*)
Change each fraction to a percent:

a. $\dfrac{3}{4}$ =   b. $\dfrac{5}{2}$ =

c. $\dfrac{3}{5}$ =   d. $\dfrac{5}{4}$ =

2. Read the directions.	Change each fraction to a percent.
3. Touch a.	
4. What is the first fraction?	Three-fourths
What do you do first to ¾?	Make it a decimal.
Do it. Make ¾ into a decimal. (*Pause.*) What decimal does ¾ equal?	75 hundredths
5. Now write 75 hundredths as a percent. (*Pause.*) What percent does 75 hundredths equal?	75%
(*Repeat steps 1–4 with remaining problems.*)	

FORMAT 14.4 Simple Ratio Story Problems

TEACHER	**STUDENTS**

PART A: STRUCTURED BOARD PRESENTATION: TRANSLATING TO FRACTIONS

1. Listen to this problem: Jill took 8 basketball shots; she made 4 of the shots. What fraction of the shots did she make? Listen again: Jill took 8 shots. She made 4 of the shots. What fraction of the shots did she make?	
2. The problem asks what fraction of her shots she made. The fraction will be how many she actually made over how many she took altogether. The bottom number tells how many altogether. What does the bottom number tell?	How many altogether
How many shots did she take altogether?	8

(*continued on next page*)

FORMAT 14.4 (continued)

TEACHER	STUDENTS

TEACHER

So I write 8 on the bottom.

(*Write the following on the board.*)

$$\frac{\quad}{8}$$

3. The top number tells how many shots she made. How many shots did she make?

I write 4 on the top.
(*Write the fraction on the board.*)

$$\frac{4}{8}$$

4. Jill took 8 shots. She made 4 shots. What fraction of her shots did she make?

(*Repeat steps 1–4 with the examples below.*)

a. Jill has 8 pencils; 5 are blue. What fraction of her pencils are blue?
b. The class has 8 students; 5 are girls. What fraction of the students are girls?
c. There are 10 apples in a bag; 6 of the apples are red. What fraction of the apples are red?
d. Bill saved $5 so far. He needs $8 altogether. What fraction of the money he needs does he have?

PART B: WORKSHEET

1. (*Give students a worksheet with instructions and problems like the ones below.*)
Write the fractions for these problems:

  a. Jane made 12 out of the 16 shots she took during the game.

  b. Alex has 15 friends; 10 of his friends live in California.

  c. Sarah won 8 out of the 12 races she ran in last year.

  d. Tim picked 30 flowers; 18 are roses.

2. Read the directions.

3. Read problem a. What should the bottom number of the fraction tell?
What number tells altogether?
Say the fraction.
Write it.

(*Repeat step 2 with several problems and then have students do rest on their own.*)

STUDENTS

4

Four-eighths

Write the fractions for these problems.

How many altogether
16
Twelve-sixteenths

TEACHER   **STUDENTS**

PART C: LESS-STRUCTURED WORKSHEET

1. (*Give students a worksheet with problems like the ones below.*)
   a. Jean ran in 8 races. She won 2 of the races. What percent of the races did she win?
   b. Ann's team won 6 out of 8 games. What percent of the games did Ann's team win?
   c. Dina got 12 out of 15 problems correct on her test. What percent of the problems did she get correct?
   d. Jill has 8 pencils; 4 of her pencils are red. What percent of her pencils are red?

2. Read problem a. The problem asks for a percent. To find the percent, first you write a fraction. (*Repeat the problem.*) What fraction do you write? (*Pause, signal.*) Write it.   Two-eighths

3. Now you change the fraction to a percent.

4. What percent of the races did she win?   25%

FORMAT 14.5   Complex Ratio Problems

TEACHER   **STUDENTS**

PART A: DETERMINING THE FRACTION

1. Listen to this problem: I'm going to tell you about the cars that a salesman sold in September. He sold 10 blue cars (*write 10 blue cars on board*) and 14 red cars (*write 14 red cars on board*) in September. What fraction of the cars he sold were red?

2. The problem asks for the fraction of the cars that were red, so the fraction will be the number of red cars sold over the total number of cars sold. What should the bottom number tell?   The total number of cars sold.

   How many cars were sold altogether? (*Pause.*)   24

   (*Write the following on the board:*)

   $$\frac{}{24}$$

   To correct: Remember: The dealer sold 10 blue cars and 14 red cars. To find the total number of cars sold, what must you do? What is 10 and 14?   24

3. What does the top number tell?   The number of red cars sold.

   How many red cars were sold?   14
   (*Write the following on the board.*)
   $$\frac{14}{24}$$

4. What fraction of the cars sold in September were red?   Fourteen-twenty-fourths

   (*Repeat steps 1–4 with several examples of both simple and complex ratio problems.*)

PART B: LESS STRUCTURED WORKSHEET

   (*Adapt Part C from the simple ratio problem format in Format 14.4.*)

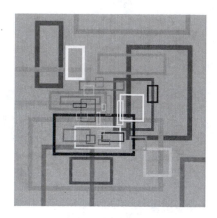

CHAPTER 15

Telling Time

Telling time is not as easy for all students to learn as teachers sometimes assume. Its difficulty is due to the number of discriminations students must make when telling time. In the following list are discriminations that, if not properly taught, tend to cause errors, especially for low-performing students:

1. Direction the clock hands move
2. Discrimination of the minute hand from the hour hand
3. Discrimination of minutes (which are not represented by the numerals on the clock) from hours (which are represented by the numerals on the clock)
4. Vocabulary discrimination; for example, when to use *after* and when to use *before*

Because of these potentially troublesome discriminations, we have divided instruction on telling time into three stages. First, students are taught a strategy for figuring out the time and expressing it as minutes after the hour. Second, when students have mastered minutes after the hour, alternate ways of expressing time as after the hour are taught, such as using a colon (8:40), quarter past, and half past. Third, students are taught a strategy for expressing time as minutes before the hour. See the Instructional Sequence and Assessment Chart for details and examples.

MINUTES AFTER THE HOUR

Preskills

The four major preskills for telling time are (a) knowledge of the direction in which the hands of the clock move, (b) discrimination of the hour hand from the minute hand, (c) counting by fives, and (d) switching from counting by fives to counting by ones, which is needed to determine the number of minutes (e.g., 5, 10, 15, 16, 17, 18, 19).

The preskill of knowing which direction the hands on a clock move is critical if students are to figure out the correct hour. A convenient way to teach students about direction on a clock is to have them fill in the missing numerals on several clocks containing boxes instead of numerals:

By doing this exercise, students can develop the pattern of moving in a clockwise direction around the clock face. In the first exercises, some of the numerals should be included as prompts on the clock (e.g., 3, 6, 9, 12). After several lessons, however,

Instructional Sequence and Assessment Chart

Grade Level	*Problem Type*	*Performance Indicator*

2a — Expressing time as minutes after the hour—minute hand pointing to a number

a.

b.

_____ minutes after_____   _____ minutes after_____

c.

_____ minutes after_____

2b — Expressing time as minutes after the hour—minute hand not pointing to numbers

a.

b.

_____minutes after_____   _____ minutes after_____

c.

_____minutes after_____

2c — Time expressed with hour stated first

a. Put an X on the line under the clock that says 7:25.

_____   _____

_____   _____

Instructional Sequence and Assessment Chart

Grade Level	*Problem Type*	*Performance Indicator*

b. Put an X on the line under the clock that says 4:03

_____   _____

_____   _____

c. Put an X on the line under the clock that says 2:53

_____   _____

_____   _____

3a   Expressing time as half past or quarter after or to the hour

○ quarter to 5   ○ half past 9
○ half past 5   ○ quarter after 7
○ 5 o'clock   ○ quarter after 8
○ quarter after 5   ○ quarter to 9

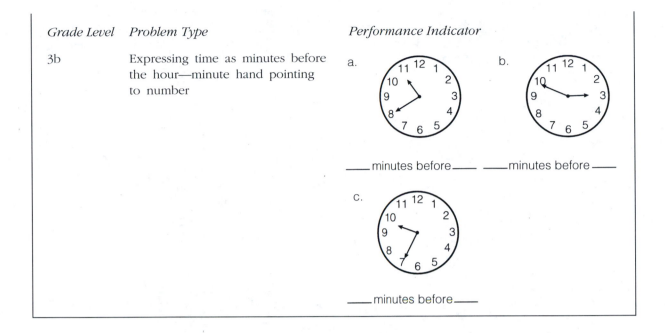

Grade Level	Problem Type	Performance Indicator

3b — Expressing time as minutes before the hour—minute hand pointing to number

a. _____ minutes before _____   b. _____ minutes before _____

c. _____ minutes before _____

these prompts should be removed, and the students should fill in all the numbers themselves. Teachers need to monitor students carefully while they work to make sure they fill in numerals in the proper direction. Teachers also can use a clock with movable hands and ask students to move the clock hands in the appropriate direction to assess student understanding of the concept.

Counting by fives is the initial way students are taught to determine the number of minutes. They are taught to start at the top of the clock, say *zero,* and then count the numbers by fives until they reach the minute hand. Later, the procedure is modified to teach students to determine the number of minutes when the minute hand is not pointing to a multiple of 5. In all procedures, however, the skill of counting by fives, or knowledge of the relevant multiplication facts, is important. Procedures for teaching counting by fives can be found in Chapter 4.

Discrimination of the hour hand from the minute hand is taught by describing each hand (the *short* hand is the hour hand, and the *long* hand is the minute hand) and then by providing discrimination practice in which students identify the hands. The teacher should present pictures of clocks and ask about each hand: "Which hand is this? How do you know it's the minute hand? Yes, the long hand is the minute hand." Commercial instructional clocks are well suited for this exercise, since teachers can manipulate the hands of the clock. The hands on the clock used for initial instruction should be easy to tell apart.

Units of 5 Minutes

The steps for teaching students to tell time by determining the number of minutes (in units of 5) after the hour is divided into five parts. (See Format 15.1.) Part A teaches students to read the hour. The teacher reminds students that the hour hand is the short hand and demonstrates how to figure out the hour by starting at the top of the clock and saying the numbers on the clock until reaching the hour hand.

Part B teaches students to determine the number of minutes after the hour. The teacher instructs students that the long hand is the minute hand and that the minute hand says to count by fives. The teacher then models and tests figuring out the minutes. The students are taught to start at the 12, say *zero,* and then count by 5 for each number, stopping at the number to which the minute hand is pointing. All examples in this format would have the minute hand pointing directly to a number.

Part C includes a board demonstration of how the strategies for determining minutes and hours are combined into a complete strategy for figuring out the time. Parts D and E are structured and less structured worksheet exercises in which the students are shown a clock and asked to write the time. Daily practice is continued for several weeks until students achieve fluency.

As a prompt to help students discriminate the hour and minute hands, we recommend that for the first several days, teachers use illustrations like the one below, in which the minute hand is drawn longer than usual. Note that in the illustration, the minute hand extends outside the clock and is written as a thin line so that it does not block students' view of the numerals on the clock.

When constructing a set of examples, the teacher must be quite careful to include a wide range of problems. In half of the clocks, the hour hand should be pointing toward the right side of the clock; on the other clocks, the hour hand should be pointing toward the left side of the clock. The same recommendation holds true for the minute hand. This helps prevent students from developing mis-rules that the strategies only apply to certain positions on the clock.

Also, examples should be arranged so that in half of the examples, the minute hand is pointing to a number larger than the one to which the hour hand is pointing. If the minute hand were pointing to the smaller number in all the examples, students might inadvertently learn that the hand pointing to the smaller number is the minute hand.

For the first week or two, examples in which the minute hand is pointing to the 12 are expressed as zero minutes after the hour. When students have demonstrated the ability to use the minutes-after strategy, the teacher can present the convention for saying *o'clock.* "When it's zero minutes after 4, we say it is 4 o'clock."

As students learn multiplication facts, they should be encouraged to use their knowledge of facts in determining the minutes rather than always starting at the top and counting by fives. The teacher explains that in figuring out minutes, each number

stands for a group of five. Therefore, when the minute hand points to 4, it is the same as four groups of five. Instead of counting, the minutes can be determined by solving 4×5.

Units of Single Minutes

After several weeks of practice expressing time with examples in which the minute hand points directly to a numeral, students can learn to express time when the minute hand is not pointing directly to a number. Note the following example:

No elaborate teaching format is required to introduce this skill. Students are told that to count the spaces in between the numbers, they count by ones. The teacher then models the process of counting by fives and switching to ones: "5, 10, 15, 20, 21, 22, 23; the time is 23 minutes after 7."

ALTERNATE WAYS OF EXPRESSING TIME

Quarter After and Half Past

The terms *quarter after* and *half past* are introduced when students master expressing time as minutes after the hour: A *quarter after* means 15 minutes after; *half past* means 30 minutes after. Teachers working with lower performing students would not introduce both terms at the same time. *Quarter after* might be introduced first. The instructional procedure consists of modeling and testing on several examples:

Summary Box 15.1
Stating Time as Minutes After the Hour

1. Students determine the hour by starting at the top of the clock and counting until they reach the hour hand. The time is stated as after _____.

2. Students determine the number of minutes after the hour by starting at the top of the clock, saying *zero,* and then counting by fives until they reach the minute hand.

3. Students practice determining the minutes after the hour.

1. Another way of saying 15 minutes after 2 is a quarter after two.
2. What's another way of saying 15 minutes after 2?
3. What's another way of saying 15 minutes after 8?

Next, an exercise in which the teacher states the time as a *quarter after* and the students restate it as minutes after is presented: "If it's a *quarter after* 2, how many minutes after 2 is it?" The same procedure is used to teach *half past* the hour. The final task consists of a discrimination exercise including both *quarter after* and *half past* the hour time:

1. What's another way of saying 15 minutes after 6?
2. What's another way of saying 30 minutes after 6?
3. If it's half past 4, how many minutes after 4 is it?
4. If it's a quarter after 4, how many minutes after 4 is it?

Using a Colon

When students are able to express time as minutes after the hour, the colon system, in which the hour is written first, can be introduced: "3:14 is read as *three-fourteen,* which means 14 minutes after 3." The procedures for teaching students to identify time that is shown by a colon involve modeling and testing how to translate the time expressed as minutes after the hour to time expressed as the hour and then the minutes after: "Here's another way of saying 28 minutes after 5: *five-twenty-eight.* What's another way of saying 28 minutes after 5?"

The teacher models and tests several more examples and then tests students on a series of four to six examples by saying the time as minutes after the hour and asking students to express it as hours then minutes after (e.g., "Tell me another way of saying 35 minutes after 4"). The teacher repeats the set of examples until students can respond correctly to all of them.

After several lessons, the teacher has students practice expressing time in a variety of ways:

> "I'll say the time one way, and then say it another way. Listen: 8:24. I'll say the time the other way: 24 minutes after 8. Your turn: 8:24. Say the time the other way." Repeat with 4:15, 7:32, 9:28.

After learning to state the time as the hour then minutes after, students also can be taught how to read and write the time using a colon. A written task like the one below, in which students are required to express the time as both minutes after the hour and as the hour and then minutes, should be introduced next.

_____ minutes after _____

_____ : _____

Times of less than 10 minutes after the hour are particularly difficult, since a zero must be added when the time is expressed both verbally and in written form. For example, 8 minutes after 6 is written as 6:08 and stated as *six oh eight.* This type of example should not be introduced until students have mastered easier ones. Several of these more difficult types should appear thereafter on worksheet exercises.

MINUTES BEFORE THE HOUR

Teachers should not introduce telling time as minutes before the hour until students can express time as minutes after the hour with accuracy and fluency. Students should demonstrate mastery by completing a worksheet of clocks with at least 90% accuracy at a rate of no more than 6 to 7 seconds per clock.

The procedure for teaching students to express time as minutes before the hour is somewhat similar to the one used in teaching students to express time as minutes after the hour. First, the teacher presents a strategy to figure out the hour, then a strategy to figure out the minutes, and then an exercise in which both strategies are applied to express the time (see Format 15.2).

The teacher first presents an exercise in which she places the hour hand between two numbers, then models and tests saying what hour it is after and what hour it is before. For example, if the hour hand were pointing between 5 and 6, the teacher would say the hour is after 5 and before 6. Next, the teacher shows students how to figure out the number of minutes before the hour. She points in a counterclockwise direction and tells the students that in figuring minutes before the hour, they start at the 12 but count in this direction (pointing counterclockwise). The teacher models and tests several examples. The next exercise is a structured one in which the teacher leads students through expressing the time as minutes before the hour.

During the first week that expressing time as minutes before the hour is presented, the minute hand should point directly to the numerals so that

FIGURE 15.1 Student Errors in Telling Time

a.

b.

c.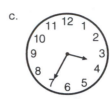

d.

30 minutes after 1   45 minutes after 8   15 minutes after 7   10 minutes after 4

all minute times involve multiples of five. Examples in which the minute hand points to a line between the numerals are introduced later. Examples should be limited to times that are 30 minutes or less before the hour (i.e., the minute hand is pointing toward the center or the left part of the clock).

DIAGNOSIS AND REMEDIATION

Errors in telling time usually are caused by component-skill errors. The remediation procedure is to reteach the component skill, then present several structured worksheet examples, then several less structured worksheet examples, and finally to provide supervised practice. Figure 15.1 shows some errors that might indicate a particular component-skill error.

In examples a and b, the student's answer is 5 minutes more than the proper time. The student is probably starting to count by fives when touching 12 instead of saying zero when touching 12. The remediation would begin with the part of the format that teaches figuring out minutes after the hour.

The errors in examples c and d may be caused by the student's confusing the minute and hour hands. If this type of error occurs frequently, the teacher presents exercises focusing on discriminating the hour hand from the minute hand (see above). If the confusion is severe, the teacher might use examples in which the minute hand is elongated to serve as a prompt.

APPLICATION ITEMS: TELLING TIME

1. Below are sets of examples prepared by teachers to use in early exercises to teach telling time as minutes after the hour. Which sets are inappropriate and why?

    Set A: 15 minutes after 8   10 minutes after 7
               10 minutes after 9   5 minutes after 7

    Set B: 13 minutes after 2   25 minutes after 4
               37 minutes after 10   10 minutes after 9

    Set C: 20 minutes after 7   35 minutes after 4
               15 minutes after 2   30 minutes after 8

2. Tell the probable cause of each student's errors.

   a. *Tom*

30 minutes after 3   50 minutes after 8   10 minutes after 11

b. *Jessica*

50 minutes after 12   20 minutes after 9   35 minutes after 5

c. *Peter*

30 minutes after 2   15 minutes after 8   50 minutes after 6

3. Specify the wording the teacher uses in correcting the first error made by each student in problem 2. The wording will be different for each student.

FORMAT 15.1   Expressing Time as Minutes After the Hour (Units of 5 Minutes)

TEACHER   **STUDENTS**

PART A: DETERMINING THE HOUR

1. (*Draw the following clock on the board.*)

2. One of the hands is missing on this clock. (*Point to the hour hand.*) This short hand is the hour hand. What is the short hand?

The hour hand

3. Let's figure out what hour the hand is after. We start at the top of the clock and say the numbers until we come to the hour hand. I'll touch; you say the numbers. Say stop when I come to the hour hand. (*Starting with 12, touch each numeral and then the hour hand as the children say the numbers.*)

12, 1, 2, 3, 4, 5, stop

4. What was the last numeral I touched?

5

(*continued on next page*)

FORMAT 15.1 (continued)

TEACHER	STUDENTS

5. The hour hand is after 5. So, the hour is after 5. Tell me about the hour.

   After 5

   (Repeat steps 1–4 with after 8.)

6. *(Point hour hand to after 5.)* Now let's figure out the hour a fast way, without counting. Look at the clock. What numeral is the hour hand after?

   5

   So tell me about the hour.

   After 5

   (Repeat step 5 with several more examples: after 9, after 2, after 6, after 3, after 10.)

PART B: MINUTES AFTER

1. *(Draw the following clock on the board.)*

2. This long hand is the minute hand. What is the long hand called?

   The minute hand

   The minute hand is very funny. It tells you to count by 5. What does the minute hand tell you to do?

   Count by 5.

3. Watch me figure out the minutes. *(Point to the minute hand.)* I touch the top of the clock and say zero. Then I count by 5 until I come to the minute hand. *(Touch the clock above 12.)* Zero. *(Starting with 1, touch each numeral as you count: 5, 10, 15, 20, 25.)*

4. Tell me about the minutes.

   25 minutes

5. Your turn. I'll touch the numerals; you count by 5. Remember to say zero when I touch the top of the clock. *(Touch the clock above 12 and then touch each numeral as the children count.)*

   0, 5, 10, 15, 20, 25

6. Tell me about the minutes.
   Yes, 25 minutes.

   25 minutes

   (Repeat steps 4–5 with five more examples: hand points to 3, hand points to 7, hand points to 2, hand points to 10, hand points to 4.)

PART C: STRUCTURED BOARD PRESENTATION

1. *(Draw the following clock on the board.)*

TEACHER	**STUDENTS**
2. We're going to figure out what time this clock shows. First we'll figure out the minutes. Then we'll figure out the hour.	
3. First the minutes. Which hand is the minute hand, the short hand or the long hand?	The long hand
4. What does the minute hand tell you to count by?	Count by 5.
Where do you start counting?	At the top of the clock
What do you say?	Zero
(*Repeat step 3 until all questions are answered correctly.*)	
5. Count by 5 to the minute hand. (*Touch the top of the clock and then the numerals as the children count.*)	0, 5, 10, 15
How many minutes?	15
I'll write the answer. (*Write 15 minutes under the clock.*)	
6. We know it's 15 minutes, but we don't know about the hour. Look at the hour hand. Tell me about the hour. (*Pause, signal.*)	After 6
7. Yes, after 6. I'll write the answer. (*Write after 6.*) That's the time the clock shows, 15 minutes after 6. What time does the clock show? Say the time.	15 minutes after 6
(*Repeat steps 1–6 with 5 minutes after 7, 45 minutes after 4, 20 minutes after 2, 25 minutes after 10.*)	

PART D: STRUCTURED WORKSHEET

_____ minutes after _____   _____ minutes after _____

1. (*Give students a worksheet that includes about six to eight clocks like those above.*)

2. Everyone touch the first clock on your worksheet. First you'll figure out the minutes, then you'll figure out the hour.	
3. Which is the minute hand?	The long hand
What does the minute hand tell you to count by?	Count by 5.
Where do you start counting?	At the top of the clock
What do you say at the top of the clock?	Zero
Let's figure the minutes.	
4. Touch the 12. Count and touch as 1 clap. (*Clap once each second.*)	0, 5, 10, 15, 20, 25, 30, 35
How many minutes?	35 minutes
Write *35* in front of the word *minutes*.	
5. Touch the hour hand. Tell me about the hour. (*Pause, signal.*)	After 4
Yes, it says after 4. Write 4 in the next space.	
6. Now tell me what time that clock says.	35 minutes after 4
(*Repeat steps 1–5 with each remaining clock.*)	

(continued on next page)

FORMAT 15.1   (continued)

TEACHER	STUDENTS

PART E: LESS STRUCTURED WORKSHEET

1. (*Give the students a worksheet with problems like the one below.*)

_____ minutes after _____

2. Touch clock a. You're going to figure out the time and write it under the clock.

3. Figure out the minutes and write the minutes in the first blank. (*Monitor response.*) How many minutes?

   20

4. Now figure the hour and write it in the last blank.

5. Read what time the clock says.

   20 minutes after 6

FORMAT 15.2   **Expressing Time as Minutes Before the Hour**

TEACHER	STUDENTS

PART A: DETERMINING THE HOUR

1. (*Draw the following clock on the board.*)

2. In telling time, you've learned to say how many minutes after the hour. Another way of telling time is to say the number of minutes before the hour.

3. Look at this clock. What hour is it after?

   4

4. The next bigger number tells you the hour it's before.
   Tell me the hour it's before.
   Yes, it's before 5. What is the hour?

   5
   Before 5

5. (*Move the hour hand between 7 and 8.*) Tell me the hour by saying what hour it is before. (*Pause, signal.*)

   Before 8

   (*Repeat step 4 moving the hand to five more positions: between 2 and 3, between 10 and 11, between 6 and 7, between 11 and 12, between 12 and 1.*)

TEACHER   **STUDENTS**

Part B: Minutes Before the Hour

1. (*Draw the following clock on the board.*)

2. Now we'll figure out the minutes before the next hour. When
   we figure the minutes before the hour, we start at the 12 but
   we count this way (*Point* ⌒) until we get to the minute
   hand. My turn: 0, 5, 10, 15, 20. It's 20 minutes before.
   How many minutes before?   20 minutes before

3. Show me which way you count to figure the minutes before
   the hour. Where do we start counting?   At the 12

   What do we say first?   Zero

   (*Move minute hand to 10.*) Tell me how many minutes
   before. (*Pause, signal.*)   10 minutes before

      To correct: We're figuring out minutes before, so we count
      this way (⌒). I'll touch, you count.

   (*Repeat step 2 with four more examples: hand pointing to
   10, 8, 11, 7.*)

Part C: Structured Board Presentation

1. (*Draw the following clock on the board.*)

_____ minutes before _____

2. Let's tell what time this clock says by telling how many
   minutes before the hour.

3. (*Point to the hour hand.*) Which hand is this?   The hour hand
   What hour is it before? (*Pause. write 4.*)   4

4. (*Point to minute hand.*) Which hand is this?   The minute hand
   How many minutes before 4 is it? (*Pause. Write 20.*)   20 minutes
      To correct: Show me which way we count when we
      figure out minutes before. Count as I point.

5. What time does the clock say?   20 minutes before 4
   (*Repeat steps 1–4 with additional times: 5 before 2, 25
   before 8, 15 before 11, 10 before 12, 20 before 5.*)

(continued on next page)

FORMAT 15.2 (continued)

TEACHER	STUTDENTS

PART D: STRUCTURED WORKSHEET

1. (*Give students worksheet with six to eight clocks. Under each clock is written _____ minutes before _____.)*

2. Let's find out what time these clocks say by finding out how many minutes before the hour.

3. Find the hour hand on clock a. What hour is it before? (*Pause, signal.*)

   Before 8

4. Now let's find out how many minutes before 8. Start at the top of the clock—remember which way to count. How many minutes before 8? (*Pause, signal.*)

   20 minutes

5. What time does this clock say?
   Fill in the blanks.

   20 minutes before 8

   (*Repeat with remaining examples.*)

CHAPTER 16

Money

The need for instruction in money-related skills is derived from their importance in daily activities. Included in this chapter are procedures for (a) determining the value of a group of coins, (b) counting change, (c) decimal notation for money, and (d) consumer skills. A more in-depth list of problem types appears in the Instructional Sequence and Assessment Chart.

DETERMINING THE VALUE OF A GROUP OF COINS

Preskills for determining the value of a group of coins include the ability to identify and tell the value of individual coins and knowledge of the 5, 10, and 25 count-by series.

Students are usually taught to identify coins in the first grade. This is a fairly simple preskill to teach, since many students will already be able to recognize several coins. A format similar to that used in symbol identification is taught for coin identification. The teacher initially models and tests the name of the coin and then models and tests its value: "This is a nickel. What is this? . . . A nickel is worth 5¢. How much is a nickel worth? . . . " For this task, the teacher can use either real coins or pictures of coins.

The penny and nickel should be introduced first. After students can label and state their values, dimes can be introduced, followed by quarters. Note that the coins are introduced *cumulatively,* which implies that students must be able to discriminate the new coin from previously introduced coins before the teacher can present a new example.

The preskill for counting groups of similar coins is knowledge of the respective count-by series. Once students have learned the count-by series, they have little trouble applying the skill to coin counting. In teaching students to count groups of similar coins for the first time, the teacher indicates the value of the coin and then models counting. For example, "Here is a group of nickels. Each nickel is worth 5¢. To find out how many cents this group of nickels equals, I count by fives. My turn." The teacher then counts by fives as she touches each coin. After modeling, the teacher tests students on counting several sets of identical coins. Worksheet exercises like the one in Figure 16.1 should follow the oral presentation.

Problems in which students determine the value of a set of mixed coins are usually introduced in second grade and contain just two or three coins. In later grades, the number of coins to be counted increases. We recommend a two-step strategy: (a) grouping like coins together and (b) starting with the coin worth the most and counting all like coins, then switching to the next lower coin in the group and counting the value of that coin. For example, in counting two quarters, three dimes, and two nickels, students would begin counting the two quarters (25, 50), switch to the dimes (60, 70, 80), and switch once more to the nickels (85, 90).

Instructional Sequence and Assessment Chart

Grade Level	Problem Type	Performance Indicator

1a   Value of single coins

= _____ ¢   = _____ ¢

= _____ ¢   = _____ ¢

1b   Determining value of groups of like coins

= _____ ¢

= _____ ¢

= _____ ¢

2a   Determining value of groups of different coins

= _____ ¢

= _____ ¢

= _____ ¢

Grade Level	Problem Type	Performance Indicator
2b	Adding dollars and cents	$1.32 $4.78 + $2.43 + $6.92
3a		
	change from less than $1.00	half dollar. The clerk gives you this change. Is it correct?

You bought a soda that costs 27¢. You give the clerk 35¢. The clerk gives you this change. Is it correct?

Grade Level	Problem Type	Performance Indicator
3b	Consumer skills: specifying change	Write the coins you would need to make 27¢. Write the coins you would need to make 79¢. Write the coins you would need to make 43¢.
3c	Decimal notation: reading and writing dollar and cents notations under 10 dollars	Write four dollars & six cents_____ Write nine dollars & thirty cents _____ Write one dollar & five cents _____
4a	Decimal notation: subtracting dollars and cents from whole dollar figures	$15.00 − 1.35 = 9.00 − 8.20 = 10.00 − 6.16 =
4b	Consumer skills: adding and subtracting whole dollars and dollar and cents amounts	Jack had $6. He spent $3.25. How much does he have left? If you had $4 and you got $2.15 more, how much would you have? Jan buys a shirt for $2.85. She gives the clerk a $5 bill. How much change does she get back?
4c	Consumer skills: determining cost of purchase for two groups of items	You buy 3 pencils for 15¢ each and 5 pencils for 10¢ each. How much do you spend? You buy 4 pens for 30¢ each and 2 erasers for 12¢ each. How much do you spend? You buy 5 pens for 15¢ each and 3 erasers for 8¢ each. How much do you spend?
4d	Consumer skills: how much can be bought with specified amount	Bill wants to buy pencils which cost 7¢ each. He has 2 dollar bills and a dime. How many pencils can he buy? Kate has 3 quarters. If spoons cost 5¢ each, how many spoons can she buy? Ray has 3 half dollars. If spoons cost 5¢ each, how many spoons can he buy?

Instructional Sequence and Assessment Chart (continued)

Grade Level	Problem Type	Performance Indicator
4e	Consumer skills: reading a price list	

Hamburger		Ice cream	
plain	35¢	cone	
cheese	50¢	small	40¢
bacon	70¢	large	60¢
fries add	20¢	sundae	
Soda		small	60¢
small	30¢	large	80¢
med.	40¢		
large	50¢		

Anna wants two hamburgers with cheese, one with fries, one without fries, a large soda, and two large ice cream cones. How much will all that cost?

Grade Level	Problem Type	Performance Indicator
5a	Consumer skills: comparison shopping— unit cost	A 6 oz. package of rice made by ABC Company costs 96¢. A 5 oz. package made by the XYZ company costs 90¢. Which package of rice is the best buy? Tell why.

Beginning with higher value coins is recommended over beginning with lower value coins, since the latter strategy more often results in a difficult counting sequence. For example, to count a quarter, dime, nickel, and two pennies, the student would count 1, 2, 7, 17, 42; counting 25, 35, 40, 41, 42 is much easier.

A preskill for counting a group of unlike coins is knowledge of addition facts in which 10, 5, or 1 is added to a two-digit number ending in zero or 5 (e.g., 70 and 10 more is ... 70 and 5 more is ...). This preskill can be taught using a model-test procedure in which the teacher models several problems and then tests students on a set of problems (e.g., 40 and 10 more, 40 and 5 more, 40 and 1 more, 45 and 5 more, 45 and 1 more, 80 and 5 more, 80 and 1 more, 20 and 10 more, 20 and 5 more).

Facts in which 10 is added to a two-digit number ending in 5 (35 + 10, 65 + 10) are particularly hard. They should not be introduced until the easier facts are mastered. Practice should be provided daily for several weeks, either orally or through worksheet exercises. If teachers use worksheets to provide this practice, they should write problems horizontally and indicate to students that they are to complete the problems mentally (not realign them vertically and compute).

To teach students to determine the value of a set of mixed coins, the teacher initially models by touching and counting the coins, and then tests, prompting students by telling the value of each coin. For example, if the problem is to determine the value of a group of coins including two quarters, three dimes, and a nickel, the teacher would start, pointing to the first quarter:

Teacher	Students
25 and (*pointing to next quarter*)	
25 more is ...	50
50 and (*pointing to the first dime*)	
10 more is ...	60
60 and (*pointing to next dime*)	
10 more is ...	70
70 and (*pointing to next dime*)	
10 more is ...	80
80 and (*pointing to nickel*)	
5 more is ...	85

COUNTING CHANGE

Two change-related skills are discussed in this section: (a) making equivalent change, which involves exchanging a group of smaller valued coins for a larger valued coin (e.g., two dimes and a nickel for a quarter), and (b) verifying the change received from a purchase. These skills are generally taught in third grade. The primary preskill for counting change is the ability to count groups of coins.

Making Equivalent Change

Giving equivalent change for a larger coin is not a complex skill to teach. However, two kinds of equivalent change exercises should be practiced. In

FIGURE 16.1 Coin Counting Worksheet

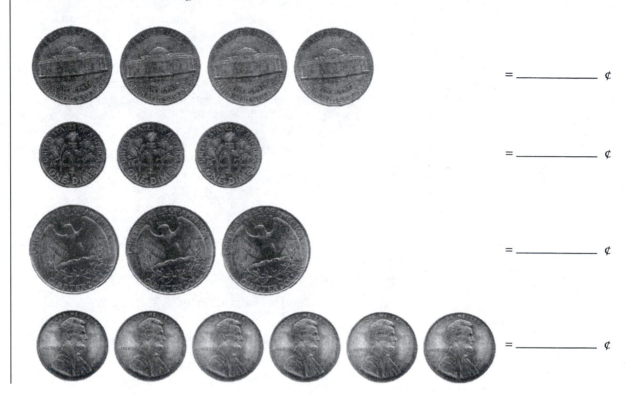

the first type, the teacher has students first identify the value of a larger value coin. Then the teacher has students determine the number of smaller value coins equal to the original coin. In this exercise, students are always counting similar coins. In the second type of equivalent change problem, the students must count a set of different coins to determine whether or not a given amount of change is equivalent to the amount stated. Both types of exercises are illustrated in Format 16.1.

Initially, coin equivalency problems should include pennies, nickels, dimes, and quarters (e.g., a quarter equals two dimes and a nickel). Larger values, including dollar bills, are introduced later.

Worksheet exercises like Figure 16.2 present a different application of the equivalency skill. In these exercises, students circle the appropriate more, less, or equal sign between two groups of coins. To introduce this exercise, the teacher leads the students in counting the coins in each group. After counting the coins, the students are instructed to write above each group its value. If the values are equal, the student is instructed to circle the equal sign. If the values of the groups are not equal, the students circle the appropriate *more than* or *less than* sign.

Verifying Change

The easiest way to verify change received is to begin at the price of the item(s) and then count the coins received as change, beginning with the coin of least value. Students then compare the number they derived to the amount given to pay for the purchase (see Format 16.2). For example, if a purchase of 36¢ is made and the student is given back four pennies

FIGURE 16.2 Worksheet on Equivalent Change

and two nickels after paying the clerk a half dollar, the student would count 37, 38, 39, 40, 45, 50. The student then knows the change given is correct, since she ends with 50¢, the value of the amount given to make the purchase.

Initial examples should be relatively easy, including small numbers of coins. Later examples can include a greater number of coins. An example appropriate for the introduction of the skill might consist of payment of 40¢ for an object costing 36¢. To verify the change in this example, students need to count only pennies: 37, 38, 39, 40. A later example might involve payment of a dollar for an object costing 36¢, for which students would need to count pennies, dimes, and quarters: 37, 38, 39, 40, 50, 75, a dollar. (See Format 16.2.)

Problems involving more than one dollar are introduced last. Note that the same strategy applies to counting change from dollars. The student counts the change to determine if the object's cost plus the change equals the payment price. For example, if an object costing 37¢ is paid for with a $10 bill, counting change would proceed as follows: 38, 39, 40, 50, 75, a dollar, 2, 3, 4, 5, 10 dollars. Again, practice is provided on worksheet exercises and through hands-on activities in which students exchange facsimiles of coins.

DECIMAL NOTATION IN MONEY

Money problems expressed in decimal notation generally are introduced in third grade. A typical problem may state that a 39¢ toy is paid for with a $5 bill and ask how much change should be given. The solution is computed by subtracting 39¢ from $5 and is expressed as $4.61. Specifying the exact coins is not an appropriate response for this problem unless the problem asks students to specify the type of change that would be given. Since many application problems call for a specific amount rather than the coins used to make change, the decimal notation for money should be introduced in the primary grades, even if general decimal instruction has not begun.

Fortunately, decimal notation for money is relatively safe to introduce before more comprehensive decimal instruction is taught. The students can be told that the two numbers to the right of the decimal tell about cents, while the numbers to the left of the decimal tell about dollars. A format for teaching students to read and write dollar figures expressed with decimal notation appears in Format 16.3. Both parts of the format are presented daily for 2 or 3 weeks. Six to eight examples should be included in each part.

Practice should include examples without dollars (e.g., $.45, $.30) and examples without cents (e.g., $5.00, $13.00). Students can be expected to have difficulty writing amounts between 1 and 9 cents because of the need to place a zero after the decimal: $7.03, $14.08. These examples, therefore, should not be introduced in the initial exercises. Concentrated practice on this type of example should be provided in later lessons. At that time, the teacher explains that there must always be two digits after the decimal when writing money figures. The teacher then models that when the number of cents is below 10, a zero and then the digit for the number of cents are written.

Story problems with money expressed in decimal notation should be introduced when students can read and write decimal notation for money. A common type of story problem that deserves special attention is illustrated below:

Jim bought a shirt for $3.62. He gave the clerk a $10 bill. How much change will Jim receive?

Jill had $6. She was given $3.50 for working in the yard. How much money does she have now?

In these problems, a dollar amount is expressed without cents after the decimal point. When working the problem, students must write the dollar amount with a decimal point and two zeroes. The critical skill of aligning the numbers according to the decimal point was discussed in Chapter 13. The teacher models working several problems of this type before assigning students to work them independently.

CONSUMER SKILLS

Three consumer skills are discussed in this section. The first, a skill taught in second or third grade, involves teaching students to pay for purchases with coins. The second, taught in third or fourth grade, involves teaching students to read price lists and menus. The third, taught in fourth or fifth grade, involves teaching unit pricing to make comparisons when shopping.

Making Purchases with Coins

When purchasing an item in a store, the student should use a strategy that allows her, as quickly as possible, to figure out the coins to give. We recommend that students begin counting with the largest value coins. For example, if a student has an assortment of coins and wants to buy something costing

28¢, the fastest way to count the exact amount is to use a quarter and three pennies. This skill can be taught by using real coins or facsimiles of coins. We recommend that the teacher introduce the rule, "When you count money to buy something, you start with the coins that are worth the most." Next, the teacher models several examples and then gives students problems to solve. The steps for teaching this skill appear in Format 16.4.

A mistake often made by students is inappropriately allocating only pennies for the value of the ones (regardless of the other coins used). For example, when counting out 38¢, students might count out 30¢ using a quarter and a nickel and then count out eight pennies instead of using a quarter (25), a dime (35), and 3 pennies. One way to prompt students to use larger coins when possible is to limit the number of pennies they are given (i.e., give students only four pennies). This procedure forces students to use nickels and dimes more wisely. As students become more adept at counting coins efficiently, the teacher can give them more pennies. Often, students will not have the appropriate coins to allow them to count an exact amount. For these situations, students must be taught to count an amount that exceeds the purchase price.

Format 16.5 teaches students to use the fewest coins to make a purchase. For example, with a purchase price of 69¢ and these coins—three quarters and two dimes—the coins that give a value closest to 69¢ are two quarters and two dimes; however, using up the larger coins is much easier, in this case three quarters.

Counting Change

Counting change is usually done by a clerk. Because most cash registers display the amount of change to give, students must be able to reach the amount using the fewest number of coins. Format 16.6 outlines the procedure for teaching that skill. The format is written just for coins. However, the format easily can be altered to teach the skill with dollars. In the adaptation, the examples would include whole dollars, and students wouldn't write letters for coins but rather the numbers that represent the bills (e.g., 20, 10, 5, and 1). Similar wording can be used: "Start with the bill worth the most and see how close you can get. Then try the next largest bill." After students have mastered change for coins

and bills separately, mixed amounts can be presented. First tell the students to figure the bills. Check their answers. Then have them figure the coins and check their answers.

Price Lists and Menus

Many price lists or menus utilize indentation systems to describe subcategories of a general group. Figure 16.3 includes a sample menu students might encounter in a fast-food restaurant. Teachers should test students on reading various price lists and menus by asking students the prices of the items represented. Teachers can then give students story problems such as: "Jerry has 2 dollars. He wants to buy a small hamburger, large French fries, and a small ice cream. Does he have enough money? If so, how much change will he receive?"

Unit Pricing

Unit pricing comparison shopping involves determining the relative cost of the same type of item when it appears in packages containing different quantities. For example, a 10 oz. bag of ABC soap costs 97¢ and an 8 oz. bag of XYZ soap costs 86¢. Which soap is a better buy? The teacher presents the rule: "To compare similar items in different sized packages, we must divide to find the unit price." The teacher then models with several examples. For example, in comparing a 6 lb. package that costs 42¢ with a 5 lb. package that costs 40¢, the teacher points out that you must find the cost per pound (the unit price) and illustrates how this can be done by dividing the total cost by the number of pounds: $42 \div 6 = 7$ and $40 \div 5 = 8$. After computing the problems, it is easy to see that the 6 lb. package is a better buy, since it costs a penny less per pound.

FIGURE 16.3 Worksheet for Reading Menus

XYZ Fast Food Restaurant
MENU

Hamburgers		*Ice Cream*	
plain—small	$ .60	cones	
plain—large	$ 1.25	large	$.60
with cheese	add 10¢	small	$.50
French Fries		cups	
large	$ .60	large	$.50
small	$ .35	small	$.30

APPLICATION ITEMS: MONEY

1. When counting a quarter, a dime, and two nickels, students count as specified below. Tell the probable cause of their errors. Specify what the teacher says to correct each student. (Assume students know the value of each coin.)

   Jill—25, 30, 35, 40
   Jim—5, 10, 20, 35

2. Tell the probable cause for each error below. Specify what the teacher says to correct each student. Jill has 5 dollars. She buys a pencil for 4 cents. How much money does she have left?

   Tom

   $$\begin{array}{r} 4 \\ \$5.00 \\ -\ .04 \\ \hline \$4.06 \end{array}$$

   Ann

   $$\begin{array}{r} 5 \\ -4 \\ \hline 1 \end{array}$$

FORMAT 16.1   Making Equivalent Change

TEACHER	STUDENTS
PART A: COUNTING SIMILIAR COINS	
1. *(Show students real or pretend coins.)* I want to find out how many nickels equal one dime. How much is a dime worth?	10¢
So I count nickels until I get to 10. What do I count by when I count nickels?	5
Stop me when I get to 10. 5,10…	Stop.
How many nickels did I count?	2
So how many nickels equal one dime?	2
(Repeat step 1 to help students figure out how many pennies are in a dime.)	
2. *(Review previously taught equivalencies.)*	
How many pennies in a nickel?	5
How many nickels in a dime?	2
How many pennies in a dime?	10
PART B: COUNTING DIFFERENT COINS	
1. I gave a man a quarter and he gave me two dimes and a nickel. Let's figure out if these coins are worth the same as a quarter. How much is a quarter worth?	25¢
Let's count the coins and see if they're worth 25¢. I'll touch. You count.	10, 20, 25
Are those coins worth 25¢?	Yes

FORMAT 16.2   Verifying Change

TEACHER	STUDENTS
1. *(Write the following on the board.)* 36¢ P P P P D Q Q	
2. *(Point to P.)* This stands for penny. *(Point to D.)* This stands for dime. *(Point to Q.)* This stands for quarter. *(Point to each letter in random order and ask)* What does this stand for?	
3. *(Point to 36¢.)* John bought apples that cost 36¢. He gave the man a dollar. We're going to count the change John got and see if it's right. We'll count from 36 and see if we end with a dollar. *(Point to pennies.)* What do we count by for these?	1
(Point to dime.) What do we count by for this?	10
(Point to quarters.) What do we count by for these?	25
4. Let's count the change. Start with 36—count. *(Point to coins as students count.)*	37, 38, 39, 40, 50, 75, 100
Did we end with a dollar?	Yes
(Repeat steps 2 and 3 with several more examples.)	

FORMAT 16.3   Decimal Notation for Money

TEACHER	STUDENTS
PART A: READING DECIMAL NOTATION	
1. *(Write the following on the board.)* $4.32	
2. Here is the way to write dollars and cents. *(Point to the decimal point in $4.32.)* This dot is a decimal point. It divides dollars and cents. *(Point to 4.)* This tells us four dollars. *(Point to 32.)* These two numbers tell us about cents. I'll read the amount: Four dollars and thirty-two cents.	
3. *(Write the following on the board.)* $3.62	
How many dollars?	3
How many cents?	62
Say the whole amount.	$3.62
(Repeat step 2 with $7.20, $.45, $6.00, $.30*)*	
PART B: WRITING WITH DECIMAL NOTATION	
1. *(Give each student a sheet of lined paper.)* You're going to write money amounts using a dollar sign and a decimal point.	

(continued on next page)

FORMAT 16.3   (continued)

TEACHER	STUDENTS
2. Listen: Eight dollars and thirty-two cents. Say that. How many dollars? Write a dollar sign, then an 8.	$8.32 8
3. Eight dollars and thirty-two cents. How many cents? Write a decimal point on the line. Then write 32.	32
4. What amount did you write? (Repeat steps 2–4 with these examples: $6.42, $.32, $4.10, $7.00, $.57, $9.00.)	$8.32

*For examples with no dollars, the teacher should model the
response on the first day the format appears.

FORMAT 16.4   Counting Coins to Reach an Exact Value

TEACHER	STUDENTS
1. Today you're going to count out money at your seats. I'll tell you how much something costs and you count out the money to buy it. When you count out money to buy something, start with the coin that's worth the most. If I want to buy something for 25¢, would I use 25 pennies or 1 quarter? Why?	1 quarter A quarter is worth more than a penny.
Right, a quarter is worth more than a penny. If I want to buy something that costs 20¢, would I use nickels or dimes? Why?	Dimes A dime is worth more than a nickel.
2. My turn. I want to buy a balloon that costs 31¢. I start with a quarter: 25, 30, 31. (Write Q N P on board.)	
3. Your turn. (Pass out coins, either real or facsimiles.) A toy car costs 28¢. Start with the coin that's worth the most and count out 28¢.	Students should put out a quarter and three pennies.
(Monitor student responses.)	
(Repeat step 3 with several more examples.)	

FORMAT 16.5   Counting Coins When You Don't Have the Exact Amount

TEACHER	STUDENTS
1. I'm going to use the coins I have to buy something that costs 56¢. (Write 56¢. Below, write Q Q Q D D D.) This is all the money I have to use. I start with the coin that has the greatest value. I get as close as I can. If I don't have the exact amount, I have to give more. I'll get the extra money back as change. Watch.	

TEACHER   **STUDENTS**

(Circle a coin each time you count.)

25, 50, 75.
I paid more than 56¢, so I'll get some change back.

2. Your turn. Point to problem a on your worksheet.

   a. 36¢ Q D D N

Start with the coin worth the most. If you don't have exactly
36¢, count more than 36. Circle the coins you'll use.
Raise your hand when you're done.

(When most hands are raised) Tell me the coins you circled.   Q, D, N

3. *(Repeat step 2 with the problems below.)*

   b. 72¢ Q D D D N N P
   c. 29¢ D D D N N P P

FORMAT 16.6   Counting Change

TEACHER   **STUDENTS**

(Write the following example on the board.)

73¢   Q
        D
        N
        P

1. When you make change, you have to figure out what coins
to use. *(Point to each letter as you say)* I'm going to figure
out how many quarters, dimes, nickels, and pennies I use
to make 73¢. I start with the coin worth the most—a quarter.
I count to get as close as I can to 73: 25, 50. I counted 2
times. So I write Q Q to show 2 quarters. *(Write Q Q.)*

Now I count dimes. I've already got 50: 60, 70. I counted
2 times, so I write D D for 2 dimes. *(Write D D.)*

Now I try to count nickels. I already have 70. I can't count
any nickels. The first time I count by 5, I get 75 and that's
too big. I don't write any N's. Now I count pennies. I still
have 70: 71, 72, 73. I counted 3 times, so I write P P P
after the last D. *(Write P P P.)*

I'm done. The answer is 2 quarters, 2 dimes, and 3
pennies—those coins make 73¢. Watch.
(Point to each letter as you count: 25, 50, 60, 70, 71, 72, 73)

2. Your turn.
(Write the following for the first problem: 48¢)

Start with quarters. Get as close as you can to 48¢. Raise
your hand when you know how many quarters. *(When most
hands are raised)* How many quarters?   1
(Write one Q after 48¢.)

Now figure out how many dimes you need to get as close
as you can to 48. Remember, you already have 25¢ from
the quarter. *(When most hands are raised)* How many
dimes? *(Write D D after Q.)*   2

(continued on next page)

FORMAT 16.6   (continued)

TEACHER	STUDENTS
Now figure out how many nickels you need to get as close as you can to 48¢. Remember, you already have 25, 35, 45¢. *(When most hands are raised)* How many nickels?	Zero (or none)
Zero nickels. If you count by 5 even one time, you get to 50¢, and that is bigger than 48¢. So you don't write anything for nickels. Figure out how many pennies you need to get to 48. Remember, you've already got 45¢. *(When most hands are raised)* How many pennies? *(Write P P P after the last D.)*	3
Let's see if we have 48¢. Start with the Q and count the coins.	

3. (Repeat step 2 with 55¢ and 82¢.)

CHAPTER 17

Measurement

CUSTOMARY AND METRIC UNITS

There are two basic measurement systems: the customary system, which is used in the United States and a few other countries, and the metric system, which is used in the majority of countries in the world.

The metric system has several advantages over the customary system. First, since the metric system uses the base-10 place value system, instruction in decimals directly relates to measurement skills. With customary units, different place value base systems are required for weight (16 ounces), length (12 inches, 3 feet), and so on. Second, in the customary system, there is no commonality among the units for various measurements, while there is commonality among the metric units. The prefixes in the metric system (*milli-, centi-, deci-, deka-, hecto-, kilo-*) are used in each area: length, weight, and capacity.

Table 17.1 includes the various customary and metric units for expressing length, weight, and capacity. Note the consistency of the metric system. The prefix in front of a unit tells the unit's relation to the base unit. At the same time, note how the various units in the customary system are different from one another.

Teachers need to check district and/or school policy regarding the extent and type of metric instruction expected in their classrooms. The question facing most teachers is not whether to teach about the metric system but rather whether both systems

should be taught simultaneously, and if not, which should be taught first. Unfortunately, there is no simple answer to this question. However, we have noticed that lower performing students are likely to confuse facts from one system with facts from the other system when both are introduced concurrently. This information leads us to recommend that the two systems be taught independently of one another, preferably at different times during the year. Low performing students should be familiar with common units from one system before the other system is introduced.

During the primary grades, measurement instruction is relatively simple. Common units and equivalences are introduced, and students use tools to measure objects to the nearest whole unit. During the intermediate grades, measurement instruction becomes more complex as less commonly used units are introduced and more sophisticated uses of measuring tools are presented. In the early grades, students measure to the nearest whole unit; in later grades, they are taught to measure partial units (e.g., $3\frac{1}{8}$ inches). Also in the intermediate grades, conversion problems are introduced in which students must convert a quantity expressed as one unit to a larger or smaller unit (5 meters = 500 centimeters).

A sequence of major skills appears in the Instructional Sequence and Assessment Chart. Though not all possible items for customary and metric units are included, each type of item appears in at least one of the two systems of units.

Instructional Sequence and Assessment Chart

Grade Level	Problem Type	Performance Indicator
2a	Customary units: length	_____ inches in a foot _____ feet in a yard About how long is a spoon? 6 inches 6 feet 6 yards About how tall is a person? 5 inches 5 feet 5 yards
2b	Customary units: weight	_____ ounces in a pound _____ pounds in a ton About how much does a cat weigh? 8 ounces 8 pounds 8 tons About how much does a car weigh? 2 ounces 2 pounds 2 tons
2c	Customary units: liquid capacity	_____ cups in a pint _____ pints in a quart _____ quarts in a gallon
3a	Metric units: length	_____ centimeters in a meter About how long is a pen? 8 mm 8 cm 2 m 2 km About how long is a car? 2 mm 2 cm 2 m 2 km
3b	Metric units: weight	_____ grams in a kilogram About how much does a pencil weigh? 75 mg 75 g 75 kg 75 cg About how much does a newborn baby weigh? 4 mg 4 g 4 kg 4 cg
3c	Metric units: capacity	_____ milliliters in a liter How much water can we put in a baby bottle? 250 ml 250 dl 250 l 250 kl How much milk would a basketball hold? 3 ml 3 dl 3 l 3 kl
3d	Customary units: length (tool—measure to nearest half-inch)	How long is the line? Circle the correct answer: 2 inches 2½ inches 3 inches 3½ inches
3e	Customary units: length (tool)—using a ruler to the nearest fourth-inch	How long is the line? 3 inches 2¾ inches 3¼ inches 2¼ inches

Grade Level	Problem Type	Performance Indicator
4a	Customary units: length conversions—inches, feet, yards	4 feet = _____ inches 2 yards = _____ feet 36 inches = _____ feet
4b	Customary units: length (tool)—using a ruler to the nearest eighth-inch	 Make an X over 2¼ Make an R over 1½ Make a T over 2⅜ Make a B over 2¼
4c	Customary units: operations—regrouping required	Circle the correct answer. 4 feet 5 inches +3 feet 8 inches 8 feet 3 inches 8 feet 1 inch 7 feet 3 inches Circle the correct answer 3 weeks 4 days −1 week 6 days 1 week 8 days 2 weeks 8 days 1 week 5 days
4d	Customary units: area—volume	What is the area of a room 8 feet long and 10 feet wide? _____ What is the volume of a box 6 inches long, 8 inches wide and 4 inches high? _____
4e	Customary units: story problems—renaming	Jill wants to make ribbons 6 inches long. How many feet of renaming material will she need to make 8 ribbons? Jill is 6 feet 2 inches. Her sister is 4 feet 10 inches. How much taller is Jill?

5a	Metric equivalencies—less common units	Circle the answer.
		A kilogram equals:
		1 gm 10 gm 100 gm 1,000 gm
		A hectogram equals:
		1 gm 10 gm 100 gm 1,000 gm
		A dekaliter equals:
		1
			10	100	1,000 |
					A milliliter equals:
					  a tenth of a liter
					  a hundredth of a liter
					  a thousandth of a liter
					A centigram equals:
					  a tenth of a gram
					  a hundredth of a gram
					  a thousandth of a gram

Instructional Sequence and Assessment Chart (continued)

Grade Level	Problem Type	Performance Indicator
		A decimeter equals:
		a tenth of a meter
		a hundredth of a meter
		a thousandth of a meter
5–6	Metric conversions	20 meters = _____ centimeters
		5000 centigrams = _____ grams
		500 kilometers = _____ meters
		3.6 meters = _____ centimeters
		46 grams = _____ kilogram
		2.7 liters = _____ deciliters

INTRODUCING THE CONCEPT

Teachers working with beginning-level kindergarten or first-grade students who have had no previous experience with measurement should demonstrate with concrete objects how to use consistent units as standards in measurement. Length can be introduced first. To illustrate measurement of length, before students are taught about abstract concepts of inches and feet, the teacher can present an exercise in which students measure the lengths of various strips of paper using paper clips as the measurement standard. The teacher demonstrates how to measure the paper strip by laying the clips along the edge of the paper and determining that the paper is "X clips long." For example, in the following illustration, the slip of paper is three clips long:

Following the demonstration, students are given the opportunity to determine the lengths of several strips of paper using paper clips.

This exercise serves two purposes. First, it introduces students to the concept of measuring a specific attribute, in this case, length. Second, it demonstrates how the units used for measurement are equivalent. The paper clips used in measuring length are always the same size.

Teachers can introduce weight measurement in the same way with a balance scale. First, the teacher demonstrates how the scale works, showing students that the weights on both sides of the scale are the same when the trays of the scale are the same height. Similarly, the teacher must show that when the weights are not the same, the side that is lower is heavier. Following the demonstration with a balance scale, the teacher introduces students to standard weights against which they can measure various objects. For example, blocks

Table 17.1 Metric and Customary Units for Measuring Length, Weight, and Capacity

Customary Units		
Length	*Weight*	*Capacity*
12 inches = 1 foot	16 ounces = 1 pound	2 cups = 1 pint
3 feet = 1 yard	2,000 pounds = 1 ton	2 pints = 1 quart
5,280 feet = 1 mile		4 quarts = 1 gallon

Metric Units			
Meaning of Prefix	*Length*	*Weight*	*Capacity*
thousandth	millimeter (mm)	milligram (mg)	milliliter (ml)
hundredth	centimeter (cm)	centigram (cg)	centiliter (cl)
tenth	decimeter (dm)	decigram (dg)	deciliter (dl)
whole	meter (m)	gram (g)	liter (l)
10 wholes	dekameter (dkm)	dekagram (dkg)	dekaliter (dkl)
100 wholes	hectometer (hm)	hectogram (hg)	hectoliter (hl)
1000 wholes	kilometer (km)	kilogram (kg)	kiloliter (kl)

that weigh an ounce can be used as the measuring standard against which other objects can be measured.

For liquid capacity, the teacher can set out a number of empty cups, present a water-filled container whose capacity is to be measured, and pour the contents into the cups, one at a time. The teacher then asks how many cups of water the container holds. Because of the potential mess involved in pouring liquids, this activity is best done as a teacher demonstration only.

PRIMARY GRADES

Common Units and Equivalencies

During the primary grades, students learn the more common units and their equivalencies. See Figure 17.1 for a table of commonly taught measurement facts. The basic procedure for introducing new units to students includes five steps. The teacher does the following:

1. Tells the function of the specific unit; for example, "Inches tell how long something is. We use inches to measure objects that are not very big. Feet also tell how long something is. We use feet to measure objects that are pretty big."
2. Illustrates the unit; for example, the teacher draws lines on the board and shows students the length of an inch or a foot. For demonstrating weight, the teacher might give students blocks weighing an ounce or a pound.
3. Demonstrates how to use measuring tools, measuring to the nearest whole unit.
4. Presents application exercises in which the students determine the appropriate tool to use when measuring an object; for example, "What unit would we use to tell how long a piece of paper is? What unit would we use to tell how long the chalkboard is?"
5. Presents an equivalency fact, such as 12 inches equals one foot.

Application exercises (step 4) and equivalencies (step 5) should incorporate review of previously introduced units from all areas. For example, if students have learned inch, foot, ounce, pound, and pint, a representative set of questions would include, for example, "What unit would we use to tell how tall a person is? What unit would we use to tell how much a person weighs? What unit would we use to tell how much a letter weighs? What unit would we use to tell how long a pencil is?"

Equivalency review might include these questions: "How many ounces in a pound? How many inches in a foot? How many pints in a quart?" Review can be provided daily in worksheet exercises. A sample worksheet appears in Figure 17.2.

In addition to worksheet exercises, the teacher should incorporate measuring tasks into daily activities. Scales, thermometers, rulers, and liquid containers should be readily accessible. Students should be encouraged to apply measuring skills with concrete objects.

The sequence and rate of instruction for measurement facts and skills must be carefully controlled. New information is introduced cumulatively. That is, a new piece of information is not introduced until mastery of prior skills and information is demonstrated. Also, review of prior information is incorporated into tasks that introduce new skills. The length units, inch and foot, are usually introduced first. Several weeks later, ounces and pounds might be introduced, and several weeks after that, pints and quarts.

When students demonstrate mastery of these smaller units, larger units (yard, ton, gallon) can be introduced. A new set of units is introduced only after students have mastered all the previous sets.

Measuring Tools

Calibrated measurement instruments include rulers, scales, thermometers, and speedometers. Every calibrated instrument is divided into segments representing specific quantities. The easiest type of instrument to read is one in which each line represents one unit. For example, on most thermometers, each line represents 1 degree; likewise, on many bathroom scales, each line designates 1 pound. Often, instruments label only some of the lines that stand for quantities:

Those instruments require students to figure out what the unmarked lines represent before they are able to read them. Instruments like the ruler and scales found in grocery stores contain lines that represent fractions of a unit (e.g., ¼ inch, ⅛ pound).

In the early primary grades, students learn to measure length to the nearest inch (or centimeter) and weight to the nearest pound (or kilogram). In the late primary and intermediate grades, students learn to measure more precisely.

FIGURE 17.1 Measurement Facts

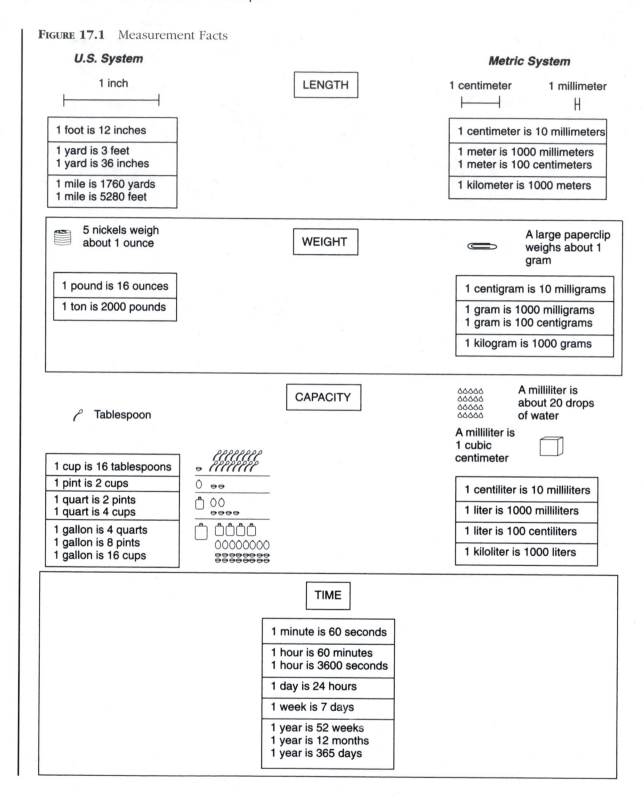

Measuring length with a ruler might be introduced first. The teacher explains that the numbers on the ruler indicate how many inches from the end of the ruler to the line corresponding to that numeral. The teacher then models using the ruler to measure several lines or objects, pointing out the need to properly align the front end of the ruler and the beginning of the line or object being measured. Finally, the teacher has the students use the ruler themselves. In order to make initial instruction more

FIGURE 17.2 Measurement Review Worksheet

Circle or fill in the answer.

1. A pencil is about 6 _____ long.	feet	pounds	inches	pints
2. A cat weighs about 8 _____.	feet	pounds	inches	pints
3. A woman is about 5 _____ tall.	feet	pounds	inches	pints
4. He drinks a _____ of milk every day.	foot	pound	inch	pint
5. How many inches in a foot?	_____			
6. How many feet in a yard?	_____			
7. How many ounces in a pound?	_____			
8. How many pints in a quart?	_____			
9. About how many pounds does a dog weigh?	2	20	200	
10. About how many feet high is a door?	8	80	800	

manageable, the teacher can give students worksheets with lines of various lengths (to the nearest inch).

For weight, the students put the object on the scale and read the number closest to the pointer. For capacity, the students fill the container with water, pour the water into a calibrated flask, and read the number closest to the water level. When teaching students to use measuring tools on which a line represents each unit but the relative value of each line is not shown:

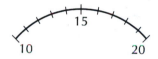

the teacher models how to count from the last given unit to the target unit. In the example below, the teacher models counting from 25, touching and counting each line—25, 26, 27, 28—to the quantity. Measuring to the nearest fraction of an inch is discussed later in this chapter.

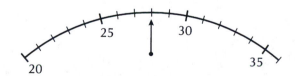

INTERMEDIATE GRADES

During the intermediate grades, the teacher follows these steps:

1. Presents and reviews all equivalencies
2. Teaches students more sophisticated uses of measuring tools (e.g., measuring to nearest ⅛ of an inch)
3. Teaches students to convert units to larger or smaller units

4. Presents measurement operations and story problems

To review previously introduced customary equivalencies, the teacher might prepare a handout, like the one previously presented in Figure 17.1, with the standard equivalencies written on it. Students who do not already know them are asked to memorize these standard equivalencies. For students who have difficulty, the teacher can present verbal exercises to review the material.

Exercises in which students identify the most appropriate unit to measure various objects follow the memorization exercise. A similar procedure should be used to review more common metric units as well.

Metric Equivalencies

In fifth or sixth grade, after decimals have been taught, exercises designed to teach students about the structure of the metric system should be presented. Format 17.1 shows the steps for teaching students the prefixes for the metric system. In parts A and B, the teacher merely presents the meaning of the prefixes. The prefixes for units less than 1 (*milli-, centi-,* and *deci-*) are presented in Part A. Note that the teacher must emphasize the *th* ending of the words *thousandth, hundredth,* and *tenth* so that students will note they are fractions and pronounce them correctly. In Part B, the teacher presents the prefixes indicating units greater than 1 (*deka-, hecto-,* and *kilo-*). Depending on the level of students, a week or more of practice may be required to teach the meanings of these prefixes. The teacher should not go on to Part C until the students demonstrate knowledge of all the metric prefixes.

Part C teaches students to use their knowledge of metric prefixes to tell the value of metric units. For example, the teacher models: Since *milli-* means a thousandth, *milligram* refers to a thousandth of a gram. Part D is a worksheet exercise in which students must find and circle the numerical representation of a specific metric unit. For example, a worksheet problem may ask for the amount that equals a centimeter, giving the following choices: 100 meters, .01 meter, .10 meter. Note that the ability to read decimal numbers is a prerequisite for this task. Daily worksheet exercises would continue for several weeks.

Abbreviations for metric units should also be introduced in a worksheet exercise. Teachers should not take for granted that students will be able to decode abbreviations. Several lessons should be devoted to teaching metric abbreviations.

Conversion Problems

This section addresses problems in which students must convert a quantity expressed as one unit into an equal quantity expressed in terms of a larger or smaller unit; for example, 3 feet can be converted to 36 inches, 2 meters to 200 centimeters.

The preskill for conversion problems is knowledge of equivalencies. Students cannot convert 5 kilograms to grams unless they know the number of grams in 1 kilogram. Conversion problems should not be taught until students know equivalencies.

There are three basic steps in any conversion problem: (a) determining whether the "new" unit is larger or smaller than the original unit, (b) determining what multiple the larger unit is in relation to the smaller unit, and (c) multiplying when converting to a smaller unit or dividing when converting to a larger unit. These steps are listed in Summary Box 17.1.

CONVERTING METRIC UNITS. Early intermediate-grade teachers should limit examples to conversions with small quantities of common units (e.g., 5 meters = _____ centimeters). In the late intermediate grades, teachers can present the conversion strategy with larger numbers. Below is a description of the procedure for teaching conversion with metric units. Before the metric conversion strategy is introduced, students should know the equivalencies of the metric units, be able to read and write mixed decimals and decimal numbers, and be able to multiply and divide by multiples of 10 by moving the decimal point to the right or the left. When dividing, the decimal point is moved to the left. For example, when dividing by 10, the decimal point is moved one place to the left ($75 \div 10 = 7.5$); by 100, two places ($75 \div 100 = .75$); by 1000, three places to the left ($75 \div 1000 = .075$). When multiplying, the decimal

---

Summary Box 17.1
Steps in Basic Conversion Problems

	Problem a	Problem b	Problem c	Problem d
1. Determine whether the new quantity is a bigger (higher order) or smaller (lower order) unit.	48 inches = _____ feet. Change inches to feet. Feet is a bigger unit.	3 pounds = _____ ounces. Change pounds to ounces. Ounces is a smaller unit.	5 kilograms = _____ grams. Change kilograms to grams. Grams is a smaller unit.	300 centimeters = _____ meters. Change centimeters to meters. Meters is a bigger unit.
2. Multiply if changing to a smaller unit. Divide if changing to a bigger unit.	Since change is to a bigger unit, division is called for. 48 inches ÷ 12 = 4 feet	Since change is to a smaller unit, multiplication is called for. 3 pounds × 16 = 48 ounces	Since change is to a smaller unit, multiplication is called for. 5 kilograms × 1000 = 5,000 grams	Since change is to a bigger unit, division is called for. 300 centimeters ÷ 100 = 3 meters
3. Determine the equivalency fact.	12 inches in a foot	16 ounces in a pound	1,000 kilograms in a gram	100 centimeters in a meter

point is moved to the right. Instructions for teaching multiplying decimals by multiples of 10 appear in Format 13.9 in Chapter 13. A similar exercise would be used to teach students to divide by multiples of 10.

Before beginning conversion exercises, the teacher should give students worksheets like the one in Figure 17.3, designed to provide practice in dividing and multiplying by various multiples of 10. The discussion in Chapter 13 on multiplying decimals by multiples of 10 specifies example types to include in worksheet exercises. Students may require several weeks of practice to develop mastery. In some multiplication problems, students should have to add one or more zeroes (e.g., $100 \times 3.5 = 350.0$). In some division problems, students should have to add a zero in front of the original digits (e.g., $3.5 \div 100 = .035$). Such examples are difficult and require modeling.

A format for presenting the conversion strategy appears in Format 17.2. As mentioned earlier, this format assumes that students have mastered the metric equivalencies (e.g., when asked what a hectogram equals, they will say 100 grams). If students have not learned the preskills, they will find the conversion exercises quite difficult and frustrating. The format contains four parts: Parts A and B teach important component skills. Part A teaches students to determine whether they are changing the original unit to a bigger or smaller unit. Part B presents the rules: *When we change to a bigger unit, we divide; when we change to a smaller unit, we multiply.* Part B concludes with an exercise in which the teacher writes sets of units on the board, such as centigram → gram, and leads the students in determining the appropriate operation.

For converting from grams to milligrams, the teacher might say, "We're changing to milligram, which is a smaller unit than gram. So we multiply." For converting from meters to kilometer, similar wording is appropriate: "We're changing to kilometer, which is a bigger unit than meter. So we divide." Teachers raised in the United States may find that learning these rules themselves requires a good deal of practice due to their own unfamiliarity with the metric system.

Part C is a structured board presentation in which the teacher presents all the steps in the conversion strategy. After the students determine whether to multiply or divide, the teacher leads them through deriving the number by which to multiply or divide. "There are 100 centigrams in a gram, so we divide by 100." Finally, the teacher demonstrates moving the decimal as a quick way of multiplying or dividing by multiples of 10. For example, determining how many grams 2,135 centigrams equal requires division, since the new unit is bigger. Students divide by 100, since there are 100 centigrams in a gram. Therefore, the decimal point is moved two places to the left, and the answer is 21.35 grams. Part D is a structured worksheet exercise. Because this exercise incorporates several difficult component skills, a great amount of practice is necessary to develop mastery.

EXAMPLE SELECTION. Four example-selection guidelines are important in teaching conversion problems:

1. In all problems, one of the units should be a base unit. The base units are grams, meters, or liters.
2. In half of the problems, the students should convert a unit to a larger unit; in the other half, the students should convert to a smaller unit.
3. In half of the problems, the quantity of original units should be a whole number; in the other half, the quantity should be a decimal or mixed number.
4. The amount the student multiplies or divides should vary from problem to problem: 10 in one problem, 1000 in the next, 100 in the next.

An example of an appropriate set of problems, following the guidelines, appears below. The answers are in parentheses.

142 centigrams = _____ grams (1.42)

9.8 grams = _____ milligrams (9800)

35 decigrams = _____ grams (3.5)

20 hectograms = _____ grams (2000)

4.35 grams = _____ milligrams (4350)

FIGURE 17.3   Worksheet on Multiplying and Dividing by 10

a. $37 \times 100 =$ _____ b. $4 \div 1000 =$ _____ c. $53.2 \times 100 =$ _____ d. $7.04 \times 10 =$ _____
e. $4.8 \times 1000 =$ _____ f. $28.5 \div 10 =$ _____ g. $72 \times 1000 =$ _____ h. $.37 \times 100 =$ _____
i. $7 \div 100 =$ _____ j. $.37 \times 100 =$ _____ k. $5.43 \times 10 =$ _____ l. $.4 \times 1000 =$ _____
m. $37 \div 10 =$ _____ n. $4.2 \div 10 =$ _____ o. $72 \div 10 =$ _____ p. $38 \div 10 =$ _____
q. $52 \times 100 =$ _____ r. $4.8 \div 1000 =$ _____ s. $400 \div 1000 =$ _____ t. $52 \div 100 =$ _____

Note that the examples shown in Format 17.2 all refer to grams. The next day's unit might refer to liters or meters. In each lesson, a different type of unit is used.

CONVERTING CUSTOMARY UNITS. Teaching students to convert quantities from one unit to another is more difficult in the customary system than in the metric system for three specific reasons: First, whereas in metric conversions the students always multiply or divide by a multiple of 10, in conversion problems with customary units, the number to multiply or divide by varies from problem to problem; converting inches to feet requires division by 12, and converting feet to yards requires division by 3.

A second reason for increased difficulty involves the procedures used when the converted unit is not a multiple of the original unit. In the customary system, the answer must be expressed in terms of a mixed number with two different units (e.g., 7 feet = 2 yards, 1 foot).

A final reason why customary conversions are more difficult is that conversions are sometimes made to a unit two or more steps removed. In the metric system, the original unit is simply multiplied or divided by 10, 100, or 1000. In the customary system, several conversions may be required. For example, to convert gallons to cups, the student must first convert gallons to quarts, quarts to pints, then pints to cups.

The sequence for introducing conversion problems with customary units should be carefully controlled, with easier problems introduced first. The three basic types of conversion problems in the customary system are illustrated below:

1. Converting a quantity of a specified unit into a quantity of the next larger or smaller unit (examples involve whole numbers only):

    28 days equal _____ weeks
    6 feet equal _____ yards
    24 inches equal _____ feet
    4 weeks equal _____ days
    2 yards equal _____ feet
    2 feet equal _____ inches

2. Converting a unit into a mixed number (and vice versa) containing the next larger or smaller quantity:

    27 inches equal _____ feet _____ inches
    19 ounces equal _____ pound(s) _____ ounces
    13 days equal _____ week(s) _____ days
    2 feet 3 inches equal _____ inches
    1 pound 3 ounces equal _____ ounces

3. Converting a unit into a unit twice removed:

    2 yards equal _____ inches
    2 quarts equal _____ cups
    72 inches equal _____ yards
    16 cups equal _____ quarts

The preskills for teaching conversion problems with customary units are knowledge of equivalents and knowledge of multiplication and division facts. Since measurement conversion tasks are usually introduced before students can divide by two-digit numbers, the teacher may choose to teach the students to count by twelves. Knowing this count-by series will help students in converting inches to feet and in determining dozens.

The format for introducing the first type of customary conversion problems (problems in which a unit is converted evenly into the next larger or smaller unit) is basically the same as that for converting metric units (see Format 17.2). The teacher has students (a) tell whether they are changing to a bigger or smaller unit, (b) tell whether they multiply or divide, and (c) tell by what number they multiply or divide. "We want to find how many ounces in 6 pounds. We're changing to a smaller unit, so we multiply. There are 16 ounces in a pound, so we multiply by 16."

The format for problems in which the conversion results in a remainder (e.g., 27 inches equal 2 feet 3 inches) is the same as for the previous type of problem except the teacher must explain what to do with the remainder. For example, in solving the problem 27 inches = _____ feet, after the students determine that 27 must be divided by 12, the teacher points out that since 12 goes into 27 with a remainder, the remainder tells the number of inches left. A structured worksheet presentation for converting from smaller to larger units when there is a remainder appears in Format 17.3.

The format for converting a mixed quantity to a lower unit appears in Format 17.4. When converting 2 feet 11 inches to inches, the teacher has the students cross out the 2 and write 24, the number of inches, above it. Then they add that quantity, 24 inches, to the 11 inches to end up with 35 inches.

Problems in which students must convert to a unit twice removed are quite difficult (e.g., 2 yards = _____ inches). The strategy we recommend involves having the students translate the quantity unit by unit. For example, in converting 2 yards to inches, the student would first convert 2 yards to 6 feet, then 6 feet to 72 inches.

Operations

This section deals with addition, subtraction, multiplication, and division operations with measurement units. As with most measurement-related skills, performing operations with customary units is more difficult than performing operations with metric units. The differences arise in problems that require renaming. Since the metric system uses a base-10 place value system, renaming presents no problems. Students merely apply the renaming skills they learned previously in decimal instruction. However, when working with customary units, there is no consistent base from which to work. The base for ounces is 16; for inches, 12; for feet, 3; and so on, so students must be taught to use these bases rather than base 10.

Addition and subtraction problems with measurement units are usually introduced in fourth or fifth grade. The operations cause little difficulty in measurement problems that do not involve renaming:

$$
\begin{array}{r} 6\text{ lb }4\text{ oz} \\ +\ 1\text{ lb }1\text{ oz} \\ \hline 7\text{ lb }5\text{ oz} \end{array}
\qquad
\begin{array}{r} 6\text{ lb }4\text{ oz} \\ -\ 1\text{ lb }1\text{ oz} \\ \hline 5\text{ lb }3\text{ oz} \end{array}
\qquad
\begin{array}{r} 6\text{ lb }4\text{ oz} \\ \times\qquad 2 \\ \hline 12\text{ lb }8\text{ oz} \end{array}
$$

$$
2\overline{)6\text{ lb }4\text{ oz}}^{\,3\text{ lb }2\text{ oz}}
\qquad
\begin{array}{r} 6.4\text{ kg} \\ +1.1\text{ kg} \\ \hline 7.5\text{ kg} \end{array}
\qquad
\begin{array}{r} 6.4\text{ kg} \\ -1.1\text{ kg} \\ \hline 5.3\text{ kg} \end{array}
$$

$$
\begin{array}{r} 6.4\text{ kg} \\ \times\qquad 2 \\ \hline 12.8\text{ kg} \end{array}
\qquad
2\overline{)6.4\text{kg}}^{\,3.2\text{ kg}}
$$

Problems that do require renaming, on the other hand, are quite difficult:

$$
\begin{array}{r} \overset{4}{\cancel{5}}\text{ lb }\overset{18}{\cancel{2}}\text{ oz} \\ -\ 3\text{ lb }\ 4\text{ oz} \\ \hline 1\text{ lb }14\text{ oz} \end{array}
\qquad
\begin{array}{r} \overset{1}{} \\ 3\text{ weeks }4\text{ days} \\ +\ 1\text{ week }\ 5\text{ days} \\ \hline 5\text{ weeks }\underset{2}{\cancel{9}}\text{ days} \end{array}
\qquad
\begin{array}{r} \overset{4}{\cancel{5}}\text{ ft }\overset{14}{\cancel{2}}\text{ in} \\ -\ 2\text{ ft }8\text{ in} \\ \hline 2\text{ ft }6\text{ in} \end{array}
$$

A preskill for renaming problems is converting units, which was discussed previously. When working an addition problem, the teacher instructs students to always start working with the smaller unit. The difficult part of addition problems occurs after students have derived a sum that includes enough of the smaller unit to form a larger unit. In the following problem,

$$
\begin{array}{r} 3\text{ ft }\ 8\text{ in} \\ +\ 2\text{ ft }\ 6\text{ in} \\ \hline 14\text{ in} \end{array}
$$

the students add 8 and 6 to end with 14 inches, which is more than 1 foot. The student must carry 1

to the feet column, cross out the 14, and write 2 to represent the remaining inches:

$$
\begin{array}{r} \overset{1}{}3\text{ ft }\ 8\text{ in} \\ +\ 2\text{ ft }\ 6\text{ in} \\ \hline \underset{2}{\cancel{14}} \end{array}
$$

The teacher leads students through sets of problems, renaming them when they must carry: "Remember, we're adding inches. How many inches in a foot? Yes, 12 inches in a foot. So if we have 12 or more inches in the inches column, we must carry a foot to the feet column."

Format 17.5 shows how to teach addition problems with renaming. The key in teaching the operations with customary units is teaching students *when* to rename and *what numbers* to use. Part A of the structured board presentation focuses on when renaming is appropriate. Part B provides practice in renaming with the appropriate numbers. Examples should include problems that require renaming and problems that do not require renaming. The examples in the format involve weight units; similar exercises should be done with length and capacity units.

After students can rename a variety of units when adding, they are given problems with subtraction. The difficult aspect of subtraction problems lies in renaming the minuend. For example, to work the problem

$$
\begin{array}{r} 8\text{ lb }4\text{ oz} \\ -\ 3\text{ lb }8\text{ oz} \end{array}
$$

students must rename 8 pounds 4 ounces, borrowing a pound from 8 pounds, leaving 7 pounds, and increasing the ounces by 16 ounces (a pound) so there are 20 ounces:

$$
\begin{array}{r} \overset{7}{\cancel{8}}\text{ lb }\overset{20}{\cancel{4}}\text{ oz} \\ -\ 3\text{ lb }8\text{ oz} \end{array}
$$

We recommend that teachers introduce this skill by first presenting problems in which a mixed unit is subtracted from a whole unit. Following are examples of such problems:

$$
\begin{array}{r} 3\text{ ft} \\ -\ 1\text{ ft }4\text{ in} \end{array}
\qquad
\begin{array}{r} 8\text{ lb} \\ -\ 2\text{ lb }5\text{ oz} \end{array}
$$

The teacher leads students through working these problems, pointing out the need to rename and how to rename: "We must borrow a foot from 3 feet. I'll cross out 3 feet and write 2. I borrowed a foot from 3 feet. How many inches in a foot?... So I write 12 in the inches column." After several days of practice, more difficult problems in which two mixed numbers are involved can be introduced. An example of a structured worksheet part of a format for subtraction problems with renaming appears in Format 17.6

Multiplication and division problems requiring renaming with measurement units are quite difficult. A strategy for working multiplication problems involves teaching the students to first multiply each unit. For example, in the problem

$$
\begin{array}{r}
5\ \text{ft}\ 7\ \text{in} \\
\times\ \ \ \ \ 4 \\
\hline
\end{array}
$$

the students first multiply 4×7 inches, then 4×5 feet, writing the products for each:

$$
\begin{array}{r}
5\ \text{ft}\ 7\ \text{in} \\
\times\ \ \ \ \ 4 \\
\hline
20\ \text{ft}\ 28\ \text{in}
\end{array}
$$

After the products are written for each unit, the students rename, converting the smaller quantity and adding:

$$
\begin{array}{r}
5\ \text{ft}\ 7\ \text{in} \\
\times\ \ \ \ \ \ 4 \\
\hline
20\ \text{ft}\ 28\ \text{in} \\
2\ \text{ft}\ \ \ 4\ \text{in} \\
\hline
22\ \text{ft}\ \ \ 4\ \text{in}
\end{array}
$$

Division problems, on the other hand, require a unique strategy. The students rewrite the quantity in terms of its lower units before working the problem. For example, in dividing 3 pounds 4 ounces by 2, we suggest converting 3 pounds 4 ounces to 52 ounces, dividing 52 by 2, which equals 26 ounces, then converting the 26 ounces to 1 pound 10 ounces.

Story Problems

Story problems involving measurement units can be introduced as soon as students have learned to work operations. The strategies are the same as outlined in Chapter 11. Following are examples of story problems:

Division
a. James has 2 feet of ribbon. He wants to make kites. Each kite needs 4 inches of ribbon. How many kites can James make?

Subtraction
b. Tania weighed 8 pounds, 4 ounces when she was born. Three months later, she weighed 11 pounds, 7 ounces. How much weight did she gain in those 3 months?

Multistep
c. Bill's plant is 4 feet tall. If it grows 3 inches a year for 5 years, how tall will it be?

Teachers should present about five problems daily for at least several weeks. When a new type of story problem appears, the teacher should lead the students through the problems. Division problems such as the one illustrated above are particularly difficult and should receive extra emphasis. Examples should include a mix of the new problem type and previously introduced types.

Measuring Tools

During the early primary grades, students are taught to read calibrated measuring tools to the nearest unit. In later primary grades, students are taught to read fractional parts of units. We discuss a procedure for teaching students to read rulers used in the customary system. Once students can read rulers, they should have little difficulty transferring these reading skills to other tools such as scales and measuring cups.

Rulers in the customary system are usually calibrated to allow measurement to the closest sixteenth of an inch. Because the different marks on the rulers tend to confuse students, a systematic approach should be taken in teaching students to measure the various fractional parts of an inch. We recommend preparing a set of rulers. In the first ruler, each inch is divided into halves. In the second ruler, each inch is divided into fourths. In the third and fourth rulers, each inch is divided respectively into eighths and sixteenths of an inch. Figure 17.4 illustrates the four rulers. A preskill for reading these tools is the ability to read and write mixed fractions.

A ruler in which an inch is divided into a greater number of parts is introduced only after students have demonstrated mastery in using the preceding ruler in the series.

A simple model-test procedure can be used to teach students to read units to the nearest half inch. The teacher points out that since the line between the numbers divides the inch into two equal parts, each line represents a half-inch. The same procedure is used to introduce rulers divided into fourths. The teacher points out that since there are four parts between each inch, each inch is divided into fourths. The teacher then models and tests, reading the ruler starting at the ¼-inch mark: ¼, ½, ¾, 1, 1¼, 1½, 1¾, 2, and so on. Note that the teacher does not initially have the students read ½ as ½. The teacher then presents an exercise in which she points to a

FIGURE 17.4 Recommended Set of Rulers

a. Marked to the nearest half of an inch

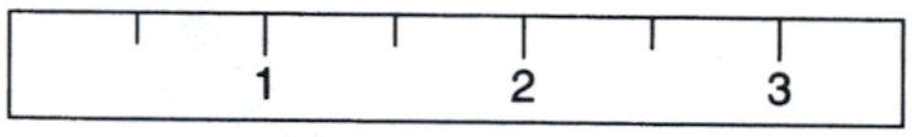

b. Marked to the nearest quarter of an inch

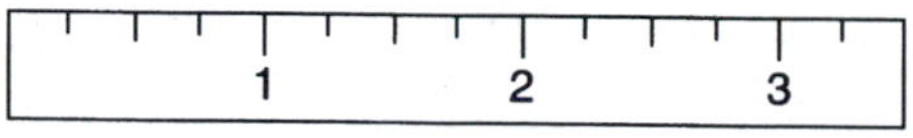

c. Marked to the nearest eighth of an inch

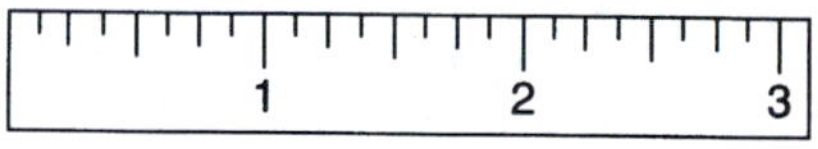

d. Marked to the nearest sixteenth of an inch (standard rulers)

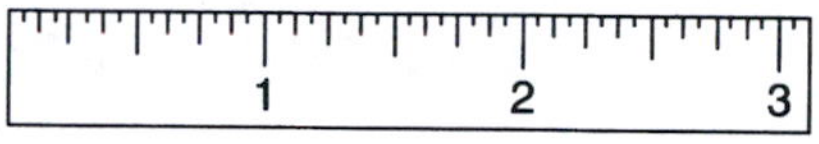

FIGURE 17.5 Worksheet Exercise for Determining Length

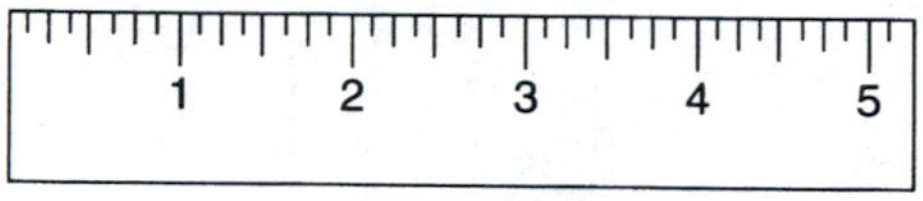

Make an X over the line that indicates $3\frac{3}{4}$ inches.
Make an R over the line that indicates $2\frac{1}{2}$ inches.
Make an S over the line that indicates $\frac{5}{8}$ of an inch.
Make a B over the line that indicates $2\frac{3}{8}$ inches.

line on the ruler and has students determine how far it is from the front end of the ruler.

When students can identify the lengths represented by various lines, the teacher can present an exercise to teach that the line that indicates $\frac{2}{4}$ of an inch also is the line that indicates $\frac{1}{2}$ of an inch. The teacher explains that the line is in the middle of the inch and so divides it into halves. The teacher explains further that when using a ruler, the length is always reported with the smallest numerical denominator. Therefore, instead of saying a line is $3\frac{2}{4}$ inches, the line is said to be $3\frac{1}{2}$ inches. A practice exercise in which the teacher has the students find the lines on the ruler that represent various distances would follow the explanation (e.g., "Find the line on the ruler that shows $4\frac{1}{2}$ inches. Find the line that shows $2\frac{1}{4}$ inches," etc.). Practice can be provided in worksheet exercises like the one in Figure 17.5.

Rulers in which each inch is divided into eighths are introduced when students (a) can use rulers in which each inch is divided into fourths and (b) have learned fraction equivalency skills. Students should have had enough practice rewriting $\frac{6}{8}$ as $\frac{3}{4}$, $\frac{4}{8}$ as $\frac{1}{2}$, and $\frac{2}{8}$ as $\frac{1}{4}$ so that they can make these conversions with ease. The teacher introduces the ruler containing eighths by pointing out that since each inch is divided into eight parts, the lines tell about eighths of an inch. The teacher then has students read the lines on the ruler: $\frac{1}{8}$, $\frac{2}{8}$, $\frac{3}{8}$, $\frac{4}{8}$, $\frac{5}{8}$, $\frac{6}{8}$, $\frac{7}{8}$, 1, $1\frac{1}{8}$, and so on.

After several days, the teacher presents exercises teaching students to express $\frac{2}{8}$, $\frac{4}{8}$, and $\frac{6}{8}$ as $\frac{1}{4}$, $\frac{1}{2}$, and $\frac{3}{4}$ respectively. The teacher reminds students that length is always reported with fractions expressed in their simplest, smallest possible terms, and then she models and tests the various equivalencies.

The same basic procedure is followed for introducing rulers in which each inch is divided into sixteenths. These rulers should not be introduced, however, until students are fluent in using the ruler divided into eighths. Daily practice over a long period is needed to develop student fluency in these skills.

APPLICATION ITEMS: MEASUREMENT

1. Write a format for introducing the yard unit. Assume students have previously learned inches and feet, ounces and pounds. Include all five steps discussed on page 381. For step, 4 write six questions.
2. Below are errors made by students on conversion tasks. For each error, tell the probable cause and specify a remediation procedure.

Ann

6 feet = <u>75</u> inches

```
 1
 12
×6
 75
```

Janet

6 feet = <u>60</u> inches

$$\begin{array}{r} 10 \\ \times\ 6 \\ \hline 60 \end{array}$$

Tim

9 yards = <u>3</u> feet

$3\overline{)9}$

3. A student says the x is over the line that shows 1¾ inches. Specify the wording in the correction made by the teacher.

4. Specify the wording in the correction to be made by the teacher.

1 foot 7 inches

$$\begin{array}{r} +\qquad 8\ \text{inches} \\ \hline \textit{2 feet 5 inches} \end{array}$$

5. For each error, tell the probable cause and specify what the teacher says to correct.

Jim

148 meters equal _____ km   *148 ÷ 1000 = 1.48*

Tina

148 meters equal _____ km   *148 × 1000 = 148,000*

6. Write a structured-worksheet presentation to lead students through working this problem. 348 centimeters = how many meters?

FORMAT 17.1   Metric Prefixes

TEACHER	**STUDENTS**

PART A: PREFIXES FOR LESS THAN 1

1. *(Write the following prefixes on the board.)*

    milli-   —thousandth of
    centi-   —hundredth of
    deci-   —tenth of
    one whole
    deka-
    hecto-
    kilo-

2. These are prefixes used in the metric system. They tell us how much of the base unit we have.

3. *(Point to milli-, centi-, deci-.)* These prefixes say there is less than one whole. What do these prefixes tell?

    (Point to deka-, hecto-, kilo-.) These prefixes say there is more than one whole. What do these prefixes say?

There is less than one whole.

There is more than one whole.

TEACHER	**STUDENTS**
4. *(Point to milli-.)* This says milli. What does it say? Milli means a thousandth of. What does milli mean? *(Repeat step 3 with centi-, and deci-.)*	Milli A thousandth of
5. Let's read all these prefixes and read what they mean. *(Point to milli-, centi-, deci-.)*	
6. *(Erase the words thousandth of, hundredth of, tenth of.)* *(Point to milli-.)* What is this prefix? What does milli mean? *(Point to centi-.)* What is this prefix? What does centi mean? *(Point to deci-.)* What is this prefix? What does deci mean? *(Point to the three prefixes in random order until students identify all three correctly.)*	Milli A thousandth of Centi A hundredth of Deci A tenth of

PART B: INTRODUCING PREFIXES (MORE THAN ONE WHOLE)

1. *(Write the following prefixes on the board.)* milli- centi- deci- one whole deka- —ten wholes hecto- —one hundred wholes kilo- —one thousand wholes	
2. What does milli- mean? What does centi- mean? What does deci- mean?	A thousandth of A hundredth of A tenth of
3. Let's read the prefixes that tell about more than a whole. *(Point to deka-.)* This says deka-. What does it say? What does deka- mean? *(Point to hecto-.)* This says hecto-. What does it say? What does hecto- mean? *(Point to kilo-.)* This says kilo-. What does it say? What does kilo- mean? *(Erase the words: ten wholes, hundred wholes, thousand wholes.)*	Deka 10 wholes Hecto 100 wholes Kilo 1,000 wholes
4. *(Point to deka-.)* What does this say? What does deka- mean? *(Repeat step 3 with hecto- and kilo-.)*	Deka 10 wholes
5. Now let's tell what all the prefixes mean. *(Point to milli-.)* What is this prefix? What does it mean? *(Pause, signal. Repeat the question in step 4 for all prefixes, presenting them in random order; give individual turns.)*	

PART C: STRUCTURED BOARD PRESENTATION

1. What does kilo- mean?	1000 wholes
2. Kilo- means 1000 wholes. So kilometer means 1000 meters. What does kilometer mean?	1000 meters

(continued on next page)

FORMAT 17.1   **(continued)**

TEACHER	STUDENTS
Yes, a kilometer equals 1000 meters. Say that.	A kilometer equals 1000 meters.
(Repeat steps 1 and 2 with millimeter, hectogram, centigram.)	
3. What does deciliter mean? *(Pause.)*	A tenth of a liter
To correct: What does deci mean? *(Repeat step 3.)*	

(Repeat step 3 with the following examples.)

dekaliter—10 liters
centigram—a hundredth of a gram
kiloliter—1000 liters
dekagram—10 grams
centiliter—hundredth of a liter

PART D: STRUCTURED WORKSHEET

1. *(Give students a worksheet with problems like the ones below.)*

    a. A kilogram equals

        1,000 grams   .001 gram   100 grams

    b. A millimeter equals

        1,000 meters   . 001 meters   .01 meters

    c. A centigram equals

        100 grams   .001 grams   .01 grams

    d. A hectoliter equals

        .01 liters   .1 liters   10 liters   100 liters

	STUDENTS
2. Look at problem a. You have to circle what a kilogram equals. What does kilo mean?	A thousand wholes
So what does a kilogram equal?	A thousand grams

3. Circle the answer.

    (Repeat steps 1 and 2 with several examples.)

FORMAT 17.2   **Metric Conversions**

TEACHER	STUDENTS

PART A: RELATIVE SIZES OF UNITS

1. *(Write the following chart on the board.)*

milligram	centigram	decigram	gram	dekagram	hectogram	kilogram
$\frac{1}{1000}$ gm	$\frac{1}{100}$ gm	$\frac{1}{10}$ gm	1 gm	10 gm	100 gm	1000 gm

	STUDENTS
2. These are the metric units for measuring weight. Milligram is a thousandth of a gram. It is the smallest unit. What is the smallest unit?	Milligram
Kilogram is a thousand whole grams. It is the biggest unit. What is the biggest unit?	Kilogram

TEACHER	**STUDENTS**

3. (*Start at gram and point to the left.*) If we move this way, we're changing to a smaller unit.

   (*Point to the right.*) If we move this way, we're changing to a bigger unit.

4. (*Point to the left.*) Which way am I changing? — To a smaller unit.

   (*Point to the right.*) Which way am I changing? — To a bigger unit

5. (*Point to centigram.*) If we have centigrams and we want to change to grams, which way are we changing? (*Pause, signal.*) — To a bigger unit

   (*Repeat step 4 with grams to kilograms, grams to milligrams, hectograms to grams, kilograms to grams, grams to decigrams.*)

6. (*Erase the board.*) I want to change centigrams to grams. What does a centigram equal? — A hundredth of a gram
   When I change centigrams to grams, which way are we changing? (*Pause, signal.*) — To a bigger unit

   (*Repeat step 5 with same examples as in step 4.*)

PART B: DETERMINING APPROPRIATE OPERATIONS

1. Here are two important rules: When we change to a bigger unit, we divide. Say that. — When we change to a bigger unit, we divide.

   When we change to a smaller unit, we multiply. Say that. — When we change to a smaller unit, we multiply.

2. What do we do when we change to a bigger unit? — Divide
   What do we do when we change to a smaller unit? — Multiply

3. (*Write on board: gram to centigram.*) When we change from grams to centigrams, which way are we changing? (*Pause, signal.*) — To a smaller unit

   Do we multiply or divide when we change from grams to centigrams? (*Pause, signal.*) — Multiply

   To correct: If we have grams and we change to centigrams, which way are we changing? If we change to a smaller unit, what do we do?

   (*Repeat step 3 with these examples: g to kg, g to mg, hg to g, kg to g, g to dg.*)

PART C: STRUCTURED BOARD PRESENTATION

1. (*Write the following problem on the board.*)

   350 centigrams = _____ grams

2. This problem says, 350 centigrams equals how many grams? We're changing centigrams to grams. What are we doing? — Changing centigrams to grams

3. Are we changing to a bigger or smaller unit? (*Pause, signal.*) — bigger

4. We're changing to a bigger unit, so do we multiply or divide? — Divide
   Yes, when we change to a bigger unit, we divide.

5. How many centigrams in each gram? — 100

(continued on next page)

FORMAT 17.2   (continued)

TEACHER	STUDENTS
So we divide by 100. Let's divide by moving the decimal. When we divide by 100, what do we do to the decimal?	Move it to the left 2 places.
6. (*Write 350 next to grams.*) If I move the decimal point two places to the left, where will it be? (*Write on board: 350 centigrams = 3.50 grams*)	Between the 3 and 5.
7. Read the problem now.	350 cg = 3.50 g

(*Repeat steps 1–5 with the problems below.*)
314 grams = _____ milligrams
(*Move decimal point 3 places to right.*)
315 grams = _____ kilograms
(*Move decimal point 3 places to left.*)
7 centigrams = _____ grams
(*Move decimal point 2 places to left.*)
18 kilograms = _____ grams
(*Move decimal point 3 places to right.*)
30 meters = _____ decimeters
(*Move decimal point 1 place to right.*)

PART D: STRUCTURED WORKSHEET

1. (*Give students a worksheet with problems like the one below.*) a. 232 centiliters equal _____ liters	
2. Read problem a. Are you changing to a bigger or smaller unit? (*Pause, signal.*)	Bigger
3. So do you multiply or divide? (*Pause, signal.*)	Divide
4. What do you divide by? Which way do you move the decimal point? How many places do you move it?	100 To the left Two
5. Write the answer. Read the problem.	Students write 2.32. 232 centiliters equals 2.32 liters

(*Repeat steps 1–4 with remaining problems.*)

FORMAT 17.3   Converting to Mixed Numbers

TEACHER	STUDENTS
1. (*Write the following problems on the board.*) a. 27 inches = _____ feet _____ inches b. 32 days = _____ weeks _____ days c. 28 eggs = _____ dozen _____ eggs d. 7 feet = _____ yards _____ feet	
2. Read problem a.	27 inches = _____ feet _____ inches.

In this problem, you have to change 27 inches to feet and inches.

TEACHER	STUDENTS

3. To work this problem, first you find out how many feet are in 27 inches, then you see how many inches are left over.

4. Are we changing to a bigger or smaller unit? *(Pause, signal.)*   Bigger

So do we multiply or divide?   Divide

5. How many inches are in 1 foot?   12

So we divide by 12.

6. 12 goes into 27 how many times? *(Pause, signal.)*   2
There are 2 feet in 27 inches. Write 2 in front of the word feet.

Do you have some inches left over?   Yes

You used 24 inches. Subtract 24 from 27 and see how many you have left. *(Pause.)* How many inches left?   3

Write 3 in front of the word inches. So 27 inches equals what?   2 feet 3 inches

(Repeat steps 1–5 for remaining problems.)

FORMAT 17.4   **Converting from Mixed Numbers**

TEACHER	STUDENTS

1. *(Write the following problems on the board.)*

  a. 3 feet 4 inches = _____ inches

  b. 2 weeks 3 days = _____ days

  c. 2 pounds 3 ounces = _____ ounces

  d. 3 gallons 1 quart = _____ quarts

2. Read problem a. This problem asks us to change 3 feet 4 inches into inches in all. First we'll find how many inches in 3 feet. Then we'll add it to 4 inches.

  (Write in. + over first problem.)

      in.+

  3 feet 4 inches = _____ inches

  What do we do first?   Find how many inches in 3 feet.

  Then what do we do?   Add 4 inches.

3. Let's change 3 feet to inches. Are we changing to a bigger or smaller unit?   Smaller

So what do we do?   Multiply

4. How many inches in a foot?   12

So you'll multiply by 12. Everybody, how many inches in 3 feet?   36

Cross out 3 feet and write 36 above it.

5. Now what do we do?   Add it to 4 inches.

6. How many inches in all? Write it in front of inches.   Students write 40.

7. Read the problem.   3 feet 4 inches equal 40 inches.

FORMAT 17.5 Renaming Customary Units

TEACHER	STUDENTS

PART A: DISCRIMINATION PRACTICE

1. *(Write the following problem on the board, with blanks for the ounces.)*

   3 lbs _____ oz
 +2 lbs _____ oz
         _____ oz

2. First, we add the ounces; then we add the pounds. How
   many ounces in a pound?   16

   That means that if we end up with 16 or more ounces,
   we have to rename.

3. I'll write numbers for ounces. Tell me if we have to rename.

4. *(Write 7 and 5 in the blanks.)*

   What's the answer for ounces?   12

   Do we have to rename 12 ounces as pounds?   No

   (Repeat step 3 with 9 + 9, 9 + 5, 8 + 9, 8 + 8, 9 + 6.)

PART B: STRUCTURED WORKSHEET

1. *(Give students a worksheet with 8–10 problems such as the ones below.)*

  a. 5 lb 9 oz   b. 4 lb 2 oz
   + 3 lb 9 oz   + 3 lb 11 oz

2. Touch problem a. Read the problem.

3. We start by adding ounces.

4. What is 9 + 9?   18

   Write 18 under the line.

5. How many ounces in a pound?   16

6. Do we rename 18 ounces as pounds?   Yes

7. Cross out 18 and write a 1 over the pounds column.

8. We had 18 ounces. We put a pound in the pounds column.
   How many ounces did we take from 18 ounces when we
   renamed?   16

    To correct: A pound has 16 ounces.

9. We had 18 ounces; we moved 16 ounces. How many
   ounces are left?   2

   Write 2 under the ounces.

10. Now add the pounds. How many pounds?   9

11. Read the whole answer.   9 pounds 2 ounces

FORMAT 17.6 **Subtraction with Renaming**

TEACHER	STUDENTS
1. *(Write the following problem on the board.)*	
5 lb 2 oz −2 lb 9 oz	
2. Read the problem.	5 lb 2 oz minus 2 lb 9 oz
3. Can you start with 2 ounces and subtract 9 ounces?	No
4. You must rename. Cross out 5 pounds and write 4.	
5. We borrowed a pound. How many ounces in a pound?	16
6. Write 16 + in front of the 2 ounces.	
7. How many ounces do we start with now?	18
8. Cross out 16 + 2 and write 18 above it.	
9. And what does 18 − 9 equal?	9
So how many ounces do you end up with? Write it.	9
10. How many pounds do you end up with? Write it.	2
11. What's the answer?	2 lb 9 oz

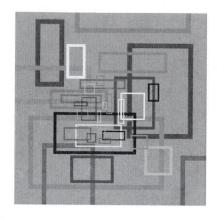

CHAPTER 18

Mathematics Study Skills: Graphs, Charts, Maps, and Statistics

An understanding of mathematics is often required to comprehend material from other content areas such as science, social studies, or health. Mathematics in content-area material often appears in the form of graphs, charts, maps, and statistics. For example, a health text might contain graphs illustrating changes in the occurrence of lung cancer and changes in the percentage of women who smoke. Questions at the end of the unit could then ask students to give the percentage of changes in smoking and in the occurrence of lung cancer from 1988 to 1998. Or a chart in a science text might give the size, distance from the sun, mass, and similar information for the planets in our solar system. A map in a history book might show the principal towns in colonial America, and a question may require students to determine how far apart they were. Obviously, students who lack specific mathematics study skills would find these items difficult. Therefore, mathematics study skills should be included in any comprehensive mathematics instructional program. Mathematics study skills discussed in this chapter include reading and interpreting graphs, reading charts, interpreting maps, and interpreting and determining statistical figures. The Instructional Sequence and Assessment Chart lists the specific problem types discussed in the chapter.

GRAPHS

A graph is a drawing or picture representation of a relationship between two or more sets of numbers. Figure 18.1 includes examples of the various types of graphs students will encounter in the elementary grades. There are four main types of graphs: pictographs, bar, line, and circle graphs.

Graphs are typically introduced during late third or early fourth grade. The first type of graph introduced is usually the pictograph, followed by bar, line, and circle graph respectively.

Two major factors determine the difficulty of interpreting line and bar graphs: (a) the amount of information on the graph and (b) the need for inferring or estimating amounts. Graphs become more complex as they show more than one set of relationships. For example, a simple line graph may show the performance of one student on a series of tasks. A more complex line graph would show the performance of several students all on the same graph with separate lines representing each student. In reading a graph with more than one set of information, the student must be able to use the key to determine which line refers to which student. Graphs with two sets of information are illustrated in Figure 18.2.

Instructional Sequence and Assessment Chart

Grade Level	Problem Type	Performance Indicator

3a   Interpreting line graphs

a. How many points did Bill score on Monday?
b. On which day did Bill score the least?

3b   Interpreting bar graphs

a. How many points did Ann earn?
b. How many more points did Ann earn than Jim?

3c   Interpreting pictorial graphs

= 10 babies born in Pinerock

How many babies were born in 1978?
a. 3   b. 40   c. 30   d. 35

How many more babies were born in 1978 than in 1979?

4a   Determining arithmetic means

Jill plays basketball. She scores 8 points in one game, 2 points the next game, 6 points the next game, and 4 points in the last game. What is her average?

4b   Interpreting map legends (simple application with whole numbers)

1 inch = 10 miles

If A is 2 inches from B on the map, how much is the distance in miles between A and B?

Instructional Sequence and Assessment Chart (continued)

Grade Level	Problem Type	Performance Indicator
5a	Interpreting complex graphs with one variable—bar graph	

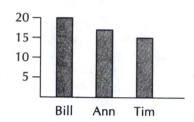

How many points did Ann score?
a. 15   b. 19   c. 17   d. 20

How many points did Bill score?
a. 20   b. 15   c. 19   d. 16

5b   Interpreting complex graphs with one variable—line graph

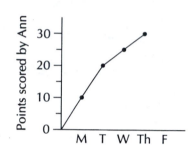

How many points did Ann score on Wednesday?
a. 20   b. 22   c. 28   d. 25

How many points did Ann score on Monday?
a. 15   b. 10   c. 9   d. 12

5c   Interpreting complex graphs with one variable—pictograph

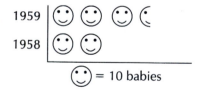

How many babies were born in 1959?
a. 30   b. 3   c. 40   d. 35

5d   Interpreting tables

Players on Taft High School Basketball Team

Name	Born	Height	Weight
Jill Hernandez	1980	5'7"	134
Tammy Smith	1981	5'4"	128
Jackie Wilson	1980	5'2"	140
Tanya Jones	1982	5'8"	132

a. Who is the heaviest player on the team?
b. How much heavier is Tanya than Tammy?
c. How much younger is Tammy than Jill?

Grade Level	*Problem Type*	*Performance Indicator*
6a	Reading Timetables	

		Bus A	Bus B	Bus C	Bus D
Lv.	downtown	9:09	9:18	9:36	9:47
Ar.	25th St.	9:14	9:23	9:41	9:52
Ar.	34th St.	9:18	9:26	9:44	9:55
Ar.	41st St.	9:21	9:29	9:47	9:58
Ar.	49th St.	9:24	9:32	9:49	10:00
Ar.	62nd St.	9:31	9:39	9:56	10:07

a. When will Bus C arrive at 41st Street?

b. How long does it take Bus B to get from 34th Street to 62nd Street?

c. What time would you leave downtown if you wanted to be at 62nd Street just before ten o'clock?

Grade Level	*Problem Type*	*Performance Indicator*
6b	Interpreting complex graphs with two sets of information—bar graph	

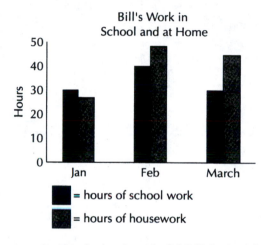

a. How many hours of school work did Bill do in February?

b. In which month did Bill do more school work than housework?

Grade Level	*Problem Type*	*Performance Indicator*
6c	Interpreting complex graphs with two sets of information—line graph	

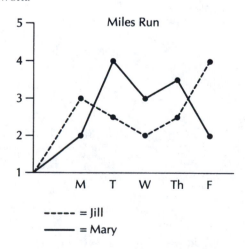

Instructional Sequence and Assessment Chart (continued)

Grade Level	Problem Type	Performance Indicator

<table>
<tr><td></td><td></td><td>a. On which days did Jill run more than Mary?
b. How many miles did Jill run on Wednesday?</td></tr>
<tr><td>6d</td><td>Calculating statistics (range, median, mode)</td><td>Mrs. James gave a test to the 9 students in her class. The marks are written below:</td></tr>
</table>

Ann	23	Monica	41
Cathy	18	Naomi	35
David	41	Paul	41
James	23	Sarah	42
		Tom	38

a. What is the range?
b. What is the median?
c. What is the mode?

6e — Interpreting map legends (complex applications with fractions)

```
  •
  C


          •             •
          A             B
  ┌──────────────────┐
  │ 1 inch = 10 miles │
  └──────────────────┘
```

a. If city C is 21/2 inches from city B on the map, how far apart are cities C and B?

Graphs also become more complex as students must infer the amount indicated. Figure 18.3 includes excerpts from four graphs. In examples a and b, the end of the bar is directly across from a mark that has no number next to it. The students must infer the number represented by the mark. In example a, there are five spaces between 20 and 30. Thus, each space represents a quantity of 2. In example b, there are two spaces between 20 and 30; thus, each space must represent 5.

Graphs become even more difficult to read when the end of the bar is not directly across from a mark, as in examples c and d in Figure 18.3. To determine the value, the students must mentally divide the space into equivalent units so that the point corresponds to a unit. In example c, the closest units are 20 and 22. The point is approximately half of the unit, so the value of the point is half of 2, or 1. Thus, the intersection point is about 21. Example d is significantly more difficult, since there is a greater difference between the numbered spaces, and the intersection does not fall at a halfway mark. To make the estimation, students must mentally divide the space into 10 equivalent units and estimate.

Pictorial graphs become more difficult when (a) each picture stands for a quantity other than one (for example, a pictograph in which each graph represents five units is more difficult than a pictograph in which each picture represents one unit) and (b) when fractional parts of a picture are shown. For example, let's say each smiling face represents 100 students, and this picture is shown.

The student must determine the quantity the last picture represents by computing one-half of 100. Even more difficult would be an example in which a partial representation greater or less than one-half is shown:

In such an instance, the student must estimate the fraction of the unit shown and then figure out the

FIGURE 18.1   Simple Graphs

1. Bar Graphs
   a. horizontal

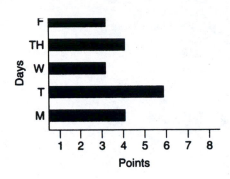

b. vertical

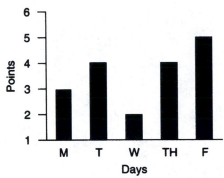

2. Line Graph

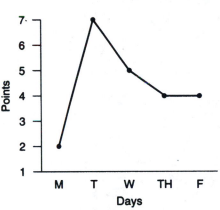

3. Pictograph

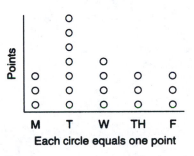

4. Circle Graph

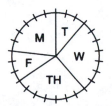

(continued)

FIGURE 18.2 Complex Graphs

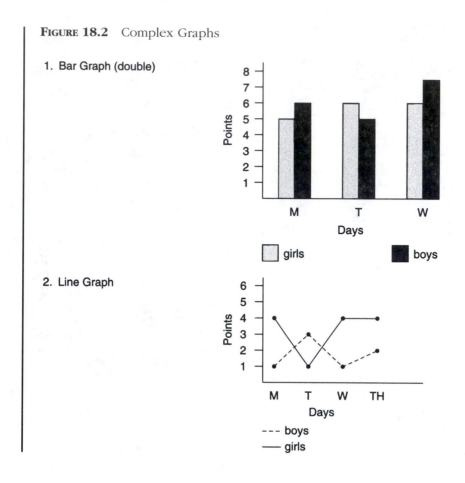

1. Bar Graph (double)

2. Line Graph

quantity it represents. In the above example, about a quarter of the face is shown; one-quarter of 100 is 25.

The sequence for introducing various types of graphs should be carefully coordinated with number reading and fraction skills so that students have mastered all component skills before being asked to read graphs. Simple graphs are introduced first. Just one difficulty factor should be introduced at a time as more difficult graphs are taught.

The teaching procedure involves modeling how to find information on the graph, using a given

FIGURE 18.3 Graphs Requiring Estimation

a.　　b.　　c. 24　　d. 40

question. For example, students may be given a bar graph that shows the number of points Sarah scored in basketball games during recess each day. An appropriate question is, "How many points did Sarah score on Tuesday?" The teacher first points out what the numbers stand for: "These numbers tell us the points Sarah scored." The teacher next points out what the letters under each bar stand for: "This M stands for Monday. This T stands for Tuesday. . . ." Finally, the teacher models how to determine how many points Sarah scored on a given day. "To find how many points Sarah scored on Tuesday, I move my finger to the T. Then I move my finger up to the top of the bar. Finally, I move my finger to the numeral across from the top of the bar. It's a 6, so the graph tells us that Sarah scored 6 points on Tuesday." The same basic procedure is used when more complex graphs are used. The teacher points out the various information shown on the graph and then models how to get information to answer specific questions.

A variety of literal questions should be included in initial examples. Literal questions ask for the amount at a particular time (e.g., "How many points did Sarah score on Monday?") or the particular time on which a specified quantity was given (e.g., "On what day did Sarah score 8 points?"). Questions calling for comparisons should gradually be included and come to represent a greater proportion of the total questions (e.g., "How many more points did Sarah score on Monday than on Tuesday? On which day did she score the most points? On which day did she score the fewest points?").

TABLES OR CHARTS

A table or chart, like a graph, specifies the relationship among sets of numbers. Reading tables and charts is frequently necessary in adult life: time schedules for buses, trains, and airplanes; financial charts dealing with income taxes, loan rates, and eligibility for benefits; instructions for recipes, medicines, and so on.

A preskill for using tables is an understanding of the concepts of row and column. Teachers can explain the terms in this way: "The lines of information going down the page are called columns. The lines of information going across the page are called rows."

The procedure for teaching students to read charts and tables follows a model-test sequence for the various parts of the table: title, headings, rows, and columns. The teacher first points out the title of the table and discusses its intent. The teacher then points out the heading in each column, discussing the type of information found under each heading. After leading students through interpreting the headings, the teacher points out how the students read across the row. Finally, the teacher models the strategy for locating information by looking for the intersection of rows and columns.

The teacher must carefully design questions that require the students to use the table. During the early intermediate grades, these questions should be literal or comparative. A literal question can be answered by simply referring to the chart (e.g., "What time does bus 834 arrive at 145th Street?"). A comparative question, on the other hand, asks the students to tell the difference between two pieces of information (e.g., "How many minutes between when bus 837 and bus 849 arrive at 135th Street?").

During the late intermediate grades, inferential questions should be introduced. An inferential question is one in which the information on the chart is used in conjunction with other information to answer a question (e.g., "During snowy weather, which bus would you take if you wanted to arrive at 125th Street at 5:35 PM?"). The chart would show two buses, one arriving at 5:34 and one arriving at 5:25. The student would have to infer that since buses travel more slowly on snowy days, taking the 5:25 bus would be better.

Format 18.1 gives steps for introducing time schedules. Part A is a structured exercise in which the teacher models and tests how to locate information on the table. To do this, the teacher should put a reproduction of the table on the chalkboard or use an overhead projector to ensure that all students can see. Students should also have a copy of the table so they can practice finding information from the table at their seats. Following Part A, students should be given worksheets containing a table and set of relevant questions to complete under teacher supervision. One or two tables should be presented daily for several weeks.

Note that in the example presented in the format, reading a bus schedule, students must first find the row containing the location of the bus stop, then look across the row for the appropriate time, and finally go up that column to find the bus they must take. Locating a row or column in a bus time schedule differs from locating information in a table where students must locate the intersection of a row and column. For example, in the following table, to find the distance from Springfield to Salem, students would find the row for Springfield, find the column that is headed Salem, and then look for the intersection to find the distance. Students should be given an opportunity to work from a variety of tables.

	Portland	*Albany*	*Salem*
Eugene	118	30	62
Springfield	123	35	67
Creswell	132	44	76

MAPS

There are many skills involved in reading a map. However, our discussion addresses only a mathematics skill directly involved in map reading: computing the distance between two points on a map.

The difficulty of computing distances on a map is affected by two factors:

1. The presence of fractional numbers. If the distance between two points is 1¼ inches and the scale says 1 inch equals 20 miles, the student must multiply 1¼ times 20:

$$1\frac{1}{4} \times 20 = \frac{5}{4} \times 20 = \frac{100}{4} = 25$$

or

$$(1 \times 20) + (\frac{1}{4} \times 20)$$

2. The relative size of the numbers. Determining the distance between two points is more difficult when each inch represents 500 miles rather than 5 miles.

The preskills for simple map problems include measuring with a ruler to the nearest inch (or centimeter) and knowing multiplication facts. For more complex map problems, students must also be able to measure to the nearest fractional part of an inch and multiply a whole number and mixed fraction.

The teaching application involves modeling and prompting students in applying these three component skills:

1. locating and reading the scale,
2. measuring the distance between two points on a map, and
3. multiplying the distance by the scale value.

Initially, map problems should involve questions in which no fractional parts of a unit are involved. Fractional parts of a unit should be introduced only after multiplying fractions has been taught.

STATISTICS

The four basic statistical concepts introduced in the elementary grades are range, mean (or average), mode, and median.

The range refers to the difference between the smallest and largest number in a set. For example, the distances that girls in Mr. Adams's class can throw the shotput are 32 ft., 29 ft., 41 ft., 18 ft., 27 ft., and 42 ft. The range is computed by subtracting 18 ft., the lowest score, from 42 ft., the highest score: $42 - 18 = 24$. The range is 24 ft.

The mean, the most commonly used statistic, is computed by adding a group of numbers and dividing the sum by the total of numbers added. For example, the mean of the numbers 24, 26, 20, and 30 is computed by adding these numbers and then dividing the sum, 100, by 4; the mean ($100 \div 4$) is 25.

The median is the middle measurement of a set that has been arranged in order of magnitude. For example, a teacher gives a test to a class of nine students and then lists the marks in order, from lowest to highest: 64, 70, 70, 70, 78, 92, 94, 94, 98. The median is the score that comes in the middle, 78. Four students scored less than 78, and four scored more than 78.

The median is relatively easy to figure with an odd number of scores. If there are 17 scores, the median is the ninth number: eight numbers are smaller and eight are larger. For 13, the seventh number is the median: six are smaller and six are larger. The median is somewhat difficult to compute for an even number of scores because the middle two numbers must be averaged. For example, if eight students score 13, 17, 19, 20, 24, 28, 31, 37, the median is computed by figuring the average of the middle two numbers:

$$\frac{20 + 24}{2} = \frac{44}{2} = 22$$

The median equals 22.

The mode denotes the most frequently occurring value in a collection of values. For example, in looking at the students' scores on the tests in the preceding paragraph, we note that one student scored 84, three scored 70, one scored 78, one scored 92, two scored 94, and one scored 98. The score that occurred most often, 70, is the mode.

Statistical concepts should be introduced cumulatively, beginning with the mean, which is the most common statistic. When students have mastered computing the mean, the teacher can introduce the range, since computing the range is relatively easy and is unlikely to be confused with the mean. The median should be introduced third, and mode last, since it is the least frequently used. The mean is usually introduced in fourth or fifth grade.

Teaching Procedure

A similar teaching procedure can be used to teach mean, median, range, and mode. The teacher defines the term, models how to figure out the particular statistic, and then leads the students through working several problems.

Sets of problems should contain cumulative review. After each new statistical concept is introduced, the teacher should present exercises in which the students apply all the statistical concepts introduced to date. For example, if range and mean had been taught previously and the median had just been introduced, the teacher should present an exercise in which the students must compute all three statistics (range, mean, and median).

Since the teaching procedure is similar for all the statistics, we have included a format only for mean, the most difficult and commonly used statistic (see Format 18.2). This format demonstrates the mechanics of determining the mean. The teacher presents two steps: (a) add the numbers, and (b) divide the sum by how many numbers were added.

When presenting the format, examples should be prepared initially so that the mean will be a whole number; that is, the sum of the quantities must be a multiple of the divisor. A problem in which the sum is 24 and the divisor is 5 would be inappropriate initially, since 24 is not a multiple of 5.

After this format has been presented for several days, a demonstration illustrating the concept of mean with a balance bar may be presented.

$$2 + 5 + 7 + 10 = 24, \; 24 \div 4 = 6$$

Next, the teacher places a fulcrum under position 6 and shows that the bar balances. The teacher summarizes by saying that the mean (6) is the center that balances the numbers on both sides.

APPLICATION ITEMS: STUDY SKILLS

1. For each pair of questions below, tell which is more difficult and why.

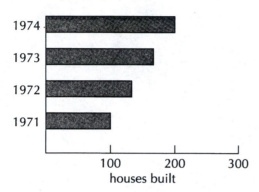

houses built

Pair one
a. How many houses were built in 1974?
b. How many houses were built in 1972?

Pair two
a. How many more houses were built in 1974 than 1971?
b. How many more houses were built in 1973 than 1972?

2. Below are three errors made by students on the problem specified. Tell the cause of each error. Specify the remediation procedure.
   Jill played in 5 basketball games.
   She scored 25 points in the first game, 15 points in the second game, 17 points in the third game, 21 points in the fourth game, and 22 points in her last game.

   What was her average?

Alex	Jill		Ramon	
25	25	19.8	25	200
15	15	5)99	15	5)100
17	17	5	17	
21	21	49	21	
+ 22	+ 22	45	+ 22	
100	99	40	100	

(continued)

3. Tell the component skills a student must have mastered to work the following problem. (*Note: A is 1¾ inches from B*)

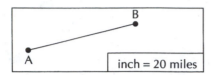

inch = 20 miles

FORMAT 18.1 Reading Time Schedules

TEACHER   **STUDENTS**

1. *(Write the following schedule on the board, or use an overhead projector.)*

     Bus Time Schedule

Locations	Bus 287	Bus 124
23rd St.	2:15	3:44
37th St.	2:25	3:54
45th St.	3:05	4:02
64th St.	3:34	4:31
76th St.	3:48	5:06

2. This is part of a bus time schedule. It tells us when buses arrive at different places.

3. Remember: The lines of information going down the page are called columns. Touch the heading for the first column. Read it.   Locations

   Under this heading are all the places that the buses stop. They stop at 23rd St., 37th St., 45th St., 64th St., and 76th St. Touch the heading for the next column. Read it.   Bus 287

   That is the number of a bus. Under this heading are all the times bus 287 will arrive at different bus stops. What time does bus 287 stop at 23rd St.? *(Pause, signal.)*   2:15

   (Repeat question with remaining locations. Repeat step 2 with bus 124.)

4. *(Point to the time schedule.)* Let's say that we want to find out what bus stops at 45th Street around 4:00. First, I find 45th Street; then I go across until I find a time close to 4 PM. Last I go up the column to find the bus number. The bus I would take to go to 45th Street at about 4:00 would be bus 124, since it stops at 45th Street at 4:02.

5. Now it's your turn. Find the bus that stops at 76th Street at about 3:45. First find the row for 76th Street. Now find the time you want—close to 3:45. *(Pause.)* What is the number of the bus?   287

   What bus would you take on 76th Street at about 3:45?   Bus 287

   (Repeat steps 3 and 4 with several questions.)

   a. How long does it take to get from 23rd Street to 45th Street on bus 124?

   b. How long does it take to get from 45th Street to 76th Street on bus 287?

   c. When does bus 287 arrive at 64th Street?

   d. When does bus 124 arrive at 45th Street?

FORMAT 18.2   **Computation Strategy (the Mean)**

TEACHER	**STUDENTS**

PART A: STRUCTURED BOARD PRESENTATION

1. Listen: Ben got 4 points on Monday, 7 points on Tuesday, 3 points on Wednesday, and 6 points on Thursday. *(Write 4, 7, 3, 6.)* We want to figure the average number of points Ben got each day. What do we want to figure out?

> The average number of points Ben got each day.

2. Here's how we figure the average. First we add, then divide the sum by how many numbers we added. First we add, then what do we do?

> Divide the sum by how many numbers we added.

3. First we add. *(Write the problem on the board.)*

$$\begin{array}{r} 4 \\ 7 \\ 3 \\ +6 \\ \hline \end{array}$$

What is the sum of 4, 7, 3, and 6? *(Pause.)*

> 20

4. The sum is 20. We added. Now we divide by how many numbers we added. *(Point to 4, 7, 3, and 6 as you say,)* We added 1, 2, 3, 4, numbers.

5. We added 4 numbers, so we divide 4 into 20. What do we divide?

> 4 into 20

How many times does 4 go into 20?

> 5

Yes, Ben's average is 5 points each day. What is Ben's average?

> 5 points each day

Did Ben score exactly 5 points every day?

> No

5 points a day is his average.

(Repeat steps 1–5 with the examples below.)
Jill scored the following points in each game: 6, 8, 9, 5, 0, 10, 4.
Tom ran these numbers of miles each day: 3, 1, 1, 7, 0, 0.

PART B: STRUCTURED WORKSHEET

1. *(Give students worksheets with several problems like the one below.)*

    Jack ran 5 miles on Monday, 2 miles on Tuesday, 4 miles on Wednesday, 0 miles on Thursday, and 9 miles on Friday. What is the average number of miles he ran each day?
    □ _____ _____ _____

2. Read the problem. What does the problem ask for?

> The average number of miles he ran each day.

3. What do we do first to figure the average?

> Add the miles.

   Add all the miles. *(Pause.)* How many miles did he run altogether?

> 20

(continued on next page)

FORMAT 18.2 (continued)

TEACHER	STUDENTS
4. What do we do after we find the sum?	Divide by how many numbers we added.
5. How many numbers did we add? *(Pause, signal.)*	5
Say the division problem.	5 goes into 20
How many times does 5 go into 20?	4
Write the numeral in the box.	
6. Now we have to write in the words. Read the last sentence. So the words we put in the answer are miles each day.	What is the average number of miles he ran each day?
What are the words that go in the answer?	Miles each day
What is the answer? Say the whole answer.	4 miles each day
Write the words.	
(Repeat steps 1–5 with remaining problems.)	

CHAPTER 19

Geometry

With Don Crawford

The geometry objectives discussed in this chapter fall into three major categories:

1. identifying and defining various figures and concepts;
2. finding the measurements of a figure, such as determining perimeter, area, circumference;
3. using logic in working with angles and lines;
4. constructing figures using an instrument such as a compass or protractor.

The specific skills to be taught can be found in the Instructional Sequence and Assessment Chart. Next to most objectives in the Instructional Sequence and Assessment Chart are one, two, or three asterisks. These asterisks indicate the use of a generic teaching procedure required for the specific skill. One asterisk indicates that the objective falls in the category of identifying and defining geometric figures and concepts. Specific teaching procedures for skills for this area are discussed on pages 411–421. Two asterisks next to an objective indicate that the objective falls in the category of finding measurements of a geometric figure. Procedures for finding these measurements are discussed on pages 421–423. Three asterisks next to an objective indicate that the objective falls in the category of constructing geometric figures. Teaching procedures for constructing geometric figures are discussed on pages 423–424.

IDENTIFYING AND DEFINING GEOMETRIC FIGURES AND CONCEPTS

Table 19.1 lists most of the figures and relationships taught in the elementary grades. The table shows the relationships among various figures and concepts. However, it is not intended to imply an order for introducing skills. A suggested order for introducing skills appears in the Instructional Sequence and Assessment Chart.

Teaching students to identify new figures and concepts is simply a form of vocabulary teaching. Three basic methods of vocabulary instruction are used to teach the concepts and vocabulary in this chapter: (a) examples only, (b) synonyms, and (c) definitions. The examples-only method is used to present vocabulary terms and concepts that cannot be readily explained by using a synonym or definition. In teaching vocabulary through examples, the teacher constructs a set of examples, half of which are of the concept (positive examples) and half of which are of a similar but different concept (nonexamples). The set must be carefully designed to show the range of positive examples and rule out possible misinterpretations. For example, when ovals are introduced, a variety of ovals should be presented to demonstrate the range of figures called ovals:

Instructional Sequence and Assessment Chart

Grade Level	Problem Type	Performance Indicator
1a	Identify circle*	Mark each circle with X.
1b	Identify rectangle*	Mark each rectangle with X.
1c	Identify triangle*	Mark each triangle with X.
1d	Identify square*	Mark each square with X.
1e	Identify interior of closed figure*	Tell me when I touch the interior of this figure.
1f	Identify exterior of closed figure*	Tell me when I touch the exterior of this figure.
2a	Identify cube*	Mark each cube with X.
2b	Identify sphere*	Mark each sphere with X.
2c	Identify cone*	Mark each cone with X.
2d	Identify the diameter of a circle*	What is a diameter? Put X on each line that is the diameter of a circle.

Grade Level	Problem Type	Performance Indicator

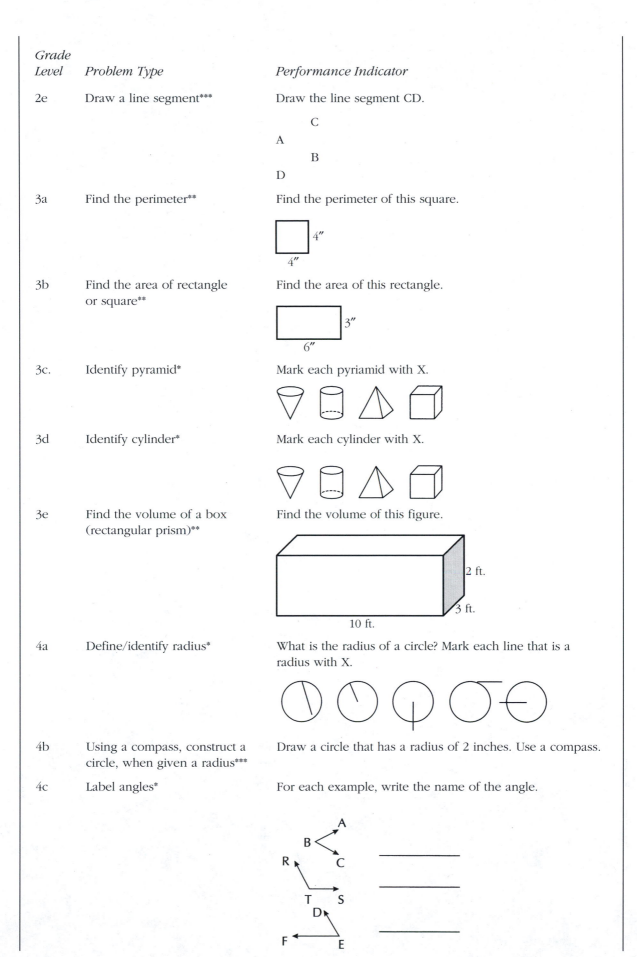

2e Draw a line segment***

Draw the line segment CD.

C

A

B

D

3a Find the perimeter**

Find the perimeter of this square.

4″

4″

3b Find the area of rectangle or square**

Find the area of this rectangle.

3″

6″

3c. Identify pyramid*

Mark each pyramid with X.

3d Identify cylinder*

Mark each cylinder with X.

3e Find the volume of a box (rectangular prism)**

Find the volume of this figure.

2 ft.

3 ft.

10 ft.

4a Define/identify radius*

What is the radius of a circle? Mark each line that is a radius with X.

4b Using a compass, construct a circle, when given a radius***

Draw a circle that has a radius of 2 inches. Use a compass.

4c Label angles*

For each example, write the name of the angle.

A

B

C

R

T   S

D

F   E

_____

_____

_____

Instructional Sequence and Assessment Chart (continued)

Grade Level	Problem Type	Performance Indicator
4d	Define degree/measure angles, using a protractor**	Measure each of the following angles.
4e	Construct angles, using a protractor***	Construct the following angles. 90° _____ 45° _____
4f	Define/identify right angle*	What is a right angle? Circle each right angle.
4g	Define/identify acute angle*	What is an acute angle? Circle each acute angle.
4h	Define/identify obtuse angle*	What is an obtuse angle? Circle each obtuse angle.
4i	Define/identify right triangle*	What is a right triangle? Circle each right triangle.
4j	Define/identify equilateral triangle*	What is an equilateral triangle? Circle each equilateral triangle.
4k	Define/identify isosceles triangle*	What is an isosceles triangle? Circle each isosceles triangle.
4l	Define/identify scalene triangle*	What is a scalene triangle? Circle each scalene triangle.

Grade Level	Problem Type	Performance Indicator

4m — Identify the following polygons:*
pentagon
hexagon
octagon

Draw a P over the pentagon.
Draw an H over the hexagon.
Draw an O over the octagon.

4n — Find the volume of a box (rectangular prism) using the formula Volume = Area of base × height**

Find the volume of a box whose base is 5 inches long and 7 inches wide and whose height is 4 inches.

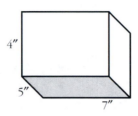

4o — Find the perimeter of various polygons**

Find the perimeter of this figure.

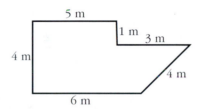

5a — Identify parallel lines*

Circle each group of parallel lines.

5b — Identify perpendicular lines*

Circle each group of perpendicular lines.

5c — Identify a parallelogram*

Cicle each parallelogram.

5d — Find the area of a triangle using the equation**

$$A = \frac{\text{base} \times \text{height}}{2}$$

Find the area of this triangle.

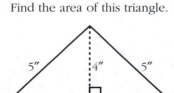

Instructional Sequence and Assessment Chart (continued)

Grade Level	Problem Type	Performance Indicator
5e	Find the area of a parallelogram using the equation** $A = \text{base} \times \text{height}$	Find the area of this parallelogram. 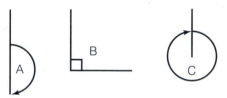
5f	State the degrees in an angle, given examples of a right angle, a straight angle, or a full circle*	How many degrees in ∠ A, ∠ B, and ∠ C?
5g	Find value of unknown component angles using facts about angles**	Find the value of ∠ B if ∠ A is one-third of a full circle. 
5h	Identify corresponding angles and that they are equal*	Identify which angle is equal to ∠ A in this diagram. 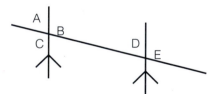
5i	Identify opposite angles and that they are equal*	Identify which angle is equal to ∠ A in this diagram. 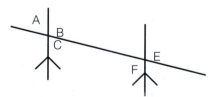
5j	Use knowledge of facts about angles to compute values of angles in a complex diagram	If ∠ A is equal to one-fifth of a circle, compute the value of angles B, C, and D in this diagram.

Grade Level	Problem Type	Performance Indicator
5k	Use equation $\pi \times D = C$ to find π, D, or C	Find the circumference of circle A and the diameter of circle B.

13 m

50″

5l	Use the equation $A = \pi \times r \times r$ to find area of a circle given the radius or the diameter	Find the area of the circle.

14 cm

5m	Find the surface area of boxes (rectangular prisms)	Find the surface area of this box.

18″

5″

6″

5n	Find the surface area of rectangular pyramid	Find the surface area of this pyramid.

15 inches   14 in

10 in

12 in

Instructional Sequence and Assessment Chart (continued)

Grade Level	Problem Type	Performance Indicator
5o	Find the surface area of a triangular pyramid	Find the surface area of this pyramid with a triangular base. 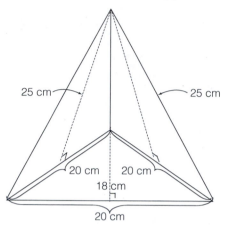
6a	Find the area of a complex figure—one with a hole or holes in it	Find the area of the wall that needs siding: 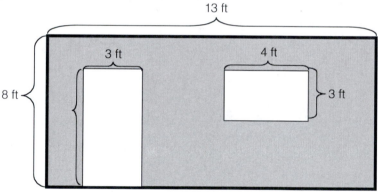
6b	Find the volume of figures that come to a point using the equation: $$V = \frac{\text{area of base} \times \text{height}}{3}$$	Find the volume of the following figures: 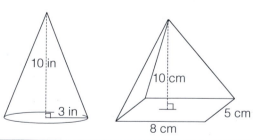

Table 19.1   Elementary Level Figures and Relationships

I. *Open Figures*

A. *Line Segment*—the shortest distance between two points (*Note:* A line extends infinitely in space in two directions.)

B. *Ray*—a line beginning at a point and extending infinitely into space

C. *Angle*—formed by two rays both of which have the same end point, which is called the vertex

1. *Right angle*—measures 90°

2. *Acute angle*—measures more than 0° and less than 90°

3. *Obtuse angle*—measures more than 90° and less than 180°

4. *Straight angle*—measures 180°

II. *Closed Figures*

A. *Polygons*—simple (no crossed lines) closed figures bound by line segments

1. *Triangles*—three-sided figures

a. Equilateral—all sides measure the same length

b. Right—contains one right angle

c. Isosceles—two sides of equal length

d. Scalene—no two sides are of the same length

2. *Quadrilaterals*—four-sided figures

a. Rectangle—four right angles, two pairs of sides with equal lengths

b. Square—four equal sides, four right angles

c. Parallelogram—two pairs of parallel lines

d. Rhombus—parallelogram having two adjacent sides congruent

e. Trapezoid—no right angles, one pair of nonparallel lines

3. *Additional Polygons*

a. Pentagon—five-sided figure

b. Hexagon—six-sided figure

c. Octagon—eight-sided figure

B. *Curved Figures*

1. *Ovals*

2. *Circles*

a. Center—midpoint of circle

b. Radius—line segment extending from midpoint to edge

c. Diameter—line that divides the circle in half

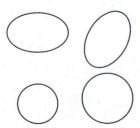

(continued)

Table 19.1   (continued)

III. *Identification of Dimensional Shapes*
  A. *Cube*

  B. *Pyramid*

  C. *Cone*

  D. *Cylinder*

  E. *Sphere*

IV. *Line Relationships*
  A. *Perpendicular lines*—lines that intersect to form a 90° angle
  B. *Parallel lines*—lines that exist beside each other without intersecting

V. *Figure Relationships*
  A. *Similarity*—having the same shape
  B. *Congruence*—having the same shape and size
  C. *Symmetry*—a figure can be folded along a line and the two parts coincide

Nonexamples should include circles so that the students will not misidentify circles as ovals. As the examples are presented, the teacher points to each example, saying, "This is an oval," or "This is not an oval," and then she tests the students by asking, "Is this an oval?"

The presentation of examples and nonexamples has been shown to be an effective way to teach geometric concepts. In a study done by Petty and Jansson (1987), students in one group were taught to identify various geometric shapes using a rational sequence of examples and nonexamples, while students in the other group were given definitions of shapes. Not surprisingly, students who were given the systematic sequence of instruction using examples and nonexamples performed significantly higher on measures of concept attainment than those who experienced the more traditional instruction.

Teaching vocabulary through synonyms involves explaining a new term by using a word or phrase already known to the students. For example, the word *interior* may be explained as "inside." Teaching vocabulary through definitions, on the other hand, involves using a longer explanation. For example, a pentagon may be defined as "a closed figure having five straight sides." Following the presentation of either a synonym or a definition, the teacher presents a set of positive and negative examples asking, "Is this a _____?"

The synonym or definition selected need not meet all the requirements of a formal definition of the concept. A teacher may initially choose a simplified definition that is not technically correct but will help the students master the concept (e.g., a rectangle has four sides and four square corners). More sophisticated definitions can be used in later grades.

Whether the concept is best taught through examples only, definition, or synonym, the teaching format consists of the same parts. Format 19.1 illustrates the basic identification/definition teaching procedure. In Part A, the teacher first models identifying several examples (if teaching by example only) or models and tests the synonym or definition. The teacher then tests students orally on a set of examples and nonexamples of the concept. Part B is a worksheet exercise in which students must use the information they have just learned. For example, after modeling and testing the definition of a parallelogram and testing students on several positive and negative examples of parallelograms, the teacher has students complete a worksheet requiring them to circle all examples of parallelograms.

Worksheets should contain two distinct sections. One section should test the application of the new definition, and the other should review concepts taught previously. This cumulative review serves two important functions. First, it helps prevent students from forgetting previously taught concepts. Second, it helps provide the discrimination practice needed when similar figures are presented. Note that student performance on the review sections of the worksheets should determine when a new concept can be introduced. Generally, new information should not be introduced until students demonstrate mastery on previously introduced information. In addition to worksheet review, extra practice should be incorporated into the classroom routine in the form of games and displays.

For example, one way for students to practice identifying figures is to use flash cards. In flash card practice, the figure is drawn on one side of a flash card and the label of that figure is written on the other side. Students study the cards and then take turns asking each other to identify the figures.

FINDING MEASUREMENTS OF GEOMETRIC FIGURES

During the elementary grades, students can be taught how to find (a) the perimeter of polygons; (b) the radius, diameter, and circumference of circles; (c) the area of squares, triangles, rectangles, parallelograms, circles, and complex figures; (d) the surface area of rectangular prisms (boxes), rectangular pyramids, triangular pyramids; (e) the volume of rectangular prisms, triangular pyramids, and rectangular pyramids; and (f) determining the number of degrees in an angle using a protractor. Recommendations regarding when to introduce each measurement skill can be found in the Instructional Sequence and Assessment Chart.

The perimeter of a polygon is the sum of the length of each of its sides. The radius of a circle is the distance between the midpoint of the circle and the edge of the circle. The diameter is a line running from one side of the circle to the opposite side through the midpoint. The circumference is the distance around the outside of a circle.

In teaching the students to measure the perimeter of a closed figure, the teacher defines *perimeter* and models how to compute it. The same procedure is used in measuring the radius and diameter of a circle.

Area refers to the relative surface occupied by a plane figure. Format 19.2 demonstrates how a teacher would most effectively teach the procedure for computing the area of a rectangle. The teacher first presents an exercise showing how a rectangle may be divided into square units by presenting an illustration of rectangles with horizontal and vertical lines drawn at the unit intervals. This illustration is critical to establish the connection between what students already know about multiplication (that one multiplies to determine the number of objects in groups of equal size) with the new skill of finding area. Note that the format uses a variety of common units such as inches, feet, yards, centimeters, and meters. Using different units enables students to generalize across problems.

The teacher points out the meaning of the term *square unit* by reference to the illustrated squares. After presenting the illustration, the teacher gives a rule for determining the area (i.e., multiply the base times the height) and demonstrates its application, computing the area of several rectangles and squares. The teacher emphasizes the need to express the answer in terms of square units (square inches, square feet, etc.).

After students have fully mastered finding the area of rectangles, the teacher can introduce exercises that require the students to determine perimeter as well as area. A sample worksheet exercise appears in Figure 19.1. The purpose of these exercises is to provide students with the practice needed to discriminate between two similar measurements.

A variety of equations can be used to teach area. However, we recommend that teachers use *base times height*. This equation is better than *length times width* because it is more closely related to the equations for finding the areas of other figures. For example, the equation for finding the area of triangles is *base times height divided by two* (see Format 19.3). If the area of rectangles has been taught as *base times height,* the relationship between the area of rectangles and triangles is easier to understand. Format 19.3 includes steps that explicitly demonstrate to students that when the area of a rectangle (base times height) is divided by two, the answer will yield the area of a triangle. This demonstration is similar to the kinds of proofs students will have to construct in high school geometry.

Once students can figure the area of both rectangles and triangles from a formula, they can easily be taught how to find the area of complex figures— ones that have figure inside them. This is the skill needed to find the area of a wall (for paint or wallpaper) that has a window or a door in it. Students learn to first find the area of the figure inside the figure, then find the area of the whole figure (the window or door), then subtract the area of the smaller figure inside the whole figure. The steps to this process are easy (see Format 19.4); however, students should be very comfortable with finding the area of both kinds of figures before being asked to do this format. As recommended in the Instructional Sequence and Assessment Chart this skill is not in-

FIGURE 19.1 Sample Measuring Worksheet

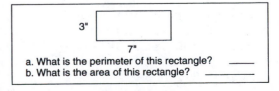

a. What is the perimeter of this rectangle? _____
b. What is the area of this rectangle? _____

troduced until half a year after students learn how to compute the area of a triangle.

The equation for finding the area of parallelograms is also base times height; it should be noted that in the case of parallelograms, this equation results in using different dimensions than those for length and width (see Format 19.5). It is easier for students to learn how to find the area of parallelograms using base times height if they have initially learned to find the area of rectangles using this equation. The format for finding the area of parallelograms also includes a demonstration of why the equation works and how it is related to the equation for finding the area of rectangles.

Using the formula base times height is an example of a big idea in mathematics instruction. This big idea unifies several disparate equations for determining the area of rectangles, triangles, and parallelograms. The big idea of base times height connects these three calculations. In addition, a very similar concept is recommended later in this chapter for demonstrating the relationships among the equations for finding the volume of solid figures.

Finding measurements of circles comes after students have learned the following vocabulary: radius, diameter, circumference and π (pi as 3.14). Students can best be taught about the constant relationship between the diameter and the circumference of a circle through the use of examples. These examples include the length of the diameter and circumference for several different circles. Using calculators, students will find that the circumference divided by the diameter always yields pi, or 3.14. Students then learn the equation *diameter times π equals circumference.*

Surface area refers to the number of square units of area on all the surfaces of a solid figure. Students can begin learning about surface area in fifth grade with exploded (unfolded) illustrations of "boxes" for which they can easily find the square units. In addition to being exploded, the surfaces that are opposite sides of the rectangular prisms should be the same color so that students can easily see that after finding the surface area of one of the matching pairs, they can multiply by two to find the area of the pair. After several lessons, students are ready to work with problems that do not show the exploded diagram. At that point, students will already understand that the faces come in pairs. They find the surface area of three sides that they can see and multiply by two for the back side of each.

Finding the surface area of other figures such as rectangular and triangular pyramids follows the same teaching procedure. The procedure begins with exploded and color-coded pairs of sides, then moves to figures in which only part of the figure is shown and the rest must be inferred.

The surface area of circles is best taught with an equation. If teachers have not yet introduced exponents, they can teach how to determine the area of a circle using the equation, π *times radius times radius.* A format similar to Format 19.6 in which the equation is given and then simply applied is the most efficient way to teach this skill.

Volume refers to the number of cubic units of space inside a figure. A procedure similar to that for teaching the area of a rectangle is used to teach students to determine the volume of a box. It is important to use a familiar term, such as box, rather than the more sophisticated term of rectangular prism, so that students are not confused by vocabulary. Once the concept of volume is mastered using the term box, then it is feasible to teach students that another term for a box-shaped figure is rectangular prism. An important preskill students should be taught before computing volume is how to multiply three numbers. Students are taught to first multiply two of the numbers and then multiply the product of those two numbers by the third.

When teaching the concept of volume, the teacher first demonstrates how a box may be divided into cubic units through an illustration of a box one unit high so all the cubic units can be seen. The teacher shows that every box has height, width, and depth. The teacher then demonstrates how multiplying the height by the width by the depth gives the number of cubic units in the figure. Then the teacher applies the equation to figures without the cubic units shown. However, the teacher must emphasize the need to express the answers in terms of cubic units.

The above recommendation for teaching the volume of a box is adequate for an initial presentation. However, a better equation is the *area of the base times the height.* This equation is taught in Format 19.6. Once students know the equation in this form, and they know the equation for how to find the area of a triangle, they can use these equations to find the area of a prism with a triangular base. They still simply calculate the area of the triangular base and then multiply by the height. The same formula works for cylinders; students are taught to find the area of the circle at the base and multiply times the height.

Finally students learn that they can find the volume of a solid object that comes to a point (e.g., cone or pyramid) by calculating the area of the base times the height divided by 3. Using the equation *area of the base times the height* is a more efficient way to teach students how to find volume than teaching students different equations for each figure.

Teaching students to measure the number of degrees in an angle requires teaching them to use a protractor. The teacher first models how to align (a) the base of the protractor and the base of the angle and (b) the vertex (point of the angle) with the center of the protractor base.

The next step requires deciding which row of numerals to read. As indicated in Figure 19.2, protractors have two rows of numerals. If the baseline of the angle points to the right:

the lower numbers are read. If the baseline of the angle points to the left, the top numbers are read:

The final step involves determining the number of degrees by noting the places at which the ray and the protractor intersect. In Figure 19.2, the intersection is at 70. Thus, the angle is 70°.

USING LOGIC IN WORKING WITH ANGLES AND LINES

Students can easily use a number of facts about angles and lines to work a variety of problems. These geometry facts are a prerequisite for more advanced geometry problem solving. Students need to know that angles can be measured in degrees, and that there are 90 degrees in a "corner" or right angle, 360 degrees in a full circle, and 180 degrees in a half-cir-

cle or a straight angle. They also need to know that the degrees in an angle that is divided into two parts can be shown as the big number in a number family; the two parts (or component angles) are the small numbers in that family.

These facts can be used to find the value of unknown component angles. Students learn to construct a number sentence or number family with a big number and the two smaller angles, which when added equal the big number. Given any two values, students can compute the third. For example, students subtract one small component angle from the big angle and obtain the other component angle.

Because students know that a straight angle is 180 degrees, they only need to know the value of one of two component angles of a straight angle to be able to figure out the other component angle. They simply construct a number sentence or number family with the big number being 180 degrees and the two smaller angles adding up to equal the big number. They subtract the known angle from 180 degrees and obtain other component angle.

After they can solve one-step problems of this type, students can learn how to solve more complex problems. First, they find the value of one of the smaller angles by working from the information given. For example, if students are given information that one of the smaller angles is ⅙ of a circle, students compute ⅙ of 360 degrees (60 degrees) to find the value of that angle. In the second step, students find the value of the unknown second component angle. Procedures for solving this type of two-step problem can be found in Format 19.7. Note that the same procedure can be used to find unknown component angles of right angles or of a complete circle.

The introduction of two additional geometric facts significantly increases the complexity of the problems students are able to solve. These two facts are illustrated in the Instructional Sequence and Assessment Chart as Objectives 5h and 5i. The first fact (Objective 5h) is that a line intersecting two parallel lines creates corresponding pairs of angles that are equal in size. In the figure for Objective 5h, angles A and D are corresponding angles of equal size. Angles B and E are also corresponding angles and therefore equal. Because this is a simple fact, the best method to teach this objective is the same method used to teach vocabulary.

The second fact (Objective 5i) is that when two lines intersect, the angle opposite any angle is equal in size. In the figure for Objective 5i, angle C is opposite angle A, so those two angles are equal. When

FIGURE 19.2   Using a Protractor

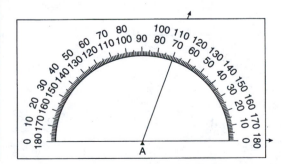

two lines intersect, they create a total of four angles, but there are only two sizes of angles, and any two adjacent angles must add up to 180 degrees.

These facts (5h and 5i) can then be used to figure out three of the four angles, if the size of one of them is known or can be computed from information given. The procedure for leading students through this type of problem is illustrated in Format 19.8. Students can build on the logic in these problems when they are presented with more complex problems, for example, problems where a line intersects two parallel lines, creating eight angles of only two sizes. These more complex problems are valuable preparation for later work on geometric proofs.

CONSTRUCTING FIGURES

Constructing figures requires the use of tools such as a ruler, compass, and protractor. In order to teach students to use such tools to construct or measure geometric figures, teachers must provide a clear model as well as sufficient, structured practice. The practice gives the teacher an opportunity to give feedback to as many students as possible. In modeling the use of a compass, for example, the teacher should emphasize the need to keep the compass upright when drawing a circle, not letting it slant. The teacher can demonstrate how circles can be drawn the "wrong way," as well as show how to correctly use the instrument.

APPLICATION ITEMS: GEOMETRY

1. Using Format 19.1 as a model, write a format for teaching the concept of parallelogram.

2. Construct a set of examples and nonexamples to use in teaching the concept of right angle.

3. Write a teaching format for teaching students to measure

   a. the perimeter of a rectangle
   b. the area of a square
   c. the radius of a circle

4. Explain the big idea that connects the methods of figuring the area of rectangles, triangles, and parallelograms and how to teach them so that students understand how the three are related.

5. Name the three steps to finding the area of a complex figure such as a wall with a window in it.

6. Explain why students should initially be taught to determine the volume of a box rather than the more correct term of rectangular prism.

7. What is the key to helping students to see from a drawing how the volume of a rectangular prism is equal to the length times the width times the height?

8. Explain the big idea that connects the methods of figuring the volume of boxes, cylinders, and rectangular or triangular prisms and how to teach them so that students understand how they are related.

9. What kind of figures must be used to initially teach students how to determine the surface area of solid figures?

10. Outline the steps in teaching students to use a protractor. What examples and nonexamples should teachers be sure to include in their demonstrations?

FORMAT 19.1   Identification/Definition—Triangle

TEACHER	STUDENTS
PART A: STRUCTURED BOARD PRESENTATION	
1. Listen to this definition: A triangle is a closed figure that has three straight sides. How many sides does a triangle have?	3
2. I'm going to point to some figures, and you tell me if they are triangles. *(Point to Δ)* Is this a triangle?	Yes

TEACHER	STUDENTS
How do you know?	It has three sides.

(Point to the following figures in the sequence shown.)

PART B: LESS STRUCTURED WORKSHEET

1. *(Give students a worksheet with problems like the ones below.)*

   a. Draw a circle around each triangle.

   b. Write the letter R over each rectangle.
      Write the letter S over each square.
      Write the letter T over each triangle.
      Write the letter C over each circle.

Look at problem a on your worksheet. Read the directions.	Draw a circle around each triangle.
2. Touch the first figure. Is that a triangle?	Yes
So what are you going to do?	Draw a circle around it.
Do it.	
3. Touch the next figure. Is that a triangle?	No
So what are you going to do?	Nothing

4. *(Have students complete the worksheet by themselves.)*

FORMAT 19.2   Finding Area of Rectangles

TEACHER	STUDENTS
PART A: STRUCTURED BOARD PRESENTATION	
1. The AREA of a figure such as a rectangle is the number of squares (such as square inches or square feet) it takes to cover the rectangle. Listen again. The AREA of a figure is the number of squares it takes to cover the figure.	
2. What is the AREA of a figure?	The number of squares it takes to cover the figure.
3. You can find the number of squares by multiplying the number of squares in each row by the number of rows. The number of squares in each row tells us the base. How many squares across the base of this rectangle?	13 squares

(continued on next page)

FORMAT 19.2   (continued)

TEACHER   **STUDENTS**

4	40	41	42	43	44	45	46	47	48	49	50	51	52
3	27	28	29	30	31	32	33	34	35	36	37	38	39
2	14	15	16	17	18	19	20	21	22	23	24	25	26
1	1	2	3	4	5	6	7	8	9	10	11	12	13
	1	*2*	*3*	*4*	*5*	*6*	*7*	*8*	*9*	*10*	*11*	*12*	*13*

4. The number of rows tells us the height. How many rows high is this rectangle?

> 4 rows

5. To find the AREA of this rectangle, we multiply the base by the height. What do we multiply to find the area?

> Multiply base × height.

6. So the equation for finding the area of a rectangle is base × height. What is the equation for finding the area of a rectangle?

> Base × height.

7. We say the answer as square units. The rectangle above has a base of 13 feet and a height of 4 feet. To find the area of this rectangle, what two numbers do we multiply?

> 13 × 4

8. Our answer will be in square units, in this case square feet. What kind of units will we label our answer?

> Square feet

9. So what is the area of this rectangle?

> 52 square feet

10. *Put this rectangle on the board:*

3							
2							
1	2	2	4	5	6	7	8

11. The base of this rectangle is along the bottom. It is measured in feet. How many feet long is the base?

> 8 feet

12. What is the height of the rectangle?

> 3 feet

13. How many square feet in the area of this rectangle?

> 24 Square feet

    Put this rectangle on the board:

2									
1	2	3	4	5	6	7	8	9	10

14. This rectangle is measured in centimeters. What is the base of this rectangle?

> 10 centimeters

15. What is the height of the rectangle?

> 2 centimeters

16. What is the area of this rectangle?

> 20 Square centimeters

TEACHER   **STUDENTS**

TEACHING THE EQUATION

1. The equation for the area of a rectangle can be written as
   (Write on board)

   Area of a rectangle = base × height. Read this equation.   Area of a rectangle =
                                                                        base × height.

2. Now let's see if you can remember this equation. *(Erase board)*

   What is the equation for the area of a rectangle?   Area of a rectangle =
                                                                        base × height.

PART B: LESS STRUCTURED BOARD PRESENTATION

1. Lets find the area of some rectangles. What is the equation
   for the area of a rectangle?

   Write on board as students say: Area of rectangle = base
                                                                        times height.

   Area of rectangle = base × height

2. Here is a rectangle.

   *(Draw this figure and label the following dimensions for base
   and height.)*

3. What is the base of this rectangle?   5 meters
4. What is the height of this rectangle?   3 meters
5. What is the area of the rectangle?   15 square meters
6. Repeat steps 3–5 by changing the dimensions on the board
   of the figure to the following:

height:	4 cm	base:	9 cm
height:	8 feet	base:	10 feet
height:	3 inches	base:	4 inches
height	1 yard	base:	2 yards

PART C: STRUCTURED WORKSHEET

Students have a worksheet with the following figures.

A.   B.

2 m   4″

    5 m.   8″

(continued on next page)

FORMAT 19.2 **(continued)**

TEACHER   **STUDENTS**

C.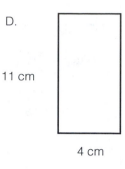

12 ft

8 ft

D.

11 cm

4 cm

1. State the equation for finding the area of a rectangle.

2. Write the equation for finding the area of a rectangle

3. Look at figure A. What is the base?
   What is the height?

4. What is the area of figure A?

5. Look at figure B. What kind of figure is that?

6. So how do you find the area of figure B?

7. Find the area of each of these rectangles

8. Check student work.

Area of rectangle = base times height.

Area rectangle = base × height.

5 meters
2 meters
10 square meters
Rectangle
Multiply base × height.

PART D: LESS STRUCTURED WORKSHEETS

Students have a worksheet with these rectangles.

A.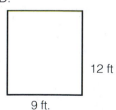

4 m

5 m.

B.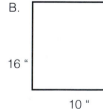

16 "

10 "

C.

7 m.

9 m.

D.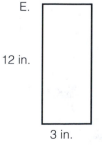

12 ft

9 ft.

E.

12 in.

3 in.

F.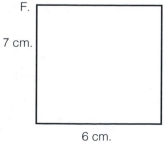

7 cm.

6 cm.

TEACHER	**STUDENTS**
1. Write the equation for finding the area of a rectangle.	Area rectangle = base × height
2. Find the area of the rectangles on this worksheet.	
3. Check student work.	

FORMAT 19.3 **Finding the Area of Triangles**

TEACHER

PART A: STRUCTURED BOARD PRESENTATION

1. *(Draw this rectangle on the board.)* What is the equation for the area of a rectangle?

STUDENTS

Base × height.

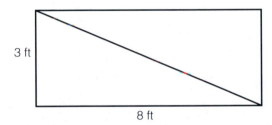

3 ft

8 ft

2. What would you multiply to find the area of this rectangle?

   What is the area?

3 times 8

24 square feet

3 ft

8 ft

3. If I draw a line from one corner of the rectangle to the opposite corner, then I have divided the rectangle into how many parts?

2

4. I have made two triangles. The area of each triangle is one part out of two parts in the whole rectangle. How do we say that fraction?

One half

5. If the area of each triangle is half of the rectangle, we can show the area of each triangle as the area of the rectangle divided by what number?

2

6. What is the equation for the area of a rectangle?

Area of a rectangle = base × height.

7. So we can find the area of the triangle the same way we find the area of the rectangle, just divided by two. Write this on the board:

$$\text{Area of the } \Delta = \frac{\text{base} \times \text{height}}{2}$$

(continued on next page)

430   Part Two / Skills and Concepts

FORMAT 19.3 (continued)

TEACHER	**STUDENTS**

Read this equation for finding the area of a triangle.

(Draw another rectangle.)

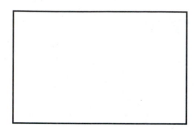

The area of a triangle equals base times height divided by two.

8. Look at this rectangle. How would you find the area?

9. Watch how anywhere I draw a vertical line, I divided this rectangle into how many rectangles? *Draw a vertical line inside the rectangle:*

Multiply base × height.

Two

I'll shade the left hand rectangle.

Draw a diagonal line in each rectangle going from the outside bottom corner to the top of the vertical dividing line. Then put the letters A, B, C, D, inside the resulting triangles:

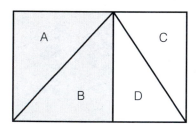

10. If I divide each of those rectangles with a line from corner to corner I have divided each rectangle into 2 triangles. The shaded left hand rectangle is divided into triangles A and B. The area of triangle A is what part of the area of the shaded left hand rectangle?

One-half

11. The area of triangle B is what part of the area of the shaded left hand rectangle?

One-half

12. The area of triangle C is what part of the area of the right hand rectangle?

One-half

13. The area of triangle D is what part of the area of the right hand rectangle?

One-half

TEACHER   **STUDENTS**

Draw heavier lines around triangles B and D.

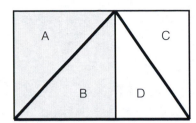

14. If I combine triangles B and D into one bigger triangle, the area of that combined triangle is what part of the area of the whole rectangle with which we started?   One-half

Yes, the area of this larger triangle is one half the area of the larger rectangle. So we can find the area of any triangle by multiplying the base times the height and then dividing that result by what number?   Two

15. So what is the equation for finding the area of a triangle?   Area of a triangle = base times height divided by 2.

Write on board as students state the equation:

$$\text{Area of the } \Delta = \frac{\text{base} \times \text{height}}{2}$$

PART B: LESS STRUCTURED BOARD PRESENTATION

1. Let's find the area of some triangles. What is the equation for area of a triangle?   Area of a triangle = base times height divided by 2.

Write on board as students say:

$$\text{Area of the } \Delta = \frac{\text{base} \times \text{height}}{2}$$

2. Here is a rectangle with a triangle inside.

(Draw this figure and label the following dimensions for base and height.)

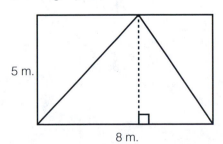

5 m.

8 m.

3. What is the base of this rectangle and triangle?   8 meters

4. What is the height of this rectangle and triangle?   5 meters

5. What is the area of the whole rectangle?   40 square meters

6. How are you going to find the area of the triangle inside?   Divided by two

7. What is the area of the triangle inside?   20 square meters

8. Repeat steps 3–7 by changing the dimensions on the board of the figure to the following:

(continued on next page)

FORMAT 19.3 (continued)

TEACHER	STUDENTS

height: 3 inches   base: 4 inches
height: 10 feet   base: 12 feet
height: 4 cm   base: 9cm
height: 8 yards   base: 10 yards

PART C: STRUCTURED WORKSHEET

Students have a worksheet with the following figures.

A.
7 m.
8 m.

B.
4 mi.
8 ft

C.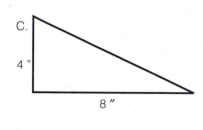
4 "
8 "

D.
11 cm
4 cm.

E.
4 mi.
2 mi.

1. State the equation for finding the area of a triangle.

Area of a triangle = base times height divided by 2.

2. Write the equation for finding the area of a triangle.

Area of the Δ =
$$\frac{\text{base} \times \text{height}}{2}$$

3. Look at figure A. What is the base?

8 meters

What is the height?

7 meters

4. Find the area of that figure.

What is the area of figure A?

23 square meters

5. Look at figure B. What kind of figure is that?

Rectangle

6. So how do you find the area of figure B?

base × height.

7. Look at figure C. What kind of figure is that?

Triangle

8. So how do find the area of figure C?

base × height divided by 2.

9. Find the area of each of these figures. Remember to use the appropriate equation for each figure.

10. *Check student work.*

TEACHER   **STUDENTS**

PART D: LESS STRUCTURED WORKSHEET

Students have a worksheet with mixed rectangles and triangles.

A.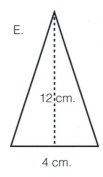

4 m.
5 m.

B.

16 "
10 "

C.

7 m.
9 m.

D.

12
9 ft.

E.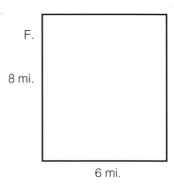

12 cm.
4 cm.

F.

8 mi.
6 mi.

1. Write the equation for finding the area of a rectangle.
2. Write the equation for finding the area of a triangle.

3. Find the area of the figures on this worksheet. Be careful to use the appropriate equation for each figure.
4. *Check student work.*

Area □ = base × height.

Area of the Δ =
$$\frac{base \times height}{2}$$

FORMAT 19.4   **Computing Area of Complex Figures**

TEACHER   **STUDENTS**

PART A: STRUCTURED BOARD PRESENTATION

1. *(Draw the following figure on the board.)*

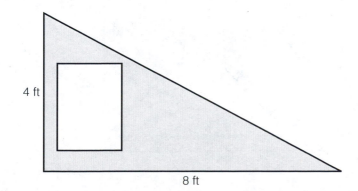

4 ft
8 ft

FORMAT 19.4   (continued)

TEACHER

The simplest way to find the area of a figure like this, with a missing part, is to compute the area of the total figure, compute the area of the missing part, then subtract the area of the missing part from the area of the total figure. What is first step to find the area of a figure with a hole in it?

2. What is the second step?

3. What is the third step?

4. To find the area of this figure with a missing part in it, what will we compute first?

5. What is the equation for finding the area of a triangle? *(Write this on the board as students say it.)*

   Area of a $\triangle = \dfrac{b \times h}{2}$

6. What is the base times the height for this triangle?

7. What is the area for the total triangle?

8. What is the second step to finding the area of this figure with a missing part?

9. The missing part in this figure is a rectangle with a base of 2 feet and a height of how many feet?

10. What is the area of the missing part in this figure?

11. What is the third step in finding the area of a figure with a missing part?

12. So we subtract the 6 square feet from what?

13. What's the area of this figure with a missing part?

STUDENTS

Compute the area of the total figure.

Compute the area of the missing part.

Subtract the area of the missing part from the area of the total figure.

The area of the triangle

Base times height divided by two.

32

16 square feet

Compute the area of the missing part.

3 feet

6 square feet

Subtract the area of the missing part from the area of the total figure.

16 square feet

10 square feet

PART B: STRUCTURED WORKSHEET

1. *(Give students worksheets with problems like the following.)*

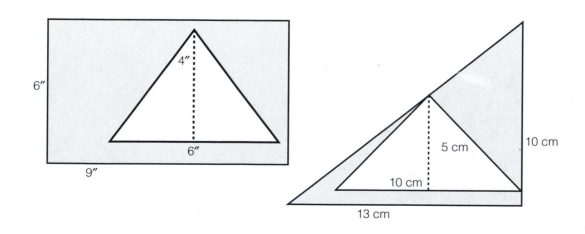

TEACHER	STUDENTS
When we compute the area of figures like these, with missing parts, what is the first step?	Compute the area of the total figure.
2. What is the second step?	Compute the area of the missing part.
3. What is the third step?	Subtract the area of the missing part from the area of the total figure.
4. So what do we compute first?	The area of the total figure.
5. Compute that for figure A.	
6. What's the area of the total figure in Figure A?	54 square feet
7. What do we compute next?	The area of the missing part.
8. Compute that in Figure A.	
9. What's the area of the missing part in Figure A?	12 square feet
10. What is the third step in finding the area of Figure A with a missing part?	Subtract the area of the missing part from the total area.
11. Compute that for Figure A.	
12. What's the area of Figure A with the missing part?	42 square feet
13. *(Do steps 4–13 with Figure B.)*	

PART C: LESS STRUCTURED WORKSHEET

1. *(Give students worksheets with problems like the following.)*

A.
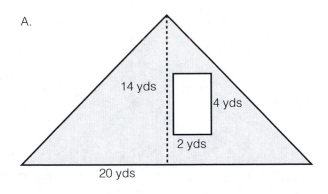

B.
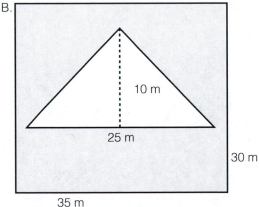

When we compute the area of figures with a missing part, what is the first step?	Compute the area of the total figure.
2. What is the second step?	Compute the area of the missing part.
3. What is the third step?	Subtract the area of the missing part from the area of the total figure.
4. Find the area of Figure A. What is the area of Figure A?	272 square yards
5. Find the area of Figure B. What is the area of Figure B?	800 square meters

FORMAT 19.5 **Computing Area of Parallelograms**

TEACHER   **STUDENTS**

PART A: STRUCTURED BOARD PRESENTATION

1. *(Draw this rectangle on the board.)* What is the equation
   for the area of a rectangle?   Base × height.

2. What do you multiply to find the area of this rectangle?   9 × 5
   What is the area?   45 square centimeters

3. Watch as I make this rectangle into a parallelogram with the
   same area. I take a triangle off of the left side and move it
   over to the right side. Have I changed the area of the figure
   or have I just moved it? *(Draw the following figure.)*   You just moved it.

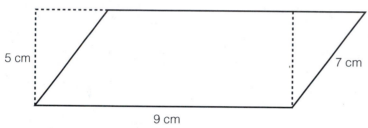

4. What two numbers did you multiply to find the area of the
   rectangle?   9 × 5

5. To end up with the same area for the parallelogram, do I
   multiply the base of the parallelogram, 9 centimeters, by   You multiply by the
   the height of 5 centimeters or by the length of 7 centimeters? height of 5 cm.

6. Yes, the equation for the area of a parallelogram is base ×
   height. What is the equation for the area of a parallelogram?
   (Write as the students say it: Area of a parallelogram =   Area of a parallelogram
   base × height.)   = the base × the height.

   (Draw another parallelogram.)

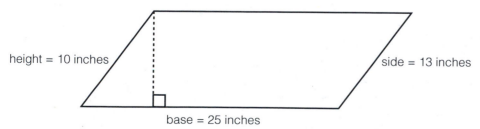

7. Look at this parallelogram. To find the area, you multiply the base
   of 25 inches times what?   The height of 10 inches

8. What is the equation for finding the area of a parallelogram? The base times the
                                                                  height.

TEACHER

PART B: LESS STRUCTURED BOARD PRESENTATION

1. Let's find the area of some parallelograms. What is the equation for the area of a parallelogram?

    (Write on board as students say: A ⟋⟍ = base × height*)*

The area of a parallelogram is the base times height.

2. Here is a parallelogram.

    (Draw this figure and label the following dimensions for base and height.)

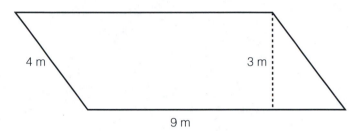

4 m   3 m

9 m

3. What is the base of this parallelogram?   9 meters
4. What is the height of this parallelogram?   3 meters
5. What is the area of this parallelogram?   27 square meters
6. *(Repeat steps 3–5 by changing the dimensions on the board of the figure to the following.)*

    height: 5 inches   side: 6 inches   base: 8 inches
    height: 10 feet   side: 12 feet   base: 20 feet
    height: 8 cm   side: 9 cm   base: 10 cm
    height: 2 yards   side: 3 yards   base: 4 yards

PART C: STRUCTURED WORKSHEET

(Students have a worksheet with the following figures.)

a.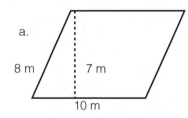

8 m   7 m

10 m

b.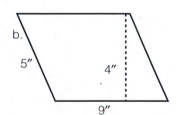

5″   4″

9″

c.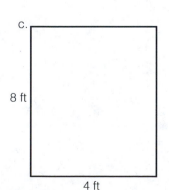

8 ft

4 ft

d.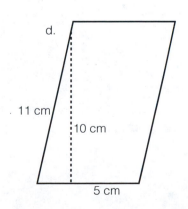

. 11 cm

10 cm

5 cm

(continued on next page)

FORMAT 19.5 (continued)

TEACHER	STUDENTS
1. State the equation for finding the area of a parallelogram.	The area of a parallelogram is base times height.
2. Write the equation for finding the area of a parallelogram.	Area $\square$= base × height.
3. Look at figure A. What is the base? What is the height?	10 meters 7 meters
4. Find the area of that figure. What is the area of figure A?	70 square meters
5. Look at figure B. What kind of figure is that?	Parallelogram
6. How do you find the area of figure B?	Multiply the base × height.
7. Look at figure C. What kind of figure is that?	Rectangle
8. So how do find the area of figure C?	Multiply the base × height.
9. Find the area of each of these figures.	
10. *(Check student work.)*	

PART D: LESS STRUCTURED WORKSHEET

   (Students have a worksheet with mixed rectangles and parallelograms.)

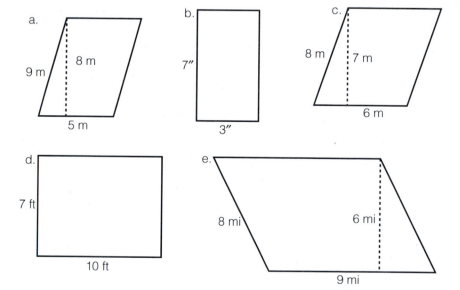

1. Write the equation for finding the area of a rectangle or a parallelogram.

   Area = base × height.

2. Find the area of the figures on this worksheet.

3. *(Check student work.)*

FORMAT 19.6   Computing the Volume of Boxes

TEACHER   **STUDENTS**

PART A: STRUCTURED BOARD PRESENTATION

1. *(Draw the following cube on board.)*

2. This is a cube. Each side of a cube is a square. Cubes
   are in the shape of dice. When you find how many cubes
   a box can hold, you are finding the volume of the box.
   When you find how many cubes a box can hold, what
   are you finding?   Volume

   (Draw this box on the board.)

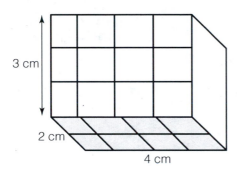

3. The equation for the volume of a box is

   Volume = area of base × height

   What is the equation for the volume of a box?   Volume = area of base ×
                                                                                                    height.

4. The base is the shaded area on the bottom. On this box, the
   base measures 2 cm by 4 cm. What is the area of the base
   of this box?   8 square centimeters

5. Yes, the area of the base is 8 square centimeters. Next we
   multiply by the height. What is the height of this box?   3 centimeters

6. So what two numbers do we multiply to find the volume?   8 × 3

7. What is the volume of this box? Remember, the answer
   must be in cubic centimeters.   24 cubic centimeters

   (Draw the following box on the board.)
   Here is another box.

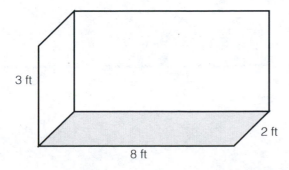

(continued on next page)

FORMAT 19.6 (continued)

TEACHER	STUDENTS
8. What is the equation for finding the volume of a box?	Volume = area of the base × the height.
9. What two numbers do we multiply to find the area of the base of this box?	8 × 2
10. So what is the area of the base of this box, in square feet?	16 square feet
	(continued on next page)
11. Once we have the area of the base, why do we multiply that by 3?	Because we have to multiply base × height.
12. What is the volume in cubic feet of this box?	48 cubic feet

PART B: LESS STRUCTURED BOARD PRESENTATION

1. Let's find the volume of some boxes. What is the equation for the volume of a box?
   (Write on board as students say.)

   Volume = area of the base × height

2. Here is a box. *(Draw this figure and label the following dimensions for base and height.)*

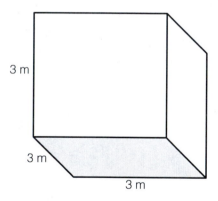

3 m
3 m
3 m

3. What is the area of the base of this box in square units?	9 square meters
4. What is the height of this box?	3 meters
5. What is the volume of this box?	27 cubic meters

6. *(Repeat steps 3–5 by changing the dimensions of the figure to the following.)*

height: 5 inches	side: 6 inches	base: 7 inches
height: 10 feet	side: 12 feet	base: 11 feet
height: 4 cm	side: 5 cm.	base: 6 cm.
height: 2 yards	side: 3 yards	base: 4 yards

FORMAT 19.7   Finding the Value of Unknown Component Angles

TEACHER	STUDENTS

1. *(Draw the following figure on board.)*

2. Angle A is the angle on one side of the straight line. Angle A is a half circle. How many degrees in a half circle?

180 degrees

3. Angle B and Angle C are parts or components of Angle A. So Angle B and Angle C added together would equal how many degrees?

180 degrees

4. So we can write a number sentence to show this. *(Write on board.)*

Angle B + Angle C = 180 degrees

5. If we know that Angle C is one-ninth of a circle, we can figure out how many degrees Angle C is and we can figure out how many degrees Angle B is. How many degrees in a circle?

360 degrees

6. Angle C is one-ninth of a circle, so to find Angle C, we multiply 360 degrees by one-ninth. That looks like this: *(Write on board.)*

$$\frac{1}{9} \times \frac{360}{1} = \frac{360}{9}$$

7. Divide 9 into 360.
   What is 9 into 360, everybody?

40

8. So we know that Angle C is 40 degrees. Now our equation says: *(Write on board.)*

Angle B + 40 = 180

9. How do we find Angle B? Do we add or subtract?

Subtract

10. Raise your hand when you have found the answer.
    How many degrees is Angle B?

140 degrees

FORMAT 19.8 **Finding the Values of Unknown Angles in Complex Diagrams**

| **TEACHER** | **STUDENTS** |

1. *(Draw the following on board.)*

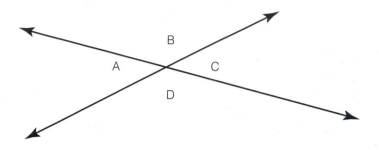

2. These four angles are made by two intersecting lines. If we know the degrees for any one of the angles, we can figure out all of the others. Angle A and Angle B are the two component parts of a straight line, or half a circle. So Angle A and B added together would be how many degrees?

    180 degrees

3. We can write a number sentence to show this. *(Write on board.)*

    Angle A + Angle B = 180 degrees

4. If we know that Angle B is one-third of a circle, we can figure out how many degrees Angle B is and we can figure out how many degrees Angle A is. How many degrees in a circle?

    360 degrees

5. Angle B is one-third of a circle, so to find Angle B, we multiply 360 degrees by one-third. *(Write on board.)*

$$\frac{1}{3} \times \frac{360}{1} = \frac{360}{3}$$

6. Divide 3 into 360. What is 3 into 360?

    120

7. Now we know that Angle B is 120 degrees. Now the equation says:

    Angle A + 120 = 180

8. How do we find Angle A? Do we add or subtract?

    Subtract

9. How many degrees is Angle A?

    60 degrees

10. What do we know about Angles A and C?

    That they are equal.

11. So if Angle A is 60 degrees, what do we know about Angle C?

    It is 60 degrees.

12. And what do we know about Angles B and D?

    That they are equal.

13. So how many degrees is Angle D?

    120 degrees

CHAPTER 20

Pre-Algebra

With Don Crawford

This chapter on pre-algebra addresses three topics: (a) the coordinate system and simple algebraic functions; (b) ratios, proportions, and word problems using these functions and; (c) other types of numbers such as prime numbers, factors, positive and negative integers, and exponents. Content also commonly found in pre-algebra courses includes many of the more complex skills found in the previous chapters on fractions, percents and ratios, geometry, and problem solving.

The specific skills addressed in this chapter are outlined in the Instructional Sequence and Assessment Chart. The number of each skill indicates the grade level at which it may first be introduced. All the pre-algebra skills listed can be taught by sixth grade if the necessary preskills have been mastered. However, in many schools, pre-algebra skills are more often taught in seventh or eighth grade.

We suggest that teachers follow the sequence of skills for each topic listed. For example, the chart for Other Types of Numbers (OT) indicates that prime numbers (OT 5a) must be taught before factoring (OT 5b). However, the four topics can be taught in any order or even simultaneously.

COORDINATE SYSTEM AND FUNCTIONS (CSF)

The coordinate system can be introduced to students as early as the third or fourth grade. At the beginning levels, students use only positive integers. Students learn that an x value is the distance of a point to the right of zero. A y value is the distance of a point up from zero. Students begin by finding the x value and the y value for given points on a coordinate system. After several lessons on finding values, students locate points on the coordinate system given the values.

Traditional algebra instruction identifies points on the coordinate system as (5,6), requiring students to remember that the first number is the x value and the second number is the y value. However, students learn the coordinate system more easily if initially they receive the points written as ($x = 5$, $y = 6$). Students will learn the order over time, but will not have to remember it at the same time they are learning about the coordinate system.

Next, students learn to complete a function table such as the following.

x	Function $x + 2$	y
0	0 + 2	2
1	1 + 2	3
2	2 + 2	4
3		
4		
5		

Teachers model applying the function to determine the y value when the x value is given. In the example above, teachers model substituting 0 for x in the function $x + 2$ to derive y ($0 + 2 = 2$; $y = 2$). After completing the table, the students plot the points on the coordinate system and connect the points with a straight line.

443

Instructional Sequence and Assessment Chart

Grade Level	Problem Type	Performance Indicator

Coordinate System and Functions (CSF)

CSF 4a Plot points on coordinate system given *x* and *y* values and reverse

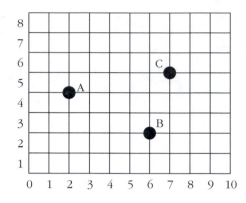

What letter is ($x = 7$, $y = 5$)?
Write the coordinates for point A.

CSF 4b Students complete a function table, plot the points found, and connect the points in a line

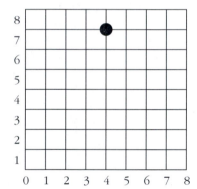

x	Function $x + 3$	Answer *y*
4	4 + 3	7
1	1 + 3	
5		
2		
3		

Complete the function table, plot the points, and connect them with a straight line.

CSF 4c Given two pairs of *x* and *y* values, students determine the function, complete the function table, and graph the points

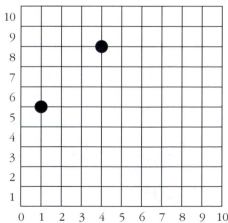

x	Function	Answer *y*
4		8
1		5
5		
2		
0		

Complete the function table, plot the points, and connect them with a straight line.

Grade Level	Problem Type	Performance Indicator

CSF 4d   Given a line on the coordinate system, students find the points, complete a function table, and find the function.

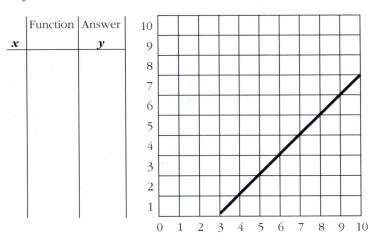

Complete the function table using the points on the line.

Ratio and Proportion (R/P)

R/P 4a   Simple ratios

The store has 3 TVs for every 7 radios. If there are 28 radios, how many TVs are there?

R/P 5a   Ratio tables

The ratio of sand to gravel in a mixture is 4 parts sand to 9 parts gravel. If there are 260 pounds in the total mixture, how many pounds of sand are there? How many pounds of gravel are there?

R/P 5b   Ratio tables problems using fractions for classes

In a factory, ⅗ of the employees were women. The rest were men. There were 890 employees. How many employees were men? How many employees were women?

R/P 5c   Ratio tables problems using fractions that compare

Abbey Hill is ⅜ as high as Howard Hill. Abbey Hill is 240 feet high. How high is Howard Hill? How much higher is Howard Hill than Abbey Hill?

R/P 5d   Ratio tables problems using percentages for classes

55% of the bagels are cheese. The rest of the bagels are plain. There are 9 plain bagels. How many cheese bagels are there? How many bagels are there altogether?

R/P 5e   Ratio tables problems using percentages that compare

Train A is 40% longer than train B. If train B is 400 meters long, how long is train A? How much longer is train A than train B?

Other Types of Numbers (OT)

OT 5a   Prime numbers

Name the prime numbers below 12.

OT 5b   Factoring

Give the prime factors for each of these numbers in this form $12 = 2 \times 2 \times 3$: 36, 27, 51

OT 6a   When the total is positive, combine several subtractions and several additions and find the answer (preskill for integers)

Find the answer to:
$0 + 18 - 12 + 6 - 5 - 4 + 9 =$

(continued)

Instructional Sequence and Assessment Chart (continued)

Grade Level	Problem Type	Performance Indicator
OT 6b	Solve problems that involve multiplication with addition and/or subtraction (preskill for integers)	a. $4 + 6 + 1$ b. $8 - 5 + 2$ $\times\ \ \ \ \ \ 4$ $\times\ \ \ \ \ \ 6$
OT 6c	Using a number line, combine positive and negative integers with either negative or positive totals	Find a. $-6 + 5 =$ b. $-4 - 2 =$ c. $8 - 10 =$
OT 6d	Absolute value	In each pair of numbers, write the one that is farther from zero: a. $-8, +5$ b. $+7, -4$ c. $-2, +9$
OT 6e	Combine positive and negative integers without a number line	a. $+2$ b. -3 c. -8 $\underline{-9}$ $\underline{-4}$ $\underline{+3}$
OT 6f	Multiply by a positive or negative integer	a. $2 + 4 - 1$ b. 6 c. $9 - 8 + 4$ $\underline{\times\ \ \ \ \ -3}$ $\underline{\times -4}$ $\underline{\times\ \ \ \ \ -7}$
OT 6g	Add and subtract positive and negative integers	a. $-4 + -3 =$ b. $-7 - -2 =$
OT 6h	Name the base and the exponent from expanded notation examples and the reverse	Name the base and the exponent for each of the following: a. $4 \times 4 \times 4 =$ b. $34 \times 34 \times 34 \times 34 \times 34 =$ c. $M \times M \times M \times M \times M =$ Write out the expanded notation problem expressed by each of the following: d. 1^4 e. D^3 f. 71^5
OT 6i	Combining exponents	Break the group of multiplied values into two groups, the part underlined and the rest. $\underline{6 \times 6 \times 6} \times 6 \times 6 \times 6 \times 6$ $6^7 = \underline{\ \ } \times \underline{\ \ }$ Combine these two terms into one: $4^5 \times 4^3 = \underline{\ \ }$
OT 6j	Simplifying exponents	Reduce the following terms: (a) $\dfrac{3 \times 3 \times 3 \times 3 \times 3 \times 3 \times 3}{3 \times 3 \times 3 \times 3} =$ (b) $\dfrac{7 \times 7 \times 7}{7 \times 7 \times 7 \times 7 \times 7 \times 7} =$

After several lessons on completing function tables, students are ready to derive the function when given two pairs of values. Initially, they are asked to choose between two possible functions that fit the first pair of values, eliminating the function that does not fit the second pair of values. After several lessons on choosing the correct function, students are ready to derive the function given at least two pairs of values. Students also are taught to plot points from the function table on the coordinates and draw a line representing the function. Format 20.1 outlines the steps in the strategy recommended to teach students how to derive a function, plot the points, and draw a line representing the function. Finally, students can be taught to derive the function when given points on the coordinate system with lines drawn through them.

RATIOS AND PROPORTIONS (R/P)

Ratios are best understood as a special kind of equivalent fraction. Therefore, a necessary preskill for ratios and proportions is the ability to find equivalent fractions. If students have not learned a procedure for finding equivalent fractions, they cannot use the strategies outlined in this chapter to solve ratio equations. The strategies for finding equivalent fractions are covered in Chapter 12.

Successfully solving ratio problems first requires that students set up the problem accurately. We recommend teaching students to write the labels in the problem as numerators and denominators on both sides of the equal sign. In the problem below, students write the labels TVs as the numerator and radios as the denominator. The students then repeat the fraction of TVs over radios on the other side of the equal sign.

> The store has 3 TVs for every 7 radios. If there are 28 radios in the store, how many TVs are there?

$$\frac{\text{TVs}}{\text{radios}} = \frac{\text{TVs}}{\text{radios}}$$

The labels provide a prompt for students to successfully identify the numbers that go on top (the ones associated with TVs) and those that go on the bottom (the numbers associated with radios). Once the numbers are written with their labels, the problem is solved using equivalent fractions.

$$\frac{3 \text{ TVs}}{7 \text{ radios}} = \frac{\square \text{TVs}}{28 \text{ radios}}$$

Next, teachers can introduce students to strategies for solving problems using ratio tables. Following is an example of how to use a table to solve a ratio problem.

> A factory makes SUVs and cars. It makes 5 SUVs for every 3 cars made. If the factory made 1600 vehicles last year, how many cars and how many SUVs did it make?

Classification	Ratio	
Cars	3	*600*
SUVs	5	*1000*
Vehicles	*8*	**1600**

The bold information in the table is provided to the students in the text. Students are to figure out the numbers in italics to answer the question in the problem.

Students can apply their previous knowledge of classification word problems to ratio problems in tables. (See Chapter 11 for a discussion of classification word problems and table problems.) Since they have already been introduced to classification word problems, they are familiar with the fact that cars and SUVs are the smaller classes and that vehicles is the big class. They know that if the two small numbers are given (i.e., cars and SUVs), they must add to find the big number (vehicles).

Once completed, the numbers in the ratio column can be used to state the ratio between any two rows. It is already stated that the ratio of cars to SUVs was 3 to 5. After determining the number of vehicles, the ratio table shows that the ratio of SUVs to vehicles made is 5 to 8 and the ratio of cars to vehicles made is 3 to 8. This information enables the students to set up a simple ratio to find the missing information requested in the question. The setup to find the number of cars made looks like this:

$$\frac{\text{Cars}}{\text{Vehicles}} \frac{3 \times (\ )}{8 \times (\ )} = \frac{\square}{1600} \qquad \frac{\text{Cars}}{\text{Vehicles}} \frac{3 \times (200)}{8 \times (200)} = \frac{600}{1600}$$

A similar setup can be used to determine the number of SUVs made.

Because students are familiar with classification problems, they also know that if the big class were known, they could find the other smaller class by subtracting. For example, if the problem indicated that the ratio of SUVs to vehicles was 5 to 9, students could subtract 9 − 5 to determine the ratio for the other smaller class, 4 cars. Setting up a ratio problem between the quantity given and the quantity requested in the problem will become routine for students.

Teachers can now introduce more sophisticated ratio tables, including those that contain fractions that represent classes. Teachers first introduce problems in which one class is a fraction: For example, ⅓ of the plants were trees. Since students know that all the plants are represented as ⅔, they can easily determine that ⅔ of the plants are not trees. The big class is always a fraction equal to one, and the two smaller classes add together to equal one. Given a set of classifications represented as fractions, students can create a ratio table using the numerators of the fractions as the ratio. The problem below is an example of this type of problem and the completed ratio table.

Three-fifths of the children in the school are shorter than the principal. If 128 children are taller than the principal, how many are shorter, and how many children are there in the school?

Classification	Ratio	
Shorter	**3**	*192*
Taller	*2*	**128**
All	*5*	*320*

Students have been taught that if $\frac{3}{5}$ of the children are shorter, then the fraction that represents *all* the children is $\frac{5}{5}$. They subtract to find out that $\frac{2}{5}$ of the children are taller. The numerators express the ratio of each of those terms. For efficiency, the format for ratio tables (Format 20.2) simply instructs students to put the numerators of the fraction family into the ratio column. Students might ask why the numerators can express only the ratio. Teachers who wish to explain why the numerators are written in the ratio column must demonstrate that when the ratios are simplified, the results are the same as the numerators. Teachers can demonstrate the process of simplifying ratios using equations similar to those below.

$$\frac{\text{Shorter Children}}{\text{All Children}} \; \frac{3/5}{5/5} \text{ simplifies to } \frac{\text{Shorter Children}}{\text{All Children}} \; \frac{3}{5}$$

OR

$$\frac{\text{Taller Children}}{\text{All Children}} \; \frac{2/5}{5/5} \text{ simplifies to } \frac{\text{Taller Children}}{\text{All Children}} \; \frac{2}{5}$$

The numerators express the ratio of each of those classes, so that the ratio of shorter children to all the children is 3 to 5, and the ratio of the taller children to the all children is 2 to 5. Once the ratios are determined, the students can find the unknown quantities by constructing a ratio between the known quantity (in this case the 128 children who are taller) and the unknown quantity (in this case "How many children are shorter?"). This is solved in the same manner as other ratio equations.

$$\frac{\text{Taller}}{\text{Shorter}} \; \frac{2 \times (\;)}{3 \times (\;)} = \frac{128}{\square} \qquad \frac{\text{Taller}}{\text{Shorter}} \; \frac{2 \times (64)}{3 \times (64)} = \frac{128}{192}$$

Ratio tables also can be used to solve comparison problems. These problems contain a sentence that indicates the basis for the comparison: *Louise was paid $\frac{5}{6}$ of what her boss was paid.* Louise is being compared to her boss. Therefore, her boss is equal to one whole, $\frac{6}{6}$. This number-family represents the completed comparison:

Difference		Louise		Boss
$\frac{1}{6}$	$+$	$\frac{5}{6}$	$=$	$\frac{6}{6}$

Once the number family is completed, students can put the numerators into a ratio table. Given any of the three values (Louise's pay, the difference, or her boss's pay), the students can construct ratio equations to determine the other two values. Here is a completed ratio table for the problem in which Louise is paid $1800 a month.

Louise was paid $\frac{5}{6}$ of what her boss was paid. If Louise is paid $1800 a month, how much more does her boss get paid, and what does her boss get paid?

Difference	*1*	*360*
Louise	**5**	**1800**
Boss	*6*	*2160*

The next type of ratio table students learn is a classification ratio table using percentages. Students are given one class as a percentage of the whole and the second class as the rest. For example, *A store got 40% of its oranges from California and the rest from Florida.* Students learn that the big class (all the oranges) is always equal to 100%. Since the big number is known (100%), this is a subtraction problem. The percentage that came from Florida is determined by subtracting (100% − 40% = 60%). Below is the completed number family that represents this problem.

California		Florida		All
40%	$+$	60%	$=$	100%

Students then put the information into a ratio table. Given the quantity of any of the three variables (total oranges, oranges from California, oranges from Florida), students can solve for the other two quantities.

A store got 40% of its oranges from California. The store got the rest of its oranges from Florida. If the store had 170 total oranges, how many were from California and how many from Florida?

California	**40%**	*68*
Florida	*60%*	*102*
All	*100%*	**170**

The ratio equation to figure out the number of California oranges is

Summary Box 20.1
Ratio Tables Using Fractions for Classes

1. Students read the problem and figure out the fraction number family.

Two-thirds of the people at the coffee shop are drinking coffee. The rest are drinking tea. If 15 people are drinking tea, how many people are drinking coffee? How many people are in the coffee shop?

	Fraction family	Ratio	Quantity
Coffee			
Tea			
People			

2. Students complete the fraction family column.

	Fraction family	Ratio	Quantity
Coffee	**2/3**		
Tea	**1/3**		
People	**3/3**		

3. Students use numerator of fraction to complete ratio column.

	Fraction family	Ratio	Quantity
Coffee	2/3	**2**	
Tea	1/3	**1**	
People	3/3	**3**	

4. Students fill in known quantities.

	Fraction family	Ratio	Quantity
Coffee	2/3	2	
Tea	1/3	1	**15**
People	3/3	3	

5. Students write ratio equation.

$$\frac{2 \text{ Coffee}}{1 \text{ Tea}} = \frac{\Box \text{ Coffee}}{15 \text{ Tea}}$$

6. Students solve ratio problem to answer question about coffee drinkers.

	Fraction family	Ratio	Quantity
Coffee	2/3	2	**30**
Tea	1/3	1	15
People	3/3	3	

(continued)

Summary Box 20.1
Ratio Tables Using Fractions for Classes (continued)

7. Students use number-family strategy to determine how many people are in the shop and complete the table.

	Fraction family	Ratio	Quantity
Coffee	2/3	2	30
Tea	1/3	1	15
People	3/3	3	**45**

$$\frac{\text{California}}{\text{All}} \quad \frac{4 \times (\ )}{10 \times (\ )} = \frac{\square}{170}$$

$$\frac{\text{California}}{\text{All}} \quad \frac{4 \times (17)}{10 \times (17)} = \frac{68}{170}$$

$$\frac{\text{Difference}}{\text{Women's}} \quad \frac{25 \times (\ )}{75 \times (\ )} = \frac{175}{\square}$$

$$\frac{\text{Difference}}{\text{Women's}} \quad \frac{25 \times (7)}{75 \times (7)} = \frac{175}{\mathbf{525}}$$

Finally, students can learn to do comparison problems using percentages. These are perhaps the most counterintuitive and difficult type of word problems. Determining the appropriate number sentence is essential to solving this problem type. Students must understand that one of the variables that is being compared will be the variable equal to 100%. For example, in the problem below, students must compare the number of women's bicycles sold to the number of men's bicycles sold. The problem indicates that fewer women's bicycles are sold compared to the number of men's bicycles sold; therefore, the number of men's bicycles sold is the variable equal to 100% in this problem.

A bike store sold 25% fewer women's bicycles than men's bicycles. (*Hint: Women's bicycles are being compared to men's, so which variable is equal to 100%?*) If the store sold 175 fewer women's bicycles, how many men's and women's bicycles did it sell?

Difference	Women's Bicycles	Men's Bicycles
25%	+ 75%	= 100%

Difference	**25%**	**175**
Women's	*75%*	*525*
Men's	*100%*	*700*

$$\frac{\text{Difference}}{\text{Men's}} \quad \frac{25 \times (\ )}{100 \times (\ )} = \frac{175}{\square}$$

$$\frac{\text{Difference}}{\text{Men's}} \quad \frac{25 \times (7)}{100 \times (7)} = \frac{175}{700}$$

OTHER TYPES OF NUMBERS: PRIMES, FACTORS, INTEGERS, AND EXPONENTS.

Primes and Factors

Successfully teaching students to understand prime numbers and factors depends greatly on their facility with multiplication facts. Students who are not fluent with their multiplication facts cannot readily determine prime numbers or the factors of a nonprime number, nor can they use the "test" to determine if a number is a prime number.

Students are taught to test by asking themselves, "Can this number be divided by something other than 1 and itself?" If the number in question can be divided by something other than 1 and itself, it is not a prime number. Teachers can have students apply this test to a list of numbers. The list should consist of half prime numbers and half nonprime numbers. Teachers instruct students to use a calculator to determine if each of the numbers on the list can be divided evenly by prime numbers less than 20 (i.e., 2, 3, 5, 7, 11, 13, 17, 19).

When adding and subtracting unlike fractions, students learn to find all of the factors of the two numerators. However, in pre-algebra, students are taught to find the *prime factors* of numbers and to represent the number as only prime factors multiplied together. The prime factors of 15 are 3 and 5 because both factors are prime numbers, and 3 × 5 = 15. The prime factors of 12 are 2, 2, 3; all factors are prime numbers and 2 × 2 × 3 = 12. The factors 2 and 6 are not *prime* factors because even though 2 × 6 = 12, 6 is not a prime number. The prime factors of 6 are 2 and 3; therefore, the prime factors of 12 are 2, 2, and 3.

Finding prime factors involves attempting to divide a number by each prime number, in order, as many times as possible. To find the prime factors of 35, students first divide 35 by 2 and 3 (the first prime numbers). However, neither 2 nor 3 divide into 35 evenly. Next, students would divide 35 by 5 (the next prime number). Since 35 divides by 7 evenly, and both 5 and 7 are prime numbers, they are the prime factors of 35.

For 36, students can divide by 2 evenly 18 times. Since 18 is not a prime number, students must continue the process of dividing until each factor is a prime number. The prime factors for 36 are 2, 2, 3, and 3 (see division below).

$$36 \div 2 = 18$$
$$18 \div 2 = 9$$
$$9 \div 3 = 3$$
$$2 \times 2 \times 3 \times 3 = 36$$

Finding the prime factors enables students to use the algebraic method of reducing fractions and "canceling." Students learn that canceling is possible because they are canceling fractions that equal one and therefore do not change the value of the fraction. For example, to reduce the fraction $^{24}/_{36}$, students find the prime factors of both 24 and 36 and then cancel the prime factors that appear in the numerator and the denominator (i.e., fractions that equal one).

$$\frac{24}{36} = \frac{2 \times 2 \times 2 \times 3}{2 \times 2 \times 3 \times 3} = \frac{\cancel{2} \times \cancel{2} \times 2 \times \cancel{3}}{\cancel{2} \times \cancel{2} \times 3 \times \cancel{3}} = \frac{2}{3}$$

Integers

Integers include both positive and negative numbers. Many students have difficulty working with negative numbers. To simplify the concept of negative numbers, we recommend that teachers use a number line. Although many students may be familiar with a number line, teachers must be sure that students understand the rule that when add, you move to the right on a number line, and when you subtract, you move to the left. Students can use the number line to easily solve problems with positive and negative integers. For example, $(-6 + 5 = \square)$ or $(-1 - 3 = \square)$. Initially, students should be given only addition combinations so that they are not confused by the appearance of both operational signs (plus/minus) and signed values (positive/negative). Limiting initial examples ensures that only one new concept is introduced at a time.

The concept of absolute value is introduced to students as "the distance from zero." Because the concept is new and difficult, the term *absolute value* is not introduced until later. Once students understand the concept of distance from zero, teachers use the concept when they instruct students to solve problems with positive and negative integers. See Format 20.3 for this strategy. The first step of the structured board presentation involves teaching students the following rules:

1. If the signs of the numbers are the same, you add.
2. If the signs of the numbers are different, you subtract.
3. When you subtract, you start with the number that is farther from zero on the number line and subtract the other number.
4. The sign in the answer is always the sign of the number that was farther from zero.

The remaining part of the structured board presentation focuses on the application of these rules. Students will need considerable practice in using the rules to solve computation problems with positive and negative integers.

Next, students are taught to multiply integers. They are first taught to multiply positive integers and multivalue numbers, such as $5 \times (7 - 2 - 3)$. Students copy the sign of each term, and using the distributive property, they multiply the positive integer and each of the values, e.g., $(35 - 10 - 15)$. After students are comfortable with such problems, they are taught a rule for multiplying by a negative integer: *If you multiply by a minus value, you write the opposite of the sign.* Using that rule, $-5 \times (7 - 2 - 3)$ would become $(-35 + 10 + 15)$. The rule is simple and efficient in that students need learn only one rule rather than the traditional four rules:

plus × plus = plus;

minus × plus = minus;

minus × minus = plus;

plus × minus = minus.

Next, students can be introduced to conventional notation for combining positive and negative integers in addition and subtraction problems (e.g., $-8 + -3 = \square$). Initially, to facilitate learning this notation, teachers may want to use exaggerated signs representing the operations (i.e., addition or subtraction). For example, the problem above could be written $-8 + -3$. Students are taught to apply two rules. First, they are taught, *The big minus sign indicates that you combine the first number with the opposite of the second number.* So −4 − −5 becomes −4 + 5. The second rule students learn is, *The big plus sign means you combine the two terms as they are.* So −4 + −5 becomes −4 + −5.

After students master the application of the rules with exaggerated signs, we recommend that they practice rewriting problems without the exaggerated signs before solving the problems.

Exponents

Writing exponents and combining exponents are skills commonly needed in complex problems. We suggest initially using expanded notation to assist students in understanding the concept of exponents. Expanded notation illustrates the relationship between repeated multiplication and exponents. Teachers provide students with several examples of repeated multiplication, such as 4 × 4 × 4 or $D \times D \times D \times D$. Using these examples, teachers explain that the number that is repeated is called the *base number*, and the *exponent* is the number of times the base number is repeated. The exponent is a little number that is written above the base number. Therefore, in 4 × 4 × 4, 4 is the base number, and the exponent is 3. This is written as 4^3.

Teachers need to provide many examples of repeated multiplication where students are asked to identify the base number and the exponent. Students should practice writing base numbers and exponents as well. Finally, students should practice writing the expanded notation when given a base number and exponent.

Combining exponents can be illustrated by presenting examples of expanded notation divided into groups. For example, $\underline{6 \times 6 \times 6} \times 6 \times 6$. Teachers point out that the examples fall into two groups, underlined and not underlined, and then use the examples to show that $6^3 \times 6^2 = 6^5$.

Similarly, expanded notation can be used to show how to simplify exponents. Simplifying exponents is just like simplifying prime factors in that the same numbers in the numerator and denominator are canceled (because they are fractions equal to 1).

For example,

$$\frac{5^9}{5^6} = \frac{\cancel{5} \times \cancel{5} \times \cancel{5} \times \cancel{5} \times \cancel{5} \times \cancel{5} \times 5 \times 5 \times 5}{\cancel{5} \times \cancel{5} \times \cancel{5} \times \cancel{5} \times \cancel{5} \times \cancel{5}} = 5^3$$

After canceling, students can determine the base number and exponent.

Summary Box 20.2
Combining Integers

1. Students use rules to determine whether they add or subtract.
   Same: Add
   Different: Subtract

   −13 + 7 = ☐
   Students determine they must add, since the numbers have different signs.

2. Students determine the number to start with based on the rule.

   Start with the number farther from 0.

   Students start with −13.

3. Students determine whether the answer will be positive or negative based on the rule.

   Use the sign of the number that is farther from 0.

   Answer will be negative, since 13 is farther from 0.

4. Students solve problem.

   −13 + 7 = −6

APPLICATION ITEMS: PRE-ALGEBRA

1. Complete the following function table.

x	Function	Answer y
0		0
1		4
2		8
3		
4		
5		

2. Construct a set of problems for use in Format 20.3 for combining integers.

3. Construct a set of examples and nonexamples for students to use in determining if a number is a prime number.

4. Explain why initial teaching and practice of the *concept* of absolute value is best accomplished using the phrase *farther from zero* rather than *absolute value*.

5. Outline the steps in teaching students to find the prime factors of a number.

6. Write a classification problem with fractions to be solved with a ratio table, and show the solution.

7. Show the solution process to the following comparison problem with percentages, using the ratio table shown.

> Ben is 35% taller than his mom. If Ben is 21 inches taller than his mom, how tall is Ben and how tall is his mom? (Hint: Ben is being compared to his mom, so who is equal to one or 100%?)

Difference	35%	21 inches
Mom		
Ben		

FORMAT 20.1 Using and Plotting a Function

TEACHER   **STUDENTS**

PART A: STRUCTURED BOARD PRESENTATION

x	Function	Answer y
1		2
4		8
3		
0		
5		

FORMAT 20.1 (continued)

TEACHER	STUDENTS

1. You have made points on the coordinate system by using a table that shows the x values and the y values. When you connect the points, you get a straight line. The reason you get a straight line is that all of the points follow the same function rule. If you're following the same rule about adding, subtracting, multiplying, or dividing the x value to get the y value, you will get a straight line on the coordinate system. Let's find the function for this table, complete the table, plot the values, and see if we get a straight line.

   The first x value is 1. What is the y value?   2

2. What would it take to get from 1 to 2? What would you add?   Add 1

3. Let's see if adding 1 will solve everything in this table. What is the second x value?   4

   What is the y value?   8

   Can you add 1 to the x value of 4 to get the y value?   No

   If adding didn't work, let's try multiplication. 4 × what number = 8?   2

   Go back and check the first values. The x value is 1. Can you multiply it by 2 to get the y value of 2?   Yes

4. So how do we know that the function is x × 2?   Because the first x value of 1 × 2 = the first y value of 2, and the second x value of 4 × 2 = the second y value of 8.

5. So we fill in the function part of this table as x × 2. What is the third x value?   3

   So what is 3 × 2?   6

   And where do we write that 6?   As the y value

6. What is the fourth x value?   0

   So what is 0 × 2?   0

   So what is the fourth y value?   0

7. Figure out the fifth y value and fill it in. What did you fill in for the fifth y value?   10

8. Now we need to plot these points. The first two points are already plotted. What is the x value for the third point?   3

   So the x value moves to the right how many spaces?   3 spaces

   The y value moves up how many spaces?   6 spaces

   Now plot that point and the two other points.

9. Connect those dots with a ruler. Raise your hand if you got a straight line.

TEACHER   **STUDENTS**

PART B: STRUCTURED WORKSHEET

Function	Answer
x	**y**
1	4
4	7
3	
0	
5	

1. Let's find the function for this table, complete the table, plot the values, and see if we get a straight line.

   The first *x* value is 1. What is the *y* value?   4

2. What would you add to get from 1 to 4?   3

3. Look at the second pair of values. Can you add 3 to the second *x* value and get the *y* value?   Yes

   What is the number sentence for those values. $4 + 3 = 7$

4. So what is the function? $x + 3$

5. Find the rest of the values. Raise your hand when you're done.

   What is the fourth pair of values? $x = 0, y = 3$

   What is the fifth pair of values? $x = 5, y = 8$

6. Plot those values then connect those dots with a ruler. Raise your hand if you got a straight line.

7. *(Do steps 4–13 using different functions.)*

FORMAT 20.2   Ratio Tables Using Fractions for Classes

TEACHER   **STUDENTS**

PART A: STRUCTURED BOARD PRESENTATION—FIGURING OUT FRACTION NUMBER FAMILIES

1. *(Put this problem on the board.)*

   Three-fifths of the bottles of glue in the store are white glue and the rest are super glue. If there are 26 bottles of super glue, how many bottles of white glue are in the store? How many total bottles of glue are in the store?

   Read the problem with students.

(continued on next page)

FORMAT 20.2 (continued)

TEACHER	STUDENTS
2. This is a classification word problem. What words tell us about the classes in this problem?	Glue, white glue, super glue
3. What is the first class named in the problem? Underline that class.	Glue
4. What is the next class named in the problem? Underline that class.	White glue
5. What is the next class named in the problem? Underline that class. *(Write this on board.)* ____ + ____ = ____	Super glue
6. Write a number sentence like the one on the board. What is the big class? Write that under the last blank.	Glue
7. So what are the two smaller classes?	White glue and super glue.
8. Where do we write those?	Under the first two blanks.
9. Do that now.	
10. Let's look at the classes one at a time. Let's start with white glue. What fraction of the bottles of glue are white glue?	$\frac{3}{5}$
11. Where do we write $\frac{3}{5}$?	Over the blank labeled white glue.
12. Do that now. Does the problem tell us what fraction of the bottles of glue is super glue?	No
13. What do we write over super glue?	A box
14. Do that now. What do we write over the big class, glue?	$\frac{5}{5}$
15. Yes, $\frac{5}{5}$. The problem doesn't say $\frac{5}{5}$. So who remembers how we know that the big class is equal to $\frac{5}{5}$?	Because the big class is all of the glue, so it is equal to one whole, or $\frac{5}{5}$.
16. The big number is given, so do we add or subtract?	Subtract
17. So what is the answer?	$\frac{2}{5}$

PART B: STRUCTURED BOARD PRESENTATION—RATIO TABLES

1. Now we are ready to draw and use a ratio table to solve problems. (*Draw this table on the board and ask students to copy it.*)

	Fraction family	Ratio	Quantity
White glue			
Super glue			
Glue			

2. We have just figured out the fraction number family. What fraction of the bottles is white glue? — $\frac{3}{5}$
3. Write $\frac{3}{5}$ in the fraction family column next to white glue.

TEACHER	**STUDENTS**

<table>
<tr><td></td><td>$\frac{2}{5}$</td></tr>
</table>

TEACHER

4. What fraction is super glue?

5. Write that next to super glue.

6. What fraction do we write for the big class of glue?

7. Write ⅝ in the fraction family column.

8. Now we are ready to complete the ratio column. We write the numerators of our fractions in the ratio column.

   What is the fraction for white glue?

   What is the numerator?
   Write the numerator in the ratio column.

9. What is the fraction for super glue?

   What is the numerator?
   Write the numerator in the ratio column.

10. What is the fraction for glue?

    What is the numerator?
    Write the numerator in the ratio column.
    (*The completed table should look like the one below.*)

STUDENTS

$\frac{2}{5}$

$\frac{5}{5}$

$\frac{3}{5}$

3

$\frac{2}{5}$

2

$\frac{5}{5}$

5

	Fraction family	Ratio	Quantity
White glue	3/5	3	
Super glue	2/5	2	
Glue	5/5	5	

11. Now we are ready to solve the problem. We are going to do that by using ratio equations. We begin by writing into the table the quantity we know. Read the problem. What quantity of glue bottles is stated in the problem?

    Write that quantity in the column across from super glue. Since we know the quantity of super glue, we call super glue the *known quantity.*

    26 bottles of super glue

12. What does the problem ask us to find out first?

    How many bottles of white glue were in the store.

13. To find the answer, we are going to make a ratio equation of our known quantity, super glue, to our unknown quantity, white glue. First we'll set up the ratio equation with the appropriate labels, then we'll fill in the known quantities

    Here's how we write the ratio equation. We start by labeling the numerator and denominator in the first fraction like this. (*Write the following equation on the board.*)

    $$\frac{\text{super glue}}{\text{white glue}}$$

    Then we write an equal sign and write the labels for the fraction on the other side. (*Write the following on the board.*)

    $$\frac{\text{super glue}}{\text{white glue}} = \frac{\text{super glue}}{\text{white glue}}$$

(continued on next page)

FORMAT 20.2 (continued)

TEACHER	STUDENTS

Now we fill in the correct ratio for the first fraction. Look at the ratio column. What is the ratio of super glue to white glue?

$\frac{2}{3}$

Complete the ratio for the first fraction. (*Write the following on the board.*)

$$\frac{\textbf{2}\text{ super glue}}{\textbf{3}\text{ white glue}} = \frac{\text{super glue}}{\text{white glue}}$$

Now we fill in the known quantity for the second fraction. Look at the quantity column and find the known quantity. What is the known quantity?

26 bottles of super glue

Write the known quantity in the appropriate fraction on the other side of the equation. (*Write the quantity on the board.*)

$$\frac{\textbf{2}\text{ super glue}}{\textbf{3}\text{ white glue}} = \frac{\textbf{26}\text{ super glue}}{\text{white glue}}$$

14. Now we're ready to solve for the quantity of white glue. Write a box by the label for white glue in the equation.

$$\frac{\textbf{2}\text{ super glue}}{\textbf{3}\text{ white glue}} = \frac{\textbf{26}\text{ super glue}}{\square\text{ white glue}}$$

We solve this by using equivalent fractions.

We are looking for a fraction equal to one. What number times two equals 26?

13

So we write in 13 over 13.

$$\frac{\textbf{2}\text{ super glue}}{\textbf{3}\text{ white glue}} \times \left(\frac{\textbf{13}}{\textbf{13}}\right) = \frac{26\text{ super glue}}{\square\text{ white glue}}$$

Here's what you should have. What do we multiply to find out how many bottles of white glue were in the store?

3×13

What's the answer?

39 bottles of white glue

15. Now we can fill in the quantity for white glue in the table. Where are we going to write 39?

In the quantity column next to white glue.

16. We now have 26 bottles for super glue and 39 bottles for white glue. How do we find out how many bottles of glue in all?

Add 26 and 39

What is your answer?

65 bottles of glue

Write that in your table and you're done.

FORMAT 20.3 Combining Integers

TEACHER	STUDENTS

PART A: STRUCTURED BOARD PRESENTATION

1. You've worked with positive and negative numbers on the number line. Here are some rules you can use to solve problems without using a number line. (*Write these on a board or on a poster.*)

TEACHER   **STUDENTS**

    1. If the signs of the numbers are the same, you add.
    2. If the signs of the numbers are different, you subtract.
    3. When you subtract, you start with the number that
        is farther from zero on the number line and subtract
        the other number.
    4. The sign in the answer is always the sign of the number
        that is farther from zero.

2. *(Write this problem on the board.)*

$$\begin{array}{r} -\ 9 \\ +\ 20 \\ \hline \end{array}$$

3. Are the signs the same or different?   Different

4. If the signs are different, do we add or subtract?   Subtract

5. We start with the number that is farther from zero. Which number is
   farther from zero, 9 or 20?   20

6. Start with 20 and subtract 9. What is the answer?   11

7. The last rule tells us how to determine the correct sign. Read the rule.   The sign in the answer is
                                                                   always the sign of the
                                                                   number that is farther
                                                                   from zero.

8. So is the answer positive 11 or negative 11? How do you know?   Positive 11.
                                                                   Because 20 is the
                                                                   number farther from zero
                                                                   and it is positive.

9. *(Write this problem on the board.)*

$$\begin{array}{r} -\ 7 \\ -\ 9 \\ \hline \end{array}$$

10. Are the signs the same or different?   The same.

11. Do we add or subtract?   Add

12. Add 7 and 9. What is the answer?   16

13. The last rule tells us how to determine the correct sign.   The sign in the answer is
    Read the rule.   always the sign of the
                                                                 number that is farther
                                                                 from zero.

14. So is the answer positive 16 or negative 16?   Negative 16.

15. How do you know?   Because 9 is the number
                                                                 farther from zero and it is
                                                                 negative.

16. *(Write this problem on the board.)*

$$\begin{array}{r} 12 \\ -\ 7 \\ \hline \end{array}$$

17. Are the signs the same or different?   Different

18. If the signs are different, do we add or subtract?   Subtract

19. We start with the number that is farther from zero.
    Which number is farther from zero, 12 or 7?   12

20. Start with 12 and subtract 7. What's the answer?   5

(continued on next page)

FORMAT 20.3 (continued)

TEACHER	STUDENTS
21. The last rule tells us what?	The sign in the answer is always the sign of the number that is farther from zero.
22. So is the answer positive 5 or negative 5?	Positive 5.
23. How do you know?	Because 12 is the number farther from zero and it is positive.

PART B: LESS STRUCTURED BOARD PRESENTATION

1. *(Write the following abbreviations for the four rules.)*
   Same: Add
   Different: Subtract
   Start with number farther from zero
   Use sign of number farther from zero

2. Here is a short reminder of the four rules for combining positive and negative numbers. Who can tell me the first rule? numbers shown are the	If the signs of the same, you add.
3. Who can tell me the second rule?	If the signs of the numbers shown are different, you subtract.
4. Who can tell me the third rule?	When you subtract, you start with the number that is farther from zero on the number line and subtract the other number.
5. And who can tell me the last rule?	The sign in the answer is always the sign of the number that is farther from zero.

6. *(Write this problem on the board.)*

$$\begin{array}{r} -5 \\ +7 \\ \hline \end{array}$$

7. Let's just talk about what we are going to do. Do we add or subtract?	Subtract
8. How do you know?	Because the signs are different.
9. What number do we start with?	7
10. How do you know?	Because it is farther from zero.
11. Will the answer be positive or negative?	Positive
12. How do you know?	Because the 7 is positive.
13. Do the problem now. What's the answer?	2

TEACHER	**STUDENTS**

14. *(Write this problem on the board.)*

$$\begin{array}{r} -\ 3 \\ \underline{-\ 9} \end{array}$$

15. Do we add or subtract? — Add

16. How do you know? — Because the signs are the same.

17. Will the answer be positive or negative? — Negative

18. How do you know? — Because the 9 is negative.

19. Work the problem. What's the answer. — Negative 12

20. *(Write this problem on the board.)*

$$\begin{array}{r} -13 \\ \underline{+\ 7} \end{array}$$

21. Do we add or subtract? — Subtract

22. How do you know? — Because the signs are different.

23. What number do we start with? — 13

24. How do you know? — Because it is farther from zero.

25. Will the answer be positive or negative? — Negative

26. How do you know? — Because the 13 is negative.

27. Work the problem. What's the answer? — Negative 6

PART C: STRUCTURED WORKSHEET

1. *(Students have worksheets with problems such as these.)*

   a. $\begin{array}{r} -\ 7 \\ \underline{-\ 8} \end{array}$ b. $\begin{array}{r} +\ 4 \\ \underline{-\ 2} \end{array}$ c. $\begin{array}{r} +\ 9 \\ \underline{-\ 13} \end{array}$ d. $\begin{array}{r} -\ 3 \\ \underline{+\ 6} \end{array}$

2. Before you do these problems, let's review the rules. What do you do if the signs are the same? — Add

3. And if you add, what sign will the answer be? — The sign of the number farther from zero.

4. When do we subtract? — When the signs of the numbers are different.

5. When we subtract, which number do we start with? — With the number that is farther from zero.

6. What sign will the answer be? — The sign of the number that is farther from zero.

7. Work the problems.

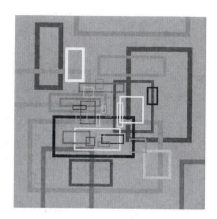

Direct Instruction Mathematics Programs: An Overview and Research Summary

Angela M. Przychodzin, Nancy E. Marchand-Martella, Ronald C. Martella, and Diane Azim, Eastern Washington University

ABSTRACT

This paper provides an overview and research summary of Direct Instruction (DI) mathematics programs, specifically *DISTAR Arithmetic I* and *II* (Engelmann & Carnine, 1975, 1976), *Corrective Mathematics* (Engelmann & Carnine, 1982), and *Connecting Math Concepts* (*CMC*; Engelmann, Carnine, Kelly, & Engelmann, 1996a). A comparison of the constructivist approach to the direct or explicit approach to math instruction was conducted. Overviews and ways in which DI math programs meet the 6 principles for improving math instruction as provided by the National Council of Teachers of Mathematics (NCTM; 2000b) are noted. Finally, a research review and analysis of DI math programs published since 1990 (yielding 12 studies) was completed. Seven of the 12 studies compared DI math programs to other math programs. Four studies investigated the efficacy of DI math programs without comparison to other math programs. A meta-analysis conducted by Adams and Engelmann (1996) was also described. Study characteristics (i.e., reference, program or program comparison, participants, research design, dependent variable(s)/measures, and results) were examined for each of the 12 studies. Eleven of the 12 studies showed positive results for DI math programs. Eight areas for future research are included.

Przychodzin, A. M., Marchand-Martella, N. E., Martella, R. C., & Azim, D. (2004). Direct instruction mathematics programs: An overview and research summary. *Journal of Direct Instruction, 4(1)*, 53–84.

This paper provides a review of DI mathematics programs including *DISTAR Arithmetic I* and *II*, *Corrective Mathematics*, and *CMC*. In addition, the constructivist approach and the direct or explicit approach to math instruction are compared. Primary emphasis was placed on the direct approach and how DI math programs meet NCTM's six principles for improving math instruction. A research review of studies published after 1990 using these programs was also conducted. Finally, areas for future research on DI math programs are provided.

OVERVIEW OF MATH STATISTICS

In our rapidly changing and technologically dependent society, we are faced with the need for a solid understanding of mathematical skills and concepts. This need is no longer limited to scientific and technical fields. Virtually every type of employment requires a more sophisticated understanding of mathematics. For example, in a 1989 report by the National Research Council, over 75% of all jobs required proficiency in simple algebra and geometry, either as a prerequisite to a training program or as part of a licensure examination. Further, in a more recent report by the Bureau of Labor Statistics (2002), estimates indicate that four of the top five employment growth fields will require a bachelor's degree in technical studies such as mathematics or computer science. Given the emphasis of mathematical skills in our society, it seems critical that our students should demonstrate basic mathematical and higher order thinking skills to be successful in present and future environments.

In 1995, the largest international study (Third International Mathematics and Science Study [TIMMS]) of academic achievement was conducted by the International Study Center (ISC) at Boston College. This study included over half a million students from 41 countries. According to the ISC's report (2001), when compared to other countries, math scores in the United States were ranked in the bottom half of the participating countries. American 4th graders ranked 12th out of 26, 8th graders ranked 28th out of 41, and 12th graders ranked 19th out of 21 countries who participated in the assessment.

The National Center for Education Statistics (2001) published its most recent results of the 2000 National Assessment of Educational Progress. In this report, known as *The Nation's Report Card,* the mathematics achievement levels of 4th-, 8th-, and 12th-grade students were assessed. The following three levels of performance were identified:

1. basic: this level denotes partial mastery of prerequisite knowledge and skills that are fundamental for proficient work at each grade.
2. proficient: the proficient level represents solid mathematical performance for each grade assessed. Students reaching this level have demonstrated competency over challenging subject matter, including mathematical knowledge, application of such knowledge to real-world situations, and analytical skills.
3. advanced: the advanced level signifies superior performance. (p. 9)

The *proficient* level is the overall performance goal for all students. Results indicated that only 26% of 4th-grade students, 27% of 8th-grade students, and 17% of 12th-grade students performed at the proficient level in math.

NCTM PRINCIPLES

Given the mathematical performance of our students on various assessments and comparisons conducted within and beyond the U.S., it seems imperative to examine how best to teach math in our public schools. The NCTM is the world's largest mathematics education organization, founded in 1920. The mission of the NCTM (2000a) is "to provide the vision and leadership necessary to ensure a mathematics education of the highest quality for all students" (p. 1). In order to accomplish this mission, the NCTM (2000b) developed five overall curricular goals for student success in mathematics: (a) learning to value mathematics, (b) becoming confident in one's own mathematical ability, (c) becoming a mathematical problem solver, (d) learning to communicate mathematically, and (e) learning to reason mathematically. The NCTM (2000b) developed *Principles and Standards for School Mathematics* as a framework for guiding educational professionals in meeting these five goals. While the Standards describe the mathematical *content* and *processes* that students should learn, the principles describe *features* of high quality mathematics education (2000b). In an earlier paper, Kelly (1994) provided examples from various levels of *CMC* to illustrate how these Standards can be met through *CMC*. This paper focuses on how the principles (vs. standards) were met by *CMC, DISTAR I and II,* and *Corrective Mathematics*. According to the NCTM (2000b), the six principles should be used to influence the development and selection of curricula, instructional planning, assessment design, and establishment of professional development programs for educators (see Table 1). It is through these six princi-

Table 1 NCTM Principles for Improving Math Instruction

The Equity Principle	Excellence in mathematics education requires equity—high expectations and strong support for all students.
The Curriculum Principle	A curriculum is more than a collection of activities; it must be coherent, focused on important mathematics, and well-articulated across the grades.
The Teaching Principle	Effective mathematics teaching requires understanding what students know and need to learn and then challenging and supporting them to learn it well.
The Learning Principle	Students must learn mathematics with understanding, actively building new knowledge from experience and prior knowledge.
The Assessment Principle	Assessment should support the learning of important mathematics and furnish useful information to both teachers and students.
The Technology Principle	Technology is essential in teaching and learning mathematics: it influences the mathematics that is taught and enhances students' learning.

ples that educators can begin to address the composite themes of high quality mathematics education.

PRIMARY APPROACHES TO MATH INSTRUCTION

There are two primary approaches to mathematics instruction. These include the constructivist approach and the direct or explicit approach (see Table 2). According to Applefield, Huber, and Moallem (2000/2001), constructivism is based on a postulate that student learning is influenced by four primary factors: (a) learners construct their own learning, (b) new learning is dependent upon students' existing understanding of the world, (c) social interaction plays a critical role in that students work in heterogeneous cooperative learning groups, and (d) authentic learning tasks are used for meaningful learning. The constructivist approach is primarily an inquiry- or discovery-oriented approach. Students are put into learning situations that allow them to "discover" which problem-solving strategies will be the most effective. Through exposure to real-life situations, students use inductive reasoning to make generalizations about mathematical concepts and problem-solving strategies. The following is an example of a constructivist lesson taken from *Math Trailblazers* (TIMS Project: University of Illinois at Chicago, 1998, p. 61).

> Recycling 100 Cans. Have the children bring in aluminum cans for recycling. The first goal might be to collect 10 cans, then 50, and finally, 100. Of course, this can be a continuing project for your class. Have the class figure out how many cans would have to be brought in by each child to reach the goal of 100 cans, or if every child brings in a can every day, how many days will it take to reach 100 cans? First, students are encouraged to brainstorm which problem-solving strategies would be most effective in solving their problem. Then, through trial and error, a solution is reached.

A second approach to mathematics instruction is known as an explicit or direct approach. In this approach, teachers help students acquire knowledge in the form of concepts, principles or rules, cognitive strategies, and physical operations (Kozloff, LaNunziata, Cowardin, & Bessellieu, 2000/2001). This knowledge is most effectively taught in the following manner: (a) teaching with clear objectives; (b) teaching concepts, principles, strategies, and operations explicitly and systematically; and (c) monitoring progress continually (Kozloff et al.). Stein, Silbert, and Carnine (1997) refer to explicit instruction as being clear, accurate, and unambiguous; therefore, the clearer the instruction, the more efficient it will be. This approach provides a comprehensive set of prescriptions for organizing instruction so that students acquire, retain, and generalize new learning in a manner that is as humane, efficient, and effective as possible. The following is an example of part of a lesson using an explicit or direct approach to instruction as provided by Stein et al. (p. 65).

TEACHER	STUDENTS
1. *(Give students paper and pencil.)*	
2. You are going to write a problem. First, you'll say it. Listen: Six plus two equals how many? Say that. *To correct: Respond with students until they can say the statement at the normal rate of speech.*	Six plus two equals how many?
3. Now we'll say it the slow way. Every time I clap, we'll say a part of the statement. *(Respond with the students.)* Get ready.	

Table 2   Summary of Two Primary Approaches to Math Instruction

Constructivist Approach	*Explicit or Direct Approach*
*Teacher presents real-life situations and facilitates inquiry- or discovery-based problem solving.	*Teacher directly teaches concepts, principles or rules, cognitive strategies, and physical operations.
*Students construct their own learning based on their current understanding of the world, usually within heterogeneous cooperative learning groups.	*Comprehensive set of prescriptions for organizing instruction to guide students' acquisition, retention, and generalization of new knowledge.
*Steps in student learning process: 1) Presented with real-life situation. 2) Brainstorm possible problem solving strategies. 3) Solution reached through trial and error.	*Three variables for effective instruction (Stein et al., 1997): 1) Effective instructional design. 2) Effective presentation techniques. 3) Logical organization of instruction
*Spiral-based curriculum design.	*Strand design.

TEACHER	STUDENTS
(Clap) Six. *(Pause two seconds; clap.)*	six
Plus *(Pause two seconds; clap.)* Two. *(Pause two seconds; clap.)*	plus two
Equals. *(Pause two seconds; clap.)*	equals
How many? *(Repeat step 3 until students appear able to respond on their own.)*	how many?
4. Now I'll clap and you say the statement by yourselves. *(Pause.)* Get ready. *(Clap at two-second intervals.)* To correct: Respond with students.	Six plus two equals how many?
5. Now write the problem.	Students write 6 + 2 = ___
6. *(Repeat steps 1–5 with three more equations.)*	

Efficacy of Direct Approach in Meeting the NCTM Principles for Improving Math Instruction

As shown in Table 1, the NCTM (2000b) recommended six principles to guide educators in making sound decisions about mathematics instruction. The direct approach to teaching mathematics is an effective and efficient way to meet these principles. Within this direct approach to teaching, Stein et al. (1997) identified three variables for effective instruction: (a) effective instructional design, (b) effective presentation techniques, and (c) logical organization of instruction. Descriptors of each of these variables follow.

EFFECTIVE INSTRUCTIONAL DESIGN. Effective instructional design consists of nine elements. First, long- and short-term objectives must by specified. Both long- and short-term objectives should explicitly state observable behaviors, performance criteria, and the conditions under which the behavior will be performed. Long-term objectives should specify exactly what students should do at the end of an educational program. The following is an example of a long-term objective taken from Lignugaris/Kraft, Marchand-Martella, and Martella (2001): "Given a worksheet with 20 addition problems up to 3D + 3D + 3D with and without regrouping, Larry will write correct answers with 90% accuracy on three consecutive weekly classroom exercises" (p. 56). On the other hand, short-term objectives are based on the component skills needed to reach the long-term goal. The following is an example of a short-term objective taken from Lignugaris/Kraft et al.: "Given a worksheet with 10 addition problems with sums less than 19 and both addends less than 10, Larry will write correct answers with 90% accuracy on three consecutive weekly classroom exercises" (p. 56).

Second, efficient procedural strategies must be designed. Kameenui and Carnine (1998) define a strategy as a set of skills used to acquire and use knowledge. To maximize student learning and instructional efficiency, it is imperative that strategies be taught to allow students to solve the greatest number of problems with the fewest possible number of steps (Kameenui & Carnine, 1998; Stein et al., 1997). The following is a number-family problem solving strategy as noted by Stein et al.:

> The number-family strategy is based on the concept that three numbers can be used to form four math statements. For example, the numbers 2, 5, and 7 yield 2 + 5 = 7, 5 + 2 = 7, 7 − 5 = 2, and 7 − 2 = 5. In a typical problem, two of the numbers in the family are provided. Students place these numbers where they belong in the family and then determine whether the missing number is obtained by adding or subtracting. The strategy is applied to word problems in that if the total number of a fact family is given, the problem requires subtraction. For example, "Kyle had two snakes. Now he has seven snakes. How many more snakes did he get?" The last sentence asks about how many more, not about the total. So one of the numbers in the problem, 2 or 7, must be the big number, the total. The phrase "Now he has 7" indicated that 7 is the total number. Students then subtract 2 from the total number; 7 − 2 = 5. Kyle got 5 more snakes. (p. 221)

Third, necessary preskills must be determined. Instruction should be sequenced so that the component skills of a strategy are taught before the strategy itself is introduced. For example, the strategy for solving addition problems and repeating addition statements should be taught before column addition problems are taught. Component skills must be mastered before students can be expected to use them as a part of a strategy.

Fourth, preskills should be logically sequenced to maximize student learning. Three sequencing guidelines are recommended when introducing new information to students. First, preskills of a strategy are taught before the strategy. For example, when teaching students to add single numbers to teen numbers with sums over 20, students must have the following preskills: symbol identification, place value, basic addition facts, and renaming. Along these lines, Carnine (1980) found that preteaching the component skills of a multiplication algorithm resulted in more rapid learning of the complex skill than teaching the components and the complex skill concurrently. Second, easy skills are taught before more difficult ones. For example, students should be taught the "regular" teen numbers 14, 16, 17, 18, and 19 before the "irregular" teen numbers 11, 12, 13, and 15. It is easier to learn the names and, therefore, the value of the number 17 ("*seven*teen"). Conversely, the number 11 is considered "irregular" and more difficult to learn ("eleven" not "one-teen"). Finally, information that is likely to be confused is not introduced consecutively. For example, students are likely to confuse the numerals *6* and *9,* so they should not be introduced consecutively.

Fifth, teaching procedures must be selected for three types of tasks: motor, labeling, and strategy tasks, because each type of task requires a different teaching procedure (Stein et al., 1997). Motor tasks, which require students to articulate a rule or to perform a precise movement, are taught using the following four-step teaching procedure: model, lead, test, and delayed test. An example of this procedure used to teach students to articulate the equality rule in addition is shown in Figure 1 (Engelmann, Carnine, Kelly, & Engelmann, 1996b, p. 50). Workbook practice provides the delayed test step in the motor task procedure.

Labeling tasks, which require students to say the word that correctly labels an object, are taught using the following three-step teaching procedure: model, alternating test, and delayed test. An example of this procedure, used to teach students how to read thousands numbers, follows (Stein et al., p. 76).

Figure 1

Example of a motor task used to teach students to articulate a rule.

EXERCISE 1 EQUALITY

a. (Write on the board):

=

- This is a very important sign that we'll use to work on hard problems. This sign is called an equal sign.
b. What's it called? (Signal.) *An equal sign.*
   (Repeat step b until firm.)
c. (Draw a circle on each side of the equal sign:)

- Here's a rule about the equal sign: You must end up with the same number on both sides of the equal sign. Listen again: You must end up with the same number on both sides of the equal sign. Watch.
- (Make 3 lines in the left circle:)

- I made lines on one side of the equal sign. Everybody, how many lines did I make? (Signal.) *3.*
- I must end up with the same number on both sides of the equal sign. So how many lines do I have to make on the other side of the equal sign? (Signal.) *3*

- (Make 3 lines in the right circle:)

- I did it. I ended up with 3 on both sides of the equal sign. So it says **3 equals 3.** What does it say? (Signal.) *3 equals 3.*
- (Erase the lines.)
d. New problem: I'm going to make little marks on one side of the equal sign. Watch.
   (Make 2 marks in the right circle:)

- How many marks did I make on one side of the equal sign? (Signal.) *2.*
- I must end up with the same number on both sides of the equal sign. So how many marks do I have to make on the other side? (Signal.) *2.*
- (Make 2 marks in the left circle:)

- I ended up with 2 on both sides of the equal sign. So it says **2 equals 2.** What does it say? (Signal.) *2 equals 2.*
- (Do **not** erase the board.)

Note. From Engelmann, S., Carnine, D., Kelly, B., & Engelmann, O. (1996b). *Connecting Math Concepts: Level A, p. 50.* Columbus, OH: SRA/McGraw-Hill. Reproduced with permission of The McGraw-Hill Companies.

TEACHER	**STUDENTS**
1. When a big number has one comma, the comma tells about thousands. Here's the rule. The number in front of the comma tells how many thousands. What does the number in front of the comma tell?	how many thousands
(Write on board: 6,781.)	
2. What number comes in front of the comma?	6
So what is the first part of the number?	6 thousand
3. *(Point to 781.)* Get ready to read the rest of the number.	781
4. Now you are going to read the whole number. *(Point to 6, then comma, then 781.)*	6,781
5. *(Repeat steps 2–4 with these numbers: 2,145 3,150 5,820 6,423.)*	
6. *(Give individual turns to several students.)*	

Figure 2

Example of a strategy task.

Basic Steps in the Short-Form Algorithm

TEACHER	**STUDENTS**
1. Read the problem.	7 goes into 238.
2. Underline the part you work first.	Students underline $7\overline{)238}$
3. Say the underlined part.	7 goes into 23.
4. Write the answer above the last underlined digit.	$\begin{array}{r} 3 \\ 7\overline{)238} \end{array}$
5. Multiply 3 × 7, subtract, and then bring down the next number.	$\begin{array}{r} 3 \\ 7\overline{)238} \\ \underline{21} \\ 28 \end{array}$
6. Read the new problem.	7 goes into 28.
7. Write the answer number above the digit you just brought down.	$\begin{array}{r} 34 \\ 7\overline{)238} \\ \underline{21} \\ 28 \end{array}$
8. Multiply and subtract to determine the remainder.	$\begin{array}{r} 34 \\ 7\overline{)238} \\ \underline{21} \\ 28 \\ \underline{28} \\ 0 \end{array}$
9. Say the answer.	7 goes into 238, 34 times.

Note. From Stein, M., Silbert, J., & Carnine, D. (1997). *DESIGNING EFFECTIVE MATHEMATICS INSTRUCTION* 3/e, ©1997, p. 204. Reprinted by permission of Pearson Education, Inc., Upper Saddle River, New Jersey.

Finally, strategy tasks, which require the integration of a series of sequential steps to form a generalizable strategy, are taught using modeling, guided practice, and supervised independent work. An example of a strategy task, used to teach students how to divide using the short-form algorithm, is shown in Figure 2 (Stein et al., p. 204).

Sixth, teaching formats are designed to specify what teachers will say and do. These formats allow teachers to focus more attention on student performance. Figure 3 shows a sample format for teaching students how to find volume (Engelmann, Carnine, Kelly, & Engelmann, 1996d, pp. 348–349).

Seventh, appropriate examples are chosen for motor, labeling, and strategy tasks. Stein et al. (1997) recommend the following for choosing these examples. Examples should involve the current strategy or a previously mastered strategy. In addition, examples of previously introduced problem types should be included. This aspect of instructional design allows students to practice the new strategy, review previous strategies, and learn to differentiate between when to use specific strategies for a variety of similar problems.

Eighth, guided practice and review are used to ensure mastery of skills. Long-term skill retention

---

Figure 3

***Example of a format for teaching students how to find volume from* Connecting Math Concepts: Level F.**

EXERCISE 5 VOLUME

Mixed Set

a. Find part 5.
• Some of these figures come to a a point. Others don't. Remember, for figures that do not come to a point, you find the area of the base times the height. For figures that come to a point, you find the area of the base times the height. Then what do you divide by? (Signal.) *3*.

b. Find the volume of figure A. Start with the equation for volume. Raise your hand when you're finished.
(Observe students and give feedback.)
• **(Write on the board:)**

> a. Area of b × h = V
>   51 × 22 = V
> $\boxed{V = 1{,}122 \text{ cu m}}$

• Figure A has a triangular base. The area of the base is 51 square meters. Times the height of 22. That's 1,122 cubic meters.

c. Figure B also has a triangular base, but it comes to a point.
• Find the volume of figure B. Raise your hand when you're finished.
(Observe students and give feedback.)
• **(Write on the board:)**

> b. $\dfrac{\text{Area of b} \times h}{3} = V$
>
> $\dfrac{27.5 \times 16}{3} = V$
>
> $\boxed{}$
>
> $V = 146.67 \text{ cu in}$

• Here's what you should have. The area of the base is 27 and 5-tenths square inches. Times the height of 16. That's 440. Divided by 3. The volume is 146 and 67-hundredths cubic inches.

d. Your turn: Work the rest of the problems in part 5. Raise your hand when you're finished.
(Observe students and give feedback.)

Key:

> c. Area of b × h = V
> $\dfrac{113.04 \times 6 = V}{}$
> $\boxed{V = 678.24 \text{ cu in}}$
>
> d. $\dfrac{\text{Area of b} \times h}{3} = V$
>
> $\dfrac{9.45 \times 3.3}{3} = V$
>
> $\boxed{V = 10.40 \text{ cu ft}}$
>
> e. $\dfrac{\text{Area of b} \times h}{3} = V$
>
> $\dfrac{254.34 \times 2.8}{3} = V$
>
> $\boxed{V = 2373.84 \text{ cu cm}}$

e. Find part J on page 361 of your textbook. That shows what you should have for problems C, D, and E. Raise your hand if you got everything right.

Note. From Engelmann, S., Carnine, D., Kelly, B., & Engelmann, O. (1996d). *Connecting Math Concepts: Level F, p. 348–349.* Columbus, OH: SRA/McGraw-Hill. Reproduced with permission of the McGraw-Hill Companies.

can be facilitated in two ways: (a) massed practice should be done until fluency and mastery are reached, and (b) systematic review should be incorporated. Dixon (1994) noted that systematic review should distribute review opportunities over time to contribute to long-term retention and automaticity of knowledge, accumulate information taught in review (after A and B are taught, A and B are reviewed together), and vary review items to promote generalization and transference.

Finally, progress monitoring procedures must take place at regular intervals. These procedures should focus on curricular objectives and should assess progress on what is actually being taught in the classroom. By knowing the specific skills that students need to master, strategies aimed at teaching those skills can be developed. An example of this type of procedure can be seen in Figure 4 (Engelmann, Carnine, Kelly, & Engelmann, 1996c, p. 22).

Figure 4

Example of CBM from Connecting Math Concepts: Level C, Teacher's Guide.

a. Open your workbook and find test 6.
   This is a test of things you've studied. You can earn as many as 20 points for doing well on the test. So work carefully.

b. Find part 1.
   You're going to write answers to problems. You'll have to move pretty fast.

c. Touch A.
   Here's the problem: 47 plus 10. Write the answer. √
   • Touch B.
   Listen: 63 plus 5. Write the answer. √
   • Touch C.
   Listen: 52 plus 4. Write the answer. √
   • Touch D.
   Listen: 29 plus 10. Write the answer. √

d. Find parts 2 and 3.
   You have 1 and a half minutes to write the answers for both parts 2 and 3. Get ready. Go.
   (Observe studdents, but do not give feedback.)
   • (After 1½ minutes, say:) Stop. Cross out the problems you didn't finish. √

e. (If students have difficulty reading items of instructions, read the material to them.)

f. Finish the rest of the test on your own. Raise your hand when you're finished.

Part 1
a. ___   c. ___
b. ___   d. ___

Part 2
a. 7 – 6 = ___   c. 9 – 6 = ___   e. 9 – 6 = ___
b. 11 – 6 = ___   d. 12 – 6 = ___   f. 10 – 6 = ___

Part 3

a. 5 ×1	b. 3 ×5	c. 2 ×5	d. 5 ×4	e. 5 ×5	f. 5 ×2	g. 4 ×5	h. 5 ×3

Part 4 Write the numerals.

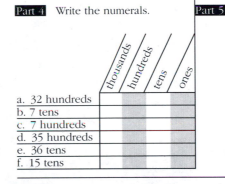

a. 32 hundreds
b. 7 tens
c. 7 hundreds
d. 35 hundreds
e. 36 tens
f. 15 tens

Part 5 Write the addition or substraction problem and the answer for each column. Then write the missing numbers in the table.

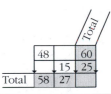

Part 6 Write a number family for each problem. Write the addition or subtraction problem and answer for each family.

a. You have □.
   You find 23.
   You end up with 97.

b. You have 206.
   You lose 13.
   You end up with □.

Part 7 Write the fractions.

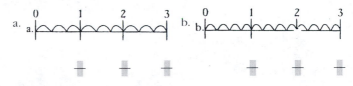

Part 8 Write the numbers you say when you count by nines.

9 ___ ___ ___ ___ ___ ___ ___ 90

Note. From Engelmann, S., Carnine, D., Kelly, B., & Engelmann, O. (1996c). *Connecting Math Concepts: Level C, teacher's guide, p. 22.* Columbus, OH: SRA/McGraw-Hill. Reproduced with permission of the McGraw-Hill Companies.

EFFECTIVE PRESENTATION TECHNIQUES. The second of three variables in effective instruction as noted by Stein et al. (1997) involves the use of effective teacher presentation techniques. These techniques involve maintaining student attention during group instruction and teaching to criterion. In order to maintain student attention, explanations should be brief and concise. Students should be given frequent opportunities to respond during instructional times (Paine, Radicchi, Rosellini, Deutchman, & Darch, 1983). Unison responding is one way to ensure all students are actively engaged in the learning process. This type of presentation technique requires the use of signals. To signal a unison response, the teacher gives directions; provides a thinking pause; and cues the response by pointing, tapping a pencil, or snapping her fingers, for example. Additionally, adequate pacing is needed. Pacing requires material to be presented in a lively manner and without hesitation by the teacher. Finally, seating arrangements should be considered. During large-group instruction, lower performing students should be seated at the front of the room to allow teachers to monitor their behavior more effectively. During small-group instruction, students should be seated in a semi-circle with lower performing or easily distracted students seated toward the middle of the group.

In addition to maintaining student attention, teachers should also teach to criterion. In order to ensure all students reach mastery, Stein et al. (1997) note that teachers must present a particular format until students are able to respond to every question or example in the format correctly. This step involves effective monitoring, error correction, and appropriate diagnosis and remediation of problems. Teaching to criterion is consistent with the Teaching Principle noted by the NCTM (2000b).

LOGICAL ORGANIZATION OF INSTRUCTION. The third variable in effective instruction as noted by Stein et al. (1997) is the logical organization of instruction. There are two primary methods to organize math instruction. One way involves a spiral-based curriculum design present in many constructivist basal math programs today. In this design, lessons focus on a single topic for a number of days. Students then revisit these topics in each successive year with greater depth. This method of curriculum design, often referred to as "teaching for exposure," allows a large number of topics to be covered briefly each year. According to Carnine (1990), the intent of the spiral curriculum is to add depth each year, but the practical result is the rapid, superficial coverage of a large number of topics each year. In fact, Porter (1989) found as much as

70% of math topics are given less than 30 min of instructional time each year.

A second way to organize math instruction is through the strand design present in Direct Instruction programs. This design includes concepts or "big ideas" that are organized around skill development strands allowing a few important topics to be covered in 5- to 10-min segments within the context of 30-min lessons. Carnine (1990) cited a number of advantages for organizing curricula around strands: (a) students are more easily engaged with a variety of topics within a single lesson, (b) strands make the sequencing of component concepts more manageable, and (c) lessons composed of several segments make cumulative introduction feasible.

Direct Instruction Math Programs

Direct Instruction (DI) programs are a strand-based approach to math instruction. They are based on the explicit or direct approach to teaching that consists of effective instructional design, effective presentation techniques, and a logical organization of instruction (as previously noted by Stein et al., 1997). *DISTAR Arithmetic I and II* (Engelmann & Carnine, 1975), *Corrective Mathematics* (Engelmann & Carnine, 1982), and *Connecting Math Concepts* (Engelmann et al., 1996a) are the three research-validated math programs published by Science Research Associates (SRA).

DISTAR ARITHMETIC I. DISTAR Arithmetic I consists of an initial placement test, 160 lessons, 140 take-home assignments, and 72 in-program mastery tests. This program is effective for students of any skill level from preschool through the primary grades. Students complete a placement test before they start the program. They are then placed into flexible skill groups. Lower performing students can complete the program in fewer than 200 school days. Higher performing students may complete the program in fewer than 108 school days. By skipping specific lessons, these students may progress as quickly as they can.

DISTAR ARITHMETIC II. DISTAR Arithmetic II consists of 160 lessons, 160 take-home assignments, three placement tests, and 15 in-program mastery tests. According to Engelmann and Carnine (1976),

> Children who have had 100 or more lessons of *DISTAR Arithmetic I* or a beginning arithmetic program other than *DISTAR* can successfully complete level two since placement tests and procedures for reviewing *DISTAR Arithmetic I* are built into the program. (p. 1)

As in *DISTAR Arithmetic I,* students complete a placement test before they start the program. They are then placed into flexible skill groups. Group membership changes based on student behavior on individual tests within daily lessons and in-program mastery tests. Table 3 shows a summary of the skill development strands for *DISTAR Arithmetic I and II.*

CORRECTIVE MATHEMATICS. Corrective Mathematics is designed for students in Grades 3 through postsecondary. The program may be used for remedial work or as a part of a developmental sequence. For example, students in Grades 4 through postsecondary can use the program for remediation if they have not yet mastered addition, subtraction, multiplication, and/or division. Students in Grades 3 through 6 who have mastered basic counting and symbol identification skills can use *Corrective Mathematics* to develop advanced addition, subtraction, multiplication, and/or division skills. The program

Table 3 *Summary of Skill Development Strands for* DISTAR Arithmetic I *and* II

Skill Development Strands	DISTAR I	DISTAR II
Rote counting	x	x
Matching	x	
Symbol identification	x	x
Cross-out game	x	
Symbol writing	x	
Pair relations	x	
Numerals and lines	x	
Equality	x	
Matching	x	
Addition	x	x
Algebra addition	x	x
Counting backward	x	x
Subtraction	x	
Dictation	x	
Facts	x	x
Story problems	x	x
Facts for symbol identification	x	
Problems in columns	x	x
Figuring out facts	x	
More or less	x	x
Written story problems	x	x
Ordinal counting	x	
Consolidation	x	
Fact derivation		x
Multiplication		x
Fraction operations		x
Length and weight measurement		x
Applications of operations		x
Negative numbers		x

consists of four basic modules (addition, subtraction, multiplication, division) and three supplemental modules (basic fractions; fractions, decimals, and percents; and ratios and equations). There are 65 lessons in the four basic modules, each with individual student worksheets. The supplemental basic fraction module includes 55 lessons; the fractions, decimals, and percents module contains 70 lessons; and the ratios and equations module includes 60 lessons. Each of the seven modules is accompanied by a minimum of 15 mastery tests as well as suggestions for remediation. Mastery tests measure students' acquisition of basic facts, operations, and story problems.

Generally, two modules may be taught per school year. The program also contains three provisions for accelerating higher performing students. First, each module contains a skipping schedule for students whose performance on mastery tests indicates accelerated progress. Second, teachers may also teach more than one lesson per day. Third, modules may be overlapped after students have completed lessons 45 or 50 of their current module.

There are two placement methods in *Corrective Mathematics*. First, teachers may administer the preskill test and the placement test that are included in each specific module. Second, teachers may administer a comprehensive placement test that surveys skills across all module areas. Table 4 shows a summary of the skill development strands for the addition, subtraction, multiplication, and division modules.

The supplementary math modules are designed to teach advanced mathematical skills. They may be taught sequentially or independently. The basic fractions module may be added to the fourth-grade curricula. The fractions, decimals, and percents module and the ratios and equations module may be added to the fifth- or sixth-grade curricula. Table 5 shows a summary of the skill development strands for the supplementary modules.

CONNECTING MATH CONCEPTS. Connecting Math Concepts (CMC) consists of seven modules or levels (*A–F* and *Bridge*). Concepts covered in *CMC* are distributed across many successive lessons to allow important connections to be made and to provide ample time to become competent at each strategy. According to Engelmann et al. (1996c), *CMC* is particularly effective with students who are at risk in mathematics. *CMC Levels A–D* consist of 120 lessons, a placement test, and a mastery test every 10th lesson. *Level A* is designed for first grade and builds on counting experiences within a variety of contexts.

Table 4   *Summary of Skill Development Strands for* Corrective Mathematics *Basic Math Modules*

Skill Development Strands	Addition	Subtraction	Multiplication	Division
Facts	x	x	x	x
Place value	x	x	x	x
Operations	x	x	x	x
Story problems	x	x	x	x

Level B is designed for second grade and makes connections between mathematical concepts and real-life situations. *Level C* is designed for third grade and places a stronger emphasis on higher order thinking skills. *Level D* is designed for fourth grade and extends students' mathematical understanding by building on the foundation of *Levels A–C.*

CMC Level E contains 125 lessons, a placement test, and a mastery test every 10th lesson. It is designed for fifth grade. Extending the concepts and skills taught in earlier levels, students analyze and solve increasingly complex problems.

The Bridge module falls between *Level E* and *Level F* and can be used for older students performing at a fifth- or sixth-grade level who have not been through *CMC Level E* and who have passed *The Bridge* placement test. It may be used as a stand-alone course in preparation for a basic pre-algebra course or, preferably, in combination with *CMC Level F* for a more complete mathematical foundation. *The Bridge* contains 70 lessons and a mastery test every 10th lesson.

CMC Level F contains 100 lessons and a mastery test every 10th lesson. It is designed for sixth grade. A placement test is not included due to the assump-

tion that students in *Level F* have either successfully completed *Level E* or have completed *The Bridge. Level F* prepares students for success in higher math. Table 6 shows a summary of the skill development strands for *CMC.*

In each of the seven levels of *CMC,* students are provided with independent work for each lesson. Teachers are provided with recommendations for remediation when students are found to be experiencing difficulties as indicated by results on mastery tests. *Structure of DI Math Programs*

DISTAR Arithmetic I and II, Corrective Mathematics, and *CMC* are structured through the use of tracks, formats, and tasks.

TRACKS. Tracks (also called skill development strands) consist of major skills or strategies. An example of a track from *DISTAR Arithmetic I* is Written Story Problems (Lessons 140–159). According to Engelmann and Carnine (1975), the purpose of this track is to teach students to solve simple, written story problems independently.

In keeping with the belief that necessary preskills must be taught prior to their use in a composite strategy, the following prerequisite skills for the

Table 5   *Summary of Skill Development Strands for* Corrective Mathematics *Supplementary Modules*

Skill development strands	Basic Fractions	Fractions, Decimals, & Percents	Ratios & Equations
Addition of fractions & whole numbers	x	x	
Subtraction of fractions & whole numbers	x	x	
Multiplication of fractions & whole numbers	x	x	
Write mixed numbers for fractions	x		
Find equivalent fractions	x		
Addition & subtraction of mixed numbers		x	
Multiplication & division of mixed numbers		x	
Reducing improper fractions		x	
Writing decimals or percents for fractions		x	
Writing fractions or percents for decimals		x	
Writing fractions or decimals for percents		x	
Finding ratios			x
Solving rate & distance problems			x
Using basic problem solving strategy for word problems			x
Using basic problem solving strategy for algebra problems			x

Table 6 *Summary of Skill Development Strands for* Connecting Math Concepts

Skill Development Strands	Level A	Level B	Level C	Level D	Level E	Bridge	Level F
Counting	x	x					
Symbols	x						
More/less/equal	x		x				
Addition/subtraction	x						
Place value	x	x	x	x	x		
Problem solving	x	x	x	x	x	x	x
Word problems	x	x	x	x	x	x	
Application: money	x						
Following directions			x				
Addition & subtraction facts							
Number relationships		x	x		x	x	x
Number family tables				x	x	x	
Measurement			x				x
Column addition		x	x				
Column subtraction		x	x	x			
Mental arithmetic		x	x	x	x		
Money		x	x				
Multiplication		x				x	
Geometry: identifying shapes, finding perimeter & area		x		x		x	
Tables		x					
Addition & subtraction number families			x				
Multiplication & division facts			x	x			
Column multiplication			x	x	x		
Division with remainders			x	x	x	x	
Estimation			x			x	
Calculator skills			x	x	x		
Equation concepts			x				
Analyzing data: tables			x				
Fractions			x	x	x	x	
Coordinate system			x	x	x	x	x
Graphs			x				x
Area			x				x
Volume			x		x		x
Time		x	x				
Statistics: range			x				
Whole number operations				x	x	x	x
Equations & relationships				x			
Decimals				x		x	x
Percents						x	
Ratios & proportions				x		x	
Ratio tables						x	x
Fraction number families				x	x	x	
Fraction operations							x
Probability				x			x
Probability geometry				x	x		
Operational relationships					x	x	x
Rounding					x		
Whole number properties					x		
Mixed number operations					x		x
Decimal operations					x		
Circles					x	x	
Angles & lines					x	x	
Geometry facts							x
Signed numbers							x
Exponents							x

written story problem track are (a) applying the appropriate strategy and solving problems in addition (introduced in Lesson 51), algebra addition (introduced in Lesson 61), and subtraction (introduced in Lesson 83); (b) writing arithmetic statements that are dictated by the teacher (introduced in Lesson 84); and (c) translating verbal story problems into written arithmetic statements (introduced in Lesson 102). Throughout each track, focus changes from teacher modeling to guided practice to independent practice.

FORMATS. Engelmann and Carnine (1975) define formats as patterns of teaching steps repeated in a number of successive lessons. A format for Counting Events and Objects from *DISTAR Arithmetic I* appears in Figure 5. Formats are maintained for three or more lessons before the focus shifts from teacher modeling to guided practice.

TASKS. A task is created by inserting a new set of numbers into a format pattern in which the wording remains unchanged. For example, the format for teaching symbol identification of the number 4 is shown in Figure 6. Notice how the wording is changed within the same format pattern to teach symbol identification of the number 2 (also seen in Figure 6). Tasks are presented in the simplest manner possible to eliminate confusion and follow a specific sequence to ensure mastery of the five program objectives. Subsequent tasks requiring similar procedures are taught in order to encourage generalization.

How DI Math Programs Meet NCTM's Principles for Improving Math Instruction

NCTM's principles for improving math instruction (NCTM, 2000b) can be met through each of the DI math programs. First, NCTM's *Equity Principle* calls for excellence in mathematics education with equally high expectations and strong support for all students. NCTM discourages "tracking" which is defined as a long-term, often permanent placement within an academic track based on perceived mathematical abilities. DI math programs use flexible skill grouping based on current levels of performance as determined by daily progress monitoring. Such monitoring consists of observations during lessons, performance on take-home assignments, and performance on in-program mastery tests. Group membership changes as dictated by individual student performance. In the *Equity Principle*, NCTM strongly encourages that expectations be the

---

Figure 5

Example of a format from **DISTAR Arithmetic I.**

TASK 4 COUNTING EVENTS AND OBJECTS Children Clap as You Count

Emphasice words in **boldface.**

Group Activity

    a. You will count and clap, pausing one second between numbers.
        Let's play a clapping game. Every time I count,
        I'm going to clap. Get ready.
        One...two...three...four.

    b. You will pause two seconds between numbers as you count.
        Your turn. I'm going to count. **You're** going to clap.
        (Pause.) Get ready. One...two...three...four. Stop.
        (The children clap as you count; they do not count.)

To correct   If the children have trouble coordinating their clapping with your counting, physically guide their hands to help them clap.

---

    c. Repeat *b* until the response is firm.
Individual Test
    Call on several children for *b.*

Note. From Engelmann, S., & Carnine, D. (1975). *DISTAR Arithmetic I: Teacher's guide, p. 22.* Columbus, OH: SRA/Macmillan/McGraw-Hill. Reproduced with permission of the McGraw-Hill Companies.

Figure 6

Example of two tasks illustrating how a new set of numbers is inserted into a format pattern, taken from DISTAR Arithmetic I.

TASK 2 SYMBOL IDENTIFICATION
Introducing a New Symbol

When you **point** to a symbol, hold your finger an inch or two above the page. **Touch** with a definite motion just below the symbol.
Emphasize words in **boldface.**

Group Activity
Do *a, b,* and *c.*

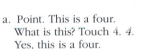

a. Point. This is a four.
   What is this? Touch 4. *4.*
   Yes, this is a four.

b. Point. Is this a four?
   Touch the dog. *No.*
   To correct: This is
   not a four.
   Is this a four? *No.*

c. Point. Is this a four?
   Touch 4. *Yes.*
   To correct: Repeat *a,* then *c.*

Repeat *a, b,* and *c* in random order until responses are firm.
d. When I touch it, tell me what it is.
e. Point to *a* or *c.* Pause. Get ready. Touch.
   Touch *a* and *c* in random order until responses are firm.
f. Randomly touch *a, b,* and *c.*
Individual Test
   Call on some children to identify two symbols.

TASK 2 SYMBOL IDENTIFICATION
Introducing a New Symbol

When you **point** to a symbol, hold your finger an inch or two above the page. **Touch** with a definite motion just below the symbol.
Emphasize words in **boldface.**

Group Activity
Do *a, b,* and *c.*

a. Point. This is a two.
   What is this? Touch 2. *2.*
   Yes, this is a two.

b. Point. Is this a two?
   Touch 4. *No.*
   To correct: This is
   not a two.
   Is this a two? *No.*

c. Point. Is this a two?
   Touch 2. *Yes.*
   To correct: Repeat *a,* then *c.*

Repeat *a, b,* and *c* in random order until responses are firm.
d. When I touch it, tell me what it is.
e. Point to *a* or *c.* Pause. Get ready. Touch.
   Touch *a* and *c* in random order until responses are firm.
f. Randomly touch *a, b,* and *c.*
Individual Test
   Call on some children to identify two symbols.

Note. From Engelmann, S., & Carnine, D. (1975). *DISTAR Arithmetic I: Teacher's guide, pp. 108, 133.* Columbus, OH: SRA/Macmillan/McGraw-Hill. Reproduced with permission of the McGraw-Hill Companies.

same for all students. DI math programs are based on specific performance objectives which all students must master as they progress through the program.

Second, NCTM's *Curriculum Principle* states that a curriculum is more than a collection of activities; it must be coherent, focused on important mathematics, and well articulated across the grades. DI math programs meet this principle by using a strand design. In this design, lessons are organized around concepts or "big ideas." According to Dixon (1994), big ideas make it possible for students to learn the

most and learn it most efficiently. Specifically, DI math programs are designed to guide students' learning of basic operations, strategies, and applications to more complex applications throughout each level and throughout each grade. Furthermore, NCTM notes that extensive field-testing should be conducted before school districts select curricular mathematics materials. DI programs have been implemented and researched in a wide variety of settings for over 30 years (Adams & Engelmann, 1996).

Third, NCTM's *Teaching Principle* states that teachers should understand what students know and need to learn and then challenge and support them to learn it well. NCTM encourages teachers to reflect on and improve their lessons with the support of colleagues within a peer coaching model. This model allows teachers to plan for maximum student success carefully. DI math programs meet this principle by providing extensive preservice training for teachers to ensure appropriate implementation and effective instructional delivery. After training, teachers are provided with coaches who conduct observations to determine areas for improvement. Coaches and teachers then work together to ensure maximum student and teacher success. According to NCTM, teachers should also be able to predict what students will do when presented with particular problems and tasks. DI preservice training, program guides, and teacher presentation books offer precorrective strategies to minimize commonly anticipated errors. DI math lesson formats also contain specifically prescribed error correction procedures; an example of this was shown in Figure 5.

Fourth, NCTM's *Learning Principle* states that students must learn mathematics with understanding, actively building new knowledge from experience and prior knowledge. NCTM recommends that elementary students should study mathematics from well-prepared teachers for at least 1 hr a day. An example of how DI math programs meet this standard can be found in *DISTAR Arithmetic I* and *II*. The teacher presents daily group instruction for 30–35 min, providing both modeling and guided practice. Students spend 20–30 min (or more, if necessary) completing independent seatwork. In DI math programs, after necessary preskills have been mastered, students also complete take-home work for added independent practice. DI math programs answer NCTM's recommendation for well-prepared teachers by using predesigned instructional formats. Teacher preparation of lessons is kept to a minimum thereby reserving valuable time and energy for focusing on student performance. Another major concern of NCTM is that students may become increasingly disengaged in mathematics instruction. DI math programs address this concern in two ways. First, higher skilled students are allowed to move as quickly through each program as necessary. In fact, Vreeland et al. (1994) found that two groups of academically talented students, who were taught using *CMC,* made gains of approximately two grade levels in 1 year on the Kaufman Test of Educational Achievement—Comprehensive Form (KTEA—C). Second, because DI math programs are strand-based, the multitopic, fast-paced formats keep students focused and motivated.

Further, the NCTM encourages conceptual understanding and problem solving skills by actively building new knowledge from experience and prior knowledge. In DI math programs, strategies are taught, rather than rote skills, in a specified order to promote generalization from previously mastered skills to new situations. According to Carnine and Engelmann (1990), explicitly taught strategies prepare students to see the total structure of a problem. DI math lessons are organized around skill development tracks or big ideas. These big ideas are introduced in small steps from one lesson to the next within each track. As concepts are mastered through massed practice, they are continuously reviewed. Similarly, the strand design of DI math programs teaches students to differentiate between situations which may appear to require the same strategic solution, when in fact, they may not. This combination of massed practice and cumulative review allows students to maintain prior knowledge while actively building new knowledge of important math concepts and strategies.

Fifth, NCTM's *Assessment Principle* states that assessment should support the learning of important mathematics and furnish useful information to both teachers and students. DI math programs address this principle by providing frequent in-program mastery tests to allow teachers to make daily decisions about individual students' progress. Additionally, with students and educators being penalized for low test scores on nationally normed achievement tests, the issue of "teaching to the test" becomes a great concern. DI math programs have been shown to have positive effects on norm-referenced test scores. Specifically, Brent and DiObilda (1993) found similar scores between DI math students and students who were taught using a curriculum deliberately aligned with districtwide standardized assessments. NCTM also suggests that perhaps multiple forms of assessment may offer more useful information in monitoring student progress. DI math programs provide several different forms of assessment including in-program mastery tests at frequent intervals, take-home assignments, and fact games.

Finally, NCTM's *Technology Principle* states that technology should influence the skills taught and enhance students' learning. Therefore, technology should be used to support the learning of mathematics, not the learning of technology. In so doing, NCTM recommends that technology be embedded in the mathematics program, rather than provided as a supplemental element. Concurrently, the National Assessment of Educational Progress (2001) report stated that eighth graders whose teachers reported that they permitted unrestricted use of calculators in class had higher average scores in 2000 than did students whose teachers restricted calculator use. In *CMC Levels C–F* students learn to use calculators to solve increasingly complex operations. For example, in *CMC Level C,* students use calculators to solve addition, subtraction, multiplication, and fraction problems. In *CMC Level F,* students use calculators to solve division problems that do not have whole-number answers and problems that multiply a fraction by a whole number or decimal. The use of the calculator in DI math programs is to support students' learning of the fundamental operations (i.e., addition, subtraction, multiplication, division) and to support their skills in using these tools when solving word problems.

Research Synthesis
on DI Mathematics Programs

The purpose of this synthesis was to survey the studies conducted using DI Mathematics Programs (SRA). Studies including *DISTAR I* and *II, Corrective Mathematics,* and *CMC* were selected using the First Search, ERIC, PsycINFO, Education ABS, and Pro-Quest databases. Descriptors included the following: Direct Instruction, *DISTAR Arithmetic, DISTAR Arithmetic I, DISTAR Arithmetic II,* direct instruction, direct teaching, direct verbal instruction, explicit instruction, mathematics instruction, *Corrective Mathematics,* and *Connecting Math Concepts.* Ancestral searches of reference lists were used to identify other possible research articles. Also, hand searches were done in the following peer-reviewed journals: *Effective School Practices, Journal of Direct Instruction,* and *Education and Treatment of Children.* Research articles in peer-reviewed journals were included for review. Articles published before 1990 were not included in this review. A total of 12 studies were analyzed in this review.

DIRECT INSTRUCTION META-ANALYSIS. Adams and Engelmann (1996) conducted a meta-analysis of DI programs including *DISTAR Arithmetic I* and *II, Corrective Mathematics, CMC,* and other DI programs. Included studies were required to have the following elements: means and standard deviations of groups, the use of a suitable comparison group, and random selection of participants to groups. Thirty-four out of 37 studies involved the active intervention of DI programs. Three follow-up studies were not included in the statistical analysis but were reviewed in a separate chapter. In a sample polling of means, 87% of the studies favored DI programs,

12% favored non-DI programs, and 1% found scores to be the same. In a sample polling of statistically significant outcomes, 64% found statistically significant differences in favor of DI programs. Finally, in a summary of the statistical analysis of math results, an effect size of 1.11 in favor of DI math programs was found in 33 of the comparisons (those studies that included a math component).

DISTAR ARITHMETIC. Table 7 shows one study using *DISTAR Arithmetic I.* Young, Baker, and Martin (1990) compared *DISTAR Arithmetic I* to a teacher-developed discrimination learning theory (DLT) program based on the first 60 lessons of *DISTAR Arithmetic I.* Participants included five students with intellectual disabilities; each scored between 35–54 on the Wechsler Intelligence Scale for Children—Revised (WISC—R). All participants had articulation problems (responses were limited to two- to three-word utterances). During the baseline phase, *DISTAR Arithmetic I* was implemented according to the program script. During baseline, average performance on mastery tests ranged from 18% to 73%, while average academic engaged time ranged from 18% to 31%. During the DLT phase, average performance on mastery tests ranged from 69% to 96%, while average academic engaged time ranged from 56% to 84%. It was further determined over 5 days during a 5-week maintenance probe that both mastery scores and academic engaged time remained higher than baseline rates. As a result, the author concluded that the match-to-sample format of the DLT phase was an effective adaptation of *DISTAR Arithmetic I* in teaching math skills to students with articulation problems.

CORRECTIVE MATHEMATICS. Three studies were found using the *Corrective Mathematics* (*CM*) program (see Table 7). First, Parsons, Marchand-Martella, Waldron-Soler, Martella, and Lignugaris/Kraft (in press) examined the use of *CM* in a secondary general education classroom for students struggling in math as delivered by peer tutors. Ten students were assigned to the learner group based on referrals by a school counselor. All had failed the lowest level of math available at that school. Nine students were recruited by the *CM* teacher, school counselors, and other high school math teachers to serve as peer tutors. All participants were pre- and posttested using the Calculation and Applied Problems subtest of the Woodcock Johnson—Revised: Test of Achievement (WJ—R). After 60 instructional days, the authors found that both learners and peer tutors experienced posttest gains in one or both areas of the WJ—R subtests.

Table 7 Program Comparison Summary Information for Investigations Involving DI Math

Reference	Program	Participants/ Characteristics	Research Design	Dependent Variable(s)	Results
Adams & Engelman (1996)	DI meta-analysis	37 studies	Meta-analysis	Overall program effectiveness	64% of studies found statistically significant outcomes in favor of DI programs. Statistical analysis of studies including math found an effect size of 1.11 in favor of DI math programs.
Young, Baker, & Martin (1990)	DISTAR Arithmetic I vs. teacher-developed DLT program based on the first 60 lessons of the DISTAR Arithmetic I program	5 students with mild mental retardation & articulation problems	Multiple baseline across subjects	DISTAR Arithmetic I placement test, teacher-designed test (including: counting, matching, selecting, numerosity, writing, & equality), & academic engaged time	Math skills scores were higher on teacher-designed mastery tests during DLT phase and across 5 days at a 5-week maintenance probe. Academic engaged time higher during DLT phase.
Glang, Singer, Cooley, & Tish (1991)	CM	8-year-old with traumatic brain injury	Multiple baseline across content areas	Math facts & story problems	Math fact rate increased but remained lower than average third graders. Story problem accuracy increased from 11.4% correct to 91.25% correct during instruction.
Parsons, Marchand-Martella, Waldron-Soler, Martella, & Lignugaris/Kraft (in press)	CM	19 students: 10 learners & 9 peer tutors	One-group pretest–posttest	WJ—R Math Calculation & Applied Math Problems subtests	Both learners and peer tutors improved in math calculation & applied math problems.
Sommers (1995)	CM	112 sixth, seventh, & eighth graders at risk for academic failure	One-group pretest–posttest	Pretest: Stanford Math Posttest: Key Math Diagnostic	Averaged 1.2 months gained per month of instruction.
Brent & DiObilda (1993)	CMC vs. Holt Math Series	189 students entering first grade: experimental group consisted of 23 stable & 76 mobile students; control group consisted of 27 stable & 63 mobile students	Nonequivalent control group	CTBS & Metropolitan Achievement Test (math subtests included: concepts/applications, computation, & total math). MAT was given to stable students only (math subtests included: computation, concepts/applications, problem solving, & total math).	Stable & mobile DI groups received scores similar to the stable control group on the CTBS, while the mobile control group scored significantly lower on the concepts subtest. The DI group scored significantly higher than the control group on all areas of MAT (only administered to stable students). Mobility had a negative impact on all students. However, mobility was more detrimental to the control groups, as evidenced by CTBS scores.

Study	Comparison	Subjects	Design	Measures	Results
Crawford & Snider (2000)	*CMC* vs. *Invitation to Mathematics*	15 fourth graders	Pretest—posttest control group	NAT: computation, concepts, & problem solving on *CMC*; CBM based on *SF*; & multiplication facts	*CMC* group made greater gains than the previous year on both CBMs and on multiplication facts test. No significant NAT posttest results noted.
McKenzie, Marchand-Martella, Martella, & Tso (in press)	*CMC Level K*	16 preschool students with & without disabilities	One-group pretest–posttest	Pre- & posttest measures included the BDI & the *CMC Level A* placement test	The BDI Total Cognitive score showed a combined effect size of .52 for students with and without disabilities. Combined scores on the *CMC Level A* placement test increased from a mean of 4.31 on the pretest to a mean of 7.69 on the posttest.
Snider & Crawford (1996)	*CMC* vs. *Invitation to Mathematics*	46 fourth graders	Pretest–posttest control group	NAT: computation, concepts, & problem solving on *CMC*, CBM based on *SF*; and multiplication facts tests	*CMC* group scored higher than the *SF* group on NAT computation subtest. *CMC* group scored significantly higher than the *SF* group on all three curriculum-based tests.
Tarver & Jung (1995)	*CMC* vs. *MTW/CGI*	119 students entering the first grade	Nonequivalent control group	CTBS mathematics concepts and applications, computation, & total math (averaged from the two subtests)	End of first grade CTBS results: *CMC* group scored higher on computation and total math but not on concepts and applications. End of second grade CTBS results: *CMC* group scored higher than the control group on all posttest measures.
Vreeland et al. (1994)	*CMC* vs. *Addison-Wesley Mathematics*	5 third-grade classrooms & 4 fifth-grade classrooms	Nonequivalent control group	ITBS Total Math (consisting of three subtests: computation, concepts, & problem solving); KTEA—C: calculation & applications subtests (Applications subtest given to only six students.) CBM problem solving test based on *CMC* & *Addison-Wesley*.	No significant change in percentile rank for *CMC* groups on the ITBS. The percentile rank change for the control groups was −15%. *CMC* third graders made gains on the KTEA—C, while no gains were noted for *CMC* fifth graders. No KTEA—C scores were available for the control groups. Academically talented third and fifth graders made better than average gains on the KTEA—C.
Wellington (1994)	*CMC*	16 first-grade classrooms & 16 fourth-grade classrooms	Nonequivalent control group	Pretest: *CMC* placement test; posttests: CBM based on *CMC* and traditional basal; district-designed mastery test	One *CMC* first-grade group and one control group showed significant improvement on the posttest. Six *CMC* fourth-grade groups showed statistical improvements on the posttest. District-designed mastery tests showed a decrease in the rate of mastery as grade levels increased.

Second, Glang, Singer, Cooley, and Tish (1991) assessed the efficacy of *CM* in teaching math skills to an 8-year-old student with traumatic brain injury. In this study, the student was also instructed using *Corrective Reading Comprehension (Level A)* to improve his reasoning skills. Instruction took place twice a week over a period of 6 weeks. After 12 hrs of instruction, the authors found that the student's math fact rate and story problem accuracy improved.

Finally, Sommers (1991) examined the effects of a comprehensive DI program in improving the overall performance of at-risk middle school students over a 2-year period. *CM* multiplication, division, basic fractions, fractions-decimals-percents, and ratios and equations mathematics modules were used in conjunction with a variety of DI reading, spelling, and writing programs. Students also used a variety of supplemental material including: self-chosen reading materials, *Journeys* (Harcourt Brace Jovanovich), *Warriner's English Grammar and Composition, DLM Growth in Grammar* workbooks, and *Heath Mathematics*. In math measures, students made average gains of 1.2 months per month of instruction (as noted by the author).

All three studies examined students with very different characteristics across various settings. In each study, authors found *CM* to be effective in increasing math skills. However, it should be noted that multiple treatment interference is a threat to the external validity of the study conducted by Sommers (1991). For this reason, it is difficult to clearly establish a causal relationship between DI programs and increases in student achievement.

CONNECTING MATH CONCEPTS. Seven studies were found using *CMC* (see Table 7). First, Snider and Crawford (1996) included 46 fourth graders who were randomly assigned to two general education classrooms. One teacher used *CMC, Level D;* the other teacher used *Invitation to Mathematics (SF)* by Scott Foresman. *CMC* students scored higher than the *SF* students on the Computation subtest of the National Achievement Test (NAT). In addition, *CMC* students scored significantly higher on both the multiplication facts test and on curriculum-based measures based on *CMC* and *SF*.

Second, in a follow-up study by Crawford and Snider (2000) both teachers used *CMC.* After 1 year of using *CMC,* the teacher who had used *SF* had students who made greater gains than the previous year on both the multiplication facts tests and on both curriculum-based measures. No significant

posttest differences were noted on the NAT subtests or Total Test scores. The authors cited several possible reasons for the lack of significant pre- to posttest gains. Some of these included (a) less than optimal implementation of *CMC*, (b) lack of alignment between the NAT Concepts and Problem Solving subtests and either curriculum, and (c) performance on norm-referenced tests are more highly correlated to reading comprehension scores than with computation scores. Although the NAT results did not reach significance, the positive results shown by the remaining data prompted the districtwide implementation of *CMC.*

Third, Tarver and Jung (1995) compared *CMC* to a program that combined *Math Their Way (MTW)* and Cognitively Guided Instruction (CGI). One hundred nineteen students entering first grade were assigned to five classrooms. One experimental classroom used *CMC,* while four control classrooms used *MTW/CGI.* The study took place over 2 years. At the end of first grade, students were posttested using the Comprehensive Test of Basic Skills—Mathematics (CTBS—M). *CMC* students scored significantly higher than the control group on Computation and Total Math but not on the Concepts and Applications subtest. At the end of second grade, *CMC* students scored higher than the control group on all posttest measures as well as on an experimenter-constructed math attitudes survey. Tarver and Jung noted positive effects for both low and high performing students.

Fourth, Brent and DiObilda (1993) compared the effects of DI curricula to those of traditional basal curricula in Camden, New Jersey. At that time, Camden was considered to have the highest percentage of children who lived in poverty in the country. The mobility rate in Camden was also higher than the national average. For that reason, this study also examined the effects of each curriculum with stable and mobile urban children. In an attempt to improve their standardized test scores, school officials had previously aligned their schools' traditional basal programs to the Comprehensive Test of Basic Skills—Form U, Level D (CTBS). This study compared *CMC* with the *Holt Math Series.* Dependent measures included the CTBS and the Metropolitan Achievement Test (MAT). CTBS total math scores were similar among stable and mobile DI groups as well as stable control groups. Both stable and mobile DI groups scored higher than the control groups on the CTBS computation subtest, while the stable control group scored higher on the concepts subtest. On the MAT, administered to stable students only, the DI group scored significantly higher than the control group on all subtests. Overall, mobility was found to have a negative impact on student achievement in both the DI and the control groups. However, scores on the CTBS indicated that mobility was more detrimental to the control groups.

Fifth, McKenzie, Marchand-Martella, Martella, and Tso (in press) examined the effects of *CMC Level K* (prepublication copy; Engelmann & Becker, 1995) on preschoolers with and without developmental delays. Participants included 16 preschoolers who attended school 5 days per week. Each preschooler completed all 30 lessons contained in *CMC Level K*. Students were pre- and posttested using the Battelle Developmental Inventory (BDI) and a curriculum-based placement test (*CMC Level A*). Results showed an effect size of .61 for preschoolers without developmental delays and .54 for preschoolers with developmental delays on the BDI. The placement test for *CMC Level A* consists of 10 questions and was given to all preschoolers. Scores for preschoolers without developmental delays increased from a mean of 4.55 correct on the pretest to a mean of 7.9 on the posttest; scores for preschoolers with developmental delays increased from a mean of 3.8 correct on the pretest to a mean of 7.2 on the posttest.

Sixth, Vreeland et al. (1994) compared *CMC* to the *Addison-Wesley Mathematics* program. Participants included 5 third-grade classrooms and 4 fifth-grade classrooms. *CMC* third and fifth graders scored higher than the control group on CBM posttest measures, based on *CMC* and *Addison-Wesley*. *CMC* third graders showed little percentile rank changes on the ITBS, while the third-grade control group's percentile rank change was −15%. No percentile rank changes on the ITBS were noted for *CMC* fifth graders. No ITBS scores were available for fifth-grade control groups. Results of the KTEA—C posttest revealed that, at the end of third grade, *CMC* third graders scored at or above the fourth-grade level. No pre- to posttest gains were noted for *CMC* fifth graders. No KTEA—C posttest scores were available for the fifth-grade control groups. This study also examined the effects of *CMC* with academically talented students. For academically talented third graders, KTEA—C posttest scores showed mean grade equivalents of 5.7 on the math calculation subtest and 6.1 on the math applications subtest. For academically talented fifth graders, KTEA—C posttest scores showed mean grade equivalents of 8.0 on the math calculation subtest and 8.5 on the math applications subtest. Overall, results were positive enough to guide the school officials' decision to use *CMC* in many of its first- through sixth-grade

classrooms. In a 1-year follow-up study, 12 classrooms, grades first through sixth, used *CMC Levels A–E*. Posttest results indicated that *CMC* students experienced gains, particularly in the higher levels of the program. These results, combined with positive teacher and parent reports, led to the use of *CMC* in nearly all first- through sixth-grade classrooms the following year.

Finally, Wellington (1994) examined the effectiveness of *CMC* for a period of 1 year in a socio-economically and ethnologically diverse school district. All 8 of the district's elementary schools participated in the study. One first-grade classroom and 1 fourth-grade classroom per school served as experimental groups. First- and fourth-grade comparison groups were also chosen from each school. The pretest consisted of the *CMC* placement test, while the posttest consisted of a teacher-designed CBM based on *CMC* and the traditional basal used by the comparison groups. Results showed statistically significant (>.05 level) differences among posttest scores for two out of the eight first-grade groups: one in favor of the *CMC* group and one in favor of the comparison group. Fourth-grade results showed statistically significant differences in favor of six out of the eight *CMC* groups. The author stated that the narrower scope of material at the first-grade level as compared to the breadth of concepts at the fourth-grade level may account for the poor first-grade results. A district-designed mastery test was also administered to first through fifth graders at the end of the school year. The results indicated that the rate of mastery (defined as 70%) declined at the higher grade levels. The results of this test combined with posttest results compelled the school district to implement *CMC* districtwide in first through fifth grades.

All seven studies found positive results when *CMC* was used. Three of the seven studies (i.e., Brent & DiObilda, 1993; McKenzie et al., in press; Vreeland et al., 1994) examined three varied populations. Brent and DiObilda specifically found *CMC* to have a positive effect on students from highly transient, low-income, minority families in an urban community. McKenzie et al. found *CMC Level K* to have positive effects on a diverse group of preschoolers that included those with and without developmental delays. Finally, Vreeland et al. found *CMC* to have positive effects for both general education and gifted students. It should also be noted that the results from three of the seven studies (i.e., Crawford & Snider, 2000; Snider & Crawford, 1996; Wellington, 1994) led to the large-scale adoption of *CMC*.

SUMMARY. In all, 12 studies published since 1990 were found using DI math programs. The majority (11 out of 12) of these found DI math programs to be effective in improving math skills in a variety of settings with a variety of students. One study (Young et al., 1990) showed positive results for a DLT adaptation based on *DISTAR Arithmetic I* rather than *DISTAR Arithmetic I* in its original format.

Future Directions for Research

Recent national and international assessments have indicated the need to implement research validated math curricula in our schools. The NCTM responded to this need by publishing its *Principles and Standards for School Mathematics* (NCTM, 2000b). These principles and standards are recommended to influence the development and selection of high quality math curricula. The research included in this summary contributed positive evidence for the use of the direct or explicit approach to math instruction using these principles and standards. However, a number of implications for future research exist.

POPULATIONS. Direct Instruction curricula are often mistakenly associated for use primarily with students with special needs (i.e., Adams & Engelmann, 1996; Schieffer, Marchand-Martella, Martella, Simonsen, & Waldron-Soler, 2002). However, 7 out of 11 studies (meta-analysis excluded; i.e., Brent & DiObilda, 1993; Crawford & Snider, 2000; Parsons et al., in press; Snider & Crawford, 1996; Sommers, 1991; Tarver & Jung, 1995; Vreeland et al., 1994; Wellington, 1994) examined the effectiveness of DI math programs on general education students. Two out of 11 studies (i.e., Glang et al., 1991; Young et al., 1990) examined the effectiveness of DI math programs with students with disabilities. One study (McKenzie et al., in press) examined the effectiveness of DI math programs on a group of students that included those with and without developmental delays. In their DI meta-analysis, Adams and Engelmann (1996) calculated the average effect size per study according to general education and special education and found similar effect sizes for both groups (.82 and .90, respectively). Further, Vreeland et al. (1994) found grade-level gains of approximately 2 years for two groups of academically talented students using *CMC*. These results indicate the need for future examination of the effects of DI math programs based on specific learner characteristics (e.g., emotional and behavioral disabilities, attention-deficit disorder, at-risk or incarcerated youth, gifted learners).

EXPERIMENTAL ANALYSIS. In reviewing the research on DI math programs, several threats to internal and external validity were found. Selection is an issue in many of the studies due to a lack of random selection of participants (i.e., Brent & DiObilda, 1993; Glang et al., 1991; McKenzie et al., in press; Parsons et al., in press; Sommers, 1991; Tarver & Jung, 1995; Wellington, 1994; Young et al., 1990). Two studies, (i.e., Crawford & Snider, 2000; Snider & Crawford, 1996) attempted to assess group equivalence and randomly assign participants. Future studies should include random selection of participants from the target population, random assignment to groups, and determination of group equivalence.

DEPENDENT VARIABLES AND MEASURES. A wide variety of norm-referenced tests were used to assess math skills (e.g., applied math, basic facts, computation, concepts, problem-solving). Six of the 12 studies (i.e., Crawford & Snider, 2000; Glang et al., 1991; Snider & Crawford, 1996; Vreeland et al., 1994; Wellington, 1994; Young et al., 1990) used CBM to determine students' level of math performance within the local curriculum. Only 4 of the 12 studies (i.e., Brent & DiObilda, 1993; Crawford & Snider, 2000; Snider & Crawford, 1996; Vreeland et al., 1994) reported using districtwide assessments as dependent measures. Our current standing on national and international assessments indicates that future research should include studies that use district and statewide assessments as dependent measures.

Two studies (i.e., Sommers, 1991; Vreeland et al., 1994) reported results as grade-level gains. According to Cohen and Spenciner (1998) and McLoughlin and Lewis (2001), such ordinal scale data should be interpreted with caution. Grade-level gains can be easily misinterpreted because the intervals in grade equivalents do not represent equal units of measurement. Therefore, according to Cohen and Spenciner, a grade-level gain of 1.0 is only representative of students who are in the average range for their grade (failing to account for individual differences). Future researchers should refrain from reporting ordinal scale data, such as age- and grade-equivalents; means cannot be calculated and, at best, only pretest medians and posttest medians (without mathematically manipulating differences) should be noted (if used at all).

FIDELITY OF IMPLEMENTATION DATA. Inherent to the design of DI programs is the use of scripted formats and training opportunities. According to Adams and Engelmann (1996), the rationale for these scripted presentations is that if teachers present an adequate set of examples with clear, consistent wording, students will learn the material with less confusion. The delivery of these programs is a key factor in their effectiveness. However, in many of the studies investigated, verification of the independent variable and experimenter effects are concerns. Seven studies provided information describing program implementation (i.e., Crawford & Snider, 2000; Glang et al., 1991; McKenzie et al., in press; Snider & Crawford, 1996; Tarver & Jung, 1995; Vreeland et al., 1994; Young et al., 1990). Future studies should monitor the implementation of DI curricula to limit experimenter effects and to increase our confidence in the fidelity of program implementation.

IMPLEMENTATION OF DI MATH PROGRAMS WITH OTHER DI CURRICULA. Three of the 12 studies (i.e., Brent & DiObilda, 1993; Glang et al., 1991; Sommers, 1991) investigated the use of DI math programs in conjunction with other DI programs (e.g., *Corrective Reading, Corrective Spelling Through Morphographs, DISTAR Language I, Expressive Writing, Reading Mastery, Reasoning and Writing*). Future studies should compare the effects of the implementation of DI math programs alone as compared to the implementation of DI math programs in conjunction with other DI curricula. On another hand, Sommers (1991) supplemented DI math curricula with other math curricula (i.e., *Heath Mathematics*), thereby making it difficult to claim that effects resulted from a single independent variable. Multiple treatment interference should be avoided by either describing the combined effects of multiple treatments or by providing only one independent variable.

CALCULATION OF EFFECT SIZES. Tests of statistical significance are often relied upon to indicate the effectiveness of a given variable. However, statistical significance data are used to provide information about whether or not results are likely due to chance. An all too common practice in research consumerism is the misinterpretation of these results. Statistical significance does not necessarily mean educational significance. In our quest to find effective math curricula, educators must consider effect size when reviewing research data. According to Martella, Nelson, and Marchand-Martella (1999), an effect size is a standardized measure of the magnitude of the differences between groups. In other words, it measures how large the differences were and can be used as an indication of educational significance. Six of the 12 studies (i.e., Adams & Engel-

mann, 1996; Brent & DiObilda, 1993; McKenzie et al., in press; Parsons et al., in press; Tarver & Jung, 1995; Wellington, 1994) included measures of effect sizes. Future research on DI math programs should include measures of effect size to reflect the magnitude of change in educational programs.

MAINTENANCE AND GENERALIZATION DATA. Two of the most important considerations in choosing math curricula are maintenance and generalization. Long-term retention of mathematical skills and strategies is critical not only for academic success, but also for future employment success. Having students show generalized skills in a wide-variety of subjects and real life situations is equally critical. Three of the 12 studies (i.e., Vreeland et al., 1994; Wellington, 1994; Young et al., 1990) included some measure of maintenance and generalization. Future DI math studies should include such data to afford educators the opportunity to examine this valuable information.

SOCIAL VALIDITY. While a great deal of emphasis is rightfully placed on quantitative measures, social validity measures are an important source of information regarding the social relevance of research questions and results. According to Wolf (1978), "a number of the most important concepts of our culture are subjective, perhaps even the most important" (p. 210). Five of the 12 studies (i.e., Crawford & Snider, 2000; Snider & Crawford, 1996; Tarver & Jung, 1995; Vreeland et al., 1994; Wellington, 1994) reported findings on students' and teachers' attitudes and opinions about DI math programs. Brent and DiObilda (1993) provided socially relevant information regarding the effectiveness of *CMC* with mobile urban children. However, given the need for effective math curricula in a variety of social contexts, future research should include measures of social validity.

CONCLUSION

The *National Assessment of Educational Progress: Mathematics Highlights,* as reported by the National Center for Education Statistics (2001), shows that 4th- and 8th-grade math scores were higher than in earlier national assessments. However, the average math scores for 12th graders declined. In addition, math scores of American students rank in the bottom half of the countries that participated in the 1995 TIMMS Project (International Study Center, 2001). Combined with the ever-increasing technological complexity of future employment, it is clear that our students are in dire need of effective math instruction.

In its *Principles and Standards for School Mathematics* (2000b), NCTM developed five overall curricular goals for ensuring student success in mathematics. First, students should learn to value mathematics. Experiencing success in mathematics helps students to value mathematics. DI math programs are designed to allow students to experience success and to know that they are experiencing success on a daily basis. Second, students should become confident in their own mathematical abilities. DI math programs are designed to develop and maintain knowledge and application of skills and concepts. As students encounter and successfully solve a wide variety of mathematical problems both in the classroom and in the real world, confidence in their own abilities increases. Third, students should become mathematical problem solvers. DI math programs provide students with the necessary tools to solve a broad spectrum of word problems and real life problems. Fourth, students should learn to communicate mathematically. DI math programs directly teach mathematical vocabulary and strategies thereby strengthening students' abilities to communicate effectively about mathematics. Finally, students should learn to reason mathematically. DI math programs teach students to discriminate between different types of problems at gradually increasing levels of complexity. The ability to discriminate between types of problems and required operations further develops students' mathematical reasoning ability. DI math programs meet NCTM's goals for student success by providing students with the confidence and skills to become effective mathematical problem solvers in both classroom and real life mathematics.

NCTM's Principles and Standards for Improving Mathematics (2000b) also provide educators with six principles for improving math instruction. As stated previously, DI math programs effectively meet these principles and result in positive academic outcomes as shown by a majority of studies included in this summary. We encourage public/private school educators and academicians to continue to investigate the effects of DI math programs in consideration of our recommendations. This line of research will continue to ensure we are using math curricula that best serve the needs of all students.

REFERENCES

Adams, G., & Engelmann, S. (1996). *Research on Direct Instruction: 25 years beyond DISTAR*. Seattle, WA: Educational Achievement Systems.

Applefield, J., Huber, R., & Moallem, M. (2000/2001, December/January). Constructivism in theory and practice: Toward a better understanding. *The High School Journal, 84* (2), 35–53.

Brent, G., & DiObilda, N. (July/August, 1993). Curriculum alignment versus Direct Instruction: Effects on stable and mobile urban children. *The Journal of Educational Research, 86* (6), 333–338.

Bureau of Labor Statistics. (2002). *Occupational outlook handbook: Tomorrow's jobs*. Retrieved April 4, 2002, from http://www.bls.gov/oco/oco2003.htm

Carnine, D. (1980). Preteaching versus concurrent teaching of the component skills of a multiplication algorithm. *Journal for Research in Mathematics Education, 11* (5), 375–379.

Carnine, D. (1990). Reforming mathematics instruction: The role of curriculum materials. *ADI News, 10* (1), 5–16.

Carnine, D., & Engelmann, S. (1990). Making connections in third-grade mathematics: *Connecting Math Concepts. ADI News, 10* (1), 17–27.

Cohen, L. G., & Spenciner, L. J. (1998). *Assessment of children and youth*. New York: Addison-Wesley Longman.

Crawford, D. B., & Snider, V. E. (2000). Effective mathematics instruction: The importance of curriculum. *Education and Treatment of Children, 23* (2), 122–142.

Dixon, B. (1994). Research-based guidelines for selecting a mathematics curriculum. *Effective School Practices, 13* (2), 47–61.

Engelmann, S., & Carnine, D. (1975). *DISTAR arithmetic I: Teacher presentation book A*. Columbus, OH: Science Research Associates.

Engelmann, S., & Carnine, D. (1976). *DISTAR arithmetic II: Teacher's guide*. Columbus, OH: Science Research Associates.

Engelmann, S., & Carnine, D. (1982). *Corrective mathematics: Series guide*. Columbus, OH: SRA/Macmillan/McGraw-Hill.

Engelmann, S., Carnine, D., Kelly, B., & Engelmann, O. (1996a). *Connecting math concepts: Lesson sampler*. Columbus, OH: SRA/McGraw-Hill.

Engelmann, S., Carnine, D., Kelly, B., & Engelmann, O. (1996b). *Connecting math concepts: Level A presentation book 1*. Columbus, OH: SRA/McGraw-Hill.

Engelmann, S., Carnine, D., Kelly, B., & Engelmann, O. (1996c). *Connecting math concepts: Level C, teacher's guide*. Columbus, OH: SRA/McGraw-Hill.

Engelmann, S., Carnine, D., Kelly, B., & Engelmann, O. (1996d). *Connecting math concepts: Level F presentation book*. Columbus, OH: SRA/McGraw-Hill.

Glang, A., Singer, G., Cooley, E., & Tish, N. (1991). Using Direct Instruction with brain injured students. *Direct Instruction News, 11* (1), 23–28.

International Study Center. (2001). *International test scores*. Retrieved April 5, 2002, from http://4brevard.com/choice/international-test-scores.htm

Kameenui, E., & Carnine, D. (1998). *Effective teaching strategies that accommodate diverse learners*. Upper Saddle River, NJ: Simon & Schuster.

Kelly, B. (1994). *Meeting the NCTM standards through Connecting Math Concepts.* Worthington, OH: SRA/McGraw-Hill.

Kozloff, M. A., LaNunziata, L. L., Cowardin, J., & Bessellieu, F. B. (2000/2001, December/January). Direct Instruction: Its contributions to high school achievement. *The High School Journal, 84* (2), 54–63.

Lignugaris/Kraft, B., Marchand-Martella, N., & Martella, R. (2001). Strategies for writing better goals and short-term objectives or benchmarks. *Teaching Exceptional Children, 34* (1), 52–58.

Martella, R., Nelson, R., & Marchand-Martella, N. (1999). *Research methods: Learning to become a critical research consumer.* Needham Heights, MA: Allyn & Bacon.

McKenzie, M., Marchand-Martella, N., Martella, R. C., & Moore, M. E. (2004). Teaching basic math skills to preschoolers using *Connecting Math Concepts: Level K. Journal of Direct Instruction, 4,* 85–94.

McLoughlin, J. A., & Lewis, R. B. (2001). *Assessing students with special needs.* Upper Saddle River, NJ: Prentice Hall.

National Center for Education Statistics. (2001). *The nation's report card: Mathematics highlights 2000.* Washington, DC: U.S. Department of Education/Office of Educational Research and Improvement.

National Council of Teachers of Mathematics. (2000a). *About NCTM: Mission.* Retrieved March 20, 2002, from http://www.nctm.org/about/mission.htm

National Council of Teachers of Mathematics. (2000b). *Principles and standards for school mathematics: An overview of principles and standards.* Retrieved November 10, 2001, from http://standards.nctm.org

National Research Council. (1989). *Everybody counts: A report to the nation on the future of mathematics education.* Washington, DC: National Academy Press.

Paine, S., Radicchi, J., Rosellini, L., Deutchman, L., & Darch, C. (1983). *Structuring your classroom for academic success.* Champaign, IL: Research Press Company.

Parsons, J., Marchand-Martella, N., Waldron-Soler, K., Martella, R., & Lignugaris/Kraft, B. (2004). Effects of a high school-based peer-delivered *Corrective Mathematics* program. *Journal of Direct Instruction, 4,* 95–103.

Porter, A. (1989). A curriculum out of balance: The case of elementary school mathematics. *Educational Researcher, 18* (5), 9–15.

Schieffer, C., Marchand-Martella, N. E., Martella, R. C., Simonsen, F. L., & Waldron-Soler, K. M. (2002). An analysis of the *Reading Mastery* program: Effective components and research review. *Journal of Direct Instruction, 2,* 87–119.

Snider, V., & Crawford, D. (1996). Action research: Implementing *Connecting Math Concepts. Effective School Practices, 15* (2), 17–26.

Sommers, J. (1991). Direct Instruction programs produce significant gains with at-risk middle-school students. *Direct Instruction News, 11* (1), 7–14.

Stein, M., Silbert, J., & Carnine, D. (1997). *Designing effective mathematics instruction: A Direct Instruction approach.* Upper Saddle River, NJ: Prentice-Hall.

Tarver, S., & Jung, J. (1995). A comparison of mathematics achievement and mathematics attitudes of first and second graders instructed with either a discovery-learning mathematics curriculum or a Direct Instruction curriculum. *Effective School Practices, 14* (1), 49–57.

TIMS Project: University of Illinois at Chicago. (1998). *Math Trailblazers: A mathematical journey using science and language arts: Teacher implementation guide.* Chicago: Kendall/Hunt.

Vreeland, M., Vail, J., Bradley, L., Buetow, C., Cipriano, K., Green, C., Henshaw, P., et al. (1994). Accelerating cognitive growth: The Edison school math project. *Effective School Practices, 13* (2), 64–69.

Wellington, J. (1994). Evaluating a mathematics program for adoption: *Connecting Math Concepts. Effective School Practices, 13* (2), 70–75.

Wolf, M. M. (1978). Social validity: The case of subjective measurement or how applied behavior analysis is finding its heart. *Journal of Applied Behavior Analysis, 11,* 202–214.

Young, M., Baker, J., & Martin, M. (1990). Teaching basic number skills to students with a moderate intellectual disability. *Education and Training in Mental Retardation, 25,* 83–93.

AUTHOR NOTE

Special thanks are extended to Bernadette Kelly and Karen Sorrentino for their comments on an earlier version of this paper. Thanks are extended to the reviewers of the *Journal of Direct Instruction* for their input into this article and also to Marcy Stein for clarifying terminology during the writing of this paper. Finally, we wish to thank Erica Eden for compiling needed resources from the backfiles of *ADI News* and *Effective School Practices.*

Frequently Asked Questions About Direct Instruction Mathematics

The direct instruction approach has been the target of many queries, controversies, and criticisms since its inception in the 1960s. Therefore, we have included this appendix to answer questions most frequently asked about direct instruction, specifically pertaining to the teaching of mathematics. The appendix is organized into two distinct sections: "Instructional Questions and Issues" and "Issues of Instructional Organization and Management." Although some of the answers to the questions can be found in the research literature, some are questions of common practice. Moreover, many are not questions at all but merely instructional issues that require collective problem solving.

INSTRUCTIONAL QUESTIONS AND ISSUES

A. How does a direct instruction approach to mathematics instruction correspond to the standards put forth by the National Council of Teachers of Mathematics (NCTM)?

The goals of the NCTM standards are

- To value mathematics
- To reason mathematically
- To communicate mathematics
- To solve problems
- To develop confidence.

Teachers using a direct instruction approach to mathematics instruction find that their teaching goals do not differ greatly from those of the NCTM. However, what teachers do find is that the instruction they design to meet those goals look different from the instruction based on recommendations made by the NCTM. For example, a direct instruction teacher carefully examines various strategies for teaching a concept or skill and chooses to teach a single strategy on the basis of its generalizability and clarity. A teacher following recommendations made by the NCTM might have students generate their own individual strategies and share them with the class. While we think generating strategies to solve problems may be an engaging activity, we know that presenting several strategies to students may confuse them. In addition, we want students to learn relationships among math concepts and, therefore, we design instructional strategies intentionally to highlight those relationships. One danger in relying on student-generated strategies is that those strategies may cause misconceptions that go undetected until students are introduced to related concepts. While we endorse the goals of the NCTM, we feel that the methods recommended to reach those goals must be examined carefully.

For a more thorough discussion of how direct instruction math programs meet the principles of NCTM, see the article in Appendix A.

B. Doesn't direct instruction mathematics result in only rote learning?

Many critics of direct instruction perceive that the approach consists of merely rote memorization of basic skills. These critics are confusing *rote* instruction with *explicit* instruction, and they may be misled due to the appearance of the instruction (e.g., use of scripted formats) rather than the instructional content. Because in a direct instruction approach, teachers are encouraged to write teaching formats prior to actual teaching, and because the formats articulate instruction in a step-by-step fashion, some educators confuse the structure of the lesson with the content of the instructional strategy. The more scripted a lesson, the stronger the perception that some form of rote instruction is being delivered.

In reality, no skills or concepts are taught by rote in a direct instruction mathematics approach that can be taught using an explicit strategy. Certainly, direct instruction mathematics includes the teaching of the counting sequence (e.g., 1 2 3 4 5) and symbol identification (6 is "six"), both of which require rote memorization. Notice, however, that the tasks of counting and symbol identification are inherently rote tasks. Programs will always contain some rote instruction, but the decision to teach something by rote is driven by the demands of the task, not the instructional designer.

Direct instruction program designers have designed useful strategies even for the teaching of basic facts. Teachers using a direct instruction approach are encouraged to teach fact number-family strategies that facilitate student understanding of the relationships among fact families and that reduce the number of facts that must be memorized. For example, the introduction to the fact family 4, 3, and 7 facilitates learning the following facts: $4 + 3 = 7$, $3 + 4 = 7$, $7 - 4 = 3$, and $7 - 3 = 4$. Instead of memorizing four isolated facts, students are taught a *strategy* for deriving facts when one of the family members is unknown. For example, they are taught when the *big number* is missing they must add, and when one of the *small numbers* is missing, they must subtract. (Note that the language of big and small numbers is used so that the strategy may be applied to multiplication and division as well as addition and subtraction.)

The point of the above example is that, despite the fact that the direct instruction *appears* as if it might be rote because of the way it is delivered, when teachers look closely at the *content* rather than the *form* of the lesson, they will find generalizable strategies. (See Chapter 1 for a more thorough discussion of strategy instruction and Chapter 6 for instruction on basic facts.) In this text, we provide generalizable strategies for many computation and problem-solving skills. These strategies promote conceptual understanding and develop reasoning skills.

C. How do you know that direct instruction mathematics strategies are effective?

The strategies presented in this book have been field-tested extensively with students of various ages and abilities to ensure that they are viable and useful. The underlying research basis for the design of the strategies was presented in Chapter 3 and again in Appendix A. The research reviewed in Chapter 3 incorporates relevant research from mathematics instruction and the teacher effectiveness literature, as well as research on specific direct instruction mathematics strategies. However, the strategies presented in this text also have been developed with feedback from students and their teachers. Teachers involved in field-testing the programs provided important feedback to those designing mathematics strategies during the development of the mathematics programs. In addition, student errors were carefully examined so that errors caused by a faulty strategy could be identified and the strategy rewritten. The development of effective strategies through feedback from field-testing is an important feature to highlight about direct instruction mathematics because of the notable absence of field-testing in educational publishing. Most commercially available programs are not field-tested with students prior to their publication. The article in Appendix A provides a research summary of direct instruction mathematics programs from which the strategies presented in this text are derived.

D. What role do manipulatives play in mathematics instruction using a direct instruction approach?

First, it is important to note that the research literature on the use of manipulatives, or concrete objects, in elementary mathematics is mixed. While some researchers have found minimal support for using manipulatives (Sowell, 1989), others have found that proficiency in using concrete representation was inversely related to proficiency in symbolic representation (Resnick & Omanson, 1987). The manipulatives themselves are neither helpful nor harmful. The way in which manipulatives are incorporated into instructional activities determine their value. Consistent with a direct instruction approach, manipulatives are most useful after an algorithm is taught. The concrete objects can be used as a means of demonstrating understanding of the symbolic representation. Many instructional programs do the opposite. That is, their initial instructional activities often require students to use manipulatives to generate or represent an algorithm before the students are taught the algorithm. The danger in delaying instruction on the algorithm is that students either fail to learn the algorithm or are unable to transfer the concrete representation to a symbolic one. That is, students can work the problem with manipulatives only and not understand how to compute the answer using only symbols.

Another potential problem with the use of manipulatives is related to the issue of efficiency. In a study involving subtraction, Evans and Carnine (1991) found that although there were no differences in proficiency levels between groups of students who were taught algorithms and those who were taught with manipulatives, there was a significant difference in the amount of time required by each group to reach a level of proficiency. The authors concluded that no matter what type of representation is used, students can gain a conceptual understanding of the problem. However, instruction takes significantly more time when initial instruction involves concrete representations.

Finally, many teachers feel that, with respect to instruction with young children, using manipulatives makes monitoring individual student performance more difficult. In Chapter 7 of this text, we recommend teaching an early addition algorithm by using line drawing instead of concrete objects. The line drawing provides students with a pictorial representation of the problem. However, even more important, the line-drawing strategy allows the teacher to examine individual student performance easily and remedy errors in a timely fashion.

E. Should teachers spend time teaching memorization of math facts?

Chapter 6 in this text provides educators with a good rationale for teaching basic math facts along with recommendations for designing math fact instruction. The reason for teaching math facts is simply that basic fact knowledge is a prerequisite for higher level computation and problem-solving skills.

When a student must stop working a problem to figure out a fact, attention is drawn away from solving the problem and directed to computing the fact. The continuity required to learn new problem-solving routines is interrupted. Fluent knowledge of math facts facilitates not only the acquisition of higher level skills, but also independence and confidence in learning.

While we advocate teaching math facts, we understand that this instruction is time consuming, especially with remedial students. Therefore, we suggest that instruction in math facts be supplemental to the teacher-directed lesson. Also, if the students require remediation, we recommend that they have a reliable alternative, such as a fact chart, to use as they are acquiring their facts.

F. Should students be allowed to use calculators in math class?

Issues regarding the use of calculators are similar to issues of manipulatives in that it is not *whether* students use calculators but *how* and *when* they use them. Teachers must make conscious decisions about the degree to which they will allow students to rely on calculators for computation. If teachers do allow calculators, they must teach students to use them properly.

ISSUES OF INSTRUCTIONAL ORGANIZATION AND MANAGEMENT

A. Is direct instruction only for low-performing students?

Because direct instruction has been effective with low-performing and special education students, educators assume the strategies are appropriate *only* for those students who are struggling with mathematics. On the contrary, we believe the strategies are effective because they are well-designed, generalizable, and clearly presented. *All* students can benefit from well-designed instruction. The mistake many teachers make when using direct instruction with higher performing students is pacing the instruction too slowly. These teachers may be providing more repetition and practice than is necessary for their students, or they may be teaching skills students already have acquired. Careful monitoring of student progress allows teachers to provide appropriate instruction for a diverse range of student abilities in the classroom.

B. How does a direct instruction approach in mathematics work in inclusive classrooms? with students with disabilities?

Most classrooms reflect a range of student ability that teachers must consider when designing and implementing direct instruction mathematics (or any) instruction. In this text, we refer to students representing the range of student ability as high and low performing students. The underlying philosophy of direct instruction is that *all* students can learn if given well-designed instruction and opportunities for practice and that high- and low-performing students differ in their need for each. Low performing students are those students who *require* (a) well-designed, unambiguous, teacher-directed instruction and (b) *more* practice opportunities in order to master the skills presented.

It is our contention that instructional models driven by location (in-class versus pullout) are overlooking critical instructional factors that are directly related to student success. We have observed excellent pullout programs and excellent in-class programs. Therefore, in our opinion, when designing services for low-performing students, including students with disabilities, the design of the instructional strategies and corresponding practice activities must be addressed prior to discussing location.

As mentioned earlier, the direct instruction strategies in this text have been demonstrated to be effective with a range of student ability. But the instruc-

tion is just one of three components necessary to ensure student success. The other two components are assessment and service delivery. The assessment component must include provisions for appropriate initial screening and diagnostic testing, in addition to a system for continued progress monitoring. Service delivery in this context refers to the systematic coordination of efforts by general and special education that includes a process of shared responsibility and collaborative problem solving.

Using the guiding principles of well-designed instruction and more practice opportunities, all teachers of students with special needs must discuss the *who, what, where,* and *how* of designing an effective program. *Who* will be responsible for teacher-directed instruction? *What* will be taught? *Where* will the student receive the instruction? *How* will the teachers orchestrate additional practice opportunities? All of the above questions are relevant to the education of low performing students.

Models for service delivery that address the components of assessment, instruction, and service delivery vary from school to school and include whole-class grouping and small-group instruction; peer, cross-age, and classwide tutoring; before- and after-school programs; and instruction delivered by parents, volunteers, and paraprofessionals, in addition to general and special education teachers. The possibilities for designing effective instructional programs for students are numerous.

References

Adams, G. L., & Engelmann, S. (1996). *Research on Direct Instruction: 25 years beyond DISTAR*. Seattle, WA: Educational Achievement Systems.

Ashlock, R. B. (1971). Teaching the basic facts: Three classes of activities. *The Arithmetic Teacher, 18,* 359.

Baker, D. E. (1992). The effects of self-generated drawings on the ability of students with learning disabilities to solve mathematical word problems. (Doctoral dissertation, Texas Tech University, 1992). *University Microfilms International,* 9238973.

Baker, S., Gersten, R., & Lee, D. (2002). A synthesis of empirical research on teaching mathematics to low-achieving students. *The Elementary School Journal, 103,* 51–73.

Barron, B., Bransford, J., Kulewicz, S., & Hasselbring, R. (1989, March). *Uses of macrocontexts to facilitate mathematics thinking.* Paper presented at the American Educational Research Association Conference, San Francisco, CA.

Becker W. C., & Gersten R. (1982). Follow up on Follow Through: Behavior-theory-based programs come out on top. *Education and Urban Society, 10,* 431–458.

Bransford, J. D., Sherwood, R. S., Hasselbring, T. S., Kinzer, C. K., & Williams, S. M. (1990). Anchored instruction: Why we need it and how technology can help. In D. Nix & R. Spiro (Eds.) *Cognition, education, and multi-media: Exploring ideas in high technology.* (pp. 115–141). Hillsdale, NJ: Lawrence Erlbaum.

Brown, J. L. (1970). Effects of logical and scrambled sequences in mathematical sequences on learning with programmed instruction materials. *Journal of Educational Psychology, 61,* 41–45.

Cacha, F. B. (1975). Subtraction: Regrouping with flexibility. *The Arithmetic Teacher, 22,* 402–404.

Cardelle-Elawar, M. (1992). Effects of teaching metacognitive skills to students with low mathematics ability. *Teaching and Teacher Education, 8*(2), 109–121.

Cardelle-Elawar, M. (1995). Effects of metacognitive instruction on low achievers in mathematics problems. *Teaching and Teacher Education, 11*(1), 81–95.

Carnine, D. (1980). Preteaching versus concurrent teaching of the component skills of a multiplication algorithm. *Journal of Research in Mathematics Education, 11*(5), 375–378.

Carnine, D. (1997). Instructional design in mathematics for students with learning disabilities. *Journal of Learning Disabilities, 30,* 130–141.

Carnine, D., Jones, E. D., & Dixon, R. (1994). Mathematics: Educational tools for diverse learners. *School Psychology Review, 23,* 406–427.

Carnine, D. W., & Stein, M. (1981). Organizational strategies and practice procedures for teaching basic facts. *Journal of Research in Mathematics Education, 12*(1), 65–69.

Christensen, C. A., & Cooper, T. J. (1991). The effectiveness of instruction in cognitive strategies in developing proficiency in single-digit addition. *Cognition and Instruction, 8,* 363–371.

Darch, C., Carnine, D. W., & Gersten, R. (1989). Explicit instruction in mathematics problem solving. *Journal of Educational Research, 77,* 351–358.

Dixon, B. (1994). Research based guidelines for selecting mathematics curriculum. *Effective School Practices, 13*(2), 47–61.

Dixon, R. C., Carnine, D. W., Lee, D., Wallin, J., & Chard, D. (1998). *Report to the California State Board of Education and Addendum to Principal Report Review of High Quality Experimental Mathematics Research.*

Englemann, S. E. (1969). *Conceptual learning.* San Rafael, CA: Dimensions Publishing.

Engelmann, S., & Carnine, D. (1991). *Theory of instruction: Principles and applications.* Eugene, OR: ADI Press.

Fantuzzo, J. W., Davis, G. Y., & Ginsburg, M. D. (1995). Effects of parent involvement in isolation or in combination with peer tutoring on student self-concept and mathematics achievement. *Journal of Educational Psychology, 87,* 272–281.

Fuchs, L. S., Fuchs, D., Hamlett, C. L., Phillips, N. B., & Gentz, J. (1994). Classwide curriculum-based measurement: Helping general educators meet the challenges of student diversity. *Exceptional Children, 60,* 518–537.

Fuchs, L. S., Fuchs, D., Hamlett, C. L., & Stecher, P. M. (1990). The role of skills analysis in curriculum-based measurement in math. *School Psychology Review, 19*(1), 6–22.

Fuchs, L. S., Fuchs, D., Kaarns, K., Hamlett, C. L., Katzaroff, M., & Dutka, S. (1997). Effects of task-focused goals on low-achieving students with and without learning disabilities. *American Educational Research Journal, 34,* 513–543.

Fuchs, L. S., Fuchs, D., Phillips, N. B, Hamlett, C. L., & Kaarns, K. (1995). Acquisition and transfer effects of classwide peer-assisted learning strategies in mathematics for students with varying learning histories. *School Psychology Review, 24,* 6004–620.

Gersten, R. (2002). *Mathematics education and achievement.* Retrieved August 6, 2002, from www.ed.gov/offices/OESE/esea/research/gersten/html.

Gersten, R. & Carnine, D. (1984). Direct Instruction mathematics: A longitudinal evaluation of low-income elementary school students. *The Elementary School Journal, 84*(4), 395–407.

Gersten, R., Chard, D., Baker, S. K., Jayanthi, M., Flojo, J. R., Lee, D. S. (under review). Experimental and quasi-experimental research on instructional approaches for teaching mathematics to students with learning disabilities: A research synthesis. *Review of Educational Research.*

Good, T., & Grouws, D. (1979). The Missouri Mathematics Effectiveness Project: An experimental study in fourth-grade classrooms. *Journal of Educational Psychology, 74,* 355–362.

Good, T., Grouws, D., & Ebmeier, H. (1983). *Active mathematics teaching.* New York: Longman.

Harniss, M. K, Carnine, D. W., Silbert, J., & Dixon, R. C. (2002). Effective strategies for teaching mathematics. In E. J. Kame'enui, D. W. Carnine, R. C. Dixon, D. C. Simmons, & M. C. Coyne, *Effective teaching strategies that accommodate diverse learners* (pp. 121–148). Upper Saddle River, NJ: Merrill/Prentice Hall.

Harniss, M. K., Stein, M., & Carnine, D. (2002). Promoting mathematics achievement. In M. R. Shinn, G. Stoner, & H. M. Walker (Eds.), *Intervention for academic and behavior problems II: Preventive and remedial approaches* (pp. 571–587). Bethesda, MD: National Association of School Psychologists.

Heller, L. R., & Fantuzzo, J. W. (1993). Reciprocal peer tutoring and parent partnerships: Does parent involvement make a difference? *School Psychology Review, 22,* 517–534.

Hofmeister, A. M. (2004). Education reform in mathematics: A history ignored? *Journal of Direct Instruction 4,* 5–12.

Jackson, M. B., & Phillips, E. R. (1983). Vocabulary instruction in ratio and proportion for seventh graders. *Journal of Research in Mathematics Education, 14*(4), 337–343.

Jerman, M. E. & Beardslee, E. (1978). *Elementary mathematics methods.* New York: McGraw-Hill.

Jitendra, A. K., Griffin, C. C., McGoey, K., & Gardill, M. G. (1998). Effects of mathematical word problem solving by students at risk or with mild disabilities. *Journal of Educational Research, 91,* 345–355.

Johnson, D. W., Skon, L., & Johnson, R. (1980). Effects of cooperative, competitive, and individualistic conditions on children's problem-solving performance. *American Educational Research Journal, 17,* 83–93.

Kame'enui, E. J., Carnine, D. W., Darch, C., & Stein, M. L. (1986). Two approaches to the development phase of mathematics instruction. *The Elementary School Journal, 33*(2), 103–115.

Kame'enui, E. J., Carnine, D. W., & Dixon, R. C. (2002). Introduction. In E. J. Kame'enui, D. W. Carnine, R. C. Dixon, D. C. Simmons, and M. C. Coyne, *Effective teaching strategies that accommodate diverse learners* (pp. 1–21). Upper Saddle River, NJ: Merrill/Prentice Hall.

Kelly, B., Carnine, D., Gersten, R., & Grossen, B. (1986). The effectiveness of videodisc instruction in teaching fractions to learning-disabled and remedial high school students. *Journal of Special Education Technology, 8*(2), 5–17.

Kelly, B., Gersten, R., & Carnine, D. (1990). Student error patterns as a function of curriculum design: Teaching fractions to remedial high school students with learning disabilities. *Journal of Learning Disabilities, 23,* 23–29.

Klein, D. (2003). A brief history of American K–12 mathematics education in the 20th century. In J. M. Royer (Ed.), *Mathematical cognition* (pp. 175–225). Greenwich, CT: Information Age Publishing.

Leinhardt, G., Zaslavsky, O., & Stein, M. K. (1990). Functions, graphs, and graphing: Tasks, learning, and teaching. *Review of Educational Research, 60*(1), 1–64.

Loveless, T., & Diperna, P. (2000). *The Brown Center Report on American Education: 2000. How well are American students learning?* The Brookings Institute. Retrieved on September 15, 2004 from www.brookings.edu/press/books/brown_report.htm

Ma, L. (1999). *Knowing and teaching elementary mathematics.* Mahwah, NJ: Lawrence Erlbaum.

Markle, S. K., & Tiemann, P. W. (1970) Problems of conceptual learning. *Journal of Educational Technology, 1,* 52–62.

Moore, L. J., & Carnine, D. W. (1989). A comparison of two approaches to teaching ratio and proportions to remedial and learning disabled students: Active teaching with either basal or empirically validated curriculum design material. *Remedial and Special Education, 10*(4), 28–37.

National Center for Educational Statistics. (2000). *NAEP 1999 trends in academic progress: Three decades of student performance.* Retrieved September 15, 2004, from nces.ed.gov

National Center for Educational Statistics. (2003). *The nation's report card: Mathematics highlights 2003.* Retrieved September 15, 2004, from nces.ed.gov

National Commission on Excellence in Education. (1983). *A nation at risk: The imperative for educational reform.* Washington, DC: U.S. Government Printing Office.

National Council of Teachers of Mathematics. (1980). *An agenda for action: Recommendations for school mathematics of the 1980s.* Reston, VA: Author

National Council of Teachers of Mathematics. (2000). *Principles and standards for school mathematics* [Online]. Available: standards.nctm.org/index.htm

National Research Council. (2001). *Adding it up: Helping children learn mathematics.* J. Kilpatrick, J. Swafford, and B. Findell (Eds.). Mathematics Learning Study

Committee, Center for Education, Division of Behavioral and Social Sciences and Education. Washington, DC: National Academy Press.

Nichols, J. D. (1996). The effects of cooperative learning on student achievement and motivation in a high school geometry class. *Contemporary Educational Psychology, 21,* 467–476.

O'Melia, M. C., & Rosenberg, M. S. (1994). Effects of cooperative homework teams on the acquisition of mathematics skills by secondary students with mild disabilities. *Exceptional Children, 60,* 538–548.

Organization for Economic Co-Operation and Development. (2004). *Knowledge and skills for life: First results from PISA 2000.* [online]. Available: www.oecd.org

Paine, S. C., Carnine, D. W., White, W. A. T., & Walters, G. (1982). Effects of fading teacher presentation structure (covertization) on acquisition and maintenance of arithmetic problem-solving skills. *Education and Treatment of Children, 5*(2), 93–107.

Petty, O. S., & Jansson, L. C. (1987). Sequencing examples and nonexamples to facilitate attainment. *Journal for Research in Mathematics Education, 18*(2), 112–125.

Porter, A. (1989). A curriculum out of balance: The case of elementary school mathematics. *Educational Researcher, 18*(5), 9–15.

Przychodzin, A. M., Marchand-Martella, N. E., Martella, R. C., & Azim, D. (2004). Direct Instruction mathematics programs: An overview and research summary. *Journal of Direct Instruction, 4,* 53–84.

Rosenshine, B. (1983). Teaching functions in instructional programs. *The Elementary School Journal, 83,* 335–351.

Rzoska, K. M., & Ward, C. (1991). The effects of cooperative and competitive learning methods on the mathematics achievement, attitudes toward school, self-concepts and friendship choices of Maori, Pakeha and Samoan children. *New Zealand Journal of Psychology, 20*(1), 17–24.

Schmidt, W., Houang, R., & Cogan, L. (2002, Summer). A coherent curriculum: The case of mathematics. *American Educator,* 1–18.

Shinn, M. R. (Ed.). (1998). *Advanced applications of curriculum-based measurement.* New York: Guilford Press.

Shinn, M. R., & Bamonto, S. (1998). Advanced applications of curriculum-based measurement: "Big ideas" and avoiding confusion. In M. R. Shinn (Ed.), *Advanced applications of curriculum-based measurement* (pp. 1–31). New York: Guilford Press.

Slavin, R. E., & Karweit, N. L. (1984). Mastery learning and student teams: A factorial experiment in urban general mathematics classes. *American Educational Research Journal, 21,* 725–736.

Slavin, R. E., Madden, N. A., & Leavey, M. (1984). Effects of cooperative learning and individualized instruction on mainstreamed students. *Exceptional Children, 50,* 434–443.

Snider, V. E. (2004). A comparison of spiral versus strand curriculum. *Journal of Direct Instruction, 4,* 29–40.

Stebbins, L., St. Pierre, R. G., Proper, E. L., Anderson, R. B., & Cerva, T. R. (1977). *Education as experimentation: A planned variation model.* (Vols. IV–A). Cambridge, MA: Abt Associates.

Stein, M., Silbert, J., & Carnine, D. (1997). *Designing effective mathematics instruction: A direct instruction approach* (3rd ed.). Upper Saddle River, NJ: Merrill/Prentice Hall.

Stein, M. L., Stuen, C., Carnine, D., & Long, R. M. (2001). Textbook evaluation and adoption practices. *Reading and Writing Quarterly, 17*(1), 5–23.

Trafton, P. R. (1984). Toward more effective, efficient instruction in mathematics. *The Elementary School Journal, 84,* 514–530.

Underhill, R. G. (1981). *Teaching elementary school mathematics* (3rd ed.). Columbus, OH: Merrill Publishing.

University of Chicago School Mathematics Project. (1995). *Third grade everyday mathematics: Teacher's manual and lesson guide.* Evanston, IL: Everyday Learning Corporation.

Van Patten, J., Chao, C., & Reigeluth, C. M. (1986). A review of strategies for sequencing and synthesizing instruction. *Review of Educational Research, 56,* 437–471.

Walker, D. W., & Poteet, J. A. (1989/1990). A comparison of two methods of teaching mathematics story problem-solving with learning disabled students. *National Forum of Special Education Journal, 1*(1), 44–51.

Watkins, C. L. (1997). *Project Follow Through: A case study of the contingencies influencing instructional practices of the educational establishment.* (Monograph). Concord, MA: Cambridge Center for Behavioral Studies.

Watkins, C., & Slocum, T. (2004). The components of Direct Instruction. In N. E. Marchand-Martella, T. A. Slocum, & R. C. Martella (eds.), *Introduction to Direct Instruction* (pp. 28–65). Boston, MA: Allyn & Bacon.

Woodward, J., Baxter, J., & Robinson, R. (1999). Rules and reasons: Decimal instruction for academically low-achieving students. *Learning Disabilities Research and Practice, 14,* 15–24.

Woodward, J., Carnine, D., & Gersten, R. (1988). Teaching problem-solving through computer simulations. *Educational Research Journal, 25*(1), 72–86.

Wu, H. (1999). Basic skills versus conceptual understanding. *American Educator, 23*(3), 14–19, 50–52.

Index